The Ministers Manual for 1986

By the same editor

Preaching
Biblical Preaching: An Expositor's Treasury
The Twentieth Century Pulpit, Volumes I and II
Surprised by God
A Guide to Biblical Preaching
Minister's Worship Manual (co-editor with Ernest A.
    Payne and Stephen F. Winward)
Learning to Speak Effectively
God's Inescapable Nearness (co-author with Eduard
    Schweizer)

SIXTY-FIRST ANNUAL ISSUE

MINISTERS MANUAL

(Doran's)

1986 EDITION

Edited by

JAMES W. COX

1817

HARPER & ROW, PUBLISHERS, SAN FRANCISCO

Cambridge, Hagerstown, New York, Philadelphia
London, Mexico City, São Paulo, Singapore, Sydney

Editors of THE MINISTERS MANUAL

G.B.F. Hallock, D.D., 1926–1958
M.K.W. Heicher, Ph.D., 1943–1968
Charles L. Wallis, M.A., M.Div., 1969–1983
James W. Cox, M.Div., Ph.D., 1984–

Acknowledgments are on page 336.

THE MINISTERS MANUAL FOR 1986
Copyright © 1985 by James W. Cox. All rights reserved.
Printed in the United States of America. For information
address Harper & Row, Publishers, Inc., 10 East 53rd Street,
New York, NY 10022. Published simultaneously in Canada
by Fitzhenry & Whiteside Limited, Toronto.

FIRST EDITION

The Library of Congress has cataloged the first printing of
this serial as follows:

The ministers manual: a study and pulpit guide. 1926–. New
York, Harper.

V. 21–23 cm. annual.
Title varies: 1926–46, Doran's ministers manual (cover
title, 1947: The Doran's ministers manual)
Editor: 1926– G. B. F. Hallock (with M. K. W. Heicher,
1942–)

1. Sermons—Outlines. 2. Homiletical illustrations. I. Hallock, Gerard Benjamin Fleet, 1856– , ed.
  BV4223.M5   251.058   25–21658 rev*
                     [r48n2]

ISBN 0–06–061599–0

85 86 87 88 89 HC 10 9 8 7 6 5 4 3 2 1

PREFACE

How can a preacher or teacher hope to hold the interest and attention of the same listeners year after year? We would say, Keep up good study habits, maintain spiritual disciplines, get out among the people, and prepare every service of worship carefully. And we would not be wrong. Such activity is fundamental.

However, people who listen to spiritual leaders need variety. Variety offers more entertainment—true! But variety also provides for the differing needs of individuals. Preachers who get in touch with ranges of experience and insight beyond their own can give their people a more nutritious spiritual diet. I once heard the poet John Ciardi commend the reading of poetry as a means of expanding experience vicariously. We could say as much for the reading, analyzing, and absorbing of the sermons and prayers of preachers. Such sermons and prayers confront us with different forms, alternative approaches, and especially with a wider and richer range of ideas. Used wisely, they can enhance the preacher's own creativity.

Here again in *The Ministers Manual* are rich materials for pastors, lay workers, Sunday school teachers, seminary students, missionaries, youth leaders, chaplains, and others.

I am grateful to many individuals and publishers for permission to quote from their material. I continue to be grateful to the trustees of the Southern Baptist Theological Seminary and to Dr. Roy Honeycutt, president, for their practical encouragement; to Alicia Gardner, office services supervisor; to Pat Powell, Janice Bittle, Trisha Schmittendorf, Eileen Long, Margo Chaney, and Rachel Tedards, who typed and proofed the manuscript; and to Clara McCartt, Kenneth Craig, and Dr. Lee R. McGlone for significant editorial assistance. I am also appreciative of the careful work of the editorial staff at Harper & Row, San Francisco.

James W. Cox
Southern Baptist Theological Seminary
2825 Lexington Road
Louisville, Kentucky 40280

CONTENTS

SECTION I: *General Aids and Resources*
Civil Year Calendars
1986

JANUARY						
S	M	T	W	T	F	S
			1	2	3	4
5	6	7	8	9	10	11
12	13	14	15	16	17	18
19	20	21	22	23	24	25
26	27	28	29	30	31	

FEBRUARY						
S	M	T	W	T	F	S
						1
2	3	4	5	6	7	8
9	10	11	12	13	14	15
16	17	18	19	20	21	22
23	24	25	26	27	28	

MARCH						
S	M	T	W	T	F	S
						1
2	3	4	5	6	7	8
9	10	11	12	13	14	15
16	17	18	19	20	21	22
23	24	25	26	27	28	29
30	31					

APRIL						
S	M	T	W	T	F	S
		1	2	3	4	5
6	7	8	9	10	11	12
13	14	15	16	17	18	19
20	21	22	23	24	25	26
27	28	29	30			

MAY						
S	M	T	W	T	F	S
				1	2	3
4	5	6	7	8	9	10
11	12	13	14	15	16	17
18	19	20	21	22	23	24
25	26	27	28	29	30	31

JUNE						
S	M	T	W	T	F	S
1	2	3	4	5	6	7
8	9	10	11	12	13	14
15	16	17	18	19	20	21
22	23	24	25	26	27	28
29	30					

JULY						
S	M	T	W	T	F	S
		1	2	3	4	5
6	7	8	9	10	11	12
13	14	15	16	17	18	19
20	21	22	23	24	25	26
27	28	29	30	31		

AUGUST						
S	M	T	W	T	F	S
					1	2
3	4	5	6	7	8	9
10	11	12	13	14	15	16
17	18	19	20	21	22	23
24	25	26	27	28	29	30
31						

SEPTEMBER						
S	M	T	W	T	F	S
	1	2	3	4	5	6
7	8	9	10	11	12	13
14	15	16	17	18	19	20
21	22	23	24	25	26	27
28	29	30				

OCTOBER						
S	M	T	W	T	F	S
			1	2	3	4
5	6	7	8	9	10	11
12	13	14	15	16	17	18
19	20	21	22	23	24	25
26	27	28	29	30	31	

NOVEMBER						
S	M	T	W	T	F	S
						1
2	3	4	5	6	7	8
9	10	11	12	13	14	15
16	17	18	19	20	21	22
23	24	25	26	27	28	29
30						

DECEMBER						
S	M	T	W	T	F	S
	1	2	3	4	5	6
7	8	9	10	11	12	13
14	15	16	17	18	19	20
21	22	23	24	25	26	27
28	29	30	31			

1987

JANUARY						
S	M	T	W	T	F	S
				1	2	3
4	5	6	7	8	9	10
11	12	13	14	15	16	17
18	19	20	21	22	23	24
25	26	27	28	29	30	31

FEBRUARY						
S	M	T	W	T	F	S
1	2	3	4	5	6	7
8	9	10	11	12	13	14
15	16	17	18	19	20	21
22	23	24	25	26	27	28

MARCH						
S	M	T	W	T	F	S
1	2	3	4	5	6	7
8	9	10	11	12	13	14
15	16	17	18	19	20	21
22	23	24	25	26	27	28
29	30	31				

APRIL						
S	M	T	W	T	F	S
			1	2	3	4
5	6	7	8	9	10	11
12	13	14	15	16	17	18
19	20	21	22	23	24	25
26	27	28	29	30		

MAY						
S	M	T	W	T	F	S
					1	2
3	4	5	6	7	8	9
10	11	12	13	14	15	16
17	18	19	20	21	22	23
24	25	26	27	28	29	30
31						

JUNE						
S	M	T	W	T	F	S
	1	2	3	4	5	6
7	8	9	10	11	12	13
14	15	16	17	18	19	20
21	22	23	24	25	26	27
28	29	30				

JULY						
S	M	T	W	T	F	S
			1	2	3	4
5	6	7	8	9	10	11
12	13	14	15	16	17	18
19	20	21	22	23	24	25
26	27	28	29	30	31	

AUGUST						
S	M	T	W	T	F	S
						1
2	3	4	5	6	7	8
9	10	11	12	13	14	15
16	17	18	19	20	21	22
23	24	25	26	27	28	29
30	31					

SEPTEMBER						
S	M	T	W	T	F	S
		1	2	3	4	5
6	7	8	9	10	11	12
13	14	15	16	17	18	19
20	21	22	23	24	25	26
27	28	29	30			

OCTOBER						
S	M	T	W	T	F	S
				1	2	3
4	5	6	7	8	9	10
11	12	13	14	15	16	17
18	19	20	21	22	23	24
25	26	27	28	29	30	31

NOVEMBER						
S	M	T	W	T	F	S
1	2	3	4	5	6	7
8	9	10	11	12	13	14
15	16	17	18	19	20	21
22	23	24	25	26	27	28
29	30					

DECEMBER						
S	M	T	W	T	F	S
		1	2	3	4	5
6	7	8	9	10	11	12
13	14	15	16	17	18	19
20	21	22	23	24	25	26
27	28	29	30	31		

Church and Civic Calendar for 1986

JANUARY

1	New Year's Day
	The Name of Jesus
5	Twelfth Night
6	Epiphany
15	Martin Luther King Jr.'s Birthday
18	Confession of St. Peter
19	Robert E. Lee's Birthday
25	Conversion of St. Paul
28	Feast of St. Thomas Aquinas

FEBRUARY

1	National Freedom Day
2	Presentation of Jesus in the Temple
	Boy Scout Sunday
	Groundhog Day
3	Four Chaplains Memorial Day
9	Race Relations Sunday
11	Shrove Tuesday
12	Ash Wednesday
	Lincoln's Birthday
14	St. Valentine's Day
15	Susan B. Anthony Day
16	First Sunday in Lent
16–23	Brotherhood Week
17	Day of Prayer for Students
	Washington's Birthday Observed
21	World Day of Prayer
22	Washington's Birthday
23	Second Sunday in Lent

MARCH

2	Third Sunday in Lent
9	Fourth Sunday in Lent
	Girl Scout Sunday
16	Fifth Sunday in Lent
17	St. Patrick's Day
23	Passion/Palm Sunday
23–29	Holy Week
25	The Annunciation
	Purim (Feast of Lots)
27	Maundy Thursday
28	Good Friday
29	Easter Eve
30	Easter

APRIL

24	Passover Begins
25	St. Mark, Evangelist
	Arbor Day

MAY

1	May Day
	Loyalty Day
	St. Philip and St. James, Apostles
4–11	National Family Week
8	Ascension Day
11	Festival of the Christian Home
	Mother's Day
17	Armed Forces Day
18	Pentecost (Whitsunday)
19	Victoria Day (Canada)
22	National Maritime Day
25	Trinity Sunday
	Memorial Sunday
26	Memorial Day Observed
30	Memorial Day

JUNE

8	Children's Day
11	St. Barnabas, Apostle
13	Shavuot
14	Flag Day
15	Father's Day
29	St. Peter and St. Paul, Apostles

JULY

1	Dominion Day (Canada)
4	Independence Day
25	St. James, Apostle

AUGUST

4	Civic Holiday (Canada)
6	The Transfiguration
15	Mary, the Mother of Jesus
24	St. Bartholomew, Apostle
31	Labor Day Sunday

SEPTEMBER

1	Labor Day
8	Birth of the Virgin Mary
21	St. Matthew, Apostle and Evangelist
28	Christian Education Sunday
	Rally Day
	Frances Willard Day
29	St. Michael and All Angels

OCTOBER

4	St. Francis of Assisi
	First Day of Rosh Hashanah

5 World Communion Sunday
7 Child Health Day
12 Laity Sunday
    Columbus Day
13 Thanksgiving Day (Canada)
    Yom Kippur (Day of Atonement)
    Columbus Day Observed
15 World Poetry Day
18 St. Luke, Evangelist
    First Day of Sukkoth
19 World Order Sunday
24 United Nations Day
25 Shmini Atzeret
26 Reformation Sunday
28 St. Simon and St. Jude, Apostles
31 Reformation Day
    Halloween

NOVEMBER

1 All Saints' Day
2 All Souls' Day
4 Election Day
9 Grandparents Day
    Stewardship Day
    World Peace Sunday
11 Armistice Day
    Veterans Day

    Remembrance Day (Canada)
12 Elizabeth Cady Stanton Day
15 Sadie Hawkins Day
23 Thanksgiving Sunday
    Christ the King
27 Thanksgiving Day
30 First Sunday of Advent
    St. Andrew, Apostle

DECEMBER

7 Second Sunday of Advent
    Universal Bible Sunday
14 Third Sunday of Advent
15 Bill of Rights Day
17 Wright Brothers Day
21 Fourth Sunday of Advent
    St. Thomas, Apostle
24 Christmas Eve
25 Christmas Day
26 St. Stephen, Deacon and Martyr
    Boxing Day (Canada)
27 St. John, Apostle and Evangelist
    First Day of Hanukkah
28 The Holy Innocents, Martyrs
31 New Year's Eve
    Watch Night

Common Lectionary for 1986

The following Scripture lessons are commended for use in public worship by various Protestant churches and the Roman Catholic church and include first, second, Gospel readings, and Psalms according to Cycle C from January 5 to November 23 and according to Cycle A from November 30 to December 28.

EPIPHANY SEASON

January 5 (Epiphany Sunday): Isa. 60:1–6; Ps. 72:1–14; Eph. 3:1–12; Matt. 2:1–12
January 12: Isa. 61:1–4; Ps. 29; Acts 8:14–17; Luke 3:15–17, 21–22
January 19: Isa. 62:1–5; Ps. 36:5–10; 1 Cor. 12:1–11; John 2:1–11
January 26: Neh. 8:1–4a, 5–6, 8–10; Ps. 19:7–14; 1 Cor. 12:12–30; Luke 4:14–21
February 2: Jer. 1:4–10; Ps. 71:1–6; 1 Cor. 13:1–13; Luke 4:21–30
February 9: Isa. 6:1–8 (9–13); Ps. 138; 1 Cor. 15:1–11; Luke 5:1–11

LENT

February 12 (Ash Wednesday): Joel 2:1–2, 12–17a; Ps. 51:1–12; 2 Cor. 5:20b–6:2 (3–10); Matt. 6:1–6, 16–21
February 16: Deut. 26:1–11; Ps. 91:9–16; Rom. 10:8b-13; Luke 4:1–13
February 23: Gen. 15:1–12, 17–18; Ps. 127; Phil. 3:17–4:1; Luke 13:31–35 or Luke 9:28–36
March 2: Exod. 3:1–15; Ps. 103:1–13; 1 Cor. 10:1–13; Luke 13:1–9
March 9: Josh. 5:9–12; Ps. 34:1–8; 2 Cor. 5:16–21; Luke 15:1–3, 11–32
March 16: Isa. 43:16–21; Ps. 126; Phil. 3:8–14; John 12:1–8

HOLY WEEK

March 23 (Palm Sunday): Isa. 50:4–9a; Ps. 118:19–29; Phil. 2:5–11; Luke 19:28–40
March 24 (Monday): Isa. 42:1–9; Ps. 36:5–10; Heb. 9:11–15; John 12:1–11

March 25 (Tuesday): Isa. 49:1–7; Ps. 71:1–12; 1 Cor. 1:18–31; John 12:20–36
March 26 (Wednesday): Isa. 50:4–9a; Ps. 70; Heb. 12:1–3; John 12:21–30
March 27 (Thursday): Jer. 31:31–34; Ps. 116:12–19; Heb. 10:16–25; Luke 22:7–20
March 28 (Friday): Isa. 52:13–53:12; Ps. 22:1–18; Heb. 4:14–16; 5:7–9; John 18:1–19:42 or John 19:17–30
March 29 (Easter Eve): Gen. 1:1–2:2; Ps. 33; Gen. 7:1–5, 11–18; 8:6–18; 9:8–13; Ps. 46; Gen. 22:1–18; Ps. 16; Exod. 14:10–15:1; 15:1–6, 11–13, 17–18; Isa. 54:5–14; Ps. 30; Isa. 12:2–6; Bar. 3:9–15, 32–4:4; Ps. 19; Ezek. 36:24–28; Ps. 42; Ezek. 37:1–14; Ps. 143; Zeph. 3:14–20; Ps. 98; Rom. 6:3–11; Ps. 114; Luke 24:1–12

SEASON OF EASTER

March 30 (Easter Sunday): Acts 10:34–43 or Isa. 65:17–25; Ps. 118:14–24; 1 Cor. 15:19–26 or Acts 10:34–43; John 10:1–18 or Luke 24: 1–12
April 6: Acts 5:27–32; Ps. 2; Rev. 1:4–8; John 20:19–31
April 13: Acts 9:1–20; Ps. 30:4–12; Rev. 5:11–14; John 21:1–19 or John 21:15–19
April 20: Acts 13:15–16, 26–33; Ps. 23; Rev. 7:9–17; John 10:22–30
April 27: Acts 14:8–18; Ps. 145:13b-21; Rev. 21:1–6; John 13:31–35
May 4: Acts 15:1–2, 22–29; Ps. 67; Rev. 21:10, 22–27; John 14:23–29
May 11 (Ascension Sunday): Acts 16: 16–34; Ps. 97; Rev. 22:12–14, 16–17, 20; John 17:20–26

SEASON OF PENTECOST

May 18 (Pentecost): Acts 2:1–21 or Gen. 11:1–9; Ps. 104:24–34; Rom 8:14–17 or Acts 2:1–21; John 14:8–17, 25–27
May 25 (Trinity Sunday): Prov. 8:22–31; Ps. 8; Rom. 5:1–5; John 16:12–15
June 1: 1 Kings 8:22–23, 41–43; Ps. 100; Gal. 1:1–10; Luke 7:1–10
June 8: 1 Kings 17:17–24; Ps. 113; Gal. 1:11–24; Luke 7:11–17
June 15: 1 Kings 19:1–8; Ps. 42: Gal. 5:15–22; Luke 7:36–8:3

June 22: 1 Kings 19:9–14; Ps. 43; Gal. 3:23–29; Luke 9:18–24
June 29: 1 Kings 19:15–21; Ps. 44:1–8; Gal. 5:1, 13–25; Luke 9:51–62
July 6: 1 Kings 21:1–3, 17–21; Ps. 5:1–8; Gal. 6:7–18; Luke 10:1–12, 17–20
July 13: 2 Kings 2:1, 6–14; Ps. 139:1–12; Col. 1:1–14; Luke 10:25–37
July 20: 2 Kings 4:8–17; Ps. 139:13–18; Col. 1:21–29; Luke 10:38–42
July 27: 2 Kings 5:1–15ab; Ps. 21:1–7; Col. 2:6–15; Luke 11:1–13
August 3: 2 Kings 13:14–20a; Ps. 28; Col. 3:1–11; Luke 12:13–21
August 10: Jer. 18:1–11; Ps. 14; Heb. 11:1–3, 8:19; Luke 12:32–40
August 17: Jer. 20:7–13; Ps. 10:12–18; Heb. 12:1–2, 12–17; Luke 12:49–56
August 24: Jer. 28:1–9; Ps. 84; Heb. 12:18–29; Luke 13:22–30
August 31: Ezek. 18:1–9, 25–29; Ps. 15; Heb. 13:1–8; Luke 14:1, 7–14
September 7: Ezek. 33:1–11; Ps. 94:12–22; Philem. 1–20; Luke 14:25–33
September 14: Hos. 4:1–3, 5:15–6:6; Ps. 77:11–20; 1 Tim. 1:12–17; Luke 15:1–10
September 21: Hos. 11:1–11; Ps. 107:1–9; 1 Tim. 2:1–7; Luke 16:1–13
September 28: Joel 2:23–30; Ps. 107:1, 33–43; 1 Tim. 6:6–19; Luke 16:19–31
October 5: Amos 5:6–7, 10–15; Ps. 101; 2 Tim. 1:1–14; Luke 17:5–10
October 12: Mic. 1:2; 2:1–10; Ps. 26; 2 Tim. 2:8–15; Luke 17:11–19
October 19: Hab. 1:1–3; 2:1–4; Ps. 119: 137–144; 2 Tim. 3:14–4:5; Luke 18:1–8
October 26: Zeph. 3:1–9; Ps. 3; 2 Tim. 4:6–8, 16–18; Luke 18:9–14
November 2: Hag. 2:1–9; Ps. 65:1–8; 2 Thess. 1:5–12; Luke 19:1–10
November 9: Zech. 7:1–10; Ps. 9:11–20; 2 Thess. 2:13–3:5; Luke 20:27–38
November 16: Mal. 4:1–6; Ps. 82; 2 Thess. 3:6–13; Luke 21:5–19
November 23 (Reformation Sunday): 2 Sam. 5:1–5; Ps. 95; Col. 1:11–20; John 12:9–19

ADVENT

November 30 (Advent): Isa. 2:1–5; Ps. 122; Rom. 13:11–14; Matt. 24:36–44

December 7: Isa. 11:1–10; Ps. 72:1–8;
Rom. 15:4–13; Matt. 3:1–12
December 14: Isa. 35:1–10; Ps. 146:5–10;
Jas. 5:7–10; Matt. 11:2–11
December 21: Isa. 7:10–16; Ps. 24; Rom.
1:1–7; Matt. 1:18–25

CHRISTMAS SEASON

December 25 (Christmas Day): Isa. 9:2–7;
Ps. 96; Tit. 11–14; Luke 2:1–20
December 28: Isa. 63:7–9; Ps. 111; Heb.
2:10–18; Matt. 2:13–15, 19–23

Four-Year Church Calendar

	1986	1987	1988	1989
Ash Wednesday	February 12	March 4	February 17	February 8
Palm Sunday	March 23	April 12	March 27	March 19
Good Friday	March 28	April 17	April 1	March 24
Easter	March 30	April 19	April 3	March 26
Ascension Day	May 8	May 28	May 12	May 4
Pentecost	May 18	June 7	May 22	May 14
Trinity Sunday	May 25	June 14	May 29	May 21
Thanksgiving	November 27	November 26	November 24	November 23
Advent Sunday	November 30	November 29	November 27	December 3

Forty-Year Easter Calendar

1986 March 30	1996 April 7	2006 April 16	2016 March 27
1987 April 19	1997 March 30	2007 April 8	2017 April 16
1988 April 3	1998 April 12	2008 March 23	2018 April 1
1989 March 26	1999 April 4	2009 April 12	2019 April 21
1990 April 15	2000 April 23	2010 April 4	2020 April 12
1991 March 31	2001 April 15	2011 April 24	2021 April 4
1992 April 19	2002 March 31	2012 April 8	2022 April 17
1993 April 11	2003 April 20	2013 March 31	2023 April 9
1994 April 3	2004 April 11	2014 April 20	2024 March 31
1995 April 16	2005 March 27	2015 April 5	2025 April 20

Traditional Wedding Anniversary Identifications

1 Paper	7 Wool	13 Lace	35 Coral
2 Cotton	8 Bronze	14 Ivory	40 Ruby
3 Leather	9 Pottery	15 Crystal	45 Sapphire
4 Linen	10 Tin	20 China	50 Gold
5 Wood	11 Steel	25 Silver	55 Emerald
6 Iron	12 Silk	30 Pearl	60 Diamond

Colors Appropriate for Days and Seasons

White. Symbolizes purity, perfection, and joy and identifies festivals marking events, except Good Friday, in the life of Jesus: Christmas, Easter, Eastertide, Ascension Day, Trinity Sunday, All Saints' Day; weddings, funerals.

Red. Symbolizes the Holy Spirit, martyrdom, and the love of God: Pentecost and Sundays following.

Violet. Symbolizes penitence: Advent, Lent.

Green. Symbolizes mission to the world, hope, regeneration, nurture, and growth: Epiphany season, Kingdomtide, Rural Life Sunday, Labor Sunday, Thanksgiving Sunday.

Black. Symbolizes mourning: Good Friday.

Flowers in Season Appropriate for Church Use

January. Carnation or snowdrop.
February. Violet or primrose.
March. Jonquil or daffodil.

April. Lily, sweet pea, or daisy.
May. Lily of the valley or hawthorn.
June. Rose or honeysuckle.

July.   Larkspur or water lily.
August.   Gladiolus or poppy.
September.   Aster or morning glory.
October.   Calendula or cosmos.

November.   Chrysanthemum.
December.   Narcissus, holly, or poinsettia.

Historical, Cultural, and Religious Anniversaries in 1986

Compiled by Kenneth M. Cox

10 Years (1976). *January 8:* Chou En-lai, premier of the People's Republic of China since its birth in 1949, dies in China. *July 2:* U.S. Supreme Court decides that imposition of the death penalty is constitutional if the underlying statute is not unfairly or arbitrarily applied. *September 9:* Mao Tsetung, founder and pre-eminent leader of the Communist Party of the People's Republic of China, dies in China. *September 30:* California becomes the first state to enact legislation allowing "Living Wills" to authorize physicians to shut off life-support systems.

15 Years (1971). *June 13: New York Times* begins publishing excerpts of the "Pentagon Papers," detailing U.S. involvement in Vietnam from the end of World War II to 1968.

20 Years (1966). *June 13:* U.S. Supreme Court hands down the *Miranda* decision, holding that the Fifth Amendment self-incrimination privilege requires careful police procedures to protect suspects' rights. *July 1:* Medicare health care program for the nation's elderly becomes effective. The Evangelical United Brethren and Methodist churches vote to merge (in 1968) as the United Methodist Church.

25 Years (1961). *March 1:* President Kennedy establishes the Peace Corps, to help improve education, agriculture, and living standards in Latin America, Asia, and Africa. *April 20:* Bay of Pigs invasion. *May:* Federal Communications Commission Chairman Newton Minow refers to U.S. television programming as a "vast wasteland," in an address to the National Association of Broadcasters.

30 Years (1956). *June 29:* Congress passes the Federal Aid for Highways Act, authorizing construction of a 42,500-mile network of roads to link major U.S. cities and leading to growth in the trucking, busing, oil, and automobile industries and to

the decline of American rail transportation. *November 4:* Soviet forces invade Budapest after the Hungarian government renounces the Warsaw Treaty.

40 Years (1946). *January 10:* United Nations General Assembly opens its first session in London, later moving to New York. *July 5:* The bikini swimsuit is introduced at a Paris fashion show.

50 Years (1936). *February 14:* The sit-down strike is pioneered by the United Rubber Workers of America, at a Goodyear tire plant. The Great Purge begins in the Soviet Union as Josef Stalin liquidates political enemies, and will take 8–10 million lives over the next two years. *July:* Jesse Owens captures four gold medals in track and field events at the Berlin Olympics before Adolf Hitler.

75 Years (1911). *May 15, 29:* In separate antitrust rulings, the U.S. Supreme Court breaks up John D. Rockefeller's Standard Oil Company trust and James B. Duke's American Tobacco Company Trust. *October 11:* Revolution begins in China that will end the 267-year Ch'ing dynasty of the Manchus and will propel China into the twentieth century. *December 14:* Norwegian explorer Roald Amundsen arrives at the South Pole.

100 Years (1886). *May 10:* Karl Barth born. *August 20:* Paul Tillich born. *October 28:* Statue of Liberty dedicated in New York Harbor, designed by French sculptor Frederich Auguste Bartholdi and presented by the French people to the people of the United States.

150 Years (1836). *March 6:* The Alamo at San Antonio falls to Santa Anna's army. U.S. religious leader William Miller publishes *Evidence from the Scripture and History of the Second Coming of Christ, About the Year 1843,* a book that will lead to the founding of the Adventist Church in 1845. U.S. clergyman Thomas P. Hunt publishes *The*

Book of Wealth: In Which It Is Proved from the Bible that It Is the Duty of Every Man to Become Rich.

200 Years (1786). *January:* Thomas Jefferson obtains a bill from the Virginia legislature ensuring religious freedom. *September:* Shays' Rebellion in Massachusetts, led by Revolutionary War veteran Daniel Shays, aims to prevent further foreclosure of farms in the country's continuing economic depression.

250 Years (1736). Pope Clement XII condemns Freemasonry. English statutes against witchcraft repealed. James Watt, inventor, born.

300 Years (1686). *July 9:* League of Augsburg, created by treaty, allies European powers against France's Louis XIV.

350 Years (1636). Harvard College has its beginnings in a seminary founded by the Great and General Court of Massachusetts at New Towne, Cambridge. *June:* English clergyman Roger Williams founds Providence, Rhode Island, a colony dedicated to the separation of church and state and to complete religious freedom, selecting the name because of "God's merciful providence" evident in that the Narragansett Indians granted Williams title to the site.

450 Years (1536). *May 19:* England's Henry VIII orders his wife Anne Boleyn executed; he marries Jane Seymour, Anne's lady-in-waiting, the following day. *October 6:* English clergyman William Tyndale burned at the stake near Brussels, after being condemned for heresy. Michelangelo begins painting "The Last Judgment" on the wall of the Sistine Chapel. Erasmus, the Dutch humanist and scholar, dies. Henry VIII of England drafts the Ten Articles setting forth standards of faith for the English church.

500 Years (1486). Girolamo Savonarola, OP, succeeds in prophetic preaching in Italy.

1600 Years (386) St. Jerome begins translation of Bible into Latin.

Anniversaries of Hymns, Hymn Writers, and Hymn-Tune Composers in 1986

Compiled by Hugh T. McElrath

25 years (1961). *Death* of Helen H. Lemmel (b. 1864), author and composer of "Turn your eyes upon Jesus" (LEMMEL); Robert Harkness (b. 1880), author and composer of "Bearing his cross for me," "No longer lonely," "Why should he love me so?" and many other gospel songs.

50 years (1936). *Birth* of William Gaither, author and composer of "Because he lives" (RESURRECTION). *Death* of Peter P. Bilhorn (b. 1865), composer of WONDROUS STORY; Gilbert K. Chesterton (b. 1874), author of "O God of earth and altar"; Percy Dearmer (b. 1867), author of "Book of books our people's strength," 'Jesus, good above all other," 'Sing praise to God who spoke through man" and translator of "Unto us a boy is born" and "Father we praise thee, now the night is over'; James Henry Fillmore (b. 1849), composer of HANNAH ("I know that my Redeemer liveth") and PURER IN HEART ("Purer in heart, O God"); John Alexander Fuller-Maitland (b. 1856), composer of LUCCOMBE ("For all the saints");

Bessie Porter Head (b. 1850), author of "O breath of life"; Lewis Edgar Jones (b. 1865), author of "Would you be free from the burden of sin"; Joseph Rudyard Kipling (b. 1865), author of "Father in heaven, who lovest all" and "God of our fathers, known of old."

75 years (1911). *Birth* of Herman Voss, author and composer of "Jesus, Savior, all I have is thine" (VOSS); Lois Horton Young (d. 1981), author of "Christian men, arise and give." *Death* of Katherine Hankey (b. 1834), author of "I love to tell the story" and "Tell me the old, old story"; James P. Harding (b. 1850), composer of MORNING STAR ("Brightest and best of the sons of the morning"); John Murch Wigner (b. 1844), author of "Come to the Savior now."

100 years (1886). *Birth* of Albert C. Fisher (d. 1946), author and composer of "Love is the theme" (FISHER) and "There's a glad new song" (REDEEMING LOVE); Charles H. Marsh (d. 1956), composer of CHAPMAN ("One day"). *Death* of John W. Hewlett (b. 1824), author of "O

Thou who dost accord us"; Joseph Scriven (b. 1819), author of "What a friend we have in Jesus."

125 years (1861). *Birth* of Katherine Hinkson (d. 1931), author of "I would choose to be a doorkeeper'; John Henry Hopkins (d. 1945), composer of GRAND ISLE ("I sing a song of the saints of God") and WESTERLY ("God the father, God the son"); first edition of *Hymns Ancient and Modern*, one of the most important hymnals of all time. *Death* of William John Hall (b. 1793), joint author of "Blest are the pure in heart"; Francis Vincent Novello, (b. 1781), composer of ALBANO ("Immortal love, forever full").

150 years (1836). *Birth* of Phillip Armes (d. 1908), composer of ARMES ("Soon may the last glad song arise"); Emily Elliott (d. 1897), author of "Thou didst leave thy throne"; William C. Filby (d. 1912), composer of FORTITUDE ("Breast the wave, Christian"); Adoniram J. Gordon (d. 1895), composer of GORDON ("My Jesus, I love thee") and CLARENDON ("In tenderness He sought me"); Washington Gladden (d. 1918), author of "Behold a sower from afar!" and "O Master, let me walk with thee"; Frances Ridley Havergal (d. 1879), author of "I gave my life for thee," "Golden harps are sounding," "Lord speak to me that I may speak," "Like a river glorious," "Take my life and let it be consecrated," and many others; composer of HERMAS ("Welcome, happy morning!"); Leighton George Hayne (d. 1883), composer of BUCKLAND ("Savior, teach me day by day"), CHALVEY ("Jesus, my strength, my hope"), ST. CECILIA ("Thy kingdom come, O God"); Jessie Seymour Irvine (d. 1887) composer of CRIMOND; Rigdon M. McIntosh (d. 1899), arranger of PROMISED LAND; Newton Mann (d. 1926), co-author of "Praise to the living God"; Thomas Pollock (d. 1890), author of "Jesus, with thy church abide," 'Jesus, Son of God most high" and others. *Death* of Johann Georg Nägeli (b. 1773), composer of DENNIS

("Blest be the tie that binds"); John Rippon (b. 1751), probable author of "How firm a foundation" and some stanzas of "All hail the power of Jesus' name"; Alfred Alexander Woodhull (b. 1810), author of "Great God of nations."

175 years (1811). *Birth* of Thomas Helmore (d. 1890), composer/arranger of VENI EMMANUEL and other plainsong tunes; John S. B. Monsell (d. 1875), author of "On our way rejoicing" and "Fight the good fight with all thy might"; William Mercer (d. 1873), translator of "How bright appears the morning star" and others; Rowland Hugh Pritchard (d. 1887), composer of HYFRYDOL; Jane Cross Simpson (d. 1877), author of "Pray when the morning is breaking"; William Hunter (d. 1877), author of "The great physician now is here." *Death* of John Antes (b. 1740), composer of MONKLAND and other tunes.

200 years (1786). *Birth* of Conrad Kocher (d. 1872), composer of DIX ("As with gladness men of old"); William Lloyd (d. 1852), composer of MEIRIONYDD ("For thee, o dear, dear country"). *Death* of John Francis Wade (b. 1710), author and composer of "O come, all ye faithful" (ADESTE FIDELIS).

225 years (1761). *Birth* of John Andrew Stevenson (d. 1883), arranger of VESPER HYMN ("Now on sea and land descending"); Joseph Swain (d. 1796), author of "O Thou, in whose presence." *Death* of Johann Ludwig Steiner (b. 1688), composer of STEINER ("O most mighty! O most holy!").

275 years (1711). *Death* of Thomas Ken (b. 1637), author of "Awake, my soul and with the sun," 'All praise to thee, my God, this night." The last stanza of both hymns is the familiar doxology, "Praise God from whom all blessings flow."

375 years (1611). *Birth* of Johannes Olerius (d. 1684), author of "Comfort, comfort ye my people."

1525 years (461). *Death* of St. Patrick (b. 389), author of "I bind unto myself today."

Quotable Quotations

1. To pay a lifelong regret for an hour's pleasure is a fool's bargain.—E. Stanley Jones.

2. Everything is funny as long as it is happening to somebody else.—Will Rogers.

3. Without miracles our prayers would simply become meaningless.—Helmut Thielicke.

4. Whether to the adoring eye of faith, the raised eyebrow of unbelief, or the scholar's lowered eyelash, the Bible remains to the imagination the most astonishing book in the world.—Geddes MacGregor.

5. I would agree that the Bible contains all the answers, at least all the significant ones. But the Bible is something like a mirror. If an ass peers in, you can't expect an apostle to peer out.—William Sloane Coffin.

6. Truth often enters by an unused, half-hidden door.—James W. Cox.

7. Christianity knows no truth which is not the child of love and the parent of duty.—Phillips Brooks.

8. No man can have a religion that elevates the secular unless within him there is a sanctuary pure and undefiled.—Harry Emerson Fosdick.

9. Belief in a cruel God makes a cruel man.—Thomas Paine.

10. The Golden Rule of itself is a dark burden which no man can bear, until Christ gathers it in grace.—George A. Buttrick.

11. The real heresies that damn a soul are not stumbles among the intellectual subtleties of theology, but to be fretful and pusillanimous under the blows of fate and the sore discipline of things.—Arthur John Gossip.

12. True faith is a very simple thing. It is believing God's Word and acting upon it.—Donald Grey Barnhouse.

13. Each time the child throws its toy out of its baby carriage it disturbs the motion of every star.—Sir James Jeans.

14. Where all think alike, no one thinks very much.—Walter Lippmann.

15. I can't believe that God plays dice with the universe.—Albert Einstein.

16. Where the Scripture is silent, the church is my text.—Thomas Browne.

17. Do not give as many rich men do, like a hen that lays her egg and then cackles.—Henry Ward Beecher.

18. We must not tie a ship to a single anchor, or life to a single hope.—Epictetus.

19. Fame usually comes to those who are thinking about something else.—Oliver Wendell Holmes, Jr.

20. In the final analysis, the question of why bad things happen to good people translates itself into some very different questions, no longer asking why something happened, but asking how we will respond, what we intend to do now that it has happened.—Harold S. Kushner.

21. The mill cannot grind with water that's past.—George Herbert.

22. Whereas most men are held back by laziness, what blocks most women is lack of confidence.—Alex Osborn.

23. The creeds of the Church are like frozen foods. They are neither palatable nor digestible until they are thawed out.—James T. Cleland.

24. When man comes to himself, he knows that evil is a foreign invader that must be driven from the native soils of his soul before he can achieve moral and spiritual dignity.—Martin Luther King, Jr.

25. Three-fourths of the people you will meet tomorrow are hungering and thirsting for sympathy. Give it to them and they will love you.—Dale Carnegie.

26. Words link together all human activities, and form a connecting bond in every human situation.—Stuart Chase.

27. Nowhere in life is the power of faith more apparent than in its capacity to make man face any experience, no matter what, with the hope that out of it some real good can come.—Daniel Day Williams.

28. There is in man a higher than love of happiness: He can do without happiness, and instead thereof find blessedness.—Thomas Carlyle.

29. Believe nothing against another but upon good authority. Nor report what may hurt another, unless it be a greater hurt to others to conceal it.—William Penn.

30. When you postpone an activity, you increase the chances of never accomplishing it, and you will be left in the future, with memories of past wishes rather than of past deeds.—Ari Kiev.

31. The man who has no inner life is the slave of his surroundings.—Henri Frédéric Amiel.

32. People who do the most seem to be least aware of it.—Gerald Kennedy.

33. The beginning of the Christian life is getting up, as you are, with your doubts and with your sins, and following Jesus; looking to Him; praying to Him, and trying to imagine how He would react to the circumstances in which you are troubled.—Donald Soper.

34. There never was a more dangerous weapon of self-destruction put into a child's hands than money.—Sam P. Jones.

35. Most men and women do not live by their arguments, but by their commitments.—Theodore Parker Ferris.

36. Since *every thought* is creative, we are creators of the world—we, along with God.—Frank C. Laubach.

37. Of nothing may we be more sure than this, that, if we cannot sanctify our present lot, we could sanctify no other.—James Martineau.

38. One cannot make just certain things a matter of conscience; either one must make everything that, as Christianity does, or nothing at all.—Søren Kierkegaard.

39. Denominationalism is always a curse when it lifts the denomination above the church universal.—Charles E. Jefferson.

40. If your head is wax, don't walk in the sun.—Benjamin Franklin.

41. Scarred men come for healing only to scarred Hands! Only a Risen Jesus with scars can understand our hearts.—Fulton J. Sheen.

42. Nowhere does one learn so well how to have faith as in the chambers of those who have known adversity—the sick, the poor, and the burdened.—Eduard Schweizer.

43. All human history as described in the Bible may be summarized in one phrase, God in Search of Man.—Abraham Joshua Heschel.

44. When one looks out on the community the test of our religion is not as much what happens inside the churches as what happens to the total life of the neighborhood.—Harry Emerson Fosdick.

45. Personal survival is a valid conclusion because it makes more sense than does its alternative, the alternative of a world of meaning which becomes meaningless at the end.—D. Elton Trueblood.

46. He who has no vision of eternity has no hold on time.—Thomas Carlyle.

47. Any theory that little by little we are approaching the brotherhood of man has to reckon that it was out of the Germany of Goethe and Brahms and Tillich that Dachau and Belsen came and that it is out of our own culture that the weapons of doom have come and the burning children.—Frederick Buechner.

48. God is certainly personal, but whether he wishes to be so in relation to the individual depends upon whether it so pleases God.—Søren Kierkegaard.

49. My memory is nearly gone, but I remember two things, that I am a great sinner, and that Christ is a great Savior.—John Newton at age eighty-two.

50. A moment's insight is sometimes worth a life's experience.—Oliver Wendell Holmes.

51. I despise theology and botany, but I love religion and flowers.—Sam P. Jones.

52. Injustice is relatively easy to bear; what stings is justice.—H. L. Mencken.

53. Properly understood, every man who truthfully desires a relation to God and to live in his sight has only one task: always to be joyful.—Søren Kierkegaard.

54. Wonder is the basis of worship.—Thomas Carlyle.

55. Faith is response. It is the wholesouled giving of life into the keeping of God who is the absolutely trustworthy source and redeemer of life.—Daniel Day Williams.

56. A man cannot speak but he judges himself. With his will, or against his will, he draws his portrait to the eye of his companions by every word.—Ralph Waldo Emerson.

57. Remember, no one can make you feel inferior without your consent.—Eleanor Roosevelt.

58. Our relationship is to a Person and not to a historical event. The event is our assurance that the Person can save.—G. Earl Guinn.

59. To be trusted is a greater compliment than to be loved.—George Macdonald.

60. God's call to obedience can be heard above the tumult, above the bands, and above the flag waving.—Clarence Jordan.

61. If anything pleasant happens to us, like peace of mind, or heaven itself, it will have to happen along the way to "the least of these" his brethren!—Paul Scherer.

62. Christ came to save and sanctify our humanity—not to make us quaint and queer.—W. E. Sangster.

63. Human beings have been most active and creative where they have believed in an active and creative God.—David H. C. Read.

64. You can never make anything out of yourself until you get a few explosions into the mixing chamber of your life: crises, difficulties, hardships, pain, suffering, opposition.—Norman Vincent Peale.

65. Nature is the living, visible garment of God.—Johann Wolfgang von Goethe.

66. Religious experience comes to us as an event that claims our entire life, by restructuring its meaning and committing us to the service of God in relation to our social world and to all mankind.—Wolfhart Pannenberg.

67. The vision of God in Christ is most vividly real in the sufferings of human personalities about us.—Wayne E. Oates.

68. To be great is to be misunderstood. —Ralph Waldo Emerson.

69. The world is God's workshop for making men.—Henry Ward Beecher.

70. The first test of a truly great man is his humility.—John Ruskin.

71. When one door of happiness closes, another opens; but often we look so long at the closed door that we do not see the one which has been opened for us.—Helen Keller.

72. It is easier to do your duty than it is to find a lie that will answer for an excuse. —Sam P. Jones.

73. Who is Jesus Christ? He is the man in whom God has not only expressed his love, not only painted it on the wall, but put it to work.—Karl Barth.

74. God in heaven, let me really feel my nothingness, not in order to despair over it, but in order to feel the more powerfully the greatness of thy goodness.—Søren Kierkegaard.

75. The Marxist finds himself in real agreement with the Christian in those two beliefs which Christianity paradoxically demands—that poverty is blessed and yet ought to be removed.—C. S. Lewis.

76. He who gives alms in secret is greater than Moses.—The Talmud.

77. In life situations involving other people, the only predictable outcome is likely to be that the unexpected will happen.—Gerard I. Nierenberg.

78. It is easy enough to believe in "a God" providing we do not much care what kind.—D. Elton Trueblood.

79. When a man comes to God, it were as if he looked from the other side of the sky, seeing the same things from another standpoint.—William M. Macgregor.

80. He who does not find little enough will find nothing enough.—Epicurus.

81. When I dig a man out of trouble, the hole that he leaves behind him is the grave where I bury my own trouble.—Henry Ward Beecher.

82. I shall pass through this world but once. Any good thing, therefore, that I can do, or any kindness that I can show to any human being, let me do it now. Let me not defer it or neglect it, for I shall not pass this way again.—Henry Drummond.

83. In war the worst men have a free hand.—Plotinus.

84. One of the lessons of history is that nothing is often a good thing to do and always a clever thing to say.—Will Durant.

85. Enjoy this world responsibly, for though you will live eternally you can never enjoy it the same way again.—James W. Cox.

86. When you are arguing against Him, you're arguing against the very power that makes you able to argue at all: It's like cutting off the branch you're sitting on.—C. S. Lewis.

87. Because a minister is free it does not follow that he has a right to proclaim from the pulpit everything he reads or everything which he happens to be thinking.—Charles E. Jefferson.

88. The transcendent difference in Christ from all who came before Him is summed up in this magic word, fulfillment. —J. Wallace Hamilton.

89. Whenever you find a man who says he doesn't believe in a real Right and Wrong, you will find the same man going back on this a moment later.—C. S. Lewis.

90. Christianity promises to make men free; it never promises to make them independent.—W. R. Inge.

91. Asking God to make you "a better Christian" by taking away your temper is like trying to make a better watch by leaving out its works.—J. Wallace Hamilton.

92. The man who bows down to nothing cannot bear the burden of himself.—Dostoievsky.

93. The only way I get at the mystery of providence is to enter into a personal relationship with him who "provides."—Helmut Thielicke.

94. If you tell the truth you don't have to remember anything.—Mark Twain.

95. No one could ever have found God; he gave himself away.—Meister Eckhart.

96. The reason for the unattractiveness of Jesus is not primarily found in him, but in his followers. It is we, who bear the name of Christian, who are in the main responsible for his rejection.—James T. Cleland.

97. What is hateful to you, do not to your fellowman. That is the entire Law; all the rest is commentary.—*The Talmud.*

98. Only the man who doubts can believe and only the man who believes can doubt.—Ernest T. Campbell.

99. Never try to reason the prejudice out of a man. It was not reasoned into him, and cannot be reasoned out.—Sydney Smith.

100. Nothing a man does takes him lower than when he allows himself to fall so low as to hate anyone.—Martin Luther King, Sr.

Questions of Life and Religion

These questions may be useful to prime homiletic pumps, as discussion starters, or for study and youth groups.

1. Should preachers read their sermons or preach without notes?

2. What is meant by the statement that Christians should be in the world, but not *of* the world?

3. Should the Bible be treated as a historical document or changed to meet perceived needs of our present world (e.g., inclusive language)?

4. When might abortion be justified?

5. Should a minister speak to issues that are primarily political?

6. Should the government be allowed to display Christian symbols on government property?

7. How can one keep one's friends while refusing to yield to peer pressure?

8. Is participation in the political process a Christian duty?

9. Is Jesus Christ more a king or a brother?

10. Will God always give us everything we ask in prayer?

11. Can we justify living above the bare necessities while millions starve?

12. Should we always make restitution for wrongs done?

13. What are the three most important things to pray for?

14. Is faith ever just wishful thinking?

15. What can personal experience tell us about God?

16. Why does God let people suffer?

17. Does harsh discipline make children better?

18. Where is heaven?

19. Is one way of worship as good as another?

20. What is the Christian's responsibility toward lower forms of life.

21. Is it mentally healthful to review one's sins?

22. Are love and justice ever contradictory?

23. How can we make holidays more bearable for lonely people?

24. What can we do to improve our devotional life?

25. How can our giving at Christmas be made more Christian?

26. In the scheme of things, is there always compensation for pain and suffering?

27. How are the sins of Christians related to their salvation?

28. How can we get rid of bad habits?

29. What are we to make of near-death experiences and reports of the life to come?

30. Can prayer make a decisive difference in physical healing?

31. What can we do to find the will of God?

32. How can we appropriately observe Lent?

33. Is premarital sex a moral issue?

34. What can we do to get unbelievers to share our faith?

35. Should the church's moneys be spent on expensive buildings and programs or used more directly to help the needy?

36. Why are religious symbols important?

37. What should happen in us when we take part in Holy Communion?

38. Does the kind of television and movies that we see affect our moral values?

39. What place does humor have in life?

40. How do heroes contribute to moral character and personal achievement?

41. What role can a significant adult (other than a parent) play in the life of a child?

42. In what ways does music contribute to our worship of God?

43. How seriously should we take tradition in the practice of our faith?

44. What do we mean by "the sinlessness of Jesus Christ"?

45. Should there be a dress code for Christians?

46. How should the idea of the body as the temple of the Holy Spirit influence what and how much we eat and drink?

47. What should be our attitude toward people who have sinned greatly?

48. Are there Christian standards of courtesy?

49. Will Christian love balance the books of ethical behavior?

50. In what sense is suffering the will of God?

51. Is beauty a friend or foe of moral goodness?

52. How can we know when God is calling us to special religious vocations?

53. Is a daily prayer time possible or practical for a modern Christian family?

54. What is the meaning of the incarnation?

55. Why did Jesus often speak in parables?

56. What is the best way to read the Bible?

57. How can the Holy Spirit help us to understand the Bible?

58. What help besides the Holy Spirit do we need to interpret the Scriptures?

59. Should we try to convert to Christianity people of a different religion who practice their faith sincerely?

60. What makes Christianity unique among the world faiths?

61. Are science and religion enemies?

62. Does God, as he is pictured in the Bible, ever seem to act like a mother?

63. What are we to make of Christians who backslide from their early promise and commitments?

64. Is the numerical success of a church a sign of God's favor?

65. How can we overcome temptation?

66. What are the values of a positive mental attitude?

67. How far should we rely on our own private judgment in religious matters?

68. Self-defense is called a "manly art," but is it Christian?

69. Is it possible to be happy all the time?

70. Is it always right to obey one's parents?

71. Who are the persons of recent times who can be fairly compared to the ancient prophets?

72. Should the church involve itself in politics?

73. What can young people do to increase the happiness of the elderly and handicapped?

74. What, to you, are the most important verses of the Bible?

75. Does self-esteem contradict what the Bible teaches on humility?

76. Is nuclear power an evil?

77. How should a church deal with difficult people?

78. Is anger appropriate to Christians?

79. How can we learn to say no?

80. Should we accept people as they are?

81. What ought to be the most "magnificent obsession" for a Christian?

82. Can a person achieve *anything* by trying hard enough?

83. Is the amassing of wealth by an individual a social good?

84. Can people really be changed?

~~5~~. Can parents love their children too much?

86. How much can we know about God?
87. When is fasting appropriate?
88. What does nature tell us about God?
89. What is the purpose of baptism?
90. When should a person confess his or her sins publicly?
91. When should we seek help with our problems?
92. What is freedom?
93. Can we do too much for people?
94. What guidelines should we follow when talking about other people?

95. Is the universe and all things in it the same as God?
96. Can people become "too smart"?
97. What is the most important thing that a local congregation can do to fulfill its ministry?
98. How important are the festivals of the Christian year—such as Lent and Easter, Advent and Christmas—in our worship and living?
99. How can our children cope with the current menace of drugs?
100. How should a Christian spend the Lord's Day?

Biblical Benedictions and Blessings

The Lord watch between me and thee, when we are absent from one another.—Gen. 31:49.

The Lord bless thee, and keep thee; the Lord make his face to shine upon thee, and be gracious unto thee; the Lord lift up his countenance upon thee, and give thee peace.—Num. 6:24–26.

The Lord our God be with us, as he was with our fathers; let him not leave us, nor forsake us; that he may incline our hearts unto him, to walk in all his ways, and to keep his commandments, and his statutes, and his judgments, which he commanded our fathers.—1 Kings 8:57–58.

Let the words of my mouth, and the meditation of my heart, be acceptable in thy sight, O Lord, my strength, and my redeemer.—Ps. 19:14.

Now the God of patience and consolation grant you to be likeminded one toward another according to Christ Jesus; that ye may with one mind and one mouth glorify God, even the Father of our Lord Jesus Christ. Now the God of hope fill you with all joy and peace in believing, that ye may abound in hope, through the power of the Holy Ghost. Now the God of peace be with you all.—Rom. 15:5–6, 13, 33.

Now to him that is of power to establish you according to my gospel, and the preaching of Jesus Christ, according to the revelation of the mystery, which was kept secret since the world began, but now is manifest, and by the scriptures of the prophets, according to the commandment of the everlasting God, made known to all nations for the obedience of faith: to God only wise, be glory through Jesus Christ for ever.—Rom. 16:25–27.

Grace be unto you, and peace, from God our Father, and from the Lord Jesus Christ.—1 Cor. 1:3.

The grace of the Lord Jesus Christ and the love of God, and the communion of the Holy Ghost, be with you all.—2 Cor. 13:14.

Peace be to the brethren, and love with faith, from God the Father and the Lord Jesus Christ. Grace be with all them that love our Lord Jesus Christ in sincerity.—Eph. 6:23–24.

And the peace of God, which passeth all understanding, shall keep your hearts and minds through Christ Jesus. Finally, brethren, whatsoever things are true, whatsoever things are honest, whatsoever things are just, whatsoever things are pure, whatsoever things are lovely, whatsoever things are of good report; if there be any virtue, and if there be any praise, think on these things. Those things, which ye have both learned, and received, and heard, and seen in me, do: and the God of peace shall be with you.—Phil. 4:7–9.

Wherefore also we pray always for you, that our God would count you worthy of this calling, and fulfill all the good pleasure of his goodness, and the work of faith with power: that the name of our Lord Jesus Christ may be glorified in you, and ye in him, according to the grace of our God and the Lord Jesus Christ.—2 Thess. 1:11–12.

Now the Lord of peace himself give you peace always by all means. The Lord be with you all. The grace of our Lord Jesus Christ be with you all.—2 Thess. 3:16–18.

Grace, mercy, and peace, from God our Father and Jesus Christ our Lord.—1 Tim. 1:2.

Now the God of peace, that brought again from the dead our Lord Jesus, that great shepherd of the sheep, through the blood of the everlasting covenant, make you perfect in every good work to do his will, working in you that which is well-pleasing in his sight, through Jesus Christ, to whom be glory for ever and ever.—Heb. 13:20–21.

The God of all grace, who hath called us unto his eternal glory by Christ Jesus, after that ye have suffered a while, make you perfect, establish, strengthen, settle you. To him be glory and dominion for ever and ever. Greet ye one another with a kiss of charity. Peace be with you all that are in Christ Jesus.—1 Pet. 5:10–11, 14.

Grace be with you, mercy, and peace, from God the Father, and from the Lord Jesus Christ, the Son of the Father, in truth and love.—2 John 3.

Now unto him that is able to keep you from falling, and to present you faultless before the presence of his glory with exceeding joy, to the only wise God our Savior, be glory and majesty, dominion and power, both now and ever.—Jude 2:24–25.

Grace be unto you, and peace, from him which was, and which is to come; and from the seven Spirits which are before his throne; and from Jesus Christ, who is the faithful witness, and the first begotten of the dead, and the prince of the kings of the earth. Unto him that loved us, and washed us from our sins in his own blood, and hath made us kings and priests unto God and his Father; to him be glory and dominion for ever and ever.—Rev. 1:4–6.

SECTION II.
Vital Themes for Vital Preaching

January 5 (Epiphany Sunday). A Motive for Contentment
TEXT: Heb. 13:5.
These most gracious words—
I. Lead us to live above visible things when we have stores in hand.
II. Lead us to present satisfaction however low our stores may be.
III. Lead us to see provision for all future emergencies.
IV. Lead us into a security more satisfactory, sure, ennobling, and divine than all wealth could bestow.
V. Lead us to reckon discontent a kind of blasphemy of God.—Charles Haddon Spurgeon.

January 12. The Dawn of a New Day
TEXT: Mark 1:1–11.
In his first public appearance, Jesus shattered prevailing expectations and inaugurated a radical new approach to the fulfillment of his task.
I. *The setting*.
(a) In John, the voice of prophecy silent for centuries rang out again in trumpet tones. Those who accepted this message submitted to baptism as a concrete expression of their new commitment. For them, John's baptism was a dramatic demonstration of repentance, an outward confession of apostasy, and a symbolic preparation for the day of redemption about to dawn.
(b) By this means, John sought to create a New Israel fit for the New Age.
(c) Jesus recognized in John the messianic herald who had come to prepare the royal way.
(d) Since Jesus clearly had not come to John as a repentant sinner, he must have come in the knowledge that he was destined to play a pivotal part in those climactic events that had now been set in motion. The Bible never says for us to be baptized either because Jesus was baptized or in the same way that he was baptized. Far from being an example to us, the baptism of Jesus seems to be totally different from the baptism that we experience. If, like the converts of John, we will turn in revulsion from our iniquity, if we will acknowledge our destitution and confess our helplessness, if we will at last go down in hope to the waters of baptism, then lo!—we will find that the Christ is there beside us! Some may look for the King in Jerusalem, but they will find him in Jordan. "A broken and a contrite heart, O God, thou wilt not despise" (Ps. 51:17). The message of Christ's baptism is that he repents and confesses and hopes *with* us and *for* us, not out of any inward need on his part but as an act of sheer grace on our behalf.
II. *The situation*. In his baptism, Jesus received divine confirmation of his strategy for delivering the wayward heart from sin. This is seen in the baptismal experience itself.
(a) The account is tersely told (v. 10), but each detail is important.
(1) "He came up out of the water" means that Jesus had now left the wilderness behind to pass through Jordan and so

16

enter the Promised Land. He had crossed his Rubicon to stand in the new age of fulfillment.

(2) The "heavens opened" suggests that in this crisis Jesus experienced an immediate and direct revelation from God.

(3) The "Spirit descending" echoes verse 8 and so indicates that Jesus will fulfill John's eager expectation of one who would "baptize with the Holy Spirit."

(b) From this point forward, he was in public view challenging all who would follow him to conquer the inner Promised Land of the human heart long ruled by Satan.

(1) The radical originality of Jesus' strategy may be glimpsed by comparing it with that of John's. John was the grim Puritan of Judaism: austere, challenging, and severe.

(2) In place of John's denunciations, Jesus set the good news of life changed from within.

III. *The significance*.

(a) The central clue to Jesus' revolutionary understanding of his mission is found in the voice from the opened heavens (v. 11). Jesus framed his impressions of God's guidance in two choice Old Testament phrases. The first quotation from Psalm 2:7, "Thou art my beloved Son," is the coronation formula of the King. The words convey God's unshakable decree that his Son shall reign in triumph and glory. The concluding quotation from Isaiah 42:1, "with thee I am well pleased," is the ordaining formula of the Servant who is sent forth to establish justice in the earth even at the cost of suffering.

(b) This combination of texts must mean that in his baptismal experience God authenticated and confirmed Jesus' growing conviction that he had been anointed as King-Messiah and Suffering Servant. This inevitably meant that, in a world of sin, his only throne would be a cross.

(c) For us, the paradox of victory-in-defeat means that we must decide whether to approve one rejected on earth but approved in heaven, one crucified in time but triumphant in eternity. In other words, as Suffering Servant, Jesus forces us to decide for or against him, not on the basis of what he has to offer, but entirely

on the basis that God has declared him to be his beloved Son, King of Kings and Lord of Lords.—William E. Hull.

January 19. Deals or Ideals?

TEXT: Matt. 4:1–11.

Because the temptations are of such pivotal importance, they are placed at the beginning of Jesus' ministry like a table of contents to all of the decisions that he made, the miracles that he worked, and the teachings that he uttered. They become for us a revealing interpretation of the man and his ministry. Because they identify the insights that Jesus determined to employ in the discharge of his messianic duties, they are of surpassing importance in guiding the formulation of a Christian strategy in our day.

I. *The first temptation* (vv. 3–4). Jesus renounced the terrible tyranny of things and refused to forsake the Cross for a bake shop. To him, the Kingdom of God could not be ordered out of a catalog, but rather must be sought for its own sake. He would live by the words proceeding from the mouth of God such as he had heard at his baptism, and he would call others to do the same, trusting God for the rest.

II. *The second temptation* (vv. 5–7). To coerce a response by spectacle, to prove his claims by cunning—these were unworthy ways to establish the sovereignty of God. Jesus did "come suddenly to the Temple" (Mal. 3:1) on another occasion, but it was not from the pinnacle of Mount Zion where all might behold his greatness, but rather from the Mount of Olives where he descended meek and lowly (Matt. 21:5). He did confront the Temple leaders, not on the clouds with attending angels, but on an ass with perplexed disciples. By this strange strategy, he invited us to learn of God, not as a result of sham and show, but rather as a result of his sacrificial service.

III. *The third temptation* (vv. 8–10). History renders a verdict on the choices that Jesus faced here at the outset of his ministry. For Judaism did decide to respond to Rome with a sword, and in less than forty years its nation and Temple were reduced to utter ruin, never to be rebuilt for two thousand years. Following the lead of their Master, by contrast, Christians decided to respond to Rome with a cross. The strategy was much slower and at first seemed more painful, but in less than three hundred years it had won the allegiance of the Empire and forged a whole new civilization that endures to this day. The way of the cross always seems to be a strategy of weakness but it possesses a power that the sword cannot confer.

IV. *His temptations and ours.* For Jesus, then, these were the temptations of inadequate messiahship. In each case, he was tempted to do a good thing, but in so doing to meet the deepest needs of humanity on too shallow a level. Thus he determined to give people, not what they thought they wanted, but rather what he knew they needed. And what of today? If we cannot seduce the loyalties of the masses by offering them bountiful prosperity or protective providence or worldly popularity, then how will they be won? There is only one way, and it is the way of Christ. It is the way of lowly service. It is the way of the cross.—William E. Hull.

January 26. The Three Good Cheers of Jesus

TEXT: Matt. 9:2; 14:27; John 16:33.

Christianity could never fulfill its claim of being the gospel for the whole world if it did not have in it this dominant element of good cheer. There is something very significant in the three occasions in the story of the life of Jesus in which he used this happy phrase, "Be of good cheer."

I. The good cheer of *forgiveness*.

(a) A sick man had been brought to Christ by four friends. It would seem quite probable that the man's sickness was directly caused by his sins.

(b) Notice how tender and generous and greathearted is the forgiveness of Christ.

(c) Christ has not lost his cheerfulness in dealing with sinners. Sin makes a man believe that he is too bad to be saved. But Jesus is ready to say, "Son, be of good cheer; thy sins be forgiven thee."

II. The second good cheer is connected with trouble and danger. It was the night when the disciples were out on the lake in the storm. In the hour of their danger he appeared.

(a) Christ has not deserted his world but is still watching over his disciples, ready to help and to save them from shipwreck. It is the great things, the spiritual realities that center in Christ, which alone can give us the support and good cheer that we need in the great emergencies and storms of life.

(b) The message of the voice depends upon its effects on the soul of the one to whom it comes. There is no voice so full of good cheer as that of Christ if we have once given our heart's affection to him.

III. The last good cheer Jesus uttered was in one of the closing conversations with his disciples, when they were very lonely and sad. The world seemed so large and they were so small; it was so strong and they were so weak. He assured them of his own triumph over the world, and that in the same faith and spirit they, too, would conquer.—Louis Albert Banks.

February 2. At Wit's End

TEXT: Ps. 107.

Have you ever lost your way, felt trapped, been ill and unsure of recovery, or in a storm at sea with survival uncertain? Then there is a word from the Lord for you in Psalm 107. "Earth hath no sorrow, that heaven cannot heal."

The first three verses are an invitation to praise by the "redeemed of the Lord." Four human dilemmas follow, each with a trumpet note refrain: "Let them thank the Lord for his steadfast love, for his wonderful works to the souls of men." God's steadfast love is unchanging, unlimited, and undeserved.

I. *The traveler* (vv. 4–7). This pilgrim was lost in the desert, wandering aimlessly. He cried to the Lord for guidance. Note the refrain (v. 8).

II. *The prisoner* (vv. 10–14). Perhaps he was shut up in the prison house of sin, or trapped by circumstances. He, too, cried to the Lord and was delivered. Jesus is the Liberator of sinners and the oppressed. The refrain is found in verse 15.

III. *Those who are ill* (vv. 17–20). The illness may be physical or emotional. In response to the psalmist's cry, God heals him. (The refrain is in verse 21.)

IV. *The sailor* (vv. 23–30). Note the vivid

phrase, "his courage melted" (RSV). When he cried for help, God became his pilot, bringing him to safety. When we are at wit's end, we should think, seek counsel, give the situation some time, and pray for the Father's help. Sooner or later we will all experience life at the breaking point (see 2 Cor. 4:8–9). Those who trust in God find his grace sufficient.—Alton H. McEachern.

February 9. The Christian Lover
TEXT: 1 Cor. 13:1–13.
I. *Love is essential* (v. 1–3).
(a) Love is essential in all our *relationships*.
(1) The home needs love as never before.
(2) The businesses—work place—need love.
(3) The social relationships of life need love.
(4) The church needs love.
(b) Love is essential is our *lives*.
(1) Without love words ring hollow (v. 1).
(2) Without love spiritual gifts are useless (v. 2).
(3) Without love sacrifice is meaningless (v. 3).
II. *Love is the energized activity of the Holy Spirit* (v. 4–7).
(a) Love does not bear the fruits of evil (cf. Gal. 5:19–20).
(1) Jealousy.
(2) Boasting.
(3) Arrogance.
(4) Rudeness.
(5) Self-seeking.
(6) Easily angered.
(7) Keeping a record of wrongs.
(8) Delighting in evil.
(b) Love is bearing the fruit of the Spirit (cf. Gal. 5:22–23).
(1) Delights in the truth.
(2) Protects.
(3) Trusts.
(4) Hopes.
(5) Perseveres.
(6) Is patient.
(7) Is kind.
III. *Love is eternal* (v. 7–13).
(a) Love is eternal because *God is love*.
(1) 1 John 4:8 "The one who does not

love does not know God, for God is love."
(2) God is "from everlasting to everlasting" (Ps. 90:2).
(3) Therefore love is eternal as a chracteristic of God.
(b) "Love never fails" (v. 8).
(1) Love never fails to meet the need of the other person.
(2) Love never fails to meet my own personal need.
(3) Love never fails because love is the fruit of the Spirit of Jesus Christ.
(c) Love is the *greatest* of the *three eternals* of the Christian faith.
(1) *Faith*, total trust in God, will abide forever.
(2) *Hope*, the anticipation of the future through Christ, abides forever.
(3) *Love*, the full realization of the incarnated Spirit of God, surpasses all.—Robert U. Ferguson.

February 16 (Lent). Lessons for the Tempted
TEXT: 1 Cor. 10:12, 13.
I. We recognize here that God suffers us to be tempted.
(a) God permits evils of which he is not the author. A man may put a great charge of powder into a gun for the purpose of ascertaining whether it is strong and can stand the test, or he may do it for the purpose of ascertaining whether it is weak, for the purpose of destroying it. So human character may be tested with friendly feelings, to try its strength, or with hostile feelings, in order to show its weakness and to destroy it. In the bad sense of the term God tempts nobody, but he suffers us to be tempted.
(b) Temptation is one of the conditions of existence in this world.
(c) Temptation is a discipline.
II. We should be afraid of temptation. There are two forms of peril against which we need to caution ourselves.
(a) It is a perilous thing to question the reality and the power of temptation.
(b) It is peculiarly perilous that we should feel a self-confident presumption that we can overcome it.
III. We must not excuse ourselves when we are tempted.
(a) We must not excuse ourselves with

the idea that it is impossible to resist temptation. Temptation becomes temptation to us only as something within us rises up to meet the allurement from without. The power from without may be mighty, and yet the man is a free man and yields to temptation only when something within him goes forth to meet that which comes from without.

(b) Again, we must not excuse ourselves as we are so often inclined to do, with the idea that our temptations are very peculiar. Of course, particular forms of temptation are mightier to one person and less mighty to another. But take the sum total, and if we saw things as the high angels see them, if we saw things as God sees them, we should never delude ourselves with that dream.

IV. Now, finally, trusting in God, we can conquer temptation. For God will help us, the text implies, both by his providence and by his grace.

(a) If you have advanced far enough in life to see the meaning of your past life, can you not look back and see how, when God's providence brought you into temptation, there has also been provided the way of escape? That is what the text implies that he will do for us if we trust in him, the faithful God.

(b) Not only by his providence but by his grace, God will help us in our temptation. If strengthened by God's grace, if filled with a hatred, a mortal hatred of sin, we struggle against it, then we shall trample temptation underfoot. We shall know the discipline of character that comes from temptation conquered.—John A. Broadus.

February 23 (Lent). Christ and His Compassion

TEXT: Matt. 9:32–38.

I. *His attitudes were all molded by divine compassion.*

(a) He compassionately described the ruin of all sinners.

(b) He compassionately desired the redemption of all sinners.

(c) He compassionately demanded the repentance of all sinners.

II. *His actions were all motivated by driving compassion.*

(a) He was compassionate in dealing with all sinners.

(b) He was compassionate in dying for all sinners.

III. *His appeals were all made from deep compassion.*

(a) Christ compassionately appealed to all who were tired.

(b) Christ compassionately appeared to all who were tired.

(c) Christ compassionately appealed to all who were thirsty.—George W. Lockaby.

March 2 (Lent). The Good-for-Nothing Christian

TEXT: 1 Cor. 1:26–31.

I. Paul begins with an accurate description of the Corinthians before their conversion (v. 26).

(a) "Not many wise" indicates their low education level.

(b) "Not many mighty" indicates their lack of real power.

(c) "Not many noble" indicates their lack of social status.

(d) Paul continues with a negative assessment of their status.

(1) Foolish and weak (v. 27).

(2) Base, despised, and "non-existent" (v. 28).

(e) Is it any wonder that the Corinthians had a problem with insecurity?

II. The Corinthians tried to solve their problem through a false estimate of their talents and gifts.

(a) Imagined themselves to be "wiser" than others.

(b) Imagined themselves to have more "spiritual power" because of their gift of tongues.

(c) Imagined their calling to be to a position of prominence rather than a position of service.

III. Often Christians will go to the opposite direction in an attempt to avoid the Corinthian error of false evaluation.

(a) Some will overemphasize their lack of talent and gifts.

(b) Some will deny any positive self-esteeem on the grounds that it is egotism.

(c) This attitude fails to understand the nature of the healthy personality.

(1) Mankind must learn to trust.

(2) Mankind must love and be loved.

(3) Mankind must perceive itself to be of value and dignity.

(4) Mankind must have an optimistic, hopeful outlook on life.

(d) From whence does this healthy personality emerge, given the brokenness so portrayed in verses 26–28?

IV. God through Jesus Christ gives to us the elements of a healthy personality and self-image (v. 30).

(a) In becoming our *wisdom*, Jesus Christ gives us *self-confidence*.

(b) In becoming our *righteousness* and *sanctification*, Jesus Christ gives us *self-esteem*.

(c) In becoming our *redemption*, Jesus Christ gives us *optimism*.

(d) We learn to *trust* as we interact in relationship with God using the attributes that he has given to us.—Robert U. Ferguson.

March 9 (Lent). Mission Possible

Text: John 19:30.

I. A mission undertaken to accomplish some specific end is not new. Indeed, the words "It is finished" that Jesus uttered on the cross also suggest that Jesus had a mission. He was not simply some wandering "holy man" peddling a few profound platitudes or an apocalyptic firebrand screaming repentance. No, he was the Son of God whose mission it was to reconcile mankind with the creator. Now that's a tremendously difficult mission.

The Gospels reveal just how difficult a mission Jesus undertook. They are a running chronicle of misunderstanding and oppression. Everywhere Jesus turned he was met by those who would not accept his message and who plotted his death. Even his own disciples frequently disappointed him by their persistent failure to grasp the true reason for his mission.

So, when Jesus uttered "It is finished," the "it" referred to the mission that he had so diligently undertaken the previous three years: a mission of teaching, healing, proclaiming, and preparing the disciples to carry on what he had begun. His part of the mission was thus coming to an end as he hung upon the cross. He had fulfilled the task for which he had been sent.

II. Yet, the mission was not over.

(a) Jesus clearly intended that the mission that he had begun should be continued by the disciples that he had so carefully trained during the course of his earthly ministry. He fully expected that they would continue the preaching, teaching, healing, and praying that had been such a part of his ministry. And, moreover, that they would continue to gather persons in discipleship to Jesus Christ. Jesus' words on the cross, therefore, remind us that the Cross was a beginning as well as an end.

(b) The disciples to whom Jesus Christ entrusted his mission were faced with the same problems that Jesus had encountered: hostility, indifference, apathy, powerlessness, and rigidity on the part of the religious establishment of their day. They, like Jesus, were sent on a "mission impossible." All objective indicators pointed to failure. The first disciples were poor, ignorant, and powerless men of humble birth. They possessed little to commend themselves to other persons—little except the gospel of Jesus Christ. Yet, despite these serious deficits, Christian history reveals that over the centuries, the "mission impossible" became the "mission possible."

(c) Why? The answer lies not in the special abilities of the disciples. It rests not in the tolerance of governments or even in the particular form of government. The "mission possible" is possible because of the Cross of Jesus Christ. The sacrifice that Christ made on the cross for our sins made possible the gift of God's grace to all persons. It is this very grace that empowered not merely those first disciples but all disciples to carry on the mission to which they had been sent by Jesus Christ—and to carry on that mission despite all manner of opposition and discouragement.

Each one of us who has been called to discipleship by Jesus Christ has a mission. It is the supreme act of faith that we take up that mission—despite the fact that it may not be the most pleasant of missions. As we undertake that mission, we are always empowered by Christ. He is always with us!

In our own time the "mission possible" lays not on the next continent, but around the corner on the next block. Perhaps the mission that Christ wants you to undertake is next door! In any case, do it! Do not allow some degree of rejection to cause you to abandon your mission or some adversity to scare you away from the task to which your Lord has set you. Perseverance is the key.

A good example of dedication to a mission is that of General Nathaniel Greene, one of Washington's generals. Washington sent Greene to North Carolina in 1780 to command the American forces against the British. The American army had been beaten several times and was outnumbered by their foes. During the year after Greene assumed command, the morale of the American army rebounded and large areas of the Carolinas were recaptured from the British. Yet, the American army in the South never won a decisive battle under Greene; however, they won the campaign. By the end of 1781, the British forces had been confined to the cities of Charleston and Savannah. Greene's explanation to Washington of this unusual turn of events read like this, "We fight, get beat, rise, and fight again." May our committed discipleship to Jesus Christ have that same determination and power— power that only our Lord can grant.— Rodney K. Miller.

March 16 (Lent). When God Comes Through in the Last Hour

Text: John 11:1, 3–6, 14–15, 23–26, 32–45.

We often have a hard time waiting for the best God has to give. God may take much longer to act than we like. Mary and Martha came to tell Jesus about their brother Lazarus and his near-to-death illness. They knew that Jesus had the power to heal their beloved brother. The Scripture says, "Now Jesus loved Martha, and her sister, and Lazarus. When he had heard therefore that Lazarus was sick, he stayed still in the same place where he was" (John 11:5–6).

How could Jesus have loved his friend Lazarus so much and yet desert him at such a critical time? Why did he wait until Lazarus's funeral before arriving at his friend's side? Perhaps Rudolf Bultmann,

the New Testament scholar, answered this question best: "Jesus' works have their own hour." Perhaps we need to realize that sometimes God comes through in the last hour.

I. Many people today would react differently to a plea from Mary and Martha to come and heal Lazarus. We probably would have, in Jesus' situation, gone immediately and healed Lazarus because:

(a) Lazarus was Jesus' beloved friend (v. 3).

(b) Healing Lazarus would have saved the loved ones a great deal of grief (vv. 31–32).

(c) Healing Lazarus would have saved Jesus from accusations that he did not care (vv. 21, 37).

(d) Healing Lazarus would have saved Jesus from the grief of losing such a close friend (vv. 33, 35).

(e) Jesus had the power to heal Lazarus (v. 21).

(f) The religious authorities wanted to kill Jesus, so a healing would have gotten Jesus in less trouble than raising a man from the dead (vv. 47, 53).

II. But Jesus chose to react according to God's will and not man's desire.

(a) Waiting until Lazarus was in the grave four days proved that Lazarus was really dead according to Jewish beliefs (vv. 17, 39).

(b) Jesus had confidence that God would raise Lazarus (v. 11).

(c) Tarrying a few days until Lazarus died gave other people an opportunity for a deeper faith (v. 15).

(d) If Jesus had intervened too soon, it would have seemed that Jesus had only human concern rather than having a higher purpose.

(e) This incident was for the glory of God, not ours (v. 4).

(f) This miracle is the final step toward God's purpose being fulfilled in the crucifixion and resurrection of Christ (12:23).

(g) Lazarus' death and resurrection pointed to eternal life through Christ (vv. 25–26).

(h) Jesus knew that waiting for his Father to act in his own time and in his own way was worth it in the end (v. 42).

III. The Bible contains various examples in which God came through in the last hour.

(a) Sarah was ninety-one years old when she had a baby.

(b) The Israelites had been in bondage in the land of Egypt for four hundred years before he called his servant Moses, at the age of eighty years, to free them.

(c) The prophet Elijah, believing that he was the only prophet who was left, was told by God when he was ready to give up that there were many more prophets who had not bowed down to the false god Baal.

(d) When Habakkuk asked the Lord when he would stop the violence and save the prophet's people, God answered, "My vision waits for an appointed time, but at the end it shall speak. If it seems slow, wait for it; it will surely come" (Hab. 2:3).

(e) God sent his Son when the time was ripe.

(f) Jesus did not die until his hour had come (Mark 14:41).

IV. God still sometimes comes through in the last hour.

(a) God may not always lift us out of the difficulties of life.

(b) God wants to teach us to follow his will and to trust his guidance, no matter what people may say and no matter what obstacles may come into our paths.

(c) God may allow certain things to happen to us in order to accomplish his purpose.

The point of this miracle is that Jesus is the resurrection and the life. Only he can enable anyone to live beyond the grave. Lazarus was a sign of the resurrection, but Jesus was the Reality. Jesus said, "Whosoever lives and believes in me shall never die."—Ronnie R. Blankenship.

March 23 (Passion/Palm Sunday). How Do We Respond to the Cross?
TEXT: John 12:20–25, 31–33.
I. The Greeks
(a) Who are the Greeks? (v. 20)
(b) Do we wish to see Jesus? (v. 21)
(c) Do we have evangelists like Philip and Andrew? (v. 22)
II. The Hour
(a) What is the hour of Jesus? (v. 23)
(b) How is Jesus glorified at the hour? (v. 23)

III. The Illustration
(a) How can a dying grain of wheat bear much fruit? (v. 24)
(b) How can losing one's life result in keeping it for eternal life? (v. 25)
IV. The Cross
(a) Does Jesus' death judge the world? (v. 31)
(b) Does Jesus' death defeat Satan? (v. 31)
(c) Does Jesus' death draw all men to himself? (v. 32)
The challenges of the Cross are as relevant today as yesterday. What is our response?—Andrew Mbama Okorie.

March 30 (Easter). The Best is Yet to Be
TEXT: 1 Pet. 1:3–9; John 20:19–30.
I. Our lessons for this morning challenge you to believe in the resurrection of Jesus Christ our Lord. They say that if you believe in the resurrection of Jesus Christ, it will make a difference in the world in which you live and the way you see yourself. Start with 1 Peter, written to encourage Christians in Asia Minor who were having a tough time of it, undergoing persecution. Peter gives them a new way of looking at the world and a new way of understanding their place in it. The resurrection gave them a grander vision of the world than they ever imagined, and it gave them a view that said their lives are of ultimate significance. We're not trapped here; we are on our way to greater life. And so what we do here on this planet is not meaningless. It has ultimate meaning. Every individual act, he says, has a repercussion in heaven. When you look at the world through the symbol of the resurrection, it's a different place.

You choose what you believe in this life, and what you choose to believe determines the quality of life that you live. What the Christian faith was doing was challenging people to believe in something grand. It challenged them to believe that this world is greater than it appears and that your life is much more important than you think.

II. They preached the resurrection not as it is so often preached in our day, as an isolated miracle in the past. They preached it as a way of seeing into the nature of reality, just like those paradigms in physics or in astronomy are used as a way of understanding the unseen reality beneath the surface of things, those images that changed the whole world because first they changed the way we look at the world. And they made it a gamble. They didn't make it easy. They didn't prove the resurrection. They didn't preach it in such a way that there would be no room for doubt. They didn't present infallible evidence and irrefutable proofs. They even wrote into the record of every Gospel—Matthew, Mark, Luke and John—that there were people who did not believe it. They even said there were no witnesses to the resurrection. That's how risky they make it. There were other documents circulating around the Church in the first century that claimed to have eyewitnesses to the resurrection, but the Church rejected them. They didn't get into the New Testament. The only documents that got into the New Testament were those that said no one saw the resurrection, only that some women happened to see the empty tomb, that's all. What they talk about is the appearances of the resurrected Christ to the disciples. They didn't see the resurrection; they saw the resurrected Christ. You see, they don't make it easy for us. They want you to take the risk of faith.

That's why John told the story of Thomas. Thomas didn't see the resurrection, so he didn't believe. When Thomas had a vision of the resurrected Christ, he then believed. But that's not the point of the story. The point is found in the last verse of the story. "Blessed are those who don't see and still believe." That's the point. Those who have faith without seeing have a special blessing. And the Epistle lesson says the same thing. Peter congratulates them on their faith in the resurrection. He says, "Without having seen him you love him and though you don't now see him you still believe in him."

III. I used to be embarrassed with talk about heaven. I'm not sure why. I think it was because heaven was something that you couldn't see, and I was raised in a culture that believed that you ought to be able to describe what you see and what you couldn't describe didn't exist, or

wasn't important. But now I know that way of looking at the world is a myth. The greater the reality, I know now, like love and freedom and life, the more you have to speak with analogy, the more you have to say, "It's something like this." And so in later years I have delighted in talking about heaven as I believe it is. I base it on what I know of Christ and what he revealed to us about God. That's what Peter is doing in this letter, incidentally. He's saying it's like an inheritance. And I like that analogy, but I prefer the analogy of the journey, because I think that that's what life as we know it now is really about. I think we always have to keep moving and keep growing in this life, and based on that, I believe that it's going to be the same in the next. And I believe that we will be welcomed there and made to feel at home there. That's how I interpret Jesus' promise, "I go to prepare a place for you."—Mark Trotter.

April 6. Not Seeing, yet Believing
Text: John 20:24–29.

This is a sermon for tough times, times when it isn't easy to believe. Many of us have these periods in our lives, sometimes long and sometimes short, much too painful to ignore.

I. The disciples didn't know what real faith-struggles were until Jesus died. You can imagine their delight when, on Easter evening as they gathered behind closed doors, the risen Lord appeared to them. Unfortunately, Thomas wasn't there that night. The others tried to tell him about their earth-shattering and faith-stimulating experience, but another's experience wasn't good enough for him.

Eventually he does confess Jesus as Lord—after he does see the risen Lord and after he is given the opportunity to touch him. Jesus' response? "Blessed are those who have not seen and yet believe."

II. It is sometimes difficult to see God when clouds from the smoldering of war block the heavens. It is sometimes difficult to see God in a church that doesn't seem concerned about the issues that really matter to us. It's sometimes difficult to see God when our life dreams are shattered, when goals we had set for ourselves get completely out of our reach and become instead hopeless illusions.

Here is a young man facing combat in a war he considers unjust, and as badly as he wants and needs to feel the presence of God he has claimed since his childhood, he cannot. But he says to himself, "I cannot see my Lord just now. I cannot feel him—yet I know he is there. I know he is here!"

This is the kind of faith Jesus was thinking of when he ended his conversation with Thomas. It was a word of challenge from Jesus and a reminder that faith is much more than believing the right things. *Faith is a refusal to turn your face from God no matter what life brings your way.*

When life blocks your view of the Lord, when you live through the valleys and shadows during which you can neither see him nor feel his presence, keep on believing. Light will come again. *Blessed are those who do not see and yet believe.*—David A. Farmer.

April 13. Belief and Toleration
TEXT: Rom. 14:13.
Character making is the object of the Christian religion, not system making.
I. What is toleration?
(a) Not charity to those who agree with you.
(b) Not simply forbearance or indifference toward those who disagree.
(c) It is accepting men for the Christ that is in their life and disposition, without scrutinizing the beliefs that they hold. A good man is taken as a good belief (see Acts 10:34, 35).
II. The grounds of toleration.
(a) Not a compliment—a favor, which in your kindness you bestow.
(b) It is simply a duty—a solemn obligation—derived from the right of men to use their own conscience and reason in matters between themselves and God.
(c) It is to be regarded, then, as a Christian attainment, like any other grace—requiring humility, self-denial of pride, lively sense of others' rights, faith that God will guide men into saving faith, if need be, by very poor paths.
III. Toleration is not possible to men who care nothing for truth—who think all doctrines alike—who believe in nothing. That is, men without convictions cannot in any just sense be said to be tolerant. But when a man does believe, values it, and then by his own sense of the sacredness of it, judges how sacred also to his brother is *his* belief, he bears a testimony that powerfully enforces the obligations of belief. True toleration tends to honor truth and firm convictions!—Henry Ward Beecher.

April 20. God Is Our Refuge
TEXT: Ps. 46.
I. The protection of God (vv. 1–3).
(a) A declaration.
(b) A description.
(c) A deduction.
II. The presence of God (vv. 4–7).
(a) An available source.
(b) An anchor of stability.
(c) An assurance of success.
III. The power of God (vv. 8–11).
(a) The power of his works.
(b) The power of his ways.—John Bowling.

April 27. Is There a Rule for It?
TEXT: Matt. 5:17–20.
Some forms of religion have unusual appeal simply because their ideas are easy to take hold of. A religion of rules and regulations has such an appeal.
I. We have to admit it—rules may be good.
(a) Rules require little thinking.
(b) Rules can produce a specific result.
(c) These facts add up to a feeling of security.
II. We have to acknowledge also that rules may be totally inadequate.
(a) Certain rules become outmoded.
(b) Rules are often misapplied.
(c) Living by rules may ignore basic motivation.
III. We need rules.
(a) The rule must be deep, growing out of something deeper than the rule itself (Jer. 31:33.)
(b) The rule must be broad, comprehending many lesser rules (Rom. 13:8b-10).
(c) The rule must be lasting, surviving all contingencies of time (Mark 13:31).
(d) We get our rule not because we seek

it: it is given to us in Jesus Christ (Phil. 1:21).—James W. Cox.

May 4. The Promise of Youth—Becoming Somebody

TEXT: 1 Tim. 1:5.

I. *A pure heart*. The apostle calls for a pure heart in the members of the church. The word *pure* here is the same word that is used for grain that has been separated from chaff; it is used for an army that has been purged of all cowardly and undisciplined soldiers until nothing is left but first-class fighting men. A pure heart refers to singleness of thought and purpose. Søren Kierkegaard called purity of heart the capacity to will one thing.

When this biblical writer appeals for purity of heart in his letter to Timothy, he is encouraging the church at Ephesus not to mix its faith in Christ with the attitudes and ideas of the surrounding culture. He is reminding them of their task of preserving a single-minded allegiance to Christ.

Paul's challenge to the adolescent church also points the way for modern youth. The young person, like the early church, faces the challenge of developing a pure heart. This purity of heart is a single-minded allegiance of Christ that tells the young person "who he is and where he's from." One author calls adolescence a process of self-definition.

How does the church help its young people to know who they are and where they're from? I believe it does this through a ministry that presents a clear vision of the Lord Jesus Christ. Jesus himself is the perfect model of one who established a decisive identity. Jesus was a loyal member of his family, yet he clearly and unashamedly established an identity apart from his family. A young person can achieve a clear definition of himself in the church only when *together* we accept the hard discipline and the often disturbing freedom of allowing Jesus to become the author and finisher of our lives.

II. *A good conscience*. Our text stresses the importance of a pure heart and then calls for a "good conscience." To have a good conscience means to be able to look at the knowledge we have of ourselves and not be ashamed of what we know. If that adolescent church of the early second century was to survive in the crosscurrents of pagan beliefs, its members had to have positive feelings of self-acceptance.

Paul understood the importance of a good conscience—a strong sense of self-esteem that would give a person an accurate moral compass. He knew that without this the Christians would lose their integrity to the propaganda of the surrounding pagan religions. By the same principle, if the young person is to achieve successfully a clear sense of personhood as an emerging adult, he must secure a vital sense of personal self-acceptance.

Jesus Christ is not only the model of the person who perfectly achieved a sense of personal identity, through his present spirit he provides the gift of personal self-acceptance. And this brings us directly to the third element on which a sound personal identity is built—*a sincere faith*.

III. *A sincere faith*. The word *sincere* literally means "without hypocrisy." Hypocrisy in religious faith occurred when an individual appeared to be religious but in God's sight was actually ungodly. Insincere religious faith was a serious threat to the adolescent church. It developed as the church struggled to preserve its integrity in pagan society. In its attempt to maintain orthodoxy, the young church sometimes lost sight of the inner religious life of its members. The result was hypocrisy—a man accepted a set of statements about the Christian faith, but in his inner life he remained unchanged.

Every young person faces the religious dilemma of those second-century Christians: Will he adopt a set of beliefs formulated by his parents or by his church and paste them on the outside of his personality, or will he become transformed by the indwelling of the Spirit of Christ in his life?

The young person has an artificial faith who only *knows about Jesus Christ*—who has a set of ideas and beliefs that he has received from parents and teachers. That young person has a genuine faith who has *allowed the Living Christ to become a part of his life*. This person knows who he is because he has a personal understanding of Jesus —the One who perfectly knew who he was.

Furthermore, he accepts himself because he is possessed by the truth that Christ cares supremely for him.—Richard L. Hester.

May 11. The Cost of a Christian Life

TEXT: Luke 14:28–33.

I. It should be understood that to become a Christian costs every sin that you have. Sins must be not only deplored and repented of in the sense that you feel sorry for and regret them, but they must be resolutely thrown overboard.

II. To be a Christian will cost you, also, the giving up of your self-righteousness. If ever a man could plead his self-righteousness, it would have been the rich young ruler. The trouble was that down at the heart, underneath all the pleasant exterior, he was proud and self-willed and would not surrender his will in obedience to Christ. Christ saves by cleansing the whole heart-fountain. Make the fountain pure, and all the streams that flow from it will be clean and sweet.

III. To become a Christian costs a public confession of faith in Christ and a brave and honest following after Christ throughout our lives.—Louis Albert Banks.

May 18 (Pentecost). The Ministry of the Spirit to the Believer

The Holy Spirit ministers to the believer in at least seven ways.

I. The Holy Spirit regenerates us (Titus 3:5). Jesus said, "Except a man be born of water and of the Spirit, he cannot enter the kingdom of God" (John 3:5). Scholars differ as to what *water* refers to in this passage, but all agree that the Holy Spirit is the agent of regeneration.

II. All Christians are baptized by the Spirit (1 Cor. 12:13). This is not an experience reserved for a select few that occurs after some unusual development in Christian growth. It is not an ecstatic experience accompanied by speaking in tongues. The baptism of the Spirit is the universal experience of all believers that unites them to the body of Christ, the church, and to Christ himself. When a person repents of sin and invites Christ to come into his or her life, at that moment the baptism of the Holy Spirit takes place. The Chris-

tian is joined to the fellowship of all the redeemed.

III. All Christians are indwelt by the Holy Spirit (John 14:17; Rom. 8:9; 1 Cor. 3:16). Upon becoming a Christian, a person receives the Holy Spirit. The Spirit lives in the life of each believer.

IV. All Christians are sealed by the Holy Spirit (Eph. 1:13, 4:30; 2 Cor. 1:20–22). This is an inner mark or identification of ownership, security, and authenticity.

V. All Christians are sanctified by the Holy Spirit (1 Cor. 1:2). Sanctification is both an act and a process. It is the act of being set apart to God and the process of growing in Christ-likeness. It culminates in glorification when we are in heaven, saved from the presence of sin.

VI. A sixth ministry of the Holy Spirit to the believer is the filling of the Spirit. To be filled with the Spirit is to be controlled by the Spirit. The two are synonymous. We always have all of him; he does not always have all of us. As someone said, "The Holy Spirit always *resides* within the Christian; he does not always *preside*." We are commanded to be filled with the Spirit (Eph. 5:18).

VII. Every Christian is gifted by the Holy Spirit (1 Cor. 12:7). A spiritual gift is a Spirit-given ability for Christian service, and every believer has at least one. There is a diversity of gifts, and no believer has all of them. Gifts are given to believers by the sovereign choice of the Holy Spirit (1 Cor. 12:11, 28). The purpose of gifts is to edify the body of Christ (Eph. 4:12). We are to be faithful in using our gifts (Rom. 12:6–8).—Arthur H. Criscoe.

May 25. The Task of the Church

TEXT: Matt. 28:18–20; 2 Cor. 5:18–6:10.

Why doesn't the church make more headway in the world? Surely nothing is wrong on God's side. However, we who represent God and who look to him for help are open to any criticisms. And the criticisms have come thick and fast—not only from those outside the church but also from church people themselves.

Now we find ourselves where the first Christians were—witnessing to a world that has to be convinced that we have something to say worth hearing. Once again we see that we are a minority fighting a secular dragon that threatens to swallow us up.

I. *The questions*. How can we know how to speak to the people of our times unless we take the time and trouble to find out the questions they are asking?

Yet is it clear that those who are searching for religion are not always conscious that it is religion they seek. Their quest may take many forms. It may express itself in the tortured questions that appear directly or indirectly in modern art, drama, or literature. Paul Tillich's approach to modern man through the "method of correlation" has much to say for it: "It tries to correlate the questions implied in the situation with the answers implied in the message."

In many creative ways both laymen and ministers discover what people are thinking.

II. *The objective*. The task of the church is to minister to the total person: it is not merely to "save *souls*'; it is not merely to help men change or adjust to their environment; it is not merely to promote mental health; it is not merely to educate people. When Jesus was on earth, he did a variety of things for people, proving that God's interest in human beings encompasses their whole life.

This concern is expressed by our evangelistic outreach, our colleges and seminaries, our publication boards, our children's homes and homes for the aged, our specialists in church and state relations at Washington, and our hospitals. Also, high-level discussion goes on continually under the leadership of denominational officials to formulate and consider new approaches to the many-faceted need of modern man.

III. *The workers*. A new staff member of a church undertook to inaugurate a program of evangelistic visitation. He called on the members of the church to visit prospects, get acquainted with them, and try to lead them into Christian discipleship. One church officer snapped, "Let him do it. That's what we're paying him for."

It used to be a man called up for military service could avoid it by hiring someone to go in his place. This cannot be done by Christians. All Christians have to fight their own battles against the foes of unbelief, secularism, and religious indifference. There may be very little that one person can do as compared with what another can do, but he or she must do *that*.

The less the church relies on paid employees to do its work and the more it involves the rank and file of its members, the greater will be the church's likeness to the church of the New Testament times, when the Christians witness was at its best.

IV. Independent campaigns to serve God are largely self-defeating and wasteful. "In unity there is strength." No individual Christian, no local church, no denomination should fail to explore every possible means of making effective the Christian witness in the world.—James W. Cox.

June 1. How Religion Gets in Our Way

TEXT: Matt. 12:1–14.

Does your religion get in the way of the good that God may want for you? Is your religion sickness, not health, to you at times? Instead of being your strength and resource, does it contribute to your distress and difficulties?

Religion gets in our way when we:

(1) make an improper separation between the sacred and the secular. We are trapped by piety.

(2) Develop rigidities that make desirable change impossible. We are snared by fixations.

(3) Become slaves to what others think of us. We are hindered by our image.

(4) Become addicted to making severe moral judgments that hurt rather than help. We stumble over our criticism.

(5) Become so uptight and defensive that our lives become unattractive and unattracting. We are entrapped by withdrawal.

Healthy religion abounds in love and thrives on service to others. Healthy religion frees persons of guilt. It lives with an open and searching mind, and it develops significant intimacy with others. Healthy religion can move among secular persons with neither compromise nor defensiveness nor pride nor withdrawal. It shares its faith with others as good news, respecting every individual's liberty and choice. It sees God through his world, not just in the confines of its own institution. Healthy religion transports us on God's highway to the fullness of life—abundant, meaningful, and eternal.—Fred W. Andrea.

June 8. The Power of Prayer
TEXT: Matt. 6:8.
I. To understand genuine prayer, one must recognize three false assumptions.

First, prayer is not an attempt to get an insensitive God to become sensitive to our problems and the real needs within the world. God is completely aware of our needs even before we ask (Matt. 6:8).

Second, prayer is not the act of reminding God what he has forgotten to do. Many people assume that if they become highly emotional, pray in a loud voice, adopt a certain posture, or use long words and compound sentences, their chances of having their prayers answered are greatly increased.

Third, prayer is not an attempt to persuade an unwilling God to act. This understanding of prayer assumes that God has a limited amount of power and is, therefore, reluctant to use this power for the benefit of individuals or circumstances, lest it be depleted. It also assumes that God can be "bullied" into doing something that he really doesn't want to do. (There is a difference between persistence in prayer and nagging.) Such an understanding is inconsistent with the nature of God, which is absolute love and absolute compassion.

II. A mature understanding of prayer must be focused upon our relationship with God rather than the gifts or rewards that he can provide for us.

One of our basic needs is the need to know God and to feel his presence in our daily life. Prayer and quiet meditation are invaluable resources in Christian life. We recognize our appreciation for God and his blessings. We confess our sins and shortcomings. We recognize our dependence upon God.

III. Four factors are essential in prayer:
First, it is important to develop a proper attitude. One must rid the mind of the distractions and preoccupations that so often interrupt the natural flow of thoughts.

Second, we should pray according to God's limits. Calvin advised persons to examine their requests to determine if a real and genuine need existed. Furthermore, Calvin believed that we share with God the responsibility for answering our own prayers.

Third, we must offer our requests in a spirit of humility. The recognition that we are not all that God intended us to be should foster a certain humility within us.

Fourth, we should expect an answer. Faith must accompany our prayer (Matt. 21:22; Heb. 11:6).

Prayer, like a close friendship, takes time to develop. Because of our different personalities, backgrounds, and styles of worship there is a wide range of viewpoints regarding prayer. Nevertheless, prayer can be a source of spiritual enrichment. In spite of the varieties of religious experience, there is one element that works for everyone—persistence!—Sam Young.

June 15. Providing the Right Model
TEXT: I Cor. 4:14–21.
I. *Primacy of being a good model.*
(a) Throughout God's Word one finds admonition to the believer to set the proper model.
(1) *Christ* is proclaimed as our model (1 Pet. 2:21).
(2) *Pastors* are called to be model (1 Pet. 5:3).
(3) *Timothy* is instructed, as a young person, to be a model to the older Christians (1 Tim. 4:12).
(b) Paul's reason for setting himself up as a model for the Corinthians was that he was their *father in the gospel* (v. 15).
(1) Paul had led them to know Jesus Christ as Lord and Savior.
(2) Other Christians would have a relationship as a *tutor*; only Paul is their father.
(c) Paul calls on them to be good models because of the *influence* that they are having.
(1) *Daily* others are being influenced by our behavior.
(2) We dare not witness wrongly for our Lord.

II. *Purpose of a good model.*

(a) It makes possible *witnessing* to the *power* of the Lord Jesus.

(1) If nothing is distinctively different, how will others know?

(2) Faultless attitudes and behavior validate the claim of Christ.

(b) It provides the means of *self-discipline* for the Christians.

(1) The most difficult task in life is to *discipline* ourselves in all areas.

(2) The knowledge that God wants his children to provide the proper example for others can give one the *impetus* to practice self-discipline.

(3) Only through the *means* of self-discipline can I *grow* to be the Christian God wants me to be.

III. *Product of a good model: Timothy.*

(a) Timothy was *Paul's true son* in the gospel.

(1) "Beloved and faithful child in the Lord" (v. 17).

(2) When imprisoned in Rome, Paul longed to see Timothy (2 Tim. 1:4).

(b) Timothy was able to *teach* the Corinthians.

(1) "He will remind you" (v. 17).

(2) "My ways" (v. 17): Paul's ethical teachings that he taught after proclaiming the gospel.

What kind of model are you setting? What type of believer are you reproducing? What legacy in the faith are you leaving?—Robert U. Ferguson.

June 22. Delight in the Will of God

TEXT: Ps. 40:8.

This psalm tells of one who has suffered, been graciously relieved, and now responds in grateful praise and grateful obedience.

I. In one sense, the will of God will always be done, whether we do his will or not.

(a) We are compelled to speak of God's will in terms applicable to our own. This is done in Scripture. There are three distinct senses in which this term is employed. First, the will of purpose; it is always done. Next, the will of desire, or wish, which is not always done—for inscrutable reasons he permits free agents to act counter to his wish. Last, will of command—the wish

of one in authority, when expressed, becomes a command.

(b) Now God's purpose, as distinguished from other senses, is not dependent upon us for accomplishment. It may be accomplished without us, by overruling and finding others willing. But God's will of desire, what pleases him, we should seek to ascertain and do. His will of command we should learn and obey.

II. We should always do God's will, even if it not with delight.

(a) We seldom, if ever, do anything with perfectly correct motives and feelings.

(b) Sometimes we cannot rise above resignation.

(c) Sometimes we may do his will with shrinking and reluctance.

(d) We should always do God's will, even if it is not a delight. And often, the painful effort will change to pleasure, the duty commenced reluctantly will become a sweet joy!

III. We should delight to do God's will. We may be led to it.

(a) By sense of right.

(b) By feelings of interest.

(c) By feelings of benevolence.

(d) By feelings of gratitude.

(e) In doing God's will, we follow the example of Jesus—seen in his whole life and declared in his own words (John 4:34). —John A. Broadus.

June 29. The Will of Witness

TEXT: Rom. 1:12–14.

The will to witness is something Paul evidenced in his life by word and deed. Everywhere and in every way Paul witnessed about his Damascus Road experience. It mattered little where he was or what he was doing, his witness was ready and real. The peculiar circumstances never destroyed his will to witness. Without realizing it, many people's witness is anchored to certain places and favorable surroundings. When this is true, the will to witness is controlled by outward circumstances rather than inner conviction.

I. The will to witness is born in the soil of conviction: By nature a witness can speak only what he or she has experienced. The experience of meeting God in a personal way on the road to Damascus was so real and so genuine that Paul could not refrain from telling of it.

The power of the gospel to bring salvation was no longer questioned, not for Jews or Gentiles. Thus he could write, "For I am not ashamed of the gospel of Christ: for it is the power of God unto salvation to every one that believeth; to the Jew first, and also to the Greek" (Rom. 1:16).

II. The will to witness gains strength in the climate of commitment: If you have genuine conviction about something, you are generally committed to it. It is the lack of conviction about either the gospel of Christ or the need of man that prevents commitment. To know either would bring you to Paul's level of commitment: "So, as much as in me is, I am ready to preach the gospel" (Rom. 1:15).

III. The will to witness achieves fruition in the warmth of compassion: Paul, in recognizing that he had something the world desperately needed, acknowledged his indebtedness to the world: "I am debtor" (Rom. 1:14). It was not that the world had helped him, but just the opposite. He had a responsibility to help the world. "Rescue the Perishing" would not have been just a song to Paul but the theme of his life. When we really care, we share!—Drew J. Gunnells, Jr.

July 6. A Radiant Certainty

TEXT: Ps. 56:9 (NASB).

I. There are many voices clamoring for our attention. But we should listen to the Psalmist.

II. The psalmist: "This I know, that God is for me."

(a) He knows that God is.

(b) He discovered that God cares.

(c) He also discovered that God is working on his behalf.

III. The effect of this knowledge of God upon the psalmist's daily life:

(a) It gave him a fine high courage.

(b) It enabled the Psalmist to "walk before God in the light of the living."—Clovis Chappell.

July 13. Ask, Seek, Knock

TEXT: Matt. 7:17.

The three imperatives ask, seek, and knock are a part of Jesus' teachings during his Sermon on the Mount. In this sermon he gives practical instruction for relating life to God and his kingdom. A key element in so relating our lives is faith. The Lord invites us to trust God by asking, seeking, and knocking.

I. "Ask, and it will be given you." This imperative bids us to have faith enough in God's love and care to ask him for our needs.

II. "Seek, and you will find." We are active participants as we diligently look for what God has for us. We seek in faith knowing that we *will* find the response from God we need.

III. "Knock, and it will be opened to you." The third imperative reminds us of opportunity. The passage of life is partitioned by many doorways. Trusting the Lord's leadership, we knock on the door before us confident that it will open to reveal the mysteries behind it.—C. Kenny Cooper.

July 20. Face to Face with God

TEXT: Exod. 3:1–17.

I. The God who cares (Exod. 2:23–25).

II. The God who purposes (Exod. 3:16–17).

III. The God who appears in the commonplace circumstances of life (Exod. 3:1–2).

IV. The God who inspires reverence and awe (Exod. 3:5–6, 13–14).

V. The God who shares his plans with men (Exod. 3:10).—James W. Cox.

July 27. A Higher Understanding of Prayer

TEXT: Luke 11:1, 5–8; 18:1–8.

If we ever learn to pray, we need a higher understanding of prayer. The disciples knew that Jesus' prayer life was unique. They knew the ritual of prayer, but Jesus knew the secret of prayer. Jesus' prayer life was vital and influential because he lived it. Our Lord unveiled his secrets of prayer in two parables.

I. What authentic prayer is not.

(a) Jesus suggests that authentic prayer is not magic.

(b) Jesus suggests that authentic prayer is not a blank check to be used for furthering our own selfish purposes.

(c) Jesus suggests that authentic prayer is not to be used only for bailing us out of hard times.

(d) Jesus suggests that authentic prayer is not answered without possible obstacles.

II. What true prayer is.

(a) Jesus emphasizes that true prayer is regular and persistent.

(b) Jesus emphasizes that true prayer is expectant.

(c) Jesus emphasizes that in true prayer we bring our needs before God.

(d) Jesus emphasizes that true prayer is answered only through sincere obedience to God's will.—Ronnie R. Blankenship.

August 3. "The Devil Made Me Do It!"
TEXT: 1 Cor. 10:1–13.

I. Temptation is a common human experience (v. 13).

(a) Every person undergoes many temptations daily.

(b) Every temptation that is succumbed to by one person is successfully resisted by others.

(c) Each person has his or her points of susceptibility.

II. Merely being religious does not guarantee immunity either to temptation or to succumbing to it (vv. 1–5).

(a) Israelites had the same experiences in the Exodus.

(1) Saw the same phenomena and miraculous interventions.

(2) Worshipped God together and were nourished.

(b) Yet, not all of the Israelites were faithful (v. 6).

(1) Some committed idolatry (Exod. 32:1–14).

(2) Some committed immorality and 23,000 died in one day (Num. 25:1–9).

(3) Some grew impatient with God (Num. 21:4–9).

(4) Some rebelled against God and were destroyed (Num. 16).

III. Only the faithfulness of God can overcome temptation.

(a) Complete reliance upon God produces the reserve necessary to triumph.

(b) God provides the strength necessary and the way of escape.

(c) The purpose of temptation is to teach us about the power of God.—Robert U. Ferguson.

August 10. The God Who Is Free . . . To Be God!
TEXT: Gen. 15:1; 22:1–14.

God for Abraham is the Interpreter of life's experiences, not the Interpreted.

I. Abraham relies on the . . . Word of God (Gen. 15:1).

(a) It is an authentic Word. God's Word versus man's word.

(b) It is an assuring Word. God's "perspective" a part of the authentic Word.

II. Abraham relinquishes himself to the . . . ways of God (Gen. 22:8).

(a) God's ways are still the best ways. What are our options?

(b) God's ways do not always make sense—they make life! Follow Abraham down the mountain, with his son, with his faith, and with his God!—C. Neil Strait.

August 17. How Does God Fight for Us?
TEXT: Neh. 4:20.

The people of Israel had been in exile. Now they were returning to their homeland, not in triumphant parades but in small bands of settlers. The joy of homecoming was shattered by the harsh realities they found. Jerusalem was in ruins. Its main defense, the wall, was a pile of rubble. Without the wall they were virtually defenseless against hostile neighbors and wild animals. Nehemiah led them to rebuild the wall.

At first, suspicious neighbors laughed arrogantly. As the work proceeded they grew increasingly angry. Their anger grew as the strength of the Israelites waned. The work was extremely hard and it was carried out in a pile of rubbish. With high resolve the Israelites continued to build the wall with a trowel in one hand and a spear in the other. As the work spread out along the wall the workers were dangerously far apart. Nehemiah then gave civil defense instructions on what to do in case of an attack. A trumpet would be sounded and everyone should rally to the sound of the trumpet. Then Nehemiah asserted with confidence, "Our God will fight for us."

We of the skeptical twentieth century do

not share his confidence. Certainly we need a divine ally today, a God who fights for us. Many are the forces that seem hostile to us. These forces make us feel that our defenses are in rubble. We need to know that when life is overwhelming, there can be the sound of a spiritual trumpet and a rallying of forces to our aid. We need the conviction that God fights for us.

There was no bloodshed there. The alliance with God was seen through the eyes of faith. If we will look at how Nehemiah was convinced that God was fighting for him, we will see how God fights for us today.

I. God fights for us by doing something with others: God helped Nehemiah through his friends. Nehemiah was cupbearer to the king, an office of honor, privilege, and trust. It was the king who first noticed Nehemiah's sadness (ch. 2). When Nehemiah explained about his homeland and its needs, the king generously gave permission and resources for the task of rebuilding. The battle was on because of a sensitive and responsive friend. God often fights for us through our friends.

II. God fights for us by doing something with our foes: Nehemiah 6:16 says that Nehemiah's enemies "perceived that this work had been accomplished with the help of our God" (RSV). His enemies were aware that God had a stake in this struggle.

This passage of Scripture puts a lot of responsibility on us. God does not take the side of those who glibly claim his presence; it is for us to choose to be on God's side, to reflect God's presence in our behavior and attitudes. Acts 4:13 tells of the early opponents of the church recognizing that Peter and John had been with Jesus. To deal with the disciples was to deal with the Christ they served.

III. God fights for us by doing something with us: Morale was low, strength was waning, and enemies were threatening. Yet astoundingly they finished the wall in fifty-two days. God did not do the work for them but they were strengthened by a sense of his presence. God always comes to his people and stands beside them. We may want to say to God: "Don't just stand there. Do something." We re-

flect our own anxiety. We feel better if we can do something for someone in distress and are usually anxious if we can only stand there. In times of sorrow, distress, or repentance, what is it that we really need? A God of fairy tales who intervenes to put Humpty-Dumpty together again or a God who stands alongside us so that we know we are not alone, enabling us to do what we need to do? God fights for us by being present with us.

Ultimately God will win his battles. Our victory depends on whose side we choose. —Jim England.

August 24. Lift Up Your Heads

TEXT: Rom. 5:1–6; 1 John 3:1–3.

I. The world's despair

(a) Everywhere there are evidences of despair.

(b) This despair can be traced to a certain rootlessness.

(c) Even some Christians have shared this spirit of the world.

II. The believer's hope

(a) Some Christians do not despair, but are radiant. They have hope! Hope is the expectation of future good. It is the common property of Christendom (Rom. 8:-28, NEB). This knowledge is the source of our hope.

(b) However, good Christians differ somewhat in their ideas of how God will bring his purposes about. Some see hope in only the next world. Others see hope realized in this world. But the truth is in both beliefs.

(c) In the face of all mysteries and doubts, Paul was sure of one thing: the love of God (Rom. 8:38–39).

(d) Beyond Paul's assurance, John was convinced that we poor sinners would be changed to reflect the very glory and character of Christ himself after all our striving (1 John 3:1–2) and that this hope would have a transforming effect upon us here and now (1 John 3:3).—James W. Cox.

August 31. Does Worship Do Anything?

TEXT: Amos 5:21; Matt. 18:20.

As some people look at the worship of the church, they see a nonsense ritual— elaborate, intricate machinery that moves earnestly but accomplishes nothing. And sometimes it doesn't! In the time of Amos the prophet, worship in Israel had become empty and vain. Why? The motions of worship were divorced from the reality of worship. The people were pleased with religion as a form, but would have nothing to do with it as a force (cf. 2 Tim. 3:5, Moffatt).

I. *Encounter*. True worship is encounter with the living God. It is coming face to face with God in a significant meeting. It is persons meeting one another for an exchange of recollections, thoughts, affections, and experiences.

(a) Every meaningful relationship in our lives has its rituals. The Bible uses figures of speech from marriage and the home to describe God's relationship to his people. God is Israel's husband: "I will betroth you to me forever" (Hos. 2:19, RSV). The church is the bride of Christ (2 Cor. 11:2; Rev. 19:7).

(b) Worship gives the worshiper the opportunity of meeting God in Jesus Christ. Jesus told his disciples that where two or three were gathered together in his name he would be in their midst (Matt. 18:20). And whoever encounters Jesus Christ in this way encounters the Father.

II. *Response*.

(a) The God we meet in worship is the God of Abraham, Isaac, and Jacob. He is the God who has performed mighty acts for his people, the God who has promised to do great things for his people forever.

(b) The God we meet in worship is the God who has fulfilled his promises by the gift of his Son Jesus Christ. All of this was and is for us. It demands a response. Whenever God comes to us in an experience of worship, it is this redeeming God who comes.

(c) God comes to us both in judgment and in mercy. He judges us to save us. He saves us to enable us to do his will. But any way we look at it, God come to us in *love*, for judgment and mercy are love in action. Therefore, we respond in love: "He first loved us" (1 John 4:19).

III. *Service to God*. When the means by which the people respond to God are presented, we worship. The reading and the preaching of the Word of God and the administration of baptism and of the Lord's Supper are acts of worship. Also, the response of the people in faith, praise, prayer, and commitment are acts of worship.

The Greek word *latreia* designates worship of God, but it also means service. God knows what we have need of before we ask him, but he still wants us to pray. He knows whether we believe in him and love him without any avowals from us, but he still wants our professions of faith and our public praise. Worship is service!

IV. *Undergirding*. The service within the sanctuary does not end the experience of worship. It is only one phase of service to God. Public worship equips the worshiper to confront the challenges that come in everyday life.

(a) The first challenge comes because the spirit of the world is at variance with the Spirit of Christ. In this time of crisis, the experience of corporate worship will stand the worshiper in good stead.

(b) The other challenge comes when the worshipers realize that they have an experience to share with others.—James W. Cox.

September 7. "The Secret Place"

TEXT: John 17:6–26; Eph. 3:14–19; 6:-18; Phil. 4:6; Col. 4:2–4.

Christians, even while caught up in the way of Christ and in fact because they are caught up in it, will sooner or later face their own needs, problems, sins, and fears —alone. They have to learn how to use their solitary hours creatively.

I. *Sources*. The practive of private devotions follows from living in community and worshiping in community. Private devotions probably did not exist before corporate worship. Private devotions are no substitute for public worship. Isn't it true that we worship and pray when we are alone because we have worshiped and prayed in the company of God's people? This is true if our private worship and prayer are genuine, for we cannot worship and pray aright unless our devotions have in them the horizontal dimension, the dimension of community.

II. *Expressions*.

(a) When we pray in private, our prayers should include all the elements of public prayer appropriate to the individual's personal need and wider concern. We should invoke the presence of God for our devotional time. We should praise God for his greatness, his goodness, and his power. We should confess our sins to him and ask his forgiveness. We should thank him for all his benefits—for health, for food, for opportunities of service, for spiritual help. We should ask him for the things we need or think we need, ask his judgment upon our petitions, and yield to his will. We should pray for persons and causes where compassion, concern, and love call for our intercessions. We should commit ourselves to the doing of God's will in our own lives, ready to assist God in answering the prayers we pray, if he so directs.

(b) Two elements in our prayers require special attention: confession and intercession.

(1) First, confession of our sins should be specific.

(2) Second, intercession, praying for others, should be specific.

III. *Aids*.

(a) We do not depend on memory alone to help us when we begin our devotions. A rich treasury of devotional materials is at our disposal. The Bible, the hymnbook, prayer books, and devotional guides offer instruction, inspiration, and specific directions.

(b) When we pray, we speak to God.

(1) When we read the Bible, God speaks to us through the Holy Spirit.

(2) Hymns make an important contribution toward deepening our thoughts about God and our relationship to him. Sometimes we can pray no better prayer than the prayer we make in the words of a deeply meaningful hymn.

(3) Moreover, the regular use of devotional guides has remarkable value. Many people spark their individual meditations with regular Bible readings suggested by denominational publications. Some go beyond this procedure and read daily from such classics at Fosdick's *Meaning of Prayer* and Baillie's *Diary of Private Prayer*.

Private devotions manifest their value in different ways in different personalities with different temperaments. One person may be very practical and matter-of-fact in his prayers and what he doe.. Another may be more mystica. person of action. And why not? not make us all alike, and there are ways to serve him.—James W. Cox.

September 14. The Blessedness of Forgiveness

TEXT: Matt. 18:21–35.

This parable reminds us of the necessity of having a genuine forgiveness that comes from the heart. Our incentive to forgive others is that God has forgiven us far more than we could ever repay.

I. A forgiving person blesses and pleases God.

(a) God is pleased when we forgive other persons because he is pleased to forgive us of all our sins.

(b) The parables of the lost coin, the lost sheep, and the lost son illustrate God's eagerness to forgive; we also should be eager to forgive others.

II. A forgiving person blesses the one whom he forgives.

(a) Most people have opportunities to forgive.

(b) We must link forgiveness with love of God and neighbor.

(c) Forgiving others allows God to work good in our lives.

III. A forgiving person is blessed.

(a) A feeling of peace and assurance comes over us when we genuinely forgive others.

(b) Forgiving others will usually cause others to be more ready to forgive you when the situation arises.

(c) Forgiveness of other persons brings us into a cleaner and purer relationship with God.—Ronnie R. Blankenship.

September 21. The Wellsprings of Character

TEXT: Matt. 5:21–30.

We all like to see a well-built house in a beautiful setting. But we know that such a house can be virtually destroyed while it still looks sturdy and handsome.

We are well acquainted with the cult of superficiality. In this cult, personality development goes no deeper than a knack for flattery, a plastic smile, or a perfunctory handclasp.

I. Outward deeds are important.

(a) Murder in various forms is one of our most serious crimes.

(b) Adultery or some generically similar act is one of our most serious social evils.

(c) King David's deplorable behavior toward Bathsheba and her husband, Uriah, exemplified both (see Gal. 5:19–21).

II. The inward attitudes are more important.

(a) The evil in human relationships orginates in the thoughts, in the imagination. Someone said, "Whatever gets your imagination gets you."

(b) Outward acts of worship are no substitute for a heart right with God (Ps. 51:16–17; Matt. 5:23–26).—James W. Cox.

September 28. Impossible Evasions

TEXT: Luke 16:13, 19–31.

There are many things we cannot avoid. Jesus said, "No servant can serve two masters; for either he will hate the one and love the other, or else he will hold to the one and despise the other. You cannot serve God and mammon."

There are other things that we can avoid. We can avoid the issue when we do not want to talk. We may sidestep when a car comes in our direction. We perhaps may retreat into shelter when we are in danger from an oncoming storm.

I. What things did Dives avoid?

(a) He avoided personal contact with anyone who was unlike himself.

(b) He avoided sincere, personal use of his life and possessions to help other people.

(c) He avoided having a personal relationship with God.

II. What things could Dives not avoid?

(a) He could not avoid death.

(b) He could not avoid facing the consequences of this life in the afterlife.

(c) He could not avoid the harm done because of the bad example he left to family and community.—Ronnie R. Blankenship.

October 5. Your Right to God's Promises

TEXT: 2 Pet. 1:1–11.

Nothing could be more relevant to our needs today than an awareness of God's promises. The promise of God stands in opposition to every negative force operating in the individual life.

I. Remember, it is *God* who promises.

II. What God has promised is essentially eternal life, that is, participation in the life of God himself (1 John 2:25).

III. Eternal life is entered into *now* (1 Cor. 2:9–10).

IV. The promise of eternal life penetrates every area of our human existence (1 John 3:2–3).

V. It should be clear to us that the promise was not made because of anything good or worthy that we have done or that we could possibly do.

VI. We enter into the blessings of God's promise through faith and works.—James W. Cox.

October 12. God Fulfills His Promises

TEXT: Gen. 17:15–21; 21:1–7.

The story of Isaac's birth is a fascinating biblical demonstration of God's faithfulness in fulfilling his promises.

I. The situation (thesis)—Genesis 17:15–21.

(a) God promises Abraham and Sarah a son.

(b) Abraham and Sarah wait expectantly.

(c) We wait on God's promises with eager anticipation.

II. The complication (antithesis)—Genesis 21:5–7a.

(a) How is God's promise to be fulfilled?

(b) Can Abraham and Sarah bear a son in their advanced old age?

(c) Can we surmount the doubts and obstacles in our lives?

III. The resolution (synthesis)—Genesis 21:1, 2, 7b.

(a) God fulfills his promise!

(b) Abraham and Sarah have a son!

(c) We are victorious over our doubts and obstacles!

(d) Jesus Christ is God's ultimate fulfillment!

Thus, God is constant and never fails. We are to believe in this faithful God who forever keeps his promises.—Andrew Mbama Okorie.

October 19. The Right Use of the Bible
TEXT: 2 Tim. 3:16–17; 2 Pet. 1:19–21.
These suggestions will steer one clear of some common dangers and help to make the Bible meaningful.

I. *The humanity of the Bible.* Keep in mind that the Bible, though it is a *holy* book, is a human book. It was written by human beings who used human language concerning human events in specific places at particular times. To be sure, they wrote of other things—of God, angels, and the unseen world. But it was men who wrote.

Many people are enthralled by the sweep of the Bible and place a high value upon it for its social, historical, and literary merit. But there is more to it than that.

II. *The inspiration of the Bible.* The Bible claims for itself that it is inspired of God (2 Tim. 3:16), that holy men spoke from God as they were moved by the Holy Sprit (2 Pet 1:21). And those who have read the Bible and lived by it have not found this hard to believe. There is something different about this book that puts it in a class by itself. One feels it "in his bones."

The same Holy Spirit leads us to the meaning God has for us in those same words today. In fact, unless the Holy Spirit gives life and actuality to the words we hear or read from the Bible, it is just like any other book for us. Therefore, "illumination" completes the meaning of inspiration.

To get a notion of the meaning of inspiration, we must look at the whole Bible—at what is actually there—and then form our definition. Any suitable definition will have to include the human element and the divine.

III. *The relevance of the Bible.* Seek to discover the relevance of the Bible. We do not make the Bible relevant to our needs —it is or it isn't! Our task is to discover in what ways it is already relevant.

The Bible deals with the ultimate issues of life—what gives life meaning and what robs life of meaning. It deals with the universal experience of death and what lies beyond. It deals with the relationship of man to God, who gives man life and who alone can overcome death. It deals with the relationships of human beings to one another and to their own selves.

Those who try to make the Bible a textbook in history, law, literature, or science miss the point. The intent of the Bible is not to present us with information—though much of the information in it is of inestimable worth. Its intent is to bring God to us, so that all of life may be transformed.

IV. *The interpretation of the Bible.* Use these practical principles as you interpret the Bible.

(a) Always try to understand the meaning of the verse by reading what goes before it and what follows it.

(b) Find out, if you can, what the entire book is about and what were the historical circumstances in which it was written.

(c) Compare the passage with other passages on the same theme. Sometimes one thought is completed by another. When thoughts seem to stand in contradiction, a consensus is needed: ask, "What is the trend of the Bible?"

(d) Let Jesus Christ be the standard by which the authority of any verse is decided.

(e) Listen for what the Holy Spirit has to say to *you.* Some issues in biblical interpretation can be settled only by the experts, those who know Hebrew and Greek and other special subjects. But most of the Bible lies before us waiting to be appropriated by any seeker of truth who has eyes to see and ears to hear.—James W. Cox.

October 26. Confidence in God
TEXT: Ps. 27.

I. God is the object of our confidence.

(a) There are hindrances to confidence in God.

(1) Presumption: failure to relate ourselves to him in such a way that he can bless us.

(2) Ignorance: failure to know what to expect God to do.

(b) The sources of true confidence in God are:

(1) God's righteous love.

(2) Our experience of the grace and goodness of God.

II. Our confidence in God should be strong!

(a) When we trust Christ for salvation.

(b) When we are tested:

(1) By temptation.

(2) By difficulty.
(3) By God's will for our life.
(4) By sorrow.
(c) When we therefore must walk by faith and not by sight.—James W. Cox.

November 2. The Happy Mourner
TEXT: Matt. 5:4.

Of all the sayings of Jesus that cause us to pause and wonder, there may be no other so radical, so far from what we consider "normal" as this Beatitude: "Happy is the man who mourns." What an odd contradiction in terms. Mourning is associated with sadness, not happiness. We reserve most of our mourning for funerals and hardly ever do you see anyone happy at funerals.

In order to understand this apparent paradox of happiness and mourning, we need to understand two things: why the happy man mourns and what is the source of his comfort.

I. He mourns for himself.
(a) His sins make him sorrowful.
(b) His unworthiness makes him sorrowful.
(c) The forgiveness of Christ gives him comfort.

II. He mourns for his loved ones.
(a) Their hurts make him sorrowful.
(b) Their blindness to sin makes him sorrowful.
(c) The love of Christ gives him comfort.

III. He mourns for the world.
(a) Its overwhelming problems make him sorrowful.
(b) Its failure to see its real need makes him sorrowful.
(c) The power of Christ gives him comfort.

Conclusion: Were it not for the forgiveness and love and power that are offered to us by Christ, we would deserve to wear the black cloth of mourning continuously, but because of his marvelous, transforming grace the man who mourns for the right reasons can truly be called happy.—James M. King.

November 9. In Jesus' Name
TEXT: John 16:23, 24.

The text is a part of our Savior's last discourse to his disciples. In order to understand it one should read chapters 14, 15, and 16 of John.

These words present four topics of reflection on prayer in Christ's name.

I. Up to this time men had not asked in Christ's name. While Christ's mediatorship, which is always the ground on which prayer is really heard, was not yet recognized, now they were taught to "ask the father in My name."

II. What is implied in asking in Christ's name?

(a) Acknowledgment of personal unworthiness. It says that a man does not expect to be heard in his own name. It is this conceit of personal merit, actual or attainable, that keeps men away from reliance on Christ.

(b) Acquiescence in the divine provision for our acceptance. Take the view presented in Hebrews. We have a great High Priest, Jesus the Son of God—he has passed into the heavens, has offered in the true sanctuary the everlasting sacrifice, which needs not to be repeated, and so he is able to save those who come unto God by him. But not only is he able to save; he has compassion on us, "touched with the feeling of our infirmities," and so on.

III. We are encouraged to ask in Christ's name. "Whatsoever ye shall ask," and so on. Of course, this must be taken with certain limitations. However, we are not left to our own judgment concerning the limitations. We are taught by the same inspired apostle who recorded the text. "If we ask anything according to his [e.g., Christ's] will," 1 John 5:14, 15. Spiritual blessings are always asked according to his will.

IV. We are told the result of asking in Christ's name. "That your joy may be full." Here is a promise of joy-full joy, even though the disciples were sorrowful. All through this discourse, he was directing their thoughts to the future, declaring that their sorrow should be turned into joy. The pious cling to religion, knowing that it can gild the clouds of life's inevitable sorrows with a heaven-sent joy.

What is the relation of prayer to joy? We might say that the very fact of communion with God is joy. Confidence of acceptance through the mediator is a source of delight. But it is by the answer to our prayers that our joy may be full.

(a) Ask for clearer practical views of justification by faith.

(b) Ask for sanctifying influences of God's Spirit, that you may be drawn near to God and kept near, filled with all the fullness of those blessings that God bestows.—John A. Broadus.

November 16. The Charlie Brown Syndrome

TEXT: Luke 23:39–43.

Most of us believe that we are one of the "little guys" on the stage of life. We lack the power and prestige that wealthy and powerful persons possess. Such persons, often in control of large businesses or governmental organizations, generally appear to get most of what they want. In turn, these very same persons have much power over the way that you and I live and often determine the prices we pay and the regulations we obey.

It often seems, moreover, that few persons in authority genuinely care about the "little guy." We feel that we are being constantly manipulated and abused. In short, we find ourselves identifying with the hero of the cartoon series *Peanuts*, the much maligned Charlie Brown. Like the comedian Rodney Dangerfield, how many times have we said to ourselves and others, "I don't get no respect!"

I. We can "adjust" to being the "little guy" in a number of ways.

(a) There is always anger. This is the road taken by all sorts of revolutionaries who battle everything that they consider to be powerful or privileged.

(b) Another form of "adjustment" is that of wallowing in self-pity. The world becomes an intractably hostile place full of those who are against us. Chronic depression and withdrawal overtake us and we can easily become involved in such destructive behavior as alcohol or drug abuse.

(c) Neither of these self-defeating responses to life really help us cope with our problems. Both are ineffective because they are based on the delusion that only our own actions will change the forces that affect our lives. In reality, there is another

force at work in our lives, and in our world, that is not controlled either by ourselves or by those with power and privilege.

II. (a) The words of Jesus to the penitent thief represent that other source of power in our world. Jesus, at the very time that he was dying on the cross for the sins of the entire world, took time to care for one insignificant man who was dying next to him. With the words, "Truly, I say to you, today you will be with me in Paradise," Jesus Christ shows us that he loves and cares for all persons, regardless of their station in life. The kingdom that he promised to the thief is open to all of us who respond to him in faith.

(b) Jesus reveals that the salvation he offers is large enough to cover all persons, but personal enough to fit the special needs of all people. Our God is thus clearly no impersonal and distant deity who reduces us to a number and who then arbitrarily imposes his will on us. His overriding characteristic is that of compassionate love.

III. Regardless of our present condition, the words of Jesus Christ help us to live with our relative powerlessness. Christ's words help us understand that our present status in life does not determine our acceptability to our God. We thus receive the hope to live our lives courageously without being crippled by bitterness and despair.

This insight, when it occurred to John Wesley, turned his life onto a new course that led to the formation of the Wesleyan Revival. At Aldersgate Street, Wesley was to receive the same sense of assurance as did the penitent thief. Welsey wrote these words of his experience that very night: "I felt I did trust in Christ, Christ alone for salvation; and an assurance was given me that he had taken away my sins, even mine, and saved me from the law of sin and death."

These words, of course, indicate that Wesley was able to place his trust in God and no longer be paralyzed by his own fears, frustrations, and anxiety. He had received at Aldersgate Street the empowering grace of Jesus Christ at the "low ebb" of his life and was ultimately able to turn personal defeat into victory through Jesus Christ.

All of us who hang on crosses of bitterness, frustration, and fear can take heart. The same grace that touched the heart of the thief, and later, of John Wesley, is very much alive today. All that we need to do to receive it is to say, with penitent hearts, "Jesus, remember me when you come into your kingdom!"—Rodney K. Miller.

November 23. Backfloating (Thanksgiving Sunday)
TEXT: Luke 12:16–31.

The newborn infant son of a pastor died three days after birth. Even the highly advanced medical technology of the medical center could not correct the congenital birth defect of the heart with which this hapless infant was born.

This unexpected and cruel tragedy has been repeated many times. All of us have known persons who have experienced similar tragedies. Maybe we have experienced one ourselves. Yet, the continued occurrence of such a tragedy reminds us that, in spite of all the precautions that we take and all the technology we possess, we are still vulnerable to tragedies of many kinds. Our lives are simply not so secure as we would like to believe.

I. Jesus was aware of human vulnerability, particularly among his disciples. He knew that our awareness of our own vulnerability, however, is the basis of anxiety —that vague, free-floating fear of the uncertainties of tomorrow.

Jesus challenged his disciples' anxiety with two illustrations taken from nature. He told his disciples to "consider the ravens: they neither sow nor reap, they have neither storehouse nor barn, yet God feeds them." In addition, he asked them to "consider the lilies, how they grow; they neither toil nor spin; yet I tell you, even Solomon in all his glory was not arrayed like one of these."

The birds and the flowers that are fed and clothed in beauty are extremely vulnerable. Jesus uses them as examples of the many common things for which God cares. If God cares so much for such vulnerable creatures as birds and flowers that have very brief lives and that are relatively insignificant, how much more must he care about human beings whom he made in his own image and into whom he breathed his Spirit, the very breath of life?

II. The message of the parable is, therefore, trust. In the very midst of an uncertain world, Jesus is asking us to trust God to care for us. Only if we can trust God will we ever have any freedom from the anxiety that can cripple and distort our lives. Jesus advises us not to worry about those things over which we have no control and about a future that is in the hands of God alone.

Only when we can trust our lives to our Lord will anxiety no longer be a problem. It is then that we are free to share with others the gifts that God has given to us and to praise and thank him for the blessings that he has bestowed upon us. When we realize that all we have and that who we are comes from God, then we no longer need to be anxious for we possess gifts that another cannot take from us.

III. We can summarize Christ's teaching on anxiety with a simple illustration. The most difficult stroke to master in swimming is the backstroke. Why? The backstroke first requires that the swimmer learn to backfloat. Now, backfloating is not particularly difficult; however, it does require that the swimmer relax. All the muscles in the swimmer's body must be relaxed. If any of the muscles are tense, then the swimmer will sink. The only way that we can keep our muscles relaxed enough to backfloat is not to struggle against the water. We must trust the physical property of a body of water to support lighter bodies on its surface.

We must have a similar trust in our Lord. Once we have learned to trust him, the anxieties of life will no longer overcome us, even in the midst of the most difficult of circumstances. Yet, trust in our Lord does not render us invulnerable or impervious to problems and heartache; however, it does grant to us the freedom to live our lives without the threat of debilitating fear and anxiety.

Thus, Thanksgiving is not merely a time when we thank God for the material comforts and the family ties that we enjoy. It is also a time to thank him for the blessings of the trusting relationship that he offers to us every day of the year through his Son, and our Savior, Jesus Christ.—Rodney K. Miller.

November 30 (Advent). Where Christ Comes
TEXT: Isa. 11:1–9.
Christ has come and Christ is coming; our task is to be ready, to be prepared. This is the theme of the Christian season of Advent.

We know that his initial coming and his presence now have brought a measure of what is to come fully when he comes again. All the best that is yet to be is already being realized to a degree where Christ comes now.

To summarize what Isaiah said: "Where the Messiah comes, God is. Where the Messiah comes, righteousness is. Where the Messiah comes, peace is." And because we know that Jesus Christ is the Messiah whom God sent, we can restate what Isaiah said: "Where Christ comes, God is. Where Christ comes, righteousness is. Where Christ comes, peace is."

I. *Righteousness*. The Messiah was seen to be the ideal king whose righteousness was grounded in revering God, thus the deep concern for and involvement with all people, even those usually not regarded. Where Christ comes, righteousness is. There is no way to conceive of his dealings with us and with all other people in a way that is less than righteous. When that righteousness has worked in our lives, then with it we will treat others rightly as we point them to him.

II. *Peace*. Because of the presence of the Messiah, paradise will be regained. Peace will be so perfect that there will be harmony in the natural order. Nature will move "backward" in the sense that it will become what it was created to be.

If natural enemies in the natural order can come to live at peace, cannot humankind learn to live peacefully among its own kind? Where Christ comes, peace is. It must be.

III. *God*. The Spirit of the Lord is given to persons so that they may be divinely equipped for demanding tasks.

God-like qualities and, more importantly, God himself are in Jesus Christ; so, where Christ comes, God is. When Christ comes into our lives, God is with us too—right now.—David A. Farmer.

December 7. The Ground of Hope
TEXT: Rom. 15:4.
People have said that where there is life, there is hope. That old adage may very well be true, but what they should go on to say is that while everyone hopes, not everyone places hope in the same thing. In this brief parenthesis in the letter to the Romans, Paul gives us some idea of the true ground for our hope.

I. The need for hope.
(a) Hope is a necessity of life, just like food and water.
(b) The only alternative is despair.
(c) It is impossible to remain neutral about the future, whether that future is the next minute or the rest of one's lifetime.

II. False grounds of hope.
(a) Our own resources.
(b) The goodness of humanity.
(c) The government.
(d) The institutional church.

III. The true ground of hope.
(a) At first glance it appears that Paul is asking us to put our hope in the Scriptures, but even the Scriptures are an inadequate ground of hope.
(b) The Scriptures point to the reality greater than any of the false grounds of hope.
(c) By foretelling our situation, Scripture encourages us to pass through this situation in hope.
(d) Even the Old Testament, Paul's only Scripture, foretells the coming Messiah and demonstrates the sovereignty of God.

Conclusion: Hope is something we all have. Think how tragic it would be to have lived your life based on a false hope. You may consider the alternatives all you wish, but they pale in comparison to the power and love of God as it has been revealed in Christ.—James M. King.

December 14. The 'Triple A' Bible—Adventure, Authority, Action
The Bible is *absent* from our churches and it does not bode well for our future.

I. *Adventure*. We will see the study of the Bible as an adventure.

(a) There is an adventure in discovering new historical facts.

(b) As we study the Bible we are listening in on a conversation. It is a dialogue between God and his people. They clash in anger. They love each other. The murder of God's son is plotted, and the murderers are forgiven. The love story between God and the human race is told, and we are allowed to listen in, and as we listen we are drawn into the greatest story ever told.

(c) To study the Bible is also an adventure in self-discovery as we come to see ourselves as God's children, as God's wayward, forgiven children, as a people especially chosen to be the object of God's eternal love, and as a people who serve a risen savior.

II. *Authority*.

(a) In the church the Bible is God's word to us and the Bible speaks to us with divine authority.

(b) The Bible loses authority when it is abused by Christians. The Puritans abused the Bible when they declared that the Bible sanctioned the execution of deranged old women whom they called witches.

(c) The Bible has authority because over the centuries it has been the experience of the church that God uses the words of Scripture to carry on his own work of saving and sanctifying his people.

III. *Action*. Perhaps the real test of the authority of the Bible is the use we make of it, if we truly let the Bible be an authoritative guide for Christian living. Often it is the stories of the Bible that sink into our souls and provide guidance for us.

The more we study the events and people of the Bible, and the more we expose ourselves to the fears and joys of the psalmist, the more we know of God's holy laws. The more we know about the life of Christ, the better we will be able to understand ourselves and to see what is really going on in our world today. And the way we behave toward each other, and what we accomplish in this life for good or evil will come out of our Bible understanding. When we become immersed in the strange and alien world of the Bible, its truth will seep into us without our being fully conscious of what is happening.

The greatest achievements of Christian living come from a people immersed in the traditions and stories of the Bible. When we breathe the spirit of the prophets and sing with the psalmists, and struggle for the gospel like Paul, then the Bible is a part of us and inevitably finds expression in daily decisions and how we live.—Stuart G. Leyden.

December 21. (Sunday before Christmas) God with Us

TEXT: Matt. 1:23.

We may not easily define the word *incarnation*, but one of the names given to the Babe of Bethlehem beautifully expresses its central meaning. "A virgin shall bring forth a son, and they shall call His name Emmanuel, which being interpreted is, God with us" (Matt. 1:23). That's the meaning and the message of Christmas: God with us!

I. *God is with us to be one of us*. Christ's humanity was real. As John wrote, he "was made flesh, and dwelt among us." He entered fully into human experience and so is able "to sympathize with our weaknesses . . . one who, because of his likeness to us, has been tested every way, only without sin" (Heb. 4:15, NEB). The men who wrote the New Testament saw Jesus as a man, but they came to know him as Savior, before whom they drew back in awe and stammered "my Lord and my God!"

II. *God is with us to feel with us*. The name Emmanuel describes the God who knew what it was to be a man. He felt what we feel—hunger and thirst, acceptance and rejection, desire for life and fear of death. He still responds to a penniless Lazarus, a prodigal boy, a doubting Thomas. He knows the demands of daily toil, the gaiety of a wedding party, the loneliness of a wilderness, and the shame and pain of a cross. He is with me when I laugh or cry or sit in silence.

III. *God is with us to save us*. He appeared among us to share our fate, to die for our sins, to be our Savior. In this same chapter of Matthew that says "they shall call His name Emmanuel," it also says "thou shalt call His name Jesus: for He shall save His people from their sins." God in Christ is with us in our guilt, "Who His own self bare our sins in His own body on the tree" (1 Pet. 2:24). God is with us to save us.

Let's close with a reference to an Easter story. It's all part of the same one Gospel you know. When the two men walked toward Emmaus, "Jesus Himself drew near, and went with them" (Luke 24:15). As you make your way toward Christmas, remember that Jesus wants to walk with you—to and beyond Christmas, to be with you, to feel with you and to save you. He is Emmanuel: God with us! —Bramwell Tripp.

December 28. When God Builds a Church

TEXT: Col. 1:15–20; Eph. 2:9–22; 1 Pet. 2:5.

Obviously, a building isn't a church, but a structure that houses God's people who are the church. The people of God are the church. We have existence as a church—we have a present and a future—only insofar as we are led and shaped and built by him.

Incidentally, when God starts building a church, it is never finished. He is always working on us. We don't wait for completion before we are functional. After a few essentials are in place, we must be usable.

I. When God builds a church, he is working on the basis of careful plans. The church isn't the result of some heavenly fantasy or a divine passing whim. This is made clear in Colossians 1:15–20.

II. When God builds a church, it is laid on a sure and secure foundation. We find in Ephesians 2:19–22 indication that the foundation of God's church centers in Jesus Christ himself, the cornerstone that both completes and holds together the whole structure.

III. When God builds a church, he uses sturdy materials. He doesn't use brick and mortar or wood and steel. God uses living stones (1 Pet. 2:5). Living stones are committed to the cause of Christ, growing, loving, serving, dependable, faithful, and flexible.

God is trying to build spiritual structures. If he does, our buildings will be wonderful expressions of his handiwork. —David A. Farmer.

SECTION III. *Resources for Communion Services*

Topic: Breaking the Bread and Revelation

TEXT: Isa. 43:1–4; 1 Pet. 1:17–23; Luke 24:13–35.

I. It rates as one of the most beautiful of the postresurrection appearances that Jesus makes. Two followers with crushed dreams and heavy disappointments trudge their way to Emmaus on that Sunday afternoon. They are suddenly joined by Jesus whom they do not recognize. They reach a stopping point, they ask the stranger to join them in a meal, and in the course of that meal he takes the bread, blesses it, breaks it, and suddenly—like the answer to a logarithm, the solution to calculus, the synthesis from the thesis and the antithesis—they see it. In my mind, I fantasize they had been at the back of the five thousand on that day he fed the masses and they watched him hold the bread in a certain way and bless it and break it and they remarked to one another then: "That was a most unique way of breaking bread, don't you think?" And when he did it this time, they remembered.

II. But that is nothing new to us. For since the beginning the Church has believed that revelation, remembrance, blessing, and intimacy with the mystery of God in Christ has come through the Communion, the Supper, the Eucharist. The names are different, but the revelation is the same. Paul in 1 Corinthians 11:23 gives instructions about the supper: "that the Lord Jesus, on the night he was betrayed, took bread, gave thanks to God (*eucharistia*), broke it, and said, 'This is my body . . .' " The early Christians took that Pauline passage and made it an essential part of the eucharistic ritual. We print it the way it has come through the centuries: *sursum corda*. "Lift up your hearts"—in thanksgiving they meant.

III. Why do we do this so often, this Eucharist, this Supper, and why is it so important? Because there is revelation in the taking of the Supper. Eyes are opened to an appreciation of something we've already known. Or something new is revealed. Or in our bowed confession we find out something about ourselves we never knew before. As with those at Emmaus, so with us, there can be a striking revelation when the bread is broken and the cup is lifted. We see things in a new perspective, if our attitude is right. If you're looking and expecting and care to see, there is another who breaks the bread and lifts the cup here today. And his presence is with you as you take today—the Body and Blood of our Lord.—Thomas H. Conley.

Topic: What Does Communion Require of Us?

TEXT: 1 Cor. 11:17–32

This table before which we are gathered has been the cause for more divisiveness than perhaps any other single thing in the history of Christianity. How ironic that the communion table should be the catalyst for such division. In the name of the integ-

44

rity of this celebration, communion—that is community—has again and again been shattered. Love has been sacrificed for integrity.

The problems at Corinth that Paul addresses revolved around this table. Corinth was a city of wide economic spread, with both very rich and very poor people living there. It seems that the upper class folks came to the Lord's Supper—which was, at this time, literally a meal—with all sorts of elaborate food and drink. The poor and the slaves, on the other hand, could muster little to bring, and sometimes all they could manage was what they could steal. Imagine, if you will, a poor refugee family amid the tailgate party at the Harvard-Yale football game. That's what it was like in Corinth.

Paul directs his initial comments to the wealthy. He says, "Don't you have a home where you can eat before you come to the Lord's Supper? All of this gluttony, this drunkenness, this display of excess in front of people who come to the Supper hungry—how can you humiliate those who have nothing?" Then Paul reminds them that this isn't merely a matter of simple courtesy. He reminds them that the unity of the meal issues from Christ's very presence in the meal. He says, remember the words of our Lord. He took bread and wine, blessed them, and said, "This is my body . . . This is the new covenant in my blood. Do this in remembrance of me." Paul reminds the Corinthians that this isn't any ordinary meal where the dictates of courtesy should prevail. He says, remember that Christ has instituted this meal and has said that he is present in it. How can we practice segregation here? How can the wealthier among us be so indifferent to the feelings and needs of the poorer among us?

But this is not the end of it. Paul then goes on with a terrible indictment. He warns, "Anyone who eats and drinks without discerning the body, eats and drinks judgment upon himself or herself." Now, whose body does Paul refer to here? Most scholars now agree that Paul is referring to the body of the believers—to the congregation. Paul is saying we must discern our congregation, our whole group, our unity. Or else we heap judgment upon ourselves by coming to this meal. What does the life of community require? Without answering this question for ourselves, our presence at this table is indictment, and not blessing. What does the life of community require?

When Paul insists on the primacy of community life, he really drives us to the primacy of love. Love—that principle, that experience, that reality that unites diverse people, expectations, and hopes, and weaves them into the wholeness of the body. Paul's hymnic plea for love—the famous thirteenth chapter of Corinthians—is intended to solve the bitter fighting at the Corinthian church. Sure, we do read it at weddings but to do so reminds us that married life might be as rocky as life in Corinth. Paul says, let love decide how we sort out our community life. There are no hard and fast rules. There are no points so critical, no integrity so important to defend that love should be sacrificed. Love bears all things, believes all things, hopes all things, endures all things. Love never ends. As for prophecy—well, Paul says today's prophetic integrity may be tomorrow's dying theological fad, but love never ends. The love in this body is the integrity to fight for.

Paul invites us to examine ourselves in light of our contribution to the unity, to the love of the congregation. And Paul's invitation also may lead us to examine ourselves in light of our contribution to the unity and love of the congregation of the entire world. We're led to examine ourselves and ask, what does love of this church require of me? What does love of this world require of me?

One way to answer this question is to bring it to the beloved. What do you require of me? Paul says, love does not insist on its own way. Love finds a way to go with the other, to find common ground on which to move forward.

As we prepare to share the elements of this table, let us consider the requirements of our community. What does Christ's body, here in this place, require of each of us? What of our gifts? What of our leadership? What of our reconciliation and moderation? What does the body require? And what about the body of Christ as it stretches around the world? What does this volatile, multicolored body require? What of our gifts, our leadership, our reconciliation and moderation? This worldwide body of which we are a member—what does it require?

Christ's body is present here. Whatever we believe—Christ is present in the elements, as a memory, as a spirit, or actually physically present—whatever we believe, these differences will no longer keep us from this table. May God grant that, finding unity here, we might carry its power with us into all of our lives.—Joanne M. Swenson.

Topic: The Lord's Presence—in Our Remembrance

TEXT: 1 Cor. 11:24.

Memory is an important asset. It is our collective consciousness, how we know who we are. The poet said that God gave us memory so we could have roses in December. That is a nice sentiment, but a greenhouse will do that.

Memory gives us a sense of history, our origin, roots, identity. By it we relive special events: birthdays, anniversaries, days of national significance. The Lord's Supper is a call to remember Christ and the cross.

I. Memory relives past events, focusing on their significance. Note the strong verbs in the account of the Supper's institution: Jesus took bread, gave thanks, broke it, and gave it to the disciples.

Recall the event of Jesus' suffering (called the passion). Hear the cries of the crowd, Pilate's protest of innocence; see Judas' dark kiss of betrayal. Listen to the crack of a whip, the thud of a hammer, a cry of anguish from the cross. Recall the towering crosses silhouetted against that angry Judean sky. Hear the sobs of his brokenhearted mother, and later those of Simon Peter.

"It was for me he died at Calvary." Thanks be to God!

II. Memory teaches who Jesus is: both son of Mary and Son of God. It recalls why he came: to show us the Father's limitless love, "to seek and save the lost" (Luke

19:10, RSV). Like the penitent thief, we want to pray, "Lord, remember me."

Memory also teaches us where Jesus is. He is interceding on our behalf at the Father's right hand, remembering us. He is indwelling believers with the Holy Spirit. Jesus is our inspiration here at the Lord's table. He is present with us in our remembrance and observance. His spiritual power is ours. Joy!—Alton McEachern in *Proclaim*.

Topic: Sacred Scraps

TEXT: Luke 16:19–31.

Albert Schweitzer was troubled. A world-class theologian, physician-surgeon of note, one of the great classic interpreters of Bach on the organ—he was all these things and more. Yet something terribly bothered him. One day on rereading our Scripture parable for today, he realized his problem: that Africa was a beggar sprawled against Europe's doorstep, and no one was doing very much about it. It was soon after this that Schweitzer left his ease of Europe for the agony of Africa.

The parable of the rich man and Lazarus is a classic of literature: so tightly knit that not one phrase is wasted. The rich man is named *Dives*, which means "wealthy." *Lazarus*, poor beggar, means, "God will help."

Every sentence adds something to Dives' wealth. He is clothed in purple and fine linen . . . he feasted—in luxury—every day . . . he is a symbol of indolent self-indulgence.

I. Lazarus is the ultimate beggar. Content to hope for a scrap of bread, he is so weak he has not the strength to fight off the street dogs who pester him and lick at his ulcerated sores of his ruined body. Lazarus does not even dream of a better future.

The wasted bread for which Lazarus hopes is itself a story. There were neither knives nor forks at table in Jesus' day. No napkins either, and in wealthy houses when a glutton finished his meal, he wiped his hands with a chunk of bread that he then tossed out to the gathered dogs and beggars who—otherwise unfed—had quite an interesting battle for possession of the scrap.

Death—as always it does—came to Dives and Lazarus. At this point, the parable shows a new seating arrangement in which Lazarus—undoutedly in enormous surprise—is carried directly to heaven in "Abraham's bosom," the plushest of all super-stretch limosines! And Dives: he grovels in the pit of hell, even more surprised than Lazarus to find where *he* is.

II. What was the great sin of Dives that has him begging a sacred scrap of Eternal Mercy and, refused that, pleading a tiniest crumb of warning of this ending so his living brothers might be spared. Even that is rejected, his sin so heavy!

The likelihood is that in life, Dives not only allowed Lazarus his scraps, but let other beggars loll around his place as well. It's a rather decent concession for a man who could have ordered the huddled humanity and hounds away. There's no indication Lazarus kicked at Lazarus in passing or was otherwise cruel in words or deeds. The sin of Dives was that he never *noticed* Lazarus, never saw him really; he accepted as a shrug of life that Lazarus—or someone else—should lie in pain and hunger at his feet while he wallowed in a belch of opulence. It was not what Dives *did* so much as what he *didn't do* that gave him hell.

Dives could look on the world's suffering and need, and feel no grief or pity that could be marshalled into help. *His was the punishment of the man who never noticed.*

III. It's difficult for most of us to find Dives' lifestyle commanding so heavy a punishment. We understand the joy of a new designer label shirt or jeans, a special restaurant meal, or a sporting event or concert that costs more for a few hours of pleasure than our grandparents earned in a week or a month—these things just show the joyous affluence of our age and that luxury is not a sin. What's a sin is glibly to overlook some needs we should be helping meet.

How many times as a child were you told to finish that horrid inedible stuff on your plate because thousands of hungry children in India were going to bed starving that night? How many times have you wished—more in frustration than charity —that someone would come to dump your platter on some infant in India? Our true caring is something larger than the disposal of the bread we wipe our hands on.

IV. Today—with Christians the world over—we share the sacred food of the Lord's table. We are royal guests, and part of the symbol of our Communion is that we taste just a bit—never overfeeding, never leaving full and uncomfortable—for this nourishes our spirit far more than our stomachs. While we share, we are obligated as well to see the misery around us, to share true food with our neighbor, to present our offerings so our neighbors in need may not simply survive, but improve: in spirit, in strength, as *neighbors*.—Milton E. Detterline.

ILLUSTRATIONS

THOSE WHO SEE AND SEEK. Christian hope is a continent of the Spirit that grows larger in the very effort to explore it. The more we traverse its valleys and mountain ranges, the less easily can it be mapped. Its roads are open only to pilgrims seeking their homeland. To them the country into which they are called is more real than the realm of shadows and deception that they leave behind. To casual onlookers the reverse is true, God's kingdom being far less tangible and dependable than the kingdoms they refuse to leave.—Paul S. Minear.

TRANSFORMATION. The grain of wheat must be ground and the grape pressed to make the flour and the wine that will be transformed into the Body and the Blood of Christ as the fulfillment of his resurrectional life captured in the Eucharist. So we, too, must also die to whatever is false in our being against our true nature as seen in the image and likeness of Jesus Christ. We must be pressed by Divine Love until there is nothing of self left so that we live now no longer as ourselves, but Christ Jesus lives in us (Gal. 2:20). It is only through such a death unto new life that Christ will be able to live within us and we will be able to go forth to bring about that abundant fruit that Christ has destined to be produced through our humble instrumentality in bringing him to many others.—George A. Maloney.

THE WINNING CROSS.   A marriage ceremony is significant in the light of what follows it. If bride and bridegroom separated after it, it would mean but little. Similarly the historic act of dying on the cross was not the redemptive factor in our deliverance, save that it was the pledge of his agelong giving of himself to us, the promise that he will never leave us nor forsake us. The historic crucifixion is to be compared with the wedding ceremony; but, to put it crudely, it is the living together with Christ after we have been drawn to the Cross that will win us from our evil ways and save us from our sins. This our Lord contracted to do. As he gave himself to the uttermost until, while still in a body, he could give no more, so now he still gives

himself to the uttermost to all who will receive him.—Leslie Weatherhead.

THE FIRST STEPS.   The first healing steps that make reconciliation possible cannot come from the rebel and the stranger. The reconciling initiative can only come from the side of God. God draws the sting of sin by exposing himself in the person of his Son to its full consequences, and by turning the cross, the fitting symbol of man's rebellion and estrangement, into the very instrument of our redemption. What more could man do to display his rejection of God than to crucify God's Son and his own representative? What more could God do to effect man's reconciliation to himself than to transform this same crowning act of rejection into the instrument of forgiving and restoring Love?—H. E. W. Turner.

SECTION IV.
Resources for Funeral Services

SERMON SUGGESTIONS

Topic: What Death Does
TEXT: 1 Cor. 15:45–48.

In 1969 a man at a hospital in Alexandria, Louisiana, "died" twenty-nine times. After each experience when his heart actually stopped beating, he was resuscitated. And he even lived to tell the story.

Due to the success of medical science in prolonging life and transplanting human organs, the question of the meaning of death has assumed new proportions. Since organs used in transplants have to be "fresh," the question of when one is actually dead has become significant.

From the Christian understanding another question is significant: What does death do?

I. *Death shows our mortality*. Philip of Macedon had a slave to whom he had given a standing order. He was to come to the king each morning of his life, no matter what the king was doing, and say in a loud voice: "Philip, remember that thou must die."

Death is a universal experience. Even the Christian is not delivered from the physical experience of death.

Death is a consequence of life. All things that live must also die.

II. *Death highlights the victory of Christ*. Jesus died too. But he achieved victory over death through the resurrection.

Jesus gave to us a whole new perspective on death. Whereas the Old Testament people feared death, Jesus showed that death was secondary to life with him.

Life does not end with death. Life as we know it ends, but he has assured continued life through faith in Christ.

By his death and resurrection, Jesus defeated sin and death. Regeneration and resurrection bring this victory to us.

III. *Death demonstrates the meaning of faith*. Death does not separate us from God. In fact, death makes possible a larger fellowship with God.

Jesus Christ has given us victory over death. Therefore, the Christian does not have to fear death. He faces death with the same faith that he faces life.—James E. Carter.

Topic: The Believer's Destiny
TEXT: 1 Cor. 15:20–23.

I. The resurrection of Jesus is rightly reported as historical fact. It happened!

Eager to settle the question about the reality of the Resurrection, Paul speaks out forthrightly as a witness who had seen the risen Lord. Paul reminds his readers that he was only one of a larger company of eyewitnessess, a company that included Peter, the other apostles, James, and more than five hundred other believers. Interestingly, although Paul was the last one to see the risen Lord in bodily form, he is usually given a dominant place as witness because he wrote so fully about his experience of seeing. So when Paul affirms that "Christ has been raised from the dead!" he is not offering a mere echo of what he heard some other noteworthy believers say. No, he is giving his own direct statement about his own direct experience.

But the resurrection of Jesus is not a fact

49

to be held in isolation. Paul therefore goes on in his statement to deal with the real consequences of that happening for us. He therefore deals with how the fact of the resurrection relates to our faith and hope, and how it affects our nature and history. Paul knew and stated what the Church must always remember: the resurrection of Jesus demonstrates the destiny of every believer. Hear again that grand declaration of our destiny as believers: "For as by a man came death, by a man has come also the resurrection of the dead. For as in Adam all die, so also in Christ shall all be made alive" (vv. 21–22).

The resurrection of Jesus is not to be understood only as a fact peculiar to his station as Son of God. It is to be understood also as historical forecast of what God intends as a consequence for all of us as believers. Paul therefore refers to the rising of Christ as "first fruits" (v. 23), meaning that the resurrection of Christ from death is the first evidence of what will happen on a larger scale later. This whole theme connects us with the great drama of redemption, with God's plan for his Church, a plan filled with sequential events and happenings. We cannot fully search out the scheme of redemption by rational inquiry; so much is understood by faith and faith alone. Meanwhile, our lives are held steady in the assurance generated from a knowledge of what he has revealed is to take place for us.

Our passage tells us that what happened to Jesus is going to happen for us. He died and rose again. We must die, and we, too, will be raised from death. Paul links this happening with the coming of Jesus in glory: "But each in his own order: Christ the first fruits, then *at his coming* those who belong to Christ" (v. 23, italics added).

II. Our resurrection therefore, is rightly announced as a future happening. And it will take place.

There is a resurrection in our future. On the basis of the passage I can claim this for every believer, for Paul was addressing a Christian congregation and was writing to strengthen each member's faith and courage to live. But I must go on and declare that resurrection is by no means limited to believers.

According to the Bible, there is a resurrection in every person's future. Just as all die, so must all be raised—and for cause. According to Daniel 12:2, "those who sleep in the dust of the earth shall awake, some to everlasting life and some to shame and everlasting contempt." Jesus taught us to expect a general resurrection when he declared that "the hour is coming when all who are in the tombs will hear his voice and come forth, those who have done good, to the resurrection of life, and those who have done evil, to the resurrection of judgment" (John 5:28–29).

The certainty of our resurrection is clear from Scripture. The question of importance is therefore to what destiny will we rise? There is one destiny for those who are in Christ. It is a destiny of glory in the presence of God and Christ. There is another destiny, an awesome one, for those who ended their lives here without having placed their trust in Christ as Savior and Lord. There is a resurrection in your future and mine. What preparation have you made for that future life?

III. When Jesus was raised from death, he had been given his most complete and exalted form, and he had entered into his most complete and exalted expression. He was experiencing what God had planned for him. We who believe are included in that plan. Resurrection will mean for us what it meant for him. It will mean a body consistent with the nature of our full life with God and the level of our new existence. It will mean the full realization of our fulfillment as children of God.

The truth about his experience is meant to influence our beliefs, our behavior, and our expectation. That truth certainly influenced the life and character of those who saw him alive after his death. Those eyewitnesses found themselves at new frontiers in their knowledge and understanding of God's work in Jesus and in themselves. And they dared to trust what was happening to them because they knew it was all connected with the reality of the Jesus they knew.

Many of us have dared to believe on him through their word, and yet our confidence in Christ now involves far more than the report that first persuaded us.

What has made Christian faith so persistent? What keeps it secure? Why do those who believe continue to do so—even in the face of arguments and assaults?

The best answer to these questions comes in the words of R. W. Dale (1829–1895), that noted English preacher who excelled in handling great themes and deep questions. Speaking eagerly on behalf of those who believe in a living Christ, Dale explained, "Whatever may have been the original grounds of their faith, their faith has been verified in their own personal experience." True faith in Christ has always been a matter of personal consciousness, and it involves real-life experiences in connection with his spiritual presence that command certainty. And where such experience is known, the influence of his own resurrection is an evident force in the mind, heart, and life.

The Resurrection means that God has broken into our old human order with a divine deed of utter newness; he has taken that closed situation we call death and shown us that it stands open at the other end—the door torn off at the hinges! The Resurrection means that we believers do not have to guess about life in the future world, nor do we have to worry about the course of nature and history as they will affect us here.

There is a resurrection in our future. These meanings are worthy of our full belief, our best behavior, and our unyielding hope. They are meanings rooted in his life and experience as God's Son and our risen Savior.—James Earl Massey.

Topic: A Funeral Meditation on Christmas Eve

TEXT: Luke 2:33–35; Matt. 2:16–18; John 11:33–36.

"And a sword will pierce your own soul also." "Rachel weeping for her children; she refused to be consoled, because they were no more." "Jesus wept."

What special word of comfort and consolation can I bring to ease the pain in your hearts?

If I were to bring merely my own feeble human words, they could never begin to fill even a portion of the void you now feel. As a minister of the Gospel, I bring to each of you in your hour of grief and sense of loss, not my own word, but the Word of God.

The Gospel does not shrink from the reality and sting of death. Even in the moment of Mary's great joy, the shadow of death is there: "and a sword will pierce your own soul also." Here in the experience of Mary, the face of death is present. Here too, we are able to understand Mary's great pain and uncertainty; for this sword of death also pierces your heart and soul. This Christmas is for you, as it was for Mary, filled with a deep darkness and sense of dread.

And your voices of grief and sorrow, your tears and broken hearts, are also reflected in the voices of the weeping mothers of Bethlehem, refusing to be consoled because their children were no more. The Son of God had been born for the salvation of the world; yet for these sorrowing mothers there was no joy at Christmas, only the aching heart and the tear-stained eyes. In the midst of all this suffering and pain, this sorrow and grief, the Gospel stands; proclaiming the birth of Christ Jesus, the Son of God, the One who would willingly bear our sorrows and griefs; the One who loves us, so that he would come to us and share our common lot; the One born in a manger, in the shadow of a cross.

The One who was born in a manger, whose life from the very beginning was surrounded by the mystery and sting of death, this One lives, this Christ our Savior lives! And because he lives he can stand by you now, in all his power and authority. He is with you. Above and beyond all others, he knows how your hearts ache; "Jesus wept." Before all others he desires to share your sense of pain and sorrow; "Jesus wept."

So here is the gift your loved one would offer you on this Christmas Eve: he asks you to let in this One who was born in a manger and lives eternally; he asks you to allow this One, this Word of God, to bring comfort and strength, to heal your broken hearts. Be gifted with the Truth that this One, this Jesus, stands beyond the dark pale of death and greets his brothers and sisters. Be comforted; know that Jesus, the great Shepherd, has walked by your loved one and with him through "the valley of the shadow of death" to bring "rest beside still waters" and to "restore (his) soul."

When, and as you are able, receive this gift from Christ Jesus, on this Christmas Eve. "Lo," he says, "I am with you always."—Albert J. D. Walsh.

Topic: That Your Days May Be Prolonged

TEXT: Deut. 5:16.

How do you measure the quality of a person's life? How do you come to understand a person's life to have been meaningful; in particular as you stand on this side of death, and he has passed over that great divide? I believe we can see the meaningfulness and the quality of a person's life most clearly when the measuring device is the Word of God. We can take this great yardstick of God's and lay it across any person's lifespan, and it will reveal the richness or the barrenness, the fruitfulness or the fruitlessness of one's life.

The commandments of God form the particular order of the measure and quality of life. These words that have thundered over the centuries with the voice that booms "You shall," 'You shall not," and "Neither shall you" point us in the direction God would have us take. These words are not meant to frighten, rather they are given out of love and concern; they reveal the pathway that leads to life and health, to joy and fulfillment. These words oppose all devices we would use to measure the value of a person's life and call our methods of measurement into question.

You could never measure the quality of R.'s life, as we so often choose to do, by the wealth and richness of his material possessions. He had little in the way of worldly goods. And we could never adequately measure the quality of R.'s life by his many friends and family members. He lived very much to himself. We could not measure the quality of R.'s life by considering the great contributions of talent and energy he left behind for all succeeding generations. He wrote no book, he passed along no great information, he made no

contribution to science. These are the values we as humans use.

In the sight of God, R.'s life was of great value and worth. Why? Because he followed the command of God, he listened to the voice that would insure a rich and full life. "Honor your father and mother." This R. did with the greatest sincerity and devotion, with fidelity and love. While we look to the great and glorious accomplishments of a person as the measure of his or her value, the Lord fixes his gaze upon the seemingly small and insignificant events, such as caring for and remaining faithful to one's parents, even to the point of self-sacrifice. It is to be the person who follows this command that God promises "prolonged days" and that all "may go well."

The divine measure, laid across the life of this man, reveals the true quality of his being in the sight of God. His days were prolonged, and it went well with R. The promises of God in this one command came to full fruit in R.'s life, and that beyond all else makes his life both meaningful and of great value! Our measurement is temporal; God's is eternal. Our measurement is limited to the material and the practical; God's penetrates to the very depth of human existence, to the heart and soul. Our measurement ends with death, which is the very point at which God's measurement on the value of human life begins.

R. has earned his place at the table in the kingdom of God, not merely through obedience but through grace. We may deem his life small and insignificant, but then again the Word of God measures our value judgment, through these words of the Lord Jesus himself: "And behold, some who are last will be first, and some who are first will be last."—Albert J. D. Walsh.

Topic: When Sorrow Comes

It is easy to offer cheap advice to those in sorrow. This sermon is not intended as advice. It is rather sharing with you a philosophy of life that I have used for many years.

I. I would point out seven "Don'ts," and then seven constructive suggestions. The seven "Don'ts" are hedges we shall put in along the pathway of sorrow to keep us from wandering into bypaths of futility and frustration.

(a) Don't think your case unique. It can be matched many times over. Sorrow is bound to hit you in some form or other in a world of this kind. With unfinished people in an unfinished world we're bound to have troubles and sorrows. The question is not their coming—the question is what they do to us when they come.

(b) Don't give yourself to self-pity. That will lead straight to introversion, and that will cause the sorrow to fester. A self-pitying self is a pitiable self. Don't allow yourself to slip into *that*.

(c) Don't give yourself to excessive grief. Many do it, thinking they are thereby showing their love for a departed loved one. It is a mistake. If the departed loved one could see you, he or she would see how excessive grief causes deterioration of the personality.

(d) Don't retail your sorrows. It may be well to talk over your thoughts with an understanding friend—to get a trouble up and out is often to relieve the pain. But don't syndicate your sorrows. Don't share them with everybody you meet.

(e) Don't resign yourself to sorrow and feel it will continue. The probabilities are that unless you keep your sorrow artificially alive, it will not continue. Time is a great healer.

(f) Don't fight against a trouble directly. Call your attention off from your sorrow by getting into constructive work for others. The clenched-fist method of dealing with sorrow fails, for it makes you tense; and when you are tense, the healing, peace-giving power of God cannot get through to you.

(g) Don't complain. If you do, your mind will look around for reasons to justify that complaint. The more you complain about things, the more things you will have to complain about.

II. I am sorry to have to start you off with "Don'ts," but they are only danger signals set up along the road to victory. We turn now to see how we can walk that road. We will work out seven steps to victory.

(a) If suffering has come to you, see whether or not you yourself are the cause of it. It may be that the universe is kicking back in suffering and frustration because of (1) your own sins or (2) your wrong attitudes to life. If there are sins in your life causing physical, mental, spiritual disruption, surrender them and lay them at the feet of Christ. Go over your life to see whether you are taking attitudes that are themselves causing disruption and suffering.

(b) But your difficulties may not come from your own sins and wrong reactions— they may come entirely unmerited. Jesus made it plain that suffering may not be a sign of sin. He said that unmerited suffering need not merely be borne; *it can be used. Determine, then, to make your sorrow make you—and others*.

(c) Remember God is doing with his sorrows exactly what he is asking you to do with yours. Since God is love, the burdens of love must fall on him. It is the nature of love to insinuate itself into the pains and sorrows and sins of its loved ones. Love takes it on itself and makes what falls on the loved ones its own. If this is true, then God is suffering in our sufferings, is hurt in our hurts, and is wounded in our sins. And what does he do with his sorrows? *He uses them*. He makes them redemptive.

(d) "Take what you have and make something out of it." Don't cry for what you haven't; take what you have and make it into something else.

(e) If you are going to do this, then learn to draw on the resources of God—learn how to pray. Go aside and in the quietness let down the bars, let go the tensions, let the healing of God go through every fiber of your hurt soul. He invades you; he heals you; he lifts you; he gives you wings; he makes you into a victorious spirit. *Provided*—and this is the point—provided you surrender your sorrow, your frustration into his healing hands. Don't hold it. If you hold it, it will fester within you. Let him have it—forever!

(f) But if God does not answer my prayers? Your faith rests not upon this, that, or the other happenings, but on something unchanging—the character of God. That always remains. Trust "in spite of" when you cannot trust "on account of."

(g) Thank God for your sorrow, even though you cannot understand it now. Into the cup of your life is going all the gladness and beauty, all the pain and disappointments, all the Gethsemane hours and the torturing moments of the cross—it is all going into the enriching of the cup of your life, the cup that you will put to the lips of others. *Then thank God for that cup.* It is richer for suffering—for suffering triumphed over. The thanks turns it all from a cruel hurt to you to a constructive healing of others through your tragedy.

You, too, can thank God for your sorrow itself, for what God is going to do *to* you and *through* you because of that sorrow. He is going to help you, not merely to bear it, but to *use* it.—E. Stanley Jones.

ILLUSTRATIONS

EPITAPH OF VICTORY.   John Newton, author of "Amazing Grace" and other hymns, was once captain of a slave ship. Christ completely changed his life. Through William Wilberforce, Newton indirectly contributed to the bill adopted by the British Parliament that abolished slavery in all British domains. The words on his tombstone describe him: "John Newton, clerk, once an infidel and libertine, a servant of slaves in Africa, was, by the rich mercy of our Lord and Savior Jesus Christ, preserved, restored, pardoned, and appointed to preach the faith he had long labored to destroy."

GOD'S INTENTION.   What, then, of the Christian hope for the individual? It is no cheap confidence in a vague something beyond death with which to quiet the fear of dissolution. It is rooted and grounded in the nature of God, in the faith that God does not let himself be defeated even by death, that what he begins he finishes. Paul says, "He that hath begun a good work in you will complete it." In Jesus Christ, God has revealed his intention for us, the life for which he has destined us, to be made in his own image. Not even for Paul was that goal reached within his lifetime. To our very dying day we "press toward the mark," being changed from likeness to likeness that we may be made

like him. Is death the final victor and not life? Is death stronger than God? Or can God be trusted to finish what he has begun? Does the great adventure reach on beyond the gates of death? If we have a really Christian hope of immortality, it is based not on what we are but on what God can do and has promised to do. The promise is Jesus Christ and he seals the promise with his Spirit.—James D. Smart.

THE DESIRE TO RECOGNIZE.   The New Testament assures us that spiritual capacities adequate to meet new situations will constantly develop. This is the clue to belief in recognition beyond death. For most Christian people heaven would be an empty and thankless boon without the possibility of recognition. Dr. J. D. Jones of Bournemouth, England, tells of a noted American preacher who in the midst of a sermon on the possibility of recognition in the hereafter suddenly cried: "What would heaven be to me without my Willie?" That spontaneous cry of a grieving father finds an echo in the heart of each one of us, even though we should each wish to mention another though equally dear name.

This desire for recognition may indeed be an instinctual longing but it is a longing that expresses an undying hope that God has implanted in our spirits. The longing is itself prophetic of a soul-satisfying response. Seldom has this been stated more tenderly than in the lines placed on Charles Kingsley's tombstone by his widow: *Amavimus, Amamus, Amabimus—* "We have loved, we do love, we shall love." Love will reign in heaven even as it blesses earth.—John Sutherland Bonnell.

THE NEW REALITY.   The kingdom of heaven is the place where evil loses its deadly power to destroy. It is the state of reality in which the victory of Jesus' resurrection is constantly reaffirmed and realized.

Heaven is also the place or state of reality in which our strength is renewed. We are comforted, in the sense of being built up and given a fresh start with new vigor and vision and drive. Many people, as they come to the end of life, grow tired and lose their courage and their desire to go on. In the kingdom of God they will find life renewed, charged with new energy and desire. Heaven is the place of rebirth. It provides the right conditions for creative new life to take place. As the Revelation of John suggests, those who reach heaven through difficulties and sorrow will never again feel hunger or thirst, or the sun's scorching heat. The Lamb who is at the heart of the kingdom, the new Jerusalem, will be their shpeherd and will guide them to the water of life, and God "will wipe away every tear from their eyes" (Rev. 21:4). We can expect to enter this new reality filled with vigor that will never wear out and ready for transformation.—Morton T. Kelsey.

GOODNESS AND GREATNESS.   A good man who is not great is a hundred times more precious than a great man who is not good.—Will Durant.

A FUNERAL PRAYER

Our heavenly Father, we know you do not play favorites. We know you do not pay attention to some people and ignore others. We also know that every once in a while—and certainly not often enough—a human being comes along and touches our lives in a very special, and a very good, way. G. was such a person. Not one of us here will ever forget him or fail to receive continuing benefits and blessings from having known him. We are all grateful to you for the life and witness of this Christian disciple. We know that he trusted you, loved you, obeyed you. He made us all want to become better persons than we are, the kind of persons we can become when your Spirit is invited and welcomed to dwell in our hearts and lives. We know that Christianity is not a story about "way back when," but an up-to-date call to live in your presence according to your Word. G. did this faithfully, and we feel the summons to do the same. Our thoughts at this service of worship are where they are supposed to be: on you, Lord. You are the One who gives us hope, and light, and joy. You are the One who breaks our bondage to sin and death. You are the One who provides us with our eternal home—the house of many mansions—and who gives us the peace that is everlasting, beyond death, and that this world can neither give nor take way. You are the One who turns our sorrow into celebration, our sadness into joy, our loss into confidence. And we thank you, and give you the praise, the honor, and the glory. Thanks be to you, God our Father, for giving us the victory, the life that is abundant and eternal: though Jesus Christ, our crucified, risen, and living Lord—now and forever.—Gordon H. Reif.

SECTION V. Resources for Lenten and Easter Preaching

SERMON SUGGESTIONS

Topic: How the World Was Won
SCRIPTURE: Col. 3:1–4, 12–17; Matt. 28:1–10, 16–20.

Matthew reports that when the resurrected Jesus appeared to the astonished disciples at Galilee, he sent them out with a commission to preach and to make disciples of all nations. He did not tell them to describe what happened in the Resurrection but to announce the meaning of the Resurrection, to interpret it. The meaning, he said, is that he is Lord, that all authority in heaven and earth has now been given unto him. That means a king has ascended his throne. The kingdom that he came to inaugurate in his own person is now established, and the disciples are back in business.

Jesus came to bring the kingdom. The Resurrection means that nothing can stop it now—not even death.

The kingdom of God was a Jewish term misunderstood by those in the Gentile world. When it was preached to those people, it had to be interpreted again.

Paul interpreted the message of the Resurrection perfectly as good news for that kind of world. It was a world that believed that human life was controlled by supernatural powers. Those powers had special names. They were called angels. We are familiar with the term *angels*. We associate it with protectors, with guardian angels. But we can thank the Middle Ages for that. In the first century angels were more the enemy than the protectors of life.

These forces were also called principalities, supernatural beings who controlled the various intermediary layers of heaven. So to live in a universe that was controlled by principalities was like living in a world in which there are a countless number of minor officials that you have to please in order to get to God. It was sort of a celestial bureaucracy that you could never penetrate.

And then there were powers, a catchall word for unnamed and unpredictable forces in the universe, each one of which could determine your life.

And as if that were not enough, there are also the celestial bodies of astrology—the sun, the moon, the stars. You had a lucky star, but there were also unlucky stars. And the height and the depth of the stars in the heaven, according to astrological charts, was how your life was determined.

To live in that kind of world was to languish in despair, to be immobilized by fatalism, and to expect imminent disaster. Listen to how Paul announces the meaning of the Resurrection to that world. He's writing to the Romans. "If God is for us, who is against us? For Christ Jesus, who died, is now resurrected and sits at the right hand of God to make intercession for us. Therefore in all these things we are more than conquerors through him who loved us. For I am sure that neither death, nor life, nor angels, nor principalities, nor things present, nor things to come, nor powers, nor height, nor depth, nor any-

56

thing else in all creation, will be able to separate us from the love of God we saw in Christ Jesus our Lord."

That was the message that won the world. It put an end to fear and fatalism and despair. It said the world belongs to God, and to nothing else. And therefore nothing else need control us in this life. The Resurrection proved it, as even the last enemy of life, death itself, has been conquered. For God has the last word, and the last word is *life*.

With that message of hope in the power of God over all the enemies of life, Christianity moved, in three centuries, from a small room in Jerusalem, to the throne of the Roman Empire. It conquered the world. Not with arms, but with hope. Freeing men and women from the fears and the superstitions that bound them in despair, that locked them in fatalism, and that led them to expect imminent disaster in their lives.

Sam Keen put it this way: "A new era had emerged (in Christian preaching). Therefore, you may be free of the binding illusion that your fate is written in the stars. The fault lies not in your stars, but in your own refusal to accept the gracious gift of human freedom." It was that interpretation of the Resurrection that freed the world.

You may believe that the world has moved beyond the first century. In many ways it has. But I will wager that while we are not in bondage to first-century superstitions, we have created an ample supply of our own. For instance, if you believe that you are trapped in any way, or that your life is over at middle age or at any other age, or you believe that you've been dealt a bad hand by fate in this life and must play life with a handicap, or that you can't get out of the rut that you are presently in, then you are in bondage to a superstition. The Resurrection revealed that God is in charge of this world. Nothing else is in charge. So if you believe in the Resurrection, you're not trapped.—Mark Trotter.

Topic: Freedom to Choose
SCRIPTURE: Luke 15:11–32.

We see in this familiar parable that free-

dom does not mean we have a license to do whatever we please. We have the freedom to choose right over wrong. By misusing this freedom we become slaves to sin.

I. There are some facts of life that we have no freedom to change.

(a) The prodigal could not help being his father's son.

(b) He could not live it up in the flesh and not demean his spiritual life and his relationship with the father.

(c) He could not stop guilt from filling his soul after he had sinned.

II. We do have freedom as to how we will react in any situation.

(a) At his father's house, the prodigal could have been contented to work and do his part, or he could choose to rebel and leave.

(b) As he lived it up in the far land, the prodigal could choose to live and to spend his money honestly, or to waste what he had.

(c) When he found himself in the pigpen of sin, he had the freedom to stay in the stench and the mud, or to return to the father.

III. We have freedom to ask God to intervene and work in our difficult circumstances of life.

(a) This wayward son had freedom to ask God to forgive him of his past.

(b) He had freedom to ask God to give him new desires.

(c) He had freedom to ask God to give him a new life.

IV. God has the freedom to choose how he will work in our lives.

(a) God is free to change all or part of our circumstances.

(b) God is free to help us to endure difficulties that cannot be changed.

The more irresponsible the prodigal son became, the less freedom he actually had. God frees us from human bondage to be the willing slaves of righteousness.— Ronnie R. Blankenship.

Topic: God Will Provide Himself a Lamb
TEXT: Gen. 22:1–8.

I. He awoke in a cold sweat, his body shivering beyond control. "What an awful nightmare. Too awful to even consider.

The sacrifice of Isaac my only son." As Abraham sat upright in his bed surrounded by the darkness, he recounted in his mind his pilgrimage with God—how God had spoken to him in another dream and told him to leave his country, his relatives, his home and launch out on a journey toward a new place that God refused at that point to disclose. That in itself was a fearful dream, even for a young man, but Abraham was an old man when God spoke to him—seventy-five years of age.

How quickly the days had flown into years. Sarah and Abraham were good parents, providing for his every need, protecting him from danger. In fact, it may have been that Abraham lived in constant fear that something might take away his beloved only son: a wild beast, a snake, an attacking desert band of nomads, a fall from a cliff—one could never be too sure, and so perhaps Abraham's whole reason for living was tied up in protecting and loving his only son. Was this not what God wanted from him? Was he not doing God's will? So then what could be the meaning of this nightmare? Abraham knew that not all dreams are the voice of God. In fact, Abraham knew all too well that only rarely was a dream authored by God and so he perhaps calmed himself, reassured himself, and went back to sleep.

II. The Scripture does not account for us what terrible struggles must have permeated the nightmarish hours before the dawn, but when the first light of day fell across the desert camp, Abraham knew what he must do. He gathered wood, tying it in a bundle, called his son to his side and, followed by two servants, set out toward a place not yet revealed by the Lord. For three days they journeyed together, and on the third day Abraham saw the place. Again the chill that cut to the marrow of one's bones returned to Abraham. "It must be done. It must be done. God has told me what to do and I must do it." Leaving the servants behind, he and Isaac carried the wood, the fire, and the knife up the mountain. When they arrived, Abraham built an altar of stones and laid the wood on top. Isaac had seen his father do this many times before. When he finished, Isaac knew that Abraham would

place a sacrificial animal on the altar, plunge his knife into it, and when it was dead, would light a fire that would completely consume it. Perhaps as he watched his father it dawned on him for the first time—"There is no animal! Father, what will be the sacrifice?" Abraham looked his only son in the face and spoke words of absolute faith. "God will provide himself a sacrifice."

But when the altar was completed and the wood laid on top, there was still no lamb, and Abraham, choking back the tears, revealed to his son that God wanted Isaac to be the sacrifice; and he would do it.

He tied his son—how hard that must have been. He lifted his body up onto the altar. He drew his sharp knife and raising it above his head, closing his eyes, and biting his lip, made ready to draw the life from the son he loved so dearly.

"Abraham stop! Do not harm your son. It is evident how much you love me for you have not withheld your son from me, your only son."

It was then that Abraham saw the ram with its horns caught in a bush. On the altar he and Isaac offered the ram and one can imagine that as on the day of his birth, there was great laughter and celebration.

Abraham named that mountain *Yahweh-jirah*, meaning "the Lord will provide." What a marvelous lesson to learn. You see, it is one thing to receive God's promise of a great inheritance, but it is a very different thing to remain confident in the promise when the night is dark and all appears lost.

No, God could not let Abraham sacrifice his only son. He stopped him. God asked him to be willing to do it, but he would not let him go through with it. That says something very wonderful about God, doesn't it? God told him, "I know how much you love me, for you would not hold back your only son."

III. We see something even more wonderful when we move nearly two thousand years forward in history to that same land and to another only son. His name was Jesus. He was an only child—not of a man but of God himself. And God loved his

Son—God could understand Abraham's love for Isaac, because God had a Son too, a Son he loved dearly. God's heart was in his Son!

For thirty-three years God's Son walked the earth. He taught his Father's message, preached about his love, healed those with twisted minds and bodies. But then one day his Son was arrested. All those who had sworn allegiance to Jesus ran away. So now, as the Scripture said of Isaac and Abraham, "they left the servants behind and went both of them together."

Through the sting of betrayal and denial, through the mockery of a trial; through the humiliation of being laughed at, spit upon, slapped in the face, beaten over the head; through the agonizing flay with a metal-studded whip; through all of that, God walked up the mountain with his Son. All the way to the top they walked together—the Father and his only Son, both sharing the same heart. What an awful time for Father as for Son. Abraham could have changed his mind, he could have said no. He could have turned around and taken Isaac safely away from the mountain. But he did not. Likewise, God could have changed his mind; he could have said, "I'll not let my Son go through this'; and he could have turned around and taken Jesus safely away. Why, he could have called ten thousand angels to rescue his only Son. But he did not.

He and his only Son, Jesus, climbed that lonely mountain of hatred and sin and agony together, all the way to the top. Just as Isaac carried that bundle of wood, Jesus carried his cross. One tradition tells us that the hill that Abraham called Yahweh-jirah had gotten another name by 30 A.D. Now it was called *Golgotha*, the "place of the skull." Once again the altar was built, this one of wood. Once again the instrument of death was raised. But this time there was no voice from heaven. No one said, "stop." This time the nails were driven, the blood flowed, the cross was raised into the sky.

Paul says it clearly, "He did not spare His own Son, but gave Him up for us all" (Rom. 8:32).

What does this tell us? That God loves you and me more than a father loves his only son. That he loves us so much that he would allow the bloody sacrifice of his only Son, so that you and I might go free from the bondage of sin and be free to have the abundant life he offers.

So when you understand how much God loved his only Son and how much he loves you and me, then what God did three days later is no surprise. He simply raised his Son from the dead. He gave him life again, and in doing so he promises you that if you will give yourself into his care as his child, then you will have eternal life too—death will not defeat you, the grave will not hold you, and you will dwell in the house of the Lord forever.

God simply moved that stone and took his Son by the hand and raised him from the dead. And together, like Abraham and Isaac, their work completed, they went home arm in arm.

"And Abraham, when he had made his sacrifice, called the name of the place Yahweh-jirah—meaning 'The Lord will provide.'"—Ben Rogers.

Series: Questions Before the Cross

Topic 1: Why Bad Things Happen to Good People

SCRIPTURE: Matt. 27:26.

Why did Pontius Pilate, the Roman governor, release Barabbas and deliver Jesus to be scourged and crucified? Barabbas was a bad man, and Jesus was a good man. Why do bad things happen to good people?

That is our question, the first of four during the season of Lent. I have called them "Questions Before the Cross," although people ask them even apart from the Cross, even apart from the Christian religion. Witness the popularity of Harold Kushner's best-seller, *When Bad Things Happen to Good People*. The Cross itself does *not create* the questions that we are going to ask, but the Cross *raises* those questions.

One of them concerns the sheer injustice of it. Why do bad things happen to good people? We ask the question not only about Jesus but about all sorts of people whom we know—good people who have never hurt anyone, who have been honest, kind, unselfish, and loving, yet whom life has treated with cruel injustice. That's not only a religious question but a human question. Yet we are going to ask it before the Cross, the supreme symbol of our religion, in the hope that if there is any answer at all, we shall find it in our Lord's suffering and death on Calvary. Why did this bad thing happen to Jesus?

I. *Our Human Lot*.

It happened because Jesus was human. From every page of the Gospels there emerges a figure whose humanity was unmistakable and authentic. His body was flesh and blood like ours with its capacity for pain, privation, and fatigue. His emotional life revealed the shifting play of love, wonder, anger, compassion, joy, and sorrow. His moral experience exposed him to evil, his social instincts led him to crave the company of friends, and his spiritual needs found him in the house of worship and at the place of prayer. Ths Bible tells us that "the Word of God was made flesh," and it uses the term *flesh* to emphasize the full humanity of Jesus, all that nature of man in which he could grow, learn, struggle, be tempted, suffer, and die.

That's why bad things happened to Jesus, and that is why bad things happen to all of us. Being good or bad has nothing to do with it, beyond the observance of a few basic rules of health. A good person may safeguard his health to some extent by taking care of his body but he cannot prevent it from being defective or breaking down any more than he can prevent his car from being defective or breaking down.

As humans we are vulnerable not only to illness and disease but also to the hazards of our environment. We live in a dangerous world, and the more civilized we make it, the more dangerous it becomes. Accidents are no respecters of persons, as Jesus pointed out when he referred to a bad thing that happened to some people in Jerusalem. Morality had nothing to do with it. Those people were human, living in a hazardous world.

The Apostle Paul had a realistic view of life. Plenty of bad things had happened to him. He might have asked, "Why should they *not* happen to good people?" As he saw it, bad things belong to our human lot with all its ups and downs.

II. *The Human Family*.

So, the Cross happened to Jesus because he was human; also because other people were human. The Cross was a bad scene, and what made it bad was the character and conduct of the people involved. Here were the priests; here was Pontius Pilate; here were the Roman soldiers.

Shall we call them wicked people? Shall we put them on trial, Nuremberg-style, and accuse them of being partners in a corporate crime? They were not conscious of committing a crime. Each acted according to what he considered legitimate motives—the priests, to protect the national security; Judas, to force Jesus to declare himself as the Messiah; Pilate, to preserve the peace of the Roman Empire; the soldiers, because they were obeying orders. He was the victim of their humanity.

Consider the tragedy that some parents have to suffer on account of the behavior and misfortunes of their children. Bad things often happen to good people not through any fault of their own but because they are members of the human family. Paul compared that family to a human body where all the limbs and organs are interrelated, so that if one member suffers, all suffer together. That's why bad things happen to good people. That's why the Cross happened to Jesus.

III. *A Conscious Choice*.

There is another reason: Jesus made it happen. He was not a passive victim on Calvary, he chose to be on the cross. Jesus didn't "lose" his life. He gave it as a conscious, creative deed. He did so by being the sort of person he was in the sort of world where he had to live.

It would have been easy enough for Jesus to escape the Cross. All he had to do was stop claiming to be the Messiah, tone down his teachings, make peace with the establishment instead of fighting it. That's what he was tempted to do at the outset of his ministry. All those expedients that the Devil held before him in the wilderness were an attempt to remove from his path the necessity of the Cross. Something had to change; he had to change, or the hearts and minds of men had to change; but as long as both remained constant, a clash was inevitable.

So it happens to every person who stands for Christ in a world that stands against him. Bad things don't just *happen* to good people. They sometimes make them happen by being the sort of people they are in the sort of world where they have to live. There is plenty to fight for and wounds to be suffered by those who choose to follow Christ in a world that is not Christ-like. That's why bad things happen to good people.

III. *The Wounded Healer*.

Let me suggest one more reason why the Cross happened to Jesus. It happened because what we call evil, pain, and tragedy play a positive, constructive, redemptive role in life. The Cross was the most positive, most constructive, most redemptive event in the world's history. Indeed, it was the ultimate paradox. Out of its foolishness came wisdom, out of its weakness came strength, out of its suffering came comfort, out of its death came life.

What we call bad things are often bad only in the eyes of outsiders. To be sure, we complain about the bad things that happen to us, but do we want a world without courage and patience and all those other fine qualities of character that bad things bring to the surface?

It is a strange fact of human experience that unhappiness has great redemptive power. Who are the really powerful people in the sense that they can comfort others and change human lives? Are they the strong and healthy, the rich and successful? No, indeed. They are the people to whom bad things have happened. Their very suffering becomes a means of healing. Such is the light that the Cross throws upon our question.—A. Leonard Griffith.

Topic 2: Is Suffering the Will of God?
SCRIPTURE: Matt. 26:39.

We are standing before the Cross of Christ, asking questions, not only about the cross itself but questions that the Cross brings into sharp focus in our minds. These are not strictly religious questions, except that two of them have to do with God. They are human questions, asked by people in all walks of life, even those who profess no conventional religious faith. Is suffering the will of God? There are several alternatives to consider.

I. *A Sign of God's Love*.

At the one extreme there is a positive answer that says yes, God did will the Cross and he does will suffering. It was part of his plan for Jesus and it's part of his plan for us. God not only wants us to suffer, he causes us to suffer—perhaps as a punishment for our sins, perhaps as a discipline to refine our characters and make us more compassionate.

You would be surprised how many people find comfort in that conviction, and they are not being hypocritical or pious. The writer of the Epistle to the Hebrews says that in causing us to suffer, God is treating us as our earthly parents treated us when we were children.

Many people want to believe that suffering is the will of God. That belief explains their suffering, gives it meaning and purpose, and keeps alive their faith in the integrity of the universe.

II. *Stop Blaming God*.

At the opposite extreme there is a negative answer that says that God has nothing to do with suffering and he certainly did not cause the Cross. That was the work of sinful men. The ministry of Jesus in the Gospel seems to deny the Divine origin of suffering. As the servant of God's will he brought every form of suffering under his sovereign control. That is the picture of God that emerges from the Gospels. Yet, having said that, we are still thrown back on our Lord's prayer in Gethsemane. Beyond any doubt he took the cup of suffering from God's hands and drained it to its bitter dregs because he believed that it was the will of God.

III. *A Meeting Place with God*.

Surely there had to be a middle ground between those two extremes. Perhaps we can say that while God does *not cause* suffering to happen, he *allows* it to happen as part of the scheme of things. At the center of life as God created it, at the heart of all reality is a principle of suffering; therefore it must come under the Providence of God. Harold Kushner says, "Could it be that 'How can God do this to me?' is really the wrong question to ask?" Many people *don't* ask that question. They don't blame God for thir suffering. They meet God in their suffering.

IV. *Obedience to God*.

Our Lord's prayer in the garden suggests one more answer to the question, "Is suffering the will of God?" The answer is yes, God may will suffering, not simply allow it but actually *will* it, in particular situations. The Cross was one of those situations. From Gethsemane Jesus went to Calvary in obedience to the will of God. He did not have to obey God's will. Accompanied by a few disciples, he could have slipped quietly out of Jerusalem. But there would be no church, no Gospel, because the Cross and Resurrection, the constitutive facts of the Gospel would never have taken place. It was not God's will that Jesus should suffer and die like a common criminal, but it was God's will that he be true to himself and fulfill his mission as the world's Savior. That's why he went to the Cross.

In that sense it may be God's will that we also have to suffer. As Christians we may sometimes find ourselves in situations where obedience to God leaves no other alternative. It may be our care of other people or our commitment to unpopular causes or our witness to Christ in a world that largely stands against him. Is suffering the will of God? We ask that question before the Cross, not because the Cross answers it but because the Cross draws our suffering into itself and therefore into its victory.—A. Leonard Griffith.

Topic 3: Why Doesn't God Do Something?

SCRIPTURE: Mark 15:33–34.

One question we *must* include in our series on "Questions Before the Cross" is the heartrending question that our Lord himself asked in his moment of extreme agony. We call it his Cry of Dereliction—"My God, my God, why hast thou forsaken me?"

Surely we ourselves would have asked that question if we had been at the hill of Golgotha on Good Friday. Why didn't God come to his rescue? Why didn't God

do something? *We* should have done something if we were God.

We ask: Where was God? Why didn't God do something? We ask that question not only about the Cross of Christ but about a great many other crosses that people have to bear. Why does God allow Christ to be crucified not only in the first century but in every generation?

We are asking that question not as unbelievers but in the context of an inherited religious faith. The Bible teaches that God is all-powerful. That's what makes him God. The Bible teaches that God is all-loving, that he watches over us and protects us just as a human parent watches over his children and protects them. So why didn't he protect his beloved Son on Good Friday? There are several answers.

I. The first is that *God could have done something*. Jesus said so in the Garden of Gethsemane: "Do you think that I cannot appeal to my Father, and he will at once send me more than twelve legions of angels?" On Calvary, when you heard the scribes taunting him to come down from the Cross, wouldn't you have prayed fiercely, "Yes, God, bring him down. You can do it. You can do anything. Save him from this horrible, shameful death!"

There is no use saying that God does not behave that way, because that's how God does behave all through Bible history. In fact, half the Bible is predicated on the mighty act whereby God delivered his people from slavery in Egypt and brought them safely across the Red Sea. Time and again he reenacted that drama, intervening in human affairs to crush the wicked and deliver his people from certain destruction.

Couldn't God step in and stop the tragedy in a manner consistent with his saving activity in history? Jesus must have believed so, or he would not have prayed, "My God, why hast thou forsaken me?" We believe so, and that's why we are not afraid to pray.

II. When we stand before the Cross and ask "Why doesn't God do something?" the answer comes back—*God has done something*. We have to remember that the Cross happened not in a vacuum but in a specific moral and spiritual setting.

The Cross took place in a setting of more than a thousand years of revealed religion. If God's people had been true to their history, they would not have crucified Christ; they would have recognized him and welcomed him and enthroned him as king.

So we must not blame God because he did not intervene to save his people from the most colossal blunder in their history. Nor must we blame God if he does not intervene to save the human race from the blunders that imperil its future today. God *has* done something. He has shown us the way we must walk and the laws we must obey if we would resolve our predicaments and realize his purpose of love and justice and peace for all people upon this earth.

He is saying to us even now, as the prophet Jeremiah said to his people, "Stand by the roads and look and ask for the ancient paths, where the good way is; and walk in it, and find rest for your souls." But God has done more than that to give us rest for our souls. He has broken into history and come where we are in One who said, "I am the way." Some Christians are so despondent about the state of the world today that they have given it up as lost and pinned all their hopes on Christ's Second Coming. The Bible itself encourages that mighty hope. Yet the Bible makes clear that God is waiting for us to come to terms with Christ's First Coming, for in his life and ministry and death and resurrection, God had done all things necessary for our salvation.

III. When we stand before the Cross and ask "Why doesn't God do something?" the answer comes back—*God was doing something*. God had not forsaken Jesus in his hour of extreme suffering. God was there on Golgotha suffering with him. The Cross had been in the heart of God from all eternity, and now he made it visible in time.

On Golgotha God *was* doing something decisive and conclusive. He was making his ultimate response to human sin. He was carrying the burden of the world's sin, and it was a burden not only of love but of judgment. The Cross was not merely the martyrdom of one man. It was the final battleground of the universe, the scene of God's last decisive struggle against all forces of evil that crucified Christ and threaten our existence. Evil was judged in Calvary. Henceforth evil has no future in God's world. It is still our enemy, but a defeated enemy, and ultimately in the power of the Cross we shall triumph over it.—A. Leonard Griffith.

Topic 4: Is Sacrifice Outmoded?

SCRIPTURE: Mark 8:34.

Is the Cross a relevant symbol for us today? The final question that we ask before the Cross of Christ is "Is sacrifice as a way of life outmoded?"

I. *Obedience*.

Sacrifice is not outmoded as long as Christianity means obedience to the mind and will of Christ. Jesus said to his disciples, "If any man would come after me, let him deny himself and take up his cross and follow me." Jesus shattered all their illusions, for he went on to say, in effect, "I am not the kind of Messiah you have been expecting, not an earthly King of power and glory, but a meek, despised, suffering Servant who must walk the way of a Cross . . . I am going to be crucified. Do you understand? I am going to die. That's how my work must be done and that's how it will have to be carried on. If you want to share in that work, if you want to have any fellowship with me and live within the circle of my friends and followers, then you must take my Cross, this principle of sacrificial love, and make it the central, controlling principle of your life."

Jesus often spoke to his disciples in those terms. He promised that they would be absurdly happy, but he promised them also a life of sacrifice. He never hid his scars to win or keep a disciple.

The Apostle Paul saw the Cross in the same way. Writing to his friends at Philippi, he declared that his supreme ambition was to reproduce in his life the events of Christ's life—"that I may know him, and the power of his resurrection and the fellowship of his sufferings, being made conformable to his death." Paul sees the Cross as an event that goes on generation after generation in the life of the church and in the lives of those who obey Christ and continue his ministry.

Shall we say that the principle is now outmoded as a way of life for Christians? If so, we have to rewrite much of the New Testament and change many of the sayings of Jesus. As long as the Cross remains central in our faith, it calls us to a life of sacrifice.

II. *Challenge*.

Sacrifice is not outmoded as long as the human heart responds to a challenge, as it does where ultimate issues are at stake. Do you think that the disciples would have responded if Jesus on his way to the Cross had promised them a life of safety and comfort? Christ offered his disciples the most dangerous and difficult task in the world.

Therein lies the appeal of the Cross. Someone said, "The most fascinating thing about Christianity has always been the Cross. Why? Because in the long run people do not respect a cheap and easy religion. They respect a commanding and challenging religion that will take all we can give and then call for more."

It challenges us at the point of our vocations—not only to full-time ministry in the church but to the choice of a career that will advance the gospel, regardless of what it costs us. The Cross challenges us at the point of our lifestyle—to live loving, caring, giving lives in this age of affluence and self-indulgence. The Cross challenges us at the point of our total commitment to Christ—the commitment of our time, energies, money, and reputation, all that we have and all that we are, for the work of his kingdom.

III. *Fulfillment*.

We can say that sacrifice is not outmoded as long as it is a way to personal fulfillment. That's what Jesus taught his disciples. After calling them to take up their cross and follow him he said, "For whoever would save his life will lose it; and whoever loses his life for my sake and the gospel's will find it."

Jesus never pretended that we can find life in any other way than by losing it. He left no doubt that only a life with the Cross at its heart and center can be radiantly and vitally Christian. Only a life controlled by his principle of sacrificial love can be a part of that larger life that he carried unbroken through death into eternity.

IV. *Redemption*.

Sacrifice is not outmoded as long as it is still a way of redemption. We know that once it was a way of redemption. We know that the world's salvation and our salvation were accomplished when Christ on the Cross cried out with his dying breath, "It is finished." We agree with the German philosopher Hegel, by no means a convinced Christian, who said in his *Philosophy of History*, "We may affirm absolutely that nothing great in this world has ever been accomplished without passion." A church that would be a saving force for Christ in society must live precisely under the sign of the Cross. The kingdom of God must still enter the world by way of crucifixion.—A. Leonard Griffith.

ILLUSTRATIONS

FAMOUS LAST WORDS. The custom of recording and remembering the last words of persons is not followed today as it was a generation or two ago. For one thing, most persons die quietly in their sleep and do not pronounce any last words consciously. But it is an interesting matter to recall some last words that have been recorded. Many of them show great courage and unshaken faith, unafraid of any amazement.

One notable last remark may not seem to display any pious mood, yet it is a word of high faith. That is the last sentence said by professor Samuel F. Upham, a man of great learning, wit, and faith and for many years a teacher at Drew Theological Seminary. When the end was near, family and friends gathered at his bedside. Someone said that Dr. Upham was already dead. Another answered, "Feel his feet. No one ever died with warm feet." Then Dr. Upham opened an eye and said: "Joan of Arc did." Those were his last words. And they were really great ones. For the wit and humor persisting to the very end were the expression of a high faith without fear.

Some of the best-known last words are those of John Wesley: "The best of all is, God is with us." Oliver Cromwell, looking at the mournful faces around his death-bed, said: "Will no one here thank God?" Both are moving declarations of a faith that never wavered.

In our own day there is that beautiful last sentence said by Dr. Peter Marshall, the Washington minister. In his biography, *A Man Called Peter*, written by his wife, she records that as he was being carried out of his house on a stretcher on his way to the hospital he said to his wife casually: "I'll see you in the morning." That night he died. But the words are a fine and true expression of Christian faith. This is what death means to a Christian: "I'll see you in the morning."

But sometimes the last words are neither noble nor words of faith. Think of the last words of P. T. Barnum: "What were today's receipts?"

Here is one on a higher level, but not high enough. William Hazlitt, the nineteenth-century essayist, said as his exit line: "Well, I've had a happy life." That showed a large spirit, with no bitter complaint. But think more deeply. Frank Swinnerton says of this last word: "Which of us, uncertain travelers as we all are on uncharted ways, could ask or say more?" The answer to the question is that multitudes have asked and said a whole lot more. It is not enough to have had a happy life.

Similar to this is the last word of Lady Mary Wortley Montague, in the eighteenth century: "It has all been very interesting." What a summary of life—"interesting!"

Contrast with that, the word of Jesus on the cross: "It is finished." He had been given work to do by his Father, and he had accomplished it. The acceptance of a great commission from God lifts life out of triviality and selfishness.

The greatest of last words are those of Jesus: "Father, into thy hands I commit my spirit." Jesus said this at the end of his life. But he also said it at the beginning of his ministry at the temptation. They are words to say at the beginning and all the way through to the end.—Halford Luccock.

CRUCIFIXION. Some wise counsel my Dad once gave me—"Son, once you have been nailed to a cross, nothing else can hurt you much anymore."—W. Randall Lolley.

THE DREAM OF EASTER. I would like to see the celebration of Easter begin at midnight as it was observed by Orthodox Christians in precommunist Russia. In Saint Petersburg, for example, the Cathedral of Saint Isaac was jammed with the faithful as they waited in total darkness for the stroke of midnight. Then as the hour struck, the guns from the fortress of Saint Peter and Saint Paul boomed their salute of the new day, the huge doors of the majestic cathedral were thrown open, candles were lit, and the choir entered and moved down the aisle singing the triumphant Easter anthem. This was a moment of intense emotion, of historic drama.—James I. McCord.

THE STRENGTH OF LOVE. During the war it was the writer's privilege to see very much of a war hospital. On one occasion a corporal showed him the photograph of a man, taking it from under his pillow and handling it with reverence and love. The minister thought it might be the photo of a brother lost in the war, but as the corporal put it into his hands he said with a break in his voice and with shining eyes, "That's the man who saved my life, sir, and he nearly lost his own in doing it." Then followed a story common enough in the war, but there could be no doubt of the bond of everlasting gratitude established between those men. The figure of Jesus towers above our human world as that of One who has established just that bond between himself and every soul. Men cannot deny that in him there was a love that sought, for their sakes, to be stronger than death or sin.—Albert D. Belden.

KEY TO THE BIBLE. It is the message of the Bible, in all its richness, that the people of our generation need. It is insufficient and misleading to present the Old Testament as the story of the growth of man's ideas about God, without the primacy of the greater theme of God's own acts and God's utterances in the events of Israel's history that makes the Old Testament what it is. It is equally misleading to present the Gospel as the conception of God taught by Jesus, without due reference to the mighty act of God himself in the Passion and Resurrection. Read in its own light, the Bible has the Resurrection as its key. Its God is the God who raised up Jesus Christ from the dead, and in so doing vindicated his word in the Old Testament and in the Cross of Christ. It is only in virtue of the Resurrection that the Bible is one, and that the message of the Bible is coherent and true.—Michael Ramsey.

THE MEANING OF SUFFERING. I talked with a man whose only child had died of a dread disease. It came upon her unexpectedly after an early life of perfect health, and she died in fearful agony. Hour by hour he sat beside her, suffering every pain with her, till he told me that in his very body he felt her physical pain. Tell a man like that there is no cross in the world, no evil, no pain! It is all in our imagination, all a state of mind! He would have good cause to throw you out of the house. As I talked with that man, he said bravely and with ringing faith, "Surely there must be a meaning in all this for me." And we soon agreed that it probably lay in the enlarging of his heart toward that which all men suffer. God forbid that we suffer, and then come out just what we always were, or reduced to the depths of self-pity and self-concern!—Samuel M. Shoemaker.

WHAT COUNTS IN LIFE. The son of a seminary teacher was critically ill in a local hospital. The diagnosis was uncertain. Surgery and the possible loss of a limb were imminent. As I started out of the room one evening, my friend said: "You know how long we had waited for the new home that we occupied six weeks ago. We had scrimped and saved on a small income for many years to have what we had wanted for so long. But it is wonderful to see how simple it would be to gladly lose the thousands of dollars we put into it, to walk out and close the door and give the key back to the builder, just to know that the little fellow here would have a chance after awhile to run and play like the rest." His smile made me know that in an hour of suffering another saint of God had discovered the things that really count in life —not cars, houses, luxuries, and large bank accounts, but families, churches, and friends, and God! You would never know if you never had to suffer!—Gordon Clinard.

SECTION VI. Resources for Advent and Christmas Preaching

SERMON SUGGESTIONS

Topic: What Do We Find in Bethlehem?
SCRIPTURE: Luke 2:15.
What will we find in Bethlehem?
I. *An event that changed history.*

How easy for us to be seduced into a celebration of Christmas that has little to do with the event we celebrate! A disillusioned pastor who felt his congregation was thinking of Christmas only in material terms threatened to prepare a realistic Christmas worship service that would include a litany to Santa Claus and a rendition of "Jingle Bells" as the offertory anthem.

While these may be a bit extreme, there is enough truth to their comments that we need to take note who would go even to Bethlehem to see the event that changed human history!

Of course, there were many in that early day who ignored what happened in the Bethlehem stable. Caesar Augustus was unconcerned when the reports reached Rome. What could the baby of a peasant born in a stable mean to the great Roman Empire? Herod, king of the Jews, became interested only when the wise men made inquiry. His interest was that of a paranoid king who was worried about someone trying to take over his earthly throne. Within the Bethlehem inn there was probably casual interest—the kind we have when any baby is born.

The event suggests to us that nobody really knows when God will move into our human life to bring hope. History has many instances when it would seem God has intervened in this fashion, but never as he did at Bethlehem. These echoed, but did not repeat fully, the event we celebrate at Christmas, the birth of Jesus. "The hinge of history is on the door of the Bethlehem stable," wrote Ralph Sockman about this event that changed all history.

II. *Good news that transforms life.*

Nearly everyone here, young and old alike, can recall at least one experience in life when good news came and completely changed the atmosphere of living.

At Bethlehem we hear and see the good news that transforms life for all of us forever. Here is the good news that we have a God who is like a loving parent. Bethlehem tells us that God cares enough for us to send us the very best—his Son! The sensitivity of truly divine love is seen here.

The good news is that God has entered into your life and mine through his coming in Christ. It would never have been enough simply to enter life as a baby and let it stand there. Some people treat Jesus only as the baby in the manger. They don't let him grow up for them and become the young man who meets us where we live. They never get to know just what God is like if they don't let the baby Jesus grow up! For it is in his life among us as a boy and young man that we come to see what God is like!

Moreover, at Bethlehem we find the

ws that God has come to us in power. Love is the significant thing, but here is love with divine power. It is this power that dynamizes our life, gives us strength to stand firm for our faith, gives us the means for bearing our witness to the faith.

That's the kind of glory we need to catch again. The splendor of God in human form is not to be equated with private possession of great wealth or with the pomp and circumstance of great empire. Christmas tells of the glory of one who lifted the fallen, healed the sick, befriended the poor and the outcast, who welcomed little children, and shunned all forms of cant and cruelty and injustice.

So, let *us* go over to Bethlehem and see this thing that has happened. There we will find an event that changed history and the good news that can change our lives into the pattern provided by God through our Lord Jesus Christ.

III. *The experience of God's real presence.*

It makes no difference who was there at Bethlehem, *if we are not there*. It makes no difference who hears the angel song, if we do not hear God's proclamation of good news. It makes no difference if the shepherds heard the message if we do not listen for it and hear it. It is of little consequence what gifts most rare were presented there, if our unique gift of love and of obedience and of trust is not there. Christ must be born in us.

No one can come near Bethlehem without the response of faith to God's gift of life and love.

This calls us to see God in the only way we can see him—through the life and ministry of Jesus. We cannot see God as we can see each other. We cannot have a picture of God as we can of Washington or Lincoln.

Many years ago the track of a three-toed dinosaur was found on top of coal strata high up on the cliffs near Grand Junction, Colorado. Nobody has ever seen the animal itself, but there they saw his footprint! No person has ever actually seen God, but he has left his divine imprint on our world in so many ways. Nature proclaims God in every aspect of its matchless beauty and creative power. But we could never know what God is like had he not revealed himself in Jesus! Jesus is not God the Father —he prayed to God the Father! But in the life of Jesus we see God more fully revealed than in any other way. And you find him in Bethlehem! You see him when you experience through your response of faith the very real presence of God.—Hoover Rupert.

Topic: Proclaiming the Good News to All

SCRIPTURE: Luke 2:10–11; Acts 1:8.

The Christmas message is a message of sharing, not of hoarding; it is a message of giving, not receiving. Luke, the author of this Christmas story, is consistent in his view that what took place on that first Christmas night two thousand years ago is a message to be proclaimed to all men. In the second volume of his literary work, the book of Acts, he insists again than the message of the good news of Jesus Christ must be shared with all: Ye shall be my witnesses—my witnesses here where you are known, and in neighboring lands, and then everywhere unto the uttermost parts of the earth. We who claim to be his people have this urgent task before us.

I. We can begin the task by following the example of Jesus himself. Christ proclaimed his message by seeking to meet every human need—physical as well as spiritual. He ministered to the total person. Jesus did heal the sick; he did feed the hungry; he did comfort the afflicted; but in all the healing and helping narratives this one message he repeats, in different form, over and over again: "Your sins are forgiven."

II. Witness bearing is another weapon that our Lord has appointed for the conquest of the world. The same message that the angel bore witness to before the shepherds, the good news of a Savior, is the same message that you and I must bear witness to today.

(a) One way of being a living witness for Christ is just that—living our lives in such a way that there can be no doubt by any with whom we come into contact where our alliance lies. Distinguishing characteristics separate the Christian lifestyle from that of the non-Christian. One of these is our view of servanthood. The Christian is not to be ruler of anyone, but servant to all. Another distinguishing characteristic is that we are to be a people of love— loving not only those who love us but even those who hate us with a passion. If these teachings are true, never will we be able to witness to "all the world" until we begin to live the gospel we preach. If we proclaim brotherhood and goodwill but practice hate and prejudice, we destroy our efforts. If we proclaim forgiveness of sin but refuse to forgive one another, we make a mockery of our message.

(b) We cannot leave out, however, the necessity of our actually sharing with others by word of mouth our personal testimony—expressing what God has done in our lives. Doesn't it make sense to believe that one reason God gave us the power to speak was that we might bear witness to him? In the quiet hush of a prayer, in the raised voice of an anthem, in the fearless pronouncement of a moral principle, we are using our voices as a witness to the world. This follows the example of the early apostles as they sought to bear the "good news of great joy" to all.

(c) The Great Commission that Jesus gave to his disciples still stands as an unaccomplished goal even after two thousand years. If there is anyone to blame for this mission not being completed, it is not God but ourselves. How are we to do it? Most of us will never travel around the world to proclaim the good news. Christ has not commanded that we all become foreign missionaries. He has commanded that we do our part in spreading the gospel. We may not be called to serve our Lord on foreign soil, but we can give our money to support the work of those who are. It is an awesome thought that God's saving acts in the world may depend, somehow, upon our being a people of prayer.—Lee McGlone.

Topic: Expectation: Agony and Ecstasy
SCRIPTURE: Isa. 9:1–7; Rev. 22:7–20.

If there is any attitude of mind or heart that is a part of the annual observance of Christmas, it is surely the attitude expectation. This sense of having something to look forward to, this sense of waiting expectantly for a special day to arrive adds richness and hope to our lives all through the year.

I. We Christians have traditionally applied a name to these days of preparation leading up to Christmas Day. We call it the season of Advent. Advent is a Latin word that means "coming." So the season of Advent is that period of four weeks before Christmas when Christians look forward to the coming of Christ into the world. It is the coming of Jesus Christ into the world that is the heart of this season. The issue is not that Santa Claus is coming to town but that Jesus Christ has come into this world, to live among us and die for us, to rescue us from sin and restore us to a right relationship with God. The issue is not expensive presents wrapped in shiny paper lying under the evergreen tree. The issue is a little baby wrapped in swaddling clothes, lying in a manger in a stable in Bethlehem, on a dark night made bright by a shining star, so many years ago.

II. There are really two ways by which we should approach this issue. One way is to share in the expectation of those who were waiting for him to come the first time. The other is to share the expectation of those who have been waiting for him to come the second time. Christ has come and Christ will come again.

(a) Look back to the people of Israel during the days of King Hezekiah, when the city of Jerusalem was surrounded by the Assyrian army. Beginning at that moment, an idea began to be passed from one generation to the next—someone was coming. No one really knew who it would be. No one really knew exactly when the person would come. They just lived in the expectation that when he came, he would do great things for Israel. The words from the prophecy of Isaiah stood at the heart of that expectation.

(1) When the prophet spoke those words, it looked as if the promise of God to the people of Israel was about to be broken and crushed beneath the chariot wheels of the enemy armies.

(2) Against that scene of dark despair, we must hear those words. "The people that walked in darkness have seen a great light. They that dwell in the land of the shadow of death, upon them has the light shined." Isaiah was telling his people that someone was coming. Isaiah did not know his name, but he ascribed to him some titles: "Wonderful Counsellor, Mighty God, Everlasting Father, Prince of Peace."

(3) As the biblical story unfolds, this expected Messiah did not come in time to defeat the Assyrians. In fact, for the Jewish community around the world the Messiah has not yet come. But the proclamation of this Christmas season, for those of us who are Christians, is that he has come. Perhaps he did not achieve what the ancient Jews had been hoping for, but our affirmation during this season is that he has come —come to preach good tidings to the poor, come to bind up the brokenhearted, come to deliver the captives.

(4) My task is to say, first of all, that for me he has come. He has come not only into the world but into my life. Has Jesus come for you? Has he come into your heart, into your mind, into the way you live your life and make your choices and set your goals and priorities?

(b) Just as crucial during these days is our expectation that one day he will come again.

(1) In Revelation 22, Jesus says to John three times: "Behold, I come." John wanted Jesus to come back, and the sooner the better. Remember where John was when he had this revelation. He was in a prison cell on the island of Patmos— there because of "the testimony of Jesus Christ," because the Roman Empire was trying to crush the faith before it blossomed. And in the last lines of Revelation, in words of agony and expectation, John cries out on behalf of the whole church: "Even so come, Lord Jesus!" But he had not yet come.

(2) Perhaps now we Christians understand how the Jews felt all of those years as they waited for one who seemed never to come.

(3) So has it been for us, waiting since the days of John on Patmos. Like the two men in *Waiting for Godot*, we seem to be waiting for someone who never comes. But my prayer remains that he come quickly. Come Lord, for we know that your coming will make a difference. Come, so that the guns of war will cease, so that the wicked will cease from troubling, so that hatred may cease, so that walls of division may be torn down, so that the kingdom of God may be fully and finally established, so that our longing eyes can see your face, so that the kingdoms of this world may become the kingdom of our Lord and of his Christ. *Come!*—Marvin A. McMickle.

Topic: Christmas Means You Belong
SCRIPTURE: Rom. 1:1–7.

I. Every ritual of belonging is surrounded by the darkness of loneliness.

(a) The warmth and light of Christmas Eve togetherness in our lives always has to contend with the surrounding darkness of isolation. Far from pushing away the darkness of our loneliness, Christmas often inadvertently allows that darkness to envelop us. Loneliness reaches its most poignant pain amid the "happy" crowd because we are so near, yet so far. How the darkness of loneliness seems to pervade even our most strident merriment.

(b) No wonder, then, that one of the controlling images in Scripture of Advent is light coming into darkness. "The people who walked in darkness," claims Isaiah, "have seen a great light." Says John in the opening of the Fourth Gospel, "The life was the light of men. The light shines in the darkness, and the darkness has not overcome it." Darkness is where you and I are alone, lost in a haunted wood, afraid of the night. Darkness symbolizes our universal condition of lostness, alienation, separation . . . loneliness.

II. But here's our hope amid the midnight of our isolation. God cares enough about you in your separation to enter your darkness and reestablish that deep-rooted sense of belonging that transcends all human relationships.

(a) Think about where Jesus was born . . . outside, in the dark. Think about where Jesus was crucified . . . outside the city, in the dark of a turbulent sky. God chooses to enter and end our isolation at two key points: *outside* and *in the dark*! God at this moment is coming outside into the dark to make connection with you. That's what Christmas is all about. Christ coming into your world of isolation.

(b) The Apostle Paul puts it another way. He describes Christ as one who "was descended . . . according to the flesh." Not flesh as in sinew, tissue, skin, muscle, and fiber. But rather flesh as in human nature, human experience. When he clothed himself in our flesh, he put on the garments of our deep sense of estrangement. Put most pointedly, to give us a sense of belonging he had no choice but to enter into our darkness.

(c) You and I are called to belong to this Christ who enters our darkness. Called to belong. Think of that! God's whole business in taking upon himself our human nature is to make it possible for you and me to be at home with him, to belong. Christmas, Christ's coming, means you belong. When you begin to get under your skin this fundamental fact that God doesn't intend to leave you alone, then some emptiness in your life will begin to be dispelled. If you sense you are in the dark, then look up at the stars. Humbling to think that he who ordered those constellations and flung those stars across the heavens cannot rest until you are reached and held close in ultimate belonging. "Lo I am with you always," promised Jesus, "even to the end."—Don M. Wardlaw.

ILLUSTRATIONS

THE MIRACLE OF CHRISTMAS. If we wish to understand the meaning of "conceived by the Holy Ghost and born of the Virgin Mary," above all we must try to see that these two remarkable pronouncements assert that God of free grace became man, a real man. The eternal Word became flesh. This is the miracle of Jesus Christ's existence, this descent of God from above downwards—the Holy Ghost and the Virgin Mary. This is the mystery of Christmas, of the Incarnation. The true Godhead and the true humanity of Jesus Christ in their unity do not depend on the fact that Christ was conceived by the Holy Spirit and born of the Virgin Mary. All that we can say is that it pleased God to let the mystery be real and become manifest in this shape and form.—Karl Barth.

CHRISTMAS JOY. We dare not let the joy of Christmas be corrupted by thoughts about the horrors of the present time and by anxiety about still greater ones that may yet come. Then the devil would have gained what he wants. With a Christianity that has no more joy in its heart he has an easy game. The only thing that he really fears are men who carry the real joy of Christmas in their hearts for against them he is powerless. All evil thrives only in joylessness.—Emil Brunner.

THE TOUCHES OF WONDER. The touches of wonder with which the Christmas story is surrounded are an indispensable part of it. I once heard Dr. Julius Moldenhawer tell of how, when he was a child, he knew so little that he believed the Christmas story, just as Saint Luke tells it. Then came a time when he knew so much—after studying higher criticism, comparative religion, and philosophy—that he could not believe the miraculous setting of the story. But now, once again, he knows so little that he believes the story just as Saint Luke tells it. What did he mean? I think he meant that if Christian faith is reached at all, it must be reached through wonder.—David E. Roberts.

GOD'S "NOBODY." Luke's sense of humor emerges at John's installation. He introduced the new minister: "In the fifteenth year of the reign of Tiberius Caesar, Pontius Pilate being governor of Judea, and Herod being tetrarch of Galilee, and his brother Philip tetrarch of the region of Ituraea and Trachonitis, and Lysanias tetrarch of Abilene in the high priesthood of Annas and Caiaphas, the word of God came to John . . . ." The Almighty dropped the "names," then appointed a "nobody." Those names included the distinguished villains who would behead his last prophet and crucify his only Son.—David A. Redding.

HE IS HERE. Dr. Stanley Jones has told a story of a little boy who stood before a picture of his absent father and then turned to his mother and said wistfully: "I wish Father would step out of the picture." Oh for a warm heart in the universe! If only the Father would step out of the picture. . . . He *stepped* out of the picture. He stepped out at Bethlehem.— W. E. Sangster.

SECTION VII. Evangelism and World Missions

SERMON SUGGESTIONS

Topic: A Witness To Give
TEXT: Matt. 28:16–20; Acts 1:6–8.

We have done a magnificent job of domesticating the Great Commission. We live with it fairly comfortably, even in disobedience. Perhaps in these days as we think of witness, one of the things we should pray for is that God would bring to us larger dimensions than we have had before of what it means to make disciples. I came with a great deal of interest to study Dr. Frank Stagg's commentary on Acts and discovered a thing I should have discovered all along; that is, that when the disciples heard this, they did not hear what we hear. They heard him say: "Ye shall receive power after the Holy Ghost has come upon you, and ye shall be my witnesses—to the Jews, who are in Jerusalem; to the Jews, who are in Judea; to the Jews, who are in Samaria; and to the Jews who are in the uttermost parts of the earth."

I would be untrue in what I feel in my heart if I did not say in the very beginning that everything good that has come or is coming into my life really has its source in one truth—that God is in Jesus Christ reconciling the world unto himself. So that the love and freedom and purpose and hope that I have is related to this. As I begin to think of what God has done for me, he ministered to me through very ordinary people. I have never seen his finger write in stone. I have never heard his voice in the thunder. Through all of these years God has allowed people to be his witness to me. Many of them at the time they were

trying to help me to see him, to love him, to trust him, to obey him, to follow him, probably had little sense of success or awareness that they were the voice of God for me.

I think, for instance, of my Grandmother Smith. During the depression my family moved to northern Illinois where my mother and father got jobs in a factory. They worked six days a week. Church was not a big thing with them in Oklahoma, and it was nothing for them in Illinois. Then Grandmother Smith came to live with us. She became God's witness to the Chafin children about church. My mother spent Sunday washing and ironing and doing all the things she could not do because of her job at the factory, and my father went fishing. It was my grandmother who suggested that perhaps I ought to enroll in Sunday school and study the Scriptures. She loved God and believed that his word and his church had something to say to life. She pointed me in that direction.

Mrs. Mason, my Sunday School teacher, first taught me the Scriptures. She would write a card when on some Sunday I decided to go fishing with my dad instead of coming to hear her teach the Bible. She was a signpost along the way of life for me, pointing me to God, the church, the Bible, and righteousness.

The thought keeps presenting itself, "Does God surround me with people who point me to him and has no one for me to influence? Does God put me in the world and constantly point me to him through the lives, the interest, the compassion, and

73

the prayers of other people, and has no place for me to witness?" The ministers on our staff are to witness. What about the rest of us? Is there some place, is there some witness, is there some person? I think so. I think that everyone who knows Jesus Christ has not only a potential for witness but probably has a field for witness that he may not be aware of. As I approach this, there are many things that I need to keep reminding myself.

I. I need to remind myself that I will never meet anyone who does not really need what God has to offer in Jesus Christ. You recall, when Nicodemus came to Jesus, with his salutation he put Jesus in a place that few men had stood (John 1:2). Jesus said to Nicodemus, "Nicodemus, there is something so wrong with everyone else in the world that unless you have a burden from above, you will not see the Kingdom; you will not understand son-ship; eternal life will evade you." In contact with the rich young ruler, the Scripture says that "Jesus beholding him loved him." He was an attractive man, a man of culture, a man of obvious intensity. Jesus said to him, "One thing thou lackest." You and I would have trouble with this, especially if Nicodemus lived next door or if the rich young ruler were in our office. If some man comes stumbling into the neighborhood, having made a complete mess of his whole life, we can see how God might help him. But when the fellow comes in and his car is longer than ours, his lot is wider than ours, his house is bigger than ours, and his position is more powerful than ours, we have a tendency to look at him as really not needing the same thing as the man who made a mess of his life. We are wrong.

Let us suppose you are on a train going from Fort Worth to Houston. You look up and getting on the train is the original flapper. She has on a mini-mini skirt. She has on more makeup than she ought to have for this time of day, or perhaps for any time of day. She is chewing gum and popping it. She comes and plops down next to you without speaking. She proceeds to dig around in her purse and takes out the last cigarette and throws the package out in the aisle. Then she takes from

her bag a popular magazine and begins reading. The thought comes to you that God could bring so many things into her life. You are not an eager beaver or a direct sort of person, so you ask about your friend who is pastor at the Field Street Church. She asks abour your church affiliation and you begin to talk. One thing leads to another, and you talk about what Christ means to you. You are proud of yourself.

A few days later you are coming back to Fort Worth, and you are thinking about this girl and wondering if what you said did any good. You are sitting there again, waiting for them to change crews, and you look up and standing in the door is her opposite. Here is a girl that someone with taste and money has taken to the best stores and dressed in the peak of style. She has bearing and poise about her. She asks if the seat beside you is taken. She sits down and takes out a lovely silver cigarette case and asks, "Do you mind if I smoke?" You say, "No." She says, "Now really, smoke offends some people. Do you mind?" By now you are saying, "Hurry up and light up!" As she lights her cigarette and offers you one, you are almost sorry that you gave it up. She takes out a magazine and says, "While I was waiting for the train, I read the most interesting article on the moral implications of nuclear testing. What do you think about that?" Right away you think, "Wow! Here's a lovely person, well dressed, and cultured and refined." And you have the most invigorating, scintillating discussion. All at once you are in Fort Worth and off the train. On the way back home you think, "You know, I never did talk to her about Christ."

Do you know why you did not bring up the subject of religion to her? Because deep down in your heart you find it really hard to believe that her problem is the same as the other girl's problem. Because you and I are so dreadfully middle-class, we think that because a person lives in a nice house, wears nice clothes, and is cultured and sophisticated he has discovered everything that God can say to him in Christ. That is not so. If we are to be a witness, we need to mark it down that whether we deal with a janitor in the building or the president of the company, we will never be in contact with people who do not need to know God in forgiveness, who do not need to know him to find purpose in their living, who do not need to know him to comfort them with their mortality and with dying.

II. I do not come across anyone who is not the object of God's love and the object of God's concern. I realize that we have a tendency to produce in the like, and so we have a tendency in evangelism to make it really a collecting of some more people who are already like us. I constantly need to go back to the Scriptures to realize that the Christian never really comes in contact with anyone who is not the object of God's love and concern.

When the disciples came back to the well of Sychar (John 4) and found Christ talking to the woman of Samaria, they were taken aback that Jesus would even be talking with this woman. Why? Because although they had walked with him, they still had not learned that you do not meet people who are not the objects of God's love. The first two or three months they were following Jesus they sang "Amazing Grace" or the first-century equivalent. They had not been in charge of the Intermediate Department very long until they began to sing "How Great We Are," and they began to look upon people as "church type" and "non-church type." We are to witness. We are to look at people, and we are to be reminded that no matter how we feel about them, these people are the objects of God's love and the objects of his concern. We will not be a good witness of God until we feel about them as he does.

III. Everyone has worlds where they are responsible and where they have some possibility of being a witness for God. I think there are times when the enormity of the task that faces us just simply tends to paralyze us. One day a dear friend of mine suggested that I needed to retranslate the Great Commission to read: "Go ye into all *your* worlds and make disciples." The real emphasis in the Great Commission is not on the word *go*, for it is better translated *going*. The real emphasis is on making dis-

ciples. So why not, in order just to get a handle on it, translate it like this: "Go ye into all your worlds and make disciples." And we do have little worlds, little circles. Some of them overlap and some are miles apart—where we go to school, where we live, where we work, where we do business, or the world of social life. These are our worlds.

You say, "Well, I've got these worlds and I know who the people are, but I am just not the witnessing type." Let me suggest that the ways of witnessing are infinite as love will create. Take the case of a woman who was a children's worker—not exactly the hot spot in the church for evangelism, you would think. She was converted in her middle forties and had very little background and training, but she had a marvelous gift from God. She loved children and through the children she loved the parents. She got to know them. She prayed for them. During the five years that I was her pastor, I baptized many young couples because this woman had witnessed to them by loving the child.

Another example is a prominent businessman in Fort Worth who was converted. He was a man who was very glib and found it easy to verbalize, but he found his new faith difficult to talk about because he was such a baby in his faith and such an old man in the community. He decided that everyone he really wanted to witness to he would bring to the church he attended. He would speak to them, shake hands with them and say, "I've found something. Go with me to this place," and he would take them. After his death I preached for a week in that church in a pre-Easter series of services. I suppose I met a score of grown men who said, "I am a follower of Jesus Christ today for one reason: That businessman brought me here, and what I felt and what I heard I knew to be true, and I responded." Not a very complicated system, is it?

A young executive attended a Christian Laymen's Forum at a seminary where he heard a faculty member discussing the new American Bible Society's translation, *Good News for Modern Man*. The faculty member said, "If the average person would expose himself to the Scriptures in an up-to-date language, he would discover God saying things to him." The young executive bought a copy of that Bible and read it. It was a very enriching experience. Now as a part of his witness he has bought copies and given them to friends and associates with this word, "I read this book the other day and it is changing my life." Then he gives one to them. You may say, "That's not much." You are right. But you would be absolutely amazed at the number of people to whom this has been a witness and a signpost.

During my second year as a seminary student I went to preach in a revival in a ranching community in eastern New Mexico. There had not been anyone new move into the community for about thirty years, and everyone who got old enough and had bus fare enough left. So that anybody who was not already a church member had been exposed to a preacher and evangelist every year for about forty years. But we made the rounds. I remember we went to see a man named Johnson, and you could just see the smile on his face as he thought, "Oh, I forgot it's the revival. This evangelist is here to try to convert me." And I tried. When I got through, he grinned and thanked me for coming—and that was it. I thought to myself, "What would it take to get to a man like this?" Living next door to him was my host who had been a neighbor some twenty-five or thirty years. He was a Godly man but not very articulate about it. During the course of this week, my host, sitting there on the back row with Johnson, became burdened for him, and he reached over and took him by the elbow and squeezed with a muscular squeeze, looked at him, and tears came to his eyes. He turned loose and turned his head and blushed, and that was it. The next morning, on the crank phone that cranked four times for my hosts' residence, came a call for me. It was Johnson. He said to me, "Kenneth, I have decided to commit my life to Jesus Christ, and if I am alive tonight when you have that service and sing the hymn, I will come forward and tell the whole church that I have decided to commit my life to Jesus Christ." Do you know why he did that? It was not because I went there and quoted

the New Testament to him. It was because someone whom he knew as a part of his world actually cared and in a very nonverbal way made it known. I wonder if you and I do not need to look around and see if there are people in our world whom God sees and we do not see. People for whom he cares. People who need to have shared what we have come to know. For I believe this is a part of God's plan for each of us to be his witness in the world.—Kenneth L. Chafin.

Topic: On Making the Wilderness Fruitful

TEXT: Mark 4:1–20.

We have probably all heard of Johnny Appleseed, the gentle wanderer who roved the countryside planting apple seeds in remote places. He believed that God had given him a mission in the wilderness to preach the gospel of love and to plant apple seeds that would produce orchards for the benefit of men and women and little children. Johnny Appleseed's whole life was devoted to making the wilderness fruitful, whether that wilderness was geographical or spiritual.

This was Jesus' mission too, to be a sower of seed in order to make the wilderness wanderings of our lives become spiritually fruitful. As he sowed Jesus gave a challenge: "He who has ears to hear, let him hear." This is a parable on hearing and heeding God's Word.

I. Hearing and heeding God's Word can penetrate the shell of the hard heart (4:15).

(a) The habit and routine of sin harden the spiritual heart.

(b) Persons with a hardened spiritual heart do not want to do anything to change for the good.

(c) The gospel of Jesus Christ can soften a hard heart, it can change a life of sinful habits, and it can give you meaning and understanding.

II. Hearing and heeding God's Word can overcome the fears of the shallow heart (4:16–17).

(a) The shallow-hearted person makes a quick and ready response to God, but he falls away just as quickly.

(b) The shallow-hearted person's spiritual life is planted in the soil of wishy-washiness that does not count the cost of following Christ.

(c) "The same heat that killed this plant should have made it flourish if it had had deeper roots" (Halford Luccock).

III. Hearing and heeding God's Word can destroy the lukewarmness of the distracted heart (4:18–19).

(a) The person with a distracted heart hears and responds to the gospel, but his life ceases to be fruitful.

(b) The person with a distracted heart has too many activities of lesser priority growing in his soil.

(c) God deserves our undivided allegiance.

IV. Hearing and heeding God's Word can cause a new heart full of abundant faith to grow in your life (4:20).

(a) Planting the gospel seed may at first seem to be hopeless and futile.

(b) But Jesus sees the bumper crop at the harvest.

(c) This encourages us not to be fainthearted in our labors.

Jesus still calls Johnny Appleseeds, just like you and me, to sow the gospel message in the wilderness of this world where people are hurting and without God. All who have ears, hear and heed this message on making the wilderness fruitful.—Ronnie R. Blankenship.

Topic: Paradise Lost and Restored
TEXT: Gen. 3:24; Rev. 22:14.

There are two ends to the history of mankind, and those two ends are separated by an unknown number of years. The first end was man's beginning. That beginning was as filled with splendor as a sunrise on a cool, crisp, clear, autumn day. Man at this end of his history was as pure as a drop of dew on the petal of a perfect rose. The other end of the history of man is the time that still lies out in the future in which God will complete his great act of love in restoring man to his paradise lost.

I. Man had a paradise but lost it. A casual study of the history of man substantiates the truth told in the book of Genesis concerning the fall of man. This truth says that man had a bright beginning but lost his goodness and right relationship wi... the Creator.

If the world had not experienced a fall in its history, we must assume that the lowest condition of man is the one from which we all have come. That, however, does not seem to be a defensible position when we consider the facts of the history of man. Even though we may see scientific and technological advances in our society, the moral and spiritual condition of man does not seem to be improving.

The loss of Eden was a great loss indeed. When man was forced to leave the Garden, a paradise existence was over. He lost a perfect relationship with God at that time. He lost a natural inner peace and purpose when he lost Eden. Man lost a right relationship with his fellowman when he was cast out of the Garden. The beautiful harmony in nature of which man was a part was spoiled at the fall of man. Life became a painful, dying experience when man lost Eden.

II. Heaven restores and surpasses lost Eden. Man, having lost a paradise Garden, is offered by God a perfect city in which to dwell. In the last two chapters of the Revelation, heaven is described as the city of God. Scripture describes this city as a place in which there is a reversal of all the evil of earth and the completion of its incomplete good.

(a) In heaven the broken relationship of man with God will be restored. "Behold, the tabernacle of God is with men, and he will dwell with them, and they shall be his people, and God himself will be with them, and be their God" (Rev. 21:3).

(b) The pain and suffering that became constant companions of fallen man will be removed in heaven. "And God shall wipe away all tears from their eyes" (Rev. 21:4). The writer of the Revelation goes on to say that the reason there will be no crying in the city of God is there will be no reason to cry—no pain, no sorrow, no death. No family escapes the problems of pain and suffering. The pain and agony associated with sick minds and bodies, broken relationships, and crushed dreams leave severe scars that have been inflicted on all of humanity by the presence and power of sin.

reat enemy of man has always .th. The best efforts of the medi- .ld have only prolonged the average span of man a few years. Death appears to be a sure and victorious enemy over fallen man. But the Scripture says that in the city of God "there shall be no more death" (Rev. 21:4). When the Son of God came to this earth and gave up his life on the cross, rising again on the third day, he crushed the head of Satan beneath his heel once and for all. With the certain defeat of Satan, death was conquered.

It is wonderful for us to behold the truth of the gospel. Our loving God draws us out of a life leading to self-destruction and leads us by his hand into a life of abundance, eternal joy, and everlasting fellowship.—Dixon Free.

Topic: World Church and Local Parish

I. Is it not clear that the concern for unity in the Church and the concern for mission stand and fall together?

(a) There have grown up two great movements, the one dedicated to world evangelism, the other to the quest of Christian unity. But basically and inescapably the two concerns are one. For the more fully the Church becomes united, the more truly is it the Body of Christ; and the more truly it is the Body of Christ, the more essentially missionary must be its spirit. The opposite is also true. The more the Church tolerates partisan, divisive, and competitive elements, the more it distorts its witness and frustrates the missionary purpose of its existence. If there is a denominational loyalty that is large-minded and noble, there is also an obdurate sectarianism that is petty and intolerable. It is one of the most hopeful signs of the times that this essential nexus between mission and unity is now being realized, and action taken accordingly—even though there may be certain sections and movements within the Church that continue to ignore it or even to oppose it.

(b) In this matter it is the younger churches that are speaking with the most unequivocal voice and applying the strongest pressure, and surely they have the mind of Christ. Surely it is manifest that it would be as wrong and futile to strive after orgnizational unity among the churches while ignoring missionary obligation as it would be to plant missions here, there, and everywhere without a single thought of the upbuilding of the new communities into the Body of Christ. It was our Lord himself who made this indissoluble bond between mission and unity clear once for all when, having prayed "that they all may be one," he added immediately, "in order that the world may believe."

II. A thoroughgoing emphasis on the essentially missionary nature of the Church will reorient all our parish activity. Every congregation ought to be prepared periodically to reexamine its own organizational life in the light of its one basic task, and to jettison or radically transform any of its activities that do not helpfully contribute to the central purpose. Christ's warfare in the world today is too critical and demanding to permit the squandering of time and effort on anything that is irrelevant to his campaign or a drag upon his mission. "Take it away! Why cumbereth it the ground?"

(a) In particular, it must be made abundantly clear that it is the layman who holds the key to the situation. The hope of the Church today lies not in any ecclesiastical strategy or clerical professionalism but in a really vigorous movement of lay religion. Never let us forget that it was not as a hierarchy, but as a layman's movement, that the Christian religion began; and one of the most urgent tasks of the hour is to fashion new channels through which the apostolate of the laity may find full and vital expression. For every church is called to be a society of witness, every church member is in the front line of the battle; and the priesthood of all believers, so dear to Reformation faith, is a fact the vast potency of which still waits to be discovered.

(b) Even our traditional modes of worship need to be brought under the searchlight of the consuming fire of Jesus' missionary passion. Why do we go to church? What are we hoping for from our attendance there? "Our feet shall stand within thy gates, O Jerusalem." Wherein lies this mysterious constraint? "If I forget thee, O Jerusalem, let my right hand forget its cunning." Do we come to church to be refreshed in our own spiritual life? Is it to be reassured and comforted against a horde of besieging doubts and fears? Is it to escape from the wilderness of the world into an oasis of recollection and peace? All this, certainly. But if it is truly in Christ's name we are worshiping, something else must be happening as well. We are being challenged. We are being disturbed. We are being burnt by the flame of Christ's terrible compassion for all the sheep without a shepherd. Our hope that the church might be to us a haven of a little private spiritual security is rudely shattered.

(c) If Christ is really present in a service —I mean, not merely being spoken of in worship as a third party who is somewhere else, but actually there in the midst—then something of the travail of his great heart over a perishing world is present too. Without this, church going can become a mere pious indulgence, and all the round of congregational activity intolerably trite and petty. If our congregational life ever becomes an end in itself, if we become introverted ecclesiastically and satisfied in our introversion, if our horizon is this society of ours, this building, this minister and people, this particular spiritual family circle, we are on the road to perdition. A hard saying, undoubtedly, but true; for where Christ comes to his own, always it is to redeem their worship from spiritual self-centeredness, always to thrust them out in loving service for the men he died to save. There is a prayer of Asa, King of Judah, on the eve of a great battle, which memorably expresses the spirit of the true worship. "O Lord our God, we rest on Thee; and in Thy name we go against this multitude." To come to rest in the Most High, and then in the strength of that experience to go out against the powers of darkness in the battle for the kingdom of the Lord—this is essential worship. This is the true missionary Church, "fair as the moon, clear as the sun, and terrible as an army with banners."—James S. Stewart.

Topic: Getting Serious about Missions
TEXT: Acts 13:1–4.

Antioch of Syria, the city mentioned in our text, was founded by the Greek leader Seleucus Nicator in 300 B.C. wh— the city Antioch for his father. Rome took control of the city, it beca— the capital of the new Roman province called Syria. The city was beautified, roads were improved, a seaport was added, and as a result the city became the third greatest city in the Greco-Roman world, being surpassed only by Rome and Alexandria. Acts 11:19–21 tells of the establishment of the Christian church in Antioch. The church at Antioch was the first great missionary church. Prior to this time, the early Christians witnessed as they were driven here and there by persecution. But now, for the first time, a church deliberately followed the leadership of the Holy Spirit in selecting, setting aside, and sending out missionaries for the distinct purpose of reaching the world for Jesus Christ. How did it happen?

I. Affirmed by proclamation. Verse 1 of the text tells us that in the church at Antioch there were "prophets and teachers." These prophets and teachers proclaimed the missionary message of the Bible.

(a) The Bible says that God is a missionary God.

(b) The Bible says that Christ is a missionary Christ.

(c) Everything that God has been up to in the world and in his church has missions as its ultimate aim.

II. Accompanied by preparation. Verse 2 says, "And while they were ministering to the Lord and fasting . . . ." But how can we prepare? Notice that the text mentions two things: these Christians at Antioch were ministering to the Lord and they were fasting. That is, they prepared by their actions and by their attitude. They had a spirit of humility, an attitude of complete dependence upon God. That is what fasting is all about. As they fasted, they forgot their own needs. They forgot their own desires. They forgot their own prejudices. They forgot themselves and were completely open to God's direction and God's design and God's dictates. When we prepare ourselves by acts of service and an attitude of servitude, that is when we will get serious about missions.

III. Accentuated by prayer. Verse 3 says, "Then, when they had fasted and prayed and laid their hands on them, they sent them away." A church that gets serious about missions is a church that is serious about prayer. Hudson Taylor said that the divine method of raising missionaries did not lie in elaborate appeals for help or in strong-arm coercion. Rather, God's plan was for earnest prayer to be given to God to call forth his laborers so that the spiritual life of the church could be deepened. When that happened, Hudson Taylor said, the people will be unable to stay home. That's what happened at Antioch, and that is what needs to happen here.

IV. Actualized by participation. The people of Antioch prayed. The Spirit of God said set aside Barnabas and Saul. And then what happened? These two men agreed to go. Verse 3 says, "They sent them away." And verse 4 says, "They went . . . . " The missionary spirit must be actualized by participation. As you think about the missionary challenge of the church, as you think about a lost world that needs Christ, ask yourself these questions: If not me, then who? If not now, then when?—Brian L. Harbour.

Topic: Reasons People Do Not Come to Christ

TEXT: John 1:1–18.

Is it not strange that the same self-revelation of God that brings salvation and light and life also hardens the hearts of the rebellious. The self-disclosure of God is offensive to the way in which people live.

People do not come to Christ because:

(1) They do not have a high enough conception of him.

(2) They think that they are too familiar with him.

(3) They do not find him presented to them in their own cultural and linguistic idiom.

(4) They cannot see through the darkness of personal despair and spiritual inhospitality.

(5) They cannot see beyond the witness or the preacher.

(6) Their habits of thought and life are too stereotyped.

(7) They do not want to make a commitment; they do not want to pay the necessary price.

Let a person go in sincere repentance and faith to the foot of the cross and what does he become? A new creature in Christ Jesus, forgiven, reconciled, with meaning and purpose in his life and on the way to marvelous fulfillment in God's will. This new life cannot come to persons through social improvement or through obedience to the law; but this regeneration comes through receiving Christ, believing on his name, relying upon him, trusting in him, and thus obtaining power to become the children of God.—Fred W. Andrea.

ILLUSTRATIONS

THE GREATEST STORY. It is related that Adoniram Judson, the great missionary to Burma, at length returned to America and was invited to a certain church to give an address. The minister and the members of the church expected an account of his intrepid labors and amazing experiences as a missionary of Christ in that Eastern land. Instead of this Judson used the occasion to preach simply about his Lord and told the story of the cross. At the end of the service the minister said to the great missionary: "Thank you for your message, Dr. Judson; but I am afraid our people were somewhat disappointed. You see, they have heard of much which has happened to you and what you have done in Burma, and they hoped to hear more of it tonight. I am afraid they expected—well, a thrilling story, such as you alone could give." "I gave them a thrilling story," replied Johnson, "the most thrilling story there is, and the greatest story that I know."—Ernest Wall.

REPENT! The comic strips make fun of the old prophet carrying his placard announcing in one word, "Repent!" Maybe we would rather laugh about it than do it. Daniel Defoe in his famous story, *Robinson Crusoe*, tells how the young Crusoe left home against the advice of his father and the tears and entreaty of his mother. When he finally saw the folly of his choice, he was too embarrassed to return home. Defoe writes of such men: "They are not ashamed to sin, and yet are ashamed to repent; not ashamed of the action, for which they ought justly to be esteemed fools; but are ashamed of the returning, which can only make them be esteemed wise men."—John S. Harris.

A WITNESSING COMMUNITY. A woman who works as a secretary commented on a particular issue to her boss. He said to her, "Did you get that idea from the funny little church you go to?" For fifteen minutes she was irritated and said nothing. Then she regained her composure and said to her boss, "I'm glad my funny little church shows." Our witness will not always be favorably received. It takes courage to be unashamed of the gospel, knowing that it is the power of God for salvation to those who accept it (Rom. 1:16). We are the fellowship of the unashamed, the unapologetic; we are the witnessing community.— Robert A. Raines.

SECTION VIII. Resources for Pastoral Care

BY WAYNE E. OATES

Topic: The Face of Jesus Christ

TEXT: 2 Cor. 4:6.

Paul says: "It is God who said: 'Let light shine out of darkness; who has shone in our hearts to give the light of knowledge of God in the face of Jesus Christ.' " We do not often meditate upon the vision of the face of Jesus Christ. Let us do so today.

We do not have any pictures, drawings, or word descriptions of the physical appearance and the face of Jesus Christ. Yet, imaginations of artists have struggled to portray his face for centuries. This is the face of a human person, Jesus of Nazareth, the carpenter's son. This is the face that on the mountain apart with Peter, James, and John was transfigured and shone like the sun. This is the face that the Apostle Paul tells us that as we ourselves with unveiled faces behold his glory, we are being changed into his likeness from one degree of glory to another (2 Cor. 3:18). This is the face upon which Jesus fell as he went a stone's throw from his disciples and prayed: "My Father, if it be possible, let this cup pass from me, nevertheless, not as I will, but as thou wilt." This is the face that Jesus' inquisitors covered, spat into, struck, and slapped, saying: "Prophesy to us, you Christ! Who is it that struck you?" (Matt. 26:67; Mark 14:65).

This being the face of Jesus Christ and all this—and more—having happened to him, what can we say of the power of his countenance in the day-to-dayness of our sometimes humdrum existence?

I. The face of Jesus Christ is a real face and not a mask.

(a) Our word *personality* comes from the Latin word *persona*, meaning mask, especially as worn by actors in Greek and Roman drama. Jesus' face was not a mask of an actor. It was not the semblance or appearance of a face. It was a face made of human flesh that bled when thorns were pushed into its forehead. The Gnostics of his day and ours would have us believe that he simply *seemed* to be human, that he did not *learn* obedience through the things he suffered. He was not believed to have had a real incarnation. He only seemed to be born of a virgin mother and acted as if he were in the flesh partaking of material nature. But the Fourth Gospel says: "The Word was made flesh and dwelt among us, full of grace and truth" (John 1:14). The First Letter of John says: "By this you know the Spirit of God: Every spirit which confesses that Jesus Christ has come in the flesh is of God . . . " (1 John 4:2).

(b) If you and I walk in the Way of Jesus Christ, we are not putting on an act, playing a "part" called "Christian." We do not do the work of Jesus Christ as a performance. We do not, as Jesus said of hypocrites, fast, look dismal, and disfigure our faces so our fasting may be seen by other people (Matt. 6:16). Rather, as our text teaches, "We have renounced the disgraceful, underhanded ways; we refuse to practice cunning or to tamper with God's Word, but by open statement of the truth, we . . . commend ourselves to every person's conscience in the sight of God." The face of Jesus Christ was "for real" and that openness demands that we reject all phoniness, play acting, grandstanding, and striking of poses of pretense. May it be said of you and may it be said of me: "That person *is* what he or she appears to be, a follower of Jesus Christ!" What you see is what you get. He or she is "for real."

II. The face of Jesus Christ is a compassionate face.

(a) Jesus focuses the gaze of his compassion upon you and me as individuals. In Mark 10:21, Jesus had just recited almost all of the commandments to the rich young man. The young man seemingly impatiently interrupted him and said: "Teacher, all these I have observed from my youth."

(b) Jesus had the option of doing what later some had been doing to Timothy when Paul told him to let no one look down upon him because of his youth. Jesus *could* have *looked down upon* him. He did not. He looked upon him and loved him with an agape love. He loved him with no self-serving needs of his own to be met. He loved him in terms of his own person as being made in the image of God. He loved him as one for whom he would later die. He loved him more than he did his own life, much more than any passing fancy or need for approval. He loved him as God loves persons.

Such acceptance and love is awe inspiring. For some it is terrifying and, as Emily Dickinson says: "They erect defense against love." This young man did this. He went away sorrowing, because he could not respond with a whole heart. Yet, Jesus' look of compassion followed him.

(c) The face of Jesus is a compassionate face. Many individuals come under that focused gaze of compassion. He was moved with compassion for the leper, stretched out his hand, touched the untouchable, and healed him (Mark 1:40–41). He saw a bereaved widow at Nain whose *only son had died*. He had compassion on her. Jesus did not look upon this widow to lust after her as a woman or to lust after her widow's money. He looked upon her with compassion as a doubly bereaved person whose husband was already

dead and her only son had just died and was being carried out. Jesus had compassion on her and brought her son back to life (Luke 7:11–15).

(d) You and I have options as to how we look upon other people, both men and women. We can look upon them to see what *they* can do for *us*. We can look upon them as means to our goals, as tools to be used in the satisfaction of our desires. Or, we can look upon them as obstacles in the way of our achieving our political ambitions. Or, we can simply look upon them as nonpersons, nonentities, as not even being there. Our faces reflect these motives and these valuings of persons.

But our finest option for looking upon persons is with compassion. Jesus looked upon crowds of persons and "had compassion upon them, because they were harassed and helpless, like sheep without a shepherd" (Matt. 9:36). The way you look at persons, conformed to the compassionate face of Jesus Christ, transforms your relationships to them. You move from self-serving to redemptive caring; you move from littleness of self-defense to empathic participation in the otherness of people's lives. You take into yourself the treasure of the image of God in them. Your face takes on the likeness of the compassionate face of Jesus Christ.

III. The face of Jesus Christ is a silent face.

(a) The silence of eternity collects itself in this face of Jesus Christ. In this awesome silence our own hearts are both comforted and confronted. The silence of Jesus' face became a deafening quietness in the last few days of his life. He had told Peter that before the cock would crow, he would deny him three times. Luke tells us that as Peter denied a third time that he knew Jesus, "while he was still speaking, the cock crowed." Then, Luke tells us: "And the Lord turned and looked at Peter" (Luke 22:61). Peter went out and wept bitterly. The silence of Jesus brought the memory of his prophecy to Peter. But did it, at that moment, bring also the promise that after Jesus' Resurrection, Peter, having succumbed to temptation himself, would have both the wisdom and compassion to turn and strengthen the other disciples? Then Herod, gladdened by the chance to see Jesus and "to see some sign done by him, questioned Jesus at some length, . . . he made no answer" (Luke 23:8–9). Then the high priest asked: "Have you no answer to make? What is it that these men testify against you?" But Jesus was silent and made no answer (Mark 14:60–61).

(b) Jesus' capacity for silence to the presence of such accusations is both a rebuke and an admonition to you and me. We always rush to our own defense. We insist on having the last word. When presented with the hurting necessities by those who seek our comradeship in their suffering, we are quick to give pat answers. When caught up in controversies, we chatter away at the latest bit of news from the front.

(c) Job had a word for us: "Worthless physicians are you all. Oh, that you would keep your silence, and it would be your teacher" (Job 13:4–5). Paul was more patient and kind when he said: "The Spirit helps us in our weakness; for we do not know how to pray as we ought, but the Spirit himself intercedes for us with sighs too deep for words" (Rom. 8:26). In that intercession, we capture a full view of the silent, compassionate, and genuinely human face of Jesus Christ who was tempted as we are and who is able to "sympathize with our weaknesses." Prompted by this vision, we can with confidence draw near to the throne of grace, that we may receive mercy and find grace to help in time of need.

IV. Finally, the face of Jesus Christ is an *intentional* face.

(a) He lived deliberately, purposively, intentionally. He was guided by an overpowering calling that shaped his direction daily. Luke tells us: "When the days draw near for him to be received up, he set his face to go to Jerusalem" (Luke 9:51). The King James Version says: "He steadfastly set his face to go to Jerusalem." Jesus' face was as Isaiah said of his own: "For the Lord God helps me; therefore, I have not been confounded; therefore I have set my face like a flint, and I know I shall not be put to shame" (Isa. 50:7). For Isaiah, for Jesus, to *set* his face meant that he was fully

persuaded that the direction he was moving was the destiny God had for him. His mind was made up. He had crossed the Rubicon. He had come to the point of no return. There was no turning back. From that point forward people have had trouble seeing the face of Jesus Christ because he is always moving in front of us as the pioneering trailblazer of our faith. He is the "point man" on our patrol in this life and the next. We can only see the back of his head, not his face. That face is always set in the direction of the Cross, a destiny we are diffident, indecisive, and too aesthetic to choose for ourselves.

(b) Consequently, our great temptation is not to deny Christ, as did Simon Peter. Our temptation is to debate and discuss, equivocate and avoid the stark destiny of the Cross toward which on that day he set his face steadfastly. As Andras Angyal says, our lifestyle of uncommitment is buttressed by getting a set of safe rules to live by "making sharp division (between us and others) with a species of desperate dogmatisms which arbitrarily overshouts doubt." But the main defense we use is indecision as a way of life. Angyal describes such a person in his book *Neurosis and Treatment* (New York: John Wiley and Sons, 1965, pp. 187, 189): "He refused to take responsibility in the sense of identifying himself with his actions and saying unequivocally, 'Here I stand.' The person is always eyeing two possibilities, choosing a little of both, but neither completely. . . . He usually feels that in avoiding commitments he leads a brave fight for personal freedom, but since he does not use it when he has it, the fight turns out to be a fight for the freedom to sit on the fence."

(c) But the time of decision comes. Circumstances have a way of pushing us off the fence. The Apostle Paul did not wait for this to happen. He redeemed the time. He forgot the things that were behind him and pressed forward toward the mark of the high calling of Jesus Christ. He did not shrink back from following Jesus Christ to the cross. He could say: "I have been crucified with Christ; it is no longer I who live, but Christ who lives in me; and the life I now live in the flesh I live by faith in the

Son of God, who loved me and gave himself for me" (Gal. 2:20).

(d) The time has come and *now* is the time for us to get off the fence, to quit fighting for the freedom of indecision. We look into the face of Jesus Christ and find our own real humanity mirrored in the flesh. We look into his face and find acceptance, affection, and compassion. His silent face prompts within us the growth of a wise and good conscience. His steadfast and intentional face sets the course of our lives and guides us unfailingly toward God's destiny for our whole lives and the meaning of each passing day.

(e) Robert Browning writes in his long poem *Saul* of how David sought to heal Saul of his despairing depression with music. He played tunes that all sheep know, tunes that would make a quail leave its mate, the wise-song of the reapers, a funeral dirge, and a wedding song. Finally, a battle song was played to the sound of Saul's name. Saul stirred and his labored breathing subsided. However, nothing completely restored "Saul, the mistake, Saul, the failure, the ruin he seems now . . . to find himself clear and safe in new light and new life." David confesses his inadequacy and says:

'Tis the weakness in strength, that I
  cry for!
My flesh, that I seek in the Godhead!
I seek and I find it. O, Saul, it
  shall be
A Face like my face that receives thee.
A Man like unto me.
Thou shalt love and be loved forever,
A Hand like this hand
Shall throw open the gates of new life
to thee. See the Christ stand!

Topic: The Daily Providence of God

TEXT: Exod. 16:4–6,11–21; Matt. 6:11, 34.

(a) In the story of the Exodus, the children of Israel, as they made their journey from the Red Sea into the Promised Land, got more and more impatient with Moses. They expressed their anger more and more to him because they did not have the kind of food that they had had when they were in bondage in Egypt. The Lord said to them through Moses, "I will give you manna in the morning; when the dew has risen you will find it. And quails will come in the evening, and you will have meat. And then you shall know that I am God." Not meat, not bread, not the enemy; *I* am God.

(b) This is the main issue in our life today: How to live our lives with foresight and planning and at the same time to live each day, in spite of its vexations, to the utmost for God. How can you and I perceive our spiritual life as a long spiritual journey, invest our lives with confidence in this day for the future? At the same time, how can we neither live in the past nor live in the future so that the present day is not totally wasted in anxiety over the future and guilt over the past? God speaks to us about different kinds of days that we have. There is a day of desire. There is a day of difficulty. There is a day of decision.

I. In the day of desire God saves us from the idolatry of our desire.

(a) The Israelites had thrown a tantrum with God. They remind me, and we remind me, of myself and yourself too, of the impatience of the grandchild of a good friend of mine who came to him and said, "Grandpa, I want this right now. I want it right in the middle of now." When we want, when we desire, we want right in the middle of now. That is our impatience. That is our hunger.

(b) Not only that, the Israelites went one step further. They not only expected it now, but they expected to have a surplus so they wouldn't have to depend upon God later. When we start building our surpluses all out of keeping with reality, this becomes greed and an idolatry of our desires. Jesus said, "Give us this day our daily bread." There is a difference in planning for the future and tending to the well-being of those whom we love and wanting it all. There is a difference between foresight and an idolatry of the surplus. In the dew of each morning's need for material necessities comes bread. In the evening of that day comes meat. Then we know that God, and not our desire, is God.

II. The day of difficulty comes and God provides us with the strength and wisdom for resolving our difficulties on a day-by-day basis.

(a) Jesus, in addressing the anxiety of our heart, says, "Do not be anxious for the morrow, let tommorow be anxious for itself." There is a difference between wise planning and being overwhelmed by anxiety. He said sufficient unto the day is the evil thereof. Suffering and loss come upon us. We lose loved ones. We feel that we cannot go on another day. We feel that we have had it. We may not be able to go on *another* day, but we can go on this day. God provides the strength for this day. There is no stress or temptation that has overcome us but that God will provide a way through it, so that we may know that he is God.

(b) There is the habit of an uncontrollable anger and temper. The maintenance of control over one's impatience and wrath is a day by day discipline. Paul put it well when he said in Ephesians 4:25, "Therefore putting away falsehood, let every one speak the truth with his neighbor, for we are members one of another. Be angry and sin not and do not let the sun go down on your wrath nor give opportunity to the devil." To control one's anger is a habit that can replace the tantrums that the children of Israel expressed. They, you and I, learn to discipline our anger day by day. We learn to put that energy into the power box of constructive activity day by day and make it produce British thermal units of energy for work to the glory of the Lord. Jesus said, "Agree with your adversary quickly while you are in the way with him. For you will in no wise get out until you pay the last farthing." The accumulation of unresolved habits that are destructive to us becomes heavier and heavier and heavier. It becomes a burdensome way of life. Our angers and our grudges become little gods before whom we bow down and worship. But when day by day we are angry and sin not, God, and not our grudges, becomes our God.

III. Finally comes the day of decision!

(a) Jesus said to Zacchaeus in the nineteenth chapter of Luke, "Today salvation has come to this house." Zacchaeus brought the desires, difficulties, and decisions of his life in eager hospitality to Jesus' entry into his life. Basic changes took place. A clear decision was made to follow the Christ. As we face the decisions about our lives, we decide whether we are going to serve God or the gods around us, as Joshua had to ask the Israelites on another occasion.

(b) We are faced with the temptation of procrastination—putting things off day by day; letting decisions go unmade until they are made for us by the passage of time. This is no plea for impulsive, unthought-through decisions. It is a plea for the more common ailment we suffer, procrastination, to come to an end. There are people who have thought for years "I will give my life to Jesus Christ someday. I will make a 180-degree turnaround in my life someday, but not today. I'm afraid of that responsibility. I'm afraid I may not be able to hold out." Faith in God is a candle put into our hands by God through Jesus Christ. If we have the courage to take the step today in behalf of our commitment to Jesus Christ, his promise is that we will have the light to take the step tommorow.

Topic: The Ministry of Encouragement

TEXT: Rom. 15:4; Acts 4:36; 11:25; 15:36; 28:15.

Each one of you has come through *your own particular storms* in life, possibly even this past week. You may have come to this place as a sanctuary from the tempest of your life at work, at home, in the community, or just within your own heart.

A gripping story dramatizes the meaning of your and my being here today. The Apostle Paul and Luke, the beloved physician, had set sail with Paul as a prisoner, from Palestine for Italy and Rome. They encountered tempestuous wind called a northeaster. All hope of their being saved was abandoned. Paul encouraged his shipmates. He said to them: "Take heart!" He was assured in his prayers they would make it to Italy. They were encouraged, and they took bread and gave thanks.

You and I have come through—or we are coming through—our particular storms. We see each other here. We thank God and take courage upon seeing each other. This is the ministry of encouragement. We encourage others in the middle of our own troubles. We are encouraged by each other. What is this ministry all about?

I. The ministry of encouragement is the practice of the priesthood of believers to each other. It consists of both receiving and giving encouragement.

(a) We are comforted by God, the Father of mercies and the God of all comfort.

(b) We become a comfort to those who are in any kind of trouble. Barnabas is our role model. The apostles gave Joseph the surname Barnabas, which means son of encouragement. In Acts 11:25, Joseph sought out Paul in Tarsus for the church at Antioch. In Acts 15:36, he stood by John Mark when Paul did not want Mark to come along.

(c) Who comforts the comforter? God does, and the fellowship of believers does. In the ministry of encouragement we put heart into each other. We lend our very being and all its strengths to each other. We "jump start" each other, a new way of looking at them.

II. We have a perennial and never-depleting source of encouragement in the Scriptures (Rom. 15:4).

(a) The Scriptures were written for our instruction, not our worship. This instruction gives us fresh angles of vision of the troubles that discourage us, a new way of looking at them.

(b) They provide both steadfastness and encouragement. The Scriptures are our anchor of reliability in a shifting, unreliable world. For example, they provide a pattern for confrontation, listening, and restoration in conflicts with other people (Matt. 18:15–20; Gal. 6:1–2).

III. Persons who are ministers of encouragement live considerately and faithfully with each other. They stand by each other when the going is rough.

(a) Considerateness is the capacity to put yourself in another person's place and respond to him or her in terms of their deepest longings.

(b) Faithfulness is staying by a person when they are ecstatic and when they are desolate, "through thick and thin." The mark of a mature person is the capacity for maintaining lasting relationships.

(c) A legend comes down to us about what heaven and hell are really like. People in hell are much as they are here except for two things—they cannot die and their elbows won't bend. When they try to eat, they cannot get food to their mouths. As a result they are constantly starving, though there is much food to be eaten. They fall into conflict with each other because they are blaming each other for their starvation. Their hunger never ends and it worsens as they fight with each other. In heaven people have the same situation, but they handle it differently. Instead of blaming each other and fighting with each other because their elbows won't bend, each feeds another with his or her outstretched arms and in turn receives food from another in the same way. Each is free of hunger and no one *has* to die. They dwell considerately and faithfully with each other.

Topic: The Better Way: The Ethic of Wholeness

Text: Matt. 5:29–30; 18:8–9.

These two verses of Jesus' teaching are pushed out of your and my attention by the glittering example of sexual lust that precedes them in the Sermon on the Mount. The same teaching is also found in Matthew 18:8–9 after Jesus interrupted the disciples' questions about "Who is greatest in the kingdom of God?" Rarely is this metaphor applied also to the lust for power! Yet, in both references, are two of the most powerful verses in Jesus' teaching, powerful because they have in them Jesus' way to health, holiness, and wholeness. Taken literally, and apart from the Spirit of Christ, they have in them a lethal message. Literalism or concreteness is a hallmark of the young child's thinking and the thinking of the mentally ill adult. When literalized, these two texts have set great tragedy into motion. I have seen acutely ill persons who interpreted this text literally for themselves. In acting upon their literal interpretation, they plucked out their eyes or they cut off their hands.

In neither instance, then—a little child's literalism or the concrete thinking of the psychotic person—can we find the better way of which Jesus speaks. To the contrary, he speaks of the worth of your and my life as a whole as contrasted with its being shaped, dominated, ruled, and ruined by a part of life, whether it is the lust for sex, power, or anything else, such as revenge. "*It is better* that you lose one of your members than that your *whole* body go into gehenna." This is an ethic of wholeness, the essence of Christ's "better way," as opposed to the self-destructiveness of permitting a segment, a piece, a part of life to destroy your and my whole life. It is rooted and grounded in the great commandment of the consecration of the whole life to God in Christ as the better way of holistic ethical living, health of being, and salvation. In this better way of Jesus Christ, you and I consecrate the whole of our being to one God, rather than this part to that god, that part to another god, and each of the other parts to as many other gods. To worship the Lord of Jesus Christ with a whole heart, free of idolatry, is the way to wholeness, integration of personhood, and healthy holiness before God and our neighbor. Jesus illustrates this better way in two situations of life.

I. *The covetousness of lust.* The first of Jesus' two specific applications of this better way, the ethic of wholeness, centered on the sexual lust of man for a woman and/or the struggle for power to be the greater in the Kingdom of God. In the Great Commandment he says a person is to love God with his whole *heart*, the seat of his emotions, wishes, and desires. He is to love his neighbor as himself. Yet, the covetous lust of a man for a woman divides and adulterates his love of God. Lust treats the woman, his neighbor, as an object, a thing, a means, not as a neighbor, a person, a being made in the image of God.

(a) When this happens, the sexual desires of a person—man or woman—take charge of the whole life. Sexual preoccupation crowds out and hinders the total life. All decisions are made with sexual intent in mind. The sexual partner, in turn, has the same thing happen to him or her as a consenting partner. However, Jesus, contrary to contemporary attempts to locate the origin of sin in *women*, fixes the prime responsibility in men—as revolu-

tionary a teaching in his day as in ours. (See Rom. 12:1–2; 1 Pet. 1:14–16.)

(b) In our present day, the horrible antithesis of such consecration splashes across our newspapers and television screens daily. Its gruesome results appear in our hospital emergency rooms. It has even broken out in day-care centers and kindergartens. I speak here of rape of women and the sexual abuse of children, both boys and girls. A worker in the rape relief center or in a hospital emergency room does not have trouble affirming Jesus' teaching that it is better that the person not have a sexual life than to destroy his or her own and other persons' whole lives with it. The sexual exploitation of women and children is terrible when found among persons who profess no religious faith. How very like the Corinthian church it is today, however, for sexual exploitation to be done in the church, by leaders of groups in the church, all in the name of sentimental, grotesque caricatures of the Christian faith.

II. *The pressure of power needs.* Jesus' second example of the metaphor of the whole life being better without a part causing the whole to perish centers upon the competitive lust for power in the church. "Who is greatest?" In his book *The Churches the Apostles Left Behind* in which he interprets Matthew 18, Raymond Brown says: "The answer to the question of who is the greatest in the Kingdom (or the church where the gospel of the Kingdom is proclaimed) is given through the example of the little child. This is not because, as romantics would have us think, the little child is thought of as lovable, or cuddly, or innocent, but the child is helpless and dependent, with no power" (p. 140). Jesus warns against scandalizing "one of these little ones" in the pell mell dash for power in the church. It is better to have a millstone around the neck and be cast in the sea. The person who causes one of these to sin is a part of the body of Christ to be severed like a hand or foot that has risen up against the common good.

(a) Readily you say that this is a two-edged sword. One can say that another who does not believe as he or she does should be cut off from the "land of the living." But there's a rub here. The Matthew account prescribes a specific, face-to-face appeal to listening and teachability as a process. If a member is offending you, go to him or her alone and see if you can get them to listen. If this does not work, take another Christian with you, and see if that person will listen. Only then do you bring the matter before the congregation or a small group of the congregation. These steps you take, if you take the Bible seriously, before you consider that person as an outsider.

(b) However, today we do not go this courageous, face-to-face way. Power-hungry people reverse the process. They go to a convention with a resolution first, then someone suggests a committee, then two people attempt to deal with the person, and the two contending persons meet face to face after all of the "little ones" have been caused to stumble. The latter is a bitter way. It does not often happen. An example of this is found in the piecemeal interpretation of the Scriptures being thrust at us today. A struggle for political power centers on the Bible. Jesus' ethic of wholeness applies here. You and I as interpreters of the Word of God, both in our understanding of the Bible and in the walk of life we live out before people, are called to see life steady and whole. We are, if we have integrity, bound by ordination, Biblical study, and prayer to declare the whole counsel of God. To take a piece or part of God's kerygma that fits our fancy and desire to rise up over the whole people of God is sin. Granted, we shall always know in part and prophesy in part until that which is perfect, complete, and whole is come. Yet, we need not become peddlers of half-truths, which Plato said are the worst form of a lie.

(c) This is especially true when we presume as I am now to stand before a people of God to interpret the Scriptures. If you ask me at this moment if I believe the Bible is unfailingly true, I will tell you: "If I can learn the whole truth of the whole Bible on any one subject that matters to the faith and practice of the Christian life, I will take it as the unfailing and eternal truth." However, if you ask me if I believe each part of the Scripture is infallible apart from the rest of the Bible, I will say that you have asked me to enter into a pact with the devil. For, as Shakespeare says, "The devil can cite Scripture for his purpose" (*The Merchant of Venice*, Act 1, scene 3, line 99). Such citing of Scripture usually hides two grains of wheat in two bundles of chaff, as Shakespeare again says. Such piecemeal interpretations on critical issues such as divorce, the place of women, and so on, are "flamingo" exegesis. The flamingo bird is fond of standing on one leg with its head under its wing to rest. The flamingo interpreter of the Scripture stands on one text and hides his or her head from the rest of the completing testimony of the Scripture as a whole.

(d) Our prayer as seekers after the whole counsel of God is that we will not rest or make peace with this piecemeal exegesis. If we are called to be ministers, we take our visions of the call of God into the discipline of three to seven years of Biblical, theological, historical, and pastoral study. We meditate on the Scriptures day and night. We refuse upon graduating to bow the knee to the golden calf of catchwords in order to capture positions of petty power on the flat earth of our little denominational scheme of things. We are committed in the name of the Lord Jesus Christ to communicate to the limits of our being the truth, the whole truth, and nothing but the truth from God's Word. We refuse to cause *one* of the little ones of Jesus Christ to stumble. For he has told us, and it is ever before us, what is the better way. The better way is to sustain the whole life than to be idolators of any part of life. We are to love no other gods before him.

SECTION IX. Resources for Preaching on Ecclesiastes

BY DWIGHT E. STEVENSON

A literary masterpiece of haunting beauty, Ecclesiastes is the most "negative" book in the Bible. Its opening "wisdom," repeated throughout as a theme is "emptiness, all is empty" (NEB). The book issues a harsh judgment: "I have seen all the deeds that are done here under the sun; they are all emptiness and chasing the wind" (NEB). More familiarly translated, this reads, "I have seen everything that is done under the sun; and behold, all is vanity and a striving after wind" (1:14, RSV).

How, then, can this book be a source for preaching? The book is a classical statement of the secular lifestyle and the secular spirit. In a remarkable book in which he comments on every verse of Ecclesiastes using a camera for his unique exegesis, Robert L. Short gives us the clue: "Ecclesiastes is human self-sufficiency stretched to its absolute limit and found sadly wanting." He throws a brilliant light on the interpreter's task with his observation, "Ecclesiastes: The Bible's Negative Image of Christ the Truth," a chapter in which he also calls the book "A Christ-Shaped Vacuum."

Following this clue, we will find the most fruitful homiletical pathway in the linkage of texts from Ecclesiastes with texts from the Four Gospels and the letters of Paul. Thus nearly every sermon will have a double text, one negative, the other positive. One states the secular question or the secular conclusion or complaint; the other states the Christian answer or insight. The resulting interplay of secular and Christian will be very instructive.

Our own secular age should find great affinity with Ecclesiastes. It may be that ours is the most secularist of all epochs since the birth of Christ. In that case, the words of this ancient book are not echoes from antiquity but beautifully articulate expressions of the soul of modernity. His very words sound as if they were crafted for our tongues.

With that interpretive foreword, we move on at once to our task.

Topic: On Coming Up Empty
SCRIPTURE: Eccl. 1:2.
"Emptiness, emptiness, says the Speaker, all is empty" (NEB).
SCRIPTURE: John 10:10.
"I have come in order that they might have life, life in all its fulness" (TEV).

Qoheleth (the Hebrew name of our author) came up empty, as a result of the pathway of life he had chosen. Christ came up empty at the very beginning of his ministry, as its very basis. The appropriate scripture is the celebrated Philippian hymn: "Have this mind among yourselves which is yours in Christ Jesus, who, though he was in the form of God, did not count equality with God a thing to be grasped, but *emptied himself*, taking the form of a servant, being born in the likeness of men" (Phil. 2:5–8, RSV).

From the autobiographical sections of his book, especially in chapters one and two, we learn that Qoheleth had little mind to be a servant. He brags, "I bought male and female slaves, and had slaves who were born in my house" (2:7, RSV). He had no mind to be a servant! On the contrary, he was—in the image of Solomon, his idol—"a king in Jerusalem." He sought to master life and to be, above all, the captain of his soul.

His trouble all along was that he did not begin on empty. He lived the affluent life and he craved everything for himself: wisdom, pleasure, fabulous achievements, untold wealth, massive power, and celebrity. Notice the critical word: "I made *myself* gardens and parks. . . . I made *myself* pools" (2:5, 6, RSV).

It will be appropriate in this sermon to quote from the book in Qoheleth's own words as he worked out his quest for ultimate satisfaction. And, in the same way, it will be essential to quote the opposing words of Jesus for insight into his "more excellent way."

How you "come up empty" makes a great difference. There are two who did it in classical manner. Which will we choose?

Topic: Like Money in the Bank
SCRIPTURE: Eccl. 7:11–12.
"Wisdom is good with an inheritance, an advantage to those who see the sun. For the protection of wisdom is like the protection of money; and the advantage of knowledge is that wisdom preserves the life of him who has it" (RSV).
SCRIPTURE: Matt. 19:16–22.
The Rich Young Man, who "went away sorrowful; for he had great possessions" (RSV).
SCRIPTURE: Matt. 11:25, 26.
Jesus' Prayer: "I thank thee, Father, Lord of heaven and earth, that thou hast hidden these things from the wise and understanding and revealed them to babes: yea, Father, for such was thy gracious will" (RSV).
Love of wisdom and knowledge as private possessions can be as pagan and as damaging as greed for money. The value that Qoheleth placed upon it was like that which he placed on money—it was a kind of property that was supposed to provide security and final satisfaction. He learned that it could not deliver what he thought it had promised. It left him feeling empty,

(1:16–17). And, instead of making him happy, it increased his sorrow: "For in much wisdom is much vexation, and he who increases knowledge increases sorrow" (1:18, RSV). Moffatt's translation puts it: "the more you know, the more you ache." Qoheleth found it a headache. Jesus, on the contrary, found it a heartache that opened him to the multitudes in a great compassion. Qoheleth, in his pride of knowledge, missed that dimension entirely.

Neither could knowledge as a possession deliver knowledge of God. "I saw all the work of God, that man cannot find out the work that is done under the sun. However much man may toil in seeking, he will not find it out; even though a wise man claims to know, he cannot find it out" (8:17, RSV).

Actually, pride of knowledge could not even deliver knowledge of the phenomenal world. That took the meekness of science, sitting down before the facts like a little child willing to learn what was not known before. Lacking that, Qoheleth thought he had seen everything and that there was nothing new under the sun.

Knowledge of God, far from being a possession, is a great reversal: we stop worrying about what belongs to us and begin considering the One to whom we belong. We acknowledge that we are *his*. Knowledge finds satisfaction not in what *we know*, but in the fact that *we are known*. This discovery is open not only to the wise and understanding under conditions of profound humility and contrition —but also to those whom Jesus called babes.

Is there, then, a positive role for knowledge that is not pagan? It is the Israelite creed that we should love God "with our mind," as well as with our heart and strength. Knowledge as quest and adventure; knowledge as the cutting edge of fellow feeling; knowledge as awareness of the divine grace bountifully poured out upon us is one of life's richest blessings.

Topic: "Mostly Fools"
SCRIPTURE: Eccl. 5:4.
"He [God] has no pleasure in fools" (RSV).

SCRIPTURE: Eccl. 7:28.

"One man among a thousand I found, but a woman among all these I have not found" (RSV).

SCRIPTURE: Matt. 5:22.

"But I say to you that everyone who is angry with his brother shall be liable to judgment; whoever insults his brother shall be liable to the council, and whoever says 'you fool!' shall be liable to the hell of fire" (RSV).

Thomas Carlyle, in his *Latter Day Pamphlets,* referred to the entire population of Great Britain in his day as "the twenty-seven million, mostly fools." Qoheleth would have approved, for he himself had concluded that most men and all women were fools.

The sages, self-styled wise men, had a rich vocabulary for fools—no less than seven Hebrew words meaning (1) untutored, ignorant, (2) stupid, (3) obstinate, (4) crude, (5) brutal, depraved, (6) mad, crazy, (7) opinionated, insolent. Thus they expressed their self-esteem and their contempt for the masses. Qoheleth's mentality is elitist. He thought of himself as well above the common horde.

Jesus thought of himself as a man of the people. He had no patience with the cynicism of the elite when they called most men fools. To call a person a fool was to expose oneself to the fires of hell, he said, in one of his sharpest words. A person who calls the masses "fools" is self-excused from doing anything to help them, while, at the same time, increasing his callousness and hardness of heart.

Jesus was realistic enough to know that "many are called but few are chosen," but he was never guilty of contempt for the masses. What he saw of them increased his sensitivity rather than hardening his heart. "When he saw the crowds, he had compassion for them, because they were harassed and helpless, like sheep without a shepherd" (Matt. 9:36, RSV). What a difference!

Topic: "Enjoy Yourself!"

SCRIPTURE: Eccl. 2:1.

"I said to myself, 'Come now, I will make a test of pleasure; enjoy yourself' " (RSV).

SCRIPTURE: Eccl. 2:10.

"And whatever my eyes desired I did not keep from them; I kept my heart from no pleasure" (RSV).

James Moffatt's translation puts it this way: "Nothing I coveted did I deny myself." This, of course, is life conducted on "the pleasure principle." It can be carried out only by one who has enough money to indulge his appetites and serve his every desire.

The irony is that a person who sets out merely to enjoy himself will develop little self to enjoy. The energy that might have gone into the development of a rich self is squandered on animal sensations. And the outcome, as Qoheleth learned, is satiety and boredom.

It is the paradox of any life that intends to be fully human that Life with a capital *L* requires self-denial. Every athlete knows this, as does any serious musician or scientist. The price of self-indulgence comes high: ignorance, lack of skill, a flabby, dissipated body, and it may even end in self-loathing.

Therefore, it comes about that the direct opposite of the pleasure principle was stated by Jesus: "If any man would come after me, let him deny himself and take up his cross and follow me" (Matt. 16:24, RSV). Does this mean life drained of happiness? On the contrary, *joy* is one of the leading fruits of the Spirit, as listed by the Apostle Paul (Gal. 5:22). T. R. Glover said that the early Christians were "all the time getting into trouble, and they were absurdly happy." What was their secret? They had discovered the larger life of living "no longer for themselves" (2 Cor. 5:15), and they had found in service their perfect freedom.

Topic: "Nothing New Under the Sun"

SCRIPTURE: Eccl. 1:4–9.

Qoheleth opens his book with the theme of emptiness and weariness, which he bases on the cycles of nature: "What has been is what will be, and what has been done is what will be done, and there is nothing new under the sun" (v. 9, RSV). Going in circles, getting nowhere.

In this philosophy of history Qoheleth was more of a Greek than a Jew. The Old

Testament as a whole sets forth a progressive view of history culminating in the kingdom of God. The Greeks, in common with many Asiatic peoples, held that history goes in cycles.

However that may be, we shall have to charge a great part of Qoheleth's pessimism to a defective lifestyle. The way he chose to take simply did not lead to an optimistic view of things, as we have seen. He was not the only writer of the late Old Testament and Intertestamental periods to have a pessimistic view of history. There we run into the opinion, often expressed, that the world is running down. 2 Baruch 85:10 is a prime example.

The regularities of nature could be read in just the opposite fashion, as Jesus showed when he observed that God sends his rain upon the just and the unjust alike, thus showing the bounty of his love for us (Matt. 5:45). And, we may ask, would Qoheleth have been more pleased if nature had suddenly become unpredictable and capricious? An earthquake or a volcanic eruption can be very unnerving!

Aside from a cyclic view of history and an enjoyment-oriented lifestyle, it seems probable that our author also lived in a relatively stagnant time, when society was undergoing little change over long decades.

How shocked Qoheleth would have been had he been able to foresee what radical changes were to break upon the world after him! A new religion, Islam, was yet to come and to change the face of the map, even to dominate his beloved Jerusalem for centuries. There were whole continents, whole civilizations, that he knew nothing about, as the age of exploration and discovery was to demonstrate. And the age of science and invention was far in the future. He could not imagine that his descendants would fly through the air and even into outer space, or talk with each other across oceans around the world in the twinkling of an eye. And, as for social change, as a slaveholder he could not have imagined the Emancipation Proclamation. Or that the major emotional problem of mankind would become "future shock," the world changing too fast to keep up with!

It is still possible, even in a scientific age, to retreat into one's own tiny little world of habit and conformity, like Solomon Grundy, "born on Monday, christened on Tuesday, married on Wednesday, taken ill on Thursday, worse on Friday, died on Saturday, buried on Sunday. That was the end of Solomon Grundy."

Yes, as we know, life can go in circles even in a world bursting with new discoveries in science, medicine, social progress, and high adventure.

In the realm of the spirit, the antidote to Qoheleth's pessimism lies in the New Testament. Jesus gave his disciples a new commandment (John 13:34). The Apostle Paul saw the coming of Jesus as the beginning of a whole new act of creation: "Therefore, if anyone is in Christ, he is a new creation; the old has passed away, behold, the new has come" (2 Cor. 5:17, RSV). The same Christian visionary saw the church as a New Humanity in place of the old warring factions of a broken humanity (Eph. 2:14–17).

The full strength of God's creation, it would seem, is far from exhausted. Given half a chance by rebellious mankind, it is only just begun.

Topic: Is It Love or Is It Hate?
SCRIPTURE: Eccl. 8:17.
"I saw all the work of God, that man cannot find out the work that is done under the sun. However much man may toil in seeking, he will not find it out; even though a wise man claims to know, he cannot find it out" (RSV).
SCRIPTURE: Eccl. 9:1.
"But all this I laid to heart, examining it all, how the righteous and the wise and their deeds are in the hand of God; whether it is love or hate man does not know" (RSV).

With all his pessimism and nihilism, Qoheleth never doubted the existence of God. *That* God is he felt assured. *What* God is eluded him. Life is a gift from the hand of God, but is it a blessing or is it a curse? He had his bad days when he felt that it might have been better never to have been born! Life is so full of trouble, frustration, and injustice!

From William P. Montague's book, *Belief Unbound*, I remember one sterling sentence: Religion is belief in "a momentous possibility . . . that what is highest in spirit is also deepest in nature."

That power, enormous power, is deepest in nature we may not doubt, especially now in this atomic age. After the dropping of the atom bomb on Hiroshima in 1945, to end the war in the Pacific, President Harry Truman broadcast his explanation that the power that had been released in the mushroom cloud over Hiroshima was "the basic power of the universe." I remember challenging that explanation in a sermon that I preached the very next Sunday. Even on natural grounds, I said, we have to believe that there is an even greater power—the silent power that harnesses this explosive energy, holds it in check, and creates an ordered world. From one standpoint every one of us has a physical body that is a walking atom bomb; but at the deeper level it is power organized into an organic whole and made capable of reason and hope, faith and love.

This we know not so much by reasoning about it as by receiving that love. Our faith is no achievement of our own. It is the result of God's initiative. It is not our search for God, but God's search for us. In order to believe that God is love, we have to know ourselves to be loved ultimately and unconditionally. That means being sought even when we are sinners. It means being loved by a divinity who takes upon himself the sins of us all.

Belief in God is belief in the momentous possibility that what is highest in spirit is also deepest in nature. Well, Jesus Christ is highest in spirit! "He who did not spare his own Son but gave him up for us all, will he not also give us all things with him?" (Rom. 8:32, RSV). "Who shall separate us from the love of Christ? Shall tribulation, or distress, or persecution, or famine, or nakedness, or peril, or sword? . . . No, in all these things we are more than conquerors through him who loved us" (Rom. 8:35, 37, RSV).

This, together with our individual creation, is God's gift to us, if we will only reach out to receive it.

Topic: Not by Bread Alone
SCRIPTURE: Eccl. 6:7.
"All the toil of man is for his mouth, yet his appetite is not satisfied" (RSV).
SCRIPTURE: Matt. 4:4.
"Man shall not live by bread alone, but by every word that proceeds from the mouth of God" (RSV) (cf. Deut. 8:3).

To work for nothing but physical food is an absurdity, yet people do it all the time. Our suburbs are filled with working couples, both working to pay for a house, but so exhausted by their work that they have to neglect their children and have no time to make a home.

Topic: "The Lust of the Eyes"
SCRIPTURE: Eccl. 1:8.
"The eye is not satisfied with seeing, nor the ear filled with hearing" (RSV).
SCRIPTURE: Eccl. 1:14.
"I have seen everything that is done under the sun; and behold all is vanity and a striving after wind" (RSV).
SCRIPTURE: 1 John 2:16–17.
"For all that is in the world, the lust of the flesh and the lust of the eyes and the pride of life, is not of the Father but is of the world. And the world passes away, and the lust of it; but he who does the will of God abides forever" (RSV).

A consumer-oriented society sharpens the lustful eye. It turns the whole world into a huge showcase of things we "must have," always tantalizing us with an unrealized fulfillment.

Topic: The Wise Fool
SCRIPTURE: Eccl. 7:16–17.
"Be not righteous overmuch, and do not make yourselves overwise; why should you destroy yourself? Be not wicked overmuch, neither be a fool; why should you die before your time?" (RSV).

Jesus, by that standard, was "righteous overmuch" and Qoheleth was right: he did die before his time!
SCRIPTURE: 1 Cor. 1:18–25.
"For the foolishness of God is wiser than men, and the weakness of God is stronger than men" (v. 25, RSV).
References
1. Robert L. Short, *A Time to Be Born—*

A Time to Die (New York: Harper & Row, 1973), pp. 101, 95, 98.

2. Thomas Carlyle, *Latter Day Pamphlets*, No. 1 (1850).

3. William Pepperrell Montague, *Belief Unbound* (New Haven: Yale University Press, 1930), p. 6.

SECTION X. Children's Stories and Sermons

January 5 (Epiphany Sunday). Something to Count On

There is a legend from China that I picked up years ago. Two surveyors were crossing a trackless desert. They had a map showing certain trees, streams, and contours of land that they were to follow. But one night a terrible storm came. They hid in a cave, and when morning came all the landmarks had been swept or washed away. They were lost. Both of them were desperate. Their maps were useless, for every landmark shown on them had been destroyed by the storm. All day long they tried to figure out a way to safety. They dared not leave that cave and slept there the second night. About midnight one surveyor ran into the cave crying out, "We're saved! We can find our way through this desolation!"

"How?" his friend asked, thinking that he had gone crazy.

"Because the stars are still there!" his friend replied.—William L. Stidger.

January 12. How God Speaks to Us

If you have a good friend, I'll bet the two of you talk together a lot. You know that being a friend means talking, but it means listening, too. We can't just talk all of the time. God is a friend, too. Talking to God is one part of prayer, and God wants to listen to us. A second part of prayer is listening to God, and God wants us to listen. Kira Whitney wrote to a devotional magazine for young people and said, "When people are done praying, ev-

erybody should listen to God to say something back to them." But listening to God isn't very easy. Autumn Warner wrote and said, "When I pray, I ask God about something and God does not talk back to me. Why not?"

It is hard to listen to God because God does not have a body or a voice like humans do. Instead, God is spirit and we have to listen to God speak inside us. When someone holds you or rocks you or gives you a hug, you feel warm and loved. When you are with God, sometimes you will feel warm and you will know that God is saying to you, "I love you." Sometimes you can listen in your imagination. You can imagine Jesus sitting and talking with you. You may ask him a question and then listen very carefully in your imagination and think how Jesus would answer you.

Duncan Whitney wrote and said, "One time I was lost in the woods and I was next to a road and I asked God for the way out of there and God showed me." Even though God does not speak to us in a loud voice, we can hear God inside us if we listen every day. Julie Finberg wrote, "I listen to God every day, all the time. God says to me: 'I love you very, very much.'"—*Pockets*.

January 19. Football Fever

Interest Object: A football.

Main Truth: Jesus is our coach who gives us instructions for life.

Scripture Text: "I can do nothing on my own authority; as I hear, I judge; and my

96

judgment is just, because I seek not my own will but the will of him who sent me" (John 5:30).

Anytime is a good time for our favorite sport of football. We enjoy watching these athletes push, bump, and struggle on the scrimmage line. It looks confusing, but the basic goal is simple. They try to run, throw, or kick the ball past their opponents for points.

On the playing field a quarterback is the man in charge. Do you ever wonder what goes on in the quarterback huddle before every play? The quarterback chooses the next play and tells his players the secret number of his chant when the ball will start moving. He gives orders and instructions. Every teammate must understand the next play and be ready to do his own job.

Then the players all line up for action. Some teammates try to block their opponents so running backs can carry the ball through the open space in the line. Or they may protect the quarterback so he can have time to throw the ball. How exciting when a player called the receiver slips into the end zone and catches the ball for a touchdown!

The quarterback is a hero for choosing the right play and making a good throw. He is the boss who runs the team there on the field.

But wait. Who is the fellow standing on the sideline with a clipboard in his hand? He points to the bench and new players enter the game as replacements. He looks very important.

Then we notice the quarterback always looks over his shoulder toward this friend on the sideline. They know each other very well. It turns out that this man is the coach and the quarterback's boss. The quarterback was simply picking plays previously planned by the coach.

No wonder the quarterback keeps looking toward his coach. He wants to be sure the real boss is pleased. If a change is needed, the coach will signal or call directions for the quarterback to relay to the team.

The coach of a football team reminds us of Jesus. I may think I am my own boss, but all through life Jesus is nearby giving en-

couragement and instruction. "I can do nothing on my own authority." "I seek not my own will but the will of him who sent me."

That is how Jesus explained his actions while on earth. He did everything the Father wanted him to do. Now we must do everything Jesus wants us to do. He is our leader.—C. W. Bess.

January 26. The Treasures of the Snow

On one winter weekend many years ago, something happened in Memphis, Tennessee, that seldom happened there. A heavy snow fell like a blanket across the city. Many people who lived in and around Memphis could not get to their churches. But they turned on their radios and heard a pastor in the city preach a very special sermon on "the treasures of the snow," words from the book of Job in the Bible. He talked about how powerful the tiny snowflake can be when it gets together with billions of others like it. But he talked about another thing that people loved especially and remembered: the snow covers black housetops with white and garbage cans with white crowns and makes trash piles gleam.

God's forgiveness is like the beautiful snowfall. It comes and covers what is ugly and makes it over into something beautiful. There is a Bible verse that says, "Though your sins be as scarlet, they shall be as white as snow." All of us need God's forgiveness, for there are wrong things in our hearts and lives. But the God who gives the treasures of the snow covers our sins with his love and forgiveness.

February 2. Guest of Honor

'Behold, I stand at the door, and knock: if any man hear my voice, and open the door, I will come in to him, and will sup with him, and he with me" (Rev. 3:20).

Six-year-old Matthew had been having more chest pains. As the hospital attendant prepared for an electrocardiogram, he explained to Matthew, "We're going to look at your heart."

The young patient immediately responded, "Oh, then you'll see Jesus."

"We'll look for him," said the attendant.

"Well, if you look at my heart, you'll

sure see him, 'cause Jesus lives in my heart," Matthew assured him.

It was a natural thing for Matthew to talk about Jesus, because Jesus is a part of his everyday life—not just someone he hears about at church or occasionally at home.—Bessie White, *Open Windows*.

February 9. A Bible for Biscuits

Senor Miguel was a shopkeeper in his small Mexican village. For a few *centavos* one could buy food from him.

One day a boy named Raymon came to the store to buy biscuits. Raymon had no money. All he brought with him was a little book that his grandmother had given him.

"Biscuits cost money," said Senor Miguel. "I cannot give them away for books. Books will not buy flour and milk to make more biscuits."

Senor Miguel, being a softhearted man, felt that he could not send the boy away empty-handed.

"I will give you the biscuits for the book," he said. "But you remember me when you have ten *centavos*. You bring them to me, and I will give you back the book. I do not need a book."

Several days passed. Senor Miguel decided to clean his stove. He came across the little book that Raymon had left. He thought: "That boy! He still owes me ten *centavos* for this book!"

Senor Miguel picked up the book. He began to read. It was an unusual book. He had never seen a book like this.

First he read from Proverbs some verses that made sense to him. Then Senor Miguel read from Psalms, and he liked those verses even better.

As the days passed, Senor Miguel read more and more in the Bible. He read from the New Testament. He read John 3:16 several times. Senor Miguel began to feel that God loved him. He read more about Jesus. He decided that if Jesus had come to die for him, he would love Jesus. He decided to do what Jesus said for him to do.

One day Senor Miguel said to his wife: "If Raymon comes back to get his book, let's ask him if we can pay more biscuits for it. I would like to keep it and read more about the man called Jesus. It is the most wonderful book in the world."—*Exploring 1*, from *Primary Leader*.

February 16. Lent and the Coming of Easter

Easter is the greatest of the special Sundays, because its mystery is greater than the rest. It is so deep and wide in mystery that it takes six weeks to get ready for it. This is even more weeks of preparation than it takes to get ready for Christmas! The time of getting ready for Easter is called Lent, and this year it began on February 12.

The Church marks the time of getting ready for Easter with the color purple. On Easter morning, the purple of Lent is changed to white, the color of celebration. You can watch the time of purple passing in your church and get ready for the change into the white of celebration on Easter morning. Churches do this in different ways, so look carefully in your own church for these colors.

Easter is the greatest mystery because it is when the Christ child of Christmas cried out from the cross to God. On Easter morning he rose from the grave. Now Jesus can be with us all today in spite of all the days that have passed since the first Easter and all the different places in which we live today.

We cannot measure Christ's presence by clocks or places. This is why we need to keep church time in a special way by the circle of the church year. The clocks and calendars in our homes and schools are very good for some things, but not for this. Church time works in an inner way among us to help us all be close to Jesus, who died and yet somehow is still with us. It helps us to be Easter people whatever time it is!—*Pockets*.

February 23. Finding Forgiveness

Molly McCormick and Angie Mutaner wrote about forgiveness. Molly said, "If I do something wrong, I ask God to forgive me and God does." That's right, Molly, God wants very much to forgive us for the things we have done wrong. God also wants us to forgive others when they do wrong to us. When you write with your pencil and make a mistake, you can always erase it and begin again. When God forgives the wrong things we have done, it is like erasing them. God loves us and wants to do that for us.

Angie wrote: "It says in the Bible to admit your sins. I do, but also sometimes I forget to admit some things but remember others. Is that a sin? What should I do?" Admitting to God the things we have done wrong is called confession. It is good to try to remember all of the things that we need to confess, but God understands if we forget sometimes. We can ask God to help us remember. It is not a sin to forget, Angie.

Here is a prayer written by Julie Grodowski:

"Dear God, thank you for my family and friends. Thank you for everything. I love you a lot. I'll always follow you. I'll try to be kind to everyone, every day. Amen."—
Pockets.

March 2. Sowing Seeds of Suggestion

A certain teacher talked one day to a class of children, telling them that they had been invited to march in a parade the next day. They were all delighted and clapped and yelled to show it.

Then that teacher began to talk of what a long, hard march it would be; of how hot the weather was; of how they would get thirsty and tired, and perhaps ill, and have to drop out of the parade. Then she asked them how many of them wanted to march in the parade, and only two hands out of twenty went up.

Then she spoke again of the patriotic purposes of the parade; of how everybody along the line would be looking at them; of how the bands would be playing, flags waving; of how proud she, their teacher, and their parents and friends would be to see them in that parade; and then she asked them again how many of them would like to march in the parade and every hand went up with enthusiasm.—
William L. Stidger.

March 9. John Woolman

John Woolman was an American Quaker who lived in the colonial period of our nation's history. Throughout his life he taught people to love God and show it in their love for one another. Woolman himself traveled throughout the southern colonies trying to get Quakers there to free their slaves. He would not eat food prepared by slaves unless he could pay them for their trouble. He would not buy things from businesses that were built on slave labor. He even refused to ride in coaches when the drivers mistreated the horses. With little help from others, he helped southern Quakers decide to free their slaves years before other southern Christians were forced to do so. John Woolman put Christ's love into action. He reminded slaveholders that they were going against the most important teaching of Jesus Christ: "Do unto others as you would have them do unto you." That is something for all of us to think about.—
Bill J. Leonard.

March 16. Take a Chance

Interest Object: A Monopoly board with chance cards.

Main Truth: Choose Jesus for a chance at eternal life.

Scripture Text: "He who has the son has life; he who has not the son of God has not life" (1 John 5:12).

People all over the world enjoy playing Monopoly. The object of this game is to make lots of money from the bank or from the other players. The winner is whoever winds up with all of the money while the losers go broke.

The game becomes very exiting when we roll the dice and move around the board. Carefully now. Don't land on property that belongs to someone else. You might have to pay high rent. Better to land on your own property.

Do you know what I dread most? Sooner or later every player lands on a chance square. When that happens to me, then I must take a chance. Some chance cards bring very bad luck. "Go to jail! Do not pass go and do not collect $200." Or "Go to the nearest utility, roll dice and pay owner ten times the value."

Whenever I land on a chance square and find myself forced to take a chance, I have a secret wish. I wish that someone would take out all of the bad risks from this stack of chance cards. They could leave all the good chances that would then cause me no fear. How fun to read "Every player must pay you $100!"

Yes, Monopoly is much like life. We would rather have choice without chance. No risks. Let's avoid any chance of something bad.

But you cannot always avoid bad things. Sometimes you have bad luck like sickness. Perhaps your best friend moves away leaving you lonely. Or you may have an automobile accident and die!

This may sound like life is just a series of aimless chances, but wait! In the most important decision of eternity, you need not leave anything to chance. You have a chance about heaven, hell, death, and life.

Jesus is the Son of God and the Savior of all who trust him. If you accept him into your life, then death is not so bad. You can have eternal life with Jesus.

Sooner or later each one of us must choose. I pray that you will make your choice on the chance of a lifetime. There is no risk in Jesus. "He who has the son has life; he who has not the son of God has not life."—C. W. Bess.

March 23. Where Are You Going?

What a wonderful sight a crowded street in a great city is! One wonders what the people are doing, where they are going, what they are thinking about. That you can't tell, but it is easy to discover two sorts of people. Those who have a purpose and those who have not. Those who have a purpose you can tell by their walk. They go straight forward. They don't stop to look in shop windows. You can tell them by their speed. They lose no time. You can tell them by their faces. They are "set." They are thinking about their business.

But there are others who drift about. They stop at shop windows. They hesitate at corners. They have no aim. They just saunter. Do you know how we got the word *saunter*? There was a time when it was a great mark of devotion to go on pilgrimage to the Holy Land, in French, *la Sainte Terre*. People helped the pilgrims on their way and some crafty people saw an easy way of living in this. They would ask for food and shelter at a house and when asked where they were going, they would say "A la Sainte Terre." People gave them food and drink and a night's shelter. But they had no intention of going to the Holy Land and people got to know it and when they saw them coming they said: "Here are more saint-terrers." So the word *saunter* was born.

Jesus set his face to go to Jerusalem, says Luke in his Gospel. He was not just out for a stroll, not caring where he went. There was purpose in his face and in his walk. Like Jesus we must set our faces to go to the city of our Heavenly King. There is a hymn that says: "Whither, pilgrims, are you going?" Have you got an answer to that? Are you going anywhere or are you just sauntering through life, out for a stroll but with no aim? An Irish song begins: "I know where I'm going and I know who'll go with me." That is a good song to sing if you are set on pilgrimage to the Heavenly City and have with you Jesus as your companion.—John Bishop.

March 30 (Easter Sunday). The Message of the Butterfly

Do you know how you felt when you saw a butterfly for the first time? Some butterflies are very beautiful. They wear many colors and seem almost to be the work of an artist. The kind called swallowtails are found all over the world. The kind we see most often in North America is perhaps the monarch. There are also the tortoiseshell and peacock butterflies.

But the butterfly was not always so beautiful. It goes through several stages. Just before it comes out of what is called the pupa case, the butterfly is a larva, an ugly, wormlike thing. But a great change takes place, and a butterfly is born.

Christians who lived long, long ago chose the butterfly as a Christian symbol, that is, as something to picture for them another thing very important to them as Christians. The butterfly reminded them of the resurrection of the Lord Jesus Christ. After Jesus was crucified and his dead body was buried in a cave, God did something wonderful and mysterious to Jesus' dead body. God changed Jesus' body into a different form. The Bible called it "a glorified body." And Jesus was alive again, but this time in a new and special way. Now Jesus was alive, never to be touched by death again. And God will sometime do something like that for us. The people who believed in Jesus and had followed him saw him several times in different places, and their hearts were filled with great joy. Then, after some time, he went to be with the Father in heaven. They did not see him with their eyes again, but his spirit lived in their hearts, and this made them brave and strong. They remembered that he had said, "Because I live, you will live also." So they faced all kind of hardship with courage. One of them, the Apostle Paul, said, "I have the strength to face all conditions by the power that Christ gives me" (Phil. 4:13, TEV).

April 6. God Is with Us

"I lie down and sleep, and all night long the Lord protects me" (Ps. 3:5, TEV).

When I was young, sometimes I would awake afraid in the middle of the night. I could hear my sister breathing as she slept a few feet away, and I felt safe again. Then I would fall asleep unafraid.

As I grew older and moved to a room of my own, I again experienced fear in the middle of the night. But I was not alone. I believed God was with me. To remind myself of that, I would pray the Lord's Prayer, and that helped me to sleep again, unafraid.

Now that I am grown, I sometimes forget that God is with me, and then I feel afraid. When I remember God is there, the fear melts away.

Any time of the day or night when we experience fear, God is with us. To feel secure, all we need to do is remember this. God's presence with us is like the sound of peaceful breathing of another close by at night; it is there, but we must remember and listen for it in order to lose our fear.
—Roxanne Rieck, *Upper Room*.

April 13. No Good Until We Use It

Luke 24:13–35, verse 32: "They said to each other, 'Did not our hearts burn within us while he talked to us on the road, while he opened to us the scriptures.'"

Interest Object: An unsharpened pencil, an unused candle, and a radio that is not playing.

Good morning, boys and girls. How would you like to take a walk down a road with Jesus? [*Let them answer.*] Wouldn't that be great? Just imagine how wonderful it would be to talk with Jesus and spend one day outdoors in the sunshine with him. I can't think of how to have a better time. People did that with Jesus. As a matter of fact, there is a story in the Bible about a couple of men who were walking down a road between towns when they were joined by Jesus. They didn't recognize him then, but they enjoyed him so much that they invited him to spend the evening at their house. Jesus taught them many things about the Scriptures, and they were amazed. They said afterwards that he had opened the Scriptures for them. It was as if they had never seen the Bible before, when really they had studied it often. But Jesus was such a wonderful teacher that he made people feel as these men felt.

We should all discover the Bible and the things that it teaches us. I brought along some things that I hope will help you to want to read the Bible and learn all that you can from it. And when you read the Bible you should read it as though you were seeing it through the eyes of Jesus.

First of all, I brought a pencil along with me. What's wrong with this pencil? [*Let them answer.*] That's right, it doesn't have a point. There is no lead. You can't write with a pencil like this. Next, I have a candle. What's wrong with my candle? [*Let them answer.*] That's right, it isn't burning and it can't give light unless it is burning. I also have a radio with me but there is something wrong with the radio. What's wrong with it? [*Let them answer.*] Right again, it isn't being played.

A pencil without a point, a candle without a flame, and a radio without sound, all are like reading the Scriptures without Jesus. Jesus is the one who makes the Scriptures happen. When you read the Scriptures or Bible and you see it or hear it as Jesus would tell it, then the Bible comes alive and it is the most wonderful book that was ever written.

The next time you sit down to read the

Bible, I want you to imagine that Jesus is talking to you and telling you the story. When you hear his voice, you will know how the men felt who took the walk with Jesus down a dusty road after his resurrection.—*The Children's Sermon Service*.

April 20. I Know Who That Is!

John 10:1-10, verse 5: "A stranger they will not follow, but they will flee from him for they do not know the voice of strangers."

Interest Object: Some taped voices that might include some of the children's parents, your voice, and the voice of a stranger to the children.

Good morning, boys and girls. Today we are going to have some fun and also learn something. I brought along my tape recorder and it has some voices on it that I think you will recognize. You must be very quiet and listen to the voices. You should only do the things that you are told to do when you know the voice that is speaking. If you hear my voice or the voice of your parents, then do what they tell you to do. But if you do not know the voice of the person speaking, then you should not do anything that they say. Sometimes some of you will know one voice and your friends will not know it because they don't know the person speaking, and you do. Let's try it.

[*The speakers should tell the children to stand up, sit down, walk two steps, and so on.*] Now I am going to play the recorder and you listen for the voices that you know and do what they tell you to do. [*Play the recorder, stop it every so often, and ask the children who moved to identify the voices. Sometimes the parents may even use the name of their child when speaking.*] You do recognize some voices, don't you? Other voices were strange and you did not obey them. That is the way it should be.

Jesus once told a story to his disciples about how sheep run away from the voice of a stranger but follow the voice of their shepherd. Sheep trust the sound of the voice of the one who takes care of them and protects them. But they are afraid of other voices because those voices steal them and hurt them.

Jesus taught his disciples that he is the shepherd for all people. He is your shepherd and my shepherd and we are like his sheep. We can trust what Jesus teaches us because he loves us and cares for us. If we listen to his voice, then we will always be safe. But if we start following the teaching of other voices, then we will be lost and hurt. A lot of teachers promise a lot of things and some of them sound good but they are false teachers and they are not interested in you but only in themselves.

Jesus is a voice that we can trust just as we can trust the voices of our parents and other people that we know. When you heard those voices, they sounded familiar and you did what they said. But when we hear strange voices, then we should stop and wait until we hear the voice that we trust.

Jesus is our leader and we should always follow him wherever he leads us. That is the way that he taught his disciples and that is the way he teaches us.—*The Children's Sermon Service*.

April 27. A Dream for God

Many years ago a young man had a dream of telling the story of Jesus everywhere in the world. When he suggested taking that good news to people, an older man said, "Sit down, young man. If God wants to save the heathen, he will do it without your help or mine."

This young man, William Carey, was a cobbler. As he worked day after day making shoes, he thought about this exciting dream of his. He preached a sermon, "Attempt Great Things for God; Expect Great Things from God." Because he believed this with all his heart, he left his own country, England, and went to India. There he spent the rest of his life teaching and preaching about Jesus who said, "Go into all the world and tell the good news."

It was several years before even one person accepted this message. But one, then another, and then many believed the good news of Jesus, until thousands upon thousands came to know Jesus because a young man with a dream opened a door.

May 4. The Greatest Truth We Can Know

One hundred years ago yesterday a

world-famous religious thinker was born in Switzerland. His father was a pastor and professor. The person we are talking about was Karl Barth. In his lifetime he wrote hundreds of articles and books. No person in this twentieth century had a greater influence on other people who made a special study of religion. Most of his writings were very deep, and some people found them hard to understand.

Once Professor Barth was asked what was the most important thing he had learned about religion. He answered, "Jesus loves me this I know, for the Bible tells me so." And he was right!

You might know all that the wisest people know about religion, yet the most important thing is that Jesus loves us, and the Bible tells us the wonderful story of that love. There is one verse in the New Testament that tells it all—John 3:16: "For God so loved the world, that he gave his only begotten Son, that whosoever believeth in him should not perish but have everlasting life."

May 11. A Wise Man

I once asked a brawny timber cruiser in the woods of Oregon whether there was any man on earth of whom he was afraid. His answer was just one word: "Nope."

I was not surprised. His huge, hairy arms thrust out of his plaid shirt sleeves, rolled up at the elbows, like the limbs of the trees that were being cut. His mighty chest threatened to split the woolen shirt with his every movement. Why should he be afraid of any man, I thought.

"I ain't afraid of no man that walks," said the giant, his stubby beard tracing out a slow grin, "but I am afraid of one woman—my wife."

Since I knew both of them, I blurted out, "But you weigh at least 250 pounds and she would stretch the scales at 110."

The grin on the big man's face grew wider, "Oh, I ain't afraid that she can beat me up," he explained, "I am just afraid of doing something that she wouldn't like. I'm afraid of her feelings—that I might hurt them."—Harold Dye, *Open Windows*.

May 18. Jesus and the Holy Spirit

Millie was very sad. She and Rhonda had been best friends for a long time. Rhonda's father had been transferred to another city. She would have to move away.

The days before Rhonda was to move were fun. She and Millie spent much time with each other. They both promised to write often. They would visit each other during summer vacations and holidays.

Finally, the day came. The moving van slowly pulled away. Rhonda said goodbye to Millie, got into the family car, and left for her new home.

Millie felt so alone and empty.

This is probably the way Jesus' disciples felt when he went back to heaven. He had been with them for forty days after his resurrection. Now, it was time for him to leave.

He promised, however, to send someone else to help them. This was the Holy Spirit.—*Exploring 2*.

May 25 (Trinity Sunday). The Shamrock

Do you know who Saint Patrick was? He is known as the patron saint of Ireland. He was a missionary who went to Ireland long, long ago to tell people who had never heard it the good news about Jesus.

Do you know what a shamrock is? It is a leaf with three petals. At one time when you look at it, it seems to be three leaves. At another time it seems to be only one leaf.

Why is the shamrock connected with Saint Patrick and Ireland? The story is told that Patrick, the missionary, was trying to explain the church teaching about the trinity, and the people could not understand. How could there be God the Father, God the Son Jesus, and God the Holy Spirit if there is only one God? Patrick bent down and plucked a shamrock and held it up for all to see. There was one leaf that was at the same time three; three leaves that were at the same time one. Then the people began to understand.

These people only *began* to understand, for the trinity is one of the great mysteries of our faith. Remember, Jesus once said that whoever had seen him had seen the Father. God the Father comes to us through Jesus, and he also comes to us through the Holy Spirit, who is God at work in our hearts.

June 1. In God We Trust

Interest Object: A handful of coins.

Main Truth: We can always trust God.

Scripture Text: "Trust in the Lord with all your heart, and do not rely on your own insight. In all your ways acknowledge him, and he will make straight your paths" (Prov. 3:5–6).

Listen to these familiar sounds as I shake something together in my hand. You recognize the sound of coins jingling in a pocket or a hand. Let's pretend we are planning a party with these coins.

As we begin our plans, I need to know something. Do you trust me? Good. Even though we are pretending, it is important that you believe me. So here is my plan.

You can take this money to the store across the street and buy some cookies for our party. But before I give you this money, I need to know something. "Can I trust you?"

After you have convinced me to trust you with my money, I will send you on your way. Don't forget to stop and look both ways before you cross the street. Sometimes a car will stop in the middle of the street with the driver signaling you that it is safe to cross. You look at him and understand what he means. But can you trust him? Surely he would not stop and then try to run over you.

After finally getting across the street and into the store, you choose a package of cookies. The brand name is on the label. Other writing offers a list of ingredients and tells how much the package weighs. Can you trust the label? Certain laws require the truth in packaging.

Finally you take the cookies to the checkout stand. The cashier rings the sales and takes the money. Now it is her time to wonder, "Can I trust that this money is not counterfeit?"

Well, by now you understand my point. In life we must do a lot of trusting. Sometimes people let us down, so we won't trust them anymore. But there is one place in life where our trust will never be disappointed.

Look on these coins. Each one says "In God We Trust." That is a wonderful truth. The Bible teaches us to trust in the Lord. Not just a little but a lot. "Trust in the Lord with all your heart."—C. W. Bess.

June 8. What a Little Can Do

When I visited Henry Ford, he invited me to dinner, and we had a long talk. He told me of his first visit to the Berry schools at Mount Berry, Georgia. Just as he was leaving, Miss Martha Berry asked him to give her a dime. Mr. Ford smiled and said, "Is that all you want? I am usually asked for gifts larger than a dime."

"A dime is all I want, Mr. Ford, but I *do* want to show you what I can do with a dime."

"What do you want to do with a dime?" Mr. Ford asked her, still smiling and a bit puzzled.

"I want to buy ten cents worth of peanuts," replied Miss Berry.

When Mr. Ford had left town, Martha Berry purchased ten cents worth of green peanuts and planted them. Several years later Mr. Ford visited her again, and she showed him the returns in money that could be directly traced to that ten cents worth of peanuts. Mr. Ford was so pleased that he gave her a new building, and two years later he gave her a whole quadrangle of beautiful Gothic stone buildings, one of the most beautiful groups of buildings in this nation.—William L. Stidger.

June 15. What Is Prayer?

Sometimes it is very hard to understand prayer. Sometimes you ask God for things and it doesn't seem that God answers you. If you pray for someone who is sick, sometimes that person doesn't get well. If you pray about a problem in your family, sometimes it doesn't get any better. If your mother or father cannot find a job and you pray, sometimes there still is no job. That is very hard to understand.

We think that God should answer our prayers in the way that we choose. But sometimes God answers our prayers at a different time. That is hard because we want the answer to happen right away. Sometimes God has a different answer, and we don't understand why. Grown-ups don't always understand either. If you have prayed and you don't understand God's answer, it helps if you can talk with someone about what has happened. Do you have someone you can talk with? Your parents can help, and so can you minister or your Sunday School teacher or a friend.

There are many things about prayer that we cannot know, but we do know that God loves us and wants to listen to us and help us. And we know that God wants us to listen, too. If we don't always understand, that's okay. After all, there are lots of things about God that we don't understand. But we always know that God loves us.

Sometimes we think God isn't answering our prayer because God doesn't talk to us in a voice that we can hear the same way we hear the voices of other people. We have to listen to God in our imagination and think about what God might want to say to us. Be very, very still and listen in your imagination to what God might want to tell you when you pray.—*Pockets*.

June 22. Great Treasures

"Lay not up for yourselves treasures upon earth, where moth and rust doth corrupt, and where thieves break through and steal: But lay up for yourselves treasures in heaven" (Matt. 6:19–20).

When I was a teenager, I lost my purse containing my comb, my cosmetics, and all the money I had. At that time I had a very small allowance and no part-time job, so for me the loss seemed catastrophic. That night I sobbed and sobbed, mourning my missing possessions.

Finally my father said firmly, "Madge, don't ever cry over money. Even when you lose every cent you have, it is not worth crying about."

I dried my eyes and stared at him in amazement. "But if money's not important, what is?"

"The love of your family and friends, your good name, your faith in God—those are important. But money? Forget it."

It is true—those things that really count are things that cannot be bought. They can be mine even when my pockets are empty.

And they are riches indeed.—Madge Harrah, *Upper Room*.

June 29. Sojourner Truth

Sojourner Truth was a black woman abolitionist who, in slavery time, traveled throughout the north telling the story of slavery and preaching the liberation gospel of Jesus Christ. The tall black woman was known for her songs and stories. She sang of the despair of her people in songs she made up herself. "I am pleading for my people, a poor downtrodden race, who dwell in freedom's boasted land with no abiding place. While I bear upon my body the scars of many a gash, I am pleading for my people who groan beneath the lash."

Once she was confronted by a man who declared, "Old woman, do you think your talk about slavery does any good? Why, I don't care any more for your talk than for the bite of a flea."

"Perhaps not," Sojourner replied, "but Lord willing, I'll keep you scratching." She kept on working for freedom even when people wouldn't pay any attention to what she did or would laugh at her for what she tried to do. Christians are people who keep the world "scratching" on the way to justice, liberation, and freedom.—Bill J. Leonard.

July 6. Noisy and Empty

"What matters is faith that works through love" (Gal. 5:6, TEV).

We used to live on Tangier Island, a small island in the middle of Chesapeake Bay. There were very few cars or trucks. Most of us got around on bikes or we walked. Every now and then, though, a package would arrive at the boat dock or the post office that was too large to carry. When this happened, I borrowed my daughter's little red wagon.

You can imagine what a racket the wagon made on the roughly paved lanes. Sometimes I could barely hear what was going on around me because of its noise. But once I put in the package, its weight would stop the rattling.

On one of these treks to the post office, a member of our church stopped me and commented, "You know, Mr. Savage, your wagon's a lot like some people's faith."

"How's that?" I asked.

"Well, it looks nice and shiny and makes

a lot of noise when it's empty. But it's not doing much work. That's like some people. Then, when the wagon's full, working, it's quiet. A lot of people are like that—quiet, but busy working for the Lord."

I asked myself how many times my faith had been noisy but not useful.—Carl E. Savage.

July 13. Listening for the Light

When the Society of Friends, or Quakers, began in England about three hundred years ago, people noticed them because of their different worship, the silent meetings. Quaker meetinghouses were simple buildings without many furnishings. They had no pulpit or organ, and the people did not follow a special order of worship. Men and boys sat on one side of the room while women and girls sat on the other. All worshipers sat without saying or singing a word, waiting for the "inner light" of God's Spirit to warm their hearts. Those who felt moved to do so might speak, but no one was forced to say or do anything.

Today, we need to learn how to listen for the still, small voice of God beyond the noise of our busy lives. Can you sit still for a few moments and think quietly about God and his love? Listen, learn, wait, seek, and hear. Hear the light that is beyond words. Hear the light even when you cannot see it or feel it.

Listen . . . the light is shining in your heart . . . can you hear it?—Bill J. Leonard.

July 20. Something Bad, Then Something Good

Wouldn't it be exciting to be invited to play in a big brass band marching down the street in Washington in front of the president of the United States? Crowds of people go to Washington every four years to share the excitement of seeing a president and vice-president take the oath of office. Anyone can watch on television anywhere in the United States, but how much more fun it is to actually be there and see it with your own eyes.

As the time drew near for the last inauguration, many young people practiced long hours and raised money so they could make the trip to Washington and march in the big parade. Then came a big, big disappointment—bitter cold weather blew into town, the coldest weather on record for an inauguration day. It was so cold that doctors thought it would be dangerous to the health of people to be outside for the inaugural ceremonies and the parade. So the ceremony had to be moved inside the Capitol, under the capitol dome, where only a small number of people could crowd in. This meant there was no parade.

Can you just imagine *your* disappointment if you had practiced so long and hard and then could not march and perform for the president? You would probably feel like crying just as many young people did when they heard the bad news.

But President and Mrs. Reagan had a great surprise for the young people! They had a very special meeting with all the band members, and the president made a speech just to them and told of his own disappointment at what had happened. Wasn't that a wonderful way to make those young people know that the president really cared about them? They could go home feeling that their time and trouble had not been wasted. This meeting with President and Mrs. Reagan really gave the band members a better opportunity to see and hear the president up close than if they had just marched past him in a band. —Patricia Parrent Cox.

July 27. How to Play the Game

We are to remember that to play the game, to play it according to the rules, and to play it our best is the sum total of what is required of us. We are certainly not here to lose the game. But no more is it required of us that we always win. Nobody can win all the time. No team is required to make so many home runs or so many touchdowns. You and I are not here to win certain results. We are here to play the game the best we can.

When the Kentucky Colonels were winning one victory after another under the leadership of Bo McMillan, the spectators used to smile to see this team go into a huddle for prayer when they came upon the field. That was something out of the ordinary. "Why do you pray?" a reporter asked one day. "Do you beg God to take the victory from your opponents and give it to you?"

"No," was the sane answer, "we do not pray to win, we pray to play. We ask God to help us to play the game in a clean, sportsmanlike fashion."—Clovis G. Chappell.

August 3. The Sign of the Fish

Several of Jesus' closest friends were fishermen. When he called them to be his disciples, they left their fishing nets and boats and went where Jesus went, telling people that God's kingdom was near and spreading the good news of God's love. Because they did this, other people became Jesus' followers too. You see, this is what Jesus meant when he first called them, saying, "Come with me, and I will teach you to catch men" (Mark 1:17, TEV).

It's no wonder that the picture of a fish —a crude drawing—became a special sign, a symbol, for Christians who lived in the years just after the time of Jesus. A Christian was someone that a follower of Jesus had caught, like a fish in a net, and had brought to Jesus. Also, the letters of the Greek word for fish were the first letters of the Greek words for "Jesus Son of God Savior." In the early days, Christians often had to meet in secret, so they used the sign of the fish to point to the place of meeting. The Christians knew what the sign meant and gathered together to worship God and to praise the name of Jesus.

Sometimes, today, you will see someone wearing a pin on a dress or a suit, and a close look will tell you that it is a fish. This shows that the person wants you to know that he or she is a Christian and is trying to obey Jesus' words, "Come with me, and I will teach you to catch men." Whether we wear a pin like that or not, we need to do the same thing: We need to try in our own way to bring other people to Jesus, so that they also can know God's wonderful love.

August 10. Where Are the Clowns?

When I was a child in Texas, we went most Januarys to the Southwestern Exposition and Fat Stock Show in Fort Worth. My favorite event was the bull riding, and with the bulls came the clowns in painted faces and baggy pants, hiding in open-ended barrels. They jumped around, fell down, and looked like they couldn't do anything but act stupid—until a rider fell off a bucking bull and then the clowns became serious as they tried to protect a defenseless, sometimes hurting, rider. They distracted the angry animal until the cowboy could get out of the way.

Gradually it dawned on me. The clowns were not there just to be funny or entertaining. The cowboys and the audience needed them desperately. In a way, Christians are like those clowns, willing to risk their lives for people who need to be protected, who are hurting, and who need the safety of a second chance. Paul was right, God *has* chosen the foolish things to shame the wise.—Bill J. Leonard.

August 17. The Day of Rest

An emergency forced me into a filling station one Sunday afternoon. A young man in a spotless uniform put the hose nozzle in the neck of the car's tank and set it for automatic shutoff. Then, he washed the windshield and every window. He opened the hood, checked the oil and water, and battery water level. For good measure, he filled the windshield washer tank.

I followed him around protesting weakly: "But I just need a little gas. You are going to too much trouble."

"Not at all, sir," he said. "I see that you are a reverend," he added, as he looked at my credit card.

"Yes," I admitted, "do you attend church anywhere?"

"I would like to, but the church people keep me so busy filling gas tanks on Sunday that I can't. Oh, no offense intended, sir," he said hastily.—Harold Dye, *Open Windows*.

August 24. The Floodwall

Many towns and villages built along rivers have been flooded again and again when heavy rains have sent the rivers over their banks. These floods have frightened people living there. They have also cost them a lot of money as they have had to clean up and repair their damaged homes.

Some places that once were often flooded are now protected by a floodwall that stands higher than the river ever rises.

Temptation to do wrong things can be like a rampaging river. It can damage our lives and can even sweep us away. It has happened to many people. But we can be protected. God helps us to build a wall so that we can be kept safe. What goes into the making of that wall?

The love of our parents and our friends helps build the wall. Learning about what God wants us to do and not to do also helps. Asking God in prayer to give us strength to do what is right and good builds the wall higher and stronger. The Bible tells us that if we trust Jesus, no temptation will come our way that is stronger than the wall he helps us build.

August 31. "You Can Trust Me"

Matthew 14:22–33; verse 29: "So Peter got out of the boat and walked on the water and came to Jesus."

Interest Object: A blindfold.

Boys and girls, I need a volunteer. Who would like to be my special helper for the next few minutes? [*Let someone volunteer or select someone.*] Now, I want to ask my volunteer a question: "Do you trust me?" You do? That's good. But why do you? Because you know me? That's right. Since you know what I'm like, you should be able to trust me. Well, I want to promise you right now, you *can* trust me. Because I'm your friend.

Now that we are sure about that, I need to have my volunteer put on this blindfold. [*Put it on him or her.*] Now, we're going to turn you around three or four times so you don't really know which way you're facing. Now, I'm leaving you to stand right there while I move over here farther away from you. Now, you are facing exactly the right direction so that, if you walk in a straight line, you will come safely to me. You won't fall down any steps and you won't trip over any other children. Will you walk to me now? [*If the volunteer hesitates, encourage him or her.*]

That's it. Keep coming. You're going exactly the right way. [*As the volunteer gets closer, stop giving verbal clues.*] There, you finally made it. Now let's take off the blindfold. How did it feel trying to make it without knowing exactly where to walk? A little scary? But you knew you were safe because I told you where to walk, didn't you?

In our Gospel lesson for today Peter had to walk a scary walk too. He was safe as long as he listened to what Jesus said and then trusted him. When he started trying to do it all by himself, he got into trouble. Jesus wants us to remember as we walk through life that we can trust him. We are safe with Jesus. But we have to listen to him always.—Mike Sherer.

September 7. Faith Needs Work

James 2:17: "So faith by itself, if it has no works, is dead."

Interest Object: A calculator.

Good morning, boys and girls. Today we are going to talk about something that all of us need to learn and understand as soon as possible. We are going to talk about faith and how to make our faith work. How many of you have heard about the word *faith*? [*Let them answer.*] Faith is something that all of us should have and use. Our faith means that if we believe in something enough, something surely will happen. If I believe that God will heal me when I am hurt, then I have faith in God as a healer. If I believe that God will make enough sunshine and rain so that the corn will grow, then I have faith that God is a grower. That is faith.

Some people think that they have so much faith that they do not have to do anything because God will do it all. They don't have to worry about anything since God will do everything. A man by the name of James listened carefully to God and gave us some answers about what people are supposed to do as partners with God. He called it working with God.

Let me show you what I mean. I have a calculator. The answer to almost any problem that I can think of that has to do with numbers is in this calculator. If I want to know how much 16 times 16 is, I know that the answer is in this calculator. I have faith that the calculator has the answer. Do you think the calculator has the answer? [*Let them answer.*] You think the answer is in there also. Do you think that the answer is right? [*Let them answer.*] You think that

Several years ago I bought a lovely vase for only a few dollars at an auction. It was very unusual in shape, with sprays of flowers painted on each side. The colors were vibrant and beautiful, and I prized it greatly.

One day I accidentally dropped it, and it broke into several pieces. I was so fond of the vase that I just couldn't scoop it up and toss it away. Instead, I carefully picked up the pieces and glued it back together. Now I use it for dried flowers. It is once again useful and beautiful.

Isn't that what God does for us? We all know people whose lives were broken and almost useless. Many of us would be beyond repair were it not for the mercy of God.

But once we cry out for help and seek pardon for our sins by accepting Christ, God picks up the shattered pieces of our lives and makes us into something new, something useful and beautiful.—June Shoemaker Libhart, *Upper Room*.

October 26. Diamond Dust

Rom. 8:16–18.

"I was passing a jewelry store in one of the big cities the other day," said George Strombeck in a *Christian Digest* article several years ago, "and saw in the window a diamond cutter. He had a pile of ugly, shapeless stones on the table by his machine. There were no sparkling blue lights, no scintillating gleams. They looked to be just ordinary stones that you would not have picked up from the pavement. In front of him was a small machine made of two disks about the size of a dinner plate. As I watched, he removed the top one and I saw six beautiful diamonds held by small, sunken clamps. The diamond cutter took out each stone and examined it carefully with his magnifying glass, then clamped it back in place. Then he picked up the box of diamond dust, the hardest cutter in the world, and sprinkled the stones liberally with it. When he had replaced the top disk, he turned on the power and it began to rotate. As I watched, I realized that he was using this diamond dust to shape and polish those dirty, ugly stones and make them scintillate and glow so they would be fit for a

girl's engagement ring. As I stood there looking, suddenly my eyes ceased to focus and a great truth took over my conscious mind. It rang like a bell. God, too, uses diamond dust to polish and shape human lives. Some of the hardships, disappointments and frustrations that have come to us are God's diamond dust.—C. Roy Angell, *Iron Shoes*.

November 2. One World

Interest Object: A globe.

When you look at this globe, you are seeing something of what our world looks like. What color do you see the most of on all sides? Blue. That is the water of all the oceans. The rest shows us the land, the continents, where people live. So there is more water than land, and that water keeps some of the continents apart. But underneath that water there is land. All of the continents like North America and Asia are connected if you go deep enough under the water. It is really one world.

It is like that with people. There are different races of people—"red and yellow, black and white," as we say in a song. In many ways we seem to be so different and so far apart. But if we go deep enough, we will discover that we all belong to one human family and one God is our heavenly Father and we have one Lord, Jesus Christ. Because this is true, because we have the same heavenly Father, we are all brothers and sisters, whether we are red, yellow, brown, black, or white; or whether we are Americans, French, Germans, Chinese, Africans, or Russians. We belong to God, and we belong to each other.

November 9. Real Riches

When my younger son was about ten, he spent a week with his grandparents and each day went to work with his grandfather. Though he would rather have been fishing or playing ball, he faithfully mowed grass, trimmed hedges, and raked leaves.

At the end of the week, his grandfather paid him for his labor. He then trudged downtown, which was about four blocks, to spend his wages.

He gave the entire amount, a whole dollar, to purchase a pair of salt and pepper shakers, which he then carefully wrapped, and upon arriving home proudly presented to me.

This gift, in the eyes of the world, would not be of much value, but to me it was priceless because I knew what it had cost my son.

Only the Father knows what it cost Jesus to give us the gift of salvation, which was everything.—Colleen Ralston, *Open Windows*.

November 16. Grow in Our Lord
Interest Object: A yardstick.

Main Truth: Our best growth is growing in our Lord.

Scripture Text: "But grow in the grace and knowledge of our Lord and Savior Jesus Christ" (2 Pet. 3:18).

Boys and girls are always growing. And that is good. You would not want to be an infant or little child all your life! So how many ways can you describe or measure growth?

A good place to start is with this yardstick. You know how. You back up to a wall and place the ruler on the top of your head. No fair standing on tiptoes. Then you move over and use the yardstick to measure your height from the floor.

Another method to measure growth is by weight in pounds. Climb upon the scales and count the pounds. You probably weigh more now than just a few months ago.

The calendar is yet another popular means to describe growth by months or years. Surely you would not forget your birthday! You have probably marked your birthday on a calendar at home. Because a birthday usually means presents and maybe even a party, you are excited when the calendar shows that your birthday is soon.

Now don't overlook one of the most obvious signs of all—when your clothes or shoes are no longer the right size. Boys and girls love to outgrow their clothes. When they get too short or too tight, then we know you've been growing.

These are different ways to measure physical growth of your body, but surely you have been changing more than just in body. What about your spiritual improvement? Every time you memorize a Bible verse or understand something new about Jesus, you "grow in the grace and knowledge of our Lord and Savior Jesus Chirst."

That is what Peter told us to do. No matter how old or smart or big we become, we must all continue to grow spiritually. Every day we can learn more about Jesus. Our love and devotion to him increases.—C. W. Bess.

November 23. An Advent Book
Do you have a hard time deciding what to give your parents for Christmas? This year you might want to write a book of yourself, an Advent Book. Buy a small bound notebook and write each date in December, one number on each page. Every day write something you would like to say to your parents. Tell them something special you want them to know, especially how much you love them. You will be surprised how fast the pages fill.

You might want to tell why Christmas is important to you. You might want to tell what you like about God's creation—rivers or lakes or mountains or flowers or trees.

Do you ever tell your parents how much you appreciate the good meals they prepare? This is a good time to tell them. Perhaps you will want to write about the things you are learning in school. Because your parents love you they like to know all about what you are doing.

Writing an Advent Book doesn't cost very much, but it will be one of the best presents your parents will receive this Christmas.—Pauline Carl Prince.

November 30 (Advent). The Christmas Wafer
Every year at the beginning of Advent, the parish church in many Polish neighborhoods sends out to its parishioners a wafer, measuring approximately two inches by four inches, on which is embossed a nativity scene. The wafer, know as *Oplatek*, is usually displayed on the dining room table for the four weeks of Advent. On Christmas Eve, the entire family gathers at the house of the oldest member to celebrate a food and blessing ceremony known as *Wigilia*, the Vigil. An extra place is set at the table to welcome a stranger or someone in need who may happen by.

The family gathers around the table, standing, as the oldest member reverently takes the Oplatek in hand, breaks off a piece, and passes it to the next family member, saying as he or she does so, "May you have wealth, health, happiness, and a golden crown in heaven." This person in turn breaks off a piece and says the blessing to the next person as he/she passes the wafer. When the last person has received the wafer, everyone listens as this prayer is said:

May your heart be as patient as the earth, your love as warm as harvest gold. May your days be full as the city is full, your nights as joyful as dancers. May your arms be as welcoming as home. May your faith be enduring as God's love, your spirit as valiant as your heritage. May your hand be as sure as a friend, your dreams as hopeful as a child. May your soul be as brave as your people, and may you be blessed.

After the prayer everyone eats his/her share of the Oplatek. Then the family sits down to be nourished by the food and friendly conversation.

May you have wealth, health, happiness, and a golden crown in heaven!—Regis Krusniewski.

December 7. Lottie Moon

Have you ever wished you could live in a different time? One lady we talk about in churches today lived a long time ago. But we remember her as if she had just left. That woman is Charlotte Diggs Moon or, as we know her, Lottie Moon.

Lottie Moon was born in 1840 and grew up on a plantation in Virginia called Viewmont. It was here that she ran and played with six brothers and sisters. It is said that she climbed every tree on the plantation "that was worth climbing." She enjoyed getting into mischief. Once when asked what the D in her name represented, she replied quickly, "Devil—don't you think it suits excellently?" She did not enjoy going to church.

She went to a seminary as girls' schools were called then. The story is told of the night before the first of April in 1855 when Lottie Moon stole up to the attic of the dormitory after all the lights were out, climbed into its tower, and tied towels and sheets around the bell so that it could not wake people up on April Fool's Day. She learned to speak several foreign languages. Just before she graduated, she accepted Jesus as her personal Lord and Savior. Only then did she learn to enjoy going to church.

After her graduation the Civil War broke out. During the war she served as a nurse. Following the war she taught school in Alabama, then in Cartersville, Georgia, where she started a high school for girls. During a regional church meeting, Lottie felt a call from God telling her to go to China. She served first in Teng-chow and later in Pingtu.

While in China she lived as much like a Chinese woman as she could. Sometimes she had to stay in houses with dirt floors, no windows and doors, and straw roofs. She carried a bedroll with her when she traveled. At night bugs and rats would bother her. However, Lottie was willing to do anything for the chance to teach Bible stories, hymns, and prayers.—*Exploring 2*.

December 14. Map or Compass?

Did you ever get lost in the woods? Maybe not. But it is easy to do. You may walk for hours, thinking you are getting somewhere, only to discover that you have been going in a circle. You come back to a place where you know you have been before. A rock, a log, or something else tells you.

What do you need to get out of the woods? A map? No, not if you are lost in the woods! What you need is a compass. A compass looks something like a watch, and when you hold it level, a hand points straight north (if you live in the northern hemisphere) to the north magnetic pole. This can keep you moving in the right direction until you come out of the woods. You won't go around in circles.

It has been said that the Bible is like a compass. When we are going around in circles, trying to decide what is right and what is wrong, whether to do this or do that, the Bible will keep pointing us in the right direction. Jesus said that the two most important things to remember when we are deciding what to do are these: Love God with everything that is in you, and love your neighbor as yourself. Sometimes, if we use the Bible as a map, we might be mixed up, but if we use it as a compass, it will always tell us that loving God and other people is the right way. The great Apostle Paul said, "If you love someone, you will never do him wrong" (Rom. 13:10, TEV).

December 21. Love One Another

One Christmas Eve when I was about ten or so, my father and I were passing Burkhart's Department Store in Cincinnati when a dirty old fellow in a tattered coat stopped me, took hold of my sleeve and said, "Young man, give me something."

I pulled my arm away, gave the man a slight push, and walked on, nose in the air.

My father stopped short. "You shouldn't treat a man like that—Christmas Eve or any other time."

"But Dad," I said, "he's a bum."

"There is no such thing as a bum, Norman," my father said. "There may be some people who haven't made the most of their lives, but all of us are still children of God."

Then he took out his skinny old wallet —it never had much in it—and he handed me a dollar. And he said, "You catch up with that man. Tell him, 'Sir, I give you this dollar in the name of Jesus. Merry Christmas.'"

"Oh, no," I said. "I can't do that." He said, "You do as I tell you, boy."

In those days you really minded what your parents told you.

So I chased after the man and said, "Sir, I give you this dollar in the name of Jesus. Merry Christmas."

The old fellow was flabbergasted. He took off his beat-up cap and bowed to me and said, "I thank you, young sir. Merry Christmas."

In that moment, his face became beautiful to me. He was no longer a bum.—Norman Vincent Peale.

December 28. Does Someone Need You?

It happened in a church. Almost everybody had left after a Sunday morning service except a small boy and the aged organist emeritus, who was ninety years old. He was trying to zip the zippers on his overshoes but was having a hard time.

The small boy, seeing his difficulty, bounded down from the chancel, stooped on one knee, and with a smile like the sunlight of all out-of-doors, zipped the overshoes of the old man, saying even as he was doing his good deed: "Mr. Booth, may I help you with your overshoes?" and finished the job without even waiting for a reply.

A keen businessman who saw the boy's deed said to the preacher: "There is a lad who has started life with a success system that simply cannot fail. He is observant. He is thoughtful and helpful. He has the spirit of service and is kindly just like the Master of us all, when he knelt and washed the feet of his disciples in the long ago. In short, the lad is a gentleman. He is more than a Boy Scout doing his one good deed each day; he has the quintessence of greatness in him illustrated in that kind act."

We not only get more out of life by doing kindly deeds, but also by having eyes to see them.—William L. Stidger.

SECTION XI. Sermon Outlines and Homiletic and Worship Aids for Fifty-two Weeks

SUNDAY: JANUARY FIFTH

MORNING SERVICE

Topic: Losing the Star

TEXT: Matt. 2:1–12.

The wise men would not be the wise men without their wondrous star. Or would they?

It occurred to me this year, for the first time in a lifetime of reading the Christmas accounts in the Gospels, that much of their journey that first Christmas was made without benefit of the star. They saw the star in the East, shining with incredible brightness over their homelands, and they saw it again as they left the palace of Herod. But in between, encompassing the vast distance from where their journey began to the few miles that marked its conclusion, they were completely without its benefit.

Talk about realism! Isn't that the way it happens with all of us? We have our moments of seeing and knowing, when the star of clarity and certainty goes before us, and then nothing.

What can we learn from these wise men and their vagrant star?

I. *Life is a journey.* (a) Life isn't rootedness and it isn't settledness. It is journey, movement, going from one place to another. The minute we think we've got it all settled, tied up, or nailed down, it springs loose on us and begins to unravel.

(b) Eventually, if you are lucky, you see that the important stance in life, the most important quality to have, is openness. It is realizing that life is gift, and that those persons receive most who are poised to receive. This is the way it was with the wise men; they followed the star that appeared in their sky. They were open and ready to be led. They knew that life is an adventure, and those who are most ready to follow see most.

II. *Faith is what we exercise in times of darkness.* (a) Faith is for the times of the journey when we can't see the star. Contrary to the pictures on the Christmas cards, the wise men traveled long miles of their journey in the dark, without benefit of the glorious star. They had to journey onward in the direction it had given them, but without its immediate aid.

(b) This too is true to life, isn't it? We spend a lot of our journeys in the dark. Again and again in life, we have a moment of great luminosity, when everything becomes clear and we feel affirmed in our choices; then the light gives way to great stretches of darkness, when we must walk alone, with only the memory of the light to guide us.

(c) And so we must all learn to wait when the star is not shining. We have seen it before; we shall see it again. But in the interim there is nothing to do but to keep going on the journey and wait until it appears.

III. *At the end of the journey is Christ.* (a) In terms of our Christian experience, at least, we may have thought he was at the beginning of the journey. But he is also at the end, in a way that is now almost too marvelous to anticipate. A journey, often couched in darkness, and Christ at the end—that is what the wise men found. And there was no question about the journey's being worth it. That is good news to those who are in a darkened phase of their life's journeys, isn't it? When you have lost the star, hold on; you will come out on the other end of the darkness, and there will be light you cannot now believe.

(b) That is what our faith is all about: He has been there all the time. Through all the darkness and all the struggles, past all the pitfalls and all the valleys, he is there. And that is what sustains all wise men—or women—on their journeys.—John Killinger.

Illustrations

THE GUIDANCE OF GOD.   One can speak of God's guidance being both explicit and implicit. There is no need to see any contradiction in this. The two kinds of guidance are complementary. I have had plenty of experience of his explicit guidance. Quite often, despite the uncertainty that always remains, I have obeyed with conviction what I have thought to be his command and afterwards have felt that I have been really inspired. But such gleams of enlightenment are pretty rare. Time and again I have been left in my perplexity. The more I realize in this way the limitations of human intelligence, even in its most enlightened and inspired moments, the more do I prefer to depend on God, asking him to lead me even if I do not see clearly where he is leading me. The Bible often employs a different image from that of the voice of God, the less intellectual image of the angel, of a mysterious, invisible presence that comes from God to guide us. We are all children in life, seeking our way, looking for a guide. We feel ourselves to be called to an adventure, to the fulfillment of a mission that we do not

know how to carry out. We suffer from our impotence to heal those we love. And God sets at our side his angels, whom we do not recognize but who guide us without our realizing it. All these angels symbolize the constant and secret intervention by God in the history of men, to guide them in the adventure to which he calls them.—Paul Tournier, in *The Adventure of Living*.

JOURNEY'S END.   At Notre Dame University, there is a great mosaic of Christ, several stories tall, on the side of the library building. He stands with his arms outspread and lifted, and is clearly visible from the football stadium. The students long ago nicknamed him "Touchdown Jesus." Touchdown Jesus. That's the gospel in a nutshell, isn't it? Jesus at the end of our journeys, at the end of all our struggles, ready to say "You made it!" And his being there makes all the journey different. Knowing he is there, we can endure our seasons of darkness, our times of pain. Knowing he is there, we can make it through the hardships. Knowing he is there, we can survive even loss and death. For we know we shall hear him say "Well done, good and faithful servant. You made it!"—John Killinger.

Sermon Suggestions

THE ATTITUDE OF FAITH.   Text: Hab. 2:1. (1) Commit your problem to God. (2) Expect an answer from God. (3) Watch and wait for the answer.—D. Martyn Lloyd-Jones.

WISE MEN REJOICE.   Gospel Text: Matt. 2:1–12. (1) Because of God's plan. (2) Because of sharing in God's plan.

Worship Aids

CALL TO WORSHIP.   "I am Alpha and Omega, the beginning and the ending, saith the Lord, which is, and which was, and which is to come, the Almighty" (Rev. 1:8).

INVOCATION.   O Lord, grant that in all our comings and goings, we may begin everything with thee, so that thy presence may sanctify our thoughts, words, and deeds throughout this new year and in all the days of our lives.

OFFERTORY SENTENCE. "And Jesus came and spake unto them, saying, 'All power is given unto me in heaven and in earth. Go ye therefore, and teach all nations, baptizing them in the name of the Father, and of the Son, and of the Holy Ghost: teaching them to observe all things whatsoever I have commanded you: and, lo, I am with you always, even unto the end of the world. Amen' " (Matt. 28:18–20).

OFFERTORY PRAYER. Receive our gifts, O God, and may they serve to proclaim the good news to the ends of the earth and to the end of time.

PRAYER. O God of eternity, you are the first and the last, the beginning and the end, the Alpha and the Omega. Yet in the vastness of what you are, you have given us our time in which to live and love and know your goodness. And within that time, life takes many turns, crosses hills and valleys, knows sunlight and shadow. Help us to know that you are God above it all and God with us in it all. We confess that we fret and even despair when the time is difficult and painful and that we are tempted to say or do some rash thing, forgetting that our times are in your hands and that both light and darkness are the same to you. Grant, O God, that we may place the most poignant hours in your hands. Help us to surrender our hurts and anxieties to your wisdom and care. Prepare us through our faithful stewardship of the appointments of your providence to carry the sometimes heavy burdens that life may bring. Deepen our joy in your service as we find ourselves partners with others in the same sorrows and the same laughter, the same adversity and the same prosperity. Give us grace to get a glimpse of your view of our lives, so that we may know that life's pluses and minuses turn out to be a magnificent plus because your greatness has filled every lack and transfigured every blessing.

EVENING SERVICE

Topic: Way Down in Egypt's Land

TEXT: Matt. 2:1–16.

I. The stable out back of Bethlehem's inn is empty now. Joseph, Mary, and the Child are gone now. The warmth of the stable has faded away and the wind blows cold through the shed. All the mystery, the glory, the wonder, the miracle of that first Christmas night have vanished, and everything appears very common now.

(a) No sooner had the wise men left and the shepherds departed than the horror of Herod's slaughter had descended upon the Holy Family, and a voice upset their calm with a command, "Take the baby and be gone to Egypt, for Herod right now is seeking to kill him!"

(b) So Mary and Joseph and the baby headed into the dark, cold night of the Sinai Desert with their few belongings. What a contrast with the scene several nights before when angelic choirs filled the air and heavenly light illumined the countryside. Now God's presence seemed to be far removed. God himself seemed distant. The Holy Family was lonely now.

(c) They must have been thinking of the wanderings of their people in the wild desert wilderness hundreds of years before. Moses had led a band of slaves out of Egypt. Though they had started out with excitement, the thrill of it all faded for them. They, too, became disappointed and longed for Egypt's glory. As with Mary and Joseph, the promises of God seemed to be in jeopardy. But the wilderness was the place where God was most faithful to his people. It was in bleak Sinai that God made covenant with his people and entered into intimate, personal relationship with them.

(d) The Holy Family and their Israelite forebears felt borne down by the monotony of it all. How does one recall the moment of glory when one feels let down and depressed? How could the Holy Family recapture the glory of Bethlehem out in the wilderness reaches of Sinai's blackness?

II. We can all identify easily with Mary and Joseph. We know something of what it is like to live in Sinai. Most of us have not seen too many stars of wonder with beauty bright. And if we did, we probably would not be impressed. Most of us have not heard angelic choirs lately. And I know that I have not run into too many wise men recently. We do not have many shepherds around here either.

(a) We know the monotony and depression that come to our lives in the desert on a vast plateau with very few mountains of spiritual ecstasy. It is easy to believe when you feel religious, when you hear angelic choirs, and when you see wonders in the sky. But most of us do not feel spiritual all the time, and believing comes hard for us in the common times of our lives.

(b) It is easy to have a warm heart when one stands in the glow of Christmas. But take away the props and see if religious faith will work in a world of business as usual. Sadness settles in quickly, and it is hard to whip up the Christmas spirit in icy January. Maybe all that business on December 25 was really false utopia designed to captivate the imagination of little children but really only superstition for mature adults.

(c) God's people have always had the experience of God's absence in the strange and unfamiliar places and circumstances of life. We have felt the mood of the children of Israel in their desert wandering when God seemed terribly absent. And so it was with the nation of Israel in Babylonian captivity. Psalm 137 records their reflections of their experience. They found themselves sitting beside the rivers of Babylon, crying plaintively, "How shall we sing the Lord's song in a strange land?"

(d) Yet even in the experience of God's absence, his presence was found to be most real. It was out of this experience that a prophet spoke of a suffering servant who would visit his people and redeem them in and through his suffering love.

III. God meets us most intimately in the living of our lives. His real visitation comes in the ordinariness of human existence. That is what incarnation means and that is what we are celebrating at Christmastide.

(a) Incarnation is real when Bethlehem comes to Sinai, when the Christ Child grows up in the desert, when faith abides day in and day out. He wants to meet you in the ordinariness of your days. Incarnation is about God's getting involved with ordinary people, ordinary flesh and blood people—like you and me.

(b) No one would deny that we need a genuine revival of the generosity and goodwill that belong to the Christmas spirit. But it is far too easy to identify the "Christmas cheer" with Christian cheerfulness. The Christ event should not be associated with a kind of childish lightheartedness. We want to keep Christmas frivolous and avoid the difficult questions of life at least at this one time of the year.

(c) Our Gospel lesson today injects the somber side into the Christmas spirit. When you think of Christmas, never forget proud, angry Herod destroying the babies of Bethlehem. The incarnation involved pain. It is almost a reminder that Calvary was only six miles from Bethlehem. The manger and the cross are part of the Christmas story. Incarnation means that God enters into the pain and agony, the dullness and drabness of our existence, and meets us most intimately in the ordinary times of our lives. In his suffering, sacrificing, saving love he embraces us.—Fred W. Andrea.

SUNDAY: JANUARY TWELFTH

MORNING SERVICE

Topic: Teach Us to Number Our Days
TEXT: Psalm 90:12.

Dear brothers and sisters, today let us turn to a portion of Scripture that may sound familiar to many of you since it is often quoted at funeral services. It is the twelfth verse of the Psalm 90: "So teach us to number our days that we may get a heart of wisdom." He who numbers his days remembers that they are counted. In other words, he remembers that he must die. To become truly wise means to get a heart of wisdom. For, in the biblical language, the heart is the very center of human life. The quality of the heart settles the question whether the whole person is foolish or wise. What, then, can we learn from this text?

I. Our days are numbered: we must die. (a) That is quite obviously true. One dies earlier, the other a little later, one perhaps after a long illness, another quite suddenly, one almost imperceptibly, another in agony. No one can escape his death. But what is the use of telling us that our days are numbered and we must die? We know it all too well already! There is no need for us to meet here and to open our Bible to get this insight. That man is mortal is somehow part of his natural history.

(b) But, according to Luther's translation, it is important to *remember* this well-known fact. Are we then urged to ponder the common knowledge of our mortal condition? That might indeed be a quite appropriate undertaking. True, we may know that everything will be over for us one day. But what does it help to reckon with *this*?

II. The message of our text, therefore, lies neither in the quite superfluous statement that we, like all mortal beings, must die nor in the questionable exhortation that *we* should attempt to remember and ponder this well-known fact. *So teach us to number our days*, the wording goes. *Teach!* This is an invocation, a petition addressed to God. It is a supplication, a prayer.

(a) As a petition, the text assumes that the chapter called death in the natural history of human life is after all worth thinking about. It reminds us, moreover, of our inability to summon the right thoughts about death into our hearts and minds, and at the same time of the urgent necessity to ponder the matter nevertheless, lest we fail to become wise, to get a heart of wisdom. Lastly, the text points to the only way out of this dilemma: to cast ourselves upon God, imploring him to give us, to grant us, to teach us to remember that we must die.

(b) God *hears* and *answers* this petition. Then we can and we may summon the

right and relevant thoughts about death. Then God himself teaches us, grants us, gives us the freedom to number our days.

III. We must go on to consider how God *hears* and *answers* this petition. To begin with, let me state it shortly and boldly: To remember, and to remember aright, that we must die is to remember that *Jesus has died for us*. (a) We may and we must know him in his suffering and death. Only then do we come to a true understanding of what our own death is all about, that truly a bit more is involved than a short chapter of our natural history.

(b) Do you know what this is, the death of Jesus? What happened? What was fulfilled at that moment? A mere necessity of nature? An accident or incident? No, the death of Jesus was a *judgment*. This is the first thing to be said and retained. It is the carrying out of a death sentence, inflicted upon Jesus instead of ourselves. *We* are judged in his person. *We* are condemned and killed in his death. Of course not we ourselves, but someone who has very much to do with us, someone who stands intimately by our side: the old man who dwells and spooks about within us all! This old man in us is judged, sentenced, and killed in Jesus' death. What Jesus had to bear in our place was nothing less than this hard and irrevocable "no", spoken by God upon this old man in us. Jesus accepted to die the death of the old man. He suffered this death in his flesh.

(c) And now our own death occurs in the power of Jesus' death in our place. Certainly only in *his* power! For no other man will ever again die this death, the death of the One judged in the place of all others. Our death happens in the power of his death, as the consequence, reflection, and sign of the divine "no," of the judgment carried out in Jesus' condemnation.

IV. But there is another and quite different thing to be remembered. What happened in the death of Jesus did not happen against us, but *for us*. (a) What took place was not an act of God's wrath against man. Quite the opposite holds true. Because in the one Jesus, God so loved us from all eternity—truly all of us—because he has elected himself to be our dear Father and has elected us to become his dear children whom he wants to save and to draw unto him, therefore he has in the one Jesus written off, rejected, nailed to a cross, and killed our old man who, as impressively as he may dwell and spook about in us, is not our true self.

(b) And now *our* own death occurs in the power of the *gracious and saving* death that Jesus suffered for our sake. Only in the power of *his* death, only as a consequence, reflection, and sign. For no other man ever suffered or will suffer death that he may mercifully redeem the whole world. In our living and in our dying, the power of the saving grace of Jesus' death for us is unfailingly at work.

V. I am at the end. Must I still explain how God goes about teaching us to number our days? Let me give you the plainest answer: God teaches us by *telling* us and by letting us *hear* of the twofold power, both killing and life-giving, of Jesus' death in our dying.

There can be no doubt: God tells us and he lets us hear. He is not found wanting. He teaches us to number our days. In all the fire of his Holy Spirit he teaches us that we must die, that Jesus has died for us.

My dear brothers and sisters, if only a spark of this fire kindles the heart of a man, whoever he is and whatever his plight, nothing is lost for him! Everything is gained! Amen.—Karl Barth.

Illustrations

SUFFERING WITH CHRIST.   If we want to share the sufferings of Jesus, who knows where and how to find them? For those who have the secret, however, how many other doors will open! Why is it that Francis of Assisi fires the admiring love of thousands, Protestants as well as Catholics, today? A recent writer on religion in poorer London has noted that the clergyman who has influence is not the zealous preacher or visitor who returns home at night to a comfortable house in the suburbs, but one who lives where he cannot help feeling all that his neighbors feel, and perhaps feeling it more deeply than they. A hard doctrine; but who can deny it the name of Christian? . . . There is no true fellowship with men if there is not fellowship with Christ; and can there be fellowship with Christ if there is not fellowship of this sort—with his sufferings?—A. E. Whitham.

DEATH COMES FOR BISHOP BUTLER. When the great moralist, the old Honest of the Episcopal Bench, was on his deathbed, he called for his chaplain and said to him: "Though I have endeavored to avoid sin, and to please God to the utmost of my power; yet from the consciousness of perpetual infirmities, I am still afraid to die."

"My lord," said the chaplain, "you have forgotten that Jesus Christ is a Savior."

"True," said Butler, "But how shall I know that he is a Savior for *me*?"

"My lord, it is written, him that cometh unto me, I will in no wise cast out."

"True," said the bishop; "and I am surprised that though I have read that Scripture a thousand times over, I never felt its virtue until this moment. And now I die happy."—Alexander Whyte.

Sermon Suggestions

THE BEST FRIEND.   Text: John 11:1–6, 19–44. (1) Jesus is a loving friend, verses 3–5. (2) Jesus is an understanding friend, verses 21–36. (3) Jesus is a mighty friend, verses 37–44.—James Braga.

ONE GREATER THAN JOHN.   Gospel Text: Luke 3:15–17, 21–22. (1) Greater in his task. (2) Greater in his source of power. (3) Greater in his identity.

Worship Aids

CALL TO WORSHIP.   "A day in thy courts is better than a thousand" (Ps. 84:10).

INVOCATION.   Grant, O God, that we may see each day of our lives in the light of this day. May sabbath glory transform every common task and sanctify all our thoughts and purposes. To this end, may thy face shine upon us as we worship thee today, so that we may acceptably serve thee tomorrow.

OFFERTORY SENTENCE.   "Christ . . . hath given himself for us an offering and a sacrifice to God for a sweet smelling savor" (Eph. 5:2).

OFFERTORY PRAYER. Our Father, you have given your dearest and best for us, yet he yielded himself up willingly to do your will and for the joy that was set before him endured the cross. May your example and his show us what love can do when it is real.

PRAYER. O God, we thank thee for morning light and evening peace; for the night in which thou hast restored our spirit's strength and the day in which thou dost lead us into a larger life; for the past from whence so much has come to bless us and for the future to which we lift our eyes in hope; for the body in which our souls are nurtured, and for the soul by which our body is glorified; for the mind that asks the mighty questions, and the spirit by which the mysteries are exalted; for truth that binds the conscience in law, and for mercy that frees it from bondage; for beauty that rejoices the eye of man and for skill that disciplines his hands; for the saint whose deeds and dreams are one, and for the sinner who hungers and thirsts beyond his deeds for benediction; for love that redeems the heart of man from fear, and for grace that sustains him in every adversity; for all thy work done in this world, we give thee thanks, O God, our strength and our redeemer.—Samuel H. Miller.

EVENING SERVICE

Topic: Getting Our Loyalties Straight
TEXT: Matt. 4:12–23.

I. The matter of our loyalties—where we place them, to whom or what we give them—stands at the very heart of the Christian life.

(a) For us, who dare confess ourselves Christian, loyalty to Jesus Christ and the kind of world we see inaugurated by Christ's breaking into our lives claims our first loyalty. Indeed, that's what the passage we read a few moments ago illustrates.

(b) When King Herod finally arrests John the Baptist, Jesus knows his time has come. The new era, the new world, the

new order, the new community, the new citizenship he calls us to can now start. We see Jesus striding across the God-forsaken Galilean countryside—a place of darkness where light needs to shine, says Matthew, proclaiming his radical message and command: "Repent for the kingdom of Heaven is at hand." He confronts Andrew and Peter. "Follow me," he commands. They leave their boats. He encounters James and John on the same shoreline fishing with their father Zebedee. "Follow me," he commands. They leave their nets. No hemming and hawing, no accommodations: a radical discontinuity in life—immediately; a realignment of loyalties—immediately; a placing of every other loyalty in jeopardy. They've gotten their loyalties straight for mission and action in the realm ruled by the love, compassion, and peace of Jesus Christ. In a vivid and telling image, Dietrich Bonhoeffer suggests those disciples "burn their boats."

II. Can we do that? Can you? Can I? Can this church? Can we "burn our boats"?

(a) I don't know about you, but those immediate responses of Peter, Andrew, James, and John strike me as a bit impulsive. That kind of drastic action doesn't appeal to most of us.

(b) Do you see? This is why the gospel of Jesus Christ has been around for so long. It continues to disrupt and stun us out of our complacency. It strikes us at our most vulnerable point. It shakes up the things we take for granted; it reshuffles our priorities; it reorders our loyalties.

(c) And our loyalty to Christ puts loyalty to our nation in a different light. Heaven knows Americans are tremendously patriotic; but we need be careful.

Must we choose sides? Can't we be loyal to our flag, and loyal to our economic system, and loyal to our president and loyal to our kids—and loyal to the new world of Jesus Christ? Good Lord, you don't want us to leave our boats. You don't make claims equal to that of our families. Can't we follow you and have it all?

III. Oh, my friends, I believe there is no one in this room who does not in his or her deepest heart want to be a disciple of Jesus —and it is not easy. Heaven knows we get up in the morning and progress through our days facing rough decisions about where best to invest our money, spend our vacations, school our kids, put our time. We face, every hour of every day, decisions illustrating the locus of our loyalties. We find ourselves in a world of trade-offs and ambiguities; of righteous decisions causing injury to others; of good choices made for the wrong reasons. Amid all this moral mush, our Lord walks by and beckons us, in frequently radical and surprising ways. Can we make ourselves available? If we can—if you and I can place ourselves in that "creative force so beautifully exemplified by Christ"—you may find yourself—I may find myself—ready, for "Christ's sake, to burn our boats."—James W. Crawford.

SUNDAY: JANUARY NINETEENTH

MORNING SERVICE

Topic: When God Hides
TEXT: John 8:59.

There is a hint of the miraculous about it as the author of the Fourth Gospel tells the story—in some strange fashion, when they got themselves stones and began looking for him, he was nowhere to be found. But you feel, as you read it, that underneath the bare record of his having gone that day through the midst of them and so passed by, there lies a deeper moral significance.

Here in the gospel was the dawn of other days, when men should be lonely through no fault of God's: In Jesus of Nazareth he had done what he could. From now on his hiding should be by nothing save by the willful distance they could still set between their world and him.

Whenever life takes to groping around dazed and uncertain as though God had gone away, you may be sure it has itself been getting its things together and deliberately or absentmindedly moving over out of his world.

I. Moving back into yesterday, for example; and he stands there forever beckoning toward tomorrow, where he lives! What if that were one of the secrets of this desolation we feel when we seem to be traveling so God-forsakenly alone? Simply that we have been following the right path but following it in the wrong direction?

(a) It's what these Pharisees had been doing. It was not that they doubted anything that had been handed down to them, or disbelieved anything. They were on the road right enough. But you see how they were headed: The only progress they were making was backward!

(b) It staggers you to stop and think how much of our own religion is like that, delving into musty records for some glimpse of a gallant Nazarene who knew how to handle life. On the twenty-fifth of December we commemorate his coming. It isn't long until Easter comes, with its flowers and brilliant anthems. It is so much easier to celebrate anniversaries than it is seriously to look for repetitions.

(c) Then, too, there was the old order of things we knew in our youth, and it was far better than this, when life was tranquil and not chaotic: We wish we could recover it, the peace that was in men's hearts. There were such tight little answers for such neat little questions, and a score of principles and ideals in economics and in government, in religion and in literature, that none but the damned ever thought of challenging. We knew what to think and where to stand.

Will *nothing* bring these moods of ours into the present, lay violent hands on them, and force them to face about? Many a backward, longing gesture has been hardened, writes Dr. Gossip, into a spectral figure, like Lot's wife on the plains of Sodom, ghastly reminders for men to point at! "Look not behind thee, neither stay thou!" It matters where you look.

It may be, if ever you lose him, that he just isn't in the place where you've been looking!

II. We must not think, however, that this is the only reason why we miss him, because we keep forever looking over our shoulders: Sometimes it's because we let ourselves run off at a tangent, facing forward all right, but fooling around with what we can *see*, and *handle*, and spread out before you for proof, like answers to prayer, as we are pleased to describe some of the things that happen to us.

(a) I know people who had found him that way and no other so long that one dull morning they lost him entirely because he didn't do their bidding! Or we like to discover him in some providential event, like the Reformation, and wrap our cloaks about us in the sweet conviction that undoubtedly he takes care of his own, until the world war comes along; whereupon a few of us grow strangely silent! Then the smile fades, and it's desperate business for some people.

(b) That happened to Jesus, you remember. There for one weird instant the waves went over him: "My God, my God, why hast Thou forsaken me?" Then he was back, as though he were a great ship you thought was foundering, and you held your breath, until she lifted out of it steadily and shed the water from her decks. When all of them were gone, and both the statistics and Providence had apparently quite marched away, he was *alone*—with God! "Father, into Thy hands I commend my spirit." That should keep you, if nothing else can, from thinking too desolately of yourself when the times are out of joint and no one stands with you. It may be then, and only then, that you'll find him!

III. Sometimes, too, we miss him because, being very practical people, with few if any traces of idealism now, and having bravely rid ourselves of everything that might seem visionary, we have set about looking for him within the realm of what we choose to call the *possible*.

(a) Most miracles are blue-penciled, and all the other things we can't understand. We shall not look there, or expect very much that is out of the ordinary. There are laws, you see, that govern so much of life. Like that coterie of friends in the book of Acts praying that Peter might be released from prison; and when he stood at the door and the maid came running in to tell them, they said to one another that she had quite taken leave of her senses. And Peter had to go on knocking! No, we are clear on that point. We shall not anticipate

anything unusual. We have arranged so that it is very difficult for God to get at us, you know; we *see through* the common things, like birth, and yesterday's happiness, and the spring. He isn't there; and the uncommon things we rule out.

(b) That's why we have so little of the spirit of pioneers, pushing on into undiscovered country; we are too much under the *tyranny* of the *possible*. If we are called on to undertake this or that by way of our Christian faith, we'll do it "if we can"; and then we hope to have some fellowship along the way of it with this Jesus of Nazareth, who, when a thing is possible, loses interest in it almost at once, if he's still the Jesus that he was, and looks at you breathlessly, with his eyes all kindling, to see whether you are going to stop with what you *can* and sit down there by yourself, or come over where he is and start what's beyond you!

IV. Where would you hide if you were God? It may help to answer that!

(a) Surely not in yesterday alone, but in today, and in tomorrow, if you wanted to keep men traveling. That certainly. Yes, there I should hide if I were God, and in that brave hour when any soul of man spreads some sail of faith and slips away from the low and level shorelines of common sense, "toward the great deeps, and the things that ought to be!"

(b) "Jesus hid himself." It may just be that he wants to beckon us by hiding! Where, in your case, do you think it most likely he'll be?—Paul Scherer.

Illustrations

PATHWAYS TO CERTAINTY. The test Jesus gave his disciples for distinguishing between opinion and reality is still a valid test today: "If any man will do his will he shall know of the doctrine, whether it be of God or whether I speak of myself" (John 7:17). The test is valid on all sides of our experiment with God. It is valid in the realm of the mind. We turn to God because he gives us answers to our ultimate questions. But we can only tell whether the answers are to be trusted by treating the world as if it were the kind of a world in which God is the basic fact. Jesus' test is valid in the realm of the emotions. God is the supreme object of worship, opening to us the possibility of a fellowship that gives joy to living and inspiration to service. Let us cultivate the habit of thankfulness. And let us do this all along the line, not simply with the bright side of life. Above all, Jesus' test is valid in the realm of conduct. God sets the standard for our actions. He reveals himself as love and requiring love in us. It is necessary only that we should act out our insight so far as it has come. If God be the truth, we shall find him most surely by holding to what seems to us true. If God be the good, we shall meet him most certainly by what seems to us right.—William Adams Brown.

GOD'S GUIDANCE.　　Because we receive detailed guidance on some things, we must not assume that we shall receive it on all things, and we must certainly not assert that we have it when all we possess are our settled prejudices or a couple of hazy ideas. The journey is still a journey of faith. Paul never hesitated to make a clear distinction between his own judgment and the directions he had received from the Lord.—W. E. Sangster.

Sermon Suggestions

PAUL'S ASSURANCE.　　Text: 2 Tim. 1:12. (1) He was sure of his Savior. (2) He was sure of his Savior's power. (3) He was sure of his Savior's power to preserve. (4) He was sure of his Savior's power to preserve to the end.—A. Skevington Wood.

A MESSAGE AT A MARRIAGE.　　Gospel Text: John 2:1–11. (1) Human resources are embarrassingly limited. (2) Divine resources are gloriously boundless.

Worship Aids

CALL TO WORSHIP.　　"Seek ye the Lord while he may be found, call ye upon him while he is near" (Isa. 55:6).

INVOCATION.　　O God, you have revealed yourself in Jesus Christ and we have set out on a path to follow him. Grant that no obscuring cloud of doubt or fear may turn us aside from that walk of faith. Even as we follow him into the unknown may we be faithful and as true seekers find the treasures of your grace that await us.

OFFERTORY SENTENCE.　　"Although the fig tree shall not blossom, neither shall fruit be in the vines; the labor of the olive shall fail, and the fields shall yield no meat; the flock shall be cut off from the fold, and there shall be no herd in the stalls: Yet I will rejoice in the Lord, I will joy in the God of my salvation" (Hab. 3:17–18).

OFFERTORY PRAYER.　　Gracious Lord, some of us have plenty; some of us have little. The fortunes of most of us change from time to time; we are sometimes up, sometimes down. Yet your love for us does not change. May our love for you never change, even when the way is hard and unpromising. Bless and use for your honor and glory the little or much that we are able to offer to you.

PRAYER.　　Eternal God, our Father, we draw near once more in awe and reverence to worship thee. Often have we besought thee to fall upon us like showers of rain. Today we beseech thee that we may retreat into the secret places of our own hearts and find thee rising there like a spring, close at hand, cleansing and refreshing. Thou art the fountain of spiritual life within us. Thou art the source of every secret aspiration, thou art in everything that lifts and liberates our souls, and as thus we come to thee in worship we pray for genuineness and sincerity. Lead from the unreal to the real.

Lead us from the unreality of this world we live in, from the tinsel of the things we touch, from its shallowness and superficiality, from all that is cheap, showy, and ostentatious in ourselves and in our fellows. Make us genuine today.

Let our faith be real. We do not ask thee to give us faith. Thou seest how much of it we have, with what carelessness and credulity we bestow it on many passing whims. Lift up our faith, we beseech thee, that it may turn toward the Eternal. Set it on things above, where Christ is. Help us to believe this day in the Highest.

Let our love turn toward the real, we beseech thee. We do not pray to thee that we might have love. Thou seest that as the skies are made for winds to blow in, so our hearts are made for love. Thou seest with what carelessness our affection turns every which way and attaches itself to all manner of things. Help us this day to love the Highest when we see it.

Turn our hopes, we beseech thee, to aims that are real. Thou knowest the expectations that throng our hearts this day, the hopes that walk up and down the avenues and alleyways of our souls. Set our hopes on things that are genuine and right. Help us to serve with our hope and devotion the will of God in our generation before we fall on sleep.—Harry Emerson Fosdick.

EVENING SERVICE

Topic: Doctrine of the Trinity

TEXT: 1 Cor. 12:4–6.

Long before 1 Corinthians was a book in our New Testament, it was a letter from a missionary to a congregation on the frontier, far from the church's hearth and home. The church had experiences for which they had no texts and problems for which they had no precedents. Some concerned members wrote to the missionary who started the church, and their questions were many, touching on marriage, divorce, litigation, support of local shrines, proper foods, leadership of women, order of worship, and the nature of a resurrected body. What a list! And among the questions was this one: What are activities of the Spirit?

I. Unlike some of us, Paul was not intimidated or thrown on the defensive by the question. He welcomed it as deserving a careful answer.

(a) In answering the letter from Corinth, Paul is not at all interested in dealing with events in the church services there as a question of whether these Spirit activities really happened. More to the point in the early church, however, was the question, did God do it? Did the Holy Spirit do it? In other words, they assumed extraordinary events occurred; the issue was whether they were acts of God.

(b) Before he can answer the question as to whether certain activities and behavior patterns are of the Holy Spirit, Paul feels the need to change the word used in the letter to him. They inquired about "spiritual things"; Paul wants to talk about "gifts." The word was *charisma*. Charisma is gift, and it is Paul's insistence that when we talk of these matters, we call them what they are—gifts of God. Apart from that association with God and grace, we might as well be discussing magic and horoscopes.

(c) And the word for Paul is plural, *charismata*; there are varieties of gifts. By its repetition it can be assumed that diversity of gifts is Paul's insistence. Perhaps the divided and confused state of the congregation was prompting some of them to wish to quiet dissenting voices, to bring order and unity to the church by demanding that all have the same gift, the same grasp of the Holy Spirit. But Paul says no. Even a quarreling church must not relinquish its diversity, opting for unity on the grounds of one common experience. And the reason? Because diversity is not a condition we tolerate, up to a point; diversity is a given in the very plenitude of God, whose grace is boundless.

(d) But what if things are out of hand? The answer, says Paul, does not lie in tighter control but in setting the experience of the church back into proper context. That context—are you ready for this? —is the Trinity. "Now there are varieties of gifts, but the same Spirit; and there are varieties of service, but the same Lord; and there are varieties of working, but it is the same God who inspires them all in everyone" (vv. 4–6).

II. My first response is: How clever of Paul! Why can't I be that quick witted? When called upon to deal with an incendiary issue, surrounded by persons with high emotional investment who have already decided the conclusion of the discussion, introduce the Trinity. One can escape before the fog lifts!

We expect more from Paul, however, and we get it. Nothing could be more appropriate to the understanding and enriching of one's experience of the Spirit than the clear association of that experience with Jesus Christ and with God. Notice also that the accent is not upon the nature of the Trinity but upon function: *gifts* of the Spirit, *service* of Jesus Christ, and *energizing* of God. Here we have doctrine with a will to do. But still the question remains: What has the Trinity to do with charismatic activity?

(a) First, let us remind ourselves that it is Paul more than any other New Testament writer who personalizes and internalizes the experience of the Holy Spirit in the church. But Paul is aware of the dangers here. A subjective experience without an outside point of reference can easily become a trap, a tender trap to be sure, but a trap of feeling, mood, intuition, sensation.

(b) Paul provides a guard against such a reduction of our faith by adding to the first article of his affirmation, "There are varieties of gifts but the same Spirit," a second: "There are varieties of service but the same Lord."

(c) And finally, Paul provides an even larger context, encompassing both Spirit and Jesus: "And there are varieties of working [empowering, enabling], but it is the same God who inspires [works in] them all in everyone."

III. Now Paul is making us think big

thoughts here. He is asking us to be aware that all worship and activity of the Christian community are responsible finally to God. No claims, real or imagined, about the influence of the Holy Spirit can justify behavior or preaching or teaching that is not appropriate to the one God, Creator, Redeemer, and Sustainer of all life. He is asking us to grasp the dimensions of the realm of the Spirit's work. If God is energizing the totality, then the arena of the Spirit's activity is too narrowly defined if it excludes any of God's creation. Those members of the Corinthian church, or any church, who removed from the list of "spiritual" concerns all issues domestic, sexual, legal, or social were, and are, in error. If the Holy Spirit means anything, it means something where people live. Paul is also allowing us to catch the hope of the final vision. That final vision was of a God who had reclaimed all things, of a time when the realm of creation and the realm of redemption would be coextensive. This is no faint wish; even now God is at work enabling the totality. The church that catches that vision is inspired by the Spirit to sing with Paul: "From God and through God and to God are all things. To God be glory forever."—Fred B. Craddock.

SUNDAY: JANUARY TWENTY-SIXTH

MORNING SERVICE

Topic: "Which Voice Will You Follow?"
TEXT: 1 Sam. 3:1–10, John 12:27–30.

I. We probably would not debate today that the voice of God has come. But does the voice of God still come? Can you and I today still hear God addressing us in some way? One of the reasons we sometimes have difficulty discerning what is the voice of God is that there are so many voices demanding our attention and calling to us saying, "I am the way of life."

(a) One of these voices today is the voice of materialism. This voice tells us that we are what we possess. What we have makes us who and what we are. Do not buy into the philosophy of life that tells you loudly and clearly that material things are the es-

sence of what constitutes authentic living.

(b) Another voice that we often succumb to is the voice that has sounded loudly and clearly for decades. And that voice is the playboy philosophy of life. This philosophy says that free sex is what really constitutes authentic living. Do not buy into that philosophy, because it is a dead-end street that will haunt us again and again with guilt and tragedy. The movies do not usually depict the outcome, the discards, and the rejects that come from that kind of life.

(c) Also do not listen to the voice that is calling us to cheap religion and civil religion. There are many voices in our land today that are telling us that religion is primarily something that we use to make us feel good. An even more distorted view is the one that equates whatever my country wants with what is the essence of religion. And so we wrap God and country in the same flag and bow down and worship both country and God at the same shrine, and we never see that this is idolatry. Do not buy into cheap religion that offers us salvation without commitment, grace without surrender, and redemption without sacrifice. Jesus calls us to take up our cross and follow him.

(d) Do not follow that voice that rings within our ears telling us that the basic philosophy of life is "meism." Selfishness is the main concern of this approach. The "meism" philosophy circulates all around us today as many constantly look out only for number one.

II. There are many voices crying to us in our land calling us to a way that is a lower way. But the voice of God is seeking to penetrate our very being and we need to listen for it.

(a) One thing for sure is said: "Learn to speak clearly and distinctly." In an age of so much "gobbledygook" and double-talk, do we not need to speak more plainly about the things of God and life? Do we not need people in politics and religion who will stand up clearly for what they believe? I hope that our young people will learn to speak plainly and distinctly in an age that avoids clear speech. Jesus Christ is the epitome of one who learned to speak clearly. They did not crucify Jesus because they could not understand what he was saying. They understood very clearly what he was saying.

(b) I hope that you will also hear the voice that comes to you saying that you are loved and acceptable to God. You notice in the New Testament that Jesus told us that God came searching after us even while we are sinners. Now that does not mean that he loves our sin. But he loves us as individuals and calls us to the very highest and best we can be with our own gifts.

(c) Listen also for the voice of God that comes saying to us that he is a God of integrity, and he wants us to have high values in the way we live and walk. It is sad today to live in a world in which the trust level has fallen so low. We need to hear God calling us to live a life of honesty, decency, and fairness in the way we relate to others.

(d) I hope that our young people will also listen to the voice that is calling them to a sense of discipline. Young Samuel had disciplined his life to respond to the call of his master. *Discipline* is an unpopular word today. Those in life who have found the most lasting values have been those who have been able to discipline themselves. Jesus has told us that his way is narrow. The broad way that leads to destruction is the way without any kind of control, without any kind of restraints. But Christ calls us to a narrow way that demands discipline.

(e) And like young Samuel, I hope we also can hear the voice of God as he calls us to a new challenge that lies before us. Samuel responded to God and met the challenge before him. There is a great, bold, exciting adventure lying before us, and I hope that you and I will not buy into the voice that says everything has already been done and accomplished. There is much left for you to do, because the greatest challenge is still ahead.

(f) There are many voices calling to us from all kinds of quarters today saying walk in my path. I hope that you will listen and determine that the true voice amid all the false voices is the voice that calls you always to the highest and best you can be.
—William Powell Tuck.

Illustrations

FROM PAIN TO PLEASURE. Be obedient to the words of Christ. Do not oppose them or argue about them. We can enjoy obeying them and profit from them now. We do not have to await future rewards. If they seem mostly burdensome and if they seem to cause no end of trouble, keep in mind that you are doing this for Christ's sake, and the pain will be pleasant. For if we always think this way, nothing will be burdensome to us, but we shall reap pleasure on every hand.—John Chrysostom.

LEVELS OF LISTENING. A Finn once suggested to me that in every conversation between two people there are always at least six persons present. What each person said are two; what each person meant to say are two more; and what each person understood the other to say are two more. There is certainly no reason to stop at six, but the fathomless depth of the listener who can go beyond words, who can even go beyond the conscious meanings behind words, and who can listen with the third ear for what is unconsciously being meant by the speaker furnishes a climate where the most unexpected disclosures occur that are in the way of being miracles in one sense, and yet the most natural and obvious things in the world.—Douglas V. Steere.

Sermon Suggestions

THE RICH CHRISTIANS.   Text: 1 Cor. 4–9. (1) The source of the riches. (2) The nature of the riches. (3) The purpose of the riches.—Robert U. Ferguson.

JESUS DECLARES HIS MISSION.   Gospel Text: Luke 4:14–17. (1) In a fitting context. (2) With a pointed message. (3) At the appropriate time.

Worship Aids

CALL TO WORSHIP.   "Behold, I stand at the door and knock: If any man hear my voice, and open the door, I will come in to him, and will sup with him, and he with me" (Rev. 3:20).

INVOCATION.   Our Father, as thy beloved Son stands at the door of our church awaiting our response to his summons, help us to fling wide the doors of our individual lives, so that his presence may bind us all together in ties of love and fellowship.

OFFERTORY SENTENCE.   "Why spend money on what does not satisfy? Why spend your wages and still be hungry? Listen to me and do what I say, and you will enjoy the best food of all" (Isa. 55:2, TEV).

OFFERTORY PRAYER.   Deepen our satisfactions, O God, with the joys of openhearted and openhanded giving. As you have given your best to us, may we seek to give our best to you.

PRAYER.   Almighty God, our heavenly Father, created by thy Word, redeemed by thy gift of Christ, and carried into the future by thy promise, we take a deep sigh of relief and come into this hour of worship for a chance to relax, a day of Sabbath rest, for it is only in thy power that the tensions and the efforts and the fears can subside, that we can rest in thy Providence, trust in thy mercy, and find ourselves renewed and revitalized by the inpouring of thy Holy Spirit. We do find that day after day we struggle to be wise as serpents and innocent as doves; we labor to be faithful servants; we grit our teeth and clench our fists as we seek to be disciples of Christ, and in this moment of worship we are invited to relax our teeth so that we might feed upon thy body and unclench our fist so that into our hands might be given the gift of fellowship and love. Thy perfect love casts out our fears and thy inspiring spirit lifts our dark spirits and renews our excitement for the common ministry we share. We thank thee for the gift of Sabbath rest, for the time of worship that relaxes and revives us, for the hymns of faith that perk us up, and for the ennobling words of Scripture that bear us up.

We thank thee for those who taught us about the joys of worship, who brought us to where we could share in the renewal of the Spirit. For our officers who have kept alive the time and place of worship; for all who have labored so hard that we might have the word of Scripture in words that we can comprehend; for those who sing so that the music of our hearts might be expressed; for those who come and give to us the gift of Christian fellowship; for those who give sacrificially so that its life might continue; for those who teach us the words so that we might hear the Spirit; for all who make this time of rest together an opportunity for discovering again the power of thy love, we give thee thanks.

We pray for thy presence and guidance. We pray for thy patience and love, for the forgiveness and grace to continue to love those who bear the name of Christian and yet bring shame and violence to it, for those who suffer under the violence of Christians as well as those oppressed by others. We pray for the sick and we pray for the well; we pray for the unemployed and we pray for the employed; we pray for the secretaries and for the managers; we pray for presidents and for janitors. We pray for bulldozer and crane operators and for the gophers; we pray for seamen and for the work at seamen centers, for offshore workers and for long-distance truckers. We pray for all those who sacrifice the ties of home and family so that we might benefit.

Be with us all: Together as thy church and apart as thy servants may we labor in the name of our common Lord, Jesus Christ.—Richard Brand.

EVENING WORSHIP

Topic: Heaven

TEXT: John 14:1–4; Phil. 1:20–26; 1 Cor. 15; Rev. 21.

On a questionnaire about worries, one member of a civic club indicated that his chief worry was whether he would go to heaven. There would be a better world and happier people if this became a more widespread concern, and concern were implemented by study, and study resulted in assurance. "For every man that hath this hope in him purifieth himself even as he is pure" (1 John 3:3).

I. When we go to the Bible, we find in different places various emphases with regard to the future life of the redeemed.

(a) At one time, we read of the immediate bliss of those who are absent from the body and present with the Lord. At another time, we read of the ultimate glory that comes through the resurrection of the body. But there should be no confusion with different phases and stages of the same general experience.

(b) The Bible does not speak of a natural immortality of man. Immortality belongs naturally to God, and he gives it to those who are in Christ Jesus. "This mortal must put on immortality" (1 Cor. 15:53).

(c) The faith of the Bible is resurrection faith, not the pagan Greek idea of a natural

immortality of man. Both Old and New Testaments affirm that there shall be resurrection; that is, the redeemed man will be a resurrected personality in a glorified body. He will be more than a disembodied spirit floating aimlessly in space or seeking another incarnation on earth. Paul wrote, "Our commonwealth is in heaven, and from it we await a Savior, the Lord Jesus Christ, who will change our lowly body to be like his glorious body, by the power which enables him even to subject all things to himself" (Phil. 3:21–22, RSV).

(d) However, we must remember the words of our Lord to the penitent on the cross: "Today shalt thou be with me in paradise." There is no long wait before one enters into a state that is "far better" (Phil. 1:23).

II. There is a great deal of mystery that surrounds the future life, for we are yet little more than unborn babes living in the womb of time. However, human experience and Biblical revelation tell us all we need to know at present about the life to come.

(a) Heaven is the fulfillment of the Lord's purpose for mankind. The designs of God, so beautiful and meaningful in their beginning and in their development, will not end in ashes and dust. Man is more than an ephemeral plaything of Deity.

(b) Heaven is a corollary of the Christian faith. Until Jesus, even the Jewish ideas of immortality were nebulous and unsatisfying. But Jesus assured us: "Because I live, ye shall live also" (John 14: 19). Immortality is life by the power and in the personal love of God.

(c) Heaven is respite from the fragmentary and imperfect, from the painful and disillusioning. It is strength and freedom for new and eternally interesting tasks.

(d) Heaven is reunion. The Savior who redeemed us and others who have poured meaning and value into our lives by their sacrifices, their love, and their companionship will be there to make heaven complete. We shall see our Redeemer as he is, and we shall know one another with complete understanding, appreciation, and love, even as God thus knows us. (Cf. 1 John 3:2; 1 Cor. 13:12).—James W. Cox.

SUNDAY: FEBRUARY SECOND

MORNING SERVICE

Topic: "Finding Forgiveness"
TEXT: Gen. 50:15–21; Luke 5:17–26.

The sermon this morning is directed to those people who need to have a sense of being forgiven. But before you exclude yourself you need to remember that all have sinned. Most of us can say that we have never committed murder, robbed a bank, nor committed rape, and therefore, we are good individuals. But who among us is free of all prejudice? Who among us in our relationships with others does not sometimes have feelings of greed, jealousy, hatred, or vindictiveness? Our sins are sometimes personal or social and sometimes both. But sinners we all are. I hope you will sense that what I am saying needs to be applied to each of us. Because none is free of sin.

Look at the New Testament story. Jesus was in town. The word had circulated around so the crowds had come from all over to hear the great teacher Jesus. He was in a home teaching. It was a very small house as most Palestine homes were. Jesus was teaching inside. There was a man who was ill. As they approached the home, they noticed that the crowd was so large that there was no way they could get through the door. The men carrying the ill man decided to go up the back stairs to the rooftop. They tore a hole in the roof, and the bed, which was nothing really but a pallet with a rope tied on each end, was lowered down through the roof to the feet of Jesus. Jesus looked at the man and said a curious thing, "Your sins are forgiven." The Pharisees were greatly disturbed by what Jesus said. Their antennas immediately went up and their thoughts began to reveal their motive for being there. Who is this man? Only God forgives sin. But Jesus demonstrated that in all honesty anybody can say your sins are forgiven, but in order that people might know that the Son of Man had this kind of power, he said to the man lying on the pallet, "Rise, take up your bed and go home." The man was cured and left praising God.

I. There are some lessons in this story that can teach us something about forgiveness. Notice first of all the faith of the man's friends.

(a) It talks here about Jesus recognizing their faith. It never says anything about the man's faith. In this passage it is revealed that the faith here is the faith of the friends who brought this individual to Jesus. We do not know if the individual had faith or not. But the chief emphasis in the passage is on the faith of the friends.

(b) When is the last time that you got so excited about the forgiveness of Jesus Christ in your own life that you invited somebody else to experience it. When? Most of us were brought to Christ first by the faith of somebody else. When have you invited a friend to meet Christ and experience the power of his forgiveness? Notice it was friends who brought this man to Jesus.

II. The passage is chiefly concerned about witnessing to the forgiving power of Christ. The scriptures demonstrate that the power was with him. This miracle is recorded in Matthew and Mark as well, to demonstrate the power that Christ has to forgive sins. For the New Testament writers, his claim was not one of blasphemy but a claim of his unique relationship to his Father. When you and I have experienced the forgiving grace of Christ, he becomes Lord to us, and God's spirit and presence ministers to us.

(a) Jesus, as recorded in this passage, asks for forgiveness for this young man's sinfulness. Some scholars have said that in some way this indicates the relationship of sin to illness. You and I must remember that in the Old Testament mind if a person was sick or had misfortune, that was a sign of sinfulness. Now today we do not regard all illness or misfortune as signs of sinfulness. But in the ancient days it was so regarded and Job struggled with that same kind of problem as his friends tried to press blame for his misfortune upon him. But there is no question that often some of our illness is psychosomatic. Sometimes illness is related to our own mental processes, our own nagging sense of guilt, our sense of resentment, our sense of jealousy, our sense of hatred, or to whatever kind of poison may be within our system that often literally does make us sick.

(b) Now do not hear me saying, please, that all illness is psychosomatic. That is not true. All illness is not in one's mind. But sometimes it is; and sometimes our physical problems are related to our own mental or emotional awareness of sins, guilt, frustrations, anger, jealousy, or whatever. Often, if they can be forgiven, released, and resolved, and relationships that have been broken are restored, then healing can take place.

III. Go further and notice that the passage indicates how strongly and how seriously Jesus takes sin. Now whether we identify completely the man's physical problem with his sinfulness, Jesus was seeking to attest to his power to forgive sins. Jesus took sin very seriously because he had seen what it had done to rupture relationships with people. Notice how often we take sin so flippantly today. We make light of it. We do not take it seriously. It becomes for us a joke until it becomes a personal problem and walks in our door or faces us across the table. We do not see the serious dimension of sin until it confronts us. But Jesus took sin very seriously.

IV. One of the central Biblical emphases about forgiveness is pardon. Jesus tells the young man that his sins are forgiven. In the story about Joseph, forgiveness is granted to the brothers even after the terrible deed that they had done to him. Forgiveness, however, is not always easy.

(a) Now there are experiences in your life and my life that we cannot undo, and the memory of them will always nag at us and haunt us. Tears from a broken heart overflow. But the ringing cry from the New Testament is that forgiveness is possible. Forgiveness provides a place of a new beginning. Forgiveness is a sense of pardon from God.

(b) The beautiful music that is sung throughout the New Testament is that God is a God of forgiveness. The New Testament church is founded on the work of Jesus Christ and his atoning grace that offers to us forgiveness and pardon. Sin and guilt are like a disease working in our life. Forgiveness brings healing and wholeness and overcomes the disease. Forgiveness is God's word that comes to us and says, "I give you another chance."

(c) The Church is telling us that God gives us another opportunity. We may botch something in our life but God comes to us and says there is a second chance. There is a new opportunity. There is forgiveness because God is a God of love and grace. "Rise, take up your pallet and go home." You have another chance at life.

(d) Luke is the only Gospel writer who gives us the version in which the young man left praising God. When the young man speaks, he praises God. Are you still praising God for the experience of forgiveness that he has given your life? Are you still marveling at the wonder of God's grace to us, such sinners we are? If you have experienced such amazing grace, then bring your friends so that they, too, might experience the marvelous grace of Christ.—William Powell Tuck.

Illustrations

HEALTH IN FORGIVENESS.   There was a woman in the hospital who all the doctors said was dying. All of them said that she would not live very long. Her illness could not be pinpointed, but they were certain she would not live long. While I was visiting her one day, she unloaded a great deal of the hatred that she had toward another person. We talked about it that day and for several days. Later she found a sense of forgiveness for the attitude that she had had toward another. Now I am going to be honest with you. I thought I was helping her to find some experience of forgiveness before she died. But the astonishing thing was that when she found that experience of forgiveness, she got well. To the surprise of her doctors and everybody, she left the hospital within a week and is still living today!—William Powell Tuck.

HE GAVE HIMSELF FOR ME.   Did you ever see yourself to be such a despicable creature that you wondered why all men did not spit upon you? You will understand the spitting scene [in the palace of Caiaphas] that night when God lets you see your own heart. There was no surplus shame; there was no scorn too much—the contumely was not one iota overdone that night. There was no unnecessary disgrace poured on Christ that night. He hid not his face from shame and from spitting for me! He loved me in my sin and my shame, and he gave himself for me!—Alexander Whyte.

Sermon Suggestions

THE PSALM OF PSALMS.   Text: Ps. 23. (1) God is our Shepherd, verses 1–4. The Lord *provides* green pastures, still pools— restoring our whole being. The Lord *guides* us in the right paths for the very honor of God. The Lord *comforts* us in our anxiety. (2) God is our Host, verses 5–6. We enjoy our Host's gracious hospitality. God's goodness and mercy pursue us. We will enjoy God's Presence: We will be where he is, forever.—Alton McEachern.

HOW DO YOU HEAR THE LORD.   Gospel Text: Luke 4:21–32. (1) With pleasure? (2) With interest? (3) With resistance? (4) With submission?

Worship Aids

CALL TO WORSHIP.   "Ye shall go out with joy, and be led forth with peace: the mountains and the hills shall break forth before you into singing, and all the trees of the field shall clap their hands" (Isa. 55:12).

INVOCATION.   God of mercy, we come to this place with expectation, believing that you will do good things for us here. We even dare hope, because of your promises, that we shall leave this place with the sense of sins forgiven, broken relationships restored, and new opportunities for service provided. So lead us by your Spirit into the truth about ourselves and the redeeming truth of your redeeming love.

OFFERTORY   SENTENCE.   "Bless the Lord, O my soul, and forget not all his benefits" (Ps. 103:2).

OFFERTORY PRAYER.   O God, you are ever giving good things to us, and we could never match your gifts. But you allow us to show our gratitude and imitate your caring as we bring to your storehouse our tithes and offerings. We bless your name and ask you to make our gifts a blessing.

PRAYER.   Lord God, we pray for peace to dwell in this place. We know peace can be here only if peace is in us who are gathered here. We know peace is not a product that can be purchased in a special store and placed on a peace platform for everyone to look at and bow down to. We know peace—true peace—is a gift and a relationship and an attitude.

We know you give us the peace we need and yearn for—the peace of the sinner with the sinless God—because in Christ, we have our Savior, who paid the price of our sins with his death on the cross, who is raised from the dead, who lives and reigns with you, at your right hand, so that we who are unacceptable are forgiven, renewed, restored.

Thanks to your love in Christ, we dare to call upon you, knowing you will hear us; we listen to you, knowing that when our hearts and minds are truly open to you, we will think some of your thoughts and discover some of your ways. You hate sin, yet you love each of us, great sinners one and all. You do forgive us. You do provide light in the midst of our chaos and confusion. You accept us as we are and change us as we need to be changed. You entrust some of your holy work to be done by sinners such as we. You invite us to your banquets, your festivals, your celebrations; you invite us to be citizens of your kingdom. You assure us that, through Christ, beyond our finite deaths there is life, life eternal and abundant and complete. What we in no way could do for ourselves, you have chosen in love to do for us. Such knowledge and assurance is too much for us! It brings us to our knees with heads bowed low; it gives us a full, healthy measure of humility; it provides us with every worthy reason to thank and praise you, and to run well the race of faith that others have run and that now you permit, even invite, us to run.

When we think of what you have done for us, our only acceptable thank you is gladly giving our lives to your service. When we think of what other people have done for us, being led by your spirit—the sacrifices they made, the nobility their lives proclaim, the principles they promoted, the burdens they carried, the hurdles they overcame, the hardships they endured, the quality of living they passed on to us who are living now—our only acceptable thank you is living in such a way that others will be blessed for good and toward God because you do accomplish a good work in us and through us.—Gordon H. Reif.

EVENING WORSHIP

Topic: One with Authority!
TEXT: Deut. 18:15–20; 2 Cor. 8:1–9; Mark 1:21–28.

I. We are enamored with authority, aren't we? We have become credentials-conscious. Training, schooling, graduations, accreditation, certification of various kinds are all attempts to answer "by what authority?"

(a) The folks of the first century were no different. They heard this new prophet, freshly baptized and newly tempted, and they at first asked about his authority. But as they listened, they sensed he had something rare and unique. For the other teachers of the law, the other scribes, rabbis, and assorted numbers of others who taught, would always quote their sources.

(b) It was almost as if Jesus had graduated from *quoting* authority to *being* authority. Jesus, increasing in wisdom and stature and in favor with God and man, stopped quoting Rabbi Eleazer and became his own authority. And everyone who heard him sensed that he had a power that was inherent within him.

II. But so what?

(a) His authority, as powerful as it was (and is) is not much without followers to acknowledge, spread, and live by his authoritative principles. And that is why in and around the edges of this passage he is calling and instructing and training his disciples, his followers. Orders without obedience are shouts in the wind. Authority without announcers is hidden and unknown. Power without its personal purveyors is nil.

(b) His authority needed obedience then. And it needs action now. Authority and action are parts of one another. Authority must issue forth in action. Action must be consistent with the authority that calls it forth. Hypocrisy is when the authority we claim has no consistent action.

(c) He really has no authority in our world except through us. We *are* the Body of Christ. Not all of it, but part of it, and if you and I decide not to respond, the part of the Body we are atrophies, withers, dies.—Thomas H. Conley.

SUNDAY: FEBRUARY NINTH

MORNING WORSHIP

Topic: The Perfect Life
TEXT: 2 Cor. 3:18.

God is all for quality; man is for quantity. But the immediate need of the world at this moment is not more of us but, if I may use the expression, a better brand of us. There is such a thing in the evangelistic sense as winning the whole world and losing our own soul. And the first considera-

tion is our own life—our own likeness to Christ. And I am anxious, briefly, to look at the right and wrong way of becoming like Christ—of becoming better men.

The verse I refer to is 2 Corinthians 3:18: "We all, with unveiled face, reflecting in a mirror the glory of the Lord, are changed into the same image from glory to glory even as by the Lord, the Spirit."

I. "We are *changed*." The mistake we have been making is that we have been trying to change ourselves. That is not possible. We *are changed* into the same image.

(a) The condition is that we reflect in a mirror the glory of Christ. The glory of Christ is in character. Do not be misled by the vagueness of that word *glory* in modern usage. We lose the force of it because we do not employ the word in current speech. When it is in your mind, substitute *character* for *glory*. "We are all, with unveiled face, reflecting in a mirror the character of Christ, are changed into the same image from character to character"—from the character a little better to the character a little better still, the character getting nobler and nobler by slight and imperceptible degrees.

(b) How to get character: Stand in Christ's presence and mirror his character, and you will be changed in spite of yourself, into the same image from character to character.

II. What, then, is the practical lesson? It is obvious. *Make Christ your most constant companion.*

(a) Five minutes spent in the companionship of Christ every morning—aye, two minutes, if it is face to face and heart to heart—will change the whole day, will make every thought and feeling different, will enable you to do things for his sake that you would not have done for your own sake, or for anyone's sake.

(b) Let me say a word or two about the effects that necessarily must follow from this contact, or fellowship, with Christ. The moment you assume that relation to Christ you begin to know what the child-spirit is. You stand before Christ, and he becomes your Teacher, and you instinctively become docile. Then you learn also to become charitable and tolerant; because you are learning of him, and he is "meek and lowly in heart," and you catch that spirit. That is a bit of his character being reflected into yours.

(c) The way to trust Christ is to know Christ. You cannot help trusting him then. You are changed. The way, therefore, to increase our faith is to increase our intimacy with Christ. We trust him more and more the better we know him.

III. And then another immediate effect

of this way of sanctifying the character is the tranquility that it brings over the Christian life. How disturbed and distressed and anxious Christian people are about their growth in grace! Now, the moment you give that over into Christ's care —the moment you see that you are *being* changed—that anxiety passes away. You see that it must follow by an inevitable process and by a natural law if you fulfill the simple condition; so that peace is the reward of that life and fellowship with Christ. Peace is not a thing that comes down solid, as it were, and is fitted somehow into a man's nature. We have very gross conceptions of peace, joy, and other Christian experiences; but they are all simply effects and causes. We fulfill the condition; we cannot help the experiences following.

IV. What a prospect! To be changed into the same image. Think of that! That is what we are here for. That is what we are elected for. Not to be saved, in the common acceptance, but "whom He did foreknow He also did predestinate to be conformed to the image of His Son." Not merely to be saved, but *to be conformed to the image of His Son.* Conserve that principle. And as we must spend time in cultivating our earthly friendships if we are to have their blessings, so we must spend time in cultivating the fellowship and companionship of Christ. And there is nothing so much worth taking into our lives as a more profound sense of what is to be had by living in communion with Christ and by getting nearer to him. And then as we go forth, men will take knowledge of us, that we have been with Jesus, and as we reflect him upon them, they will begin to be changed into the same image.—Henry Drummond.

Illustrations

DOING THE IMPOSSIBLE.   John Henry Jowett told of an epitaph that he found on a tombstone in a small church cemetery in a tiny village. A local woman who had spent her life recklessly in service was remembered by the words "SHE HATH DONE WHAT SHE COULDN'T." Her actions were a commmentary on the commitment of her life. What we give or do not give makes a statement about our real priorities, too.—Roger Lovette.

BEYOND DUTIES AND RULES. Though Christianity seems at first to be all about morality, all about duties and rules and guilt and virtue, yet it leads you on, out of all that, into something beyond. One has a glimpse of a country where they do not talk of these things, except perhaps as a joke. Everyone there is filled with what we should call goodness, as a mirror is filled with light. But they don't call it goodness. They don't call it anything. They are not thinking of it. They are too busy looking at the source from which it comes. But this is near the stage where the road passes over the rim of our world. No one's eyes can see very far beyond that.—C. S. Lewis.

Sermon Suggestions

WHEN LOVE PREVAILS. Text: Luke 6: 27–38. (1) The demands on us are difficult. (2) The example for us is inspiring. (3) The rewards to us are astonishing.—James W. Cox.

HOW TO SUCCEED IN EVANGELISM. Luke 5:1–11. (1) In our own wisdom we fail. (2) By the Lord's wisdom we are challenged. (3) When we obey the Lord, we succeed.

Worship Aids

CALL TO WORSHIP. "Ye shall be holy: for I the Lord your God am holy" (Lev. 19:2).

INVOCATION. O God of perfect goodness, give us today a vision of your true self, that we might be renewed by your forgiving love and challenged by your demanding righteousness.

OFFERTORY SENTENCE. "Now as you excel in everything—in faith, in utterance, in knowledge, in all earnestness, and in your love for us—see that you excel in this gracious work also" (2 Cor. 8:7, RSV).

OFFERTORY PRAYER. Our Father, in this time of offering, grant that we may translate our spiritual gifts into worthy tokens of your grace, to the end that what we are may be reproduced in the lives and service of all those who are touched by what we are and do.

PRAYER. O Lord our God! We come into thy presence with the heartfelt request that thou wilt accept us, granting us no rest until we are willing to rest in thee —that thou wilt fight against us and for us until thy peace reigns in our hearts, our thoughts, and conversation, in our very being and in our living together. Without thee we can do nothing; with thee and in thy service we can do all things.

Be present and active today, especially everywhere where thy church gathers together. Be with the sick and dying, all who are destitute, oppressed, or have gone astray, so also with those who rule, who mould public opinion and hold in their hands the means of power. Pour out thy love to oppose rampant hate, thy reason to oppose unreason; oh, that from thee might flow not merely a trickle but a torrent of justice to oppose so much injustice! But thou knowest better than we what is best for us and the world—ultimately destined, as it is, for thy glory.—Karl Barth.

EVENING SERVICE

Topic: The Essence of Christian Character

TEXT: 1 Cor. 13:1–3.

I. Paul is not alone in his powerful stand in support of the essential quality of love for the Christian life. Can you imagine, or perhaps you may have experienced, work without love, marriage without love, parenthood without love, power without love, law without love, or the church or a god without love? Paul suggests to us that the highest Christian virtues are null and void apart from love. Not that the gifts of the Spirit in speech, in prophecy, understanding, knowledge, and faith are small or unimportant, but they do not stand alone! The essence of Christian character is the deep well of God's love for us, expressed through us.

II. This revelation is strange because it

reveals what we already know. If we could love one another, we could end the problems of crime, war, divorce, and perhaps even a whole catalog of physical and emotional illness. When Jesus brought together Leviticus 19:18 and Deuteronomy 6:5 in answer to the question of the greatest commandment, he was saying nothing new. Perhaps he was speaking in terms of a new possibility. The problem is not so much our awarensss of the essential quality and power of love but our ability or will to be loving.

III. Paul's hymn is not a "how-to" instruction kit on the art of Christian love so much as it is a call to priority and a word of identity for God's kind of love. At bottom, this is our greatest need. The practical element in the poetry is locating the starting line. To a church that is torn by conflict and competition, immaturity and immorality, Paul identifies the essential quality in the Christian life. The Corinthians are so intense on elevating themselves to greatness that they have missed the first step. Not unlike the Twelve contending for the best seats in the kingdom of God, these Christians forgot the meaning of true greatness. In the kingdom of God, which is not so far removed from the human world in which we strive, Christian love makes the difference between being and nothing.

IV. The hymn still sounds a clear and relevant note in our lives. We do not suffer from a lack of talent. Even in the area of Christian graces, we are a gifted people. Of all of the ages of humankind, we are the best equipped, the best educated, and the most powerful, yet we continue to sound like a noisy gong or a clanging cymbal.— Larry Dipboye.

SUNDAY: FEBRUARY SIXTEENTH

MORNING SERVICE

Topic: Getting in Touch with Your Self
TEXT: Gen. 3:22–32; Luke 15:17.

The story of Jacob at the brook called Jabbok is one of the greatest stories of all literature. During the night, a stranger came and wrestled with him. They struggled for hours, heaving and grunting and sighing. "What is your name?" asked the stranger. "Jacob," he answered, with none of the deception of years ago. Jacob tried to get the stranger's name, the way we try to hold a dream that is fleeting, but the stranger was gone, and Jacob said, "I have seen God face to face."

Do you see the human drama in that? A man has worked hard all his life, building a fortune and establishing a dynasty. But he is restless and ill at ease, and wants to get in touch with his roots again. He comes back home, and in a night of fear and desperation, has a dream or an experience that cuts to the very core of who he is. And when it is over, it is as though heaven itself has touched him and shown him the future. "I have seen God face to face."

I. We do get out of touch with ourselves and our pasts, don't we? The days come and go, the years pile up, and we lose contact.

(a) Being out of touch with our selves eventually makes us sick. Some of us become greedy and rapacious. Others become bitter and resentful and even violent. We become unnatural selves, selves that don't behave the way selves ought to behave.

(b) Sometimes, if we are fortunate, something happens to bring us back to our selves. An illness. An accident. The loss of a job. Failure in school. The breakdown of a marriage. An insight grasped in the theater or in church or in reading a book. A sense of desperation, like that experienced by the young prodigal when he finally "came to himself" and decided to go home.

II. The Bible does not hesitate to brand such experiences of getting in touch as spiritual. Something of a spiritual nature occurs when we manage to break through the clutter of our lives and make contact again with our deeper selves. "I have seen God face to face," said Jacob when it happened to him. It is like coming home to the Father, said Jesus in his story of the prodigal son.

(a) In a sense, Jesus' whole ministry was an invitation to people to get in touch with their truest selves again. We must become like little children to enter the kingdom of heaven, he said—that is, we must get back beyond the complications and paraphernalia of existence to the innocence and joy of our simpler selves. To some, this is threatening. They are afraid of getting in touch. So people opposed Jesus. They hid behind law and tradition, and denied their feelings. And finally they crucified him so he would stop reminding them of their truest selves.

(b) Jacob's name was changed in his encounter. It had been Jacob, which meant "supplanter." Not a good name. A name implying trickery and deceit. It became Israel—"prince of God." And that too is the way it is with all of us who get in touch with ourselves at the deepest levels. We find out that we are princes and princesses of God. Sons and daughters of the Most High.

(c) How about you? Are you in touch with your self? If you aren't, there is no better time to get in touch than right now. The angel of God is probably wrestling with you at your own fording place, your own personal Jabbok. And the blessing only comes after you wrestle.—John Killinger.

Illustrations

NO MORE FEAR.   Amy was the rich child of divorced parents. Her mother, needing to blame someone besides herself for the divorce, blamed Amy. When Amy was only three, her mother threatened to cut her into stew meat. Amy was terrified and hid under the bed. As a young woman, Amy married a wealthy man and went everywhere in a chauffeur-driven Rolls Royce. She was divorced and remarried, this time into the European jet set. There was nothing she wanted she could not have—except peace of mind. She developed painful, crippling arthritis. It became so bad that she had to have both arms in a sling, and her daughters combed her hair and fed her. The psychiatrists said it was psychosomatic, induced by a sense of guilt for her mother's unhappy life. Her European husband tired of her illness and divorced her for another woman. Alone, broken in health, and miserable, she had a conversion experience. Then, as a sense of God's forgiveness flooded over her, her body began to overcome the arthritis. She felt renewed as a person, in touch with herself again.

She went back to the house where she had lived as a little girl and entered her old bedroom. There was the bed under which she had hidden when she thought her mother was going to cut her up into little pieces. She sat on the bed and a mysterious thing occurred. She had the feeling that she was sitting in God's lap and he was rocking her as his little girl, and she heard him say, "Amy, you don't ever have to fear again."—John Killinger.

THE DIVINE CALL.   Who has ever given up a privilege without being forced to do so, except in response to a spiritual call? In his search to discover the motive forces of human behavior, Freud saw at first only the pleasure principle. Everyone has now recognized the important role that the principle plays in all human actions, from the most selfish to the most generous. But it is impossible to satisfy all one's desires in this world, and Freud himself recognized and described a second principle, that of reality. Reason, it says, bowing to the limitations of reality, imposes renunciation of unattainable desires. What escaped Freud was that there is a third principle, the divine call, which leads to quite other renunciations. —Paul Tournier.

Sermon Suggestions

HOW TO BECOME A CHRISTIAN.   Text: Acts 19:23. Simply, believe in Christ.

(1) Credit the historic record of his life. (2) Believe that Jesus was what he claimed to be. (3) Believe that Jesus did what he said he came into the world to do. (4) Believe that Christ means precisely what he says: "Him that cometh unto me, I will in no wise cast out."—David James Burrell.

LED BY THE SPIRIT, TEMPTED BY THE DEVIL. Gospel Text: Luke 4:1–13. (1) Bread is good, but not ultimate. (2) Power is necessary, but not without perils. (3) Trust in God is obligatory, but not without presumptions.

Worship Aids

CALL TO WORSHIP. "Behold, the Lord's hand is not shortened, that it cannot save; neither his ear heavy, that it cannot hear" (Isa. 59:1).

INVOCATION. As thou art reaching out toward us, as thou art listening for our cries, give us grace to confess our sins, trust thy love, obey thy will, and in true worship praise and glorify thy matchless name.

OFFERTORY SENTENCE. "If you will obey my voice and keep my covenant, you shall be my own possession among all peoples; for all the earth is mine, and you shall be to me a kingdom of priests and a holy nation" (Exod. 19:5–6).

OFFERTORY PRAYER. We thank thee, O God, that thou hast given to us, thy people, a special role on earth—thy earth. May we fulfill thy purpose by our prayers, our offerings, and our very lives, so that thy truth and love may be known by people everywhere.

PRAYER. Walk with us, O God, in the plain paths where the day-by-day routine settles down to a test of private perseverance, unheralded by the accolade of praise or bright reward. If the heavenly vision grows dim and our hearts are weary in well doing, lay thy hand upon us and steady our steps that we may press onward, even in darkness, toward the light ahead. If we are alone and the task seems more than we can do, or if done, not at all welcomed by the world, reveal thy presence at our side that we may labor with thy help. Turn us from the dreams of far glory to work in the commonplace circumstances of this mortal world, and disclose to us the miracle of thy grace in unexpected places. Even so, may thy will be done on earth as it is in heaven, through Jesus Christ our Lord.— Samuel H. Miller.

EVENING SERVICE

Topic: We Must Confront Evil
TEXT: Matt. 5:29.
Jesus spoke with disturbing clarity on the matter of evil. To be rid of it, we must do something about it. No one has ever conquered anything by evasion. We want here to confront ourselves with the subtle ways in which we are blinding ourselves to this fact of evil.

I. To begin with, we are constantly endeavoring to be rid of it by romanticizing it.

(a) The matter of juvenile delinquency is a fertile illustration. Now delinquency is real. It is a bitter fact that is giving concern to all who are in any way related to youth. We believe that by calling it youthful buoyancy we have softened it. We believe that by saying that adolescence is carving out a new future for itself we have rationalized it. We have done nothing of the sort. After all our romanticizing, glamorizing, and rationalizing, the evil is still here.

(b) It is only a stone's throw from delinquency to divorce. Both are frequently cradled in lack of personal discipline. Now divorce is assuming dangerous proportions. The American home is being torn to pieces. The moral and social foundations upon which we have stood in the past are being broken asunder. How will you glamorize that?

(c) It is only a short step from delinquency and divorce to moral and spiritual indifference. There is a heartrending relationships among these three. We have glamorized spiritual indifference by saying that everyone has the right to live his own life, that we have no leave to foist our opinions upon others, and that morality and religion are matters of personal decision and personal convenience. The results of this so-called broadmindedness and generosity of spirit have been a decay in the character of our people.

II. Look now at another way in which we have endeavored to rid ourselves of this ugly fact of evil. We have sought to do it by giving evil an intellectual aspect.

(a) We have been clever in this matter. We have spoken of evil as aberration, or abnormality, or more often as simple maladjustment. In doing this, we believed that the stain of ugliness had been removed from evil.

(b) There is a moral paralysis that the physician cannot cure. There is a distortion of intention that no neurologist can untwist. There is a sinfulness that no psychology in the world can explain away. It simply will not do to change the creed from "I believe in the forgiveness of sins" to "I believe in the forgiveness of abnormality."

III. We have a third method of escaping from the reality of evil. We clothe it as the new freedom.

(a) We have pictured ourselves as brave men and women bent on a grand adventure in new living. We have eulogized this so-called freedom by claiming that new men in a new generation must divorce themselves from the silly conventions of a less enlightened day and that they must discard the annoying restrictions of discredited religious codes.

(b) But see what has happened to us. In our endeavor to find freedom, we have toppled over whole traditions, and we have discarded the hard-earned moral values of our people. All moral values have been dearly bought and in our careless crying for freedom, these moral values—bought with poverty, sweat, blood, and broken hearts—are being discarded.

(c) In the end, when we are free from these conventions and restrictions, from what are we free? These people who are so free, are they not prisoners of their desires, prisoners of time, prisoners of little things? This new freedom has given us neither freedom nor dignity. In this day we need to relearn the fundamental principles that there cannot be freedom without discipline.

(d) Now we are in a way becoming an undisciplined generation. We must confess that a gospel of unyoked individualism is gripping our hearts. We want what we want when we want it. We give free bent to our emotions. The fruit of it all is unhappiness within ourselves and conflict within society.

(e) So, in the end, after all our subtle and clever ways to disguise evil, it is still with us. If we really want to be rid of it, we must learn to stand up to it. We must take seriously the counsel of Jesus, "If thine eye offend thee, pluck it out." This, to be sure, is a severe remedy, but it is this remedy and health or it is something else—and what this something else is all of us know deep in our hearts.—Arnold W. Lowe.

SUNDAY: FEBRUARY TWENTY-THIRD

MORNING SERVICE

Topic: Six Ways to Tell Right from Wrong

TEXT: 1 Tim. 1:12–13.

Our thought starts with the plain fact that it is not always easy to tell the difference between right and wrong. Today I propose talking about this matter with homely practicality to my own soul and to yours. So this morning I invite you to no airplaine trip into the lofty blue but to a practical land journey as we set up six homely guideposts to the good life.

I. In the first place, if a man is sincerely perplexed about a question of right and wrong, he might well submit it to the test of *common sense*.

(a) Suppose that someone should challenge you to a duel. What would you say? I would advise you to say "Don't be silly!" As a matter of historic fact, dueling, which was once a serious point of conscientious honor, was not so much argued out of existence as laughed out. The common sense of mankind rose up against it, saying "Don't be silly!" So Jesus, in his parable of the rich man who accumulated outward things but cared nothing for the inward wealth of the spiritual life did not say "Sinner!" but "Fool!"—"Thou fool, this night thy soul shall be required of thee: then whose shall those things be, which thou hast provided?"

(b) What we are saying now is that this is a healthy thing for a man to say to his own soul before somebody else has to say it to him. That is the first test and—alas!

—twenty years from now somebody here this morning, listening to this and paying no heed to it, will be looking back on life and saying bitterly, "God be merciful to me, a fool!"

II. In the second place, if a man is sincerely perplexed about a question of right and wrong, he may well submit it to the test of *sportsmanship*.

(a) Now, the essence of sportsmanship is that in a game we do not take for ourselves special favors that we deny to other players but, making the rules equal for all, abide by them. In daily life that means that a man should always consider what the results would be if everybody acted on the same principle as he does.

(b) The golden rule, my friends, is a grand test. Husband and wife, parents and children, employers and employees, black and white, prosperous and poor, Occident and Orient—what if we did not cheat? What if we did as we would be done by? What if we played the game?

III. In the third place, if a man is sincerely perplexed about a question of right and wrong, he may well submit it to the test of *his best self*.

(a) Notice, I do not say to his conscience, for the conscience merely urges us to do right without telling us what the right is, but deeper than conscience and more comprehensive is this other matter, a man's best self. For, of course, no one of us is a single self. How much simpler life would be if we only were! There is a passionate self, reaching out hungrily for importunate sensations, good, bad, and indifferent. There is the careless self taking anything that comes along, excellent and vulgar, fine and cheap. There is the greedy self in whose eyes an egoistic want blots out all the wide horizons of humanity beside. But deeper than all these is that inner self where dwells the light that, as the Fourth Gospel says, lighteth every man coming into the world.

(b) Be sure of this, that if, in large ways or small, any one of us does help to ennoble our society and build a better nation for our children and their children to be born into, it will be because we have taken our secret ambitions up to the tribunal of our finest self. There *is* something in us

like a musician's taste, which discriminates harmony from discord. There *is* something in us like a bank teller's fingers, which distinguish true money from counterfeit.

IV. In the fourth place, if a man is sincerely perplexed over a matter of right and wrong, he may well submit the question to the test of *publicity*.

(a) What if everybody knew what we are proposing to do? Strip it of secrecy and furtiveness. Carry it out into the open air, this conduct we are unsure about. Suppose our family and friends knew about it. Imagine it publicly talked of whenever our name is mentioned. Picture it written in the story of our life for our children afterwards to read. Submit it to the test of publicity. Anybody who knows human life with its clandestine behavior understands what a searching and healthy test this is.

(b) Things that cannot stand sunlight are not healthful. There is a test for a perplexed conscience. How many here do you suppose would be affected by it? Imagine your behavior public.

V. In the fifth place, if a man is perplexed about a question of right and wrong, he may well submit it to the test of *his most admired personality*.

(a) Carry it up into the light of the life that you esteem most and test it there. My friends, it is the beauties and the personalities that we positively have loved that set for us the tests and standards of our lives. Why is it, then, that conduct that seems to some people right seems to some of us cheap and vulgar, selfish and wrong? It is because for years we have known and adored the Christ. There is a test for a perplexed conscience. Carry your behavior up into the presence of the Galilean and judge it there.

(b) If someone protests that he does not propose to subjugate his independence of moral judgment to any authority, not even Christ's, I answer, "What do you mean by authority?" There are all kinds of authorities—ecclesiastical, creedal, external, artificial—against the imposition of whose control on mind and conscience I would as vigorously fight as you. But there is one kind of authority for which I hunger, the insight of the seers.

VI. In the sixth place, if a man is perplexed about a question of right and wrong, he may well submit it to the test of *foresight*.

(a) Where is this course of behavior coming out? All good life, my friends, depends upon the disciplining of clamorous and importunate desires in the light of a long look. We Christians who are trying to be intelligent long since gave up our belief in hell, but one suspects that many of us, throwing over the incredible and picturesque impossibilities of that belief, have dropped also a basic truth that our forefathers carried along in it. Every man who picks up one end of a stick picks up the other. Aye! Every man who chooses one end of a road is choosing the other. Aye! Every course of behavior has not only a place where it begins but a place where it comes out.

(b) We really do not need to be so perplexed about right and wrong as we sometimes are. To be sure, there is nothing infallible about all this. Goodness is an adventure and "time makes ancient good uncouth." Nevertheless, the test of common sense, of sportsmanship, of the best self, the test of publicity, of our most admired personality, of foresight—these are sensible, practical, high-minded ways to tell right from wrong. I call you to witness that in all this I have not been imposing on you a code of conduct; I have been appealing to your own best moral judgment. Alas for a man who neglects that! For though, as in Paul's case, one may come out at last to a good life, it is a bitter thing to have to look back and say, a blasphemer, and a persecutor, and injurious—such was I—ignorantly.—Harry Emerson Fosdick.

Illustrations

USING GOD. There is no nausea on earth like that which is provoked by the hackneyed churchy chirps that herald readiness for whatever form of wickedness may be in the offing: "God will provide"; "The Lord is with us"; "I feel guided to accept the challenge"; "As a God-fearing man I am reluctantly forced to the conclusion that my duty is . . . ." The more diabolical the evil proposed, the more needful it is, of course, to invite God's public patronage of it.—Geddes MacGregor.

MOTIVATION. Charles Allen tells of his boyhood days and playing baseball. He relates, particularly, a tight game in which he got a long hit. He said: "I was running around the bases as fast as I could, but I seemed to gain added strength when I heard (my father) shouting above the crowd, 'Come on home, Charles, come on home.'"—C. Neil Strait.

Sermon Suggestions

MAXIMUM LIVING. Text: Luke 6:38. (1) There is no realm in which the danger of the minimum becoming the maximum is greater or more disastrous than that of religious faith. What we should bring is not a maximum of credulity but of venture, of personal response to the best we have known. (2) This maximum-minimum scale comes close to us in our relation to people. It is a truly Royal Journey to go from a spare minimum to a maximum in the sharing of ourselves with others, not as an obligation but as a direct way into the abundant life.—Halford E. Luccock.

WHO WILL BE SAVED. Gospel Text: Luke 13:22–30. (1) The desire for salvation. (2) The terms of salvation. (3) The recipients of salvation.

Worship Aids

CALL TO WORSHIP. "O send out thy light and thy truth: let them lead me" (Ps. 43:3).

INVOCATION. As we meet to worship thee, O God, we look to thee to dispel the darkness that lurks in our hearts, the folly by which we so often let ourselves be guided. Chart our paths for us and shine upon our ways with true wisdom.

OFFERTORY SENTENCE. "Blessed are they that do his commandments, that they may have right to the tree of life" (Rev. 22:14).

OFFERTORY PRAYER. Our Father, you have created us; you have watched over us with love all our days; you have opened to us the gates of new and abundant life. Grant that in our living and in our giving we may be guided not by law but by love.

PRAYER. We thank you for the four seasons, for winter's own reasons holding us close to home, close to life's pulse of death and life, life's bare-branched clarity and simplicity, baring to us even our breath; where your cold knows no pity, no warmer, wind-hidden side. Warm then your own the more with creaturely caring the one for the other.

We pray for people behind bars. We thank you for ministries to them. Make us a little more a force for good, a voice of reason; as citizens just and humane, as a people of God, fellow thieves of the goodness of God, in the same boat, glad to help.

Rehabilitate us all from any Roman circus spirit of thumbs down and from sin that does beset us every one.—Peter Fribley.

EVENING SERVICE

Topic: The Privacy of Piety
TEXT: Matt. 6:1–6, 16–18.

It's tough going in the private world of piety. Others may not understand what you are doing, or that you're even doing anything. And you, yourself, may at times not understand what you're doing, or if you're "doing" anything.

I. What is it about piety that requires privacy? Jesus' words here remind us that there is always the danger of hypocrisy in pious acts done publicly. Goodness harbors a tendency to hide from being seen or heard, lest it become tainted with self-righteousness. When goodness appears openly, it is no longer goodness, although it may still be useful as organized charity or as an act of solidarity.

II. Lent is a time of piety. And so, it is essentially a private time. How will we remain faithful to our private Lenten practices? We may make promises to ourselves to pray more, but who will remind us to keep them? Jesus' words here in Matthew

remind us: In our privacy is the God who sees in secret. God is present in our private moments. In fact, it is God's presence that transforms loneliness to solitude. In the privacy of our piety, we are not alone. We are known and loved by God who sees in secret.

(a) What is God like? Are we sure that we want to share our privacy with God? Does God become like some inescapable parent who holds us accountable for the things we said we would do in Lent? Does God become a heavenly taskmaster? Jesus says three times in our Gospel passage, "Your Father who sees you in secret will reward you." Your God, Father and Mother, will reward you. Jesus does not say, "Your Father, who sees you in secret, will badger you." No, the promise that is held up is that of a reward.

(b) Lent is a funny time. We tend to think that in Lent we are going to give God something. But, does God need anything? Perhaps Lent is yet another time when God seeks to give to us. We know that God gives to us at Easter, at Pentecost, at Christmas. Isn't Lent that time when we try to even up the tally? Jesus' words, however, confound our reflex to even the score. When we pray, when we fast—God returns, God gives back. If we think of Lent as a time of making recompense to God, Jesus reminds us here, it can't be done. Each time we seek to give to God, God gives back, rewards us even more.

III. These are the promises of the private encounter with God. God will meet us, changing loneliness to solitude. God will hear our prayers, see our giving, visit our acts of piety. And God will answer our giving with God's own giving to us. Although piety and goodness may seem fragile in their inherent secrecy, God will be our witness. And though the solitariness of prayer may seem threatening and unknown, God will be our guide. God will be the touchstone, too big to hold, the wellspring, too gushing to dam up, the reality too present to describe in words. These are the promises of God.

(a) There is an essential, private quality to the practices of Lent. The practice of charity, of prayer, of potential acts like fasting—all require a kind of secrecy to preserve them from the dangers of hypocrisy. But they also require the secrecy of solitude with God. Without God's witness, charity, prayer, and penance may seem unreal or meaningless. Without God's presence at our side, we have cut ourselves off from the wellspring of charity, of prayer, of penance. God is the essential companion in the privacy of piety.

(b) And God is the essential companion in making sense of what Lent is all about. To understand the gift of Christ's death and resurrection, we must go to the *gift*-giver. We must enter the privacy of solitude with God, for understanding the meaning, the reality, of the crucifixion and resurrection.—Joanne M. Swenson.

SUNDAY: MARCH SECOND

MORNING SERVICE

Topic: Finding God in Unlikely Places
TEXT: Exod. 3:5.

This morning we study the kind of person who, in difficult situations, does not lose God but finds him. We start far from here, out in the wilderness of Sinai some thirty-two centuries ago, where Moses, facing a desperate situation, heard the divine voice say: "The place whereon thou standest is holy ground." He was in an unpromising place, and it was news to him when amid the sagebrush and the sand, the arresting message came that *that* was holy ground.

Far from being merely thirty-two centuries old, that scene is here in this congregation now. We find God in life's lovely things. Yes! God is in life's lovely things, but sooner or later all of us come to the place where, if we are to find God at all, we must find him in a wilderness. Today we all need that insight. Not only does life land each of us in an unpromising situation, but our whole era is tragic, desperately tragic. How does one find God here? Yet some of the most momentous discoveries of God in history have been made in just such situations.

I. What went on inside Moses that made possible his discovery of holy ground in the wilderness?

(a) First, he found something to be angry at. He had been brought up as the son of Pharaoh's daughter, living a soft life, a playboy, it may be, at the royal court, but as maturity came on he began to be angry. How he must have fought against it, this disturbing indignation against something intolerably wrong, the slavery of his people! The more he grew up, however, the angrier it made him, until one day, seeing a Hebrew slave beaten by an Egyptian taskmaster, he was so incensed that he slew the taskmaster.

That was foolish. That did no good, but at least it could no longer be said that Moses was a playboy. He was angry at something unbearably wrong. That was the beginning of the real Moses. His anger needed harnessing, but it was basic to all that followed.

Need I expand the application of this to ourselves? Look at our world! It is hard to find God here, we say. Well, we can start. We can see the evil here that ought to arouse our indignation. We can see the everlasting right here calling for our backing and support. We can at least quit our moral apathy and wake up to the momentous issues of right and wrong in our community, our city, our nation.

(b) This start, however, led him to a second stage: Moses in the wilderness confronted Moses. He had never had such a searching look at himself before. To confront oneself in a wilderness, to be told that there is divine opportunity is a soul-searching experience. Tackle yourself, God said to Moses.

Of course, Moses at first backed off from that. Who was he to do anything about the Egyptian situation? He shrank from God's formidable call at first, but not finally. He *confronted* himself until he *dedicated* himself. He found his vocation in the wilderness. That is the gist of it. By God's help, he would be Moses. A divine voice had said to him in a wilderness, "The place whereon thou standest is holy ground."

(c) God is saying that to someone here

today about some situation—personal, domestic, social, national. It is dreadful, we may be thinking. Yes, but if a situation is dreadful, then there is need. Tragedy is simply need spelled with different letters, and so opportunity to help is there. So the great souls have found holy ground in unlikely places; they have found their vocation there.

II. We come to grips with our central theme, however, when we follow Moses' experience to a deeper level. In this encounter with right against wrong, in this self-dedication for his people's sake, he came face to face with God. Whatever may have been his idea of God, it is clear from the record that he had not in the least expected to meet his God there. What kind of situation was that in which to encounter God?

(a) Many of us are precisely in that state of mind. We habitually talk of God in terms of love, beauty, goodness so that when we face a situation in our personal experience or in the world at large where love, beauty, goodness are singularly absent, we lose all sense of God. "Where is he?" we ask. If the *only* God a man has is a God who thus is seen in the lovely things of life, then when he finds himself in some tough, dismaying experience in a desert where beauty, goodness, and loveliness are absent, where has his God gone? In days like these I need the God who encountered Moses in the wilderness.

As a matter of historical fact, some of the most memorable encounters with God in history have been of that type: Moses in the desert; the great Isaiah in Babylon; Job, out of his tragic calamity. As for the New Testament, there is Calvary. My soul! Crucifixion is not lovely. Who, casually looking on, would have thought God there? But countless millions since, with hushed and grateful hearts, have seen that Calvary was holy ground. It is no accident, I tell you, that man thus finds in tragic situations some of his profoundest insights into the divine. Soft occasions do not bring out the deepest in a man—never!

(b) I do not know where this truth hits you but for myself, now in my elder years, I bear my witness. My deepest faith in God

springs not so much from my Galilees, where God clothed the lilies so that "Solomon in all his glory was not arrayed like one of these," but from times when the rain descended and the floods came and the winds blew and beat, and God was there so that the house fell not. You know the familiar argument that the world is such a mess, its evil so senseless and brutal, that we cannot believe in God. Well, the world's evil is a great mystery. It raises questions that none of us can answer, but over against the souls who because of the wilderness surrender faith in God, I give you today the souls who found him in the wilderness. They are a great company.

III. Now a brief final word. When any man thus finds God in unlikely places, one may be fairly sure that he first found God in some likely places. Some beauty touched his life, some love blessed him, some goodness made him aware of God. If you have that chance now to discover the divine, don't miss it! It's not easy to find God in unlikely places. Start now by finding him in a likely place. Beauty, goodness, loveliness are here, nobility of character, unselfish sacrifice, moral courage, and lives through which a divine light shines like the sun through eastern windows. And Christ is here too, full of grace and truth, in whom we see the light of the knowledge of the glory of God. Find God in these likely places that you may find him in the unlikely places too.—Harry Emerson Fosdick.

Illustrations

THE WIT TO WIN.   Our strength grows out of our weakness. The indignation that arms itself with secret forces does not awaken until we are pricked and stung and sorely assailed. A great man is always willing to be little. Whilst he sits on the cushion of advantages, he goes to sleep. When he is pushed, tormented, defeated, he has a chance to learn something; he has been put on his wits, on his manhood; he has gained facts, learns his ignorance, is cured of the insanity of conceit, has got moderation and real skill. The wise man throws himself on the side of his assailants. It is more his interest than it is theirs to find his weak point. . . . In general, every evil to which we do not succumb is a benefactor. —Ralph Waldo Emerson.

CREDO. I believe in the sun, even when it is not shining; I believe in love, even when I feel it not; I believe in God, even when he is silent. (Words found written on the wall of a cellar in Cologne after World War II.)—Geddes MacGregor, *The Sense of Absence*.

Sermon Suggestions

WHEN THE GUEST TURNED HOST. Text: Luke 10:38–42. (1) Martha intended him only to be a guest, but this could not be. (2) Christ came indeed to accept kindly hospitality but even more to bring his saving gifts. (3) Mary first sat at Christ's blessed table, and Martha no doubt soon followed.—R. C. H. Lenski.

"UNLESS YOU REPENT." Gospel Text: Luke 13:1–9. (1) A gracious call to conversion. (2) A merciful postponement of judgment.

Worship Aids

CALL TO WORSHIP. "And Jacob awoke out of his sleep, and he said, 'Surely the Lord is in this place; and I knew it not'" (Gen. 28:16).

INVOCATION. Almighty God, break through the hardheartedness of someone here today. Remove the scales from blind eyes. May we all know your presence in love, in goodness, and in power.

OFFERTORY SENTENCE. "What doth it profit, my brethren, though a man say he hath faith, and have not works? Can faith save him?" (James 2:14).

OFFERTORY PRAYER. Our Father, we know that there are many cries of need that go up every day and every hour— there are the lonely, the sick, the homeless, the prisoners, the poor; there are institutions that depend on our generosity; there are especially the spiritually destitute who need our love and the message of a Savior who cares and forgives. May our giving be a response of genuine faith that always comes to expression in action and not only in good wishes and prayers.

EVENING SERVICE

Topic: Sin and Forgiveness
TEXT: 1 John 1:8–10.

The apostle is making an earnest, vehement protest against living in sin, when one professes to be Christian. God is Light, and in him no darkness at all—to say therefore that we have fellowship with him and walk in darkness is to lie.

But here must arise in the mind of even the earnest Christian the thought that he has sinned, even though with all his efforts he has striven to walk only in the light. The apostle regards this state of mind and calls attention to the provision for pardon of our sins. In the midst of such arguments and precepts occurs the text.

Suppose one stood up before an audience such as this to speak of innocence and excellence and merited felicitation. How utopian! You would call him a fool or a maniac. But I come but to speak of sin and salvation. Hear then for your soul's salvation, hear for eternity.

I. The evils of denying that we are sinners.

(a) To do this is to deceive ourselves.

(1) Some foolishly make professions of sinless perfection.

(2) Unconverted men are often unwilling to face self-examination and delude themselves.

(3) It is a delusion. God's Word, here and elsewhere, declares we are sinners. Our own conscience condemns us. Some object here that their consciences do not condemn them. To some extent this may be true; the conscience may be stupefied and perverted through result of previous errors and misconduct. It is lamentable to be deceived about anything—most of all about this.

(b) To deny that we are sinners is to make God a liar.

(1) Because he has expressly and repeatedly declared it. In Romans, chapter 3, the Apostle Paul has gathered dark fragments from many a monument of wickedness

and combined them into one mournful mosaic, that he might give at least some faint representation of human guilt.

(2) All the arrangements of the plan of salvation presuppose the sin of men, of all men, of every man. Will you call God a liar? If not, then you are a sinner. Unless we are forgiven, we perish. Let us confess our sins—inwardly, as to God.

II. The provision God has made for our forgiveness.

(a) This is consistent with God's justice. This is through the mediation of Christ. Christ is our advocate, our propitiation.

(1) Is the vicarious death of Christ itself consistent with God's justice? Perfectly, when we remember that it was voluntary—"No man taketh it from me; I lay down my life of myself." All the noblest acts of heroism with which Christianity adorned have been of this character—self-sacrifice for others' good. Is his death capable of being accounted for on any other principle? Why could not this cup pass from him?

(2) Does Christ's propitiatory death re-move the obstacles to forgiveness? So God's Word declares in John 2:1, 2 and Romans 3:24–26. This atoning death manifests at once God's displeasure with transgression, and his mercy to the transgressor—condemns sin but saves the sinner. Thus if we confess our sins, we may be forgiven for Jesus' sake.

(b) But God is pledged that they shall be forgiven. It is of his mercy, his favor—gratitude so far as we are concerned—but he has pledged himself—his faithfulness to his promises is involved, his equity in fulfilling his engagements. These promises of God's Word, though they may be familiar, are hope of forgiveness.

Come then, to God! Do not deny that you are a sinner, but confess your sins and seek forgiveness. God's fidelity to his pledged Word is the assurance that he will forgive. Yea, will cleanse from all unrighteousness—will treat us at once as if we were not unrighteousness, and will gradually correct and remove our personal unrighteousness, until at last we shall be perfectly holy in heaven.—John A. Broadus.

SUNDAY: MARCH NINTH

MORNING SERVICE

Topic: Victory Over Death

TEXT: 1 Cor. 15:56, 57.

In this passage the idea of victory is brought to bear upon the most terrible of all—a Christian's enemies. It is faith here conquering in death.

I. That which makes it peculiarly terrible to die is asserted in this passage to be guilt. We lay a stress upon this expression—the sting. It is not said that sin is the only bitterness, but it is the sting that contains in it the venom of a most exquisite torture. And in truth, brethren, it is no mark of courage to speak lightly of human dying. It is mockery, brethren, for a man to speak lightly of that which he cannot know till it comes.

(a) Now the first cause that makes it a solemn thing to die is the instinctive cleaving of everything that lives to its own existence. It is the first and the intensest desire of living things, to be. Now it is with this intense passion for being that the idea of death clashes. Let us search why it is we shrink from death. This reason, brethren, we shall find, that it presents to us the idea of *not being*. When we die, we are surrendering in truth all that with which we have associated existence.

(b) The second reason is not one of imagination at all, but most sober reality. It is a solemn thing to die, because it is the parting with all round which the heart's best affections have twined themselves. And therefore it is that when men approach that period of existence when they must go, there is an instinctive lingering over things that they shall never see again.

(c) Another pang that belongs to death is the sensation of loneliness. We die alone. We go on our dark, mysterious journey for the first time in all our existence, without one to accompany us. Friends are beside our bed, but they must stay behind. Grant that a Christian has something like familiarity with the Most

High *that* breaks this solitary feeling; but what is it with the mass of men? It is a question full of loneliness to them.

(d) And yet, my brethren, with all these ideas no doubt vividly before his mind, it was none of them that the apostle selected as the crowning bitterness of dying. "The sting of death is sin." Now there are two ways in which this deep truth applies itself. There is something that appals in death when there are distinct, separate acts of guilt resting on the memory. But, my brethren, it is a mistake if we suppose that is the common way in which sin stings at the thought of death. My Christian brethren, this is the sting of sinfulness, the wretched consciousness of an unclean heart.

II. We pass to our second subject—faith conquering in death. There is nothing in all this world that ever led man on to real victory but faith. Faith is that looking forward to a future with something like certainty that raises man above the narrow feelings of the present. Ours is not merely to be victory; it is to be victory through Christ.

(a) In the first place, it is the prerogative of a Christian to be conqueror over doubt. Now Christ gives us victory over that terrible suspicion in two ways—first, he does it by his own resurrection. We have got a fact there that all the metaphysics about impossibility cannot rob us of. In moments of perplexity we look back to this. The grave has once, and more than once, at the Redeemer's bidding, given up its dead. It tells us what the Bible means by our resurrection—not a spiritual rising into new holiness merely. It is that, but also something more. It means that in our own proper identity we shall live again. Make that thought real, and God has given you, so far, victory over the grave through Christ.

There is another way in which we get the victory over doubt, and that is by living in Christ. Doubts can only be dispelled by that kind of active life that realizes Christ. And there is not faith that gives a victory so steadily triumphant as that. Live above this world, brethren, and then the powers of the world to come are so upon you that there is no room for doubt.

(b) Besides all this, it is a Christian's privilege to have victory over the fear of death. It is the easiest thing to represent the dying Christian as a man who always sinks into the grave full of hope, full of triumph, in the certain hope of a blessed resurrection. Brethren, we must paint things in the sober colors of truth, not as they might be supposed to be, but as they are. Often that is only a picture. Every day Christ's servants are dying modestly and peacefully—not a word of victory on their lips; but Christ's deep triumph in their hearts—watching the slow progress of their own decay, and yet so far emancipated from personal anxiety that they are still able to think and to plan for others, not knowing that they are doing any great thing. They die, and the world hears nothing of them; and yet theirs was the most complete victory. They came to the battlefield, the field to which they had been looking forward all their lives, and the enemy was not be found. There was no foe to fight with.

(c) The last form in which a Christian gets the victory over death is by means of his resurrection. It is a rhetorical expression rather than a sober truth when we call anything, except the resurrection, victory over death. We may conquer doubt and fear when we are dying, but that is not conquering death.

And, my brethren, if we would enter into the full feeling of triumph contained in this verse, we must just try to bear in mind what this world would be without the thought of a resurrection. Until a man looks on evil till it seems to him almost like a real personal enemy rejoicing over the destruction that it has made, he can scarcely conceive the deep rapture that rushed into the mind of the Apostle Paul when he remembered that a day was coming when all this was to be reversed. A day was coming, and it was the day of reality for which he lived, ever present and ever certain, when this sad world was to put off *forever* its changefulness and its misery, and the grave was to be robbed of its victory, and the bodies were to come forth purified by their long sleep.

(d) And now, to conclude all this, there are but two things that remain to say. In the first place, brethren, if we would be conquerors we must realize God's love in Christ. Believe that God loves you. He gave a triumphant demonstration of it in the cross. Never shall we conquer self till we have learned *to love*. Christian life, so far as it deserves the name, is victory. We are not going forth to mere battle—we are going forth to conquer.

Lastly, there is need of encouragement for those of us whose faith is not of the conquering but the timid kind. Victory is by faith, but, O God, who will tell us what this faith *is* that men speak of as a thing so easy, and how we are to get it? You tell us to pray for faith, but how shall we pray in earnest unless we first have the very faith we pray for?

(e) My Christian brethren, it is just to this deepest cry of the human heart that it is impossible to return a full answer. All that is true. To feel faith is the grand difficulty of life. But, brethren beloved, we can say "Look up," though we know not how the mechanism of the will that directs the eye is to be put in motion; we can say "Look to God in Christ," though we know not how men are to obtain faith to do it. Our polar star is the love of the cross. Take the eye off that, and you are in darkness and bewilderment at once. Let us not mind what is past. Perhaps it is all failure, and useless struggle, and broken resolves. What then? Are you in earnest? If so, though your faith be weak and your struggles unsatisfactory, you may begin the hymn of triumph *now*, for victory is pledged. "Thanks be to God, which"—not *shall* but—"*giveth* us the victory through our Lord Jesus Christ."—Frederick W. Robertson.

Illustrations

GETTING READY.   W. C. Fields, the famous comedian of another era, lay dying in a hospital. He was not known to have any religious affiliation or sentiments. When his friend and drinking companion, John Barrymore, equally famous as an actor, came to see Fields in the hospital, he found him reading the Bible. Barrymore expressed surprise. In explanation, Fields said to his old friend, "When

the fellow in the yellow nightshirt comes, I want all my bets covered."—Charles U. Harris.

THE UNSEEN COMPANIONSHIP.   Was it empty rhetoric when David Livingstone said it was not just himself who went tramping through darkest Africa—it was David Livingstone and Jesus Christ together? Was it fever or delirium when Samuel Rutherford wrote to a friend from prison, "Jesus Christ came into my cell last night, and every stone flashed like a ruby"? Was it credulity or distortion of fact that made a great scholar of this generation say, after visiting a friend in the Christian ministry who had worked himself almost to death in a Midland slum, that in that poor room he encountered Christ—there was his friend living in that hell, and there was Christ beside him?—James S. Stewart.

Sermon Suggestions

THE WAYS OF THE TEMPTER.   Text: Matt. 4:1–11. (1) The tempter appeals to: a bodily appetite; an obscure nervous feeling; ambition, which is wholly of the mind. (2) He proposes: a useful miracle; a useless miracle; a gross sin. (3) He seeks to excite: distrust of God; presumptuous reliance on God; worldly-minded abandonment of God.—John A. Broadus.

MODERN PRODIGALS.   Gospel Text: Luke 15:11–32. (1) Going away from God. (2) Suffering apart from God. (3) Rejoicing in return to God.

Worship Aids

CALL TO WORSHIP.   "The Spirit and the bride say, Come. And let him that heareth say, Come. And let him that is athirst come. And whosoever will, let him take the water of life freely" (Rev. 22:17).

INVOCATION.   Almighty God, thou who didst raise Jesus Christ from the dead, touch the dead and dying elements of our lives and usher us into the abundant life that thou hast promised to those who love thee. Remove from our hearts any destructive fear of the future, whether of the life that now is or of the life that is to come. Let our openness to thy Spirit and our worship of thee give thee access to our hearts, our homes, our work, and our play.

OFFERTORY SENTENCE. "A man's life consisteth not in the abundance of the things which he possesseth" (Luke 12:15).

OFFERTORY PRAYER. O God, we know that we cannot live by bread alone, but there are those who will not live because they have no bread; and there are those who are already dead in trespasses and sins because they have not received the bread of life. We bring you our offerings, that some may have bread and that some may have your quickening word. Bless us all as we give, and bless those whose hunger is satisfied and whose spiritual need is met because we care.

PRAYER. Stir us, Holy God, to see thee in the refugee, the depressed, the hungry, the haughty, the naked in body or spirit. Open our eyes to see poverty beneath diamonds of glitter or wealth of spirit beneath raiment of rags and treat each need with the wisdom of Christ. Let us not walk by on the other side of need because the problems are larger than our commitment. O thou, who hast ordained that in the resources of faith we can know no poverty of soul thou canst not meet; embolden us to walk where others might take pause, to bind up the wounds of the broken, to visit the prisoner in mansion or jail, to speak the Word of Life where in debauchery or misery it is most needed, to continue always to shed the light of the gospel where others have given up, because the kingdom of God knows no bounds and Christ did never renounce the cross!—E. Lee Phillips.

EVENING SERVICE

Topic: You Ought to Tell Somebody
TEXT: Mark 5:1–20.
There are two miracles in our story for today. The first one is the account of the demon-possessed man being restored to health and peace by Jesus. One has to look closely to catch the second miracle. It centers around the dramatic moment in the narrative when Jesus has been told to leave the neighborhood and has started to get into the boat. The man who had been possessed looked first at Jesus and his disciples as they were preparing to depart. Next he looked at the people of the neighborhood who had urged Jesus to leave. A moment of panic threatened a relapse into manic behavior and in desperation the madman or the former madman begged Jesus, "Let me go with you!" But, can you believe it, Jesus refused and said to him, "Go home to your own folk and tell them what the Lord in his mercy has done for you." And the next sentence says, "The man went off and spread the news in the Ten Towns of all that Jesus had done for him; and they were all amazed."

The miracle I'm interested in is the mysterious action of God by which a person commissioned to "go and tell" can move from a sense of utter panic to the place that he or she responds even to the point of enjoying the opportunity to tell his or her story. The miracle is one greatly needed. For many Christians are paralyzed at the thought of telling others about their encounters with the Spirit or the life transforming experiences that radically altered their outlook on life. They'd prefer to cherish these moments like private property. But what if the sharing of our personal experiences of transformation and deliverance may be the means whereby others come to know the living power of Christ?

I. Let us look again at the reasons the man was so threatened by the command of Jesus, "Go home and tell what has happened to you." Racing through that man's mind were thoughts, the logic of which would be this:

(a) "You had better go with Jesus. To return home would reveal that you are still crazy." Just what the man had seen that day was enough to warn him: The one who had healed him was sent away by his neighbors. They preferred their swine at the expense of his peace of mind. Then his mind went back into the horrible past. They had taken him away from his family.

They had tried to bind him with chains. They had left him in the mountains and tombs. Once again, his mind raced forward.

(b) "Will my wife receive me? Will she accept my embrace without fear? Will my children be able to call me daddy again? Will the neighbor's children run when they see me coming? Will they believe I have changed? Will they change from fear and suspicion to acceptance?"

Well, all these thoughts flashed through his mind and in such a situation like that, Jesus tells him, "Go home and tell what has happened to you." For a moment he wanted to shout out, "Jesus, why would you heal me and then send me back into that hell again?" But then, the second miracle of which I have been speaking took place. How, we do not know. What occurred?

II. What we do know is that the man went and he told. And in the telling of that story he developed a love for the sharing of his story. I think we can piece together what might have participated in the kindling of that love for the telling of the story. Let's interview this man. Let's walk with him on his way to another of the towns where he went to tell his story.

(a) "Sir, you really seem to love what you're doing. Would you mind sharing with us how you've come to find such meaning in the sharing as you do?"

(1) "Well, it's been a growing thing. At first I was scared to death, but I had no choice; Jesus said, 'Go and tell.' So I found strength from somewhere to get started. And then I discovered the power in the sharing of that story.

(2) "Let me say a word about what the telling of the story did for me. In the early stages the telling freed me from focusing on my scars and wounds; you remember the chains and being left in the mountains and crying and all that stuff? It didn't seem to matter so much, however, as I told my story. And I also saw that the sharing gained for me a new identity. They stopped referring to me as the madman and called me the man touched by Jesus. And of course, let me mention how easy it is, after a madness like mine, to wonder if one will fall back into the former condi-

tion. But I find that as I tell my story I experience a reinforcement of confidence in the strength of my new wholeness. And the telling of the story calls me to moral and spiritual responsibility also. It reminds me not only of who I am but also what I must do to be responsive to the gift of healing. It slowly dawned on me that my sharing the story did something important for Jesus who had healed me. I think they said he speaks of it as the kingdom.

(3) "I remember now the day Jesus healed me. I remember how the people sent him out of the region because of what had happened to the swine. His disciples didn't like that and urged Jesus not to leave: Don't let them run you away, they seemed to suggest to him. But Jesus seemed to know something they didn't know. In sending me back to my friends and neighbors to tell the story of what Jesus had done for me, it was as if the power of his presence was in some strange way wrapped up in the retelling of his mighty deeds.

(4) "At first I was not aware of it, but as I continued to share my story, I sensed being a part of a larger process. I saw that the needs of the people and my story seemed to be made for each other. My experience came to be nothing more than just a pilot project, a kind of preview of coming attractions—coming attractions of importance for all creation. I told my story and as I told it I felt accompanied by a presence—something from beyond: The Holy Spirit came and worked in loving power as I kept telling that story."

(b) "Well, thank you, sir, for sharing your story with us."

And brothers and sisters, something about that story has challenged me. What about you? Has Jesus touched your life with transforming and renewing power? Do you know something about the way signs of the kingdom of God have been manifested in your life, your home, your church, your community? Perhaps the kingdom needs your story to open the way of peace and love for your friends and neighbors. Or even you may need the strength today that is stored in a story of your past encounter with the living Christ. Tell it to somebody and see what it may do for you. But more importantly, the Spirit of God is at work to bring wholeness to individuals, our communities, and our world. May the Spirit count on your life's experiences or faith encounters as an instrument of God's peace. Are you ready to be used as an agent of salvation or empowerment?—James A. Forbes, Jr.

SUNDAY: MARCH SIXTEENTH

MORNING SERVICE

Topic: The New Covenant
TEXT: Jer. 31:31, Heb. 8:6.

I. Behind the religious quest in every age lie three elemental needs of the human spirit. These are, first, a moral imperative—some authoritative guideline for character and conduct, a standard to deal with our innate awareness of responsibility and obligation; second, a divine fellowship—the longing for a living presence in the unseen, a transcendent reality beyond this transient material world; third, an inward cleansing—the chance to make a new beginning, when sin has corrupted the standard and broken the fellowship, leaving an angel with a flaming sword barring the road back to Paradise.

(a) God's first covenant with Israel had three basic factors, corresponding closely to these perennial demands. The covenant met the demand for a standard with the law. "Here is your norm," it said to Israel. "By rendering obedience here, you will settle the question of responsibility, and peace and prosperity will follow." Further, it met the demand for a divine fellowship with the priesthood. For the function of the priest was precisely to be a link between the human and the divine. He would penetrate behind the veil and bring back news from the beyond; and thus the fellowship between God and man would be established and preserved forever. And last, it met the demand for cleansing with the system of sacrifices that reached their zenith in the Day of Atonement, the great *Yom Kippur*. By perpetual repetition right on to the end of time, perpetual pardon would be secured, and the shadows accumulating around the conscience dissipated like mists before the dawn.

(b) Is this remote from twentieth-century man's concern? Not in the least, in fact, would it not be true to say that there is something in all of us that is more at home with the old covenant than with its fulfillment in the gospel? The law: There is a certain satisfactoriness about having a code to keep, a dictated standard to observe, especially in these days when so many inherited standards have been dissolved by the acids of modernity. The priesthood: There is a considerable relief in the thought of being able to deal with God in some other way than by personal encounter. Religion by proxy is so much less disturbing than direct confrontation. The Day of Atonement: It can be comforting to confide in the apparatus of religious ordinances and observations, if indeed these can somehow help to secure the divine favor and thus lift life's burdens and heal its wounds.

(c) But even in Israel awkward questions kept arising. The law was indeed the gift of God and the norm for the people's life. But was the law itself perhaps just a symbol of man's fallen estate and therefore impotent to redeem? Again, how could the priest, himself a mortal man, a sinner like all the rest, bridge the gulf and bring men to God? Once again, could the Day of Atonement, constantly requiring to be repeated, really salve a guilty conscience? How could its slain beasts and altars splashed with blood save the sinner from his sin?

II. All this fermenting dissatisfaction came to a head with Jeremiah. "Days are coming," he heard a voice from heaven say, "when I will make a new covenant with Israel." A new move was impending from the side of God, a new strategy to revolutionize history and to reveal the cosmic patience of the Almighty. Three points the oracle stresses.

(a) Regarding the externalism of law, the inwardness of the divine word: "I will put My law in their inward parts, and write it in their hearts." Here is the assertion that the world cannot be redeemed by statutes, nor evil eradicated with a Decalogue. The constant desperate struggle to observe the prescribed conditions of obedience could only minister to self-righteousness, thus rivetting the shackles of sin more surely on the soul. But now God's delivering grace is going to penetrate to the hidden seat of human frustration and capture the last bastion of pride and corruption.

(b) Regarding the derived and mediated character of priestly religion, the immediacy of the divine fellowship: "They shall teach no more every man his neighbor, saying 'Know the Lord': for they shall all know me, from the least of them unto the greatest." No more secondhand dealing with God through imperfect intermediaries; there can be no verve or luster in a faith shining with a borrowed light. That must give way to the directness of touch and the sureness of vision that come when heaven and earth authentically meet and heart can speak with heart.

(c) Regarding the inefficacy of cultic sacrifice, the initiative of the divine forgiveness: "I will forgive their iniquity, and I will remember their sin no more." For the perpetually repeated sacrifices, with their crassly material symbolism, could never break into the doomed and vicious circle that sin's self-propagating power inexorably creates. But one day God would take the initiative and make obsolete all such vain oblations by one eternal offering. This would be the all-sufficient amnesty for sin, through the everlasting mercy of the Lord. "The day is coming," said Jeremiah.

III. "The day has come," declares the writer to the Hebrews, quoting the Jeremiah oracle in full. Christ in his own person is the new covenant.

(a) See how the vision came true. The inwardness of the divine word—this is made actual in Christ. For what Jesus does is to de-externalize the norm for life and character and inscribe it on the heart. He does this by himself becoming the norm, so that those who are united to him by faith and interpenetrated by his Spirit are lifted into a realm of devotion where life ceases to be regarded in legal terms at all. Law has been transmuted into love.

(b) The immediacy of the divine fellowship—this also is made actual in Christ. For here is a High Priest, untouched by sin, eternal, who not only stands on the side of men in complete and utter self-identification, representing them to God, but also stands absolutely on the side of God, to bring him to men. Thus the veil is rent in twain from the top to the bottom. The unbridgeable gulf is bridged once and for all.

(c) The initiative of the divine forgiveness—this, too, is made actual in Christ. For now—and this is what makes Christianity such a miracle to crown all miracles—the oblation is not man's but God's. It is God who makes the offering in the person of his Son. The cross is the one true altar, the defeat of the devil and the atonement of the world. And the resurrection seals the act of reconciliation.

(d) One thing remains to be added. Such a covenant—unilateral though it is, the product of sheer unmerited grace—clearly carries obligations. God's mighty deed for us in the blood of the everlasting covenant must elicit our vow to God in the dedication of life. And because the cross and the resurrection are unique and unrepeatable and once for all, the commitment they demand is irrevocable. "Let us therefore go forth," says the writer to the Hebrews, "forth to Jesus outside the camp." So shall we ratify our calling as the community of the new covenant. And so we shall go journeying on—pilgrims, strangers, sojourners all of us, with no continuing city here but seeking one to come—on to our true home, "the city which hath foundations, whose builder and maker is God."—James S. Stewart.

Illustrations

THE DIVINE INITIATIVE. In every man there is something of God, which Christ claims. Loyalty to that claim means new strength of character, new power to serve men, new peace of heart with God; it makes of life a fascinating adventure, with somebody caring for us all the way. If we go on, we shall win through, though we stagger under a cross, for in death as in life, we belong to God. There we have the upward dynamic of spirit.—H. Wheeler Robinson.

GIVE ALL TO LOVE. Too few of us pour this anointing oil on the relationships of our daily lives. We cannot afford to forget that the superb charter of kindliness includes salespersons, our own domestic help, the garage mechanic, and the tailor who presses our clothes. Too many of us deal in high-sounding platitudes about the "brotherhood of man" but exhibit an ugly class consciousness by treating the janitor as though he belonged to an inferior breed. "I call no man charitable," said Thoreau, "who forgets that his barber, cook, and hosteler are made of the same human clay as himself." We are destroying our own peace of mind when we make dictatorial or bad-tempered aggressions upon the dozens of human beings who help turn the complex wheels of our society. The brotherhood of man will work better when we take the time, patience, and *love* to discover what our fellowman looks like, to learn his name and to regard him as a human being.—Joshua Loth Leibman.

Sermon Suggestions

WHO IS GOD. (1) God is real, not just an idea in our minds. (2) God is concrete, not something abstract. (3) God is "transcendent," not simply the order of nature around us. (4) God is "personal," in the sense that he knows. (5) God is "caring." —Elton Trueblood.

THE MORALITY OF FORGIVENESS. Gospel Text: John 8:1–11. (1) Forgiveness addresses universal need. (2) Forgiveness motivates for better conduct.

Worship Aids

CALL TO WORSHIP. "Let everything that hath breath praise the Lord. Praise ye the Lord" (Ps. 150:6).

INVOCATION. O God, who from everlasting to everlasting art the same, who

lovest us with an undying love and changest not; open us in this hour of worship to the power and majesty of thy glory and thus fit us on earth with a view of the eternal, that we might do the work we are called to do and give thee the praise.—E. Lee Phillips.

OFFERTORY SENTENCE. "The Lord is good to all: and his tender mercies are over all his works" (Ps. 145:9).

OFFERTORY PRAYER. These are our blessings, God: health to enjoy, food to eat, friends to cherish, work to do, faith to practice, life to live, hope to carry through our days and beyond. Receive now these gifts we bring from the largesse that surrounds us, for they but speak a portion of our gratitude for life in thy love.—E. Lee Phillips.

PRAYER. O thou great Father of all! we draw near to thee as disobedient children, to confess our wrong, and mourn over it, and pray for deliverance from it. We beseech of thee that we may live worthy of our relationship to thee. We are thy sons. We are adopted into thy family. We are much loved and much forgiven. We are borne with, and helped, every day and on every side. Grant that every feeling of honor and gratitude and love may conspire to prevent our receiving all thy mercies, so many, and so precious, and returning nothing but disobedience.

Forgive the past, and inspire the future. Grant that we may never be discouraged. If there be any that have begun to walk the royal way of life, and are perplexed and hindered, and see little of growth in themselves, still let them go forward. Grant that none may look back and count themselves unworthy of eternal life. And we pray that thou wilt quicken the conscience of everyone. Give a new and deeper sense of guiltiness. And grant that men who are named of thee may judge of their conduct and their character, not by human laws but by the higher law of God. And so, by that spiritual and inward measure may we measure their thoughts and their feelings and say, from day to day, "Against thee and thee only have I sinned and done this evil in thy sight." And so we beseech of thee that thou wilt raise us step by step above temptation, until at last we are prepared for that higher land where they sin no more and are tempted no more and rejoice together forever.

Bless the word that shall be spoken today. Bless the servants of thy sanctuary here. May we take with us the spirit of Sunday into the week. May we be able to praise the Lord. While we are *diligent in our business*, may we know how still to be *fervent in spirit*. May we know how silently to teach men. and grant that so long as we live, we may be willing and abundant laborers in thy cause.—Henry Ward Beecher.

EVENING SERVICE

Topic: When You're in the Doldrums
TEXT: Ezek. 37:5–10, John 3:1–17.

I used to wonder why anyone like Nicodemus, so successful in this world, would ever go to Jesus. He had everything. And now I know. He had reached that point in his life when you realize that what you have is not enough, and to get more only deepens the emptiness. It was a kind of honesty that led Nicodemus that night on a path he never thought he would ever take, to visit Jesus, to ask him "How can I find new life?" And Jesus said, "Truly, truly, I say to you, unless one is born anew he cannot see the kingdom of God." Nicodemus asked, "How can a man be born when he is old?"

Jesus doesn't say this, but I want to point it out anyway. I want to suggest that that is probably when it will happen—when you grow old. It's been pointed out that so many people raised in the Church at late adolescence or early adulthood leave only to come back to the Church when they are older. Sociologists point out that they are coming back because they are now faced with their mortality, the reality of their own death. But that has not been my experience as a pastor. I have observed that people return to the Church when they get older not because of the fear of their death but because of the emptiness of their lives.

I. This text has come to be of singular importance to many Christians in our time. It's sort of a benchmark of what it means to be Christian for them. It's a source of the term "being born again," so popular in our time. So we do well to examine it rather closely.

(a) And I point out to you first that this is the only place in the New Testament where that term appears. It's only to Nicodemus that Jesus said, "You must be born again." To other people he said different things. Do you think Jesus would have said the same to you?

(b) Let's look at it. What it means to be born again is to·be found in the formula, "Unless one is born of water and the Spirit he cannot enter the kingdom of God." To be born of water certainly refers to baptism. It means baptism, and baptism means starting over. Beginning with the honest admission that my life is not the way I want it to be, and I want it to be better than it is now.

(c) That is what being born of water means. In the other Gospels it's called repentance. In Matthew, Mark, and Luke it's called repentance, which means turning around, going in a different direction, beginning again. If there's anything that you can do to yourself to begin again, it is being honest about the life that you are living. Whatever it is and however it happens, honesty is the first step in being born anew.

II. And the second lesson from this text is that it comes by the Spirit, and the key to understanding that is the words "The Spirit blows where it wills," which means that you don't know how it's going to happen or when it's going to happen.

(a) I am amazed at the variety of ways the Spirit works in the lives of individuals. But I tell you this. It will most often come through the influence of another person's life, in ways that the other person will not even be aware of.

(b) It is amazing, the variety of ways the Spirit works in your life. However it happens, whenever it happens, there is one thing that everyone who has experienced it testifies to, and that is, it is nothing that you did. It is a gift. In the words of John's Gospel, "It comes from above."

III. We don't know what eventually happened to Nicodemus, but the evidence is that because he came to Jesus he could not leave him, and neither did Jesus leave Nicodemus. And if that happens, in time the Spirit will blow, and you will be born anew.—Mark Trotter.

SUNDAY: MARCH TWENTY-THIRD

MORNING SERVICE

Topic: The Second Word

TEXT: Luke 23:36–37; Matt. 5:7.

There were three crosses on Calvary, three fellow convicts hanging side by side. Two of them fell below society's standards. One of them rose above the accepted standard. He, too, was a criminal and had to pay the price of his social nonconformity. Unusual goodness may be equally an offense with unusual badness.

I. We know the charge against Jesus. It was nailed to the cross for all to see and to read: *Jesus of Nazareth, the King of the Jews* (John 19:19). But why were the other criminals condemned to death?

(a) One of the two was angry, indignant, consistently self-centered. He picked up the jeers of the soldiers; "If you are the King of the Jews, save yourself" (Luke 23:36–37), and he gave it a new twist: "Are you not the Christ? Save yourself and us!" *And us!*

(b) The other rebuked him. He was evidently conscious of a difference between the cause of their crucifixion and the reason for Jesus' execution. This criminal is often referred to as "the penitent thief." But one wonders in what way his plea was primarily a confession of sin? Was it not, rather, an affirmation of confidence? This fellow sufferer on the central cross *was* the Messiah, the inaugurator of the kingdom of God. The criminal caught on to the idea late and vaguely. And Jesus promised him more than he asked: "You don't have to wait until the kingdom is established; 'Today shalt thou be with me in Paradise.' " This is mercy in action, the mercy that is the desire and ability to give comfort to the most undeserving.

(c) What is Paradise? What does Jesus mean by Paradise? We do not know. Sheol (or Hades) is the abode of the dead. Gehenna is the suburb of Sheol appointed for the punishment of the wicked. Presumably, Paradise is the suburb of Sheol reserved for the blessed, the accepted of God. Jesus promised that malefactor more than he asked for.

(d) There were three crosses on Calvary. One criminal died *alongside* Jesus; the other died *with* Jesus. There is an eternity of difference in the two prepositions.

II. "Today shalt thou be with me in Paradise."

(a) Isn't it what we would have expected our Lord to say? His answer on the hill of Golgotha goes along with a statement he made on another hill, on the Mount of the Sermon. There he said: "Blessed are the merciful" (Matt. 5:7). Why are they "blessed"? Partly because "they shall obtain mercy." But, more basically, because by being merciful, they are behaving like God. This deed of mercy on the cross is in line with our Lord's whole ministry.

(b) A person is merciful when he feels the sorrow and misery of another as if it were his own. Jesus was interested in sinners, not because of their merit but because of their misery. Our Lord was not in strange company on the cross; he had frequented with sinners all his life. He once said: "Him who comes to me I will not cast out" (John 6:37). Why wouldn't he get rid of them? Because he believed that his Father had sent them. So his job was to accept them. He was utterly convinced that God is merciful, and to be like God is to be merciful.

III. What does this say to us? Believe it. Believe it. Believe it. Oh, I know many of us don't want to believe it. Why should a criminal, and presumably a sinner, be granted Paradise at the fifty-ninth minute of the eleventh hour? There is only one reason: Jesus said he would, and he said it because mercy is *the* attribute of God. Christianity is, as someone has said, "the religion of all poor devils." For never forget that we don't get into heaven because we are good. We get into heaven because God is good. Thanks be to God.

IV. Do we ever long for a patron saint, a personal saint, a junior-varsity saint? May I suggest this criminal, who is known as Dismas? He is the patron saint of thieves and robbers and, I read somewhere, of outfielders in baseball! Bishop Sheen has suggested that the last thing he stole was Paradise. May I dare correct a bishop? Dismas did not have to steal Paradise; he received it as a free gift of grace from a fellow criminal who had the right to make the gift. The offer is still open.—James T. Cleland.

Illustrations

CHRIST BORE IT ALL.   "Behold the Lamb of God, who carries away the sin of the world." What happened was that all the sins, the offenses, mistakes, confusions, and perversities of the whole world in all generations and in all countries (including our own!) were loaded upon him as if he had made himself responsible for them. What happened was that he did not complain at the sight of this sea of horrors and did not protest at the unheard-of demands made upon him but instead took all this load willingly upon himself and let our sin be his sin, our grief his grief. What happened was that he carried all this load: "Carried it up to the cross," as we read in another place. What happened was that, by dying on the cross, he carried the load away, removed it, and did away with it—and *set free* the world and all of us from it.—Karl Barth.

THE LORD OF YOUR LIFE.   By the sending of his Son Jesus Christ, *God himself* draws near to you, discloses himself to you and bestows his life upon you, making himself Lord in your lives. But not a Lord according to your conceptions of lordship and not as you yourselves wish to govern and rule. God made himself Lord by becoming a servant, by washing his disciples' feet, by being obedient unto death, even unto the

death of the cross, in such a way that he the righteous and the sinless one loaded himself with the curse of sin for your sakes, for you—unrighteous and sinful men—that you might no longer be crushed by the power of sin. Whoever believes in this crucified Lord, whoever accepts the action of God by which he takes this condescending way in order to meet and find us who live so far below him, . . . then God in Jesus Christ becomes the Lord of your life.—Emil Brunner.

Sermon Suggestions

HE DIES, HE *MUST* DIE.   Text: Luke 24: 26. (1) Could any but a crucified Savior *reveal* our sins? (2) Could any but a crucified Savior *save* us from our sins? (3) Could any but a crucified Savior meet us in our agony?—W. E. Sangster.

HOW JESUS CAME TO JERUSALEM.   Gospel Text: Luke 19:29–40. (1) He entered confidently. (2) He entered humbly. (3) He entered in the name of God. (4) He entered to the sound of rejoicing.

Worship Aids

CALL TO WORSHIP.   "Blessed be the King that cometh in the name of the Lord" (Luke 19:38).

INVOCATION.   Enter, O Christ, the sanctuary of our hearts. We fall down before thee; we worship thee; we spread garments in adoration before thee and sing the hosannas that hail thee Lord of our lives. May it always be so, lowly Nazarene, Savior of all.—E. Lee Phillips.

OFFERTORY SENTENCE.   "For God so loved the world, that he gave his only begotten Son, that whosoever believeth in him should not perish, but have everlasting life" (John 3:16).

OFFERTORY PRAYER.   So great a God, so great a love, so great a gift, so great a salvation, so great a life, so great a destiny —how our hearts are overwhelmed by thy goodness. May others, through us, catch a glimpse of what thou art, and thus may they also come to know the greatness that surrounds thy name.

PRAYER. Eternal Spirit, thou unseen source of peace and power, we worship thee. Oft we have strayed from thy straight path, walking not kindly with one another, or humbly with thee, or honorably with ourselves, afraid of that which we should not fear, and seeking that which we should not desire. We come to thee for thy correction and redemption. Arise within our hearts, thou fountain of all grace, with cleansing pardon, healing strength, steadying resource, and overflowing joy.

Father of light, we bless thee for the brave men and women who have gone before us, by whose example we have been heartened and from whose sacrificial living we have profited. We bless thee for the duties of life, its loyalties and obligations, its responsibilities and tasks, from which if thou wilt sustain us in faithful stewardship, satisfying meaning and purpose shall flow into our living. We bless thee for the love of our friends, the beauty of our homes, the entrustment of children, and for every window of affection and goodwill through which light falls upon our lives.

Especially, we remember, with the gratitude of those who have been redeemed, the life of him who for our sakes died on Calvary. We confess our infidelity to him, we who like ancient Jerusalem have often welcomed him with protestations of loyalty, and ere the week ended have crucified him. Amid the waywardness of a violent world, that has denied his faith and forsaken his way, we turn afresh to him. To whom else can we go; he has the words of eternal life. Grant us a fresh vision of his way of living, a resolute decision to let him be our Master, and a new willingness daily to take up our cross and follow him.— Harry Emerson Fosdick.

EVENING SERVICE

Topic: Live and Help Live
TEXT: Exod. 20:13.

If I were to ask you, "What is the number one problem in your business, your home and your neighborhood?", you would probably answer, "Human rela-

tions." Getting along with each other, functioning side by side, day by day is one of life's great challenges. How well we can do that determines our destiny.

I. *Thou shalt not kill.*

(a) May it be quickly said that this statement has nothing to do with capital punishment or warfare. Other scriptures in the Levitical laws deal directly with those problems. This is not a cheap, one-shot answer to abortion or euthanasia. Each of these painful situations has to be worked out individually, praying for God's wisdom and applying the principles of love and sanctity for life.

(b) Bible scholars agree this is a prohibition of murder. The Hebrew verb implies "violent and unauthorized killing." There is a vast difference between murder and killing. If this commandment were to be taken as a blanket prohibition of killing, then it would be wrong to kill insects, snakes, dangerous beasts, and rabid dogs.

(c) More is intended here than a prohibition against taking life. It is an encouragement to help each other save life.

II. *Attitudes toward others.*

a) Now, here is a hard-hitting truth that, if caught cleanly, will blister more than your hands (see Matt. 5:21–24). In the mind of God, murder is more than an act, it is an attitude. You face the judgment of God when you allow hateful anger to cloud your relationship toward another. You stand accountable for a severe sin if you ever hold contempt in your heart against any person. To call another person a "worthless fool" is to invite for yourself the fires of hell, warns our Lord.

(b) There is a positive side of this commandment. It does not mean that we are to live and let live, but we are also to live and help live. When God walked this earth as a man, he was our example of compassion for the needs of all others. Not only did he condemn a murderer but also the ones who walked by without helping a wounded brother. The foundation of this commandment is that God values every person as much as he values me. This rule of living means that we see everyone as he does.

III. *Love God and others as yourself.*

(a) Now we begin to see the great wisdom of our Lord's summation of the Commandments: "*You will love the Lord your God . . . and you will love your neighbor as yourself.*" Perhaps we don't pay enough attention to the last phrase of that statement: "as yourself." This commandment is asserting that, neither by act nor attitude are you to take your own life. It is true that suicide is forbidden by God. We did not create our life and we don't have the right to take it. The very fact of life carries with it an obligation to live. We must leave in God's hands how he judges this violation

of his law. He is love and knows all the circumstances and mental conditions and responsibility.

(b) There are more ways to commit suicide than by taking your physical life. You can have a wrong attitude toward yourself. By forgetting that you are a special, unique creation of God, you can kill your potential. Just as hatred of others is a serious sin, so is hatred of self. It is to the best interest of everyone that you be a happy, productive person, enjoying to the fullest all God made you to be.—Frank Pollard.

SUNDAY: MARCH THIRTIETH

MORNING SERVICE

Topic: Easter Living

TEXT: Matt. 28:1–10; Col. 3:1–4.

There is an excitement and joy to Easter that is undeniable. I am sure you can sense something of the uniqueness of this tremendous day. Little children feel the excitement. Even as we grow older, we sense that this is a special day. We have the stirring Easter music, the beauty of the cross and of the Easter lilies, the power of the Scripture, and the good news of the greatest victory to inspire us.

I. Without Easter, only despair.

(a) The New Testament makes it clear that the alternative to Easter is not pleasant. Without Easter, life is like a land caught in the grip of unending winter. Until Easter it seemed the darkness and the cold were winning and would ultimately prevail. Do you realize that when you start reading the Bible, you read in Genesis, chapter 1 about a good and loving God who created a magnificent universe and a beautiful earth? At the end of chapter 1, verse 31, we read, "And God saw everything that he had made, and behold, it was very good." Then turn just two pages and let your eyes fall on the words of chapter 6, verses 5 and 6: "The Lord saw that the wickedness of man was great in the earth, and that every imagination of the thoughts of his heart was only evil continually. And the Lord was sorry that he had made man on the earth, and it grieved him to his heart." How did things

go wrong so quickly? Human beings rejected the sovereignty and authority of God. They sought to establish their own power and prestige. The result was to release an avalanche of evil and chaos. Turn over page after page and you see the cruelty of kings, the betrayal of false prophets, constant demands for luxury and comfort of the people, and hostility toward God. The darkness deepened. The chill was terrifying. Finally the people were carried away into captivity. The temple was destroyed. The whole situation seemed to be an utter chaotic failure.

(b) God, however, was not defeated! He came himself, personally to enter human history. The Gospel of John says simply, "And the Word became flesh and dwelt among us." (John 1:14). He taught good news that God was a loving, compassionate father. He seemed to be pushing back the darkness and turning the tide of the relentless advance of the night. Then the political and religious leaders decided that his life could not be tolerated. He went through the mockery of a trial and was nailed to a cross between two criminals. When he died that terrible Friday on a cross located on a skull-shaped hill outside Jerusalem's walls, it seemed to be the ultimate triumph of evil and the power of darkness. He was then taken to be placed in a borrowed tomb, where a great stone was rolled in front of the door. The seal was set, and the guard was placed. People went home from the cross in despair. The disciples were hiding in terror. His friends knew that the cause was totally lost. Without Easter, life is like a country bound in endless winter.

II. Easter makes a difference.

(a) It made a difference to devastated women. On the first day of the week, while it was still dark, Mary Magdalene, the other Mary, and the other women went early to the tomb. They were going to complete the preparation of the body of Jesus for final burial. They had no thought of the resurrection. They were worried about only one matter—"Who will roll away the stone for us from the door of the tomb?" (Mark 16:3). When they came around the last corner to that lovely garden where the tomb was cut from solid rock, they saw that the stone had already been rolled away. A shining stranger was seated there and he said to them, "Do not be afraid; for I know that you seek Jesus who was crucified. He is not here; for he has risen, as he said. Come, see the place where he lay. Then go quickly and tell his disciples that he has risen from the dead, and behold, he is going before you to Galilee; there you will see him." (Matthew 28:5–7). They were terrified! As they ran back to Jerusalem with fear and great joy, they met Jesus. They fell before him and worshiped him. They rushed back to tell the disciples, who refused to believe. This is the summary of the apostolic response to Easter, "but these words seemed to them as an idle tale, and they did not believe them" (Luke 24:11). Slowly, gradually, the resurrection reality began to dawn upon the disciples. John says that on the evening of the first Easter, Jesus came and stood among the disciples and said, "Peace be with you" (John 20:19). The resurrection possibility began to touch them and set them free from their terror and their defeat.

(b) Years later, Paul was writing to a small church at Colossae about the power of Easter living. It was a church that was troubled by false teachers and false doctrines. In the letter, Paul made an amazing statement. He said, in effect, that God did not stop Easter with Jesus. He just launched it. As he defeated sin and death and raised Jesus from the dead, he is still doing the same today. Listen again to

chapter 2, verse 13. "And you, who were dead in trespasses and the uncircumcision of your flesh, God made alive together with him, having forgiven us all our trespasses." Now I want you to visualize three words of Scripture painted or projected in huge letters across a wide screen just behind me. These three words *together with him* summarize the message of Easter. Let me share with you what I am hearing. It is exciting. I was once dead in my sin and trespasses. I was frozen in the darkness of my guilt and my own death. The God who raised Jesus has offered me the possibility of a new being, resurrection reality, and a new existence—*together with him*. That is my Scripture for Easter living. These are the three words I want you to take with you—*together with him*. I was dead and called it living, but I was not living at all.

(c) I am impressed also with another verse in Colossians. It is chapter 3, verse 3: "For you have died, and your life is hid with Christ in God." Some of us know what it is like to face the apparent certainty of death. Easter announces that our lives are not out of control, that the world is not out of control. There is One stronger than any of the chaotic and destructive forces. We realize that something of our pride and arrogance dies within us, but our authentic existence, our real life, is hid with Christ in God. Paul goes on to say, "When Christ who is our life appears, then *you also* will appear with him in glory" (Col. 3:4). Notice how once again Easter draws a circle and includes us in. I am included in the rsurrection reality.

III. Receive and believe.

(a) What is our response to this amazing Easter possibility? I believe it is to *receive* and *believe* the Easter gospel—then to *extend* and *expand* Easter living. But it was the will of Jesus that his followers should believe and know his victory. You remember his words to Thomas, "Put your finger here, and see my side; and put out your hand, and place it in my side; do not be faithless, but believing" (John 20:27). As we receive the Easter message, then we are a part of the communication of the reality of transforming hope. We are to be numbered among those who extend and expand the Easter reality.

(b) Easter is the good news that he is risen! Outwardly your life may appear unchanged. Still, Easter means that deliverance is on the way. The night of endless winter will end! The overpowering runaway will be controlled. Sin and death have been defeated! The future is open. "And you, who were dead in trespasses and the uncircumcision of your flesh, God made alive together with him" (Col. 2:13). You are alive! Receive your life! Rejoice in your life! Live your life! Go forward to claim your Easter possibilities that are before you! Go forth to live in gratitude, praise, and joy! Let us dare to be a people of hope in an age that has given up in despair. Let us be a people who demonstrate the possibility of Easter living. Let us dare to be a people who share Easter joy and hope.—Joe A. Harding.

Illustrations

THE JOYOUS SECRET.   I was privileged to become acquainted with a great Scottish Presbyterian preacher, Dr. Murdo Ewen MacDonald. He was the chaplain for the American prisoners of war during World War II and was greatly loved by our soldiers. He told about how he learned about the invasion of Normandy and of D day. Early in the morning an American shook him awake, shouting into his ears, "The Scotsman wants to see you—it's terribly important." MacDonald says that he ran over to the barbed-wire fence that separated the British and the American camps, where MacNeil, who was in touch with the BBC by underground radio, was waiting for him. He spoke two words in Gaelic—"They have come!" MacDonald then ran back to the American camp and began waking up the soldiers. He said again and again, "They have come! They have come!" The reaction was incredible. Men jumped up and started to shout. They hugged each other. They ran outdoors. They rolled on the ground in joy. The Germans thought they were crazy. They were still prisoners. Nothing had outwardly changed. Inwardly, however, they knew everything was different.—Joe A.

Harding, with acknowledgements to Chevis Horne.

CAN ONE RISE FROM THE DEAD?   Does not the very fact that he was born in a stranger's cave and buried in a stranger's grave prove that human birth and death are equally foreign to him? Look about at nature. Is not the springtime the Easter Day of the Good Friday of winter? Has not all death within itself the germs of life? Does not the "falling rain bud the greenery"? Does not the falling acorn bud the tree? Why should all creation rise from the dead and not the Redeemer of creation?—Fulton J. Sheen.

Sermon Suggestions

JESUS LIVES!   Text: Matt. 28:1–20.
(1) A fountain of joy for you this Easter morn. (2) A source of strength for you in your entire life. (3) A stream of grace for you in the Holy Communion. (4) A wellspring of hope for you in the face of death. · —R. C. H. Lenski.

"AT EARLY DAWN."   Gospel Text: Luke 24:1–10. (1) A visit and a disappointment. (2) A vision and a recollection. (3) Return and recital.

Worship Aids

CALL TO WORSHIP.   "And the angel answered and said unto the women, Fear not ye: for I know that ye seek Jesus, which was crucified. He is not here: for he is risen, as he said. Come, see the place where the Lord lay" (Matt. 28:5–6).

INVOCATION.   Almighty and everlasting God, you and you alone have brought us to this moment. It was by your might that Christ was raised to life. It was by your grace that we were saved. And it is by your providence that we have gathered for worship today. Help us so to celebrate the resurrection of your Son that it becomes a living reality in our hearts and souls.—James M. King.

OFFERTORY SENTENCE.   "He that spared not his own Son, but delivered him up for us all, how shall he not with him freely give us all things?" (Rom. 8:32).

OFFERTORY PRAYER. Our Father, as you have freely given us all that we have and lovingly made us all that we are, we now freely and lovingly give back to you the substance of our lives. Forgive us where we have been selfish. Ever remind us that it was from the poverty of the cross that we gained the richness of life. Accept these gifts as a token of our sincere worship, for we do love you and earnestly seek the furtherance of your kingdom.—Timothy E. Madison.

PRAYER. "And they went out and fled from the tomb; for trembling and astonishment had come upon them; and they said nothing to any one, for they were afraid" (Mark 16:8).

O Christ, we have buried your resurrection under lilies because an open grave strikes terror in the heart and embarrasses the intellect. Flowers hide the awkwardness of our Easter celebration. We are more comfortable finding you in nature than among people. When streams tickle the earth into the grand smile of spring, and the same rush of life that surges from root through stem drives through our veins, then with ease we sing, "Fairest Lord Jesus, Ruler of All Nature." But after the blossoms' glory and plump fruit's ripeness, when there is a November funeral and earth's arteries are freezing shut, then the lily will not save us. We need more than a ruler of nature. We need the conqueror of death. We need you, our risen Lord. Let not spring's sun delude us with its transient warmth, but let the seasonless power of your resurrection fill us with everlasting life.—Thomas H. Troeger.

EVENING SERVICE

Topic: Confession of an Average Church Member

TEXT: Mark 9:14–29.

I have always been grateful for this man who was honest enough to say, "Lord, I believe; help my unbelief." That is the perpetual cry of the average church member today. I'll bet I know some of the thoughts running though your minds. I know them because I have had them too, at various times in my life. And, with your permission, I want to try to speak to some of them.

I. Some of you, I imagine, are saying "I know religion is important, but I never seem to feel very religious." True religion is a discipline. It is a way of life, and the more of life that is included in it, the more it shapes us into the persons we want to be. What you have to do is commit yourself to the religious way of life, even to the things you do not feel like committing yourself to, and then one day you wake up and find that your whole being has been molded by the commitment.

II. "But the music and creeds seem so old-fashioned and out of tune with my world," you may say. Perhaps; that is because religion has a lot of tradition in it. The creeds we say are usually based on the theological commitments of people who lived sixteen or seventeen centuries ago. The hymns were written by people who lived in our religion's past. They have been cherished, through the years, by the people whose lives have been shaped by them. But future Christians will use them as part of the living, growing tradition.

III. "I try to pray," say some of you, "but I can't. It doesn't seem to work for me." That is not at all unusual. Many Christians have difficulty praying. Prayer, like everything else in religion, is a practice. It is not something you do well at first or something you do well occasionally. You have to learn to pray. You learn to be quiet before God and listen to God, instead of trying to talk to God all the time. It isn't going to God with requests; it's going to God and making a gift of yourself.

IV. "The church is always asking for money," you say. "I give what I can, but I can't understand why some people give thousands of dollars a year to an institution." Giving is like everything else in being a Christian—if you only felt that you were a real part of things or had a deep life of prayer, you would truly wish to have a larger share in the program of the church, both here and around the world. I would suggest that giving more sacrificially can help you to feel that you are a vital part of the church. Most people who complain about the emphasis on stewardship forget that Jesus talked more about money and how we relate to it than almost any other subject.

V. "I know my problem," you say. "I don't feel that I really count in the church. I'm a nobody." If there is one place in the world where one ought to feel that he or she truly belongs, it is in the church. The church wants to be different. Believe me, it does. We know you're important to God, and we want you to be important to us too.

VI. "The church is full of hypocrites." Sad to say, you are probably right about that. The word *hypocrite* means "one who

wears a mask," and we all wear masks at one time or another. Part of what we're trying to do in the church is discover what our masks are and how to live without them. We worship God together and study the Word together in order to see what true humanity is and how we can conform to it.

VII. I've called this sermon "Confession of an Average Church Member." It's terrible to be average at anything—to sit on the bench or not be chosen on the team. If the Spirit is speaking to you now and saying "move in, move in," won't you do it? Say "Lord, I believe, help my unbelief," and then help it yourself by moving in where faith has its best chance to grow.—John Killinger.

SUNDAY: APRIL SIXTH

MORNING SERVICE

Topic: Scandals of Faith
TEXT: Matt. 8:2, 10.

These Gospel lessons, as a rule, seem so neat and simple. And they aren't at all. There is nothing here for anybody, unless we are ready and willing, before we do anything else, to run headlong into what the New Testament calls the "scandal" of the Gospel, the stumbling block that is hidden away for us in almost every passage.

I. Take for instance what this leper says. "Lord, if thou wilt, thou canst make me clean." There is no gettng around it, that does take the power for granted and leave the will in the realm of the uncertain. The power is there. God is almighty, isn't he? But what about the willingness? He could if he would.

(a) Our ancestors felt that way about him in the primeval forests of Europe. The Jews should have known better, but often they felt that way too. Why else were they forever trying to get on the right side of him? So they prayed and worshiped and fasted and offered sacrifices. The whole Old Testament is nothing but the long record of how God tried his best to get people to quit that. Only to have us still "lobbying around in the courts of the

Almighty," as another has put it, looking "for special favors." We want something, and you may be sure we shall go on plucking at his sleeve, pestering him for it. He can if only he will.

(b) What we've got on our hands is an almighty but reluctant God; and down here on our heathen levels we are out to persuade and cajole and maneuver him. There is a source from which all blessings flow, and we are in this business of being Christians not without some effort to turn it on if we can. The trouble is that just now, and we can't understand it at all, the faucet seems to be stuck!

(c) There was one dark moment even in Jesus' life when there seemed to be nobody anywhere who cared enough to keep his grip on things. And sooner or later we face it. The God of the mathematicians and geologists, the God of the astronomers and historians, can go hang then. We want help. Disaster strikes—disease, flood, hurricane, war; a very drunken debauch sometimes, from one end to the other, of poverty and homelessness and hunger and death. And we try to pray, but it does no good; so we try to read the riddle and can make no sense of it. So— multitudes who can't quite make up their minds to give their minds over to mindless chance say, "If your God is almighty, he isn't good. There is no other way to explain it." And we undertake to smile bravely and answer, "O yes there is: God so loved the world"—until it comes our turn to remind him that we too are still here and that things have gone terribly wrong with us, as well as with these other people, and will he not please do something—please! He could if he would.

II. The only way out of it is into another scandal on the next higher level. Let me lay it in front of you without any decoration. You say that if God is almighty, he isn't good. What if I should come right back at you and say that if God is good, he isn't almighty? You have to rescue God's power at the expense of his love, or you have to rescue his love at the expense of his power. And in that you will come nearer the truth, shudderingly nearer! If there is anything at all in this Jesus, we shall have to say to him not what the leper said, "Lord, if thou wilt . . . ," but "Lord, if thou canst . . . ." There is something in him that looks far more like powerless love than like loveless power.

(a) Two thousand years ago, the people in Palestine were faced with that dilemma and decided not to put up with it. Power that seemed lacking in love was not so hard to understand; but love like this that was lacking in power—they could not swallow that. So they nailed it to a cross and wagged their heads and said, "If thou be the Son of God, come down!"

(b) And that's what the New Testament means. Loveless power isn't the problem there; the problem is powerless love. Give anybody just one glance at it, and that's what he would say. Whatever else God is, you can count on him, first, last, and all the time, to be willing, eternally willing, willing before ever we begin to worship him, willing when the prayer hasn't even formed itself yet in our thought.

(c) Bethlehem and Calvary mean that there are places in the human heart where power cannot come; only weakness can get in. Quarrels can't be stopped until we are ready to stop them. There are people who can't be made good because they do not want to be made good. The wickedness of evil lives can't be kept from hurting the innocent; airplanes can't be kept from dropping bombs that fall on children; shells can't be kept from bursting and killing somebody we love. It is not God's might we need to ponder. We need to ponder his weakness. He has to put up with no end of contradiction in order to let you be a person, in a world where courage is possible, choices are pretty grim, and faith is a clean adventure far and away on the other side of spoon-feeding!

(d) It is the love of God that's unconditioned; we condition his power. "Lord, if thou wilt . . . "? Not at all! "I will. Wilt thou?" And to the blind man, "What wilt thou that I shall do unto thee?" And to the impotent man by the pool of Bethesda, "Wilt thou be made whole?" And over Jerusalem, once more at the last, his lamentation: "Thou that killest the prophets and stonest them which are sent unto thee, how often would I have gathered thy children together, even as a hen gathereth her chickens under her wings"—"how often would I . . . , and ye would not!"

III. So have we moved from the power that seems lacking in love to the love that so often seems lacking in power—and never is! The primary and ultimate scandal of the Christian religion is the power-in-love that will not devote itself to our ends.

(a) Take for example the centurion in this same chapter. Observe that neither his reputation nor what he had done came into focus for Jesus. What was said about him made no impression. It was said that he was worthy, and it wasn't just gossip. But what was the centurion's own estimate of himself? He said to a Jewish rabbi, from over Nazareth way, "I am not worthy that thou shouldest come under my roof."

And Jesus listened—"He is worthy," others said; "I am not worthy," said he—but Jesus paid no attention to any of it. Jesus was looking at something else entirely, at the only thing that mattered, and there was a light in his eyes. He had come upon a faith that was of itself enough to be almost a miracle in that land of timid and doubtful and suspicious folk, where he himself had grown so heartsick for it. He hailed it as if it were something he had been looking for everywhere, high and low, and suddenly in this out-of-the-way place had stumbled on it: "I have not found so great faith, no, not in Israel."

(b) It's all he looks for in any of us; at times he seems unbearably careless about the rest: only something in you and me that will keep saying a resounding yes to him everyday we live, to him and to all the contradictions that life can throw in the way; pressing on as far as we can see, and when we can't see any longer, going it blind! Do you have an idea that it's easy for him to fashion that kind of faith in anybody? It won't take much out of you, you think? This ruthless love, which so often can do so little about the hazards without ceasing to be love, and so has to do something about you—or cease to be power!

(c) And when he has wrought in you enough faith to receive whatever he has in mind, beyond there is the still costlier gift of the faith that will accept it that can gaze straight into the eyes of some gray messenger of sorrow, asking "What blessing then do you bring?" All along in Job, from the drawn-out bitterness of his heart, through the lurid flashes of blasphemy on his lips, you can watch that kind of faith being shaped by those great compassionate hands.

(d) That isn't loveless power, and it isn't powerless love. It's something more disturbing than either of them. It's the power-in-love—in love with us!—that spares neither itself nor its object, like a potter with his wheel, day after day, turning out a human soul.—Paul Scherer.

Illustrations

UNFINISHED EASTER. If anyone asks why this very religious generation is not battering at the doors of the churches instead of wandering through the corridors of the occult, gathering in charismatic groups, or taking the mystic road to Katmandu, my answer would be that, on the whole, we have failed to present the gospel as a living experience. We have become reporters of the religious experience of others from Abraham to Bonhoeffer, rather than catalysts of the living Christ. Instead of bringing people into vital contact with him and conveying the excitement of life in the Spirit, we have tended

to offer what I might call an ABC of theology and an NBC of current affairs. We are suffering from the blight of the secondhand—honoring someone else's God, interested in someone else's Jesus, keeping the gospel as one removed from the center of our lives. So Easter may become nothing more than an exercise in religious nostalgia to the sound of trumpets.—David H. C. Read.

THE RISEN LIFE. Life in the Spirit is the earnest of our inheritance yonder. Listen on this matter to that great Asiatic Christian now gone home to God, Dr. D. T. Niles of Ceylon. "The resurrection that awaits us beyond physical death will be but the glorious consummation of the risen life which already we have in Christ." "The risen life we have already." Of D. T. Niles himself that was manifestly true—you could not know him and not see the risen life there.—James S. Stewart.

Sermon Suggestions

THE NAME ABOVE EVERY NAME. Text: Acts 2:36. (1) The name Jesus is the name of the Man, which tells us of a Brother. (2) "Christ" is the name of office and brings to us a Redeemer. (3) "The Lord" is the name of dignity and brings us before the King.—Alexander Maclaren.

BELIEVING WITHOUT SEEING. Gospel Text: John 20:19–31. (1) Christ's good intention for us—peace. (2) Christ's power for us—the Holy Spirit. (3) Christ's blessing in us—faith.

Worship Aids

CALL TO WORSHIP. "Then said Jesus to them again, Peace be unto you: as my Father hath sent me, even so send I you" (John 20:21).

INVOCATION. Lord Jesus Christ, your peace has enthralled us and stilled our fears. Strengthened with might by your Spirit within us, may we be ready to hear your voice and go with you where you will lead us. So let our worship be listening as well as speaking.

OFFERTORY SENTENCE. "Go into all the world," says the risen Lord, "and give the good news to everyone" (Mark 16:15, the New Testament in Basic English).

OFFERTORY PRAYER. Loving Father, we know that you want our hearts more than anything we have and we would give them to you. We know that miracles are wrought through our tithes and offerings, and we bring them to you. Use us where you lead us, and use our money as it goes representing our devotion and love.

PRAYER. Out of all our doubts and out from our cares, we come, O thou blessed God of light and of consolation! How much do we need thee! Left to ourselves, how helpless we are! We have proved our own power. We have proved what we can do for joy and what for purity. We have proved our hours of strength, and we have proved also our hours of weakness. And we know no longer because thou hast said it, but because we have felt it and proved it, that without thee we can do nothing. Our whole hope, then, is in thee. By thy power we are strong. Without that power we are emptiness and nothing.

Accept our thanks for such measures of experience as we have had. Had we but opened the door, thou wouldst have come in. Now thou hast stood speaking peace to us upon the threshold. Grant us that knowledge and that will by which we may persuade thee to come in and abide with us. Come, we beseech of thee, to dwell. Come not to sit at the evening meal, and as our eyes begin to be enlightened, vanish away from us. Come to break bread and to tarry. Come to make our morning joy, our noonday strength, and our evening gladness. Come, O thou whom our souls need; thou whom we have been taught to love; thou whom, loving, we cannot forget to love. Come and chide, rather than severely rebuke. Come and show the mercy of pain, if pain be the medicine. Come and show thy lenient hand in chastisements and disappointments. Only let us know that thou art about us, thinking of us, calling us by name, dealing with us, and let us know that we are sons, and all shall be well. Grant unto us, we beseech of thee, more and more to enter into the fellowship of communion; to learn thy secret hiding place; to find thee out from day to day, in light and in darkness. May we rejoice more and more in lifting up our thoughts to thee. May we see more of thy processes in nature and more of thy nature in society and life. May we behold thee in all the powers that are exercised upon the earth. We pray that we may rejoice in the Lord and be strong in the God of our salvation.—Henry Ward Beecher.

EVENING SERVICE

Topic: Turned on or Tuned in?

TEXT: John 20:1–31.

The twentieth chapter of John's Gospel helps us to clarify our perceptions about the Christian life of faith. Most of us live ordinary lives—lives marked by a mixture of defeats and victories, doubts and faith, temptations and strong-willed convictions. Christian life is not primarily gauged by the level of one's feelings. The beauty of John 20 is that individual needs are met. Jesus always met the needs of individual persons as he encountered them. The advice of the risen Lord to Mary and to Thomas illustrates this.

I. To some Jesus says, "Do not cling to me."

(a) Mary may represent for us one in quest for Jesus. She responded to him using the old title—Rabbi—that she had used often back in Galilee when things were simpler. She was thinking how wonderful it was now that things were going to be the same again. In Mary's cry is the longing for the "good old days." Mary thought she could now resume following Jesus in customary ways. Now that he was alive again, she could go back to relating to him in the former ways; things would be like they were before.

(b) But Jesus was showing Mary that his permanent presence is not by way of appearances but by way of the Spirit who was coming. Hear Jesus saying to Mary, "Do not cling to me. Do not think that you can get so religiously turned on that you can hold me and possess me and have my companionship as of old. There are new realities to which you must adjust. Things will never be the same again. Now go tell the disciples. . . ."

(c) And so it is that Jesus is speaking to everyone: "If you are too wealthy, too secure, too assured of your own place, too certain of your own faith, too satisfied with the status quo, too nostalgic—then you need to hear Jesus saying: 'Do not cling to me.' " For Jesus summons us to take some risks. He calls us to be on a journey, taking up our own cross and following him daily. He calls us to be on a pilgrimage for him and for God's people. For we, like Abraham, are called to go out, not knowing where God will send us.

(d) Jesus never allowed one of his followers to retreat into an easy peace and security. Indeed, he sent his disciples out on a mission to deal with unpredictable problems and even to face death. Christianity can never be the faith of those who selfishly are concerned for their own emotional and physical security. "Do not cling to me."

II. But Thomas had needs different from Mary. To Thomas Jesus says: "Thrust your hand into my side."

(a) Christianity is for the shattered and the broken. It is for both the weak and the strong. It is for those of little faith. It is for those, like Thomas, who do not have an intimate experience with Jesus where they hear him call their name. Christianity is for common, ordinary folk who struggle with doubt and temptation. Christianity is not exclusively the property of those who reside on the highest mountaintop or who are plunged into the deepest valley, but Christians by and large are a people of the plain of life's ordinary days.

(b) When we need to be prodded into action and activity, when we need not to be clinging to Jesus as a two-year-old clings to the legs of his mother, then Jesus speaks to our need, saying "Take up your cross and follow me." And when we need to be comforted and assured, even as a child requires the love of hugging embraces, then we hear Jesus invite us to thrust our hands into his side; we hear Jesus call us to come to him as we labor and are heavy laden.

(c) If Mary was turned on, Thomas was tuned in. Thomas was the discriminating one who could not let his emotions run wild. Perhaps he was a gloomy Christian, a person of a moody temperament. He also had an inquiring mind. He reacted stongly to the senseless suffering of Christ. We should be thankful that Christians are not all alike! We are not all as turned on as Mary nor as gloomy, reflective, and thoughtful as Thomas.

(d) We can learn from Thomas's example to be honest and open with our doubts, and we can learn to maintain personal fellowship with those who believe. Thomas suffered when he was absent from the gathering of Jesus' disciples. So Christian life and Christian doubting ought not to be a private affair but a corporate sharing together. What he found was infinitely greater than Mary's sentimental babbling of all the old titles and the yearning for old paths. Greatly more profound than Mary's simple "Rabbi" is Thomas' confession: "My Lord and my God!" The way of useful doubting is the way by which the doubter finally comes to say "Lord, to whom shall we go? You have the words of eternal life."—Fred W. Andrea.

SUNDAY: APRIL THIRTEENTH

MORNING SERVICE

Topic: Follow Thou Me

TEXT: John 21:22.

"What is that to thee? Follow thou me."
You may have one kind of lot in this life of discipleship and someone else may have another; and you may be puzzled by that, and may want to ask all sorts of questions about it, and about God's will, and all the mystery of the crosses of this life. But you can't expect to answer all these questions, and that is not the main thing. The main thing is loyal discipleship. "What is that to thee? Follow thou me." Let me try to translate that challenge in three different ways that will fit ourselves.

I. *Never mind your perplexities, but follow Christ.*

(a) There is many a young heart that,

when it hears Christ's challenge, does just the thing that Peter does in that scene—begins to ask questions. Now sometimes these perplexities are not genuine perplexities at all but merely excuses, convenient evasions, a sort of red herring drawn across the trail, because it is far easier to raise questions and difficulties than to rise up and follow Christ.

(b) With many people, however, it is not that low dishonest kind of questioning but very genuine doubt and perplexity about the truths of religion. Many young people pass through that discipline, and those who have been through it know very well what a painful desolating experience it is —to want and long to believe in God and to build one's life on religion, and yet to be tormented with perplexity and uncertainty as to whether it really is all true. Now what can be said to a man in that situation? Well, of course, you have to face your doubts and perplexities quite frankly and honestly and try to think them out and get light on them. But the great and salutary and reassuring lesson is this: It is not just by thinking it all out that light comes, and you do not have to wait until you have thought it all out (or you would have to wait forever). You can go on bravely in the path of duty and purity and love. So much of Christ is plain to you, and so far you can follow him with your eyes wide open. And if you are perplexed about this and that, Christ says: "What is that to thee? Follow thou me."

II. *Never mind what other people are doing, but follow Christ.*

(a) In this vivid scene, when Peter is challenged to follow Christ, he begins to talk about the other disciple. There is something so straight and personal about Christ's challenge: Why should not the other disciple have as hard a challenge? There is something so lonely about this business of making up his own mind to follow Christ.

(b) There are many ways in which people still try to evade Christ's challenge by looking at other people. Some do it by criticizing other people—pointing at the faults of Christians, pointing at the misdeeds and hypocrisies of people who profess to be Christ's followers, and making

that an excuse for not following Christ themselves. Then there are some who hesitate about following Christ wholeheartedly because they do want company and they don't want to make a lonely choice or to go further than their friends and comrades. I say to you all, and especially to those of you who are young—never mind what other people are doing, but follow Christ.

III. *Don't be merely a member of the Church, but be a follower of Christ.*

(a) Now there is nothing on earth greater than the Church. It is part of the very essence of the gospel. Its fellowship is near the heart of the Christian life. And yet, it is quite possible to be "churchy" without being truly religious or Christian. "Churchianity" is not Christianity. And we are sometimes in danger of confusing them.

(b) It is a sound message still for all Church-folk, whether ministers or people. Do all for Christ. Go deeper than all human fellowship, deeper than all mere churchmanship, listen to the voice of God in Christ, and do all for him. "What is that to thee? Follow thou me." And if the Church is going to be a true, live Church of Christ in this coming day and generation, it will be because its men and women, like you and me, and above all because its young men and women, growing up out of childhood, hear for themselves the call of Christ, and rise up to follow Him.—D. M. Baillie.

Illustrations

STEP INTO THE STREAM!   God is wanting you and drawing you, exactly as you want your little son to get up and take his first steps, and you give him your hand. Two things may make you hesitate: the fear that you will not "stick with it," or something you don't want to give up. You know you can't be fully in the stream of this world, with its many false values, and also in the stream of God's grace, even though you'd like to be in both. But how little do the things we give up appear, after the great experience has happened! You may feel a bit awkward slithering down the bank where you have been sitting for so long, first getting your toes wet, and then slowly getting wet all over. There is no swimming for people who only wade, and there is no enjoying the full stream of the grace of God for those who hang onto the roots and bushes on the bank and never let themselves go. Let yourself go entirely. Let the water in the stream hold you up, instead of relying on your willpower. Reservations and delays and sins have held you back long enough. Get in, and let the stream of the grace of God wash and buoy and carry you along. Let self-effort drown beneath those waters!—Sam Shoemaker.

LOVE DOES THINGS.   Love can never sit by contentedly and see the one it loves perish. It has no choice but to forget itself and seek to do something to remedy the situation. At the risk of its own destruction, it rushes into the burning building to rescue the trapped child. At the endangering of its own life, it nurses tenderly the loved one who has become the victim of a contagious and deadly disease. Love always acts to prevent its beloved from perishing. It dies in the attempt sometimes, but it acts.—Roy H. Short.

Sermon Suggestions

THE GOLDEN CALF.   Text: Exod. 32:19–20. (1) The weakness. (2) The sin. (3) The judgment. (4) The remedy.—Suggested by Clayton Williams.

"THEY CAUGHT NOTHING."   Gospel Text: John 21:1–14. (1) Disillusionment prevailed: They went back to their former occupation. (2) Defection foundered: They did not succeed on their own. (3) Decision triumphed: They obeyed and their fortunes changed.

Worship Aids

CALL TO WORSHIP.   "And Jesus said unto them, Come ye after me, and I will make you to become fishers of men" (Mark 1:17).

INVOCATION.   Our Father and our God, we have begun our discipleship of thy Son.

If we have been following afar off, bring us, by all that we do here today, closer to him, so that we may become what all Christians should be—people who help others come to know you and love you and serve you.

OFFERTORY SENTENCE.   Jesus said, "He that findeth his life shall lose it: and he that loseth his life for my sake shall find it" (Matt. 10:39).

OFFERTORY PRAYER.   Lord, we come with so much while others have so little. Send our portion to those most in need that like good seed it will grow and flourish and blossom into the fruit of the Spirit, through him who is the first fruit of the kingdom.—E. Lee Phillips.

PRAYER.   O God: You have taught us to pray for one another; to give thanks, to confess, to intercede. You have taught us in the prayers of Scripture and of the saints and in the prayed lives of all faithful people.

Hear us, then, as we turn to you. Where we ask wisely and in faith, grant us our petitions. Where we ask foolish things, be kind. Where we sadly omit, fill in. Where our deepest-felt words Godward are between the lines, listen carefully. For ours is not a praying age and we are not a deeply praying people.

Hear our prayers of thanksgiving: for many good spirits that give us strength; for strong ties of human caring; for families that are very close; for people whose quiet humor clears the air; for persons enthusiastic about life, themselves, and all that is decent and fine; for the rare gift of common sense.

Hear our prayers of supplication, O God. Our best is flawed, incomplete. Only by your light do we see light. In the best of lives there is another side and much to tell. Without your mark of mercy our burden is more than we can bear. Hear us, then, and help us. We confess, O God: that we are too busy; that we are set in our ways not only of good but of wrong and of half-heartedness; that physical illness troubles us more than spiritual illness; that we say and do awful things to one another and hurt one another deeply and regularly.

Hear, O God, our prayers of intercession. Hear and help us in caring for one another. We pray, O God: for loved ones in nursing homes; for those ravaged by old age, "bare ruined choirs where late the sweet birds did sing"; for persons looking for work; for persons lonely, depressed, angry; for all undertaking some new thing. —Peter Fribley.

EVENING SERVICE

Topic: Christ the Renewer
TEXT: John 8:1–11.

I. The great aspect of sin is this: It completely corroded and disintegrated that which God made complete and whole.

(a) As man was made in the image of God, he was a whole man, he was an integrated man, he was a man who lived a life in the light of God, not in the darkness of selfishness, in the corrosion of hatred, loneliness, or prejudice. He was a whole man in a whole society, the center of which was God himself. That was man as created; that was man as God intended him to be.

(b) But we are *not* what we were intended to be until redeeming Love comes our way. That's why Christ is at the center of renewing the man. Here we are dealing with the tremendous power of God that can integrate the disintegrated; that can bring the fragmented men and women out of the fragments and create a whole man, a whole woman, a whole society.

II. Let's look at the incident in John, chapter 8—the woman who had been caught in adultery. The religious authorities—the Pharisees and scribes, the keepers of the Law—had caught this woman in the act of adultery and dragged her to the Temple to deal with her.

(a) As they dragged her along, there was beautiful orthodoxy in what they were doing, but there was no love in orthodoxy. It was a religion without mercy, without feeling, without love and without understanding. That kind of authority has no authority to renew her. The best they can do is to treat her like an object, a thing.

(b) We are talking about life corroded, life burdened to the core because that's exactly what sin is. This woman has missed the target for living. She has been taken advantage of by her weakness, and by humanity. And that's exactly what sin does. It's an exploitation, a misuse of humanity. Tell me, who could, on earth, put those pieces together? Let us see how the Lord deals with her.

(c) He turns to the crowd and says, "Anyone among you who has never committed the same sin or desired to commit that sin, let him throw the first stone." And they discovered that they too were fragments, that they too were as guilty and as bad inside as the woman was bad outside. And one after another, they walked out of the room, they quietly disappeared. The woman was still standing in the center. And Jesus said to her, "Woman, where are they? Has no one condemned you? Neither do I condemn you. Go and sin no more." No more judgment, no more condemnation, but renewal.

(d) Remember, you don't shock him. The renewer is here to deal with men and women who are just what they are. You are not necessarily respectable in his sight, but if you are what you are, you simply can sit at his feet as you are. Take heart. The renewal is for you. Christ is the renewer. —Festo Kivengere.

SUNDAY: APRIL TWENTIETH

MORNING SERVICE

Topic: The Lord of Death
TEXT: John 11:1–44.

Are we to view death as the ancient Greeks who saw death as the liberation of our souls from the prisons of our bodies? Or are we to take the fatalistic view that sees death as the archenemy of man who will eventually destroy us forever? Or are we to take the Christian view—that death is an enemy, but it is an enemy that has been conquered by Christ and now is under his control? It is comforting to know that the Lord whom we serve in this life, the one who exercises his authority while we live, shall also be in control when we die. Such is the case in the story of Lazarus.

I. The account of Jesus' reaction to the death of Lazarus is a highly personal account. Lazarus is unknown outside the Gospel of John, but we are assured that he was one whom Jesus loved. Jesus had personally exercised his authority in Lazarus' life. Now he would exercise his authority at his death.

(a) Just as Lazarus was personally and intimately known by Jesus, we too are assured that Jesus is our constant companion as we face the tragedies of our own lives, and as someday we face death itself. Every aspect of our lives is open to the loving scrutiny of our Heavenly Father. It is absurd to assume that Christ, who has been by our sides in every other experience of life, will abandon us at the experience of death. God forbid!

(b) We are told that as Jesus approached the tomb where Lazarus lay, he was overcome in a moment of emotional overflow. He "groaned" in his spirit, uttering untranslated sounds. He was deeply troubled; he shook himself. Then we read, "Jesus wept." The cause for this unusual display of emotion on the part of Jesus is open to debate. The picture of Lazarus's death, I feel, confronted Christ with the grim reality of his own looming death. The thought of it was enough to shake him.

(c) Shaken though he was, he was not defeated. When his "hour" did finally come, his desire was not to do his own will, but to do the will of the Father. And so, voluntarily Jesus gave his life. He died. As we face our own enounter with death, we may do so with complete knowledge that our Lord, the one who has personally shared in this event and overcome it, is with us.

II. Though there is great comfort in being assured of Christ's personal authority over death, we don't have to wait until we die to know that comfort. Christ's authority over death is already a present reality.

(a) If I have any criticism of the religion of my grandparents' day, it is that their religion was too much other-worldly in its view of life and death. Life on this side of the Jordan was simply to be endured so that we may enjoy security and happiness in the sweet by and by. What a tragedy it is when we Christians fail to see that life in Christ begins with our initial earthly experience with him and not with our final earthly experience with him.

(b) The people of God have already experienced victory over death. We live today with Christ, and so shall we forever. However, in viewing Christ's present authority over death, we must not forget the future dimension of the age to come. We have life today, but in the final consummation of the ages we shall experience the grandeur of God's blessings in a way far above our present understanding. We stand in the hope of a better day.

III. Christ's authority over death is also exercised *eternally*.

(a) Philosophers have for centuries sought to understand the nature of man's ultimate existence. Various men of intellect have projected their understanding of life in fatalistic terms. Others have seen man as a part of some great cosmic soul; when we die, we return to this cosmic soul until we find another body in which to live and are reincarnated. Our identity as a person is lost and is caught up in the cosmos.

(b) Neither of these two views of ultimate, eternal existence satisfy me or give me hope. But we can find the answer in the Holy Scriptures. The one word John uses more than any other to describe what Christ gives to us is *life*. "In Him was life, and the Life was the light of men." "Just as the Father has life, even so He gave to the Son also to have life in Himself." "I am the Bread of Life," he says. But he did not selfishly keep this life to himself. He would lay down his life and take it up again, so that we too might have life. He is the Good Shepherd who lays down his life for his sheep. He has come that we might have life and might have it abundantly. The Gospel of John ends with the concluding remarks that "this has been written that you may believe that Jesus is the Christ, the Son of God; and that believing you may have life in His name."

(c) The enemies of our Lord searched the Scriptures, for in them they thought eternal life could be found. Jesus traced the source of eternal life to himself: "That whosoever believes in Him should not perish, but have eternal life."

(d) Death is not something in which we are always spectators. It is an event in which we shall all share. The difference in bravely facing our own deaths and waiting in dread for this awful moment is what we believe about Jesus Christ. We believe he is Lord now. We believe he is Lord forever.—Lee McGlone.

Illustrations

BROUGHT TO LIFE.   A. M. Chirgwin quotes the modern example of Tokichi Ishii. Ishii had an almost unparalleled criminal record. He had murdered men, women, and children in the most brutal way. While in prison he was visited by two Canadian women who tried to talk to him through the bars, but he only glowered at them. In the end they abandoned the attempt to speak to him; but they gave him a Bible. He began to read it. He read on until he came to the story of the Crucifixion. He came to the words: "Father, forgive them, for they know not what they do," and these words broke him. "I stopped," he said. "I was stabbed to the heart, as if pierced by a five-inch nail. Shall I call it the love of Christ? Shall I call it his compassion? I do not know what to call it. I only know that I believed, and my hardness of heart was changed." Later, when the jailer came to lead the doomed man to the scaffold, he found not the hardened, surly brute he had expected but a smiling, radiant man, for the murderer had been born again. Literally Christ brought Tokichi Ishii to life.—William Barclay.

FINAL ASSURANCE.   Not only can we be sure that life in the world beyond will be vastly different, we can also be sure that God is in control, that God is Lord—first, last, and always! The God who created man from the dust of the earth, so that man became a living soul, can also out of the dust of our earthly existence create an eternal existence. "Thanks be to God who

gives us the victory through our Lord Jesus Christ" (1 Cor. 15:57, TEV). The risen Christ is "the guarantee that those who sleep in death will also be raised" (1 Cor. 15:20, TEV).—James W. Cox.

Sermon Suggestions

CHRISTIANS MUST BE CHILDLIKE.   Text: Matt. 18:1–6. (1) Not in mind and speech (1 Cor. 14:20; 13:11). (2) In humility and freedom from jealousy (cf. 1 Cor. 14:20). (3) In teachableness and submission to divine authority (cf. Eph. 6:1).—John A. Broadus.

FAITH IS A GIFT.   Gospel Text: John 10:22–30. (1) To those who belong to Christ. (2) Who prove their faith by following him. (3) And who are protected by the Father's power.

Worship Aids

CALL TO WORSHIP.   "I am the resurrection, and the life," said Jesus. "He that believeth in me, though he were dead, yet shall he live" (John 11:25).

INVOCATION: Hear us, O Lord, as we praise your name. Quicken our hearts by the power of your Spirit as we worship you. Call forth from us in this hour the best we have to offer you. Motivate us by the strength of your love to love you and all mankind. Descend upon us, O Lord, that we might see the glory which is Christ Jesus, our Lord and Savior.—John Jones, Jr.

OFFERTORY SENTENCE.   "Truly, truly I tell you," said Jesus, "unless a grain of wheat falls into the earth and dies, it remains a single grain; but if it dies it bears rich fruit. He who loves his life loses it, and he who cares not for his life in this world will preserve it for eternal life" (John 12:24–25, Moffatt Translation).

OFFERTORY PRAYER.   O God, who out of love created all things, give us now thy Spirit to love and give our all to thee. We know that thou art self-sufficient, yet thou hast taught us that it is more blessed to give than to receive. We have been receiving precious gifts from thee since the beginning of the week; and now, O Lord, that we want to show our gratitude, help us to give cheerfully and generously for thy kingdom's work here on earth. Above all, help us first to give ourselves to thee in all sincerity and then use us mightily in the world that thou lovest and for which thy Son, our Savior, died.—Abayomi Lawal.

PRAYER. We draw near to thee, our Heavenly Father, with gratitude and with thanksgiving. At thine hands we have experienced bounties innumerable, joys more than we can tell, mercies inexpressible. What tongue can speak of the kindnesses that thou hast manifested toward us, by the great realm of nature, which thou hast ordained to serve us and which is the minister of thy bounty; by all the blessings that thou hast sent into life through society; and by all the overrulings of thy providence by which the events of every day have conspired together for our good; but, above all, by thine own precious self, by Jesus, our Master and companion, and by the power of the Holy Ghost, through which we commune with thee and by which our life is lifted up above the flesh and holds sacred and blessed companionship with thy life? By all our thoughts, by all our affections, by every spiritual sentiment, we are brought into this companionship, and are the sons of God in very deed.

Oh! that there were in us that spirit that should make manifest more gloriously the power of God on the human soul. Oh! that, since we are sons, we might show ourselves princes, that, going forth, our faces may shine, and that men may know where we get our inspiration; where our comfort comes from; whence are all the gifts by which we are made strong in our combat with grief, with temptation, and with wickedness in high places.

We pray, O God! that thou wilt comfort any that are beginning this life and that see men as trees walking. Touch their eyes again. Grant that they may see clearly. May all those that are striving to follow thee but that see the discrepancy between their ideal and their real life, and mourn over it, be comforted and encouraged to persevere.

We beseech of thee that those who are tempted and carried by gusts of passion out of the way and find themselves disheveled and turned upside down, like men that are whirled in the tempest, may not give up in despair but gather again their energies and attempt once more to walk the royal way. Let none, having once put his hand to the plow, turn back. May no one count himself unworthy of eternal life.

Oh! that every one of us might behold the coming glory and be inspired with the thought of the joy and dignity to come. May every one of us take hold of present duty. And though we are filled with weaknesses and are conscious every day of sins, though infirmities multiply themselves without number on every side, though our whole life is illiterate, untaught, in things spiritual, yet may we look forward, and "*press* forward, toward the mark for the prize of the high calling of God in Christ Jesus."—Henry Ward Beecher.

EVENING SERVICE

Topic: "Heaven and Earth Are Shaken
TEXT: Heb. 12:25–29.

What do we see in the drama of our time? Has our world been left to the mercy of vast, impersonal forces that bear down upon us with unrelenting fury? If God is there, why does he not show his hand?

Our text reminds us that God is there. Not only is he there, he is doing something. There is divine purpose in the midst of this cosmic catastrophe. If we miss this, we become blind leaders of the blind who walk in the fearfulness of an uncertain tomorrow.

I. There is no way to properly interpret misery of man without seeing majesty of God.

(a) The writer and the readers of the Hebrew epistle knew what comes to man as time runs out in an era. Their estate was as uncertain as ours. Steadily and inevitably, terrific change was forced upon them. Judah gasped and went down in the death struggle with Rome. The sacred ritual of the Temple was swept away. That holy and beautiful house was burned and the abomination of desolation strode into the holy place. The whole earth shook and faith trembled with it. Where now was God? What now of his promise? Did he not know that the heathen were raging? Did he not care that the people imagined a vain thing? Is tragedy stronger than hope?

(b) The answer came in strange and daring fashion. God has not forsaken thee; rather it is he that hath done this! He is the author. And if it should seem incredible that he should thus shake his own temple, just remember that he will yet shake his own heavens. When man elevates himself against God and God's laws, God reestablishes the balance between himself and man.

How easy it is to lose sight of God. How casually we drift into a way of thinking that makes God a prisoner of the universe. This is what Toynbee is trying to say to us in his interpretation of history. Nations rise, flourish, grow fat, and settle down in ease. Then some hand shakes the kaleidoscope through which they view life and a new pattern evolves. It is God working a work in eternity.

II. Why does he thus shake down the heavens that canopy our ways? He does so in order that those things that can be shaken might be shaken.

(a) I would be possessed of anxiety neurosis, too, if the roots of my life had gone as deeply into the present world order as have the interests of most professing Christians. We may have joined in singing "this world is not my home," but we have consistently refused to believe that there is down here no continuing dwelling place. Aren't we about ready to listen to the Word of the Lord? It's not easy to ignore the prophets, but so far we've succeeded admirably (see Isa. 24:18–20).

(b) The Bible speaks repeatedly of the beginning and the end of the world. It may not fit your particular scheme of things, but no fair-minded interpreter of the Bible can successfully ignore scores of passages that teach it (see Mark 13:25, 31; Rev. 6:13).

Think you that I am guilty of the unpardonable sin of interpreting poetic metaphor as historical reality? Then I will ask you to consider one additional reference. In one of the later books, Second Peter, we find these words, "and the elements shall melt with fervent heat, and the earth also and the works that are therein shall be burned up" (2 Peter 3:10). Beloved, if this ever was vision, it is no longer such.

It has rather the sound of modern physics in it. Indeed this is the burden of men of science. One would almost conclude from our present attitude that God has not revealed himself in Chirst; and we must, therefore, learn of him from philosophers and scientists.

I am not condemning science for its knowledge—I condemn it for its idolatry, for its subtle idolatry, for the purpose of persuading us that this earth is the place for the establishment of the kingdom of God and we ourselves are well able to do it.

God has again shaken the earth; and if our hearts are set on those things that can be shaken, we are destined to go down with it (see Ps. 102:24b-27).

III. From before the foundation of the world God purposed an eternal kingdom. Creation's plan is subservient to God's eternal kingdom.

(a) There was a time when the world did not exist. There will be a time when it will no longer exist. There never was a time when God's redemptive purpose did not exist. And of his kingdom there shall be no end. Now, our text states that God "shakes not the earth only, but also Heaven . . . that those things which cannot be shaken may remain. Wherefore we receive a kingdom which cannot be moved. . . ." Thank God for this word!

(b) Every shaking of any earthly kingdom but moves us closer to the time of Christ. Empires wax and wane, but towering o'er them all one sees the figure of the eternal Son of God. The mob at his feet may rage. They may gamble again for the remains of his kingdom. They may go home and forget that he ever lived, but that Man on the cross will yet haunt them down a thousand million years.—Carl Bates.

SUNDAY: APRIL TWENTY-SEVENTH

MORNING SERVICE

Topic: How to Live a Full Life
TEXT: Acts 6:5.

It is a fair assumption that we all want to live full lives. After all, we only have one chance. Now, to see what this can mean to us and do for us, we are to look closely at the attractive character of Stephen, one of the heroes of the early Church. In the profile given of him, the word *full* is used several times. He is described as "a man full of faith and of the Holy Spirit . . . full of the Spirit and of wisdom . . . full of grace and power." The key to it all is that he was "filled with the Spirit." Here was a man whose life was posssessed, controlled, disciplined by the Spirit of God. All that he was and did came as the by-product of this tremendous experience. This is how to live a full life! How does this fullness of the Spirit express itself? What does a full life in the Spirit mean in practical terms? What is said of Stephen here can and should be true of all of us.

I. One sign of the Spirit-filled life is *faith*.

(a) Stephen is described as "full of faith." Everybody has some faith and lives by it. To talk of faith as a fortuitous gift that some people possess and others don't is absurd. Faith is woven into the very fabric of life itself and is an integral part of it. The question is not whether or not we shall live by faith, but rather by what faith we shall live. The atheist believes that there is no God and that the Universe is therefore ultimately meaningless—and lives and dies by that faith. The Christian believes that God is and that in Christ he has visited and redeemed us—and lives and dies by that faith.

(b) Fullness of faith in this connection is betting your life on God! It is trusting him absolutely, totally committing your life to him, for better, for worse, at all times, and in all circumstances. When we have such faith, we may be affected by temporal conditions, but we are not determined by them. We are determined by our unwaver-

ing faith in the God of the Scriptures and of Jesus Christ. We know that nothing, literally nothing, in life or death can separate us from his love.

(c) Fullness of faith in this connection is also getting things done for God! Faith is a dynamic, exciting power. Great believers are great achievers. You see, fullness of faith is not a matter of natural endowment, of an optimistic temperament, or of a credulous nature. It is a gift of God the Holy Spirit, the by-product of his presence with us.

II. A second sign of the Spirit-filled life is *wisdom*.

(a) Stephen is described as "full of wisdom." And wisdom is as invaluable as it is rare. It must be distinguished from knowledge. Modern intellectuals, with all they know about science, politics and current affairs, the physical universe, the physiological and psychological constitution of human nature, may be very conscious of their intellectual superiority. But they have to be reminded that they may still lack wisdom.

(b) Wisdom is moral insight, understanding, discernment, a sense of what is vital. The wise know more than facts; they know how to apply them and use them. The wise have sagacity in the affairs of life and in personal relationships, a sagacity rooted in moral integrity and spiritual sensitivity.

(c) This is often seen where understanding the Bible and Christian truth is concerned. Knowledge of Hebrew and Greek, of Biblical literature and doctrine is no infallible guarantee of spiritual wisdom. The Holy Spirit is our teacher here, as Jesus promised. Spiritual things are spiritually discerned.

III. A third sign of the Spirit-filled life is *grace*.

(a) Stephen is described as "full of grace." *Grace* is the loveliest word in the Christian vocabulary. The Greek word is *charis*, and in pre-Christian days it was used to describe the charm of a lady, the grace of a speech, the favor of a king. In

Christian usage, it describes the free, unmerited, saving love of God. What a tribute when our lives merit being called "full of grace"!

(b) To be "full of grace" is to have a charming manner. When Stephen was attacked and falsely accused by his enemies, we read that "gazing at him all who sat in the council saw that his face was like the face of an angel." The beauty of Jesus was seen in him, the charm of his Master. This graciousness is not merely external polish, a carefully manicured product of a charm school.

(c) Moreover to be "full of grace" is to have a forgiving spirit. Stephen was martyred, stoned to death for his fidelity to Christ. And his dying prayer was an echo of his Savior's prayer on the cross: "Lord, do not hold this sin against them"—a magnificent expression of magnanimity! To be gracious is to be forgiving, even as the grace of God has forgiven us.

IV. One more sign of the Spirit-filled life is *power*.

(a) Stephen is described as "full of power." This faithful, wise, gracious man was no weakling. He had experienced the fulfillment of Jesus' own promise: "You shall receive power when the Holy Spirit has come upon you." The Spirit empowers—mentally, morally, physically, spiritually. In the power of the Spirit, Stephen, like the apostles, witnessed. In that power we, too, are enabled to communicate our faith today.

(b) Further, in the power of the Spirit, Stephen endured. No hostility, no threat of death, could deflect him from his loyalty to Christ and the Church. He had the stamina to see through to the end the commitment he had made. And endurance is a quality to be prized in any realm of life—even above enthusiasm. The real test that separates the sunshine soldiers from the seasoned warriors is endurance. CONCLUSION

V. You can live a full life! That's the message of Pentecost. The Spirit has been given. Let him fill you with his spirit, with faith, wisdom, grace, and power. For that is a full life indeed. And it is all yours for the taking now.—John N. Gladstone.

Illustrations

MORE THAN CONQUEROR. There was an outstanding Scotsman at the end of the last century named Henry Drummond. His impact on the student life of Edinburgh, and far beyond, was enormous. He had critics who dismissed him as a "character," claiming that he had achieved distinction, not through merit but through a happy combination of fortuitous circumstances. A well-to-do home, a handsome appearance, a facile pen, an easy, talented platform manner—these, not character, explained his popularity, they said. But tragedy came to Drummond. In his early forties, he was smitten by a mysterious disease of the bones and lingered on for two years in excruciating agony. Yet, this dying man continued to exude the same grace the same indomitable optimism, the same unruffled equanimity. The critics were silenced. This man endured. He was more than conqueror!—John N. Gladstone.

SEEKERS AND FINDERS. Many different species of birds fly along the California deserts. Some make wide circles in search of food and never find anything to eat. Then there is that inspiring miracle we call the California hummingbird. He jets over the wasteland and spots a bright flower blooming on a remote cactus. He dives down, spearing the blood-red heart of the sweet desert blossom and drinks his honey. When others find nothing to eat, the hummingbird finds a flower.—Robert H. Schuller.

Sermon Suggestions

THE FIVE STAGES. Text: John 14:6. The Way is Christ, the Person, embodying the kingdom of God. The stages through which we pass in getting from our ways to the Way are: (1) Contact. (2) Conflict. (3) Conversion. (4) Cultivation. (5) Contribution—E. Stanley Jones.

REFLECTED GLORY. Gospel Text: John 13:31–35. (1) The command to love. (2) The example of love. (3) The evidence of love.

Worship Aids

CALL TO WORSHIP. "Ye shall go out with joy, and be led forth with peace: the mountains and the hills shall break forth before you into singing, and all the trees of the field shall clap their hands" (Isa. 55:12).

INVOCATION. "God of grace and God of glory," help us to look in the right places for fulfillment and joy. Let us begin the quest with you and trust your wisdom, so that when the days of opportunity are past we go out with joy and be filled with peace. To this end, make this a time of beginning for some and a time of beginning again for others.

OFFERTORY SENTENCE. "Give, and it shall be given unto you; good measure, pressed down, and shaken together, and running over, shall men give into your bosom. For with the same measure that ye mete withal it shall be measured to you again" (Luke 6:38).

OFFERTORY PRAYER. Dear Lord, as we think today about the hurt and pain of a hungry world, make us hungry for a word from you. Even though our stomachs are full, may we feel a need that goes deeper than any physical hunger, a need to be in a right relationship with you. We come now with an opportunity to re-establish that relationship, to reopen our lines of communication with our Maker and our Lord. We thank you for another such chance and pray that we might seize it in such a spirit of gratitude and worship that we all might be blessed.—James M. King.

PRAYER. Father, Source of our hope, we thank you for the blessings you have given us. We thank you for the privilege of worshiping you. We have not earned the right to know you. We not only fall to the temptation of sin, we even seek out sin. But even as we confess that we are unworthy, we are aware of your outstretched arms as a loving father welcoming one home from the far country. What is man that you are mindful of him?

Lord, give us the wisdom, the will, and the courage to share the love that you have given us with others. Help us to love our neighbor, to give ourselves willingly in your service.

There are those who would be with us today in this place but they could not. For those traveling we ask your protection. For those who are suffering we ask for your healing touch and the peace that only you can give. We know that, even in the midst of the tribulation of this world, Jesus has overcome the world.—Norman Brown.

EVENING SERVICE

Topic: Light for a New Life
TEXT: John 9:1–41.

I. A magazine advertisement showed the picture of a man groping his way along. The caption read, "Eyes that grope in a fog that never lifts." Blindness! That is our condemnation. We have been born blind—spiritually. And we remain blind until something drastic happens to us.

We can see well enough to do those things that pander to our physical appetites. We develop keen aptitude for walking in darkness. Sin loves darkness and thrives in it.

II. How did we become so blind to the better things, the higher, the eternal? It is fascinating to speculate. We can blame it on our parents. We can blame it on fate—"That is just the way we are!" A convicted criminal was found to have a tattoo on his body that said, "Born to go to hell!" But these speculations are unprofitable. Some of our best psychiatrists have given up on the technique of ferreting out a patient's past as a means of cure. What is going on now and what can happen in the future hold the key. Our very blindness may become an occasion for an amazing work of God.

III. Jesus Christ, the Light of the world, has come to take away our darkness, to heal us of our blindness. And it happens. What he came to do gets done when individuals begin to cooperate with him. Something real occurs with the first feeble efforts, but it is a growing experience— from one degree of faith to another.

IV. The new life in the light is not always

easy to live. Faith in Jesus Christ brings about a new way of looking at things. The old passes away and something new appears. New attitudes and new habits take hold. Then complications develop. The new believer now finds himself at odds with some individuals, groups, and institutions. He no longer fits in exactly. Instead of being shaped by his environment, he becomes—potentially—a shaper of it. He may, of course, with the best of intentions, with an abundance of zeal, become a bit impatient and short-tempered with his "adversaries." In any case, life will not always be easy. Persecution for one's faith is not limited to countries where the government is by policy antireligious or atheistic. There are subtle ways of trying to bring into line people who do not think as their opponents think. They may not be formally excluded from anything but only ignored and treated as nonpersons. Some people have been driven to suicide by this kind of exquisite torture. Others, however, have grown in faith and service as they have met opposition creatively, whether that opposition has come from persecution or from some form of temptation.

V. What makes the difference? It is the continual help of the one who takes away our blindness. In the hour of greatest need—as when the man who had been born blind was excluded from the synagogue—Christ comes to us. We may experience his presence in the Eucharist or in another high hour of private or public worship. Or we may sense his presence as we remember his "lo, I am with you always." Or some friend or stanger may appear with an unexpected word that blesses. So, walking "in the light as he is in the light" is a day-by-day possibility, difficulties and temptations notwithstanding.—James W. Cox, *Word and Witness*.

SUNDAY: MAY FOURTH

MORNING SERVICE

Topic: The Magnificently Varied Grace of God

Text: 1 Pet. 4:10, Phillips Translation.

You would recognize at once the Greek word Peter uses here in talking about gifts and grace. It is *charisma*. In Christian usage, *charisma* doesn't refer to an elite minority, one here and one there who exudes a mysterious quality of charm. It refers to all who believe, all who love and serve our Lord Jesus Christ, all who truly belong to the Church, which is his body, and know the power of the Holy Spirit. A charisma may take many different forms. There is nothing set or stereotyped about it. The grace of God is magnificently varied. I would like to explore with you some of these varied expressions.

I. In the first place, the Christian charisma expresses itself *in personal salvation*.

(a) The greatest of all the gifts of God's grace is salvation. Salvation means health and joy and peace. Now, you can't earn this, win this, buy this. It is a gift to be received in penitence and faith. So, every Christian believer rejoicing in the gift of saving faith is a charismatic Christian.

(b) We are to be faithful dispensers of this gift. This means that a primary emphasis of the Church must always be evangelism, sharing the good news of salvation with a lost, gone-wrong world. All our sincerest efforts are a misplacing of energy unless they lead to faith in him who can save both the individual and society.

II. In the second place, the Christian charisma expresses itself *in vigorous thought*.

(a) As with faith, so with reason—it is a gift of God's grace. Unexamined prejudices are among the greatest enemies of the Church and lead to all kinds of divisions and disturbances. Vigorous, honest thought is the answer.

(b) To be sure, Christians vary in their mental capacities. But we should thank God that there are among us faithful stewards of the gift of reason, scholars to shape our theology, expound and interpret the Scriptures, and equal the best thinkers outside the Church. It is our duty to honor their work, to sit at their feet and learn from them. All of us, whatever our natural capacities may be, are under obligation to love the Lord our God not only with our hearts and souls and strength but also with our minds.

III. Again, the Christian charisma expresses itself *in forgiving love*.

(a) Forgiveness is at the very heart of the gospel. The very essence of the good news we have believed and declare is that God forgives sins through Jesus Christ, and we are to be forgiving people.

(b) Forgiveness is never cheap. The cost of our forgiveness to God was the precious blood of Christ. It is the cost of forgiveness, a cost so prodigious and enormous that makes it moral and moves us to saving penitence. It is also difficult to forgive and, in our own strength, often impossible. But this forgiving love is a gift of grace, a *charisma* of God; and we must pray for it. It is the most powerful therapeutic gift in the world, and let loose, it will bring healing and hope to people and nations.

IV. In the fourth place, the Christian charisma expresses itself *in unselfish service*. "Serve one another with the particular gifts God has given each of you. . . ."

(a) The New Testament insists that every Christian has a charisma. For too long we have thought of gifts in terms of the spectacular, the dramatic, the obvious. All service ranks the same with God. A healthy Church is one that unites a great diversity of gifts in the fellowship of the spirit for the glory of God.

(b) A Christian charisma is a gift that grows. I have seen this happen wonderfully in our own Church. Ordinary people have begun serving, timidly, hesitantly, and they have grown in stature and ability under the burden of responsibility. The Spirit of Christ has enabled them and transformed them. It can happen to you, if you are willing to discover, discipline, and dedicate the gift that is in you.

V. Once more, the Christian charisma expresses itself *in generous giving*.

(a) *Grace* means the self-giving love of God in Christ for a race both lost and loved. Our impulse to give is of God—a *charisma*.

(b) There are some dreadfully false theories about giving circulating among some Christians. Supremely dreadful is the idea that if we give to God, he is sure to favor us and make us more prosperous than the nongivers!

(c) No! No! How each of us gives as God prospers us is a decision between ourselves and God. But we should make the decision in the light of his generosity to us, as "faithful dispensers of the magnificently varied grace of God." God asks no more and no less—that we should be faithful. "It is required of stewards that a man be found faithful." The capacity to be a generous, faithful giver is in itself of God, a gift to be coveted and sought. And no gift brings with it a greater blessedness and inner contentment.—John N. Gladstone.

Illustrations

AN EXPENSIVE LOYALTY.   In an English parish church there is a memorial tablet to a Cavalier soldier who gave generously of his money to the Royalist cause and in the end gave himself. This tribute to him is carved on the tablet: "He served King Charles with a constant, dangerous, and expensive loyalty."—John N. Gladstone.

A DIVINE COMPULSION.   The finest words for that compulsion, I think, are to be found in *King Lear*. In one scene the banished Duke of Kent returns in disguise to take service with King Lear, and this dialogue takes place:

LEAR: What wouldst thou?
KENT: Service.
LEAR: Who wouldst thou serve?
KENT: You.
LEAR: Dost thou know me, fellow?
KENT: No sir, but you have that in your countenance which I would fain call master.—Halford E. Luccock.

Sermon Illustrations

WAY OF BLESSING; WAY OF WOE.   Text: Luke 6:17–26. (1) The God-centered way brings blessing. (2) The self-centered way brings woe.

THE FIRST RETURN OF CHRIST. Gospel Text: John 14:23–29. (1) He comes to dwell in those who keep his word. (2) He comes to continue his work as Teacher. (3) He comes to bring his special peace.

Worship Aids

CALL TO WORSHIP. "The joy of the Lord is your strength" (Neh. 8:10).

INVOCATION. Father-God, we are here this morning because we know you to be the one true, living God. Our faith in you has caused us to gather together, and we ask that this faith that has brought us thus far be multiplied as the product of our worship. We look to you today for the assurance of your presence. Lead us this week in an awareness of being your children, teaching us to respond to your will in every appropriate way.—Cindy Johnson.

OFFERTORY SENTENCE. "It is in God's power to provide you richly with every good gift; thus you will have ample means in yourselves to meet each and every situation, with enough and to spare for every good cause" (2 Cor. 9:8, NEB).

OFFERTORY PRAYER. Our Father, we know that we can give only what we have. You have always endowed us with some gift of providence or grace that we can offer on the altar of the church's stewardship. Receive, we pray, what we bring to you in love and gratitude.

PRAYER. Lord, make us instruments of your peace. Where there is hatred, let us sow love; where there is injury, pardon; where there is discord, union; where there is doubt, faith; where their is despair, hope; where there is darkness, light; where there is sadness, joy. Grant that we may not so much seek to be consoled as to console; to be understood as to understand; to be loved as to love. For it is in giving that we receive; it is in pardoning that we are pardoned; and it is in dying that we are born to eternal life. —Attributed to St. Francis, *The Book of Common Prayer*.

EVENING SERVICE

Topic: How to Treat Sinners
TEXT: Matt. 9:9–13.

I. We may feel more justified than ever in taking a hard line with "sinners." We are sick of the kind of permissiveness that puts a halo of approval on many vices. Perhaps we have been victims of violence or a family member has been drawn away into a destructive pattern of life and has hurt us deeply. Why should we add our influence to an already negative force among us and compound the ills of our society?

II. We remember that the Apostle Paul said, "You must put to death, then, the earthly desires at work in you, such as immorality, indecency, lust, evil passions, and greed" (Col. 3:5, TEV). But we easily forget that he also went on to say, "And you yourselves at one time used to live among such men, when your life was dominated by those desires" (Col. 3:7, TEV). Too easily we may forget our own past. On the other hand, we may be like the elder brother in Jesus' parable of the prodigal son: totally unsympathetic because we, unlike others, have not been strongly tempted to commit sins of the flesh.

The sins of the Pharisees were greater than those of the tax collectors and sinners. Henry Drummond once said, "The very fact that the world sees the coarser sins so well is against the belief that they are the worst. The subtle and unseen sin, that sin in the part of the nature most near to the spiritual, ought to be more degrading than any other. Yet for many of the finer forms of sin society has yet no brand. This sin of the elder brother is a mere trifle, only a little bit of temper, and scarcely worth the recording."

III. Not one of Jesus' first disciples was from among the Pharisees, if we except Nicodemus, a secret disciple. They were from "the people of the land," not from the religiously elite. The Apostle Paul was first Saul of Tarsus, a Pharisee. Before he became a servant of Jesus Christ, he had to be shaken to his foundations and rebuilt. He had to come to the place where he would admit that he was the "chief" of sinners, so that he could say, even of himself, "if any one is in Christ, he is a new creation; the old has passed away, behold, the new has come" (2 Cor. 5:17). Christianity, then, requires love rather than ritual; acceptance of the sinner, in spite of his sin. Sometimes achieving this attitude comes "through many tribulations."

IV. The teaching of the Old Testament, the example and teaching of Jesus, amd the experience and teaching of the Apostle Paul suggest that we who are trying to be Christian ought to be charitable toward those whose lives have been and are being wasted by all kinds of wrongdoing. Karen Horney, a renowned psychiatrist, said that in psychiatric practice the therapist must *accept* the patient as a person but does not have to *approve* of his behavior. Both individuals and nations often need such treatment.

Lord Shaftesbury, the English social reformer, walked up to a man being released from prison for the nineteenth time, shook the man's hand and said, "Ah, Maynard, we'll make a man of you yet. We'll make a man of you yet." Years later the man testified, as he recalled the incident, "That was forty-three years ago come Michaelmas, and I've never seen the inside of a prison cell since."

How shall we as a nation deal with former enemy nations and nations that are or that we imagine to be enemies? D. T. Niles, the Christian statesman/minister from Ceylon, said, "Treat a man as a brigand, and he will act as a brigand."—James W. Cox, *Word and Witness*.

SUNDAY: MAY ELEVENTH

MORNING SERVICE

Topic: Consecrated in the Truth
TEXT: John 17:19.

My text is a part of one of Jesus' prayers, and it clearly shows the deep concern he had as he talked to God on behalf of those who were his disciples. Jesus was praying that his followers would be "consecrated in truth" or, in other words, settled in righteousness and faithful in service.

I. Jesus expected his voluntary death for the disciples to have certain effects upon them. Jesus wanted to see his disciples confirmed in grace, fully involved in God's will as he had taught them to be. He wanted them to be faithful and fruitful in carrying out the purpose for which he was about to die.

(a) So Jesus solemnly set himself to face death on their behalf. A sense of concern prompted his deed while a sense of destiny filled his mind.

(b) But Jesus saw wider horizons than the immediate present, and he saw a wider circle than the immediate disciples. Thus he said to God, "I do not pray for these only, but also for those who believe in me through their word" (John 17:20). That includes us.

(c) Jesus knew that through his followers he could further spread the saving word, he could reach more people, and he could bless more lives. Jesus wants us all consecrated in truth, confirmed in right living, and prepared for faithful service for God in his name.

II. As followers of Jesus, you and I are heirs to the effects of this prayer.

(a) Jesus wants us to be confirmed in his grace and governed by *his* interests. He wants us all to experience the influence of his life.

(b) He wants to engage our full attention, motives, thought-life, and energies. He wants to retain our conscience. He wants to inform our faith and direct our will. This is what the rest of the New Testament calls *sanctified living*.

(c) Jesus wants to lead us all beyond a simply human performance in which selfishness and sin hinder our lives. He wants us to know and follow the principles and perspectives by which he lived and worked.

III. Jesus used himself in the interest of others—you, me, everyone.

(a) Our Lord's desire is to see us help others in his name. No believer or church can live in his full pleasure apart from this higher allegiance, this focused concern to live and work for the sake of others.

(b) Both the individual Christian and the local church must forever remember that sacrifice is inherent in living a consecrated life.

IV. Our text shows us how Jesus viewed his commitment to God. He gave himself with thoughtful resolve. He acted in love.

(a) When did you last review your commitment? When did you last take inventory of your concerns, your motives, and your deeds? If you have not done so lately, I ask you to do it now.

(b) We all know that an uncommitted life is an unproductive life. Uncommitted persons do not look beyond themselves because they serve only themselves; they do not carry a burden for our Lord's will, nor do they live by that will.

(c) Jesus wants us committed. Jesus wants us all confirmed in grace and freed from the circle of limited, selfish concerns. Jesus wants us to be like him—consecrated in the truth and useful to God and helpful to others.

V. It is time for committed, consecrated living.

(a) If we are to please God, if we are to be saved, we must be committed persons. If we are to prevail in this unbalanced, unheeding, uncaring, unreasonable, unsafe, and ungodly society, we must live consecrated lives.

(b) Being consecrated in truth means that we will act at all times in accordance with what is godly, with what is expedient, with what is helpful, and with what is essential to further the ministry of Jesus.—James Earl Massey.

Illustrations

A UNITY OF SERVICE. Doctrinal rigidity cannot heal us. Our beliefs, or at least our interpretation of our beliefs, have always been imperfect, for the church is not only a society of forgiven sinners, it is also a society of deluded sinners. The first men who followed Jesus followed through faith, not knowing very clearly who he was, yet trusting his word. "Follow me, and I will make you fishers of men" (Matt. 4:19). Everything that they came to believe about him they learned in fellowship with him. Even at the cross

and after the Resurrection there were times when the apostles disagreed, (that is, Peter and Paul).

There real faith came through action. Theirs was a unity of service. Our unity will be restored as we put down our prideful pretention to omniscience and personal adequacy.—Charles A. Trentham.

A COMPELLING VISION. No artist is great who simply draws lines and applies colors according to the rules of some textbook; he must have those fascinating and tormenting visions of beauty, as well as unquenchable longing to see his vision become visible on canvas or audible in an inspired orchestra. There is no great scientist without a passion for research, no great philosopher who is content with the history and criticism of his field but fails to be a consecrated devotee of truth. Only from the soil that in some real (though not literal) sense is soaked with blood will the loveliest flowers and the ripest fruits come in their perfection. "He that loseth his life, he alone can really save it."—Herbert Welch.

Sermon Suggestions

THE RENEWAL OF CREATION. Text: 2 Pet. 3:13. (1) There is an obvious need for it. (2) The expectation of it is rooted in a present experience of change. (3) The only world that will satisfy the child of God is that in which his Father's will is known and done.—Andrew C. Zenos.

THE SCOPE OF CHRISTIAN UNITY. Gospel Text: John 17:20–26. (1) It is modeled in the unity of the Father and the Son. (2) It is a gift to the believing church. (3) It reaches out to the unbelieving world.

Worship Aids

CALL TO WORSHIP. "Consecrate yourselves today to the Lord" (Exod. 32:29).

INVOCATION. Because we have praise to offer, thanks to give, friendships to repair, and service to you and to one another to render, we would present ourselves to you. Strengthen our weak desire; correct our many mistakes; and give us a clear vision of your will for our lives.

OFFERTORY SENTENCE. "Keep your life free from love of money, and be content with what you have; for he has said, 'I will never fail you nor forsake you' " (Heb. 13:5, RSV).

OFFERTORY PRAYER. Our Father, grant that through love of thee and love of one another we may always be masters of our gifts and our achievements and mastered by none of them, to the end that we might serve thee supremely.

PRAYER. We pause in sacred memory, O God, to lift our thoughts of gratitude for those who mothered us—who shared with us the warmth of their bodies when we first ventured forth in thy universe, who shared with us their affection when life lay hostile about us, who shared with us their love when the world was too much with us, who shared with us themselves when we felt the heaviness of living. And now bless those who today guide the fate of thy children. Take away their heaviness of heart when their dreams are shattered; remove their anxieties when problems fall thick upon them; ease their frustrations when the days' events prove exhausting. Stay beside them as they listen in the darkness of the night for returning footsteps; bulwark their spirits when the patter of many feet would shatter their poise; strengthen their hearts when helplessness takes over and they feel their labors are in vain. When irritating problems would tempt them to lay down their tools, when the daily annoyances would take away their high resolves, and when the cries in the night would weaken their spirits, remind them of their high obligations and the joys at the end of the road.—Fred E. Luchs.

EVENING SERVICE

Topic: The Spectrum of Caring
TEXT: Prov. 31:25–31; Rom. 12:1–2; Luke 1:26–32; John 19:25–27.

The gospel lessons today show the broad spectrum of caring that is needed. Mary is before us today from that first burst of joy, pregnant with Jesus, Son of God, to be Savior of the World, to that bloody cross humped up against a blackened sky, a crucible where he was hanged by the collusion of forces and powers still with us today. Mary maintained a mother's caring all the way through her son's life. And that's the point, the virture, the spectrum of caring.

I. Caring has always to balance the promise with its reality.

(a) The promise at pregnancy has to be weighed against the disappointment at death. The balanced spectrum of caring must always move from beginnings that are so sweet and simple to those tough crosses that appear on the hills of our individual lives.

(b) So, the spectrum of caring is still an inherent part of the mothering, nurturing of today. Indeed, the nurturing of mother church has to face some of these same changes and tasks.

II. The spectrum of caring has to take into account the changing roles of the mother who discovers she is first woman. Women today are being deluged by what they should think, feel, do, be. Some women feel guilty because they enjoy, like, are fulfilled by being wives, mothers, homemakers. The only *must* today is the *must* of being who you are and want to be.

III. The spectrum of caring also has to understand the concept of interpretation of life to children. The fact is we don't protect our kids from anything today. The trick is to interpret to them what is a sane and caring approach to the world about them. They will see and hear it all. Our task as parents, even as Church, is not to try to shield as much as it is to interpret once things are seen and heard.

IV. The spectrum of caring as a mother today keeps in perspective the primary relationship with husband. The "one flesh" concept is not the parent-child concept, it is the husband-wife concept. W. M. Brodie, who has for years worked with emotionally disturbed children, says, "that, when the parents were emotionally close, more invested in each other than either was in the child, the child improved. When either parent became more emotionally invested in the child than in the other parent, the child immediately and automatically regressed. When the parents were emotionally close, they could do no wrong in their management of the child. The child responded well to firmness, permissiveness, punishment, talking it out, and other management approaches. When the parents were emotionally divorced, any and all management approaches were equally unsuccessful."

V. The spectrum of caring uses memory to hold us in moments of hurt. I can imagine Mary's standing before the cross and having quick flashbacks and vignettes, episodes when Jesus was a boy, growing up in Nazareth. Memories help us keep the balance, don't they? They take us away for a moment from the immediacy of hurt. They provide us respite.

VI. The spectrum of caring also runs the risk that care will have to be given with no promise that anything of worth will ever be given back.

(a) That is the heart of most of our disappointments, isn't it? Mothers or no, our most frequent form of frustration is that we don't get back enough for what we've given.

(b) I'm sure Mary wanted Jesus to become successful, be well received. And if she was there for the triumphant entry, her hopes went sky high, only to have them crash to earth by the end of the week. But there was a grand moment of gratitude. Jesus commended her keeping to John. He couldn't give her all that she wanted or expected, but gratitude he did give. Gratitude sometimes makes up for a host of frustrations. We don't always fulfill one another's expectations, but we can at least be grateful and express that in our lives.—Thomas H. Conley.

SUNDAY: MAY EIGHTEENTH

MORNING SERVICE

Topic: An Antidote for Apostasy
TEXT: John 15:26–27; 16:4b-11.

I. Falling away from faith in God has been an aspect of human behavior almost since the beginnings of time. The people of Israel, for example, were notorious for their apostasy, and the Old Testament contains the writings of the many prophets who sought to bring Israel back into relationship with their God.

(a) The very real danger of apostasy also exists for Christians. In fact, Jesus Christ himself saw that possibility even during the course of his earthly ministry. Indeed, as he prepared to depart from his disciples, he warned them of the difficulties that they would encounter. Aware that they could not alone cope with the hostility that would be directed against them, Jesus guaranteed his disciples another source of strength and comfort—the Holy Spirit.

(b) This Holy Spirit, moreover, would confirm, in the hearts of the disciples, all that they had learned and experienced during their association with Jesus. They would be convinced beyond all doubt of the revelation of God through Jesus Christ and assured of his subsequent return. In short, the coming of the Holy Spirit would place the Christ even into such a faithful perspective that the disciples would be able to persevere in *any* hostile environment.

II. The Holy Spirit was not merely available to those first disciples who personally knew Jesus.

(a) He is also available to all who call themselves disciples. We, who are members of the twentieth-century Church, still have need of the Holy Spirit to help sustain and strengthen our faith in the very face of the pressures of life in a modern technological society. The same forces that challenged the faith of the early Christians challenges our faith today. Indeed, with the increasing complexity of the twentieth-century world, there probably exist even more temptations to apostasy than existed in past centuries.

(b) Thus, like so many Christians over the centuries, we are often tempted to "fall away" from faith by taking the path of least resistance. Authentic faith in Jesus Christ places responsibilities upon us regarding the way we live and how we use our resources. Christ bids us to love one another and our neighbor. All of these aspects of the Christian life tend, whether we like it or not, to separate us from friends and relatives who tend to do what they want when they want to do it.

III. Contrary to our well-rehearsed excuses, "falling away" from Christ does hurt. Quite apart from placing ourselves in mortal danger of God's judgment and punishment, apostasy hurts not only ourselves but many others as well. We are no longer influenced by the revelation of God through Jesus Christ in our relationships with other persons.

(a) Consequently, we can fall into the most brutal and self-serving kinds of behavior. Throughout the history of the human race, particularly since the time of Christ, the most violent and brutal men have been those who have little sense or experience of God.

(b) So, be strong in your faith through the Holy Spirit. Let no person cause you to "fall away" from Christ by dangling in front of you the easy path of least resistance. Allow the Holy Spirit of God to reinforce in your hearts and minds the revelation that *is* Jesus Christ—a revelation that leads to life and away from the way of worldly compromise and apostasy that leads only to sin and ultimate death.—Rodney K. Miller.

Illustrations

DEEP ROOTS.   I tried to remember who I was, where I'd come from, and where I was going back to. And if you do that, everything will work out all right.—Harry S. Truman.

CONFUSED BY TRUTH ITSELF.   The Christian who lives in an age of hydrogen bombs, interstellar communication, space capsules, nuclear power, and political revolutions must remember that the simple faith of childhood is often challenged by doubt. It is never easy to live in such a world. One day a student came to my study in the university, and there was bewilderment written all over his face. He said to me, "I have just come from a lecture where I learned something that I never thought possible, and the professor pulled the rug out from under my life." Then he said, "I wish I had never heard it." It is much more comfortable and agreeable to accept everything that is put before you, whether food or facts: Ask no questions, and just swallow. There is a popular cliché: I have made up my mind, don't confuse me with facts.—Joseph R. Sizoo.

Sermon Suggestions

WHY WE ACT THAT WAY.   Text: Luke 9:39 –49. (1) Because of the way we were taught. (2) Because of our insight into ourselves or the lack of it. (3) Because of the "set of the soul." (4) Because of our attitude toward Jesus Christ.

WHEN THE HOLY SPIRIT COMES.   Gospel Text: John 15:26–27; 16:4b-11. (1) He bears witness to Christ. (2) He does the work of Christ.

Worship Aids

CALL TO WORSHIP.   "The Lord searcheth all hearts, and understandeth all the imaginations of the thoughts" (1 Chron. 28:9).

INVOCATION.   O God, who on this day taught the hearts of your faithful people by sending to them the light of your Holy Spirit: Grant us by the same Spirit to have a right judgment in all things, and evermore to rejoice in his holy comfort; through Jesus Christ your Son our Lord, who lives and reigns with you, in the unity of the Holy Spirit, one God, for ever and ever.—*Book of Common Prayer*.

OFFERTORY SENTENCE.   "Offer to God a sacrifice of thanksgiving, and pay your vows to the Most High" (Ps. 50:14).

OFFERTORY PRAYER.   Lord, where our hands are closed, open. Where our hearts are shut, pry. Where our resolve is weak, prod. Lead us to give as we have received, that we may live as we know we ought, through him who gave his life to open us to life abundant.—E. Lee Phillips.

PRAYER. "Jesus (is) the mediator of a new covenant, whose sprinkled blood has better things to tell than the blood of Abel" (Heb. 12:14, NEB). The blood of Abel, Lord, stains our hands and cries out from the ground. It smears the pages of our defense budget. It throbs as a red memory in our grey conscience. It clots the arteries of love between black and white, the strong and the weak, the rich and the poor. We need a transfusion of Christ's life. The same pulse of grace that beat in him must beat in us. The same love that surged through him must surge in us. O God, may our lives be marked by Christ's blood and not Abel's, by forgiveness and not revenge, by peace and not war.—Thomas H. Troeger.

EVENING SERVICE

Topic: Take with You Words
TEXT: Hos. 14:2.

The Old Testament prophet, Hosea, was talking to his own nation about repentance, but he could have been talking about all of life and each one of us. "Take with you words," he said. Whatever else we take, we shall certainly take—words! Words are the vehicles of our thoughts, the outlet for our ideas. And words are charged with tremendous power. They can hurt or heal, pacify or inflame, inspire or depress. The words we take and speak do tend to betray who and what we are. We shall all speak and write thousands of words throughout the years. But few or many, what words should we take with us? I make three suggestions.

I. Take with you words of *praise*.

(a) Now, true praise is not something to be given lightly or glibly. It makes demands, if it is to be worth giving and receiving. It demands magnanimity. Magnanimous people are big people, generous in outlook, able to soar above pettiness and jealousy. Littleness cannot praise or congratulate. It begrudges another's success, prosperity, gifts.

(b) It demands sincerity. Praise that is in fact blatant flattery, designed only to curry favor, or given when it is obviously not merited is better not spoken. It can even have the reverse effect.

(c) It demands a principle of selection. Some people instinctively look for faults and weakness in anything and anybody—and find them. Others look for virtues and strengths—and find them.

II. Take with you words of *encouragement*.

(a) There is never a shortage of people or circumstances to pour cold water over us and our most strenuous efforts. This world is full of depressors.

(b) Words of encouragement are contagious. Faith elicits faith. Encouragement gives fresh nerve, self-confidence, the will to persevere. Our society is hurting for what has been called "the little loves"—words of hope and encouragement spoken in due season, removing the burden of insufficiency, releasing unsuspected unused gifts.

(c) It is particularly important to speak these words to children and young people. Here we need to be lavish in encouragement. Never worry about keepng them humble. Life will look after that!

III. Take with you words of *witness*.

(a) Many of us are extremely reticent here. We are Christians, but silent Christians. In our place of business, school, the club, few know where our central loyalty is to be found. How can they? We never talk about it. We keep our faith in Christ and the church as dark as possible. What is more, we have a good excuse for so doing. "I let my life speak," is the classic excuse. "I try to live the Christian life rather than talk about it." The truth here is that actions do speak louder than words, and an inconsistent life will nullify our pious phraseology. Whose life is so good that our mere example, alone, is a sufficient witness? It is precisely because our lives are not good enough that we must also have the courage to witness by word. Precisely because we do falter and fail we must be ready to speak of Christ and acknowledge our allegiance.

(b) To be sure, speaking the word of witness calls for tact and a proper sense of the occasion. Courtesy, good taste, and common sense are against the militant witness who accosts all and sundry with the blunt question "Are you saved?"

(c) But avoiding such pitfalls, we should

not hesitate to speak a good word for Jesus Christ, to share our love for his church, to articulate the personal convictions we live by and will die by. A word of witness, spoken naturally, sincerely, and lovingly, may have eternal significance in the life of another. "Take with you words" of praise, encouragement, witness.

IV. But we must complete this injunction of Hosea. "Take with you words and return to the Lord: say to him, 'Take away all iniquity: accept that which is good and we will render the fruit of our lips.' " The prophet is underlining two needs. There is the need for *repentance*. Then there is the need for *meaningful action*. In other words, we will reinforce our words with deeds. We will give meaning and credibility to what we say by what we do. Our actions will conform to our words. It comes to this. Our words are terribly important. Our actions are equally important. What God had joined together, let no man put asunder.—John N. Gladstone.

SUNDAY: MAY TWENTY-FIFTH

MORNING SERVICE

Topic: But If We Suffer with God
TEXT: Rom. 8:16–17.

People in the midst of darkness are not primarily concerned, if at all, with argument and complaint. What they seek lies in another direction altogether: someone to help them out of their trouble. And so it is that we look not for arguments to satisfy the inquiring mind but for resources to sustain the fainting heart. And through a window of faith we see beyond the valley to the hills from whence cometh our help. Paul says, "Provided we suffer with Christ we may also be glorified with him." Suffering obviously is news of evil report, we say. Sometimes it is altogether tragic. But seen through the window of Christian faith this report begins to make sense, for if we suffer with God then suffering can be the occasion for good news.

I. First of all there is good news in the discovery that, as we suffer with God, *he suffers with us*.

(a) This is not good news just because "misery loves company"; misery does not love company that well. No, in God's suffering we encounter something more than misery loving company; there is real soul therapy—great spiritual healing in the companionship of a God who shares our deepest grief, our sharpest pain, our darkest despair. For one thing it assures us that in the vast scheme of life we have not been abandoned or forgotten in the dale of trouble. For another it encourages us to discover that God does not willingly afflict us or complacently stand by as a spectator. Whatever we suffer, he suffers with us.

(b) Talk to the ones who have come up through the vale of sorrow and their word is always the same. Although we may never understand *why* we suffer, it removes that suffering from the realm of meaningless affliction if God bears it all with us. At the very least, it is a comfort to know that someone, God above all others, understands. At the very highest, all things become new in the assurance that come what may, nothing can separate you from God's love, that his love never sees you enter any valley alone but goes there with you, that there is nothing in all creation that you and he together cannot see through in triumph.

II. Moreover, there is good news in the discovery that, suffering with God, we can make an offering of our suffering.

(a) Psychologically this is healing: not to have to stand and "take it," like a passive pincushion, receiving all the shafts of pain that life drives into us. Inwardly, if we can offer our pain and sorrow and anguish to God, we have marvelously transformed suffering. No longer is it our master but our gift. The primary thing is never the physical distress, or the mental turmoil, or even the spiritual anguish, but rather the inner response that the soul makes to these outward influences.

(b) Thus, suffering, whether from divine retribution for sin, or suffering from sorrow, or pain from natural cause, can be offered as a sacrifice to God as a means of serving him. It was through suffering that

Christ became one with his Father's will. Suffering, you see, can become a challenge and an instrument of God's love.

III. Then suffering can be good news if it leads us into closer knowledge and fellowship with God.

(a) Always one of the first effects of suffering is to strip away life's outer defenses. The security we have come to feel in the things with which we have surrounded ourselves is suddenly gone. Values suddenly assume their proper dimension, as though the fog in which we dwelt had in that moment lifted and the near and distant scenes taken their true size and shape. This indeed is one of the purposes that suffering may serve, that it forces us to let go of luxuries, toys, playthings, gadgets of which we have grown too fond, forcing us back upon God until we find in him our only abiding security and stronghold.

(b) Of course, not automatically does this follow in the train of suffering. Some people grow bitter. Others, when forced to let go of health, or success, or hearts dear to them, do not seek the covert of God's wings but escape into private worlds of the unreal. A soul drooping in the deep gloom of suffering is no witness to the glory of God. But suffering must first be faced in all of its reality, and its ministry received. Then, and only then, if we suffer with God we find him as we never could find him in the sunlight of perfect composure or placid peace.

IV. Suffering is good news if it leads us through pain to larger sympathies and closer bonds with fellow children of God.

(a) Suffering, if it is self-enclosed, all dammed up within the soul, may indeed become a poison to the soul. There is no gospel in such affliction, no gospel in mere suffering for the sake of suffering. But again, with Paul, if we suffer with God then pain becomes for us what it was for Christ: a way into the heart of God's family.

(b) Through my pain I can take my stand beside pain-filled hearts in all the places of the earth. On the cross Christ endured pain, not just for himself; he suffered there *with* and *for* all men. We speak altogether too casually about "bearing our crosses." Notwithstanding, in a profound way suffering can become for us a cross if we accept it with God and if it leads us to suffer with all men as Christ was doing on the cross.—Robert E. Luccock.

Illustrations

REVELATION IN A DEATH CAMP.   We were at work in a trench. The dawn was grey around us; grey was the sky above; grey the snow in the pale light of dawn; grey the rags in which my fellow prisoners were clad, and grey their faces. I was again conversing silently with my wife, or perhaps I was struggling to find the reason for my sufferings, my slow dying. In a last violent protest against the hopelessness of imminent death, I sensed my spirit piercing through the enveloping gloom. I felt it transcend that hopeless, meaningless world, and from somewhere I heard a victorious yes in answer to my question of the existence of an ultimate purpose. At that moment a light was lit in a distant farmhouse, which stood on the horizon as if painted there, in the midst of the miserable grey of a dawning morning in Bavaria. *"Et lux in tenebris lucet"*—and the light shineth in the darkness.—Viktor E. Frankl.

A CURIOUS FACT.   The Christian doctrine of suffering explains, I believe, a very curious fact about the world we live in. The settled happiness and security that we all desire, God withholds from us by the very nature of the world: but joy, pleasure, and merriment, he has scattered broadcast. We are never safe, but we have plenty of fun, and some ecstasy. It is not hard to see why. The security we crave would teach us to rest our hearts in this world and oppose an obstacle to our return to God: a few moments of happy love, a landscape, a symphony, a merry meeting with our friends, a bath or a football match have no such tendency. Our Father refreshes us on the journey with some pleasant inns but will not enourage us to mistake them for home.—C. S. Lewis.

Sermon Suggestions

THE TRINITY IN HOLY SONG.   Hymn Text: "Come, Thou Almighty King." (1) We pray to God the Father. (2) We sing praises to God the Son. (3) We adore God the Spirit. (4) We worship the blest Three in One.—Andrew W. Blackwood.

THE WAY OF SALVATION.   Gospel Text: John 3:1–16. (1) Being right with God requires a new birth. (2) The new birth is not a human achievement. (3) Faith in Jesus Christ brings about this new birth.

Worship Aids

CALL TO WORSHIP.   "The Lord is near to all who call upon him, to all who call upon him in truth" (Ps. 145:18, RSV).

INVOCATION.   Almighty and everlasting God, who hast given unto us thy servant's grace, by the confession of a true faith, to acknowledge the glory of the eternal Trinity, and in the power of the divine Majesty to worship the Unity: We beseech thee that thou wouldest keep us steadfast in this faith and worship, and bring us at last to see thee in thy one and eternal glory, O Father; who with the Son and the Holy Spirit livest and reignest, one God, for ever and ever.—*Book of Common Prayer*.

OFFERTORY SENTENCE.   "Thou art worthy, O Lord, to receive glory and honor and power: for thou hast created all things" (Rev. 4:11).

OFFERTORY PRAYER.   Our Father, you have invited us to come boldly to your throne of grace. We thank you for this privilege. We come now to give, from hearts of gratitude, our gifts to you. Use them to extend your kingdom in the hearts of people, and use us to be faithful in every area of life that through our lives as well as our gifts, people shall come to know Jesus, whom to know aright is life eternal.—J. Patrick Hash.

PRAYER.   "For a thousand years in thy sight are but as yesterday when it is past, or as a watch in the night" (Ps. 90:4). Eternal God, in whose sight a thousand years are but as yesterday, may we let go of the past and bravely face the future. May children who are reluctant to grow up put behind them childish things and reach toward adulthood. May people who are conscience-stricken by deep wrong release their guilt and accept your forgiveness. May couples whose first bloom of passion has faded persist in their loyalty and their love. May people who are ill dream not only of former health but trust in your healing spirit to mend and restore. May people who are dying know that as you were with them through birth and life, so you will be with them through death and beyond. Though the calendar changes, let us with confidence remember that in all generations you have been our dwelling place, and though we are swept away like a dream, you shall be God from everlasting to everlasting.—Thomas H. Troeger.

EVENING SERVICE

Topic: Riot or Revival?
TEXT: Acts 17:1–15.

It seems that everywhere Paul went either one of two things broke out: a riot or a revival. Two episodes from Acts are perfect examples. When Paul preached in Thessalonica, a riot broke out; when he preached in Berea, a revival broke out. What were the factors that made for such vastly different reactions to Paul and the gospel he preached?

I. It needs to be pointed out that there were many similarities between these two cities.

(a) Both of these cities were Greek cities.

(b) Each of these cities had a Jewish community, and in both cities Paul began his ministry in the Jewish synagogue.

(c) Paul used the same technique in both cities. He tried to show from the Old Testament that the Messiah had to suffer. This was a major hurdle, because for most Jews the concepts of Messiah and suffering were diametrically opposed, except for the hope that the Messiah would inflict suffering upon the hated Romans. Then Paul set about to show that Jesus had, in fact, fulfilled the role and that he was, therefore, the Messiah. I would not be surprised to find out that he preached the same sermon in both cities.

II. The difference is to be found in the

kinds of people to whom Paul preached.

(a) The Thessalonians were closed-minded. They didn't want to learn anything new. They were classic defenders of the status quo. It was the Thessalonians who charged Paul and Silas with "turning the world upside down."

(b) As closed-minded as the Thessalonians were, just so open-minded were the people in Berea. In fact, "open-minded" would not be a bad translation for the word translated "noble character." The Bereans were not afraid of new ideas. They were not so committed to the status quo that they were afraid to change.

(c) The general attitude toward life that the people in both of these cities manifested can be seen specifically in their attitudes toward Scripture. The Thessalonians refused to study the Scriptures with an open mind. They were convinced they already knew what it said; they didn't have to look and see. If they were wrong in their interpretation, they didn't want to know. Not only did the Thessalonians have a closed mind, they had a closed Bible. The Bereans on the other hand had an open Bible. So it was that they "received the message with great eagerness and examined the Scriptures every day to see if what Paul said was true." The Bereans treasured the Word of God and were willing to change their lives to match their new understandings of it, rather than trying to change their understandings to match their lives.

III. All of this seems to raise the question of why, generally speaking, we have neither riot nor revival in the church today?

(a) For all intents and purposes, most of us have neither closed minds nor open minds; our minds are in neutral. No riot or revival for *us*. We don't want anyone to think we are some sort of religious fanatic or something.

(b) Likewise, when it comes to the Bible, we don't really have a closed Bible or an open bible; we have no Bible at all. The fact of the matter is we don't know what the Bible says and we don't really care.

(c) The reason we have neither a riot nor a revival today is that we have no enthusiasm for our faith. There was a riot in Thessalonica because the people there were enthusiastic for the status quo. There was a revival in Berea because the Bereans were enthusiastic for the truth. There is neither today because we don't get exicted about anything.—Randy Smith.

SUNDAY: JUNE FIRST

MORNING SERVICE

Topic: Where Christianity Begins
Text: Matt. 7:13–27.

I. Christianity began in a very special way—in the life and teachings of one who lived in the Holy Land.

(a) The first disciples were very practical men who had been plucked out of the very practical process of making a living one way and another and had been set on a strange and wonderful mission. This had happened because of one who said, "Follow me!" Follow him they did—but with questions and doubts forcing themselves to the surface all along the way.

(b) Never one to demand blind faith, Jesus took them apart and taught them the meaning of discipleship. He did this through what we know as the Sermon on the Mount. They must have been thunderstruck at its austere demands—even as we are now. Few things could be clearer or more certain than that the writer of this Gospel as well as the early church expected Christians to begin here—with these teachings as guides to their daily life. Their witness was to be the life they lived in faithfulness to these teachings.

II. I find myself wondering whether people like us have the courage to let our Christianity begin in the Sermon on the Mount. Yet I confess that if it does not begin there, I do not know where else to say it takes its rise.

(a) This proposal for the salvation of men and history amounts to this: (1) To be saved, man must seek a new foundation for his life in the will of God, (2) To be saved, a society must seek a new foundation for its laws, conventions, and total life in the righteousness of God. Such a proposal was laughed to scorn by the self-styled realists of Jesus' day—a fate that it has suffered almost uninterruptedly for nineteen centuries.

(b) He challenged men to take their stand on three basic principles.

(1) When Jesus affirmed that God is the supreme fact in life and history, he was echoing the centuries-old faith of his forefathers. God is the Creator, Sustainer, and Redeemer of the world. No absentee Deity, his will for life is the deepest truth about it and should be sought with all diligence. When man puts his trust in God and is able to keep it there, he becomes invulnerable to "the arrows of outrageous fortune," finding in God the strength he needs for living in adversity as well as in prosperity.

(2) It follows, then, that all men are the children of God—rich and poor, good and evil, ill and well, joyful and sorrowful, white and colored—all are his children. This, I suppose, is one of our greatest needs—to know ourselves to be the sons of God.

(3) Implicit in the conviction that God is the supreme fact in life and history and that all men are the children of God is the claim that life is a divine trust. Life, everyday living, is a dealing with God. Life is our truest word to and from God. For Jesus, words, as words, did not carry much weight. The deed—that is the real revelation of a man's faith. Our possessions and human relationships are sacred in the exact sense that they involve the divine intention as truly as our own. But the kingdom of God must come first in a man's thought and life if he would correctly appraise himself and his work. When a man worries so much about food and clothing that he forgets the purpose of life itself, he has not kept first things first.

(c) How well we know that the human situation rapidly becomes intolerable unless life is treated as a divine trust. Treat other persons or races or nations as means to our end, as instruments in purposes that serve our own welfare, and to the extent that we are successful, we make revolutions inevitable. Yet the illusions nourished by power, wealth, and position continue to darken our awareness of this fact. The ability to enforce our will on others through military power is such an impressive fact today that we are turning to it as a kind of guarantor of security.

III. Not for a moment did our Lord seek to hide from his disciples the costliness of such convictions.

(a) The transformation of life and history plainly implicit in them calls for more than a verbal proclamation of them; they had to "come alive," to become incarnate in the lives of men and in history before they could become the way of salvation. He made it clear that one could know the vocabulary of religion, could say, "Lord, Lord," yet now know or be known by its transforming.

(b) Where does Christianity begin? In loyalty to Jesus Christ as the revelation of God's will for man's life; in belief in his teachings; in commitment to him as our Lord and our Leader. And in fellowship with those who followed him to the mountaintop to hear the sermon and then down into the valley to meet the challenge of daily human needs. As we do this, we will be like the wise man who built his house on a rock.—Harold A. Bosley.

Illustrations

CHRIST IS DIFFERENT.   There is no reformer or preacher today who believes that he is the incarnation of the ideal. At best, most of them would say that they were signposts pointing to a heavenly Jerusalem but in no case that they were the city itself. It is in this that Christ differs from all of them. While Socrates was saying, "Wait for another," Christ was saying, "I am here. The Scriptures are fulfilled in your ears." While Buddha refused to be a lamp to guide the poor dying Ananda, Christ was saying, "I am the Light of the world." While Confucius refused to see in himself a personification of his ideal of sinlessness, Christ was saying that he was Life and Resurrection. While the prophets of Israel pointed beyond themselves, Christ proclaimed himself as the Expected One of the Nations.—Fulton J. Sheen.

THE VITAL TURNING POINT. I know a marriage that is going on the rocks today because the initial wholeheartedness was wanting. Many a nominal Christian, also, is dull and lackluster because he has never even tried to surrender himself to Christ completely. We begin by surrendering to Christ as much of ourselves as we can, to as much of Christ as we understand. But our pride resists surrender to anybody, even to God. William James called self-surrender "the vital turning point of the religious life." Our performance will never come up to our promise, but we need the initial promise as the lasting guide for our subsequent living.—Samuel M. Shoemaker.

Suggestions

THE THREEFOLD CERTAINTY. Text: 1 John 5:18–20. (1) The Christian is emancipated from the power of sin. (2) The Christian is on the side of God against the world. (3) The Christian is conscious that he has entered into that reality that is God. —William Barclay.

FINDING GENUINE FAITH IN UNLIKELY PERSONS. Gospel Text: Luke 7:1–10. (1) This faith shows itself in good works. (2) This faith shows itself in humility. (3) This faith finds fulfillment in total reliance on Jesus Christ.

Worship Aids

CALL TO WORSHIP. Jesus said, "Blessed are they which do hunger and thirst after righteousness: for they shall be filled" (Matt. 5:6).

INVOCATION. Holy God, by whom the meek count suffering but for a while, and the peacemakers count tribulation but for a season; open and restore our flagging spirits to the resources of thy counsel. Stir us to new devotion; guide us in deeper prayer; seal us in the love of Christ by which we are being redeemed. Even now, Lord, even now.—E. Lee Phillips.

OFFERTORY SENTENCE. "I appeal to you . . . brethren, by the mercies of God, to present your bodies as a living sacrifice, holy and acceptable to God, which is your spiritual worship" (Rom. 12:1, RSV).

OFFERTORY PRAYER. Father, we thank you that because of Jesus we can be part of the family of God. Thank you for loving us and caring for us. Thank you for blessing us with your abundant riches. Activate us to love, care, and bless others in your name. May our gifts come from cheerful givers, who have assurance that the offering will be used to bring others to you. that they may be a part of your family.— Dan W. Parker.

PRAYER. Life-giving Lord, Were there no days of sunlight when rain has washed the land and the green earth stands ankle deep in dew; Were there no nights when moonlit beauty weaves a magic of delicate light across the brow and cheek of all who walk in its glow; Were there no hours when quiet hushes the heart and joy fills the soul and triumph in faith is known; Were there no moments when in the clutches of sorrow we are held securely in the Everlasting Arms and the love of friends; Were there no time in which to make up for past failures and shape future resolves from Divine pardon; Were there no events to challenge us, to inspire and motivate and draw the finest from us; Then we would be poor lost pilgrims, aimless, purposeless, dejected, and adrift. Yet in Thy grace, O Lord, we are recipients of all these gifts and more. Let our gratitude merge with resolve into a commitment of joy. Then may our rejoicing be full and our service fruitful, through the Christ of the ages.—E. Lee Phillips.

EVENING SERVICE

Topic: Don't Preach at Me!
TEXT: Ezek. 2:1–5.
As I studied this passage from Ezekiel, I began to see here reasons why Ezekiel preached under frustrating circumstances and why I continue to do the same. Let me share them with you.
I. *I preach because of what God has done for me personally.*
(a) If God had not done something for

me, then I would have no basis for preaching. If I have had no personal experience with God, then for me to try to preach would be like trying to feed the hungry out of an empty basket.

(b) Ezekiel had much the same experience. When he encountered the very presence of God, as recorded in the first chapter, he fell down on his face before God. Throughout the book of Ezekiel, God refers to the prophet as "son of man." But, in spite of the fact that Ezekiel was a "son of man," God loved him and called him to stand before him.

II. *I also preach because it is what God has called me to do.*

(a) I'm sure that Ezekiel was just as amazed as I was when the Lord said to him, "Son of man, I am sending you to the Israelites. . . . Say to them, 'This is what the Sovereign Lord says.'" At that moment Ezekiel joined the ranks of those whom God had called to the task of proclaiming the Word of the Lord.

(b) Let me quickly point out that none of us who have responded to God's call have any reason for pride. As God constantly reminded Ezekiel, we are all "sons of man."

(c) Preaching is never easy. It wasn't easy for Ezekiel or any of the other prophets. It is not easy for the conscientious preacher today. But we all know what Paul meant when he wrote: "When I preach the gospel, I cannot boast, for I am compelled to preach. Woe to me if I do not preach the gospel!" (1 Cor. 9:16). I preach because God had called me to preach.

III. *Finally, I preach, not in spite of the fact that we are a rebellious people but because of it.*

(a) That rebellious streak makes preaching more frustrating. Some people never seem to see the personal significance of the message. But even more frustrating than those who never see the personal application of the sermon are those who like to wallow in the sermon. There are always those who talk about how much the sermon really hit them, but nothing ever happens. They never change. They just come back the next week to be hit again.

(b) But, in spite of all our defenses against the Word of God, all the ways we try to avoid the implications of the gospel in our lives, I must keep preaching. For, as Paul put it, "the message of the cross is foolishness to those who are perishing, but to us who are being saved it is the power of God" (1 Cor. 1:18).

(c) In spite of the fact that preaching consists of one son of man proclaiming the Word of God to other sons and daughters of man, in spite of all the weaknesses involved both in proclaiming and in hearing, preaching is still the release of the power of God for the salvation of mankind. We are not saved by preaching; we are saved by our faith in Jesus Christ and his work of grace. But preaching is how God has chosen to proclaim to the world what he has done and what he can do if we will respond. Therefore, I preach because we are rebellious, because we need to be confronted constantly by the gospel of Jesus Christ.—Randy Smith.

SUNDAY: JUNE EIGHTH

MORNING SERVICE

Topic: Why Did Jesus Die?
TEXT: Rom. 5:8.

Why did Jesus die? That sounds like a simple question, but it is really a complex one—several questions in one. I want to take up three questions in turn, leading on from the simplest to the deepest.

I. *Why did they get him put to death?*

(a) Undoubtedly it was because they regarded him as a dangerous teacher, a he-

retical rabbi, a false prophet. They were very orthodox and conventional; but this new rabbi from Nazareth, who had never been properly trained, was unorthodox, unconventional, outspoken, not very careful about their ancestral religious traditions, not a very strict Sabbatarian, as they understood it, and not very particular about the company he kept.

(b) The very first thing that turned the religious leaders against Jesus and shocked them more than anything else was his attitude toward sinners, his way of mixing with sinners. These people were beyond the pale of religion, and no self-respecting rabbi would be seen talking to them. But Jesus seemed to be more interested in these people than he was in anybody else, and he practically said that God was too.

(c) Now all that was genuinely shocking to the religious leaders, the Scribes and Pharisees. Jesus seemed to be subverting all moral distinctions, lumping together the good and the bad, saying to notorious sinners: "Your sins are forgiven." So that is the answer to our first question.

II. *Why did Jesus himself choose to die?* But did he choose the cross?

(a) We must be very careful about that, because that has sometimes been said in quite false and artificial ways. One imaginative modern writer has pictured the matter as if Jesus deliberately planned to get himself crucified. Other people have often thought of Jesus as setting out in life with the perfectly clear knowledge of a divine plan of salvation by which he was to die on a cross to make atonement for the sins of the world; so that from the start he accepted the cross as a thing that was "according to plan." Surely that is too simple. The ordeal he had to face was much harder than that. He had to go forward in the dark, walking by faith, and not by sight.

(b) And what darkness it became, when it began to be clear that his own people were turning against him and plotting his death! That was not a climax according to plan. Nay, rather, we know from the Gospels that when Jesus saw it coming, he shrank from it with horror, and that even up to the night before his crucifixion he hoped and prayed that somehow it might not come.

(c) Then did he not choose the path of the cross? Yes, indeed he did. He was not a helpless victim. There was a choice before him, and he went on with his eyes open. He *could* have saved himself. He could have done it. And yet, of course, he couldn't do it, couldn't even for one moment begin to dream of doing it. Why not? Because it would have meant giving up his mission. And above all, that would have

meant giving up the sinners, giving up his shocking habit of being "a friend of publicans and sinners."

(d) So, you see, whatever else we may have to say about the meaning of the death of Jesus, it is manifestly true in the plain historical and local sense that he died for sinners, the sinners of his own immediate environment, the "lost sheep of the house of Israel" in his own time. It was his love for these sinners that brought him to the cross. And that is our second answer to the question: Why did Jesus die?

III. *What was the meaning of the death of Jesus in the eternal prupose of God?*

(a) When Jesus' own followers looked back and pondered on that dreadful event, what did they make of it? In the whole history of human thought there is nothing more extraordinary than this: that the crucifixion of Jesus made people think of *the love of God.* You might have expected these followers of Jesus to lose all faith in the love of God. In all ages good men had been asking agonized questions about the terrible things that were allowed to happen in this world.

(b) But that was not what happened. What happened was very different. It was this. When they thought of Jesus going to the cross in his love for sinners, they said, "God must be like that." Nay, but they said even more than that, something still more wonderful. Not simply "God must be like Jesus," but "God was in Jesus" when he suffered and died for sinners.

(c) That is why Jesus died. Jesus died on the cross because it was God's will to come right into our sinful fallen human situation, and, incarnate in a man, to bear upon himself the sin of the world.—D. M. Baillie.

Illustrations

THE CRUCIFIED GOD. The uniqueness of Jesus Christ concerns more than his person. His incomparable work on the cross is also unique. This means that Christ, as divinity, entered into the human condition, taking upon himself the sin and guilt of the world (2 Cor. 5:19). He was more than a prophet or holy man. Christ was also a sin bearer and mediator between God and humans. He was not only the model or example but also the Savior of a fallen humanity (1 Pet. 2:18–19).

The idea of Jesus as the crucified God is a stumbling block to Jews and folly to Gentiles (1 Cor. 1:23). Maharishi Yogi refuses to consider that Christ ever suffered or that Christ could suffer. Maharishi teaches that through transcendental meditation a sinner very easily comes out of the field of sin and becomes a virtuous person. Muhammed taught that Jesus was never crucified but that another took his place. Buddhists, too, find it difficult to come to terms with the crucified Christ. So we see that there is a great gulf between the Christian view of Christ's vicarious or sacrificial work and the view of other religious or cultic groups. [See Donald G. Bloesch, *Essentials of Evangelical Theology*, Vol. 2 (Harper & Row p. 248).]

The incarnaton of Christ exists for the atonement. The atonement achieved on the cross was a deed done to save us from it and its consequences. Christ lived for us and he died for us, doing for us what we could not do.—John P. Newport.

BEYOND EXPLANATION. One of the most moving scenes in English literature comes at the end of Dickens's *Tale of Two Cities*. The carts were rumbling through the thronged streets of Paris to the guillotine. In one of them there were two prisoners: a brave man who had once lost his soul but had found it again and was now giving his life for a friend, and beside him a girl—little more than a child. She had seen him in the prison and had observed the gentleness and courage of his face. "If I may ride with you," she had asked, thinking of that last dread journey, "will you let me hold your hand? I am not afraid, but I am little and weak, and it will give me more courage." So when they rode together now, her hand was in his; and even when they had reached the place of execution, there was no fear at all in her eyes. She looked at the quiet, composed face of the man beside her and said, "I think you were sent to me by Heaven."

What is the Christian answer to the mystery of suffering? Not an explanation but a reinforcing presence, Christ to stand beside you through the darkness, Christ's companionship to make the dark experience sacramental.—James S. Stewart.

Sermon Suggestions

GOD'S MERCY IS OUR ONLY HELP. Text: 1 Tim. 1:12–17. (1) For our task of keeping the faith. (2) For our task of worshiping God. (3) For our task of service in the church.—Richard R. Caemmerer.

FROM DEATH TO LIFE. Gospel Text: Luke 7:11–17. (1) Through the Lord's compassion. (2) Through the Lord's authority.

Worship Aids

CALL TO WORSHIP. "The Son of man came not to be ministered unto, but to minister, and to give his life a ransom for many" (Mark 10:45).

INVOCATION. Father, we are here today as your servants, often unwilling servants, always inept, but servants nonetheless. Show us in this hour how we might best serve you. Show us how we can move beyond the petty concerns of our own lives to a concern for our fellow human beings. Help us to be willing to serve regardless of the consequences. And on this Sunday when we focus on the cross of Christ, give us a willingness to accept the crosses that you intend for us to bear.—James M. King.

OFFERTORY SENTENCE. "I count all things but loss for the excellency of the knowledge of Christ Jesus my Lord" (Phil. 3:8).

OFFERTORY PRAYER. Our Father, the more you teach us of the meaning of Christ and his cross, the more we see our life, our achievements, and our possessions as means to service and less as ends to themselves. Teach us more, our Father, and give us the will to pattern our lives after his self-giving.

PRAYER. We praise thy name, the only wise God and our Father through Jesus Christ, for thou art worthy of praise. The whole earth is full of thy glory, and thy creation will continually magnify thy holy name. Therefore, we say in one spirit, Holy, Holy, Holy, Lord God Almighty, thou who wert, art, and will be from generation to generation, glory be to thy name.

And now O Lord, we beseech thee to accept our praises and to answer our petitions that we shall bring before thee not because of what we are but because of what Christ Jesus has done for us on the cross at Calvary. Father, we want to confess our sins and we ask for forgiveness of every known and unknown sin that we might have committed against thee and our fellowmen. Cleanse us, O God, of all doubts and faithlessness and help us in the power of thy Spirit to walk aright so that the joy of thy salvation might be multiplied in us.

Immortal Father, we lift thy church before thee. May the power of darkness never overcome thy church. We know that many of us Christians have not lived up to thy expectation. We have not loved one another as thou hast commanded us; we have not witnessed as thou hast told us; and yea, we have not worshiped thee in Spirit and in truth, nor have we sought thy* face with all our heart and soul. We humbly beseech thee, O Lord, to have mercy upon us.

There is none here without any problem. Thou who made us dost know us better than we know ourselves. We therefore beseech thee to attend to our needs according to thy grace and riches in glory. We need thy peace in this world of hate so that we may act with goodwill toward our enemies.

Father, thou art the potter and we are the clay. May thy will ever prevail, not ours. As thou dost bless us, so may we be of blessing to others, that our light may truly shine to thy glory alone.—Abayomi Lawah.

EVENING SERVICE

Topic: How Much Do You Think You Owe?

TEXT: Luke 7:47.

Love grows out of forgiveness. The greater the forgiveness, the greater the joy and gratitude, and out of that gratitude and joy comes greater love. If one knows, takes an honest look at the depth and magnitude of her own sin, and then receives the total and gracious forgiveness of God, the redeeming power of God's love, then she will not but love like this woman in Luke.

I. But somebody always wants to take a truth and stretch it to the absurd and make it a falsehood.

(a) If gratitude is greater the bigger the debt, maybe we ought to run up a big debt so we can be even more grateful. If God's love is more fully celebrated by those who experience more forgiveness, then maybe we ought to sin more often so we can be forgiven more.

(b) It is different from our experience of grace and forgiveness because those who have acknowledged themselves as sinner and seek and receive God's loving forgiveness always acknowledge that the debt is bad enough without having to add anything to it. The person who suggests that we ought to go out and sin a little more so that we can enjoy forgiveness a lot more has not fully looked into the face of his own sin. And that logic distorts the nature of our problem.

II. So we have this historical event and this story in Luke's Gospel. Jesus is at supper with Simon the Pharisee.

(a) Simon seems to have invited Jesus the way that some peoole always want to invite to social gatherings the "in" people at the time. And then this woman came in and made a spectacle of herself and Jesus. Anointing him with valuable perfume, washing his feet with tears, and drying them with her hair. Simon is outraged—not so much by what the woman did as by the fact that Jesus did not object. The whole passage demonstrates a contrast between two attitudes of mind and heart. Simon's approach was formal, objective, rational, detached. He treated Jesus with just enough respect to keep it polite, but with just enough omissions of niceties to keep it from becoming pleasant.

(b) Simon had his fixed notions of reality. He was conceited enough about those notions to think that Jesus would see things the same way. Simon saw only a fallen woman, a sinner, scum, worthless; Jesus saw a human being, a sinner pardoned and forgiven, a person changed and given a new life.

(c) The woman was conscious of nothing else but her need and, therefore, was overwhelmed with gratitude and love for Jesus who had already opened to her the doors to life more abundant through the grace of God.

III. The greatest of sins is to be conscious of no sin; but a sense of need will open the door to the forgiveness of God because God desires to see his creation be and live in relationship with him in love and fatih. He will redeem us.

(a) There is only one sin that shuts us off from God, and it is the very thing we prize the most in our society—our sense of self-sufficiency. Even God can't give us what we do not want and will not recieve.

(b) It isn't a king we need, not at the last. And it isn't a judge, not in the deep places where we come. In the deep places it is a Savior that we need. And Jesus offers to be that Savior.—Richard C. Brand, Jr.

SUNDAY: JUNE FIFTEENTH

MORNING SERVICE

Topic: Our Homes—and God

TEXT: Matt. 7:11.

From all things in earth and heaven, which would you choose as the best sign for God? The sun, perhaps, for the sun is a source of life. A flower, perhaps, for God is beauty; but a flower soon withers. A cross? Yes! Then what did Jesus choose as sign for God? Fatherhood (or motherhood) and a home. That Christ should choose the home as the sign for us is a clue to the meaning of life.

I. (a) What has home (chosen by Jesus as a sign for God) to teach us about death? The answer is instant. Would any worthy parent snuff out a child's life? Would any worthy parent say, "I have so many: one more or less does not matter"? Why should we make God a crueler image than man? Concerning eternal life: "If ye then being evil know how to give good gifts, how much more . . ."!

(b) What about hell and the judgment? That Jesus should choose the home as the symbol of eternity throws light on that issue. No wise parent would always shield a child from the consequence of selfishness. That kindness would not be kind; it would be ruinous indulgence. All right; we must say that there ought to be a judgment both here and hereafter. Any wise home has its rigors but is still home.

(c) Jesus believed, with immense daring, that a worthy home is the best symbol of God. That fact has bearing on a man's faith.

II. The symbol is a clue also to the strategy of life.

(a) What is the focus from which the alien world is subdued into the kingdom of God? Some would say "an army." Brute force or "a world government." What *is* the creative center of our world? Suppose it were the home!

(b) Consider certain plain facts about a home. Children are (or ought to be) the fruit of the rapture of love. Thus children became precious. It is fairly certain that any state system of raising children will break, sooner rather than later, on the prime fact that pain and love make the family a unit by nature, and probably (aside from the church) earth's most enduring loyalty.

(c) Consider again how wisdom is nourished in a home. There are three generations—children, parents, and grandparents. Thus there can be a bequest of experience from older to younger. Stress that fact: Parents have learned something about food, and they pass along the information to their children. Have they learned nothing of God? They should not "sell out" to the nonsense of letting a child choose his own religion at the age of twenty-one. Nobody has his own religion: God is one God. No religion can be just chosen: It is not a necktie, but the main artery of a man's neck. So in a home there can be, and should be, a bequest of experience (not with coercion but in love) from older to younger. At the same time there should be the gift of venture, a reminder that the world is in continuous change, from the younger to the older.

(d) Thus the cruciality of the home. It should set its stamp on the world. It—the home—should determine cities, not business. So the home should determine business (that must become a home), government, penology, factory systems, and education; for the home is the sign of God.

(e) Do I need to add that the home is the best thing any man or woman can build? Perhaps God will ask us hereafter, when we tell him that we think we did fairly well in building a successful business or a successful church, "but what about your home?"

III. (a) That Jesus should choose the home as a symbol of God is our condemnation, for homes are broken by quarreling and death, and even the best home fails all who live in it. This fact Jesus recognized even while he chose the symbol: "If ye then, being evil. . . . " When there is no redemption for the home, all homes, and thus all men and women, are lost.

(b) Young men and women in a flush of marriage ardently believe that they can decide terms of faith on their mutual devotion. A home cannot thus live, any more than a man could live by eating his own fingers.

(c) "To them that ask him": Most homes do not ask. In most homes family worship has disappeared. Tragedy might be moderated if the people within the home prayed as individuals, but individual prayer is largely forgotten. But I would beg you: Be among them "that ask him"!

IV. Thus church and home are forever linked, the church being the earthly prophecy and foretaste of that eternal home in which all true earthly homes are held. "If ye then, being evil, know how to give good gifts unto your children, how much more shall your Father in heaven give good things to them that ask him."—George A. Buttrick.

Illustrations

A FATHER'S FORGIVENESS. Lachlan Campbell in the Bonnie Brier Bush was the stern old Calvinistic elder who sat in judgment on the theology of the Glen. He straightened out the minister who slipped in a bit of compassionate heresy that seemed to minimize the awful sovereignty of God. His daughter Flora at last rebelled against the harsh regime of her home and ran away to London. The elder was no less severe upon his own; he related her fall at the next meeting of the Session, and with his own lips moved that her name be stricken from the church roll. But afterward he got a glimpse of the New Testament; he had been locked up in the Old. He had always said "Jehovah," but now he learned to say "Our Father." He caused a letter to be written to his erring daughter asking her to come home and assuring her of forgiveness. Then the stern old man, thinking his daughter would return at night, lighted a huge parlor lamp that was kept for show, and placed it at the window. "And every night till Flora returned, its light shone down the steep path that ascended to her home, like the divine love from the open door of our Father's house."—Charles R. Brown.

A CHILD SHALL LEAD THEM. A clerical friend was on a Pullman car. He found himself with men who were returning from the races. Their language was shockingly irreverent. Their conversation showed that nearly all of them had been gambling. When the time for retiring came, a little boy was made ready for his berth. The tiny fellow stood in the aisle of the sleeper, clad in his pajamas. Ere he climbed into his bed the child looked doubtfully about, as if he were hesitating. Then he overcame his timidity, knelt at the side of the berth, folded his hands, and began to pray in a childish treble, heard all over the car, "Now I lay me down to sleep." For a time profanity ceased; all talk of bets won or lost died into silence. The eyes of the hardened men grew moist with tears. One tough fellow pointed to the kneeling child and said, "I would like to know what that little chap has that I have lost." For a few moments those "lewd fellows of the baser sort" found themselves in the presence of Christ because they were in the presence of a child's heart.—Edwin H. Hughes.

Sermon Suggestions

OUT OF THE MOUTH OF BABES.   Text: Matt. 21:15–16. (1) Would-be wise men often show folly by despising the young. (2) Children sometimes see religious truth more clearly than prejudiced adults. (3) The praise of children is thoroughly acceptable to God. (4) The piety of children ought to touch hard hearts and silence malignant opposers of the gospel.—John A. Broadus.

LOVE AND FORGIVENESS.   Gospel Text: Luke 7:36–8:3. (1) A great debt. (2) A mighty savior. (3) An abounding gratitude.

Worship Aids

CALL TO WORSHIP.   "As kind as a father is to his children, so kind is the Lord to those who honor him. He knows what we are made of; he remembers that we are dust" (Ps. 103:13–14, TEV).

INVOCATION.   Our Father, through your infinite goodness we find ourselves once more in your house and in your presence. Help us to stand before you just as we are and claim nothing except your compassion and rich promises. As we see and feel our sin in the light of the cross, give us discernment to see sin as you see it and then to confess and forsake it.—J. Patrick Hash.

OFFERTORY SENTENCE.   "Bless the Lord, O my soul, and forget not all his benefits" (Ps. 103:2).

OFFERTORY PRAYER.   For the warmth of the sunshine, the fragrance of the flowers, and the laughter of children we give thee thanks. We know that all good and perfect gifts come from thee. No measure of gratitude could express the debt of love we owe for the gift of thy incarnate son, yet we implore thee to accept these meager tokens as symbols of our devotion to thee from this time forward.—Michael Berryman.

PRAYER.   We praise thee, O God, for the little children given into our keeping. For their purity of heart, their constant simplicity, their natural and trusting affection, and for the wonderful comfort and joy they bring to us, we praise and bless thy glorious name. Continue, we beseech thee, thy protection of them; and grant to us such a measure of thy Spirit that we may work together with thee for their good.

We remember before thee the many children who are now denied a fair chance in life, all who are hindered by a bad environment, all who are made to toil at an early age, all who are unwanted, neglected, and ill-treated. Make haste, O Lord, for the help of these thy little ones. Suffer us not to add to their burden or to leave them without a champion for their cause. Fill us with thy holy wrath toward the things whereby they are bruised and afflicted, and by thy great compassion bring us swiftly to their aid. All which we ask in the name of him who took little children in his arms and laid his hands upon them in blessing, thy Son Jesus Christ our Lord.—Ernest Fremont Tittle.

EVENING SERVICE

Topic: The Seduction of King David
TEXT: 2 Sam. 12:1–14.

It is in the spirit of a people thirsting for the grace of God that I want to talk about the encounter between King David and the prophet Nathan. Granted disgrace is exposed in our text, but the discerning eye will catch a glimpse of something much more important at work in this story. There is an unfolding of the inner workings of grace by which God lures us into our own fulfillment and mission.

I. I want to suggest the first thing that grace does. There is something about grace that manages to penetrate protective defenses.

(a) Grace could not help very much unless it could do this. For there is a human proclivity toward covering up so that we can protect ourselves against an insensitive and uncaring world. Defense mechanisms have a valuable role, but if we major in such efforts to defend ourselves we end up shutting out God's creative possibilities. So it is significant in the inner workings of grace to see that grace knows how to get through to us. Grace knows how to get a hearing. Grace manages to get items placed on the agenda of our hearts. David came to understand that this issue, raised by Nathan the prophet, must be dealt with. It was not so much that he now had a sense of disgust at just being caught; it was not simply because he felt that he was in trouble because of his image. No, something of grace had delivered him to the condition of genuine conviction. Grace penetrates protective defenses and gets the agenda on the hearts of those who are so touched by grace.

(b) But what is the issue with which grace was working here? What is the issue under consideration in the life of David? Well, how we answer that question depends on whether we are interested in the sordid details of the king's disgrace or whether we are still able to focus on the inner workings of God's grace. Grace is not interested so much in the sordid details of our behavior. Human beings tend to look on outer appearances. But grace will always look at the heart. So then in that moment when Nathan said unto him, "David, thou art the man," immediately David recognized something. He recognized—"I have sinned; it is not my behavior that's really the basic problem, it is my character. It is not my libido, it is not my image, it is not my ego; it's my heart— I've got heart trouble"; he recognized that.

(c) But something else had happened to David, and this is the significant thing: He recognized that his behavior and his character were like having a blood clot at the base of his brain that would lead to his heart, and his life would be as good as gone without some kind of intervention. This happens as an act of grace. For you see, we all are like David: we can't see ourselves until we are shown our selves; as a pastor I learned this. Often in preaching about love, I could hear myself speaking in tones of hate. Or are there those of you who may try to defend yourself against feminist charges and discover, just as they thought, you still had sexist proclivities? Or even people who like to prove that they are clear of all racial feelings sometimes find grace helping them to see. Oh yes, the

problems are still there. So grace works not only to penetrate protective defenses, but grace identifies the defect in the character.

II. But grace does another thing: It releases redemptive options.

(a) After Nathan had left David, Nathan waited for a long time to see whether the king would destroy him. Each day that passed without armed couriers from the king seemed like a day of grace. But grace doesn't leave us with judgment alone. Grace goes to work beyond judgment to release the redemptive option. You see, grace sees the defect, but grace sees something else. Grace sees in David resourcefulness. He is a man of talent. Grace sees that this man has been assigned a place in the plan of God. Grace understands that this is a man who has experienced the reality and power of God, one who has declared the Lord is my light and salvation. Grace sees that here is a man who has an earnest desire to be faithful to God. So grace sent not an agent to destroy David but sent Nathan and his story as a means of enablement, as a means to set David free from his covert sins, so that he could be ushered forth to new possibilities. This happens to us in worship. It happens sometimes at work—a friend sees through the facade. Sometimes a poem penetrates our defenses, sometimes a sunset reveals that which is dark in our character; that is the nature of grace. So it is an act of grace that made David say to Nathan—"Nathan, I have sinned." Where did those words come from? They came from the inner workings of grace.

(b) I've preached about the inner workings of grace because it's always obvious to me that grace is at work in our lives. But I trust that David's exerience will open our eyes anew so that we may see grace even when our failures have been discovered and say amen to its beneficent workings within us. Brothers and sisters, it is not always a mark of defeat and destruction when our shortcomings are seen; if grace is at work in that moment of exposure then we too, like David, may discover that the grace was simply setting us free to become men and women after God's own heart.— James A. Forbes, Jr.

SUNDAY: JUNE TWENTY-SECOND

MORNING SERVICE

Topic: Overcome Evil

TEXT: Matt. 6:9–13.

We are all agreed that we must get the best of evil and not allow it to get the best of us. The Lord of life put this prayer upon our lips—"Our Father who art in heaven, deliver us from evil." The main question before the house has to do with the method. How can we best overcome evil?

I. We are told to overcome evil with evil.

(a) The Hebrews tried that method in their early social legislation. "An eye for an eye, a tooth for a tooth, a life for a life." They claimed divine sanction for it, because these laws are prefaced by a "Thus saith the Lord." The method, however, did not produce good results. Jesus put upon it the stamp of his disapproval. We cannot overcome evil with evil.

(b) The nations have tried it. Military experts claim that the only way for a nation to have peace is to increase its armament and become so strong that no other nation will ever dare to attack it. We see at once the futility of it as a general method. Where would we come out if every nation tried to increase its armament until it became stronger than every other nation? The mad race in increased armaments leads inevitably to financial, political, and moral bankruptcy. Men do not build a social order fit to live in, or one that will stand, by returning evil for evil.

II. We are told to overcome evil with good. This is what might be called "the higher resistance." Why not try that method?

(a) We are not to be passive in the presence of evil—we are not to take it lying down. We are to do something about it, and the best thing we can do is to do good. Our minds go back to "that green hill far away, outside a city wall, where the Lord was crucified, who died to save us all." What was he doing? He was not looking down to bemoan his fate. He was looking up to say, "Father forgive them"—they are ignorant—"they know not what they do." Has any other scene in the whole history of mankind ever gone so far toward overcoming evil as that scene?

(b) Does anyone believe that evil is more powerful than good, that Satan, however we may construe that term, can overcome God? Look back through the facts of history. Have those outbursts of violence accomplished any permanent good that might not have been had on much better terms? They have usually meant merely the transfer of power from the oppressor to the oppressed, who in turn became oppressors themselves, when the turn of the wheel had brought their opponents into their power.

(c) We have tried hatred and violence—why not try patience and consideration, friendliness and cooperation, in our industrial and our international disputes? Why not try an honest, persistent effort to get the other man's point of view and to show some decent respect for his ideas, even when we do not agree with them?

III. But the cynics will say with a sneer, "You cannot overcome evil with good because you cannot change human nature."

(a) "Oh, but we can!" The thing has been done repeatedly. It is being done now all over the world. Human nature is being changed steadily and a renewed human nature will build a world order wherein righteousness and peace and goodwill shall stand fast and bear rule. In the long run and over wide areas of human experience, righteousness and peace have a survival value that those other qualities lack; therefore the future belongs to them. The only way to overcome evil with a victory that will last is to overcome evil with good.

(b) We hear much these days about the superiority of realism over idealism. Some of it is sensible talk and some of it is just empty chatter. The master was no sentimental dreamer. He combined realism with idealism. He knew what was in man and needed not that any should tell him.

He knew that men lie. He knew that men can be mean and hateful. He knew that men can be cruel and vindictive. Yet he faced all those facts with an idealism that would not accept defeat. "Ye are the light of the world," he said to a small group of plain people like ourselves. In that light we have seen light and have been able to find our way about.

(c) If I did not believe that good is more powerful than evil, that God can and does put down Satan under his feet, I should have no gospel to preach. The gospel is the good news that God is with us and for us, that the kingdom of heaven is at hand if we will only have it so. We may well believe that his way is the only way that we can ever conquer evil.—Charles R. Brown.

Illustrations

MAKING NEW FRIENDS. Dr. Henry C. Link says that he and one of his neighbors never became acquainted until their dogs staged a fight. Dr. Link's dog wore a muzzle; his neighbor's did not. The dog without a muzzle seized a leg of the other. Only when Dr. Link kicked and choked him and twisted his tail did the dog open his jaws and release the leg. The rescue occurred in the presence of the neighbor who was the owner of the attacking dog. The two men became acquainted. Dr. Link sagely remarks that what living near each other for six months did not accomplish, the dogs brought to pass in five minutes! —Karl Ruf Stolz.

PERSISTENT GOODWILL. In the Norwegian story, *The Great Hunger*, a certain farmer had an enemy across the way whose land adjoined his. The two men had not always agreed about line fences and the encroachment of one man's stock on the other man's land. This enemy had treated the farmer with bitterness and scorn.

There came a year of famine when all the farmers in that region felt the pinch of want and this enemy had no grain that spring with which to sow his fields. Early one morning, before it was fairly light, this farmer went to his barley bin and found that he had only a bushel of grain left for the needs of his family. He poured it all into a sack and went out and climbed over the fence and sowed his enemy's field with the very last of his own grain. When he came back his wife met him, smiling through her tears. She understood—she too had gotten up early, that she might share with her husband in showing that enemy the spirit of Christ. There is something mightier than enmity. Persistent goodwill changes enemies into friends.— Charles R. Brown.

Sermon Suggestions

CHRISTIANS ARE WELL OFF EVEN IN SUFFERING. Text: 1 Pet. 4:1–6. (1) Suffering can be an armor against sin. (2) Suffering moves us to commit ourselves to God who judges rightly. (3) Suffering leads to an ultimate victory.—Gerhard Aho.

THE WAY OF THE CROSS. Gospel Text: Luke 9:18–24. (1) The lifestyle of the Christ. (2) The lifestyle of Christ's followers.

Worship Aids

CALL TO WORSHIP. "God's love has been poured into our hearts through the Holy Spirit which has been given to us" (Rom. 5:5b, RSV).

INVOCATION. Our Father, make our hearts to be channels through which your love goes out to all people. Forgive our sins of blind prejudice and smoldering grudges that keep that love from finding a way to those who need it. Have your way with us.

OFFERTORY SENTENCE. "Let your light so shine before men, that they may see your good works, and glorify your Father which is in heaven" (Matt. 5:16).

OFFERTORY PRAYER. Our Father, we thank thee for opportunities to put our best desires into action: for families that have been formed, for churches that have been established, for schools that have been founded, for missions that have been undertaken, for hospitals that have been built, and for all concrete expressions of a human and Christian spirit. Now wilt thou consecrate our tithes and offerings to the end that the life of each of these institutions may be continued and strengthened and that thy name may be glorified.

PRAYER.   O thou who guidest every one of us, thou who knowest every one of us and in what little shallop or seagoing craft of greatness we are, we give thee all our thanks that we cannot drift beyond thy love and care. We thank thee for the perpetualness of thy mercy, for the sweetness of the belief that is perennial from the blossoms of thy love. Great God, make its appeal to us this morning so that we shall rally all the forces within ourselves, so that deep shall cry unto deep, water shall cry unto sky, deep answering unto deep—God and man in one sweet and holy confederation of forces; the partnership of divine and human that we know in our Lord and Savior, Jesus Christ.—Frank W. Gunsaulus.

EVENING SERVICE

Topic: The Gift

TEXT: 2 Kings 2:1–15; Eph. 4:1–7, 11–16; Mark 6:45–52.

The issue raised in this gospel lesson today is this: What is the gift? And is it enough? For me the gift here is not a miracle of walking on the water. The gift is rather the presence of the Christ with the disciples in the boat.

I. Walking on the water is a bit theatrical at three in the A.M. He had already turned down being a sign-Messiah and refused to whip up miracles for the Pharisees and Scribes. And if he was going to calm the storm, why not do it from on shore without the walking part? He surely didn't need to stir their faith. They were with him and he never used signs to inspire faith anyway. Further, if he did that for these sailors and not for all sailors in trouble, you have a problem with a mother of a lost sailor asking him in Galilee: "I heard you saved your boys from a storm. Where were

you four night ago when my boy drowned out there?" And that's my greatest problem with a walking-on-the-water miracle. It makes a promise that doesn't square with our experience.

II. And his presence with the disciples, his "be not afraid," which is the real gift here, pales into insignificance beside footprints in the waves and the suddenly calmed winds. Hard acts to follow—wave walking and wind calming. So, we might ask, "Is presence all? Is presence enough?" Those are the real questions.

(a) If we mean, Is his presence enough to radically change a situation, no not always—perhaps not even sometimes. What happens when he climbs into our boat and the storm swamps our craft and drowns one of our loved ones?

(b) If we mean, Is it enough to protect us from harm or ill, or evil or temptation, again the answer is no. What happens when Jesus climbs into our boat and says, "fear not" and the heart condition doesn't improve, and the cancer doesn't go away, or the child dies, or a loved one suffers, or the bankruptcy comes, or the lightning destroys the house we've lived in for twenty years?

(c) The problem with Jesus' walking on the water and calming the storm is that it becomes a promise, conscious in us or not, and we expect that to happen to us as well. We're disciples, too. Dropouts in the Christian faith, or those who keep their names on the roll from which to marry and bury family, come from these expectations. There is a disappointed expectation in every dropout I've ever encountered, either with (1) the God whom they thought promised something and didn't deliver, or (2) with the people of God whom they thought promised something and didn't deliver. A religion that can survive unrewarded virtue can survive anything, but not many of us have that!

III. For me, to put faith in either of these two events as miracle—walking on water or calming the storm—raises expectations that cause us trouble.

(a) But there is more here. The gift here, the miracle here, the event of note here is his word: "Take heart. It is I. Do not be afraid." Here is the release from fear and I do not care whether the one who gives me this release was wading in or walking on the water. It doesn't matter.

(b) In relationship to fear, there are two basic ways to live our Christian lifestyle. One is under legalism—prohibitions, restraints that are repressive—and fear reigns here. In this style of life Jesus walks with us if we're good; big brother is around but he's watching us, not walking with us. We have anxiety and worry about whether we will slip and fall and what will happen to us if and when we do.

(c) But there is another way to live our Christian lifestyle. Living under the gospel and not under legalism is the way to hope. Here we become free to give ourselves over to someone, something and not be concerned about the conformity or uniformity of the results.

IV. The gift is not a gift of miracle. Not enough to go around, obviously. The gift is gift of presence *and* the release from fear, release that comes in community. Jesus rounded out the community when he got to those in the boat. Is that all—his presence? Is it enough? You bet. Presence is *all* there is. Presence is everything there is. It *is* the gift. The gift.—Thomas H. Conley.

SUNDAY: JUNE TWENTY-NINTH

MORNING SERVICE

Topic: Praying with Power

TEXT: Eph. 6:18.

The context of our verse is the description of the spiritual battle that Christians are called to wage against the power of evil. In Ephesians 6:10–12, we see the enemy against which we must wage our spiritual battle. In Ephesians 6:13–17, we see the equipment we must wear as we wage this battle. Then, in Ephesians 6:18, we see the energy by which the victory is to be won, and that energy is the power that comes from prayer. And it can be for us. We, too, can experience that power if we can understand the adverbs and pronouns of prayer.

I. First, there is the *whoever* of prayer. When Paul gives the command to pray, he is implying that this command can be followed by every believer. One of the most exciting truths in the New Testament is that through Jesus Christ we have been given access to the Father. Whoever wants to can come before God in prayer and fellowship with him. The recognition of that fact is the first step in praying with power.

II. Second, we see the *whenever* of prayer. Paul says that we should "pray at all times."

(a) This great truth is repeatedly sounded in Scripture. In 1 Thessalonians 5:17, the Bible says, "Pray without ceasing."

(b) How often we admonish our people to set up a certain time and place for prayer. And I believe that is important. But I do not want us to so emphasize the need of a special time and place for prayer that we miss the repeated biblical injunction to pray at all times. When we go through each day of our lives with a prayer constantly on our lips, always on the verge of a prayer, then we will have taken the second step toward praying with power.

III. Third, consider the *wherever* of prayer. There are two ways of answering that question.

(a) We can answer the question *geographically*. It is remarkable to notice the varied geographic locations in which some biblical prayers were offered. Geographically, you can pray anywhere.

(b) But there is another way to answer the question "where?" and that is to answer it *spiritually*. Paul says that we are to "pray at all times in the Spirit." The prayer that prevails against evil, the prayer that promotes the cause of God, the prayer that provides spiritual power is prayer given by a Christian who is living and walking in the Spirit!

(c) As a Christian, you have dwelling within you the very Spirit of God. If you will begin to listen to the Spirit and love the Spirit and live in the Spirit so that you may pray in the Spirit, then you will have taken the third step toward praying with power.

IV. Fourth, there is the *whatever* of prayer. About what should we pray?

(a) Paul answers that question in our text when he says, "With all prayer and petition."

(b) Whatever the invading anxiety is in your life, you can go up before God and spread it out before him. When blessing comes, you can thank God. When burdens come, you can seek God's assistance. When you have failed, you can ask for God's forgiveness. When you have succeeded, you can praise God for his help. When you don't know what to do, you can ask God for his guidance. You can pray to God about everything.

(c) When we come to the point in our communication with God where we realize that nothing is outside the scope of his concern and nothing is beyond the reach of his power, then we will have taken the fourth important step toward praying with power.

V. Above all, it is important that we pray with the right end in mind.—That is the *wherefore* of prayer.

(a) Notice how Paul puts it in verse 19 of our text, "and pray on my behalf, that utterance may be given to me in the opening of my mouth, to make known with boldness the mystery of the gospel."

(b) That is the wherefore of prayer. We are to pray so that the gospel may be more effectively communicated to those who have not heard. The ultimate purpose of prayer is that we may become so sensitive to his presence and so in tune with his purpose that we can be used to spread the message of God's love to the world.

(c) The primary focus of prayer is not on us. It is on God, and on his presence and his purpose and his proclamation and his plan.—Brian L. Harbour.

Illustrations

FREEDOM IN PRAYER.   In prayer we refuse to accept as ultimate what appear to be the fixed conditions of the world, because we believe that these conditions are not ultimate. They have a temporary validity within the purpose of God, but they are in the end subordinate to his love. We do not yet know what love can or cannot

achieve. Our faith prompts us to pray, in Kierkegaard's phrase, even "for the impossible." Prayer "is a form of expectation" (M. Nïdoncelle). It is the growing point in the divine-human encounter. It is participation in new creation.—Peter Baelz.

TO TRANSFORM THE WORLD.   We have enough Christian people to transform the world right now, if only their thoughts were always on Christ's side. But they suppose their thoughts are their own, and so a large part of their thinking cancels out the rest of their thinking. We need to mobilize the minds of the men of goodwill so that they will form a mighty *mass attack of good thoughts*. Then we altogether will tip the scales the other way, will lift the world to a new high, in spite of the selfish little thoughts of mean people. Here is a principle most people need: Fix your thoughts upon what ought to come to pass and not upon the things you dislike. Let the things we oppose die of neglect. For we help everything we think about—even when we are thinking against it.—Frank C. Laubach.

Sermon Suggestions

THE SIX STEPS OF THE GOSPEL.   Text: Mark 10:46–52. There are six main steps in the Christian gospel. We see each of them clearly illustrated in the story of Jesus and Bartimeus. (1) First, there is the need. (2) Second, there is the awakening of our belief in Christ and our desire for him. (3) Third, we must ask for Christ's help. (4) "And Jesus stood still," we read. That is the fourth step. (5) The fifth step: "And he, casting away his garment, rose and came to Jesus." We do want Christ, but there are some other things we are unwilling to let go. (6) The story of Bartimeus ends: "And immediately he received his sight, and followed Jesus in the way."—Charles L. Allen.

WHAT JESUS' FOLLOWERS MUST BE WILLING TO DO.   Gospel Text: Luke 9:51–62.

(1) Renounce comfort and security. (2) Establish spiritual priorities. (3) Pursue the will of God relentlessly.

Worship Aids

CALL TO WORSHIP. "I was glad when they said unto me, let us go into the house of the Lord" (Ps. 122:1).

INVOCATION. O Almighty God, who pourest out on all who desire it the spirit of grace and of supplication: Deliver us, when we draw near to thee, from coldness of heart and wanderings of mind, that with steadfast thoughts and kindled affections we may worship thee in spirit and in truth; through Jesus Christ our Lord.—*Book of Common Prayer*.

OFFERTORY SENTENCE. "Give unto the Lord the glory due unto his name: bring an offering, and come into his courts" (Ps. 96:8).

OFFERTORY PRAYER. It is to you, dear God, that we look for the strength and courage to do what is right. We know that you are a God of justice, and we pray that you help us to live our lives in a just manner. Free us, O God, from selfishness, from hate, from prejudice, and from idolatry, so that we might live in the freedom of sharing, of loving, of equality, and of walking humbly in your service. Take our gifts, O Lord, and bless them and use them in the struggle for justice. In the name of the just God we pray.—John W. Neal.

PRAYER. O thou who hast gathered us out of sundry places and bound us by the grace of thy spirit in the communion of this church, bless us as we pray together and for one another, that we may be mindful of the burdens borne invisibly, of the sorrows not seen but heavy on the heart, of the sins unknown but deep within inner shame. Let us not lift casual, thoughtless prayer to thee, but standing at the deep center of our own need grant us the grace to stretch our hands to those who worship with us, that with one accord we may all seek that strength which is beyond us but never withheld from any in need. Whether it be health of body, clarity of mind, or peace of soul, turn us with ready lives to kneel at our neighbor's need, that in all things we may be faithful to our Lord, thy

Son, who came not to be ministered unto but to minister.—Samuel H. Miller.

EVENING SERVICE

Topic: The Liberating Christ

TEXT: Col. 3:1–11.

This text has a relevance for us if we would be released from all lower allegiances and realize the higher life "which is being renewed in knowledge after the image of its creator." From what does he set man free?

I. Christ sets men free from the claims of crass materialism.

(a) Every Christian feels the pull of the material world. How can we escape it? The materialism of any age may become a deadly foe to the Christian spirit. Things may be temporal but they are also tangible and an undue preoccupation with them is apt to overshadow the "unseen and spiritual" world.

(b) That is why Jesus spoke of riches, not as wrong in themselves but as a possible enemy to the Christian life. The philosophy of comfort and ease, encouraged by material possessions and the greed for gold, robs men of any appetite for spiritual realities.

(c) Things have a definite value. But things must be made subservient to the great spiritual ends of life. Actually the Christian lives in one world while he lives in another. Not for a moment does he ignore the reality of this mundane life. Rather he brings the eternal into time and infuses his earthly task with spiritual purpose.

II. Christ also liberates men from the tyranny of the "flesh" (vv. 5, 9–10). Who has not experienced that sharp inner conflict between good and evil?

(a) Men have reacted to this inner struggle in various ways. Some have accepted the ascetic ideal. Others have adopted a philosophy of pleasure and have yielded to bodily appetites. Still others have regarded the body as sacred, the temple of the Holy Spirit, and have endeavored to subordinate it to spiritual ends.

(b) The Christian ideal calls for the most radical denial of self. The flesh-dominated life must be dug out by the roots and destroyed! The ugly sins described by the apostle have been condemned by the church in every age. Every moral detour leads to inner degradation and outward degeneration.

(c) The apostle, however, draws up a new catalog of sins (v. 8). There are subtle sins, sins of the disposition, that are as evil as the gross sins of the flesh. Who has not encountered persons who are orthodox in letter but most unchristian in attitude and speech? Are not bitterness, hatred, gossip, slander, ill will, and foul thoughts among the cardinal sins from which Christ would set us free? Our disposition must be changed until it becomes like that of the master's.

III. Our redemption is not complete, however, until Christ has liberated us from the corrosion of an unexamined prejudice (v. 11).

(a) There are national lines that separate men from each other. Yet Christianity crosses geographical boundaries. Christian people, regardless of national background, can clasp hands in brotherly fashion. Christ destroys the barriers.

(b) There are racial barriers. Prejudice is not particular; it sits at home in the heart of any person who will offer it a home. Jesus never felt that it was enough merely to talk about improving relations between the races. He took steps to demonstrate the spirit of brotherly kindness and friendly helpfulness.

(c) Men erect religious barriers. Denominational pride can become a serious sin. I am a Baptist, both by "birth" and by reflection. In my own mind, I have satisfactory reasons for my beliefs and commitments and an abiding gratitude for our religious heritage. But a man's deepest convictions need not lead him to regard with darkest suspicions the professed faith of earnest men in other denominations. We have one thing in common: Christ! The world needs him, not our varied interpretations of him or our differences of opinions about him.

(d) Christ has set us free! He makes us new men; he gives us a new hope; he plants a new love within us; he turns our faces toward a new home.—Nolan P. Howington.

SUNDAY: JULY SIXTH

MORNING SERVICE

Topic: The Story of Two Giants

TEXT: 1 Sam. 17.

One of the most unforgettable stories in the Old Testament is the story of David and Goliath. David was hardly more than a boy, too young to go off and join the army with his older brothers. David, however, was dauntless and went to the king. "I will go and fight the Philistine," he said. Saul saw that it was idle to protest, and said, "Go, and the Lord be with thee." Thus lightly clad and with virtually no weapons, he went out to meet Goliath. Then David, lithe, nimble, free to move, slung a stone. It hit Goliath in the forehead and stunned him; he fell to the ground and David went and killed him. The last line of the story reads, "And when the Philistines saw that their champion was dead they fled." That is the story —primitive, crude, bloody, dramatic, stirring a mingling of legend and history. The wonder of it is that across the years it speaks to us today.

I. The first thing that it says to us is that there are always men like Goliath in the world, giants who threaten the peace of the world, men who by their mere massiveness hold the world in the grip of fear.

(a) There have always been giants like Goliath, and there are now. We need not name them. But we must remember that these destructive giants have never come to a good end.

(b) We do not know why there are giants continually disturbing the peace of the world. All we know is that it is so, and to remember it now gives us a perspective that we greatly need. It reminds us that we are not unique.

II. The second thing the story says is that in the great conflicts all the good is not on one side, or all the evil. The struggle is not between a sheer brute and an innocent, idealistic youth. Both men could be cruel; both were cruel. Both would kill, and one did kill.

(a) Let us put this down in black and white. In the great issues of life it seldom happens that all the good is on one side and all the evil on the other. The good is almost always tinctured with evil, and the evil is seldom, if ever, entirely devoid of potential good.

(b) In my opinion, there is nothing that would do more to strengthen the spirit of America than for mature Americans to be able to say that America has not always been right, is not always right now, but we believe that it is on the right track, and that in the issue we face, it represents the greater good, and therefore we gladly take our stand on its side. The more we love it, the more critical of it we must necessarily be.

III. The third and, I think, the most significant thing that the story has to say to us is that David was a giant too, but a very different kind of giant. Goliath was a giant in the traditional sense. He was a giant in size and weight. David was a new kind of giant, a giant in intelligence and spirit. His strength was in his faith and not in his fists. He won the contests not by his physical prowess but by what you might call, even though it seems a rather sophisticated phrase to use about David at this point, his spiritual power.

IV. The thing that haunts me now, and the reason why I have gone back to this old story, is this: It seems to me that we Americans are trying to wear the armor of our opponent. We are being tempted from every side to match our might against his, pound for pound, bomb for bomb, and so outmaneuver him at his own game. Competition is a good and legitimate thing in life, but none of the really great things in life have ever been accomplished by people who were doing it from the sheer ambition to get there first.

(a) I feel sure of two things. First, the day of the old weapons is over and gone. Nuclear energy has made all explosive weapons obsolete, for the simple reason that they are too effective to be practical. Even if it were not so, it is more and more evident to me that the great contests in life

are ultimately won by those with the greatest intelligence and faith.

(b) *Intelligence*. We are letting ourselves be told that we can win by bombs and bases, so we are making more and more of them to the neglect of other things that alone can make us strong. We ought to know better than that.

(c) *Faith*. I am perfectly aware of the danger that we see in a man who rashly identifies his will with the will of God. By faith I mean now the things you put your trust in, the things you reach for, the things that shape your character, or more precisely, your loyalty to those things.

(d) America is a giant in the world today; there is no question about that. The question is, What kind of giant shall we be? Shall we be the old-fashioned, traditional giant, putting all our trust in our weight, our size, and our money? Or, shall we be a new kind of giant who realizes that as history moves on, new strains develop and in the long run the victor is always the one who has the intelligence and the faith?—Theodore Parker Ferris.

Illustrations

WORD AND DEEDS.   Knowing that the disembodied, unformed Word is no Word at all, we shall again let the Word be flesh so that the love of God is expressed through our changed lives in a language others can understand. We shall recognize that social involvement is not an optional matter of ethical obedience but a condition of being in communion with God at all. We shall understand that to be hid with God in Christ is not to wallow in glossolalia but to be rightly involved in community. We shall quit singing, "Far away the noise of strife upon my ear is falling . . . Safe am I within the castle of God's word retreating . . . For I am dwelling in Beulah Land" and start singing, "Rescue the perishing; care for the dying; snatch them in pity from sin and the grave," and "Where Cross the Crowded Ways of Life."—Foy Valentine.

THE MIRACLE OF SELFLESSNESS.   Out of Nothing he creates Something. Out of the End he creates the Beginning. Out of self-ness we grow, by his grace, toward selflessness, and out of that final selflessness, which is the loss of self altogether, "eye hath not seen nor ear heard, neither have entered into the heart of man" what new marvels he will bring to pass next. All's lost. All's found. And if such words sound childish, so be it. Out of each old self that dies some precious essence is preserved for the new self that is born; and within the child-self that is part of us all, there is perhaps nothing more precious than the fathomless capacity to trust.—Frederick Buechner.

Sermon Suggestions

ONWARD CHRISTIAN SOLDIERS! Text: Matt. 10:5–15. Our mission to the lost: (1) The scope (vv. 5–6). (2) The strategy (vv. 7–8). (3) The seriousness (vv. 9–15).—William E. Hull.

GUIDELINES FOR CHRISTIAN WORKERS. Gospel Text: Luke 10:1–12, 17–20. (1) Consider the challenge. (2) Follow the rules. (3) Be prepared for both failure and success.

Worship Aids

CALL TO WORSHIP. "If the Son makes you free, you will be free indeed" (John 8:36).

INVOCATION. Grant, O Lord, that we cherish all our lawful freedoms, but that we, above all, cherish the freedom in Christ from the slavery of sin. Today help us to see that even while we pursue one freedom we may lose that most important freedom of all.

OFFERTORY SENTENCE. "No servant can be the slave of two masters; for either he will hate the first and love the second, or he will be devoted to the first and think nothing of the second. You cannot serve God and Money" (Matt. 6:24, NEB).

OFFERTORY PRAYER. O God, if our hearts are curled around our money, relax that idolatry and help us to worship only you, the only true God. Bless us both in our adversity and in our prosperity, so that neither of them will turn us away from you.

PRAYER. God of our fathers, their stay in trouble, their strength in conflict, their guide and deep resource, we worship thee. Be thou to us what our fathers have said thou wert to them, a fortress, a high tower, a refuge in the day of trouble. We, too, are tossed about by the vicissitudes of life and the uncertainties of fate. We need security. We long for peace. We would find the things that endure. We need strength greater than our own.

Our fathers have said that thou wert to them a pillar of cloud by day and of fire by night, that thou didst lead them, thy word a lamp unto their feet and a light unto their path. Be that to us. We, too, are pilgrims and pioneers still launching out on stormy seas for lands unknown. Each day is an adventure. O God of the pilgrims and pioneers, lead us in paths of righteousness for thy name's sake.

Our fathers have said concerning thee that thou wert to them the captain of the well-fought fight, that thou, the Lord of Hosts, didst gird them with the armor of the Lord and arm them with the sword of the Spirit. Be that to us. We, too, must fight. Contentions rise up within us, and adverse circumstances rear themselves hostilely against us, and we need the courage that our fathers knew. Be thou to us the Captain of the Host. And at the end of the long day grant that we, too, may say, I have fought a good fight.

Our fathers said thou wert their friend, the unseen companion of their pilgrimage, in whom with utter trust they could confide. Be that to us. We, too, need friendship. Blessed be thy name for earthly friends who by their love make life beautiful. Yet the day comes when we would see through earthly friendship into the divine care and feel the everlasting arms beneath us. O Father of the faithful, in the day of need we, too, like our fathers before us, would speak unto thee as a man speaketh with his friend.

God of our fathers, we pray thee today for the nation that the fathers founded. We thank thee for the heritage that has come down to us, bought by other toil and other tears than ours. For great character, that has been woven into the fabric of this nation, blessed be thy name! For great leaders who in crucial times thou hast lifted up to direct our paths, blessed by thy name! Help us today with vivid vision to see the heroes of old who feared thy name. Steady our hands to grasp the torch of the nation's righteousness, which they bequeathed to us. Make stable and wise our minds to understand the high entrustment, that the light of this people may not fail.—Harry Emerson Fosdick.

EVENING SERVICE

Topic: Proclaiming Life and Liberty
TEXT: Luke 4:16–21.

Jesus began his preaching ministry with a sermon about life and liberty. Jesus was eager to see life lived under changed conditions and he promised a liberation from all that restricts God in our lives. His text was Isaiah 61:1–2, an Old Testament passage familiar to all his hearers in their hometown synagogue. When Jesus finished preaching, the people knew that his sermon had been planned with them in mind, that he had spoken to help them experience God's will and provisions for their lives. It was a message of great magnitude, practical meaning, and appeal. It was a message to help his hearers realize that God still acts to help people deal with the staggering weights and burdens imposed upon them by circumstances, frailty, and sin.

God still helps us because he honors life and promotes liberty. As Paul has reminded us, "The God who made the world and everything in it . . . himself gives to all men life and breath and everything" (Acts 17:24–25). Your life and mine are more than biological accidents. The life we have is a gift from God, something of personal value to be honored, protected, and enhanced. Jesus came to tell us this and to help us live as responsible and thankful souls.

I. *Respect for life*. Some of us live in nations that have a high view of human life and whose statements of purpose have been influenced by the biblical views about human worth. It is comforting to have such a heritage, and certain holidays provide the people of our nations with opportunity to remember and be renewed by the spirit of that heritage.

(a) We Christians should not forget the prophetic role of the church in shaping such a heritage in so many lands. The church has influenced many of our nations, helping them through the biblical view about the worthiness of life. That influence must continue because so many other influences are constantly at work, undermining human life as God intended it for us. The church at its best honors God, witnesses about Jesus Christ, and lives in the will of God by promoting justice, human welfare, and the dignity of liberty for all. In so doing the church must sometimes raise its voice and rally its strength against the selfish designs of big business, institutionalism, nationalism, secularism, and racism.

(b) Like Jesus, the church must promote life and liberty. We who follow Jesus must be concerned about divine honor, moral splendor, and the importance of persons. We must make the message of God's love heard, sounding the golden trumpets of the gospel.

(c) This week is that time of the national calendar when we are asked to reflect upon the national purpose as spelled out in the Declaration of Independence and the federal Constitution. My reflection reminds me about those trained and conscientious preachers who helped to frame our national documents—godly leaders who courageously called upon all of the people to invest life, fortunes, and sacred honor in the awesome task of nation building. Sad and sorry things have since happened in our national life, to be sure; but the way we began still judges and reminds us of the high vision of our founding leaders.

(d) The time of our beginning was also that time in our nation when ministers of the gospel had to express themselves at least twice a year on the subject of civil government. This usually happened just before a major election. The wisdom of this should be apparent: religious insights *should* influence civil order and social process. Rightly expounded, the Word of God promotes civil order, personal worth, and a just social process. Let anyone study the historical books of the Old Testament —especially Exodus, and the prophetic books such as Isaiah and Jeremiah and Amos—and that person gains a clear understanding that biblical faith always views life and liberty as blessings from God, and seeks to promote and preserve them.

II. *A life of deliverance.* Jesus did come preaching about life, but he stressed life of a particular quality. He talked about—and offered—deliverance from every deterrent to inward freedom. So he called his hearers to a new birth, to repentance, renewal, forgiveness of sins.

Jesus called hearers to follow him and receive "abundant life." The church rightly honors life in general; but like Jesus, we especially proclaim and promote a certain life in particular. That life is one of holiness, wholeness as it is seen in Jesus. This is life on a redeemed level. This is life with power to handle decisions rightly. This kind of life results from having a changed character through the renouncing of sin and willful disobedience to God. This new life encourages sharing and it generates concern for others. We must never forget that the quality of our contribution to the lives of others is influenced by the quality of the life we put into it. This is something more than mere

"good works"; it is a matter of working with God to bless life and promote liberty. It is the life Jesus lived. It is the very incentive for his death.

III. *Freedom from fear.* Jesus preached about life and liberty, offering us freedom from the fear of death. As in our own day, his was a time when people had considerable questions and fears about death and dying. The words of Jesus speak meaningfully to this generation increasingly preoccupied with questions about our morality.

(a) For each one of us each day is part of a death march; we are all headed for a listing in the obituary column of some community newspaper. Both in sickness and in health we are never free from the awareness that our time here is short, and that a boundary mark awaits us at some point on the road in the future.

(b) Jesus came preaching life and liberty. We humans were meant for something other than oppressive conditions and restrictive fears. We were meant to have wholeness of life, freedom from a burdened conscience and a sin-filled memory. His work leads to life beyond realized failures and the fear of judgment. And the promise was that it could all happen for the hearer right then and there. Thus came the word of Jesus about it being "the acceptable year of the Lord."— James E. Massey.

SUNDAY: JULY THIRTEENTH

MORNING SERVICE

Topic: A Plea For Patience
Text: Rom. 8:25.

Whatever the world in general may think of it, patience occupies a high place in the New Testament list of virtues. And Christian patience is not a dull, negative passivity, waiting for something to turn up. It is a strong, active virtue. It is more like what we mean by endurance, perseverance. It means holding on tenaciously when the going is tough, plodding doggedly on while others are giving up the game and the outlook seems hopeless. Let

me make this plea for patience by posing three rhetorical questions.

I. First: *Are you patient with yourself?*

(a) The hardest battle on the hands of most of us is the battle with ourselves. Much of our irritation and impatience with others is a projection of our own feeling about ourselves. We tend to give ourselves a lift by dragging someone else down.

(b) The committed Christian is acutely aware of this fight. What disappoints us in our moments of ruthlessly honest self-examination is the slowness of our growth in character. Long after our decisive encounter with Christ the same sordid sins continue to haunt and harass us.

(c) What we have to understand is that the Christian life demands patience—a steady, unwavering perseverance. There is no such thing as "instant sanctity."

(d) Are you patient with yourself? There is no limit to the heights of character we can reach, no limit to the victories we can achieve, if we will wait patiently and walk humbly with God. To be sure, a victorious Christian life is gloriously possible. Our fathers knew it. You and I know it. Therefore—we work and wait for it with patience. Are you patient with yourself?

II. Here is the second question: *Are you patient with the Church*?

(a) It is fashionable to be impatient with anything institutional today, and not least the Church. Impatience with the Church is as old as the Church. The radicals and the reformers have always been in evidence in every age. And rightly so! But the posture of protest should never be adopted without the patience of love. Shouldn't we have a lover's quarrel with the Church, remembering that love is patient?

(b) We must be patient with the Church's hypocrisies. No Church is what it ought to be, by a long shot. There is a yawning gulf between the actual and the ideal. What Church is there anywhere, of any denomination, where the gospel is consistently and radiantly embodied? We overlook the fact that God builds the Church out of the rough material of human nature. It is to the Church's glory, not shame, that it welcomes sinful, struggling, weak, slow, ungracious people. The Body of Christ consists of an unpredictable and often unattractive mix of fallible but believing hearts.

(c) We must be patient with the Church's traditions. An institution as old as the Church has inevitably gathered around itself powerful traditions, creeds, ceremonies, customs. There are ways of thinking, worshiping, serving which, having been accepted as agreeable to the Word of God and having proved themselves in experience, have been passed on from one generation to another. There is, of course, nothing sacrosanct about some of the traditions of the Church. A new and changing day demands new methods, new images. The point is that such adjustment is always a slow and painful process. Change must certainly come—but how can it come effectively except as a reward to the patience of love?

(d) We must be patient with the Church's decisions. They are not always our personal decisions. Unfortunately, they are not always God's decisions. It is obviously more difficult for a community to decide what is the Christian thing to do in any given situation than it is for an individual.

III. Once more: *Are you patient with God*?

(a) Many of us are wrestling with God, baffled by his reticence, impatient with his slowness. We are in a hurry, and God isn't. So we bombard heaven with our passionate prayers and complain that God is an ever-absent help in time of trouble.

(b) So we wrestle with God. But we had better hope to lose! The very greatness of God is in his long-suffering. The majesty of God is in his mercy. The power of God is in his patience. Where would any one of us be if it were not for the divine love that breathes deeply and waits patiently?

(c) Christian patience is rooted in the conviction that God's time is always the best time, the right time, the only time. No one who believes in him will ever be disappointed. You cannot force the hand of a God who chooses to make his appeal to men from a cross on a hill, who could smash us by his power yet rather stoops to win us by his love!—John N. Gladstone.

Illustrations

THE HOPEFULNESS OF CHRIST.   A pagan writer, speaking of the age in which the gospel was given to the world, describes it in words that would be hard to match for pathos and for poignancy. *Moritur et ridet* is his sentence—it laughs with the death rattle in its throat. It was an age that, for all its boast of conquest and all its inheritance of art and culture, had sunk into the deadness of despair. Then on that world, strangely and unexpectedly, there was breathed the hopefulness of Jesus

Christ. And light stole back again into a thousand eyes, and life leaped up within a thousand hearts, till men began to feel that they were saved, not only by a love that bore the cross; they began to feel that they were saved by hope.—George H. Morrison.

WAITING FOR UNDERSTANDING. I am imagining a tiny ant creeping along the front of this pulpit and coming to this break in the cushions, and finding it a real problem to know how to cross the gulf here, where my finger is, and get home in time for supper, and I am realizing that he does not even know that he is in the pulpit of the City Temple! He has never heard of the City Temple! Poor little insect! What does he know of London, or England, or Europe, or the world, or its place in space? Honestly, without diminishing man's importance to God because he is a loved object, our *mental* grasp of things is probably as fractional as an ant's grasp of the world. If the majesty and wisdom and power of God are infinite, as we glibly say, is it any wonder that I cannot understand what he is doing? Indeed, it is amazing that the One who had the greatest insight and saw farther than any of us could tell us with his divine authority, "You *will* understand afterwards," and that Paul by faith could say, "I shall know fully."—Leslie D. Weatherhead.

Sermon Suggestions

HASTENING LOT.   Text: Gen. 19:15.
(1) The righteous need to be hastened. (2) The sinners need to be hastened.—Charles Haddon Spurgeon.

WHAT MADE THE GOOD SAMARITAN GOOD. Gospel Text: Luke 10:25–37. (1) He did not use Scripture to justify hardness of heart. (2) He responded at once with true humaneness. (3) He looked to the victim's continuing welfare.

Worship Aids

CALL TO WORSHIP.   "I wait for the Lord, my soul doth wait, and in his word do I hope" (Ps. 130:5).

INVOCATION.   Our Father, we come to this place from our often frantic activities, bent as we are to run ahead of you, sometimes ignoring your commandments, sometimes taking matters into our own hands that could be better left up to you. Quiet our racing pulse and restore our jaded spirit as we once again try to put our trust and hope in you.

OFFERTORY SENTENCE.   "I know thy works, and thy labor, and thy patience" (Rev. 2:2).

OFFERTORY PRAYER.   When we have labored on with patience, O God, the reward has come. The joy of honest toil and the products of what we have done have added to our sense of meaning and belonging. Grant that those who have no satisfying work or who can no longer work may not feel that life no longer has meaning or that they are now only in the way. Help them to know that you and we do not forget what they have done in the past and to know that their presence among us is a precious gift of your providence.

PRAYER.   Patient God, we thank you for time; for our life together; for time over coffee; for kids' time, listening to their music, talking; for lives intertwined through common tasks; for the inns and resting places of the human spirit, times, holy places, special people—where we take a breather, a restaurant or coffee shop, a kitchen table, a corner at work.

Adorable God, we thank you for the liturgy of our common round, the shape of specialness gracing ordinary days like lilacs about a dilapidated home: an evening out, a weekend away, hunting or fishing, a ball game, needlework, a good book. We give you thanks for new faces; forbid it that we should assume they shall find something of worth and warm us and ours. May we be among them as ones who serve. May we be of some use. We pray for people faithfully tending others, that they may find a pace they can hold, that they may endure, that they may laugh, that they may believe beyond the grave.—Peter Fribley.

EVENING SERVICE

Topic: The New Manna

TEXT: Exod. 16:2–4, 9–15; Eph. 4:17–25; John 6:24–35.

I. Hungry for meat and steady food to sustain them on their way, the Israelites prayed and fussed and complained about their status on the trek to the Promised Land.

(a) "Give us meat." And the quail came. But what they didn't know was that in this part of the world the quails always came. Quails in that part of the world winter in Africa and migrate northward in the spring in vast flocks. It is an exhausting flight, done in stages, and we are told that when the birds alight to take a rest, they are so exhausted they can easily be picked up. But in this ordinary event the Hebrews see the sacred, the hand of God, the deliverance of the Almighty.

(b) It was the same with the manna. For many years it was thought that the manna was a substance produced from the tamarisk bushes. In fact, in early Christian centuries, some Greek monks lived in the Sinai on the sweet manna from the tamarisk bushes. More recently, we have discovered that the manna is really produced in the desert regions by an insect *najacoccus serpentinus*.

A chemical analysis reveals that the manna contains a mixture of three very basic sugars with pectin. The sap from the tamarisk bush, on which these scale insects feed, is rich in carbohydrates but very low in nitrogen. In order to acquire and keep enough nitrogen for their metabolism to operate properly, the insects have to consume an enormous amount of the sap. The excesses pass from the insects in honeydew excretions and the dry desert air changes these into drops of sticky solids. They turn whitish yellow and can be collected and eaten, even today, to sustain life. In the ordinary event, the sacred is seen.

(c) While we have clearly outstripped calling the manna and the quail "miracles," we still have the need to do what the Hebrews did, namely, to find in the ordinary the presence of the sacred. Burning bushes, falling quail, and a substance so

mysterious they called it *"manhu"* ("What is it?") we can explain, but the need to find the sacred in the ordinary is still with us.

II. And if we do not develop that kind of spiritual sensitivity, then we find ourselves in the same boat with those in *John* 6, the Gospel lesson today.

(a) They were looking at him who was flesh-and-blood sign of God's grace and presence and they were asking him for a sign of God's grace and presence. "What sign can you give us that would prove God's here?" The fact that he was man, the ordinary, the everyday, caused them to stumble and they were unable to see in him the sacred.

(b) "Let God knock us off our feet and we will believe." Isn't it enough that a man stands before them who heals broken hearts, inspires confidence from inferior spirits, and makes acceptable the outcasts, drowns fear in floods of love, and knits up the unraveled wounds of the human dilemma?

(c) Aren't these miracles in the mundane? Isn't this the sacred in the ordinary? Isn't this God in the pedestrian? Yes. If we have the eyes to see. The sacred in the ordinary. *The new manna for the journey of life is the vision to see the divine in the daily and the holy in the humdrum, the godly in the gabble.*

III. And if we understand that, then we will go out to be the sacred in the ordinary, be the new manna, be the light to the world, a city set on a hill, the salt of the earth, the leaven in the lump.

(a) If we do not understand it, we will wait for him to do something else. Show me a sign. I wrote somewhere a few years back:

"So much hope is spent in waiting—waiting for Godot who never shows; waiting for Messiah if you're Jew, waiting for *Parousia* if you're Christian, waiting for the end of the world if you're one of those. So much hope is spent in waiting." But the new manna is like the old. It is not meant for the keeping. It is meant for daily use. If we save for tomorrow what was meant for using today, it spoils.

(b) Or if we do not wait we may make another error: We try to turn the ordinary into the sacred. We try to make entertainment worship; we try to make our workaholism divine by claiming it's for the family; we make our prejudices biblical (God made Cain black; the Jews killed Jesus; such-and-such a denomination is closer to the Bible). Either waiting to use tomorrow what was meant for use today or trying to turn the ordinary into the sacred instead of seeing the sacred in the ordinary can spoil the manna.

(c) We are saints, believers who see the sacred in the ordinary and become the new manna. With a little courage we become the new manna for the world.—Thomas H. Conley.

SUNDAY: JULY TWENTIETH

MORNING SERVICE

Topic: Faith—the Source of Christian Victory

Text: 1 John 5:4.

I. (a) Faith seems to be the weakest weapon in our arsenal. It seems so to us because we have so little of it and also because faith, in itself, appears to be like a tender, fragile plant easily bruised and destroyed.

(b) Of course, faith comes highly recommended. Many people have highly praised it—people ranging from religious mystics to men of business to scientists. A faith of some sort is necessary in every realm of life. But the sort of faith John writes about in his letter has to do with that elusive quality Jesus spoke of when he said, "If ye have faith as a grain of mustard seed, ye shall say unto this mountain, Remove hence to yonder place; and it shall remove; and nothing shall be impossible unto you" (Mt. 17:20). It is the sort of faith the advertisements point to—showing a family kneeling in prayer and saying, "Give them a faith to live by." Faith then is presented to us as the way through our mountainous problems—the way to family solidarity and world peace.

(c) But it is easy to see that faith is seriously challenged. The faith of Jesus himself was sorely tried. When he was crucified, his enemies hurled at him the words, "He trusted in God; let him deliver him now, if he will have him: for he said, I am the Son of God" (Mt. 27:43). And there was the man who spoke to me after a worship service. He referred to some recent disasters that had shocked and saddened thousands. Then he fairly shouted at me, "How can God let little children burn up and blow away?"

II. In view of all this, what do you think of this audacious claim by John: "This is the victory that overcometh the world, even our faith"?

(a) This man has obviously seen a great deal of life—its temptations, its hatreds, its cruelties, its demonic forces. And he views the world as an enemy of man and an enemy of God. He is not thinking now of the world of sunsets and songs. He is not thinking of the world as the writer of Genesis thought of it when he said concerning all creation: "And God saw everything that he had made, and, behold it was very good" (1:31). He is thinking of the world of wild lust and towering pride, the world of darkness and death. To him the term "the world" describes "The sum of all the forces antagonistic to the spiritual life."

(b) But this man sees faith—the weakest thing in the world—as the conqueror of life's most formidable enemies. Suffering and death are no longer a threat when faith prevails. Dostoyevsky, the Russian novelist, as a political prisoner knew the bleakness, the loneliness, and the terror of Siberia. But he wrote to his brother: "In the penitentiary, I ended up by discovering men, real men, profound and beautiful characters." The crucifixion of Jesus Christ and all the creative benefits that have come from it and its everlasting value as the paradigm of all true heroism—this seen by faith is more than victory. "Surely the wrath of man shall praise thee," sang the Psalmist. Does this not mean that the power of human sin is broken? Nothing that man can do will finally frustrate the gracious purpose of God. Evil always overreaches itself and plays into the hands of God, who somehow turns it to good. The cross is the proof of that. And faith takes hold of the victory within that truth.

(c) Obviously, this is a special kind of faith. It is not a superficial optimism. It is not Polyanna's belief in the innate goodness of all men. Therefore, it is not mere faith in the future or mere faith in man. At bottom, it is faith in God. But let me put it in a simpler and a more practical way: the faith that overcomes the world is a certain way of looking at Jesus Christ. It is a certain way of relating ourselves to him. It may be as simple as the matter of hearing Jesus Christ saying to you, "Follow me," and then of leaving all to follow him.

III. Now what does this add up to?

(a) It means that life has a new reference point in Jesus Christ. "If any man be in Christ, he is a new creature: old things are passed away; behold, all things are become new" (2 Cor. 5:17). That is the way the Apostle Paul expressed it in one place. In another place, he wrote: "If ye then be risen with Christ, seek those things which are above, where Christ sitteth on the right hand of God. Set your affection on things above, not on things on the earth" (Col. 3:1–2).

In other words, life can never again be quite the same for one who has been gripped by a vital faith in God as God is revealed in Christ. Suffering, because of Christ, loses its emptiness and takes on meaning. Death, because of Christ, loses its nihilistic gloom and is filled with hope. Evil, because of Christ, loses its power and is overcome in a new hunger and thirst after righteousness.

(b) Therefore, faith is the most practical and urgent reality in human experience. It offers the way out of all the dead-end streets of our lives. It finds its perfection as it is focused on Jesus Christ the Son of God who, we are told, is "the author and finisher of our faith" (Heb. 12:2).—James W. Cox.

Illustrations

SERVING GOD.   We are to serve God. How we do this will depend on each one's personal vocation. God calls us to serve him in different ways. One factor is common to all of us. Everything human, except sin, has a new significance since God became man. Jesus Christ lived the ordinary life of a carpenter of his day in Nazareth, and by doing so he has made holy all ordinary things and activities. When you work, for example, the Father is reminded of the fact that his divine Son once worked too; when you sit around chatting to friends, the Father remembers that his Son did the same. This may sound just a bit naive on a first reading, but think about it. It is an idea rich in consequences, for it means that whatever we do (except, always, what is sinful) looks different to the Father than it does to us. You have that floor to sweep. Nothing very dramatic in that. God sees more than the sweeping. He sees it as a service of him, and this because his Son did that kind of thing for thirty years of his life. Almost nothing has been recorded of those years lived by Our Lord in the family at Nazareth. As news value they are of no consequence, but where it truly matters those years are precious indeed. And so it is for all of you. Your daily work is your daily service of God. To make that service a loving one adds to it, both in giving honor to God and in the joy you will experience.—Basil Hume.

GROWTH IN GRACE.   The new life participates in the power of God. We do not do it all. We share in a working that is beyond our sight and our power. Our moment in time is the heir of all previous moments and of what God has accomplished in them. We are deceived by the appearance that everything is dependent upon our efforts. But the tides and powers that shape our destiny and to which we add our mite of freedom and creative decision have been running for all the ages. It follows that what we actually do is largely invisible to us. What we actually do is what our life becomes as it influences the ongoing history. We share in a destiny we can but faintly envision. We participate in a task that occupies God for eternity.—Daniel Day Williams.

Sermon Suggestions

THE HIGHEST PRAYER.   Text: Exod. 32: 32.

(1) Surely the highest prayer is when we pray for another, a friend or an enemy. (2) To pray for another is to think of God and our friend together, and of ourselves in relation to both. (3) Our prayer for others must be specific, persistent, patient.—Joseph Fort Newton.

THE DESIRABLE AND THE ESSENTIAL. Gospel Text: Luke 10:38–42. (1) We pour our strength into many things that are good but expendable. (2) We give little attention to what is both good and indispensable. (3) Christ calls us to rearrange our scale of values.

Worship Aids

CALL TO WORSHIP. "Ye shall seek me, and find me, when ye shall search for me with all your heart" (Jer. 29:13).

INVOCATION. Bring our straggling thoughts and vagrant affections to a focus today, O God, so that we may not only find you but also rejoice in your presence.

OFFERTORY SENTENCE. "Now he who provides seed for sowing and bread for food will provide the seed for you to sow; he will multiply it and swell the harvest of your benevolence, and you will always be rich enough to be generous" (2 Cor. 9:10, NEB).

OFFERTORY PRAYER. Our Father in heaven, we would not be so calculating as to look for a reward for every good deed, but we would pray that somehow we could see that the more we give, the more we want and have to give, not so much for our own enjoyment as for the help it will be to others and the honor it will bring to you.

PRAYER. Lord, God, if we have all things except a right relationship with you: Can we be satisfied? We are adopted children on this planet, but when we separate ourselves from That One who lovingly, eternally adopts us—you, God—we most assuredly do not become satisfied persons. When we reject, for whatever reason, your acceptance of us in Christ we create our own abandonment: We are left to ourselves, and in this there is no satisfaction at all. For indeed our hearts, our basic beings, remain mysteriously but permanently restless, empty of satisfaction, until we rest ourselves in you and your care and your guidance. Accepting any other kind of satisfaction is dangerous, hazardous, to our health and to our humanity! Many people could feel satisfied when they hung the Only Sinless, Perfect Human Being on a cross! How uncomfortably true it is: People satisfied by the wrong things and in the wrong ways are capable—in the name of being satisfied—of bringing havoc and hurt to a wounded world crying out for love and reconciliation.

You alone, God, are our confidence and strength. You alone make it possible for us to be greater than our sin, more than our corrupted selves. You take us home where otherwise we would be lost. You give us purpose where otherwise we have no reason for being. You get us outside of ourselves where otherwise we see ourselves and others and all things through the blind confusion of a sinner's eyes. And you satisfy us completely because we know that in all things you work for good with those who love you and who are called according to your purpose. We do love you. We thank you for calling us.—Gordon H. Reif.

EVENING SERVICE

Topic: Good News for the Exhausted
TEXT: Isa. 40:30, 31.

Some people imagine that the Christian gospel is exclusively for down-and-outs. Thank God the gospel is for the down-and-outs! Where else can beaten men and women go but to God their Father and Christ their Savior? The Christian gospel, however, is also for the up-and-coming. It is capable of challenging and engaging men and women in their physical, moral, and intellectual strength. We certainly need to hear the good news for the exhausted! Now, this good news that comes to us through the great Hebrew prophet involves a principle and a promise.

I. Look, first, at the *principle*. "But they who wait for the Lord shall renew their strength. . . . " The principle is this: The answer to our human exhaustion is in God.

(a) Only as we learn to wait on him can we hope to overcome it. No human situation is hopeless if God is taken into account—and God is waiting for us to wait on him! He is waiting for us to realize that when we reach the end of our tether, he is there at the end.

(b) Waiting in the biblical sense is emphatically not a passive, negative attitude. It implies *an attitude of dependence on God.* The sad thing is that this dependent attitude toward God often comes only after we have been brought low.

(c) Waiting on the Lord also implies *an attitude of obedience to God.* To wait on God is to open our minds and wills to his instructions and to obey them. This obedience is costly. It demands the renunciation of our own stubborn will and determination to please ourselves. We get in step with God's purposes in history and for our own lives, discovering that in his will is our peace.

(d) Waiting on the Lord, again, implies *an attitude of expectancy from God.* How big is our faith when we worship and pray? What do we expect from God? Expect great things from God, for he is able and willing to give them.

II. Now look at *the promise.* "They shall mount up with wings as eagles, they shall run and not be weary, they shall walk and not faint." It is a threefold promise— "mount up," "run," and "walk."

(a) We are promised, first, *the gift of a true perspective.* Waiting on God gives us eagles' wings to fly high, to rise above the normal level of vision, and, therefore, to see things in true perspective. It is no exaggeration to claim that much of our exhaustion can be traced to one factor—our lack of vision, our shortsightedness, our loss of perspective. Our desperate need is to climb above the family, the job, the local church, contemporary politics, the present failure. The wings of an eagle will help us see the days in relation to the years, the years to the centuries, the centuries to eternity.

(b) We are promised, next, *the gift of a disciplined passion.* "They shall run and not be weary." In the Bible, running is a symbol of a great devotion, a passionate enthusiasm. This passion is indispensable to life, to service, to the Church. The kingdom of God urgently needs passionately committed men and women to run the errands of God in our time. But it must be disciplined passion! Otherwise it will soon grow weary and fade away.

(c) We are promised, finally, *the gift of a stubborn perseverance.* "They shall walk and not faint." There is a sense in which to mount up with wings is easy—our high moments are exhilarating experiences. To keep slogging on, day after day, year after year, until "the shades lengthen and the evening comes, the busy world is hushed, the fever of life is over and our work is done"—this is perseverance.

(d) These are difficult days. There is no shame in being exhausted. But it is a shame to stay that way when God wants to give us so much—a true perspective, a disciplined passion, a stubborn perseverance. He is waiting for us to wait on him! —John H. Gladstone.

SUNDAY: JULY TWENTY-SEVENTH

MORNING SERVICE

Topic: The Secret Followers of Jesus
TEXT: John 19:38–42.

Joseph of Arimathea was a disciple "secretly," for fear of the Jews. And so was Nicodemus. How many others, one wonders, were also secret followers? Make no mistake about it, there are many, and always have been. We would like to be followers openly—to speak for him in the marketplaces of life, to witness by our piety and devotion—but we do not dare.

I. Poor Joseph and Nicodemus! We sympathize with them.

(a) Two men of distinction, members of the most august body of Jewish men in all the world. What would their colleagues think if they knew that Nicodemus had visited Jesus secretly at night or that he and

Joseph entertained the possibility that the Galilean might really be the Savior of the world? What would the masses think?!

(b) Life can be terribly complex at times, can't it? And those with most responsibility find it most complex. It was easy enough for the disciples to follow him—they were simple men, men with few friends, men without political alliances. But Joseph and Nicodemus were well connected. They had others to think about. They had the entire country to think about. That's the way it is with us, isn't it? It's all right for the young and the ill-connected to be fully committed to Jesus. But those of us who are older and more involved and deeply respected—we have to be careful, don't we? Joseph and Nicodemus were disciples secretly because they had areas of their lives where Chist wasn't welcome. And we are the same way!

II. Joseph and Nicodemus's biggest problem, of course, was that they couldn't decide what they really believed about Jesus.

(a) If they had believed for sure that he was the Messiah he claimed to be, and that many of the people said he was, they would certainly have thrown in their lot with him and taken the consequences, whatever they might have been. But they weren't sure. They were clever enough to understand all about delusions and that sort of thing. Suppose Jesus was mistaken about himself and that he wasn't really the Messiah. Then where would they be? They would have stepped into a ship with no bottom it it! They had to try to befriend him secretly while maintaining their appearance and work as members of the Sanhedrin. In their position, they couldn't afford to do more. The leaders of society have to be cautious.

(b) Again, we understand, don't we? Most of us are never really sure of what we believe. There is so much at stake that we seldom take the time or spend the effort to decide what we truly believe. We can't afford to make a mistake, to make a wrong move. So we're committed to not making any drastic moves at all.

III. But something happened to Joseph and Nicodemus. That is the truth to which our text witnesses. Something

shocked Joseph and Nicodemus out of their secret discipleship into open discipleship. When they beheld Jesus on the cross, they knew where their loyalties really lay. They couldn't remain secret followers any longer.

(a) It isn't any wonder, is it? There isn't anything in the world like the cross of Christ for bringing out the true loyalties of people. And Joseph and Nicodemus, seeing and hearing all, were wrenched as they had never been wrenched before. He *was* the Christ, and they had failed him. He *was* the Messiah, and they had waited too long to acclaim him. Suddenly, though it was too late, they made their move. Having lingered in half-belief while he was alive, they came to his side in death and asked permission to take down his poor, broken body and bury it in a tomb.

(b) It is amazing what they risked by doing this. There were strict laws in their religion. Anyone who touched a dead body must go through long and elaborate cleansing procedures before observing a holiday. Passover was upon them—the most blessed feast of the Jewish people. And these two leaders of the people would be unable to participate. They were defiled, accursed, by touching the body of a criminal. There would be no more secret of their discipleship, for now everyone would know. They were signing their own resignations from leadership in the Sanhedrin. Their loyalties to the Galilean were now declared! They had lost more than the disciples of Jesus themselves; they had given up their very positions to acknowledge him.

(c) Joseph and Nicodemus were changed by looking at the cross. They traded their secret discipleship for an open discipleship. What about us? Will we be changed too?—John Killinger.

Illustrations

TOO LITTLE RELIGION.   We go on with the balancing act year after year, trying to hold on to Jesus in church and hold on to our own selfish principles in school or business or wherever it is we spend most of our time in the world. We're like the old black sister whose pastor said of her that she had just enough religion to make her miserable at the dance hall but not enough to make her happy in prayer meeting. We're caught in the middle and determined to stay there.—John Killinger.

ON THE WAY TO VICTORY.   When Jesus wills to become our Lord, he can come quietly and naturally. Things may simply go awry in our calling, in our marriage, or in our relationship with our children. Then we sulk, complain, and become bitter. But one day we discover that something went completely wrong in our life and obviously has to be different. Then weeks, even years pass and nothing miraculous happens. We battle with ourselves, sometimes succeeding, sometimes losing. We are not changed with a single stroke. Perhaps we even find ourselves often defeated, despairing, and more distraught than ever.

But Jesus never lets us go. "Do good to those who hate you," he says. "You cannot serve God and mammon," he says. "Every one who looks at a woman lustfully has already committed adultery with her in his heart," he says. "Do not be anxious about tomorrow. Consider the lilies of the field," he says. One of these sayings, which perhaps we could not even repeat correctly, will not let us alone. And Jesus becomes Lord over us. Perhaps he has to fight for his place as long as we live. So much else clamors to become mightier than he. Yet he will never forsake us. Thus our heart knows in all confusion and temptation, "Jesus is Lord!" He affirmed me and forgave me long before I knew it. Therefore, I may joyfully come to grips with whatever is not yet pleasing to him. The Holy Spirit lives in us simply, not displaying exceptional piety, but very practically and very concretely.—Eduard Schweizer.

Sermon Suggestions

THE FACTS OF LIFE—AND DEATH.   Text: Job 14:14. (1) The Bible recognizes the reality and finality of death. (2) Belief in eternal life is a consequence of belief in God. (3) Eternal life is a gift. (4) Eternal life can be described as rebirth, John 3:3. (5) Eternal life is a possibility here and now.—Robert McAfee Brown.

PRAYER—FROM BEGINNING TO END. Gospel Text: Luke 11:1–13. (1) An approach to prayer. (2) An attitude for prayer. (3) An assurance in prayer.

Worship Aids

CALL TO WORSHIP.   "I say unto you," said Jesus, "Whosoever shall confess me before men, him shall the Son of man also confess before the angels of God" (Luke 12:8).

INVOCATION.   Embolden us in our faith and witness today, O God, and may our honest confession of love to you give strength to those who are struggling to make their life count for you. Help us to do good works without shame and embarrassment and apology, and so may we glorify your name.

OFFERTORY   SENTENCE.   "Each   one should give . . . as he has decided, not with regret or out of a sense of duty; for God loves the one who gives gladly" (2 Cor. 9:7, TEV).

OFFERTORY PRAYER.   As we present our offerings today, a host of your children pass before our vision: the unbelieving, the weak, and the mature; the sick, the pain-wracked, and the dying; the lonely, the doubters, and the despairing; the hungry, the content, and the gluttonous; the lay person, the preacher, and the missionary. Give us the grace to see that what we give may be a symbol of our caring and an actual touch of love for them, and so may we give gladly, knowing why we give.

PRAYER.   Almighty God, Father of all mercies, we your unworthy servants give you humble thanks for all your goodness and lovingkindness to us and to all whom you have made. We bless you for our creation, preservation, and all the blessings of this life; but above all for your immeasurable love in the redemption of the world by our Lord Jesus Christ; for the means of grace and for the hope of glory. And, we pray, give us such an awareness of your mercies, that with truly thankful hearts we may show forth your praise, not only with our lips but in our lives, by giving up our selves to your service, and by walking before you in holiness and righteousness all our days; through Jesus Christ our Lord, to whom, with you and the Holy Spirit, be honor and glory throughout all ages.— *Book of Common Prayer*.

EVENING SERVICE

Topic: Turn to Me and Live
TEXT: Luke 11:13.
Something we really need and what many Christians are longing for is a spiritual renewal, a true awakening. But how can we arrange for a lasting revival? How can we prompt the Holy Spirit to renew Christ's Church? If a renewal will be granted to our churches, it will no doubt be through prayer. Prayer meetings and prayer conferences are the need of the moment. When speaking about renewal, I think of various aspects of both Christian life and church life:

I. *Renewed worship*.
(a) It is one of the greatest blessings of this country that Americans are still going to church. But why is it that we regularly attend church services? Is it the good old tradition, just a habit? Or do we go to church for no other reason but to worship the Lord?

(b) I always feel that if the Lord really is present in the church, something must happen. I must hear him speak to my heart. I will see him change people. I will see people recognize his presence and I will hear them lift up their voices to praise and glorify his name. Their prayers will not be filled with hollow phrases and ritualistic formulas, rather everybody will empty their heart before the Lord and will speak in new terms.

II. *Renewed discipleship*. We are accustomed to saying "Lord Jesus." But do we mean it? Do we accept his Lordship?

(a) Real prayer is some kind of a revolutionary act. I have crucified my "ego" and I surrender my life to the Lord Jesus. Real prayer is a confession of weakness and helplessness. I cannot do a thing. I must let the Lord Jesus act on my behalf. I depend on him! On his grace! Real prayer is

a confession of faith, the practice of faith. I trust in him, that he rules, he fulfills his plan, he will be near to help and comfort me. Such faithful prayer will help to overcome any of today's resignation.

(b) But such prayer must be practiced every day. It's that kind of "walking and talking with Jesus," listening to his voice and his commands. For true Christians prayer can be a real public witness. Do we recognize that the saints always were ordinary people, "people like you and me"— but praying people?

III. *Renewed fellowship*.
(a) Fellowship is more than just being together and saying "hello" at the coffee hour. Real fellowship means to care and to share. We have to come to learn that the Lord Jesus Christ is just as much at work today as he was at the time of the apostles. We only need to have our eyes and ears open to recognize him and his great deeds.

(b) Fellowship in prayer—the sharing of experiences with Christ and the spiritual togetherness before the throne of God— will strengthen our faith, will encourage the brethren, and will help to build the kingdom of God.

IV. *Renewed service*.
(a) Prayer and practical work always go hand in hand. Prayer always connects action and meditation. It is the bridge to the Lord's double calling, "come" and "go."

(b) It is only by prayer that we learn what the Lord wants us to do. There are so many possibilities, there are such great needs, there is an enormous mission field.

(c) However, we as individuals are not called to do everything that needs to be done. God wants to use each of us: the individual, the pastor, the missionary, the church member—even the local church— is asked only to do what the Lord wants us to do. That is why the Lord first says "come" before he tells us to "go." Prayer is some kind of "issue of orders!'

(d) There is a famous altar in Czechoslovakia showing Christ without arms, reminding us that we are his arms to serve the world. Christians therefore not only pray "Thy will be done"—they ask their Lord: "What do you want me to do?"— Gerhard Claas.

SUNDAY: AUGUST THIRD

MORNING SERVICE

Topic: Inseparable Love
TEXT: Rom. 8:38, 39.

Let us remember Paul's fightings within and without and then we can form an estimate of this text of ours with the assurance it expresses of that love of God from which nothing is able to separate. With a voice whose tones are like the music of the choir invisible the great apostle chants the confidence of his faith.

I. We will dwell for a moment on the ground of Paul's confidence. *It is the love of God in Jesus Christ.*

(a) The secret of this triumphant faith, this power that enabled him to rise above all evil, was not his own love of God but God's love of him. I know there is much in our world that shrieks against that high truth. I know it is easy to feel that man is so little and feeble that he must be beneath the care of God. In the school of Christ we have been taught that service is the greatness of man. It is also the greatness of God. His very life consists in the ceaseless giving of himself to his children.

(b) Thus the ground of Paul's confidence is not only God's love but God's love *which is in Jesus Christ our Lord.* The apostle believed that the love of God is the ultimate fact in the universe, and that nothing exists of sufficient potency to overcome the purposes of that all-conquering love.

(c) How did the apostle arrive at this conclusion? Well, he might have pointed out everything gracious and beautiful and good in human nature, and said the Maker of that must be better than that; it must all be an expression of the graciousness and beauty and love of God. The apostle might have easily referred to these things. But he had become convinced that the same Jesus who went about doing good, who healed the sick, who cleansed the lepers, who died upon a cross, that that same Jesus came into his life and so transformed him that he went forth to save in the name of

his love. That same Jesus persuaded him that nothing could separate from the love of God the children he had redeemed. And that same Jesus is the ground of our confidence too.

II. In the next place we will notice that Paul conjures up all the terrors that afflict the soul, all the enemies of faith and assurance, all the things that destroy confidence; and then he challenges them to do their worst.

(a) "I am persuaded that neither death nor life." The order may seem strange to us. On reflection we will all admit that death is not the great separator, but life. Life separates but death unites. Life is made up of guests that come and go; life is made up of greetings and farewells. But in the love of God we may triumph over life. Life is a stormy season, but the love of God is the sun that breaks through the clouds and floods the landscape with longed-for light and heat.

(b) "Nor angels, nor principalities, nor powers." Consider a man who starts out in the morning with his heart set upon the service of God, but before the day is half done something has happened within the strange mechanism of body and spirit in which he lives, and everything has gone wrong. He feels the day has been handed over to the powers of darkness, and he finds it all but impossible to believe in the love of God. Let all such be assured that God's love cannot be defeated by angels or principalities or powers.

(c) "Nor things present, nor things to come." In this phrase the apostle refers to Time, that strange enemy to faith. How often Time has robbed men of assurance. Disappointments check our hoped-for progress. The optimism of earlier days gives way and the tendency both spiritual and mental is in the direction of a mild kind of pessimism that is as harmful as a drop of poisonous acid in a glass of pure spring water. I venture the assertion that it is impossible for any man to go on from decade to decade and keep a cheerful temper and a trusting heart without that series of uplifting thoughts that it is the privilege of inseparable love to furnish.

(d) "Nor height, nor depth, nor anything else in all creation." If Time cannot prevail against God's love, neither can Space. In the earlier days of life on this planet people had small sense of space. The earth was flat and over it was "that inverted bowl we call the sky." But by and by the science of astronomy revealed other worlds beside the little one we inhabit. And I am but one soul among the countless millions in all these worlds. To believe that God can care for me, with my obscure life, my petty trials, my little human loves and desires—who has not felt a chill passing over his heart as he has raised the problem with himself? In the light of this revelation we know that height or depth matter not; up or down, it is all the same. Not even space can keep me from him for he is love.—W. A. Cameron.

Illustrations

ACCEPTANCE—IN SPITE OF. . . .   I once knew a young man who was struggling with a very serious problem; he carefully tried to conceal the struggle from his best friend, because he was afraid that if the friend found out, their friendship would be ruined. But at last the young man could stand it no longer, so he went to his friend and told him the whole story. And the friend replied: "I've known about it all along, and I've liked you in spite of it." As you can imagine, that young man went away with a tremendous burden lifted from his shoulders. He had exposed the worst about himself, expecting to be rejected; and he had come away—accepted. —David E. Roberts.

INSEPARABLE LOVE.   In his "Reminiscences of Frederick Denison Maurice" Mr. Haweis relates this incident: "I remember asking him one day, 'How are we to know when we have got hold of God? because sometimes we seem to have got a real hold of him, whilst at others times we can realize nothing.' He looked at me with those eyes which so often seemed to be looking into an eternity beyond, whilst he said in his deep and tremulously earnest voice, 'You have not got hold of God, but he has got hold of you.'"—W. A. Cameron.

Sermon Suggestions

THE MESSAGE OF THE NEW TESTAMENT. (1) *Fulfillment*. The Proclamation opens with an announcement that the long-expected climax of the history of God's people has arrived. (2) *The Story*. The fulfillment took the form of a series of events, which are recounted as they were handed down by the first witnesses. (3) *The Consequences*. The outcome of the events narrated was the emergence of the church itself as the new "Israel of God." It was marked as such by the gift of the Spirit. (4) *The Appeal*. The Proclamation led up to an appeal to the hearers to give their personal assent to the "Good News."—C. H. Dodd.

THE PERILS OF WEALTH.   Gospel Text: Luke 12:13–21. (1) It often divides families and society. (2) It often becomes an obsession and a measurement of value. (3) It often promotes fleshly indulgence. (4) It often leads people to miss the true riches.

Worship Aids

CALL TO WORSHIP.   "The Lord is good, a stronghold in the day of trouble; and he knoweth them that trust in him" (Nah. 1:7).

INVOCATION.   Lord God, if it is easy to worship you when things are going well for us, some of us should have a great time of worshiping you today. If it is essential to worship you when our lot in life is difficult, full of hardships and hurts and hassles, some of us will go way beyond playing games with you and focus our attention on you most sincerely and completely. If it is eccentric to worship you in a world that considers you just one more superstition, a vain imagination, a relic of the past, an obstacle to real progress, some of us will do very well what the world calls nonsense and foolishness. If it is ennobling to worship you when our understanding of ourselves is poor and pathetic, some of us will discover much better who we are by giving you the affection and adoration and allegiance that belong to you because you are our only God and we are, through Christ, your precious children.

May all the avenues that bring us to the Throne of Grace see us traveling earnestly forward, not standing still, or going backward, or wandering wayward, so that, worshiping you in spirit and in truth, our delight may be in you, and your joy may be in us.—Gordon H. Reif.

OFFERTORY SENTENCE. "What is good has been explained to you, man; this is what Yahweh asks of you: only this, to act justly, to love tenderly and to walk humbly with your God" (Micah 6:8, *The Jerusalem Bible*).

OFFERTORY PRAYER. Lord God, Yahweh, may our offerings reflect what you ask of us in all of life: May our giving be fair, considering what we have received; compassionate, considering your love for us; prayerful, considering the many worthy causes in which these offerings may be used.

PRAYER. We thank thee, Father, that back of all the mystery and the change there is love, above every hostile circumstance, brooding over the narrowed lives of thy children, a love that forever wills and orders and shall conquer. From it we have come into the world; to it we make our stumbling, halting way back. Teach us to choose the paths it chose, nor trust ourselves to any other, willing rather to fail by love than to win by the loss of it.—Paul Scherer.

EVENING SERVICE

Topic: Four Tests of Successful Living
TEXT: Luke 12:16–21.
Jesus was speaking about a certain man who had said to himself, "I will pull down my barns, and build greater." We resent Jesus' implication that this man was a fool. He was successful, but was he foolish? After all, that is our philosophy of success:

to pull down barns and build greater; to look to the day when we can say to our souls, "Take thine ease, eat, drink, and be merry." To many people success is something tangible. They think that they can measure it economically and socially. To them it is money; it is accomplishment; it is a name written in bold letters; it is something vivid; it is being masterful; it is pushing obstacles out of the way; it is crowding men to the sidelines; it is riding the crest of the years; it is possessing things that yesterday were only dreams.

I. To us success lies in the thought that through the years we have made some spiritual progress.

(a) We feel more deeply; we understand more readily; we are moved more quickly. We have learned to put first things first. This was the meaning of successful living as far as Jesus was concerned. What is of primary importance in our lives? What do we seek first? What do we want most? In the answer to these questions lies joy or sorrow. What do we desire first for ourselves and for our children? In this answer lies the success or failure of the soul. What answer would we have given to these questions yesterday? What answer can we give today?

(b) What progress have we made in meeting the challenge of life? We are not immune because we are wise or clever or influential. Have we discovered something along the road that helps us to stand our ground? Have we found weapons for the soul, so that our peace is not in danger?

II. To some of us success lies in the conviction that we are living as we want to be remembered.

(a) That is a perilous thing to say, for it touches every corner of the heart. We cannot rewrite the history of our own years. Each of us writes his or her own biography, and there is a terrible finality about it. Is that the way we want to be remembered?

(b) One has to be a good father to be remembered as a good father, with a patience as long as the years. One has to be a good mother to be remembered as a good mother, with an understanding as deep as the sea. One has to be a good teacher to be remembered as a good teacher, giving wings to children's thoughts. One has to be a good Christian to be remembered as a good Christian, losing himself utterly in the thought of Christ's being. We will be remembered as men saw us in the day of remembrance. Now to live that way!

III. To some of us success lies in the feeling that this is the way we would live life all over again.

(a) How easy it is to become reminiscent and nostalgic. To live life over again! One does not say that without joy or without fear. There were the mistakes that still haunt us. There were the pools of sorrow by which we waited for the light of day to break. And now to look back upon life and be able to say, "I would do it again." That is the soul's triumphant moment.

(b) Oh, yes, let the heart be honest, there is the regret that we were not better men and women, that we served unreadily and loved too little. And this regret: that we waited so long before we let Christ become a power in our lives.

IV. To some of us success lies in he warm knowledge that we shall leave the world a better place than it was when we found it.

(a) Our world may be small or our world may be large. It may be hemmed in by four walls or it may circle the globe. But whatever it is, is it a better world because of us? The most powerful possession we have is the influence we wield upon others. The influence is the invisible but ineradicable tracing of our words, our characters, our habits upon the hearts of others. Here is a touch of earthly eternity.

(b) All of us leave some imperishables. Most things our parents left us were at our mercy. But they left some imperishables. They are in our veins; they are in the turn of our thoughts; they will be in our children. Life will repeat itself. Most things we shall leave will be at the mercy of others. Wisely or foolishly, they will do with them as they please. But we will also leave something imperishable. What will it be? Will it be some moral frailty, or will it be some spiritual strength? Will it be a sense of integrity, or will it be our faith? Nothing can destroy that. That is not at anyone's mercy.—Arnold H. Lowe.

SUNDAY: AUGUST TENTH

MORNING SERVICE

Topic: Marching Off the Map

TEXT: Heb. 11:8.

This ancient and dim figure of Abraham leads a procession that in some measure we all join. It is the Big Parade of our time, indeed, of every time. We are conscripted into an expedition beyond familiar landmarks, a thrust outward into new and uncharted territory.

I. Our world has marched off many maps, and new ones must be drawn, maps that are more true to the realities of the present situation. Our world has marched off old maps in every realm.

(a) We are even getting a new map of the sky from the 200-inch telescope on the top of Mount Palomar in California. There is a new heaven and a new earth. It makes a difference, not only in astronomy but in thinking about man's place in the cosmos.

(b) The medical profession has marched off old maps of medicine. It sounds reasonable! Think of the new maps, of what has been and may be accomplished with sulfa, penicillin, streptomycin and all their relatives, if the game is allowed to go on, without being stopped by atomic darkness.

(c) There is no need to elaborate the obvious. We have marched off the map of scientific certainties. That map filled in with heavy black lines the dictum of Francis Bacon, that "the application of science to invention will tend to perfect man's estate." That old confidence reached its peak in the High Priest of Progress, Herbert Spencer, with his holy dogma of the inevitable upward and onward. One of the real spiritual assets of our time is the deepening of the suspicion in the minds of multitudes, that Superman is a moron.

II. Every day makes it clearer that the world has marched off the map of competing national sovereignties.

(a) The major issue was pictured sharply, though unintentionally, in a pamphlet issued by the Unites States War Department a few years ago. It had the alluring title, *What To Do If an Atomic Bomb Falls*. There were ten points. I remember only one, the first, but that was a stroke of genius. It said, "Keep calm!" That is a masterpiece. An ordinary man would not have thought of that. It must have taken at least a three-star general. If an atomic bomb falls, we will all keep calm—permanently! But if we get disturbed enough about it beforehand, it may not need to fall.

(b) We must stand against the upsurge of mere emotion, which has become such a turbulent flood in our day. To give way to blind emotion is always the devil's line of least resistance.

III. Certainly the world in our century has marched off the map of economic certainties. Every day it becomes more impossible to build a fence around anything —people, war, wealth, poverty, disease, welfare, liberty. In all these, the world is an unfenced field. Fence building is a futile employment, when nations have been pushed into tight propinquity, which will be either frightful or beneficent. We have done wonders with the mechanical arts of addition and multiplication of production. We have done too little with the ethical art of division. We have done a little about *short* division, splitting up the produce of earth among small groups. The problem of survival depends on *long* division, among the whole human family. Maps drawn in the eighteenth and nineteenth centuries offer no safe guidance.

IV. Abraham walked west with faith in God, faith in a power beyond a human map.

(a) The pilgrimage of many minds in this generation is exemplified in that of C. E. M. Joad, of England. In the 1920s he wrote jauntily that the next fifty years would administer the *coup de grâce* to Christianity. He conceded, generously, that a few of the English cathedrals woud be kept open for the entertainment of American visitors. But by 1949 he had learned a different language. In his book *Decadence*, he wrote: "Man's further advance depends upon the inpouring of divine grace which is vouchsafed to him by the Divine Author of his being."

(b) A great word that—*grace*. And a timely one. It is more than a "charming" word. It is a word of salvation, for an individual, for every group, for the world. It has marked up within it the map of the eternal world of God's purpose and love. There is no faith, no hope and prayer so pertinent to our life as this, "The grace of our Lord Jesus Christ be with you all."— Halford E. Luccock.

Illustrations

GOD'S NAME AND GOD'S NATURE.   God's name and God's nature are Love. God is no respecter of persons in his love. He loves all men alike. He loves the meanest man in America, as well as he loves the best man in America. He loves the most abandoned sinner in every community, as much as he loves the holiest saint. I will go further and say God loves the poor lost sinner more than he loves the saint. You ask me where I get that doctrine, and I tell you that I get it from the lips of Christ himself. "What man of you, having a hundred sheep, if he lose one of them, doth not leave the ninety and nine in the wilderness, and go after that which is lost, until he find it?"—Sam P. Jones.

"AND THEN SOME."   A retired business executive once was asked the secret of his success. He replied that it could be summed up in three words: "and then some." "I discovered at an early age," he said, "that most of the differences between average people and top people could be explained in these three words. The top people did what was expected of them— and then some. They were thoughtful of others, they were considerate—and then some. They met their obligations and responsibilities fairly and squarely—and then some. They were good friends to their friends—and then some. They could be counted on in an emergency—and then some."—Myron J. Taylor.

Sermon Suggestions

SUFFERING. Text: Prov. 3:11, 12.
(1) Do not think little of pain, denying its existence or its providence. (2) Do not think so much of your pain as to let it crush you. (3) Suffering is reception into sonship (2 Cor. 4:17). (4) Learn also to think of suffering without reference to your benefit, theocentrically—as an act of blind obedience to one whose purposes need it and to whom you are not blind; as required by a holiness far beyond you or your holiness, but in which your holiness is included.—P. T. Forsyth.

SPIRITUAL SIGNS OF GOD'S KINGDOM. Gospel Text: Luke 12:32–48.
(1) Generosity. (2) Preparedness. (3) Faithfulness.

Worship Aids

CALL TO WORSHIP. "I pray thee, let me go over, and see the good land that is beyond Jordan, that goodly mountain, and Lebanon" (Deut. 3:25).

INVOCATION. O thou who didst lead thy people by a pillar of cloud by day and a pillar of fire by night, push back the horizons of our faith and let us look with steady eyes and willing hearts for new disclosures of thy will for our lives. Infuse us with thy Spirit and pour into our hearts thy love, so that wherever we go and whatever we do we shall please thee.

OFFERTORY SENTENCE. "He that findeth his life shall lose it: and he that loseth his life for my sake shall find it" (Matt. 10:40).

OFFERTORY PRAYER. Our Father, our truest life is in doing the things that you would have us do. Help us to look for the abundant life, not so much in material things as in the increasing wealth of things spiritual—in love, joy, and peace.

PRAYER. Our Father, we fear that we often begin our prayer with petitions for ourselves, and put our daily bread before thy kingdom, and the pardoning of our sins before the hallowing of thy name. We would not do so today, but guided by our Lord's model of prayer, we would first pray for thy glory; and here, great God, we would adore thee. Thou hast made us and not we ourselves. We are thy people and the sheep of thy pasture. All glory be unto thee, Jehovah, the only living and true God.

With heart and mind, and memory and fear, and hope and joy, we worship the Most High. It well becomes us to put our shoes from off our feet when we draw near to God, for the place whereon we stand is holy ground. If God in the bush demanded the unsandalled foot of the prophet, how much more shall God in Christ Jesus?

With lowliest reverence, with truest love, we worship God in Christ Jesus, uniting therein with all the redeemed host above, with angels and principalities and powers.—Charles Haddon Spurgeon.

EVENING SERVICE

Topic: The Man Who Overcame Depression

TEXT: 1 Kings 19:11–12.

The average man may be depressed by trivial things that the man like Elijah would never notice. It is at least a kind of indirect tribute to a great soul that it is capable of being touched by great despondencies— by despondencies, that is, that a man will only be exposed to when his loyalties are so large that it is not with petty personal fortunes, but with the grand issues of universal right and wrong that he is grappling. Understanding, then, the kind of depression by which Elijah had been overcome, let us go forward to think of the way God dealt with him to help him overcome it.

I. In the first place, it is as though the Lord had regarded Elijah with a kind of divinely humorous compassion. According to the narrative it is said that God sent an angel to lead Elijah to a cake baked on the coals and a cruse of water. It is as though God were saying to him: "Elijah, the trouble with you is that you are hungry, and so you are out of sorts. What you need is something to eat, and I am going to give it to you."

(a) How true that is to the working of God. He has made us not as disembodied spirits but as souls whose growth and fulfillment must be accomplished in conjunction with these material bodies and this material world in the midst of which we dwell.

(b) Let us take care, then, that in our thought of religious loyalties we never make these so airy and remote that they become dehumanized. Our ability to serve God greatly must in the long run be founded upon a sensible regard for those things that keep men in everyday health and strength.

(c) Surely, then, we cannot as religious people be indifferent to the material fortunes of people anywhere. How can we expect that people will be anything else but doubtful and depressed if they are hungry?

II. The second thing God did was to rouse Elijah to his need for action.

(a) As Elijah stands there at the mouth of a cave, with the awful solitude of the rocky canyons and crests of the mountains below him and around him and above him, there comes a mighty wind. After that there came an earthquake. And after the earthquake there came a fire. And then, as Elijah stood still at the mouth of the cave, and as he wrapped his face in his mantle, there came to him a different revelation. It was a still, small voice. It was the quiet, inescapable sound of conscience speaking in his soul.

(b) How true to all deep human experience that immortal picture is! So often and instinctively men who, like Elijah, have given their best effort to some great enterprise and then, in a moment of emotional reaction, plunged into a terrible doubt about it all, have desired just what Elijah desired.

(c) But presently men begin to see, as Elijah saw, that this is not the answer. The inescapable quietness of God presses home to their hearts with a deeper question. The real world, the world of men's beliefs and motives and choices, that inner world out of which alone any moral order that is to last must rise, cannot be shaped by wind or earthquake or fire. It must be created by the power of human souls that

will be obedient when God sends them out to manifest his spirit. "What doest thou here, Elijah?" That was the question he had to answer first.

(d) Let all men and women remember this in their hours of doubt and depression. "It shalt be told thee what thou shalt do." Thank God for the voice of the practical conscience within us that fulfills that promise. A great deal about the future may be still dark; but if you know of some one thing that obviously you must do, you are on the way of being saved.

III. But there was still a third thing that God had to do for Elijah. He helped him overcome his sense of isolation.

(a) For one of the things that lay heaviest on Elijah's heart was the feeling that he was alone. It is a terrible thing to feel morally and spiritually solitary.

(b) To Elijah in the wilderness bowed down by *his* sense of isolation, there came the voice of God saying: "Yet have I left me seven thousand in Israel, all the knees which have not bowed unto Baal, and every mouth which hath not kissed him." Seven thousand! Where had they been, and why had Elijah not known of them? Well, they had been there in Israel all the time; but they had never taken the trouble to tell Elijah what they thought and felt. They somehow assumed that he would know, and they never stopped to think how much it might matter to him if he did know.

(c) Was that characteristic only of the men of Israel in that far-off past? Always and everywhere there are the few moral and spiritual leaders who champion the ideals that the best men want, the men who stand for refinement against vulgarity. If the Elijahs in the field of education, or in politics, or in the Church are not to be driven into the wilderness, the seven thousand in Israel who have not bowed the knee to Baal had better let them know that they are there.

(d) Your doubt and your depression can vanish when your sense of isolation vanishes. When you remember that great company of the witnesses of God in every age who strengthen you by their comradeship, you will know you cannot fail.—Walter Russell Bowie.

SUNDAY: AUGUST SEVENTEENTH

MORNING SERVICE

Topic: The Evangelist—Philip
TEXT: Acts 8:35.
I. "Then Philip opened his mouth."
(a) That is exceedingly hopeful. One of the tragedies of many who are in the Church today is that of the closed mouth. We open our mouths to eat. We open our mouths to buy and sell. We open our mouths to gossip. We sometimes open our mouths to criticize. But too few of us open our mouths to preach Jesus.
(b) That indicates courage. It is only a few days since Philip has seen a very ugly murder that was committed because a certain friend of his insisted upon opening his mouth. If young Stephen of the clear head and shining face and Spirit-filled heart had only keep silent, he would not have been mobbed.
(c) That speaks also of spontaneity. Philip was not simply driving himself to preach. He felt that he could not help speaking. His testimony would have been that of some of his fellow disciples: "We cannot but speak the things that we have seen and heard."
II. Who was Philip?
(a) He was not one of the apostles. Philip was a layman. When the apostles decided that it was necessary that seven men be elected to look after the temporal affairs of this infant church, Philip was one of the men chosen. He was chosen for the lowly task of serving tables. Yet we remember this man today not so much because he was a competent businessman as because he was a Spirit-filled and effective evangelist.
(b) Philip conducted a successful revival in Samaria. He was used of God in preaching to the multitudes. But doubtless if you had talked to him near the end of his pilgrimage, he would have told you that the most useful part of his ministry had been his work with the individual. And this type of preaching is possible for every one of us. All of us cannot proclaim God's message from the pulpit. But there

is not one but can preach Jesus to the individual. Preaching Jesus to the individual is the privilege of every Christian. Not only is this the privilege of every one who is a follower of Christ, it is also his solemn responsibility. Because we can preach Christ, therefore we ought to preach him. And because we ought to preach, we are by no means guiltless if we refuse to do so. Such was the conviction of Philip. He took the command of his Master to preach the gospel to every creature seriously.
III. But how was it that the Lord was able to use him for this particular preaching mission?
(a) He could do so because Philip was obedient. He was open to Divine guidance. Philip was engaged in a great revival in Samaria when the message came to him to leave this city with its populous streets and rejoicing multitudes. While the shouts of those being won to Christ were yet in his ears, he was ordered to set out for a desert country miles away. It looked like a very foolish thing to do. But Philip obeyed. So Philip set out from Samaria and journeyed south. He did not know exactly the purpose of his journey, but he was sure that his Lord was not sending him upon a fool's errand. After quite a long journey, Philip reached the forks of the road. He came into the highway that led down from Jerusalem to Gaza. Just up the road yonder he saw a chariot coming surrounded by a retinue of soldiers and servants. A great man was approaching. Of that much he was sure. And then the Spirit spoke within his heart: "Go near and join thyself to this chariot." It seemed a strange command. There were dozens of good reasons for his refusing to obey. What response did Philip make to the command of the Spirit? He obeyed. He refused to be frightened by the position of the Ethiopian. Philip was enthusiastic and wholehearted in his obedience. He ran fleet-footed on the errands of his Lord. And as he thus went running toward the

chariot, I dare say that he was praying earnestly that the Lord would give him an opening.

(b) Philip knew his Bible. The Evangelist was within hearing distance. The Ethiopian was reading aloud. And when Philip heard what he was reading, he had to hug his heart to keep it from leaping from his bosom. The words were entirely familiar to him. There was not another passage in all the Word of God that Philip would have been quite so glad to find the Ethiopian statesman reading as the one he was reading, which was none other than the fifty-third chapter of Isaiah. "Pardon me, but do you understand what you are reading?" and Philip's face was so radiant and so eager that the great statesman felt at once that here was one who knew. "No, I do not understand," he answered. "How can I except some man teach me?" Christ uses men for the salvation of other men. He seems shut up to that method. If there is not "some man" to teach, then the seeking soul will not be won. A message must have a messenger. An evangel is of no avail without an evangelist. "How can they hear without a preacher?"

(c) He knew his Lord. Then this statesman who did not understand invited Philip into his chariot. And they reread this marvellous passage together. And the Ethiopian was asking Philip a question. "Of whom is the prophet speaking? Of himself or of some other?" In other words: "Who is this that was wounded for our transgressions? Who is this Lamb of God that taketh away the sin of the world? Who is it that is able to deal adequately with sin in your life and mine?" Who indeed? Preacher, do you know? Sunday School teacher, do you know? Member of the official board, do you know? Who is it that saves? Parents, with your responsibility of training young lives for God, do you know? Philip knew. "And he began at the same Scripture and preached unto him Jesus." And while Philip was yet speaking a light broke upon the darkened face of the African statesman. He entered upon the blessed experience that, thank God, is for all men in all times and in all climes. This man who was on his way from church with his heart yet hungry then and there found the Bread of Life.

IV. Now, let me remind you that it was not simply by accident that this needy statesman and this Spirit-guided evangelist met that day at the forks of the road. God's hand was in it. I dare to believe also that it is not by mere chance that you and I have met at the forks of the road this morning in God's house. I dare to believe that God has put me in the path of some of you to keep you from going away and missing the thrill of the knowledge of Jesus Christ. I dare to believe that he has thrown this message this Sabbath morning across your path to keep some of you from the tragedy of a wasted life.—Clovis G. Chappell.

Illustrations

BUT! Abraham was old and Sarah was barren, *but* they became the parents of a people. Pharaoh was strong and Egypt was mighty, *but* they could not stand against Moses. Uzziah was dead and Israel was leaderless, *but* Isaiah could point to a throne in the heavens. Jesus was crucified and his tomb sealed, *but* he is today the Prince of Life. The church had not many mighty, not many rich, *but* it withstood the power of Rome.—Daniel T. Niles.

MESSAGE AND MISSION. Generally teachers of theology and pastors are skeptical of evangelists, and evangelists are skeptical of teachers of theology and pastors. Evangelists feel that teachers of theology and pastors often obscure the simplicity of the gospel with a lot of technical and theological language. Teachers of theology and pastors often feel that evangelists oversimplify the gospel and offer a "cheap grace." In spite of this, we cannot separate evangelism and theology because they are never separated in the Scriptures. Message and mission are so interwoven in the Scriptures that they cannot be separated. An example is the message and mission of Christ. Who he was, what did he come to do, and what he said are so intermixed that we cannot talk about one without talking about the other.—John F. Havlik.

Sermon Suggestions

THE RICHEST HILL ON EARTH.   Text: 1 Cor. 8:11. (1) The cross of Calvary is a reality through which we see the nature of God. (2) We never see Calvary in its full meaning until we see ourselves in it. (3) We do not really see the cross until we see it as a way of life for ourselves.—Halford E. Luccock.

CHRIST AND CONSEQUENCES.   Gospel Text: Luke 12:49–56. Where Christ is at work: (1) Division, in some degree, is inevitable. (2) Destruction is threatened. (3) Deliverance is available.

Worship Aids

CALL TO WORSHIP.   "How beautiful upon the mountains are the feet of him that bringeth good tidings, that publisheth peace" (Isa. 52:7).

INVOCATION.   Redeemer God, as we are saved by the power of the gospel, set on fire and equip us today with the truth and love behind that message to go from this place to be, all of us, your evangelists.

OFFERTORY SENTENCE.   "They that be wise shall shine as the brightness of the firmament; and they that turn many to righteousness as the stars for ever and ever" (Dan. 12:3).

OFFERTORY PRAYER.   Gracious God, if money can be used to bring people to the Savior, if money can be used to teach those who have found him, if money can be used to provide services to the community of faith and the larger community, then bless these gifts to those ends, we pray.

PRAYER.   Forgive them all, O Lord: our sins of omission and our sins of commission; the sins of our youth and the sins of our riper years; the sins of our souls and the sins of our bodies; our secret and our more open sins; our sins of ignorance and surprise, and our more deliberate and presumptuous sin; the sins we have done to please ourselves and the sins we have done to please others; the sins we know and remember, and the sins we have forgotten; the sins we have striven to hide from others and the sins by which we have made others offend; forgive them, O Lord, forgive them all for his sake, who died for our sins and rose for our justification, and now stands at thy right hand to make intercession for us, Jesus Christ our Lord.—John Wesley.

EVENING SERVICE

Topic: For the Glory of God
TEXT: John 9:24; 1 Cor. 10:31.

The meaning may surprise you. So common is the expression "Give God glory" or "Glory to God on high" that the meaning is unquestioned; it is assumed that we are saying something like "Praise God!" In reality, the Biblical phrase "Give glory to God" is a Hebrew idiom meaning "Confess your sins." The New Testament words of Jewish leaders to the man whom Jesus healed of blindness meant the same when they said, "Give God the praise." This was a command to confess. It is as though the Jewish leadership was demanding that the healed man admit to being an imposter. "Give God the glory by speaking the truth" was the thrust of their words, "the truth" for them being that Jesus had not been the healer or that the man never in fact had been blind.

Not to be lost or minimized in all of this is the praise element that ordinarily is thought to be the meaning of glorifying God. That implication surely is present as well, following upon the basic meaning of confession. Honor and dignity rightly are accorded God; it is fitting that human beings praise God for infinite goodness and perfection. We recognize divine majesty, power, and worth through our worship and also our discipleship. We affirm the moral excellence of God when we act to glorify his name. Yes, there is praise inherent in following Saint Paul's admonition, "Whatever you do, do all to the glory of God."

I. Let us give thought to the act of confession. What is it, exactly? It really is a tool of self-knowledge. It is a way of standing apart from ourselves and testing our strengths and weaknesses. That kind of discipline will not be everyone's, but it suggests an avenue of approach. It provides a way for self-examination, and confession has self-examination behind it.

(a) We have to recognize that this is far from easy for most people. The reasons are not hard to find. Who among us wants to be wrong, or make a mistake, or violate a trust? When it comes to serious moral or ethical breaches of behavior, the immediate human plea is "Not guilty!"—so eager are we to avoid the stigma of having erred, and so anxious are we to escape the consequences.

(b) It yet remains true that confession is good for one's soul. Indeed, it is the only approach to sin that can initiate cleansing and healing. Confession is the first step toward a new heart and right spirit. It brings us immediately before God whose power it is to sanctify our souls.

II. Truly, God is glorified by our opening of mind and heart to him. The divine mercy can then be bestowed, the divine holiness can be imparted. Moreover, God is praised through such actions on our part. Praise belongs to God.

(a) One of the great insights of Hebrew religion (to which we are heirs) is that praise—to avoid being self-praise—must begin with gestures of contrition. As persons humble themselves before God, they are setting aside all vain glory, all self-boasting. They have focused instead upon the Exalted One, the Lord most high and holy. *Praise* is the word to describe this response.

(b) There is an Old Testament proverb that says, "A man is judged by his praise." The probable meaning of this thought is that a person is tested by the praise heaped on him by others. And we do extend praise, each to the other. But a second meaning also might be found in these words, the idea that a person is judged by what he praises. Each individual is evaluated by what he or she worships and holds to be of highest worth. All of this is to say that praise is important, and the direction of praise deserves careful thought. Above all other objects or subjects, praise belongs to God. That praise is given as we do whatever we do for the glory of God.—John H. Townsend.

SUNDAY: AUGUST TWENTY-FOURTH

MORNING SERVICE

Topic: "On Transplanting Faith"
TEXT: Ps. 137, John 6:66–67.

Psalm 137 is one of those psalms that comes out of the traumatic experience of the Jewish race in their exile in Babylon. One might say that they were homesick. Like college freshmen who have never seen the inside of a dormitory, these Jewish exiles just could not make the adjustment to the new environment. For one thing, God seemed so far away. It was easy to worship God in the temple in Jerusalem, but Babylon was such a different place. Not only were they far from home, but their whole theology was riddled with holes. They had to rethink their entire religion, and they had to do it in a pagan place five-hundred miles away from home. Who can wonder that these discouraged exiles hung their harps on the willows and

plaintively asked, "How can we sing the Lord's song in a strange land?" But the problem that the exiles had is a perennial one. How does one transplant faith from the sanctuary to the world of work and play, politics, marriage, business, television, pornography, and mobility? Are we able to sing the Lord's song in a strange land? What kind of Christian witness do we bring to the various worlds in which we live and move and work and play? My primary concern today is with students and their need to take the name of Jesus with them into the strange new world of academic life and fuller adulthood.

I. Why is it that so many students "lose their religion," as we say? Young adults who were involved in their local church take no part in the religious activities on the campus. What is wrong?

(a) In every generation students have been caught up in cynicism and doubts, and for the most part, this has been a healthy effort to think through religion and to find a personal faith. It seems to me that doubts and uncertainties are healthy and necessary if one is to have an intelligent faith. But one must make sure that after he has played with all the philosophies and experimented with other religions, he can come full circle and say with Peter, "Lord, to whom shall we go? You have the words of eternal life."

(b) But what really disturbs me is that some never question religion. There are some people who never get over their naive doubts and never grow up religiously. They go through all their lives assuming that the Bible is a volume of superstitions, that the church is full of hypocrites, that ministers are less than intelligent, that faith is a hindrance to knowledge of the truth, and that the world can be explained meaningfully and adequately in materialistic and scientific terms alone. So many students go through their whole life thinking that religion really does not matter—that it is one of life's options: One can take it or leave it; that this is not a life or death proposition.

II. Well, what is it that keeps students from "singing the Lord's song" in the strange land of academic life?

(a) Traditional religion is one thing—the kind of religion that many students inherit from their parents. This kind of religion tries to protect young people from the harsh realities of the world. Predictably, when these same young people become young adults and are exposed to the harsh realities of the world on some campus, traditional religion wilts like a flower in the heat of the desert.

(b) Another kind of religion that just will not hold water is the kind that "just believes." People who have this kind of religion assign to God anything that they cannot understand, and they never really make the effort to penetrate life's mysteries.

(c) Then there is the religion that is all sentimentalism. Religion that is all emotion and feeling and watery-eyed sentiment just will not survive the long haul. Christian discipleship is more than singing tearfully "Where Ever He Leads I'll Go" but refusing to go down the road to minister to those with real, pressing human needs.

(d) Then there are those who believe in a kind of general religion. They may be interested objectively in the phenomenon of religion, but they definitely do not care for religious institutions, the church, the Bible, ordinances, and prayer. They like to study but they do not want to become committed.

(e) Then there is the kind of religion that tries to escape from life's pressures and problems, to be a refuge in the storms of life. This leads some observers to say that all Christians must somehow be emotionally immature since they cannot face life, since they cannot cope with the circumstances of their living, since they cannot manage their life situation.

(f) Perhaps we cannot "sing the Lord's song in a strange land" because our religion is too puny. We would do well to lose these brands of religion because they represent the kind of thinking that destroys the religious life of so many students.

III. Well, what is the right kind of religion, the kind that will enable us to "sing the Lord's song in a strange land"? What we need is a faith for all seasons. Such a faith is a personal faith. You see, that is what is so beautiful about the soul searching of young adults. They're passing from the inherited religion to a real and vibrant personal faith.

(a) A faith for all seasons is one that deals honestly with the significant questions in a person's life. A meaningful faith, a faith for all seasons, is a growing faith that is open to new experience. The kind of Christian faith that is for all seasons is not afraid of new circumstances and truth but embraces all of life and seeks to understand it in the light of faith.

(b) This faith is not threatened when men discover that the earth is round instead of flat. This faith is not shattered by scientific discoveries. This meaningful faith is not linked to the age of rocks but is bound to the Rock of Ages.

(c) The kind of faith that is for this season and for all the seasons of your life does not provide you with all the answers, but it does enable you to live out the questions of your existence. God does not promise to give us all the answers; he promises to be with us. He promises to keep on giving himself to us.

(d) How do you "sing the Lord's song in a strange land"? How can you "sing the Lord's song" in the emerging chapters of your life? Jesus stands alongside you—to keep you at your best. Open yourself to the fullness of his saving, sustaining presence, and be alive in this season and always.—Fred W. Andrea.

Illustrations

INTO A STRANGE LAND. The hour is coming for everyone of us when we shall have to go forward into a strange land, into a region that we have not explored as yet, into that Unknown Country from which travelers do not return. In that hour it will be Jesus Christ or nothing. All the wealth of the world, however evenly it might have been divided by that time, cannot make it otherwise. Therefore let's take our Christian faith with us and sing the song of confidence and courage. "Yea though I walk through the valley of the shadow of death, I will fear no evil, for thou art with me." The Lord of hosts is with us. The God of Jacob is our refuge. I know whom I have believed and I am persuaded that he is able to keep that which I have committed unto him. Be strong and of good courage, the Lord thy God, he it is that goeth with thee; he will not fail thee nor forsake thee." Let's sing it, blithe, radiant, undaunted, let come what may!—Charles R. Brown.

DOUBTING OUR DOUBTS. Most Christians know about the faith of the great believers but not about their inner struggles. Listen to William Lyon Phelps in his autobiography: "My religious faith remains in possession of the field only after prolonged civil war with my naturally skeptical mind." That experience belongs in the best tradition of the great believers. John Knox, the Scottish reformer—what a man of conviction! Yes, but remember that

time when his soul knew "anger, wrath and indignation, which is conceived against God, calling all his promises in doubt." Increase Mather—that doughty Puritan—what a man of faith! Yes, but read his diary and run into entries like this: "Greatly molested with temptations to atheism." Sing Luther's hymn, "A mighty fortress is our God," and one would suppose he never questioned his faith, but see him in other hours. "For more than a week," he wrote, "Christ was wholly lost. I was shaken by desperation and blasphemy against God."—Harry Emerson Fosdick.

Sermon Suggestions

THE GREAT EMIGRATION. Text: Heb. 11:16. (1) The things we are leaving: Old misconceptions of God himself. Our old superstitions. The old motives in Christian service. Our old conceptions of religion. (2) To what we are journeying: A better understanding of our Bible. A realization of human brotherhood. The ideal social life. The day when the kingdoms of this world will become the kingdom of our Lord and of his Christ.—W. W. Weeks.

WHO ARE THE SAVED. Gospel Text: Luke 13:22–30. (1) Situation: Salvation is a universal need. (2) Complication: Some will not find it who expect it. Others will find it that some expect to miss it. (3) Resolution: Seek the right way and be prepared for unexpected company.

Worship Aids

CALL TO WORSHIP. "Thus saith the Lord, The heaven is my throne, and the earth is my footstool: where is the house that ye build unto me? and where is the place of my rest?" (Isa. 66:1).

INVOCATION. Eternal God, our heavenly Father, all things, all places, all persons belong to thee. There is no escaping thee if we would; there is nowhere that we cannot find thee if we seek thee. We believe that thou art here, among us.

Strengthen our faith to believe that thou wilt be with us wherever circumstances may lead us.

OFFERTORY SENTENCE. "Some people spend their money freely and still grow richer. Others are cautious, and yet grow poorer. Be generous, and you will be prosperous. Help others, and you will be helped" (Prov. 11:24–25, TEV).

OFFERTORY PRAYER. O Lord, we offer up unto thee everything that is good in us, although it be very small and imperfect, that thou mayest amend and sanctify it. Make it pleasing and acceptable unto thee, and always perfect it more and more. And bring us also, who are often lazy and unproductive, to a good and blessed end.—After Thomas à Kempis.

PRAYER. Deepen us down, O God, until we are one with our life. Shut us in from all distraction and unreality. Grant us no exit for escape, but where we are living, there meet us face to face. In the midst of confusion, where circumstances overwhelm us, burdened by the sheer weight of our private world, we stand waiting for thee. We know our failures and our successes that are so much like failures, and we know our need of thee. Without thee, O God, our life is empty; indeed worse than empty, for the emptiness is filled with naught but noise and the desperate fury of meaningless gestures. Somewhere in the midst of the wilderness let the bush of glory burn; somewhere amid the realities of life let thy benediction be revealed. We wait for that which thou alone canst give.—Samuel H. Miller.

EVENING SERVICE

Topic: The Narrow Way
TEXT: Matt. 7:13–14.
Jesus taught that life is a matter of either/or—being here or there, being up or down, being good or evil. Jesus did not preach any moral in-betweenness; he always drew moral distinctions. He also candidly warned people about the sad consequences of choosing the worst. That is what our text is all about.

I. Two companies of people are described in the picture drawn from our text: The one, on the broad way behind the wide gate, is large; the other company follows the narrow lane behind the slender gate, and the single-file movement of its members gives it the appearance of a very small band.

(a) Jesus warned that the larger group proceeding on the broad way was headed toward ruin. That group is a noisy crowd. The crash of merriment fills the air as its members fumble along thoughtlessly in fun and dangerous pleasures. You know about crowds: The mood in a crowd is often one of excitement; impulses are free from restraints and reactions are sometimes primitive and gross. Crowds are seldom interested in meanings. The picture Jesus painted here with words should frighten us because the people in that crowd are moving down the wrong road.

(b) But Jesus commended the second group! Its members are not influenced by the suggestion of the crowd or by a selfish spirit of imitation. Everyone on the path of life moves intelligently, reverently, and with an understood purpose. It is a group of disciplined, decided, guided persons; it is a group of obedient believers who are ready for the dangers and trials along the way.

(c) This word picture from Jesus gives us an essential warning. We are reminded that there are two ways to live, and there are those eternal consequences from the way we humans live our lives. If we live foolishly without regard for God on the one hand, we cannot expect to have a good end. We are clearly told that we will surely not have his company at the end of our days. But there is on the other hand another way to live. It is a way of great promise—and it makes great demands upon us.

II. "The way is narrow."

(a) The early church understood and expected that right living in an evil world would not be easy. They understood what Jesus meant when he said that "the way is narrow."

(b) Some later Christians have mistakenly applied this verse to much that is largely outward. Jesus was not speaking about narrow customs when he advised that "the way is narrow." Now to be sure, customs are sometimes involved and affected by the demands of the Way, but conformity to customs is not in itself the proof that we are Christians. Jesus himself revolted against a narrowness present in his own day. In his statements to certain scribes and Pharisees, Jesus even ridiculed their narrowness. He condemned the narrowness of "straining out a gnat and swallowing a camel" (Matt. 23:24).

III. What was Jesus talking about when he said that "the way is narrow"?

(a) Jesus meant that Christian living is a way of disciplined living. The way is narrow in that our life and living must be according to the plan of God for us. The way is narrow in that we are restricted to what is meaningful for us in the sight of God. On *this* Way, we are limited to being and doing what is right.

(b) The broad way, the way that leads to. destruction, is spacious. It has no fences; it has no restrictions; one can carry on that broad way anything and everything desired—including vices and binding and blinding habits.

(c) The narrow way will allow and admit only the self as corrected and trained by God's standards. This means a will that is kept always under spiritual discipline. It means governed emotions that trained in love for God. All these are involved in the soul's singular destiny. The Way is narrow because everything matters for us, since the whole of life should be under one divine will.

IV. The narrow way demands the forsaking of cherished sins. It demands the submission of a pampered self. It demands the renouncing of a wrong lifestyle. It demands a full commitment to righteous living. The way of Jesus is narrow because belief in him calls for an utter abandonment of ourselves to him and the utter forsaking of all half-gods. The narrowness of the Way to which Jesus pointed involves the utter pledge of the soul.— James Earl Massey.

SUNDAY: AUGUST THIRTY-FIRST

MORNING SERVICE

Topic: When the King Refuses
TEXT: Matt. 20:21–22.

I. May I remind you of the facts?

(a) According to Saint Matthew, the mother of the sons of Zebedee, that is Salome, came asking for chief places for her two sons in Christ's kingdom. Perhaps they got their mother to make this request on their behalf. After all, she was the sister of Jesus' mother and she did help the apostolic band. But whatever the reason, I used to despise James and John for this. I used to count them the fathers of all those ecclesiastical "place seekers" whom I despise. But I have changed my mind. Not about place seeking in the Church, but about James and John. What I think they wanted was not a comfortable seat but a spectacular piece of service. They wanted to burn themselves out. They wanted a task of outstanding size. After all, they were men of action. They had energy to spare. They longed to call down fire from heaven and sweep in the kingdom of God. And what had they been offered? Following Jesus around villages! Watching him heal the sick! Witnessing his restoration of the weak-willed! "O Master," they cried in effect, "let us *do* something for thee." "O mother Salome, you bid Jesus let us do something for him." And so she goes, not without maternal pride, I think, "Grant that these my two sons may sit, the one on thy right hand and the other on thy left in thy kingdom."

Now here is a remarkable fact. She wasn't rebuked by Jesus! She did not, as far as we are told, receive any answer at all! I know some commentators suggest the mother didn't ask at all. Saint Matthew only put that in out of reverence for James and John; but I doubt it. Anyway, James and John received the answer. Maybe Jesus saw it was a "put-up job." And the answer they received hurt. It hurt terribly. Jesus said, "Ye know not what ye ask." It hurt because they thought they knew very well. But his next words cut deeper still.

"Those two places are reserved for others." Doubtless they retired crestfallen. They had offered for heroic service in Christ's kingdom, and they weren't wanted! Doubtless Salome, their mother, went away crestfallen, too. Her two sons weren't wanted!

(b) Did it ever occur to you, I wonder, that God might not want our service? That's a new view of the sovereignty of God. I cannot say it occurred to me till I considered this Scripture. We grow so accustomed to the idea that all the calling to God's service is on God's side and all the refusing is on our side; but the Bible has a knack of turning upside down preconceived notions. Sometimes God does not want our heroic service. Our allegiance? Yes, God always wants that. But quite often nothing startling from us, nothing life-giving, nothing tremendous, only patient following in the routine acts of life; going to the city, working patiently and coming home by the same bus.

I think this is difficult. I think it is far easier to live the heroic life when you are out in the limelight, when people will notice what you say and observe what you do. My heart goes out to James and John. I know how they felt. It is so much easier to live the Christian life when we are called to some big and challenging task. But when we are called to occupy some insignificant platform in life, or scarcely any platform at all; when young people have to stay at home to look after aged parents, when routine jobs occupy so much of our waking hours and we are growing older without seeing the sunny parts of the earth, then it is we grow rebellious against the smallness of our lot. I say I sympathize with James and John, more especially when their offer went unaccepted.

II. (a) Is this why our Lord wasn't hard on these two men? But the other disciples were. The Scripture says, "They were moved with indignation." They certainly read the question of James and John as place seeking. And on that account were given corrective teaching by Jesus. He showed that there have to be leaders in the Christian Church; but there is a difference between leadership there and leadership in the world. In the former, it is a primacy of service. He who is accounted great is he who does most for other people, not he for whom other people do much. In the Church, the supreme leader should be the supreme servant. And if he thoroughly understands this he can seek a chief place. Jesus understood it. He had a chief place, but it meant service unto death, or, as he put it, "Even as the Son of Man came not to be ministered unto, but to minister, and to give his life a ransom for many."

Do I have to remark on that word *ransom*? Only because it has played so large a part in theological theories of the atonement. But do not ask the question to whom the ransom was paid and the phrase will not yield difficulties. Straightforwardly it means Christ's primacy is supreme because he gave his all for our redemption, even his life.

(b) Come back to James and John. Come back to their mother's request: "Command that these my two sons may sit, one on thy right hand, and one on thy left in thy kingdom." Come back now and look at these men with all the resentment and indignation and envy taken out of your eyes. Learn instead this lesson about unanswered prayer. Salome asked, "Command these places for my sons in thy glory." And Jesus refused. He did not answer that prayer. He said those places were in fact already allotted. He also added, "Ye know not what ye ask." And this is what I am inclined to think, that whenever God does not answer our prayers, it is because we do not know what we ask. And here you have it in black and white: "Command that these my two sons may sit, the one on thy right hand and the other on thy left in thy glory" (Saint Mark's word). But the day came when, standing by the foot of Christ's cross, Salome saw what coming in his glory was. It was crucifixion. And to think that she had asked *that* for her two sons! How she must have wanted to tear the tongue out of her mouth! There *was* one on his right hand! and another on his left! Malefactors they were, dying in agony! Oh, if only she had known! But Jesus knew. Therefore he did not grant her request. Perhaps that is why he does not always answer our requests. We do not know what we ask. But God does.

And I am sure some reader has prayed to God with all his heart, "O God, let me out, let me out, I cannot stand this routine another day. I shall scream if I see that wretched office desk again." And God has said no to our prayer; and we've had to go back and the routine has had to go on. But we shall be making the mistake of our lives if we are sullen in consequence. We know not what we ask. We may have been asking for crucifixion without knowing it.

(c) Once more we look back at these men. We don't know exactly what happened to John. But we do know what happened to James. With bewildering brevity the end of his life is described in the book of the Acts of the Apostles. "And Herod killed James the brother of John with a sword." Did Salome remember then? Did she remember how Jesus had said, "Ye shall drink of my cup and be baptized with the baptism that I am baptized with." Jesus had been baptized in blood. Did Mary mother of Jesus run to Salome her sister then? "They did it to my son, now they have done it to yours." Did they sit long hours each trying to comfort the other? We do not know. But this we know. James did in the end get what he asked. Perhaps he was ready for it. And some day for us God may grant our prayer though he denies it now. We shall be ready then. But till then we must be patient, very patient, believing that God knows best what we can manage.—D. W. Cleverly Ford.

Illustrations

THE DAYS OF THY YOUTH.   Youth is more willing to make decisions that call for changes in life. Youth does not have as much at stake as age from the standpoint of the involvement of others. Such considerations may make it well-nigh impossible for one so to positionize himself that he can hear God's call after youth has passed. Age often refuses to be found "in the way" so the Lord can speak. Some years ago, President Hutchins, then head of the University of Chicago, spoke to a high school graduating class. He startled the boys and girls—no doubt pleased them also!—by stating that they were probably nearer the truth than they would ever be again. He

felt that life would tame their spirits and dull their vision until they would rationalize and compromise their ideals.—J. Winston Pearce.

ARE YOU ABLE?   Let's look at the four absolutes of Chairman Mao, then see how we can adapt and use them for good rather than evil:

1. *Absolute acceptance (commitment)*. The Chinese were to begin with a total commitment of the mind to a certain way of life. It was foundational, a prerequisite.

2. *Absolute dedication*. This means making the Chinese way of life your number one priority, committing your life to it, and being willing to die for it.

3. *Absolute discipline*. Taking charge of your lifestyle, disciplining mind and body, health and study habits. All for the sake of the cause.

4. *Absolute action*. More than acceptance, more than dedication, more than discipline, more than believing in and talking about it, but acting upon your conviction. Doing something about it. Daily. Living it, doing it, fleshing it out on the firing line.

Of course, we are diametrically opposed to the target of all these absolutes, but let's look at them again in the light of our own goals, wanting to live for Christ and enjoy his peace by living out his divine paradoxes that seem to contradict everything we've ever been taught about success.—Pat Williams and Jerry Jenkins.

Sermon Suggestions

THE FOOLISHNESS OF GOD.   Text: 1 Cor. 1:12, 25, RSV. (1) There was a divine foolishness about his birth. (2) There was a divine foolishness about his silent years. (3) There was a divine foolishness about the conduct of his ministry. (4) The foolishness culminated in the cross.—J. D. Jones.

PROTOCOL FOR BANQUETS.   Gospel Text: Luke 14:1, 7–14. (1) For guests: If you are not presumptuous, your proper worth will be recognized and rewarded. (2) For hosts: More importantly, if you recognize the proper worth of the outsiders, your "love will be vindicated."

Worship Aids

CALL TO WORSHIP. "Let us draw near with a true heart in full assurance of faith" (Heb. 10:22).

INVOCATION. Within these walls let holy peace,
  And love, and concord dwell;
  Here give the troubled conscience ease,
  The wounded spirit heal.
May we in faith receive thy word,
  In faith present our prayers,
  And in the presence of our Lord
  Unbosom all our cares.—John Newton, 1769.

OFFERTORY SENTENCE. "Though I have all faith, so that I could remove mountains, and have not love, I am nothing" (1 Cor. 13:2).

OFFERTORY PRAYER. O Lord, let the outworking of our faith find its way to expression in support of loving service to all the causes dear to your heart, whether at home or abroad.

PRAYER. O Lord, we remember with sadness our want of faith in thee. What might have been a garden we have turned into a desert by our sin and wilfulness. This beautiful life that thou hast given us we have wasted in futile worries and vain regrets and empty fears. Instead of opening our eyes to the joy of life, the joy that shines in the leaf, the flower, the face of an innocent child, and rejoicing in it as in a sacrament, we have sunk back into the complainings of our narrow and blinded souls. O deliver us from the bondage of unchastened desires and unwholesome thoughts. Help us to conquer hopeless brooding and faithless reflection, and the impatience of irritable weakness. To this end, increase our faith, O Lord. Fill us with a completer trust in thee, and the desire for a more wholehearted surrender to thy will. Then every sorrow will become a joy. Then shall we say to the mountains that lie heavy on our souls, "Remove and be cast hence," and they shall remove, and nothing shall be impossible unto us. Then shall we renew our strength, and mount up with wings as eagles; we shall run and not be weary; we shall walk and not faint. —Samuel McComb.

EVENING SERVICE

Topic: Christian Humility
  TEXT: Luke 14:1, 7–14.

The Pharisees were very careful to fulfill the commandments of the Law and to practice the ritual regulations that governed worship, food preparation, diet, dress, and interaction with gentiles. Such matters as table fellowship, ritual cleanliness and ceremonial status were of paramount importance to the Pharisaic Jew of the first century A.D.

I. Although there is nothing inherently wrong with these sorts of religious practices, the Pharisees misused and misunderstood them. They used their scrupulous religious practices as a basis for excluding other persons from their fellowship, and they fully expected that God would "reward" them, above all others, for what they believed to be exemplary behavior and practice in the sight of God. Persons who did not conform to the Pharisees' expectation came to be considered "outcasts" and "sinners."

(a) Thus, the zealous Jewish laymen, known as the Pharisees, who had arisen 150 years before Christ to reform and purify Judaism, had succumbed—by the days of Jesus—to the evil influence of pride and exclusiveness. This pride was evident on many public occasions. Most Pharisees evidently believed that, because of their exemplary religious practice, they should be given seats of special honor—higher than those accorded to other persons.

(b) Jesus, however, blasted the pretentions of the Pharisees when he said, "When you are invited by anyone to a marriage feast do not sit down in a place of honor. . . . For every one who exalts himself will be humbled, and he who humbles himself will be exalted."

II. Most Christians once believed that Jesus simply told the Pharisees this parable about "humility" in order to reveal to them their bad manners. Jesus, however, was not dispensing good social advice in this parable. His words have little to do with proper "dinner party etiquette."

(a) The interaction of host and guest in the parable deals with an aspect of man's relationship with God. God, in the person of Jesus Christ, is inviting men and women to the Messianic feast upon his return. However, the only way to respond to his invitation is by the renunciation of any claim or merit of one's own. Salvation then is God's unmerited gift to us—something the Pharisee had to learn and a reality that put him in the same position as those he had scorned as outcasts and sinners.

(b) Yet, the humility with which Jesus Christ asks us to approach our God is not simply accomplished through grudging toleration of the outcast. The fact is that our final acceptance in the Messianic banquet depends on our acceptance of others now. Jesus brought that point home when he said to his Pharisee host, "But you give a feast, invite the poor, the maimed, the lame, the blind, and you will be blessed, because they cannot repay you." In other words, if we forgive and accept other persons, then God will forgive and accept us. This is humility in the Christian sense. It is not purely a passive virtue, but it is highly active and needs to find expression in the lifestyle of every Christian.

III. Humility then is not sackcloth and ashes and a gloomy face. It is the recognition that our salvation depends upon a God who sees all of us as his children. He wants us to acknowledge his gift of salvation to one another and to share that gift. He enjoins us to put away the false pride and sense of accomplishment that separates us one from the other.—Rodney K. Miller.

SUNDAY: SEPTEMBER SEVENTH

MORNING SERVICE

Topic: The Gospel and Our Work

Text: Ps. 90:16–17; Matt. 20:1–16.

This parable is not an economic tract, although some people have tried to press it in that direction. There are some great religious truths that we can draw from the parable for our work.

I. One of the things we need to understand in this story is that the men who were sitting around the marketplace were not being depicted as lazy. This was the place where individuals were supposed to go when they did not have a regular job or trade of some kind or did not own land. The marketplace was the spot for workers to gather who wanted to work. Maybe a new beatitude could be coined in which we might say, "Blessed are those who give others work because they give them self-respect."

II. It is interesting also to observe the attitude reflected in the men who had worked.

(a) Notice the anger that one man feels toward another when he thinks he should have received more wages. Think about how often that happens in our work rela-tionships today. In this parable one man becomes angry because the owner seeks to pay another the same wage for less work than he had done.

(b) In our society today, there is no question that one's attitudes toward his or her work often indicate the kind of work we do.

(c) Our work requires of us responsibility and commitment to do the very best that we can while we engage in it. In the eyes of God, if each does his work to the very best of his ability, that work before God is equal.

III. One of the unfortunate things in our society is that sometimes people view work as a curse. Many believe that work is the curse that God placed upon us at the fall of Adam and Eve. But this is not the biblical attitude toward work. When you read the Genesis account carefully, you find that in the story man was placed in the Garden to till the garden before the curse was given. Man is set to work naming the animals and caring for the garden. Man/woman are involved in work as cocreators with the Creator. Work is not a curse but a blessing. Work is a gift to us from God who invites us to engage with him as his workers in the world.

IV. When we reflect on this parable, we want to declare quickly that it seems so unfair for God to be like this. One of the central truths that comes from this parable is that God is extravagant in his generosity. God does not love us more because some of us work harder, or because some of us have superior minds, or superior backs, or superior jobs. God's love to us is an expression of his grace and is not dependent upon our own efforts to earn it.

V. It is also interesting to observe in this parable that the men work with the opportunities that they have. "Why are you standing in the marketplace idle?" they are asked. "Lord, no one has given me work to do," they respond.

(a) Some people do not have greater opportunities because they simply have not had doors open for them. But whatever doors of opportunity open before us, small or large, each of us is to use abilities and talents he or she has to the very best of one's ability.

(b) All of us do not have the same opportunities nor the same abilities. If you give the very best to God with what you have, in God's sight it is of equal worth. We serve God and labor in our work, not for reward or recognition from him. We cannot separate the sacred and secular, because God is involved in our work and in our worship. We worship through our work and work through our worship.

VI. God who is the Creator loves us and seeks to have companionship with us.

(a) Our only real compensation for our labor, we are told through this parable, is God's companionship. Jesus told this parable right after Peter and the others had wanted to know what rewards they would receive for following him. For those who labor long and hard, this parable might sound unfair. Jesus declared that one could not say that only those who labored long count with God. We cannot pile up merit before God or win his favor. Our relationship to God is not purchased; it is a gift.

(b) It is God who is generous and loving. He is extravagant. If we are concerned because some brother comes into the kingdom late and is loved graciously by God, the problem is not with God but with

us. If we are jealous because a sister or brother is received by God when he or she is elderly and experiences the grace of God, then the problem is not with God but with us. We respond, hopefully, to God's extravagant goodness toward others not begrudgingly but with thankfulness that not only they but we have not been treated as we deserve but according to the graciousness of God.—William Powell Tuck.

Illustrations

DEFINING SIN CORRECTLY. We mislead ourselves and deaden our consciences by thinking of the sins of the flesh as being only gross and carnal sins, for the violent revulsion we feel at such so-called fleshly sins is apt to make us unduly lenient to our own more respectable failures. But Scripture rather disconcertingly puts them all on a level and includes them all under the title of the flesh. The scriptural writers call all the underside of our nature, all the egotistic, self-seeking side *flesh*, and all the upper side in which God alone can dwell *spirit*. From this point of view it is just as much of the flesh to be hectoring and self-assertive, say, to an employee as it is to commit adultery. Both kinds of conduct fall to the side of the flesh and its weakness.—Herbert H. Farmer.

AN ATTITUDE OF IDENTIFICATION. The late Gordon Allport helped me with this. He pointed out that we can learn to respect people as persons and identify with them by an imaginative extending of our own rougher experiences in the direction of the problems we encounter. For instance, I may never have stolen $100,000, but I can remember stealing a stapler from a major oil company over twenty-five years ago when I was starting my business career. The uneasiness, the rationalizations —I can extend all the feelings in my own imagination and understand "another" thief much better. As a matter of fact, as I look back I can see that I have not encountered any sins or failures in other people that I could not imagine myself being involved in to some extent under some circumstances.

And I think that is the key to the most

helpful attitude for a Christian in producing creative change in the world—to realize that in some way we can walk in almost anyone's shoes—as God did in ours—in order to learn to respect them and identify with them in the midst of their sins and stupid mistakes, which in God's eyes aren't much different from ours. And because *we* are personally experiencing the healing forgiveness of God and have this to bring to others, we have a way to help that can lead to deep and lasting changes in their total lives.—Keith Miller.

Sermon Suggestions

CHRISTUS CONSOLATOR. Text: Matt. 11:25–30. (1) None greater ever offered to comfort us. (2) None gentler ever called us to himself. (3) None richer ever promised us so much.—R. C. H. Lenski.

WHAT A FOLLOWER OF JESUS HAS TO DO. Gospel Text: Luke 14:25–33. (1) The desire—seen in the crowds (v. 25). (2) The dream—expressed in the parables (vv. 26–32). (3) The demand—described in the challenge (v. 33).

Worship Aids

CALL TO WORSHIP. Jesus said, "I must work the works of him that sent me, while it is day: the night cometh, when no man can work" (John 9:4).

INVOCATION. Almighty God, Creator of all things, as you established the rhythm of work and rest, so may we find in the different pace of this special day something of your wisdom. Cause our adoration, our confession of sin, our thanksgiving, our petitions, our intercessions, and our renewed commitments to prepare us for faithful labor in your world.

OFFERTORY SENTENCE. "Be ye steadfast, unmovable, always abounding in the work of the Lord, forasmuch as ye know that your labor is not in vain in the Lord" (1 Cor. 15:58).

OFFERTORY PRAYER. We know, O Lord, that no offering is too small or too large if it truly represents our faithful stewardship. So we come to you as we are—honestly—and as we hope to become, asking your blessing upon what we bring.

PRAYER. O God, whose blessed Son was once carpenter at Nazareth; we pray to thee for the workers of the world. Cheer with thy presence those whose labor is wearisome and joyless, and receive into thy protection those who work in dangerous trades. Look in thy compassion upon all who are exploited or any way ill-treated, and make haste for their help. Give of thy wisdom to all who are in positions of trust, and beget in them a most lively sense of obligation. Rebuke those who through love of money or lust for power would betray their fellows, and in thy great mercy restrain them. Raise up able and unselfish leaders both among those who toil and among those who employ and direct the labor of others; that human industry may be brought under the rule of love, which is the law of life; and that so there may be daily bread for all, and for all the opportunity of growth in mind and heart and soul.—Ernest Fremont Tittle.

EVENING SERVICE

Topic: The Deliverance of Israel

TEXT: Ezra, Nehemiah, Haggai, Malachi.

There are times in life for all of us when it seems that hope is all we have left. So it was for Israel as she floundered in the throes of Babylonian captivity. God's holy city had fallen. God's chosen people had been defeated. It was a time of deep despair and serious soul searching for the Jews. For God's chosen people to be captives in a foreign land, removed from the temple, deprived of their freedom, and divided from their brethren was a humiliating experience indeed. But God was not through with Israel yet. The books of Ezra, Nehemiah, Haggai, and Malachi tell how the people were restored to their land, not all of Israel, but a remnant of the faithful, and it was through them that God would continue to unfold his redemptive drama. In the story of the deliverance of Israel, we see two important insights to apply to our lives today.

I. The first lesson of the experience is that forgiveness is God's final word.

(a) God's final word is "Come now, and let us reason together . . . Though your sins are as scarlet, they will be as white as snow; though they are red like crimson, they will be like wool" (Isa. 1:18).

(b) There are those of you who read this who need nothing more than to experience the forgiveness of God. You have failed God. You have yielded to temptation. You have sinned. And over and over and over again you have been hearing God's first word of judgment on your sin. You need to move past that initial step and hear God's final word, "I will forgive."

(c) How can you get in on this forgiveness? We find an answer to that question in 2 Corinthians 7:9–10. Paul contrasts two kinds of sorrow over sin: worldly sorrow and godly sorrow. Worldly sorrow simply means regret. That is not enough. This godly sorrow is not just feeling bad about your sin. This godly sorrow means feeling so bad about your sin that you don't want to do it anymore. Godly sorrow leads to a changed attitude toward God and toward the sin and that leads to forgiveness. To get in on God's forgiveness, you have to regret your sin, release your sin, and repent of that sin and then return to God's plan.

II. There is a second lesson here in this account of the deliverance of Israel: Forgetfulness is man's fatal weakness.

(a) What happened to the remnant of Israel when they returned to their land of promise? Did they rearrange their priorities? Did they rally around God? Did they renew their faith? A few of the Israelites did these things for a short period of time. The tragic truth is that very soon the Israelites had returned to the same practices, purposes, and perversions that had led to their earlier fall.

(b) The people of Israel were once again delivered by their God and restored to their land. But no sooner had the dust settled than they forgot about God's love, they forgot about the honor due his holy name, they forgot about the life to which they were called, they forgot about the love they were to have for each other. They forgot. That was their fatal weakness.

(c) How often we forget. In our prosperity, we forget our dependence on God. In our poverty, we forget the blessings of God. In the daily tasks of life, we forget who we are. When life is against us, we forget whose we are. When establishing our schedules, we forget why we are really here. Forgetfulness! In our day, as in the days of the restoration, this is man's fatal weakness.

III. That is why in both the Old and New Testament, God calls us to remember.

(a) God's final word to his people in the Old Testament, in Malachi 4:4, is to remember. "Remember," God said, "the law of Moses My servant, even the statutes and ordinances which I commanded Him in Horeb for all Israel."

(b) This week, as you live out your lives, as you relate to other people, as you spend time with your family, as you confront temptation, as you face the challenges of each day, remember!—Brian L. Harbour.

SUNDAY: SEPTEMBER FOURTEENTH

MORNING SERVICE

Topic: A Fool Farmer and the Grace of God

TEXT: Mark 4:3–9.

I. (a) "A sower went out to sow," said Jesus. You hear the story and you think to yourself, what a dumb, dumb farmer! Can you imagine any farmer stupid enough to sow seed in a thornbush, a rock pile, or right down the center stripe of an interstate? The parable is laughable, almost as silly as the Christian Church sowing seed of the gospel! We may not have tossed God's word into thornbushes, but we've certainly preached Good News in mighty odd places.

(b) Of course, if anyone's a fool in the parable, God's the fool! For has not God commanded our speaking? Has he not told us to go to every nation, to cover the world with his Word? And God doesn't seem to care whether anyone listens or not. He doesn't compile lists of "hot prospects," or recommend evangelizing only where there's enough cash to build a church. God says "preach," and his command is unconditional. He wants us, his people, out of our stained-glass buildings and into the world, speaking. God has commanded us to preach Good News—everywhere. So, if there's a fool in the parable, the fool is God.

II. (a) Well, be honest: Results are less than impressive. How few do respond. Here we've been preaching the gospel for twenty centuries and the world's only about eight percent Christian (or twenty-three percent by the most exaggerated figures. Ed.) Rock, thorn, and highway: At least the parable understands the odds. Nowadays nobody, but nobody, seems to want to hear the gospel—particularly in America. Maybe we aren't desperate enough, hungry, hurt, or hard-up enough to hear the gospel. Twentieth-century America seems rocky soil indeed. Rock, thorn, and highway! Be honest: We preach the gospel but results are scarcely impressive.

(b) So, how easy it is to become discouraged. How easy to lose heart. When nobody's listening, who wants to speak? Perhaps that's what's happened to us Main Line Protestant Types: Because nobody seems to listen, we've quit speaking. When was the last time you actually talked to anyone—even your own family—about the God you believe in? When? When the world seems tone-deaf to the gospel, we turn off. Instead of scattering seed, we've kept our church lawns well mowed. How easy, oh how easy it is to become discouraged, to lose heart.

III. (a) But hold on! Hey, take a look at the end of the parable: There's going to be a harvest. Look, thirty times, sixty times, a hundred times—a harvest! God takes our foolish leftover, throwaway seeds and turns them into triumph. There's a harvest coming: Someday every knee shall bow and every tongue confess that Jesus Christ is Lord to the glory of God the Father. No idle dream, it's promised word of the Lord, and the Lord keeps his word; someday it shall be! Thirty, sixty, a hundred times over; there's going to be a harvest. ✚

(b) So, guess what? Agenda for the Church: Speak the gospel and trust God; trust God and speak the gospel. What else is the Church for, but to spread the Good News? Shall we spell it out: Your church does not exist to spruce up your morals. God may not be much interested in what we call "morality." The Church does not exist to teach your children religion: Christian faith may not be "religion." Your church does not exist to provide Christian fellowship; you can rub human fur against human fur almost anywhere. No, the Church lives to preach the gospel! That's what a church is for: to name God into the world. Somehow you'd think we'd want to spread the news, news of God's good, undeserved grace in a world that seems so graceless. What else is a church for? So, agenda for the Church: Trust God and speak the gospel, speak the gospel and trust God. ✟

(c) Where do we live? Well, between the stammer of our speaking and the grace of God. God wants us to name his name into our conversations, so folk will know God is and believe. Stammer, blush, but dare to speak. "Between the foolishness of speaking and the grace of God. . . . " A good place to live, dear friends: only a step to the kingdom of God.—David G. Buttrick.

Illustrations

† THE INVISIBLE SEED.   The seed is in the soil; it sprouts; nothing will stop it. The harvest is as excessive as was the failure of the farmer depicted at the beginning of the parable. The yield reaches sixty, even one hundred grains for one. And once more the summons of Jesus comes to us: "He who has ears to hear, let him hear." Something happens, something grows where God begins to reign. Perhaps it is still completely hidden, so that we doubters see only stone, birds, and bushes. They are there, visible and big as life, although the green shoots of wheat can hardly be seen. But they will bear the sixty

or one hundred grains, while the enormous strata of rocks, and the billows of bushes head high, and the noisy birds will bear no fruit. So it is with the reign of God. —Eduard Schweizer.

 HOW IT BEGINS. A cartoon showed a big city apartment, filled with plants. There was philodendron around the curtain rods, ivy on the walls; there were buckets, pots, ashtrays all filled with plants; everywhere, the place looked like a jungle. In the middle of the room a little lady was explaining to her neighbor, "Would you believe it all began with one African violet!" We laugh, laugh for joy. For God will take our foolish seeding of the gospel and turn it into miracle. There's harvest promised! Someday the fur-capped Russian and the Detroit wino and the New York City subway crowd and the Indiana farmer will all come together in one glad gang before God: It shall be. —David G. Buttrick.

Sermon Suggestions

BARNABAS—"SON OF ENCOURAGEMENT." Text: Selections from Acts. What is it that sets persons like Barnabas apart from the rest of us? Vision, the ability to see what is hidden from the rest of us. (1) He sees a gift to give where others see a profit to keep (4:36–38). (2) He sees the future saint where others see the former sinner (9:26–27a). (3) He sees grace for all where others see grace for the elect (11:23). (4) He sees the potential for steadfastness where others see the reputation of irresolution (15:37–40).—James M. King.

GOD'S PERSISTENT QUEST. Gospel Text: Luke 15:1–10. (1) Commences in a sense of loss. (2) Continues despite all discouragements. (3) Concludes with fulfillment and rejoicing.

Worship Aids

CALL TO WORSHIP. "God purposely chose what the world considers nonsense in order to shame the wise, and he chose what the world considers weak in order to shame the powerful" (1 Cor. 1:27, TEV).

INVOCATION. Lord, without thee we can do nothing; with thee we can do all. Help us by thy grace not to fall; help us by thy strength to resist mightily the very first beginnings of evil, before it takes hold of us; help us to cast ourselves at once at thy sacred feet, and lie still there, until the storm be overpast; and, if we lose sight of thee, bring us back quickly to thee, and grant us to love thee better, for thy tender mercy's sake.—E. B. Pusey.

OFFERTORY SENTENCE. "Who hath despised the day of small things?" (Zech. 4:10).

OFFERTORY PRAYER. Compared to the wealth of nations, O Lord, what we give here today is small. Yet we believe that the gospel that shook the ancient world to its foundations is still powerful and that our tithes and offerings can be used by you to make the world once more take notice of your power and know your love. So bless our little and make it much.

PRAYER. God of the ages, our God, great are the works of your hands and of your heart. As we meditate on what you have done and what you are, we are filled with wonder and awe. As we reflect on what we have done and what we are, we have to confess that because of our own self-will we have not allowed you to do in and through us all that you desire to see in our lives, and our shortcoming is ever before us. Forgive us, O God; deepen our desire to glorify you in every aspect of our lives. May your name be hallowed within our family relationships, at our work, in our recreation, among our friends, in the community of believers, and in our private thoughts. Lift us above our frequent discouragement and occasional despair by a renewed and renewing sense of your purpose working out in history despite all hindrances and apparent failures.

EVENING SERVICE

Topic: Triumphant Living
TEXT: Col. 2:6, 13–15.
Isn't it wonderful what happens when life begins to turn in a positive and con-

structive direction? There are three great certainties, three great dynamic positive facts that Paul shares with the Colossians that are foundational for victorious living.

I. The first great certainty for triumphant living is this—in Jesus Christ, and him alone, fullness of life is available here and now (vv. 9–10).

(a) The Greek word for fullness is *pleroma*—it means more than enough. Notice that the word is used twice. There is fullness of God's revelation and fullness of life in Jesus Christ.

(b) The cults call into question the adequacy of Jesus for the fullness of life. Dig deep enough and you will discover that the cult teaches that something more is needed. Paul says, "Not so!" Jesus is not just one of a series of teachers, leaders, or revelations. He is unique. There is nothing missing. There is absolutely nothing of authentic existence that I can ever know or discover that is missing in Jesus Christ.

II. The second great certainty is this—in Jesus Christ God has not only given us fullness of life—he has also given us fullness of forgiveness for all our sins (vv. 13–14).

(a) There was a humiliating custom in the ancient world of publicly listing a person's debts. This was done on a scroll, listing the amount owed, and to whom the money was owed. Sometimes a poor man would have a wealthy friend who would pull the nail out, fold the paper over, and write his name across the back of the paper; then he would drive the nail back in through the paper and cancel the debt by taking it upon himself.

(b) Paul saw something like that as he looked at the cross. The cross reveals the tragic depth of your sin and mine—but even more the cross reveals the heart of God, who takes our debts, our sins, and cancels the bond that stands against us, nailing it to the cross. No one else can do that.

III. There is still a third great certainty for triumphant living. We have fullness of triumph and victory (v. 15). The Greek word for triumph is *thriambeuo*, which invoked not just an image or picture of victory but also the celebration of the power of the victory—the joyous procession! "He disarmed the principalities and powers and made a public example of them, triumphing over them in him" (Col. 2:15).

(b) In our text the triumphant one is no Roman general. He is none other than Jesus himself. He is more than the Nazareth carpenter now, more than the Galilean teacher, more than the great physician, and even more than the long-awaited Messiah. He is the triumphant victor before whom all creation bows. He has won the ultimate battle; and he has defeated and disarmed, not just a few sinners but the principalities and powers. The ultimate source of evil is now revealed, in public example, as defeated and powerless before Jesus Christ.—Joe A. Harding.

SUNDAY: SEPTEMBER TWENTY-FIRST

MORNING SERVICE

Topic: You Must Ask

Text: Luke 7:36–50.

To be forgiven by our Lord means saying that we *are* sorry for what we have done. In short, forgiveness depends upon our seeking of repentance.

I. The sinful woman who anointed the feet of Jesus is an example of a person who was sorry for what she had done. Although she spoke not a word, her actions spoke loudly of her desire to be forgiven and of her change of heart. Repentance was thus her active search for the forgiveness that only our Lord can give.

(a) This woman's act of repentance was not lost on Jesus. In typical fashion, he compared the woman's act of humble repentance with the fine home and self-assured demeanor of Simon the Pharisee. Despite the obvious superficial differences between the woman and Simon, both were sinners. The woman was a more obvious sinner, but Simon was also a sinner.

(b) The difference between these two sinners, however, was that the woman repented of her sin while Simon did not.

Jesus seems to suggest, in his subsequent parable of the two debtors, which follows the woman's anointing of his feet, that because the seriousness of Simon's sins were of less magnitude than those of the woman, he was more inclined to sweep them under the rug and to feel that they were of little consequence. In short, Simon seems to have had the attitude that he had his life under control to the point that he did not need to lean on God for much. Thus, since he obviously felt little need to be forgiven by God, he was little inclined to forgive others. In the words of Jesus, "but he who is forgiven little, loves little."

II. Although some of us may have been in the position of the sinful woman at some point in our lives, most of us are usually in the position of Simon the Pharisee. We try to lead "respectable" lives doing those things that tend to stabilize and care for our families, homes, and community. Most of us are careful to avoid grossly immoral, illegal, or bizarre behavior—things that would place us in direct conflict with other persons. In short, we are expert in leading the middle way of life.

(a) How easy is it then not to ask God for forgiveness? This is particularly true when we know that we have committed no major or mortal sin. Like Simon, we tend to ignore the little stuff; however, like Simon, we run the risk of losing our ability to forgive other persons.

(b) By regularly turning to our God to seek forgiveness, for even those minor infractions of God's law, we experience anew God's reconciling and restoring love in our lives and the peace and wholeness that only he can grant through his Son, Jesus Christ. Having experienced his love ourselves, we can then share that love as we share the experience of forgiveness with other persons.

(c) Jesus, in the house of Simon the Pharisee, demonstrated the reality of God's forgiveness and challenged Simon the Pharisee to lay aside his mask of self-righteousness and turn to God in repentance. Moreover, Jesus demonstrated that forgiveness is merely one facet of the love that God shares with his people.

III. Thus, to receive forgiveness we must acknowledge—in word or deed—that we have done something wrong and that we are sorry for it. In short, we must confess our sin, something that is extraordinarily difficult and painful to do because it places our pride and ego on the line and makes us realize that we are not faultless or perfect.

(a) Yet, to confess is really a form of catharsis—to rid ourselves of those things that run counter to what we want to be and to open up the process of inner and outer healing. A simple example of the importance of confession and the search for forgiveness is found in marital counseling. Whenever I as a pastor counsel a couple having marital problems, I know that they are beginning to make progress when one can turn to the other and say, "Honey, I'm sorry." This is usually reciprocated and the relationship often begins to heal. The ability to say "I'm sorry" is an indication that pride has been overcome and that love has prevailed.

(b) Jesus Christ challenges each of us in that way. Overcome pride. Let love prevail in our relationship with God and our relationships with other persons. Then, and only then, can we not only experience God's forgiveness but also share with our fellow human beings.—Rodney K. Miller.

Illustrations

DO WE ALWAYS KNOW ENOUGH TO ASK? An Oriental sage aptly exemplified this art of detachment when relating his neighbor's attitude. His Chinese friend had one horse and one son. When his horse strayed off, his friends came in and sympathetically said, "We are sorry that you have had such bad luck." The farmer calmly replied, "Was it bad luck?" A few days later the horse came home, bringing three wild horses with him. "We rejoice with you in your good fortune," his neighbors remarked. "Is it good luck?" the Chinese man replied. When questioned about his lack of sorrow and elation, he explained that his only son, while riding one of the wild horses, fell and broke his leg. The neighbors again expressed sympathy. The farmer then pointed out that the broken leg was not bad luck, since a war broke out and because of his injured leg the boy was not called into service. And on it goes. What is bad and what is good?—Roy O. McClain.

THE ART OF PRAYER. The art of prayer must be learned, for reservoirs of power are at our disposal if we can learn this art. "If we learn it"—that is the rub. People expect results without any practice of the art. We would deem a person foolish who stepped up to a musical instrument only occasionally, expecting to tune into music and become the instrument of music without long training and practice. The little son of a missionary bought a mouth organ in India and came home in tears: "That man cheated me. There is no 'God Save the King' in his mouth organ." We just as foolishly believe we can get ready-made results without the practice of prayer.—E. Stanley Jones.

Sermon Suggestions

COMMAND AND PROMISE. Text: Deut. 1:6–8. (1) "You have stayed long enough" (v. 6). (2) "Advance," (v. 7). (3) "See, I have given you this land" (v. 8).—C. Neil Strait.

YOUR MONEY AND YOUR LIFE. Gospel Text: Luke 16:1–13. (1) The canny wisdom of the world (vv. 1–8). (2) The neglected wisdom of the kingdom of God (vv. 9–13).

Worship Aids

CALL TO WORSHIP. "The eyes of the Lord are upon the righteous, and his ears are open unto their cry" (Ps. 34:15).

INVOCATION. We come to you, O God, because you call us to come. We pray to you, because you invite our prayers. You assure us that we are not only heard but that our prayers will be answered, though sometimes in ways we do not expect. Help us to be as open to your will as you are open to our cry.

OFFERTORY SENTENCE. "Let us . . . always offer praise to God as our sacrifice

through Jesus, which is the offering presented by lips that confess him as Lord. Do not forget to do good and to help one another, because these are the sacrifices that please God" (Heb. 13:15–16, TEV).

OFFERTORY PRAYER. Lord, we are a people who earnestly want to do what is good in your sight. That is why we pray to you: We want to do good and we want you to reveal to us what that good is. Doing good is for us a necessary response to the matchless goodness you have shown us, in so many ways, and especially in the person of Christ our Lord. We simply cannot behold your goodness in the land of the living, we cannot be recipients time and time again of your blessings, without having a hunger and a thirst to do good, as you make that known and possible. It is our way of saying a humble and joyous thank you. It is also our way of not being selfish: We who have been given so much because you are such a caring, sharing, loving God —we want to relate to one another and to others in a manner that, however slightly, reflects your love and goodness to us. Even in our darkest and most disobedient moments, you stayed with us and did not desert us. When we needed you most and deserved you least; indeed, when we were your enemies, you did not forsake or forget or fail to forgive us. So, with overwhelming gratitude to you for all that we can in no way ever repay, accept these offerings, and us, in the work of your church, the ministry of reconciliation, the kingdom of love, the gospel of Christ.—Gordon H. Reif.

PRAYER. Father . . . Father—for this is the manner in which our Savior and Lord taught us to address you. He knew, even as you know, how like children we are. We thank you for your fatherly care, your ever-present love. We thank you for your fatherly counsel, your willingness to guide us. We thank you for your fatherly gentleness, your patience with us. We are but dependent children . . . innocent, trusting . . . ah, Father, if that were but the whole story. . . . We are rebellious children too —against your revealed will. We are selfish children—insisting on our rights, neglecting the needs of others, refusing to accept responsibility for the weak. We are unforgiving children—intolerant of others, cruel, unmerciful, unloving. Father, forgive us for Jesus' sake. Even now, Father, other members of our family need you. For the sick we ask your healing. For the grieving we ask your comfort. For rejoicing parents we ask your grace. We ask wisdom for those confronted with decisions, courage for those who are confronted with need. Help us to help them. Your larger family claims our attention, Father. Do not allow us to be isolated here. Prod us into wider witnessing. Constrain us by your love.—J. Estill Jones.

EVENING SERVICE

Topic: Life in Christ
TEXT: Phil. 1:21.

So much was Paul's life tied up with Christ that he could say, "For me to live is Christ." What he meant was that if Christ were to be taken out of his life, there would be nothing left. But what did he mean when he said, "Christ is life for me?"

I. Paul meant first of all that Jesus Christ was the initiator of life. His life began with Christ.

(a) Paul expressed this thought many times but nowhere as beautifully as in the second chapter of Ephesians: "And you were dead in your trespasses and sins in which you formerly walked according to the course of this world. . . . But God being rich in mercy, because of his great love with which he loved us, even when we were dead in our transgressions, made us alive together with Christ" (Eph. 2:1–5).

(b) The thing we need to be most afraid of today is not that our life will end but that it shall never have a beginning. Only Christ can fill the emptiness of man's soul. Only Christ can bring life. Only Christ can lift man out of his sin and set him on a new pathway.

II. He also meant that Jesus was the ideal of his life, the goal toward which he moved.

(a) Again this idea is expressed in many places by Paul but nowhere as clearly as in 2 Corinthians 5:15, "He died for all, that they who live should no longer live for themselves but for him who died and rose again on their behalf." Paul did not live for himself. He lived for Christ. Christ was the ideal, the purpose of his life.

(b) Your values, your goal, your purpose, your ideal will determine how you look at life, how you react to life, and how you live life. And I believe that every person fits either into Philippians 1:21 or Philippians 2:21. Philippians 1:21 says, "For me to live is Christ." Philippians 2:21 says, "They all seek after their own interests, not those of Christ Jesus." Where do you fit? What are you living for? There was no question about where Paul fit. Life not only began with Christ but it existed for Christ. Christ was his ideal.

III. Paul would add that Jesus is not only the initiator of his life and the ideal of his life but also the inspiration of his life.

(a) That's what Christ was to Paul. And nowhere is it more clearly expressed than in Galatians 2:20. "I have been crucified with Christ, and it is no longer I who live, but Christ lives in me; and the life which I now live in the flesh I live by faith in the Son of God, who loved me and delivered himself up for me."

(b) Paul said, "He lives in me." And he gives me the stimulus, the motivation, the power to press on toward the goal. He is my inspiration.

IV. He also means that Christ is his insulation in life. He protects us from everything that seeks to destroy us.

(a) Nowhere is this more beautifully declared than in Romans 8:38: "For I am convinced that nothing can ever separate us from his love. Death can't and life can't. The angels won't, and all the powers of hell itself cannot keep God's love away. Our fears for today, our worries about tomorrow, or where we are—high above the sky, or in the deepest ocean—nothing will ever be able to separate us from the love of God demonstrated by our Lord Jesus Christ when he died for us" (Living Bible).

(b) Our lives are hidden with Christ in God (Col. 3:3) and nothing will ever be able to separate us from him. That is what Paul was saying. And because of the presence of God in our lives, we know that we will make it through whatever we have to face.—Brian L. Harbour.

SUNDAY: SEPTEMBER TWENTY-EIGHTH

MORNING SERVICE

Topic: Our Shaken World and the Unshaken Kingdom

Text: Heb. 12:26.

What is shaking our world in these world-shaking days? It would help us to know.

I. We can hardly believe that any machine has us in its grip.

(a) Our modern tumult is *not* new; always our world is shaken. We speak of the changeless stars, but if we could look long enough we would see that stars are sputtering candles. Any mountain range is only a ridge on the rind of a slowly drying orange—or should we say lemon?

(b) Man changes more swiftly than the stars or hills. Every item in our body, except the enamel on our teeth, dies and is renewed every five or seven years. Is any argument needed that man's works also disappear as certainly as autumn leaves?

(c) Yet we do not learn. All things move, like shadows. The changes may dismay us unless we remember that change is the law of life.

II. But whose law? The Bible declares that God shakes not only the earth, but heaven; not only wicked empires, but even the Temple. So chaotic were New Testament times that men were then sure that some final cataclysm was at hand. The Craftsman, they were convinced, was about to sweep clear his workshop to make a new beginning or else destroy history once and for all.

III. The shaking of our world is not without purpose. The whole creation is in change and often in tumult "that those things which cannot be shaken may remain" and that our life may there be built.

(a) But where is the unshaken kingdom? The unshaken kingdom is within us. We see it glinting through the moving panorama of things about us, like a mountain seen through driven mist. Laws change, but right abides; theologies are rewritten in every generation, but God endures. Our half-truths come and go, but truth is never shaken. Where is the unshaken kingdom? Glinting through the changes of the changing world.

(b) Where is it? Revealed in Jesus Christ! That we know, not alone because he promised, "Lo, I am with you always," and not alone because others have testified that he is near, but because the fixed point of light in us glows whenever we think of him. He is not only "the Rock of Ages," but the Rock of Eternity—the "kingdom that cannot be shaken."

IV. God is shaking our world, using even wicked men for his purposes; and God will shake all life until the eternal shines clear of the cumbering dust of the temporal. So? So that we may learn to live in his enduring will.

(a) Sometimes history appears to be still. But even then the stillness is deceiving, and those same clouds can quickly become tempests by which the very mountains are torn out by the roots. How shall we preach and teach? In what mood and by what power? Only the Bible could ever give this kind of answer: "Wherefore we receiving a kingdom which cannot be shaken, let us be *thankful*." The Bible does not bid us be thankful *for* violent change, but it does bid us be thankful *in* it. Why? Because God has set eternity in our hearts in the Lord Christ, and because change throws into bright relief the unchanging treasure.

(b) In that thankfulness "serve God acceptably." That is to say, a man must preach and live now in witness to that which does not change. Always he must so live, but gladly now when change provides a foil for his solid testimony.

(c) "With reverence and godly fear." Now more than ever—worship! The Church stands amid the rubble of a changing world. Its buildings may not stand, but it stands—the congregation of lowly souls who through prayer find the unchanging Lord.

V. Wise are we if we have learned that all things *made* by God are shaken, while all souls *born* of God abide. It does not greatly matter what changes come in the outer world, for bones and muscles and houses and cash will be shaken. For God is always shaking "the things that are made. . . . that the things which cannot be shaken may remain." Wise will we be if we live in one world and visit in another—if we live in the abidingness of God and visit for a while in the changing earth.—George A. Buttrick.

Illustrations

REAL SECURITY, REAL LIFE. Jim N. Griffith tells a story of his mother and father. They were killed in an accident. The day after the double funeral the family began the painful task of going through their personal belongings. Griffith says, "Opening their Bibles, we found an old church bulletin with a printed questionnaire from their pastor asking that they write down what Christ meant to them. My dad had written in that scrawling manner of his: 'I am sixty-eight years old—Jesus Christ is my security.' Mother, left-handed, had written in her familiar penmanship: 'Jesus Christ means life itself to me.' "

THE THINGS THAT REMAIN. These are the burning fires: Cross! Ordeal! These are the eternal destroyers that are in this world by God's will to mash all that will mash, to crush all that will collapse, to burn out all that will burn, to purge out all that is false, to destroy in you everything that can die. The tangibles perish. The things that you see cannot endure, but everything that does last lasts through ordeal; every human institution that survives survives out of crisis; every human value goes on existing *after* the cross that tests it. *Everything eternal comes out of a crucible.*—Carlyle Marney.

Sermon Suggestions

THE INCOMPLETENESS OF LIFE. Texts: 1 Cor. 13:12; Phil. 3:12; 1 John 3:2. (1) Incompleteness of knowledge. (2) Incompleteness of achievement. (3) Incompleteness of character. (4) The complete man Jesus.—J. D. Jones.

WHAT IF THE RICH MAN . . . Gospel Text: Luke 16:19–31. (1) Had really seen the poor man? (2) Had carefully listened to the teaching of Scripture? (3) Had prudently looked beyond the present moment?

Worship Aids

CALL TO WORSHIP. "In the shadow of thy wings will I make my refuge" (Ps. 57:1).

INVOCATION. How great thou art! Thou who hast created the heavens and the earth, who indeed cannot be contained in temples made with hands, we invoke thy presence with thy people today. Expand our horizons to the far reaches of thy world. Intensify our consciousness of thy love, speak to us clearly of thy will.—J. Estill Jones.

OFFERTORY SENTENCE. "Provide for yourselves purses that don't wear out, and save your riches in heaven, where they will never decrease, because no thief can get to them, and no moth can destroy them. For your heart will always be where your riches are" (Luke 12:33b-34, TEV).

OFFERTORY PRAYER. Look into our hearts, O God, and tell us what we love. If we love you little, help us to love you more. If we care too little about the people around us, help us to be more concerned. If we are too much wedded to the things of this world, free us from our idolatry and set our hearts on the enduring riches of your kingdom.

PRAYER. Lord, shake the earth with the power of God. Oh! that the heathen lands may hear the Word of God and live. But first convert the church, and then thou wilt convert the world. Oh! deal with those that depart from the faith and grieve the Holy Spirit. Bring them back again to their first love, and may Christ be fully and faithfully preached everywhere to the glory of his name. Now forgive us every iniquity; now lift us beyond the power of every sin; now lift us to pray and praise; now make the home full of sacred power, and, last of all, come, Lord Jesus.—Charles Haddon Spurgeon.

EVENING SERVICE

Topic: God-Made Men or Men-Made Gods

TEXT: Exod. 20:1–2, 4–6.

The outward appearance of this commandment is a prohibition of images; the chief concern, however, is with how we worship God. Whereas the first commandment told us *whom* to worship, this commandment tells us *how* to worship him.

I. The pagan said that God could be known best by having sacred rocks, trees, animals, carvings that represented him.

(a) But the danger involved here is that inevitably when idols or figures are used, there is a great tendency to forget that they are only symbols, and men tend to worship the symbol itself.

(b) Although most of us would feel that we are safe on this commandment—the erection of idols is not limited to pagans in the past. It may be true that the age of graven images is past, but the age of making gods is ever with us.

(c) Idolatry's other name is materialism. Although we do not make our gods into little, squat figures, we nonetheless strive to make things provide us with the source of satisfaction that can come from God alone.

II. The Jews contributed a second way by which man tries to make God real. Their answer was that God met them in their religion and more specifically in the temple.

(a) To the Jews the temple with its Holy of Holies was the place where God met them. But somewhere along the way they failed to understand who God really was. They thought they could control God. They thought of God as being in a box. They thought they had him all confined.

(b) But even this view had its dangers. If the Temple was where God stayed, then when they were away from the temple they could not worship God. This, of course, had some advantages. As long as they had to go to Jerusalem to worship God, this meant that they could live like they wanted to when they weren't worshiping him.

(c) Again the similarities between the past and the present are so obvious. The decision with which we are faced is not whether we shall be religious or irreligious, but which religion we shall choose. Our problem does not deal with making images of God. We are not as crass as that. Our problem is worshiping the wrong image of God.

III. The Christian replies that the Incarnation is the only way God makes himself known.

(a) Jesus said: "He that hath seen me hath seen the Father" (John 7:15). "I am the way, the truth, and the life; no man cometh unto the Father but by me" (John 14:6).

(b) This second commandment, when understood in the light of the Incarnation, stands out in brightness and clarity. We are not to make idols because they fail to show us God. Instead we are to come to God through Jesus Christ for he alone is the way to God, the truth of God, the life with God.—James E. Taulman.

SUNDAY: OCTOBER FIFTH

MORNING SERVICE

Topic: Who, Me?

TEXT: Matt. 16:13–23.

Part of the New Testament's genius lies in its perceiving major characters as representative. No one conveys this representative quality of New Testament characters more than Peter.

I. Our church memory focuses on him as we try to understand what faithful discipleship entails. The New Testament incidents magnifying Peter are not simply isolated personal transactions two thousand years ago—interesting, perhaps, but simply biographical trivia. Hardly! These incidents symbolize the issues, the choices, the decisions faced by Christians and by churches for generations, as we encounter and convey Christ in this world. Peter's confession, Peter's good intentions, Peter's dismal failures, Peter's moral myopia, Peter's lying for fear of his life, Peter's fleeing, Peter's triumphant faith: All of these describe tensions and choices facing everyone who would confess Jesus as the Christ.

II. We begin by looking at one of those revealing New Testament incidents. Jesus invites Peter to join in his ministry.

(a) With crowds eager to hear him, Jesus commandeers a boat and goes out into the lake to speak to them. When he returns, he discovers a boatload of weary fishermen, exhausted from a night's work and nothing to show for it. Jesus encounters them and insists they head out again into deep water. Peter protests: "Master, we have been at work all night; we've searched every shoal; we've cast our nets into every underwater canyon; we've taken nothing."

(b) Sound familiar? The early church sees in that passage a reflection of its own miserable failure to gain adherents. Who of us who loves a church doesn't understand this discouragement?

(c) And that kind of discouragement stretches across any number of our lives. Oh, the things that get us down in the face of life's great adventure! And we certainly know how to make ourselves miserable. We can say with Peter, "Lord, we have worked all night and taken nothing."

III. Or take that event reflected in our lesson this morning. Remember Jesus' question, "Who does this people say that I am?" The answers identify him with the best the Jewish religious tradition offers. "Who do you say I am?" he continues. And Peter answers with the churches down the ages, "You bear the new age of justice and peace; you are the Christ." No sooner does Peter confess this than he blunders into total misapprehension of the Master's Christhood and finds himself labeled no better than Satan.

(a) Do you see what's happening? Jesus tells Peter loyalty to Christ may lead to crucifixion. And Peter answers, "Oh no, Lord, not you. Let's stay clear of crucifixion. You're a winner, Jesus. Following you doesn't mean risking trouble, or controversy. We'll follow you so long as you remain a celebrity, on good terms with everyone."

(b) Right here, we discover the major obstacle to our hope for the world. It is not atheists or communists. It's not necessarily the generals or oil barons; the drug dealers, or politicians on the take. The primary obstacle to Christ's new age is Christians: Loyal confessor one moment, sell-outs, without batting an eye, the next. As Pogo put it, "We have met the enemy and it is us."

(c) Oh, friends, can we remain loyal to Christ amid all persuading us the kind of world God promises can be brought about at no cost to our own status, or income, or privilege, or power? That kind of persuasion is outright deception. Be careful. The New Testament ascribes to it a simple expletive: "Out of my sight, Satan; for yours is the way, not of God, but to this world."

IV. Oh, Peter, how human you are. Noble on the one hand but, oh, so vulnerable. My soul—nobility, vulnerability: How well the New Testament knows us!

(a) And yet—and here is "the Beauty Part"—as well as the New Testament knows us, the towering, indisputable, incredible power of our hope lies in Jesus choosing Peter-types to convey his gospel to the world. Do we mean Jesus calls the likes of Peter—yea, the likes of you and me —with all our failures and blindnesses, all our false starts and dead ends, all our hollow promises, mixed motives, and chaotic priorities—Jesus chooses the likes of us to bear the tidings of Love's new world? Believe it! Christ takes us as we are; Christ remains true to us in our weakness; Christ loves us through our self-centeredness, undergirds our mediocre faith, and promises to embrace us as we pursue a mission of joy and peace.

(b) That's the gospel! That's our faith. That's our hope. And ultimately, stumbling, yearning, noble, vulnerable human beings that we are, that gospel enables us to rejoice with Peter, as he writes to that blessed little band in the maturity of his faith: "Blessed be the God and Father of our Lord Jesus Christ! By his great mercy we have been born anew to a living hope through the resurrection of Jesus Christ from the dead."—James W. Crawford.

Illustrations

STRENGTHENED BY TESTING.   How vividly I recall a long-cherished day when, with a companion who knew intimately trees, birds, and flowers, we inspected a giant oak that had met disaster in a frightful storm. My friend carefully counted the rings on the end of a log sawed from the trunk of the tree and announced the oak was 250 years old. Then he called my attention to a strange scar that ran halfway across the heart of the sawed-off end of the log. "Sometime in the first fifty years of its long life," he explained, "this tree was injured; it is likely that another tree was driven against it with such violence as to mar this tree permanently, but the injury did not stunt its growth, so strong and sturdy it became, as it battled with storms, snow and ice for two and a half centuries."—Edgar DeWitt Jones.

DEPENDING ON GOD.   He calls me, he entrusts me with a task. What a support for me! To receive a mandate, to be invested with a function is always a powerful support to a person. How much more so when we are conscious that the mandate comes from God! Then even timid people find themselves possessed of indomitable energy. My friends sometimes tell me that I am too pessimistic. But though I am pessimistic about mankind, I am optimistic about God. I depend on him and on his astonishing resources. I am not persecuted as Jeremiah was, but like him I was timid, hesitant, uncertain, and I am well aware of my weakness. I do not know what to say to all the people who bring me their dilemmas, for they seem to me generally to be insoluble. But I become quite different the moment I believe I can see what God's will is. I can face any obstacle. Of course I am often mistaken, I can never be certain. There is such a disproportion between God and me! But it is the same God who will afterwards be able to make me understand where I went wrong, and who has taught me that it is better to make a mistake with conviction than to remain always in doubt.—Paul Tournier.

Sermon Suggestions

THE BELIEVER WHO KNOWS TOO LITTLE. Text: Matt. 16:22–23. (1) Prejudice often prevents his understanding the plain teachings of revelation. (2) Conceit often leads him to set his own judgment above God's teaching (cf. 1 Cor. 4:6). (3) Presumptuous ignorance often makes him hinder the cause he tries to help. (4) Strength of will and warmth of heart often render his ignorance more harmful. (5) Therefore, his honest opinions and well-meant advice must sometimes be utterly rejected by others. (6) Further instruction and experience may make him a pillar in the church (Gal. 2:9).—John A. Broadus.

WITHOUT AN EYE TO REWARD.   Gospel Text: Luke 17:1–10. (1) When temptations come, both tempter and tempted have responsibility (vv. 1–4). (2) Through faith, the "impossibility" of forgiving the offender is possible (vv. 5–6). (3) Forgiveness is the Christian's obligation, not an option (vv. 7–10).

Worship Aids

CALL TO WORSHIP.   "Praise ye the Lord. Praise the Lord, O my soul. While I live will I praise the Lord: I will sing praises unto my God while I have any being" (Ps. 146:1–2).

INVOCATION.   Restore unto us the joy of thy praise, O Lord. Fill us with the gratitude that befits thy wondrous deeds and gifts, and bring our lives into line with our thanks and praise.

OFFERTORY SENTENCE.   "Each tree is known by its own fruit. . . . The good man out of the good treasure of his heart produces good" (Luke 6:44a, 45a, RSV).

OFFERTORY PRAYER.   Make our hearts right, O God, so that our stewardship may be right. Or, make our stewardship right and then let love fill the vacuum of our need.

PRAYER.   O our Father! reach forth thine arms, and take us that have fallen to the ground, up above our weakness, higher than our own strength can carry us. Lift us into the sphere where thou dwellest, that our thoughts may also partake of the sonship that we have; for thou dost no longer call us servants, but friends. Blessed God, if we are thy friends, show forth to us this morning this relationship. May we understand it by the consciousness of friendship in us. May we know thee by that which rises within us to call for thee. Let the echo of thy nature sound in us. Let there be something that we shall long to say, Father. May there be that in our hearts that shall hunger—hunger for love greater than that which one man can give to another. We have tried the world, and we bless thee for it. There are many joys in it. There is much in it that makes us wish to live. And all the sweet friendships of life—how they are clothing us as with a garment! And how hast thou ordained praise in the household and in the individual heart! And how hast thou caused the very natural world round about us to smile and bless us! And yet, who of us is satisfied? What bounty ever left us without a yearning and longing for something more? Is it that we have come from heaven and these dim dreams of lost glory come back? Or is it the intimation of thy Spirit —the earnest of our inheritance? Is it not that thou dost, by the Holy Spirit, strive in us, making prayers for us with groanings that cannot be uttered and making supplications in us? Art thou not drawing us toward thyself as the real supply of the soul? Thine is love that perfects itself. Thine is a companionship that leaves nothing to be desired—that still lifts us, excites our imagination, and more than fulfills every ideal. Thine is a companionship that never wearies. There are no pauses in it. We are never with thee conscious of divine weakness. There are no flaws in that perfection of nature that thou bringest to us. Now, grant, we beseech of thee, more of that help by which we may live as seeing him who is invisible. We pray that we may enter into the divine life; that we may find food for our souls, joy in our solitude, consolation in our bereavements, light in our loneliness and darkness, strength when we are unstable, and

courage in the hour of fear. Grant that still —in all moods, in every necessity, in the soul's deepest and innermost want, though inarticulate—we may find thee all in all.—Henry Ward Beecher.

EVENING SERVICE

Topic: The Discipline of Submission
TEXT: Phil. 2:5–11.

I. Christ came "out of the ivory palaces into a world of woe." He, finding himself in the form of a servant, emptied himself of divine prerogatives and became obedient, even to death on a cross.

(a) Jesus taught, "Blessed are the meek. They shall inherit the earth." The word *meek* meant the God-controlled. Blessed are those who place God at center. Blessed are those who commit themselves first and foremost to God's will and to God's kingdom.

(b) If the teachings of Jesus were not enough to teach submission and not arrogance, then the example of Jesus would. He was a man for others. He was the suffering servant who gave himself a ransom for many.

II. The gospel is at heart quite simple. You can boil it down to a single concept. The invitation of Jesus is so clear a child can grasp it. He simply said, "Come, follow me." But the gospel is also a many-faceted thing. Following Christ is the most demanding challenge you will ever take on. He also said, "Learn of me." You will spend the rest of your life doing that.

(a) The teachings and example of Jesus are an affront to our pride. We don't really like it. We might as well be honest and admit it. We would rather think of him as the King with majesty and glory rather than riding into Jerusalem on a jackass. The cross has been a scandal and always will be a stumbling block to many.

(b) Men think they're free but are really in bondage to sin and death. And heaven's demand comes as a jarring word. It is not always a welcome word. Heaven's demand is what the allies required of the Axis powers during the Second World War—unconditional surrender. You see, as surely as salvation cost Christ his life, it will cost us our precious will and pride.

III. What do you suppose would happen if everyone of us should give God all there is of us? If God should have all you are, this group alone could change our world, impact our city, and carry high the banner of Christ near and far.

(a) What does it mean to surrender one's life to Christ? It means in the first place that we experience the forgiveness of our sins. He forgives us, and we enter into relationship with God. It means joy, it really does.

(b) Surrender means a life of obedience and growth. God changes us from within, transforms our attitudes. We get to the point where we value other persons as important instead of seeing them as stepping stones or irritants. We can rejoice in their success. We can be touched with their sorrow and disappointment.

(c) What does it mean to surrender our lives to Christ? Heaven save us from the competition within a marriage that contributes strife, heartache, and alienation. "Be subject to one another for the sake of Christ" (Eph. 5:12). What a needed word from God for every couple. We can have a "co-archy" where Christ is Lord.

IV. Jesus took the world's standard of greatness and stood it on its head. Many businesses are organized on the theory of a pyramid, and the higher you climb toward the apex, the nearer you get to the top, the more people you have under you, the more power you exert. Jesus flipped the pyramid upside down. Jesus' diagram of greatness is that the nearer you get to the apex, the more people you carry in love, the greater responsibility you have for others. It's just the opposite of the world's standard. You don't swagger into the kingdom—you bow, you surrender, you submit your will to the Father's.—Alton H. McEachern.

SUNDAY: OCTOBER TWELFTH

MORNING SERVICE

Topic: God Wrestles with a Rascal
TEXT: Gen. 32:24.

Every Sunday morning here we thank God for the "means of grace"—not for its definition. Among the means of grace is the Bible. And it comes to us chiefly through stories, very human stories, very human stories of people like us "standing in the need of grace."

I. Enter Jacob. This is our story for this morning. Let's forget that he was what's called a "patriarch."

(a) The Bible introduces him as a very ordinary person with an even more than ordinary allotment of original sin.

(b) Already, as we read, we have a feeling that we're not going to like Jacob. By all our standards of judgments, Esau is the man for our money. To us it seems incredible that God's choice could fall on the weasly, pushy, insinuating, jealous, ambitious, and unscrupulous cheater who was his mother's pet. But grace was waiting in the wings.

II. If this cameo of Jacob as a rascal seems overdrawn, let me remind you of a few incidents in his career that are set down in evidence against him.

(a) There was that business about the birthright. A birthright was enormously important in those days. So Esau had the birthright—and Jacob was jealous. One day he saw his chance. Esau came back exhausted from the hunt, desperately hungry. "Give me some of that" he said, "I'm worn out." "All right" said Jacob, "and by the way there's one condition: You give me your birthright." Esau was the kind of young man who lived for the day and never worried about what might happen when his father died. "I'm dying of hunger right now," he said, "and what use is a birthright to me? Take it."

(b) Smart work for Jacob, but there was worse to come. For the next story tells us about a devilish piece of trickery. In those days not only a birthright but a father's blessing was of immense, supernatural value. And this story finishes with the despairing cry of the older brother: "Hast thou but one blessing, my father? Bless me even, me also, O my father. And Esau lifted up his voice and wept." There was no blessing, and Esau is left with a burning hatred for his treacherous brother, and swearing revenge.

(c) After this it is not surprising to find Rebekah arranging for Jacob to be packed off for a vacation with his uncle Laban. Does it surprise you to realize that it was on that journey, and to this cowardly rascal, that there was given a vision of God that has been sealed into the memory of Jews and Christians for over three thousand years? It was a man with all this on his conscience who spent a night alone in the desert with a stone for a pillow and dreamed of that great ladder with the angels of God ascending and descending upon it. Could anything more plainly tell us that the grace of God is not bestowed as a reward for the righteous but as gift for the sinner?

III. The story we heard this morning comes as a climax, a gracious climax, to his adventures away from home. The vision at Bethel finds its counterpoint in the strange event at the ford of Jabbok.

(a) It is one of the most mysterious tales in the whole Bible. The factual background is plain enough. Jacob is on his way home with a huge caravan of oxen, asses, camels, and loot that he had tricked out of his uncle. He comes to the river Jabbok and suddenly he hears alarming news: Esau his brother is coming to meet him with a force of four hundred men, the last person in all the world he wanted to see. His reaction is typical—to try to buy off his brother. While waiting for his brother's response, he crosses the Jabbok with his family, then prepares for a sleepless night by the riverside.

(b) "And Jacob was left alone"—yes, alone with his conscience. That comes to all of us at times, doesn't it? That's why we may at times do anything to avoid being alone. He was alone—and his brother he had robbed of the birthright and the blessing was within range, plus four hundred warriors. Where was the God of Bethel, the God of the mighty promise? This time he came in a curious form.

(c) "There wrestled a man with him until the breaking of the day." Who was this mysterious stranger? There are a thousand questions to be asked, just as we have a thousand questions about the operation of the grace of God. This is the "dark night of the soul," the time when conscience catches up, when the thought of God is more alarming than comforting, when there seems no escape from the consequences of our folly and our sin. But before the dawn came up and the stranger disappeared, Jacob knew who that stranger was: "I have seen God face to face, and my life is preserved."

IV. The God of the Bible is not a God who dwells serenely in heaven smiling on the good and blistering the bad. He is a God who wrestles with a rascal. His grace is not bestowed as a payment for services rendered but as the surprising eruption of his love at the very point of our despair. We know only too well that the world is not divided into the good and bad, period. There is a rascal in everyone of us, and it is when we admit it—perhaps even in such a dark night of the soul, that we are most likely to find that "amazing grace." And that's when the wrestling angel may choose to bestow his blessing, the dawn comes, and we are saved by grace.—David H. C. Read.

Illustrations

WHAT WE WANT. A picturesque short story puts the truth vividly. A man killed in an auto accident awoke in a strange, silent place. "Is anybody here?" he cried. Instantly an angel stood before him, "What can I do for you, sir?" The man asked what he could have. "Anything you like," the angel replied. "That is, anything except one," the angel added. "There is no pain here, no struggle, no want." The man was delighted. "Fine," he said. "Take forty years off my life; I have come to the right place." And it was done. Then followed a list of things he wanted, and everything he asked was granted. After a time he got tired of getting everything he wanted when he wanted it. He was so bored he could not go on. "I want something to do," he said, "some effort, even pain. I'd rather be in hell than be here." The angel was startled, and replied, "Where do you think you are? This is hell!"—Joseph Fort Newton.

INCREDIBLE CHANGE. In 1843 a senator stood up in the chamber of the United States Senate and, speaking of the hope of some that there might be a transcontinental railway that would make Oregon a valuable territory, he said, "To talk about constructing a railroad to the western shore of this continent manifests a wild spirit of adventure that I never expected to hear broached in the Senate of the United States." That is one way of looking at things. Some months ago, I saw a moral failure, a downright moral failure, so thoroughgoing that he stood in imminent peril of the law and, so far as visible facts were concerned, there was no more chance that he could ever be anything except a failure than there was, in the senator's mind, a possibility of a transcontinental railroad. Today, however, that man is distinctly not a failure. In these last few months he has staged one of the most splendid moral recoveries it has ever been my privilege to see, and the secret of it all was getting over to him Christ's way of looking at life.—Harry Emerson Fosdick.

Sermon Suggestions

TAKE THE "IF" OUT OF YOUR RELIGION. Text: Mark 9:22. (1) Disappointments and defeats put an "if" in our faith. (2) That "if" eats like a canker sore and keeps us weak. (3) Only the power of Christ can remove the "if" and restore full faith.—Chalmer E. Faw.

THE CHRISTIAN'S DUTY TO BE THANKFUL. Gospel Text: Luke 17:11–19. (1) Because God cares. (2) Because God's caring is shown in his action. (3) Because God's action brings a full salvation.

Worship Aids

CALL TO WORSHIP. "Cast all your anxieties on him, for he cares about you" (1 Pet. 5:7, RSV).

INVOCATION. Our heavenly Father, we come to you with many worries, some of us even with a sense of constant dread. Strengthen our faith, so that we can experience a new birth of freedom and serve you with confidence and joy.

OFFERTORY SENTENCE. "Each one, as a good manager of God's different gifts, must use for the good of others the special gift he has received from God" (1 Pet. 4:10, TEV).

OFFERTORY PRAYER. O God, give to us the gift of love, and the gift of giving will not be too hard to get.

PRAYER. Your Spirit has called us together. Indeed your spirit has called us all to serve you, and we gather to make that service significant. We are at best unworthy servants, lonely and frightened, weak and threatened, strong and confident, aggressive and assured, pious and pretentious. Forgive us, Father, and help us. We love you because you have taught us how to love; you have taught us the meaning of love; you have loved us. We praise you for your goodness and grace, for your majesty and mercy. We thank you for the promise of revival. Teach us what revival is, Father, the refreshing rain in a desert land, the stern judgment in an apathetic company. Oh, Father, clear away the cobwebs of complacency, alert us to the challenge of commitment, call to us again and again. Help us to respond in love and loyalty.—J. Estill Jones.

EVENING SERVICE

Topic: The Pleasures of Piety
TEXT: Prov. 3:17.
Some have thought it wrong that Christianity should appeal so much to the desire of happiness—most men, on the contrary, dislike its requirement of self-denial. As objections, a French preacher has well said, we might leave them to refute each other. But then both statements are true—and religion herein corresponds with human nature as we find it. Men in general have a conflict between feeling of interest

and of duty—desiring gratification, yet feeling that they ought to deny themselves. Religion proposes to reunite and harmonize these so that the desire for happiness may be satisfied with holiness; that not only interest in fact, but men's *feeling* of interest, may coincide with duty—and while denying themselves all unlawful gratification, they may have new desires, whose gratification shall afford real happiness. Religion should make us happy, for love is the fulfilling of the law, and love is happiness. Religion may properly appeal to our desire for happiness, because we cannot exercise love to others without self-love. Selfishness, the perversion, the caricature of this, is wrong, but self-love is a necessary part of our nature, indispensable to our loving others and thus indispensable to religion.

Condescending to our infirmities and seeing that men have lost the relish for holiness, God appeals to their relish for happiness. If attracted by this, they may then be less averse to holiness. But observe, there is no compromise—it is not by the offer of sensual pleasures, here or hereafter, that we would attract men to religion. We do not say that you can be religious and still enjoy the pleasures of sin. We do insist that you can be religious and still have pleasure. It would not do if happiness were the sole object in seeking religion—but it may attract and other elements enter in afterward.

Take this, then, as the subject of the sermon—"Religion Affords Happiness" or "The Pleasures of Piety."

I. The influence of piety upon those objects and relations that are commonly thought to contribute most to happiness.

(a) Influence upon length of days. How does religion contribute to this? Even conscientious care, even strong religious principle, fails to save many persons from neglect of health; but what would become of them without such principles?

(b) Influence upon reputation. Consistent piety secures respect and confidence. Those who are religious should refuse to compromise with others. They may be annoyed, even vexed, at your refusal, yet in their hearts they will honor you. A firm, decided stand is easiest to maintain and at the same time most reputable.

(c) Influence on riches. I cannot speak of this, any more than the former topics, at length. Riches do not of themselves make a man pious—they often, though not always, have a contrary effect. Piety does not necessarily promote wealth—but it must always have that tendency. It deters from vices, and vice is commonly expensive. It enjoins and encourages those virtues, which are promotive of wealth, as frugality.

(d) Influence upon our social relations. Affection of kindred and friends is enhanced by piety and mutual duties are performed better where there is piety. Piety gives a greater disposition to forgiveness and to self-sacrifice. It sheds a new luster over the brightest home, bestows an added joy upon the most loving hearts.

II. The new sources of happiness that piety opens up within us. Piety opens up many new sources of happiness.

(a) Trust in providence. Rather than "trusting to luck" or trusting merely to the uniformity of the laws of nature, we place our trust in a personal God who governs all things by his powerful Word. How immense the importance to our happiness of regarding the doings of providence as the work of our Father.

(b) Peace of spirit. This grows out of reconciliation with God. How often the happiness of the impenitent is marred by thoughts of his dangers as the enemy of God. But reconciliation with God, what a ground for peace of spirit—appropriating all the gracious promises, resting upon them, delighting in them. Then we may be able, by God's grace helping, to attain peace of conscience.

(c) The enjoyment of religious exercises. Piety makes our worship, both public and private, pleasant. In seasons of private prayer and in Scripture reading, truth comes with unwonted clearness and preciousness.

(d) Self-sacrifice for the good of others.

(e) The hope of eternal blessedness.

Let it not be said then that religion would destroy happiness. It confers the highest happiness in life, the only happiness in death and in eternity.—John A. Broadus.

SUNDAY: OCTOBER NINETEENTH

MORNING SERVICE

Topic: Relying on Our Spiritual Resources

TEXT: Phil. 4:13.

The Apostle Paul was either cursed with arrogance, or he was a man endowed with a triumphant faith in the power of God. This is the conclusion to which we must come when we hear him say, "I can do all things through Christ which strengtheneth me."

I. With the exception of the generation that produced the Renaissance, there has never been another generation endowed with as much confidence in itself as ours.

(a) We have boundless faith in our ability to accomplish things. We are unwilling to set any limits to what we can do, nor are we ever satisfied with anything we create. This confidence in ourselves has acted like a generator urging us on and on. So much is this true that we have become boastful. The very moment, however, we leave the material scene we lose this confidence. Here is none of the assurance that helped us to create our present civilization. Here we are not boastful; here we are not certain of ourselves; we are diffident.

(b) We seek to explain this difference by saying that the world of things is the world of reality, whereas the world of spiritual things is a cobweb of filmy dreams. This is a fallacy. Indeed, it is a tragic fallacy. Whatever takes place within us is real. So we come back to this immortal sentence: "I can do all things through Christ which strengtheneth me."

II. The Apostle Paul relied on spiritual resources.

(a) There is nothing vague about these resources. They can be clearly defined. Let us put it this way: One of the most satisfying experiences in life was to have a good family doctor. It was a relief to know that at any time during the day or during the night a call would bring him to your side. He always proved himself more than a healer to the body.

(b) Why cannot our relationship to God be like that? To turn to him not merely in time of extremity but when the sun shines upon the way and when good things are about us in abundance.

III. How do we lay hold upon the resources? Where is the key that unlocks the door?

(a) Why, we hold it in our hands when we pray. Never do we need to know this more than when we feel ourselves drained of confidence to cope with our circumstances. There is something so deep in prayer that few of us have ever fathomed. When prayer becomes the atmosphere in which we live day after day and so becomes a pervading mood, it shapes the pattern of our thoughts and inclines us toward certain actions.

(b) We begin to understand what Paul meant when he said that "we wrestle not against flesh and blood, but with the powers of darkness and the spiritual hosts of wickedness." Prayer becomes energy. It is dynamic. It shifts the scenery amidst which we play out our lives. But prayer not only changes things—that, of course, is what most of us want of prayer. Prayer weaves traits and ideas into the fabric of our character. We sometimes say that Christianity must reveal itself as a practical force in everyday life; it must feed the hungry and bring about social reforms. It must do all of that, but first of all it must change us and link us to the very destiny of God himself.

IV. One of the most sustaining resources in our spiritual adventure is the recognition that we need God.

(a) We need him as a light so that we may see our road. We need him in our thoughts so that they may build the kind of world in which it is good to live.

(b) We need God because we are intellectually inadequate. That should make us humble. We have enough intelligence to fashion wonderful things. We can go far intellectually, but only so far. We can only create so much, and then we must reach out for something we do not possess ourselves.

(c) We have not reached the end of our spiritual resources until we come to know that God needs us. I do not know of any other thought that can give a man such dignity and reason for his existence. God is God, and there is no abridging his power and there is no dimming his wisdom. But in the world of our moods, our joys, and our sorrows, what is it God ever does without you and me? Is there some wrong to be righted? How will he do that without you? Is there some fear to be allayed in a troubled heart? How will he do that without you? God does need us.—Arnold H. Lowe.

Illustrations

IN THE LORD IN THE WORLD.   We need to revise and clarify the opinion we have formed about ourselves, about our position and importance in the world. Not that such things call for expiation, as though they were evil. What they require is to be possessed as though we did not possess them. We should realize that all we have comes from God and exists only for his sake. The approach to this ideal is simple: the cross. We must agree to travel through a tunnel in order that the light given us may really be from God and not from the flesh and provide material for service and thanksgiving rather than for carnal, even though legitimate, enjoyment. Here is the crux of Christian living. It necessitates a second birth—not merely that of baptism that did not cost us much, but that of a genuine "conversion," namely, of a thoroughgoing reappraisal of all the values of our whole life. It cannot be accomplished without the cross, nor without those little sacrifices of which Saint Teresa of Lisieux has given us better understanding. We do not really set out on this way of "self-stripping" of life through death, which is the way of our Lord Jesus, unless we include all those little matters which, in actual fact, keep on the alert our will of belonging not to ourselves but to the Lord (cf. Rom. 6:10–11; 14:18).—Yves Congar.

ANSWERED PRAYER.   George Müller, the founder of an orphanage in Bristol, England, in the last century, relied on God by means of prayer to supply the resources necessary to maintain his orphanage. He did not advertise or plead for money, but the needs were always met. In the year 1844, he recorded this in his journal: "Aug. 6.—Without *one single penny* in my hands the day began. The post brought nothing, nor had I yet received anything, when ten minutes after ten this morning the letter-bag was brought from the Orphan Houses, for the supplies of today.— Now see the Lord's deliverance! In the bag I found a note from one of the laborers in the Orphan Houses, enclosing two sovereigns, which she sent for the Orphans, stating that it was part of a present which she had just received unexpectedly, for herself.—Thus we are supplied for today."

Sermon Suggestions

THE PRESENCE AND POWER OF THE GOSPEL. Text: Col. 1:6. (1) The *presence* of the gospel—in you and in the world. (1) The *power* of the gospel—bearing fruit (Gal. 5:22) and growing. (3) The *purport* of the Gospel—the grace of God in truth.— Edwin C. Dargan.

GOD MAY ANSWER BY NOT ANSWERING. Gospel Text: Luke 18:1–8. (1) God wants to bless us. (2) Circumstances are often against us. (3) We may have to wait patiently though actively. (4) Giving up is the easy way. (5) God may bless us most richly in our waiting.

Worship Aids

CALL TO WORSHIP.   "O come, let us worship and bow down: let us kneel before the Lord our maker. For he is our God; and we are the people of his pasture, and the sheep of his hand" (Ps. 95:6–7).

INVOCATION.   Almighty God, who made the heavens and the earth, we raise our voices in celebration of your creation. When we behold the brilliant colors of autumn and feel the blowing of the winds, we are reminded of your power and strength. When we observe the birds and animals preparing for winter and experience the blessing of rain, we are reminded of your wisdom. When we hear the voices of little children and feel the presence of those who care, we are reminded of your goodness and love. As we gather to worship this hour, we seek your presence and blessing, not because we are deserving but because you are a loving God. We come before you praising your name and expressing our thankfulness in our songs and in our prayers.—Kay M. Byrd.

OFFERTORY SENTENCE. "My God shall supply all your need according to his riches in glory by Christ Jesus" (Phil. 4:19).

OFFERTORY PRAYER. Our Father, we need our daily bread, but we need the bread of heaven more. As you continue to offer us the heavenly manna, may our willingness to share the bread of earth deepen and increase.

PRAYER. We bless thee, our Father, that thou hast made known to us thine existence; that thou hast made known to us the joyful tidings of thy relations to us, and thy feelings; that thou hast called thyself Father, and so assured to us all the blessings of the household in love. We rejoice now without fear; not without regret and sorrow, because our unworth perpetually chides us. Yet so great is thy kindness and thy love, that not all our conscious defect can keep us from joy in the Holy Ghost. Certainty of the future does not lie in our continuance but in the greatness of thy watchful care; in thy faithful mercies; in that redeeming love, stronger than death, by which we have been gathered, and nourished, and instructed, and disciplined, and built up into the holy faith. And our confidence is in thee. In thee, O God! we shall be steadfast. In thee alone are we safe. And now we pray that, standing between the earth and the heaven, the earthly influences that are seductive and ruinous may grow less and less potent with us, and that all celestial influences that lift us high above the senses, and higher every day, may prevail, and that we may become more holy. Grant that the beauty of holiness may be ours.

May our light so shine that it shall seem beautiful to men. May we have this unconscious power. May we be like thee. May we not only go about doing good, and for the sake of doing good, but may our example, all unbeknown to ourselves, lead men to virtue and holiness.—Henry Ward Beecher.

EVENING SERVICE

Topic: The Suffering Servant
TEXT: Isa. 53.

Isaiah's prophecy gives us one of the best descriptions of Christ in his role as redeemer. Nowhere in Scripture is his summary of the Suffering Servant equaled. What do Isaiah's truths say to our contemporary living? Let's probe a bit further to see what his writing yields.

I. Isaiah pictures the *Exalted Servant*.

(a) That the world will hear about the Christ is God's intent and command to his followers. Before men will listen there must be someone to speak an authentic word that gets their attention. God's exalted Son was one who would, in time, move to center stage of history's unfolding drama and claim the spotlight.

(b) But his ascending to center stage is not the ascending of a star—it is the ascending of a Servant. And herein is his uniqueness. And out of it came exaltation, acknowledgement, worship, followers.

II. The most vivid picture Isaiah gives us is the *Rejected Servant*. Isaiah 53 is a masterpiece of literature. But its bitter message is that God's Son is rejected by the very people whom he tried to help. It is not alone a rejection of a moment or a generation—it has characterized the ages.

III. Isaiah also gives us the picture of the *Atoning Servant*.

(a) If there is one truth that surfaces out of Isaiah 53 it is that God has paid our price by his son and purchases atonement for us through his death. And it is all for us, who stand in our sin, without merit and without anything to give.

(b) Atonement for us means that God, through Christ, saw beyond our sin, saw beyond our ugliness, our unlovableness, our rebellion, and died that we might be redeemed, restored, reconciled. Sin had discarded us; it had put the scars of its following on us; the flaws from disobedience were evident. But redemption is God coming to us, in his Son, and touching all the scars and flaws with atoning healing, lifting life to possibility and hope.

IV. The final picture Isaiah gives us is one of triumph—a *Conquering Servant*.

(a) God's plan, from sin's inception, was to bring man back to himself, into fellowship, into redemptive relationship, into freedom, into a reconciled state with the Father. Isaiah's chorus of victory shares with us that suffering has won the day and God has won a mighty victory.

(b) All this—for us—is the message of Isaiah 53. But it is only ours when we invite the Suffering Servant into our arena of agony to be Savior. To turn him aside is to add another chapter to his rejection.—C. Neil Strait.

SUNDAY: OCTOBER TWENTY-SIXTH

MORNING SERVICE

Topic: Saints in Strange Places

TEXT: Phil. 4:22.

This is a very wonderful word. Who are these "saints of Caesar's household"? We may get at the answer if we remember that there was a church at Rome for a considerable period before Paul passed though the gates of the Eternal City and wore the humiliating badges of her sovereignty on his fettered wrists. Our text tells us that it is they who send a message of good cheer to their fellow Christians in Macedonia. If we will but listen they will send a message to us across the gulf of the centuries.

I. The saints of Caesar's household teach us that the Christian life can be lived and a high order of Christian character developed in the midst of unfavourable surroundings.

(a) If genuine religion could flourish at Rome and within range of Caesar's palace, it can flourish anywhere. And yet there were saints in Caesar's household! The gentle river of Christian love flowed from the precincts of imperial lust and tyranny; the flowers of Christian grace decked the sepulchre, breathing fragrance amid scenes of corruption and death.

(b) Circumstances do differ, and some circumstances are more favourable to Christian growth than others. In some families it is a great deal easier than in others to maintain a healthy spirituality. Instead of deploring our surroundings and assuring ourselves that our failure comes from the lack of opportunity, if we were to make the best use of what we have and bend our forces to changing evil into good we should make such spiritual progress as we never dreamed of making. If we were so minded we might use some of the most unlikely things in the formation of a noble character.

II. The saints of Caesar's household remind us that the Christian life can be lived and loyalty to Christ maintained in the face of persecution.

(a) It is highly probable that Paul was tried by Nero in person. It meant something to be a Christian in Rome when the Church was young and yet there were Christians in Rome—yea, in the household of Nero himself.

(b) Christ foresaw that his followers would have to go through persecution and suffering if they were to be loyal to his truth. When he opened his lips on the mountain, he said, "Bless'd are they which are persecuted for righteousness' sake for theirs is the kingdom of heaven." How deep and high is the optimism that lies behind these words! What insight had this teacher who could emphasize the pains and penalties of discipleship and could yet see the glorious issue of it all. Wherever the fires of hatred have burned against the truth, they have purified it always, but defeated it never.

(c) And how often that stone has been hurled by those who should have known better. Men professing to be religious have persecuted and reviled and said all manner of evil aginst those who could not pronounce the same religious formula as themselves. They have burned heretics and anathematized men of science, and written slanders against humble seekers after truth. The history of the Church is red with the blood of men who were driven to death by the bigotry and intolerance of those who have professed the name of the generous Jesus.

III. The saints of Caesar's household proclaim the reality of Christian communion.

(a) They send a message of greeting to their fellow Christians in Philippi, whom not having seen they loved because of their common faith in Jesus Christ. In drawing them into fellowship with himself Jesus drew them into fellowship with all the saints of God. Faces set alike toward heaven, and hearts set alike in the things of the kingdom, insure an increasing fellowship and love. When saints fall asunder and become alienated from one another it is not because they are Christian; it is because they are so imperfect in their Christian character. It is because they are so imperfectly developed that the disciples of Jesus are led to entertain ill feelings toward one another.

(b) How slow the Church has been in learning this lesson! That company of early Christians that amazed the Roman Empire by meeting the fury of hate with a new kind of love puts us to shame. Of the failures of the Church none has been as tragic as its failure in fellowship. They were poor and few and weak, but they set themselves undismayed to challenge the might and wealth and sin of imperial Rome. They succeeded because they knew the value of fellowship.

(c) I like to remember that these saints that sent that message across the sea to Philippi and though dead are still speaking to us, belonged to the humbler walks of life. The saints of Caesar's household were of the plain heroic breed. Their names are known alone to God. Yet they are one with us, for the unity of the Church has never been broken. Here is an apostolic succession indeed! Here is the communion of saints!—W. A. Cameron.

Illustrations

FROM WEAKNESS TO STRENGTH. One of the most notable interviews I have had in the last twelve months was the case of a man who found himself facing the greatest opportunity of his career. Should he not succeed, his failure would be spectacular and irretrievable. There was no apparent reason why he should fail. I said that there was no "apparent" reason. Deep down in his heart, however, this man knew that success was impossible, not because he lacked ability, but an inner weakness made him a lion shorn of his strength. Some day all men would know his dreadful secret. In desperation he sought help. Like a great light breaking upon his darkness came the word of God. "My grace is sufficient for thee, for my strength is made perfect in weakness." Day by day rejoicing in a strength greater than his own, he would say: "When I am weak, then I am strong." What had been an appalling weakness in his life now became the point of firmest resistance.—John Sutherland Bonnell.

A SECRET CHEMISTRY. There is no flower more beautiful than the white pond lily. It is firmly rooted in the mud and slime at the bottom of the pond, but it rises above its origin like a white robed angel and is so superior to its environment that we wonder concerning the magic with which it appears to be endowed. If you were to look at the seed and were to examine its offensive surroundings you would declare that such a product from such a habitation would be impossible. But by a secret chemistry beyond the reach of our understanding it extracts from the discouraging mud a very miracle of beauty. It has a distinct and lofty purpose in view, uses whatever will aid it in the accomplishment of that purpose, and unerringly rejects all else.—W. A. Cameron.

Sermon Suggestions

A MYSTERY BECOMES A REVELATION. Text: Col. 1:27. (1) The excellence of the gospel—gloriously rich. (2) The extent of the gospel—not for Jews alone, but for all. a. "Christ in you"—by faith, love, obedience. b. "The hope of glory"—of personal excellence, blissful surroundings, triumphant truth.—Edwin C. Dargan.

MISUNDERSTANDING GOD.   Gospel Text: Luke 18:9–14. (1) We may be too proud of ourselves to understand God. (2) We may be too despairing of ourselves to understand God. (3) However, it is those who cast themselves utterly on God's mercy who come to understand him and his ways with us.

Worship Aids

CALL TO WORSHIP.   "Let us, then, always offer praise to God as our sacrifice through Jesus, which is the offering presented by lips that confess him as Lord" (Heb. 13:15 TEV).

INVOCATION.   O God, we belong to you, and you care for us. As we contemplate your goodness, our hearts well up and overflow with praise. Accept our worship, as we seek to worship you in spirit and in truth.

OFFERTORY SENTENCE.   "They shall not appear before the Lord empty-handed; every man shall give as he is able, according to the blessing of the Lord your God which he has given you" (Deut. 16:16–17 RSV).

OFFERTORY PRAYER.   Gracious Lord, we would appear before you either with empty hands or empty lives, yet however much we give seems too little in view of the amazing gift of your Son. Forgive us the stinginess of life and possessions, for the sake of him who loved us and gave himself for us all.

PRAYER.   Our Father, we thank thee for all thy people who have gone before us and have taught us by noble example, and we thank thee even for those whose bad example has warned us. May neither example and its lesson be wasted on us. Whatever suffering they have known in life, whether through their own folly or through their faithfulness, may they not have lived in vain. Through thy grace, spare us the pain and dishonor to ourselves, to others, and to thee, that a self-centered life would bring. Help us to find the abundant life and share it with others and so bring glory, praise, and honor to thy holy name.

EVENING SERVICE

Topic: Cultivating Solitude
TEXT: Ps. 46:10.

"Be still and know that I am God." Jesus calls us from our loneliness and busyness to his solitude and peace. We do not need to nurture silence and solitude. We do need periodically throughout the day to be still and know that he is God.

I. We live in a noisy world, and the noise can get to us after awhile. This can be a prelude to real problems. Fatigue can be a warning sign. Jesus, too, was "wearied," the Scripture tells us. We may experience the loss of perspective. When minutia and mole hills are blown up into mountains, we lose our sense of perspective. We become easily annoyed or ready to explode at the drop of a pin.

II. Life, even in the midst of noise, can get terribly lonely. It's possible to be lonely in a crowd, to be lonely at a party, to be lonely while surrounded by friends and even family members.

(a) Loneliness is something universal. It cuts across all age groups. It cuts across all socioeconomic groupings. Success is lonely. Pain is lonely. Leadership is lonely. We experience loneliness in the midst of our busyness and noise.

(b) Loneliness is inner emptiness, but solitude is inner fulfillment—silence, peace, contentment. Jesus is our example. Look at him in his ultimate solitude. It was called Gethsemane, that beautiful little olive grove with its ancient trees. Jesus, in the midst of busyness and the worst loneliness any man has ever experienced, had contentment. He found a solitude of Gethsemane that gave him an inner peace and that he would later bequeath to his disciples, including us.

III. Let me suggest some steps toward solitude. There are times when we need to turn aside, to step back, to stand apart, to get out of the stream, stand on the bank, and measure the flow.

(a) Focus first on nature, the beauty of spring flowers, the brilliance of sunlight after the rain. Center down for a time on the world about you. Drink in its beauty. Become at one with nature, the beauty of the world our Father has made.

(b) Then center for a moment on yourself, getting in touch with your own humanity, confessing your sins, receiving the Father's pardon, learning to value yourself as someone who is made in the image of the Creator. God made you. You're significant. You're unlike anyone else in all the earth. You have worth, importance to God.

(c) Now focus for a moment on God. Put both feet flat on the floor and lay your hands on your lap, palms upward; then take three deep breaths and relax. Now concentrate on the majesty of God.

(d) Focus on the beauty of nature. Focus on yourself. Focus on God. Focus on other people. No one is an island. All about us there are people bearing burdens and hurts. There are those who need our word of encouragement.—Alton H. McEachern.

SUNDAY: NOVEMBER SECOND

MORNING SERVICE

Topic: Round About by Way of the Wilderness

TEXT: Exod. 13:17, 18.

I. A straight line is the shortest line between two points; but it's not always the best road to travel!

(a) In the old days, when you left New England, or Virginia, or some other state along the Atlantic seaboard for the West, as so many of our ancestors did, you took a horse or two and a covered wagon and followed the river beds, skirting the mountains, winding in and out as the land lay. It took you months to make the trip, but you learned a good deal en route. You overcame many hardships and weathered many privations. When you arrived, if you did arrive, you weren't just the same person who set out: You had been equipped by the journey itself and hardened into some sort of fitness for your new life on the prairies.

(b) Today, you step into an airplane. You follow a much straighter line. You fly as the crow flies, and it takes you only a few hours. But the trip does you no good! You're just as feeble-minded in Los Angeles when you get out as you were in New York when you got in; no more, no less. You've saved time and covered ground; but what of it? You haven't added anything much to your fund of usable experience. Other things being equal, you'd be just as well off if you were back where you started!

(c) Now the fact is, of course, that these

Israelites simply weren't ready for the Promised Land. If they had been led there promptly and directly, they would have been slaves still, precisely as they were when they came out of Egypt. And between a slave by the Jordan and a slave by the Nile, there wasn't much choice. What they needed was time in which to become a nation. The shortest road was not for them the best; there was no use traveling it. There was more, much more to be had round about through the way of the wilderness. Some day, when they arrived, they'd be fit.

II. It's a necessity with which we are often faced, this business of going around.

(a) Anybody who has ever lived close to life will tell you that trying to save time by taking shortcuts is one of the most perilous things folk do. It's the distilled wisdom of a good many ages that keeps warning us against this too great eagerness of ours to get somewhere without being very careful to fill up the spaces in between! There is a sort of immediacy about the American character that only succeeds in turning most of us into mushrooms that spring up overnight, when we were really intended to be oaks!

(b) Shall we keep holding this in view then, as one of the simple, profound truths that help to shape all human destiny? Jesus came face to face with it in his own person, as he stood yonder on the threshold of his ministry, and a voice whispered: "Cast thyself down; for it is written, he shall give his angels charge concerning thee; in their hands shall they bear thee up, lest at any time thou dash thy foot against a stone." There was the dark and sinister suggestion that he get on with it: to clutch all his faith in his hands and with one wild hazard show the crowds loitering in the temple courts what mighty things this God could do! To win them at a stroke, without the years and the pain, and the dust, and the cross at the end! But he kept shaking his head and looking distantly into the future, his lips moving quietly: "Not near! Not near! Round about through the way of the wilderness!'

III. I wonder if that has anything to say to you and me here today? There are experiences aplenty that are quite like the desert. I wonder if they are God's way round?

(a) I suppose that nobody has been having exactly a smooth time of it lately, though I hope we aren't exaggerating the roughness. That would be just blind folly and ingratitude, to magnify a few normal difficulties and a little average hardship, and call the sum of it a desert, when really it was nothing more than a cross-country hike! But we have known something of life's apparent sternness, haven't we? How carelessly it seems to narrow us down sometimes and take things away that we thought quite necessary. The income we used to have is the least of it. Maybe it's the health we had, or the hope we had, or even some love we had. And it's gone now. And the road is lonelier and there hardly seems to be anything much worth having anywhere on the horizon.

(b) It's the postponements we seem unable to bear: that we should have to wait for marriage and friendship, for experience and success, and whatever plan God has; that we should have to wait for everything to ripen as he wants it. Would it save us anything, do you think, to remember then that maybe after all it's God's road we're on, and as often as not that road is long and by the way of the wilderness.

IV. You won't misunderstand me, will you? It isn't any mood of contentment I've been commending to you: that a man should settle down with a sigh in this wretched world, or in the midst of his own failures, and do nothing but wait. That's a silly caricature of the truth. I am just hoping against hope that some of us may learn to wait better while we work!

(a) Because that's the only way to the kind of victory that God meant for human souls to have! Not the kind you are after necessarily. The kind he's after! There are in the Bible no foolish promises for faithful people, halfway along some unwise course they have chosen for themselves, that things will turn out at last as they had planned.

(b) It may just be that you and I are in this world, not so much to achieve something as to be something; and by that means, not another, to help bring the kingdom of God among men. I am not amazed at the time that takes. Being something always does take time; and tears, they may be a part of it; and broken hopes, and bitter delays. But surely, it is not these things that matter. What matters is the stature of the soul that comes through them.—Paul Scherer.

Illustrations

LOVE'S SLOW WISDOM.   There is a touching story of a simple Christian in America at the time of the American Revolution, named Peter Miller. This good man had one enemy, who hated him so bitterly that he once went so far as to spit in his face. Miller bore this insult quietly and without any attempt to take revenge. Later, when the war with Britain began, Miller's enemy took the British side and was said to have acted as a spy for the British. He was caught and sentenced to be hanged. Miller went to General Washington and begged him to spare the life of the condemned man. Washington replied that in such times it was necessary to deal most severely with spies and traitors. "Otherwise," he added, "I should cheerfully release your friend." "Friend!" replied Miller, "he is the only enemy I have." Washington was so deeply impressed that he signed a pardon, and Miller arrived just in time to save his enemy.—Stephen C. Neill.

PLAYING TO WIN.   Dr. Hutton, editor of the *British Weekly*, tells us that on the golf links at St. Andrew's the higher grade of caddie is something of a dictator. He hands you the proper club, gives you the direction, and then awaits in silence the event. One day a stranger, unacquainted with this delightful tyranny, reached the tee for a dog-leg hole, which had to be negotiated circuitously. The caddie handed him a club, and said, "You play on that tar-roofed shed, away there to the left." "Would it not be better," objected the stranger, "to go straight for it?" To which the caddie retorted, "You may play in any direction you like; I was only suggesting how to play in order to win the hole."—Paul Scherer.

Sermon Suggestions

A TRILOGY OF CONSOLATION.   Text: Col. 2:2. (1) Mutual love. (2) Intelligent faith. (3) Growing knowledge.—Edwin C. Dargan.

FROM THE SYCAMORE TREE TO THE TREE OF LIFE.   Gospel Text: Luke 19:1–10. (1) A detested men. (2) A determined man. (3) A delivered man.

Worship Aids

CALL TO WORSHIP.   "Trust in the Lord with all thine heart; and lean not unto thine own understanding. In all thy ways acknowledge him, and he shall direct thy paths" (Prov. 3:5–6).

INVOCATION.   Because of our lack of faith and commitment, O God, we are like wandering sheep. We need thy guidance. Help us to seek, above all, thy kingdom and thy righteousness, so that everything in time will fall into its proper place and our lives will glorify thee.

OFFERTORY SENTENCE.   "With a freewill offering I will sacrifice to thee; I will give thanks to thy name, O Lord, for it is good" (Ps. 54:6).

OFFERTORY PRAYER.   How can we fittingly thank you, Lord, for burdens lifted, suffering assuaged, sins forgiven, life renewed, differences reconciled, and hopes restored? We bring to you now a token of our gratitude and love, and we pray that because of what we do others also may know your goodness.

PRAYER.   Heavenly Father, from your vantage point of eternity look afresh into our time—this time—time that you have given to us. You have come into our lives with your love. We have learned to love from that invasion—that incarnation. You know all about us—you know us better than we know ourselves. Teach us to be perceptive and thereby sympathetic with one another. Forgive us, Father, for our waste of time and opportunity. Forgive us the facades of hypocrisy, the masks of pretense. Help us to be honest with ourselves and with one another. We love you, Father, because you first loved us. We love one another and pray for one another. Some of our family suffer, Lord. Free them from their discomfort. Some of us are anxious, Lord. Calm our fears and strengthen our faith. Some of us are in the sorrow of bereavement. Send your Spirit of comfort. How grateful we are, Father, for this good day and this opportunity to celebrate your sovereignty as your servants.—J. Estill Jones.

EVENING SERVICE

Topic: The Fool Hath Said "There Is No God"
TEXT: Ps. 14:1.
I. *The fool.* If you will read Psalm 14 and Psalm 53, you will find that the Scripture, as all literature, pays great attention to the word *fool.* The fool has said in his or her heart there is no God, no meaning, no consequence, no significance. There is nothing.
(a) *God's fool.* Now this is the mastery of foolishness—to make the fool in us God's fool, not the world's fool. My goal is to persuade you to surrender that folly in your life to the creative power of God rather than to have you succumb to the temptations of the world and become the world's fool.
(b) *The atheist-fool.* There is no believer like an atheist. The atheist believes there is no God. He cannot prove it anymore than I can. He believes it in the face of a beautiful day like today. The majesty of

history and the pain of humanity that brought music, art, and architecture as well as order, democracy, hope, and gallantry. He wipes them all out. He says, "There is no God." What presumptive evidence. It is a gambler's choice.

(c) *The agnostic fool.* An agnostic says, in the comfort of his club, "I don't know." What does he mean, "He doesn't know"? He means, "I do not believe that it is possible to know." That is all he is saying. More church people are probaby apathetic, have no feeling. What they say is, "I believe, but I do not feel. I do not care to feel. I do not believe that there is feeling, so therefore, I pull the drapery of life around me and shield my soul and believe I can make my own meaning out of my years as I go through."

II. *Challenging the fool.* When you deal with your friends who say jocularly over a drink, "I am an atheist," try saying to them, "You believe more than I do! You believe in your presumptive humanity that you can take this glorious history and this marvelous universe and say with egocentricity, 'There is no God.' You have no proof." My friends, I do not believe anyone is a sincere atheist. I believe he or she is more "anti-theist" and should be challenged then to fight the God idea, to work against God. Then you will not be so apathetic in your response because the interaction in life and spirit will be a strong one. Anti-theism means that we frustrate the movement of God's spirit within us.

III. *What we know about God.* I have to say, as we move ahead, that coming to clarity about God is understanding that he is beyond our full knowing. We know only in part. We can only respond to the signals that we have, and in that response there is the honesty and existential quality of every modern young man or woman.

(a) *The fantasy of God.* The God most men and women say that they do not believe in doesn't exist! The God that men and women tell me all week long that they do not believe in, the kind of God they describe that they do not believe in, does not exist. Their description is a child's fantasy. The Eternal Creator, who loves and hopes and yearns and struggles and gave his only begotten son in human form that

we might get a handle on it, patiently deals with us in all kinds of ways. But, we blank him out with our prejudicial, limited, false pictures of God.

(b) *The revelation of God.* You know, if you ever met God face to face, you would be scared stiff. That is why God always comes incognito, quietly at Christmas in a stable or with dirty sandal feet at Easter's pilgrimage to a bloody old cross, like a common criminal to a borrowed grave, in little churches across the world, in faithful men and women here. God brings it down to size so that you can handle it and waits for you to come to the point where you can say, "Oh my God, how great thou art!"

God has chosen the foolish things of the world to reveal himself so that no man or woman should be proud before him. Therefore, I urge you to acknowledge in humility the fool in each of us. We stand amazed before God. We acknowledge God in order that we may believe life. We believe without knowing. You believe in order to act. We act in order to confirm and to understand.

IV. *The shadow of the fool.*

(a) I was thinking of all things we take for granted. Breathe deeply for a moment. Oxygen. Where do you get it? Light? Food comes out of the chemistry of the mud. The nuclear fire of all the basic elements. Gravity. Think what would happen to an airplane if they pulled gravity out. We would be lost in space. Explain gravity to me or magnetism, light, oxygen, food, water, fire, or love, faith, hope, joy, and peace! All these basic assumptions sustain our daily lives, but the fool rattles his little bell and says, "I do not believe there is a God." More truly, it should be said, "I am agnostic to God, the creator, supplier, master of my life. I will be the master of my own fate." And God says, "Thou fool, you shall die," and every mortal knows this shadow.

(b) Acknowledge the mystery of God. You believe in order to find God. You probe. You knock. You look. You seek. You ask. You walk. You stumble. You fall and get up. The Lord loves you and keeps you on your way.

(c) The final act of coming to God is the clarification of commitment, which simply means you surrender your innermost fool, the ambiguity, the dark side of human nature, and you let him take charge of it. You allow a new attitude to come, a new scale of values. You take concrete steps to come nearer God. "Draw near to God and he will draw nearer to you." Run away from God, and he will appear to run away from you. It is a reciprocal responsiveness.— Bryant M. Kirkland.

SUNDAY: NOVEMBER NINTH

MORNING SERVICE

Topic: Blessed Are the Immature

TEXT: Eccl. 1:1–9; Eph. 4:11–16, RSV; Luke 18:15–17, NEB.

The disciples were mature men, and they didn't like what they saw. Jesus was on his way to Jerusalem where there was bound to be a showdown with the religious and political authorities. This was what they would say was "men's business" calling for careful planning, profound discussion, and mature and experienced judgment. And now here was Jesus held up by a mob of women with babies and toddlers. They had not the slightest idea of the great issues that would be raised in Jerusalem. All they wanted was for Jesus to stretch out his hand and touch their children. Ignorance; superstition; kid's stuff—that's what it was. So "they rebuked them." And Jesus rebuked the rebukers. It is one of those moments when we find Jesus at odds with his disciples. That's why I find it challenging today. Don't we claim to be his disciples? Are we sure that we understand him much better than the twelve who were with him then? Hadn't they left their own homes and their children because of the urgency of Jesus' call? And now Jesus was angry because they were clearing the way for him. Whose side are you on?

I. "Blessed are the immature." Is this what Jesus is saying? Yes, I believe it is— but not if by "immature" we mean those who refuse to grow up, those who act like infants when they are teenagers, or like teenagers when they are middle-aged.

(a) This sermon is not designed to encourage those who are dodging their responsibilities as adults by childish behavior. I have come to believe that much of the art of discipleship lies in growing into the childlike spirit and growing out of the childish.

(b) It is when I contemplate the way in which maturity is being defined in our modern society that I want to rise and shout: "Blessed are the immature!" For increasingly the maturity that is being commended to us in our culture is nothing other than a cynicism, a sophistication, an attitude of "you can't change my mind; you can't win me over to any cause; I've seen it all before." It is assumed that to be mature one must reject all ideals, scorn the expression of emotion, be skeptical about moral standards and grandly aloof from religion.

(c) Maturity in a secularist society means little more than an adjustment to the prevailing atmosphere of cynicism and distrust. It has become a mark of maturity to expect the worst from our neighbors, to stand aloof from any religious or political engagement, and to criticize any kind of enthusiasm. "The kingdom of God belongs to such as these," says Jesus—all, whatever their station in life, who greet each day with a childlike vision, trust, and hope.

II. The Bible rings with this response to the grace of God, and the figure of Jesus rises from its pages as the embodiment of the childlike spirit.

(a) The passage just before our text in Matthew's Gospel is the story about the Pharisee and the publican at prayer. Here is the mature religious man. He has reached his moral goals: "I am not as other men are, extortioners, unjust, adulterers, or even as this publican." And here with his face to the ground is the tax collector with the grace to recognize that religiously and morally he is destitute: "God be merciful to me a sinner." An immature prayer? Yes, and that's why we never get beyond it in our earthly passage.

(b) We heard this morning from the writer of the Book of Ecclesiastes. I think God let this book slip into the canon to remind us of what life looks like to a man who has settled into the genial cynicism of religious old age. He has seen it all. "Remember now thy creator in the days of thy youth" he says at the end of his book, but someone might have reminded him that it's not a bad thing to remember him in old age, as the years close in, and catch the infection of the creative Spirit of God, the "light that shines more and more unto the perfect day."

(c) What a difference when we hear from Saint Paul rejoicing in the new perspective of those who have met the risen Christ and had their horizons lifted to the dimension of eternal life. All cynicism, all spiritual fatigue, all loss of hope is swallowed up in the vision of the Christian community pressing on to that distant and magnetic goal, the maturity that awaits us in heaven.

III. "Blessed are the immature." Nothing is more paralyzing for a Christian or a Christian church than the belief that we are already mature—or as mature as we believe we can ever be.

(a) The mature Christian is the one who knows that he or she is still immature. Paul was not the only apostle to understand this truth. What does Peter say to the churches that were mature enough to listen to his letters? "As newborn babes," he wrote, "desire the sincere milk of the word that ye may grow thereby."

(b) Are we growing? Or have we settled down to the kind of maturity we thought we reached some years ago? Have we kept alive the thought of a heavenly maturity that beckons us on no matter what age we are, or have we been infected with the cynicism that blows from the closed world of a secularized society? To the childlike spirit God offers the nourishment that keeps us growing—the Word of life that reaches us through Scripture, the private and the common prayers through which this new life flows, the invigoration of worship in spirit and in truth, and these sacred symbols of the Body and Blood of him who said: "Blessed are those who know their need of God; the kingdom of heaven is theirs." —David H. C. Read.

Illustrations

CHILDLIKE FAITH.   I shall not soon forget hearing that lovely young girl from one of our college campuses, a summer missionary to Hawaii. As she stood early in the morning to read the morning watch, she told us of an old lady who was constantly talking about her confidence in Christ, her assurance that she was held in the hand of Christ until, one morning, a cynic said to her, "Suppose Christ should let you slip through his hand?" And she smilingly said, "But that could never be for I am a part of his hand."—Charles A. Trentham.

THE SIN OF PRIDE.   The Greeks feared above all things the state of mind they called *hubris*—the inflated spirits that come with too much success. Overweening in men called forth, they thought, the envy of the gods. Their theology may seem to us a little unworthy, but with the phenomenon itself and its effects they were only too well acquainted. Christianity, with a more rational theology, traces hubris back to the root sin of pride, which places man instead of God at the center of gravity and so throws the whole structure of things into the ruin called judgment. Whenever we say, whether in the personal, political, or social sphere, "I am the master of my fate; I am the captain of my soul," we are committing the sin of pride; and the higher the goal at which we aim, the more far-reaching will be the subsequent disaster.—Dorothy L. Sayers.

Sermon Suggestions

UNION WITH CHRIST.   Text: Col. 2:19. (1) Nourishment supplied. (2) Strength imparted. (3) Increase made.—Edwin C. Dargan.

EQUAL TO ANGELS.   Gospel Text: Luke 20:27–38. (1) All of us wonder about the life to come. (2) The future life will be different from this life. (3) God will be the same, and the difference will be glorious.

Worship Aids

CALL TO WORSHIP. "Grace be unto you, and peace, from God our Father, and from the Lord Jesus Christ" (Phil. 1:2).

INVOCATION. O God, whose blessed Son came into the world that he might destroy the works of the devil and make us children of God and heirs of eternal life: Grant that, having this hope, we may purify ourselves as he is pure; that, when he comes again with power and great glory, we may be made like him in his eternal and glorious kingdom, where he lives and reigns with you and the Holy Spirit, one God, forever and ever.—*Book of Common Prayer*.

OFFERTORY SENTENCE. "Thine, O Lord, is the greatness, and the power, and the glory, and the victory, and the majesty: for all that is in the heaven and in the earth is thine; thine is the kingdom, O Lord, and thou art exalted as head above all" (1 Chron. 29:11).

OFFERTORY PRAYER. Exalted Lord, gracious Lord, loving Lord, we belong to you and all that we claim as our own is truly yours. Grant that by our knowing this we may give good account of our stewardship.

PRAYER. Our Father, for so Jesus taught us to address you, we thank you for your love—not limited to a group of men long ago, not confined to our fathers and our mothers, not even restricted to those of us who gather here. Your love, Father, extends to men and women, both young and old, to boys and girls—children who are dependent and teenagers who are trying desperately to grow up. We thank you that you have loved us and our families. We love you, Father, with all our heart, with all our soul, with all our strength, and with all our mind. Help us to use heart and soul and strength and mind for your glory. They are all yours—by your gift of life and by our stewardship of them. Help us, Father, to love one another—the older and the assured, perhaps dogmatic; the younger and the immature, perhaps frivo-lous; the insecure and lonely, perhaps clinging vines; the suffering and the sorrowing, perhaps unattractive; the confident and the certain, perhaps contemptuous. Our love for you, beloved by you, draws us together; our loyalty to your cause binds us together. Help us to help one another, for Jesus' sake. Grant your Spirit to those who grieve, your healing to those who suffer, your presence to those who are distressed. We subject ourselves afresh to your Spirit and ask your cleansing from our sin. Set us apart for your service, Father, separate us from anything that separates us from you.—J. Estill Jones.

EVENING SERVICE

Topic: A Message Without Frills

TEXT: Ps. 130:1–8; 1 Cor. 7:20–23; Mark 1:14–20.

I. We sometimes think it would be romantic to live in Jesus' day when he was molding disciples and founding the church. But that was no picnic. And we who have a difficult task before us need to remember that.

(a) The Jews were under Rome's thumb and Israel was looking for someone—anyone—to deliver them. Desperation breeds opportunists and there were dozens of prophets vying for Messianic privileges.

(b) John the Baptist was in prison for pointing his finger at King Herod for seducing his brother's wife and making her his own wife after he had put away the wife he already had. Jesus had to begin his ministry having been recommended by a man who was now in prison. In terms of political preaching, this was a no-frills time.

(c) It was not a very "up" time to begin a ministry. But Jesus did it. He came proclaiming good news, the kingdom of God, which means the rule of God is at hand, he announced. Another way to put that is: "What God's rule in a human life looks like can be seen in me. Look at it. It is at hand!" The bad news was that the folks needed to turn away from their sins. And that was no time for repentance either.

(d) "We aren't free, we're a repressed people, we're unfulfilled and you want us to give up all our sins, too? Come, Jesus, this is the wrong time to be asking." You see what I mean? We stand squarely in the midst of a Christian history that is no stranger to hard times. The founder of it all started "good news" in a no-frills time.

II. But there is an initiative to be taken by us because an initiative has already been taken toward us. The good news of the gospel is given before the request for repentance. The kingdom is here. Turn and receive it. It is not the other way around. We have tended to make it so. We have tended to say shape up and God will love you, you can then be his, you will then receive his grace. That's not the way it is.

(a) It is just the other way around. When you know the love and acceptance of God, then you turn not because you have to under threat of punishment but because you want to under promise of power. God with his grace takes the initiative. We respond to the good news and then take the initiative to make that good news, in its thousands of facets, available to all who are in God's world.

(b) What I've just said is basic to why we raise money here. Don't forget it or siphon it off into a practicality that forgets its reason for being. Stewardship and financial campaigns are often trivialized because they get too far removed from their biblical and theological base. Remembering who took the initiative first and the call that resulted and the answer that evolved are vital when we take our pen in hand to sign that pledge card.

III. There is a story to be told. Not all the Body of Christ tells it in the same way. Every church tends to believe it has a bit more of the truth, perhaps. But the medium is the message. The way the story is told is the story.

(a) We tell the story to and for all persons here: black, white, male, female, young, old, rich, poor, well-fed, hungry; peaceful and confused, lazy and workaholic, despaired and hope-filled. The church of Jesus Christ in this place is open to all.

(b) It is a story of hope, that no matter how sinful we have been or are, regardless of our crimes and failures, there is forgiveness and care given here. It is a story of power, that all of us have within us powers we have not yet touched and can handle that power with our hands when we model after the Christ. It is a story of faith, that we who are the wounded can become healers. It is a story of mission, that beyond these walls there are hungers and needs that would overwhelm us if we walked out into them on the front porch today.

IV. The ten percent has lost favor with many. It's been loaded with "have to's" and guilt and a host of other invalid reasons for giving.

(a) We make no promises about accrued blessings or increased profits or anything else with that story. I still believe that voluntarism is the only way to be responsible stewards and that when we understand our history, the story to be told, the initiative God has taken, we will give "as God has prospered us."

(b) But there are those in our midst who think they don't count. Their mite, their pledge, their giving can't possibly make that much difference. One person, one pledge, one gift is vital.

(c) It all started with a no-frills message: The kingdom of God is at hand, turn and receive it. Now it has evolved into a history no stranger to hard times, a purpose for giving, a story to be told, an initiative to be taken. Remember that when you are called on to pledge. Remember.—Thomas H. Conley.

SUNDAY: NOVEMBER SIXTEENTH

MORNING SERVICE

Topic: It All Begins in Your Head
Text: Exod. 20:17.

I. *As a man thinketh in his heart so is he.*

(a) This commandment recognizes the titanic truth that for you all good and bad begins in your head. Your life will be a success or a failure in direct proportion to that which you desire.

(b) What does "covet" mean? It means to desire earnestly. Now it is an amoral word. It does not say that it is a bad thing to covet. Paul tells the Corinthian Christians to covet the best gifts. In the Sermon on the Mount Jesus said: "Blessed are they which do hunger and thirst after righteousness for they shall be filled" (Matt. 5:7, KJV).

II. *Coveting the right standing with God.*

(a) When our Lord tells us to be contented with what we have, he is simply warning us not to let life's furniture make a fool of us. He is not telling us not to do better.

(b) It is not coveting or desiring earnestly that is forbidden here. What is expressly forbidden is desiring earnestly your neighbor's property or his wife, or her husband.

(c) As Jesus applies this principle to Christian living, he goes deeper. He combines our desires for things with the First Commandment—thou shalt have no other gods before me. In so doing, he warns that desiring things more than desiring right standing with God is one of life's largest blunders.

III. *Man's worth is not measured in dollars.*

(a) In a society like ours, when we talk of standards of living, it means nothing about standards or living. When we talk about how much a man is worth and speak of only how much he has, then there is the danger of the acquiring of money and its derivatives becoming the consuming passion of the best days of life. This is a sin.

(b) We need to pay heed to what Jesus said about Christian principles of possessing. They are found in Matthew 6:19–21: "Lay not up for yourselves treasures upon earth, where moth and rust doth corrupt, and where thieves break through and steal: But lay up for yourselves treasures in heaven, where neither moth nor rust doth corrupt, and where thieves do not break through nor steal: For where your treasure is, there will your heart be also" (KJV).

IV. *Three principles of possession.*

(a) *Temporary holdings do not constitute real riches.* That which can be lost is not really owned. Even to the rich the grave brings bankruptcy. Here our Lord says, "Because I love you I do not want you to spend your short but valuable lives piling up temporary treasure. Haven't you lived long

enough to learn that just about the time a man says, 'I've got it made,' time runs out on him? Don't you know that life's treasures are always being eaten by the moths of depreciation, wasted by the rust of inflation, and stolen by the thousand and one varieties of thieves that inhabit this earth. Temporary holdings do not constitute real riches."

(b) *Eternal investment is wisest,* "but lay up for yourselves treasures in heaven." God wants us to possess. He wants us to have, but he wants us to have the best. Hear him say, "If you keep your fortune on earth, you have made a fortune and stored it in a place where you cannot hold it. Make your fortune, but store it in a place where you can keep it. Invest it in the kingdom of God and let it draw interest compounded throughout eternity." Is money that important? Why all this musing about so mundane a matter as money?

(c) *We always look after our investments.* "For where your treasure is there will your heart be also." Your treasure is not of the greatest importance, but what it does to your heart is important. This is why the love of money is called the root of all kinds of evil. It can pull you down to a low level and change your life to a frustration of temporariness where your every desire, every move, every joy is directly related to the condition of your bank account or the stock market. But if invested in heaven, it can anchor your soul. Fix your attention on the eternal and keep your heart in the condition God wants it, and it will give you peace and happiness.

V. *Covetousness leads to sin.* Covetousness will lead you down an unhappy trail. It leads to a decaying of character. If the supreme desire of your life is just to get things, especially things that others have, then it will lead you to become a liar, it will lead you to adultery, it will lead you to theft. It destroys the opportunity for life's best. I guess the greatest problem of all is that if you want only material things, you sink to the level of things, and you miss so much of what it means to be made in the image of God.

VI. *Overcoming covetousness.* Our Lord reminds us that it is never enough just to drive the thought out. You must put in a positive one. You don't say, I'm not going to think about it, or you are going to be thinking about it.

VII. *Contentment in Jesus Christ.*

(a) The Apostle Paul was an extremely ambitious man. Yet he's the one who later made the statement "I have learned to be content in whatever state I have found myself."

(b) The greatest problem with the things of this world is that they crowd God out of your life. Jesus said in the Sermon on the Mount, "No man can serve two masters, you cannot serve God and mammon."—Frank Pollard.

Illustrations

ACQUISITIVENESS. It was taught in the name of Rabbi Meir: When man enters this world his fists are clenched tight, as if to say: "The world is mine. I shall soon hold it all within the grasp of my hand." When he leaves this world, his palms are wide open, as if to declare: "I have not inherited a thing from the world."—William B. Silverman.

FOR THE SAKE OF OTHERS. We may understand very little about the meaning of Jesus Christ, but at least this much we know: A human life has been lived on this earth that no longer centers in or revolves about its own self but gives itself away for the sake of others. If we live in this atmosphere even slightly, then a desire that would ruin the life of my wife or my children can never be right under any circumstances. Or how could I hoard money or possessions until I had completely dispossessed and destroyed others? Or how could I still let myself be so enslaved to good food or drink that nothing else could compete?—Eduard Schweizer.

Sermon Suggestions

SEEKING THE THINGS ABOVE. Text: Col. 3:3. (1) Complete separation, as by death, from worldly things. (2) New life in Christ stored up; not yet in full view.—Edwin C. Dargan.

TRIBULATION TIME. Gospel Text: Luke 21:5–19. (1) The problems described (vv. 5–17). (2) The Protector implied (v. 18). (3) The perseverance required.

Worship Aids

CALL TO WORSHIP. "We have not a high priest who is unable to sympathize with our weaknesses, but one who in every respect has been tempted as we are, yet without sin" (Heb. 4:15, RSV).

INVOCATION. Lord God, we are here this morning because we want to go somewhere we have not yet been. We want to come into your presence and receive your marching orders for us this particular day. We want your Spirit to touch our hearts, releasing us from our sins nd fears, from all the things that cripple our discipleship and hasten our departure from your lordship. We want your Spirit to touch our minds so we may receive a vision that is in harmony with your will and in keeping with living not for ourselves alone but for you and your kingdom of righteousness. We know you are not going to tell us—right now—all we need to know for the rest of our lives or give us all the courage we need to be faithful to you during our earthly journey. We know you are not now going to clear up all the mysteries we face and are going to face. We also know, however, you will not ignore the pleas and the petitions we bring to you out of humble and grateful and adoring hearts. We know you will indeed give us enough light, enough strength, enough resolve to travel faithfully through this day—if we ask for those things earnestly and sincerely. Life on this earth is sacred, because you, God, are holy, and because we, God, by your grace, are your people. We may not do a single thing better than anyone else, but if all that we do is done for you, our reasons are right. And you are happy, and so are we.—Gordon H. Reif.

OFFERTORY SENTENCE. "Keep your life free from love of money, and be content with what you have; for he has said, 'I will never fail you nor forsake you'" (Heb. 13:5, RSV).

OFFERTORY PRAYER. Almighty God, you sent your Son Jesus Christ to reconcile the world to yourself: We praise and bless you for those whom you have sent in the power of the Spirit to preach the gospel to all nations. We thank you that in all parts of the earth a community of love has been gathered together by their prayers and labors, and that in every place your servants call upon your Name; for the kingdom and the power and the glory are yours forever.—*Book of Common Prayer*.

PRAYER. O Lord, Uncreated Light, near, yet far away, magnificent in mercy, plenteous in grace, generous in love: We pause to worship thee, who are holy beyond our comprehension yet real enough for us to love and adore with the unique awe due thy holy Name. We confess our shortcomings and sins: criticizing when we should have kept quiet; speaking when we should have listened; dividing truth to suit our purposes instead of heeding truth to edify our souls, waiting for opportunities instead of creating them, hoping for maturity instead of claiming our gifts and joining in to do our part. We have mocked, divided, and chided. We have forgotten, faltered, and failed, and we ask, loving Lord, forgiveness for our sins and the pardon only the cross provides: Cleanse our souls.

As we remember the past, loved ones gone on, deeds done, glad moments bathed in the beauty of retrospect, bind up what we have known of the past to grace us in the present. As we experience the present, grant us strong hearts and sound minds to do our ethical best in representing Christ Jesus in this place. If we do nothing else, let us show forth the love of Christ in the present. As we look to the future and recall the sending of the dove of thy Holy Spirit on Pentecost, let thy Spirit descend on us that our future, informed by the past and anticipated in the present, may be wedded to thy precious will. Then lead us where thou wilt, direct us as pleases thee, fill us as honors thee, redeem us as magnifies thee, use us as delights thee. And cleanse us with the undeniableness of thy Presence until all we have been, all we are now, and all we hope to be, proclaim a Creator God, a Savior Son, and a Guiding Spirit, that come what may cannot be denied and in heaven's light will never pass away.—E. Lee Phillips.

EVENING SERVICE

Topic: Total Christian Stewardship
TEXT: 2 Cor. 8:1–9.
I. The Christians in Macedonia were, by and large, very poor. Because the region was highly exploited by the Romans, most of the people, whether Christian or not, were poor. But, no doubt, it was even worse for the Christians. Of them Paul said, "They have been severely tested by the troubles they went through . . . They are very poor."

(a) Paul was in the process of collecting an offering from the Gentile Christians throughout Asia and Greece to relieve the suffering of the Jewish Christians in Jerusalem. No doubt he also wanted to bring the two great arms of first-century Christianty—the Jews and the Gentiles—closer together.

(b) But when Paul thought about the Macedonians and the dire straits that they were in, he wondered if he should ask them for help. Well, maybe they could give a little bit. But what they gave, in Paul's words, "was more than we could have hoped for!" But not only did they respond more generously than Paul could have imagined. Do you know what they did? Hold on to your seats, because you are *really* not going to believe what else Paul said. He said, "They begged us and pleaded for the privilege of having a part in helping God's people in Judea."

II. Paul also makes it clear that there was a totality about the stewardship of the Macedonians. They realized that there was much more to real commitment to God than giving money. You have to give yourself. And so it was that Paul could say of them, "First they gave themselves to the Lord; and then . . . they gave themselves to us." In other words, in whatever ways that were open to them, they gave themselves to God and to one another. And because they had given of themselves, they were able to give their money. You see, money was not a substitute for giving themselves; it was an extension of giving themselves.

III. But a question echoes through my brain when I read about those Macedonians. That question is, "How? How could they give as they did?"

(a) There can be little doubt that there were several factors that contributed to the Macedonians' ability to make what seems to us to be a superhuman sacrifice. But Paul, in his usual way, gets to the very heart of the matter in the ninth verse: "You know the grace of our Lord Jesus Christ; rich as he was, he made himself poor for your sake, in order to make you rich by means of his poverty."

(b) There you have it: "the grace of our Lord Jesus Christ." What is the grace of Jesus Christ? Paul goes on to explain what he meant. He said that Jesus, who was rich, became poor so that we could be rich even though we were poor. Jesus willingly gave all that richness up and came into the world to have nothing—not even by earthly standards, much less compared to what had been his. And he did it all so that you and I who have nothing might be rich.

IV. If all your treasure is in the things of this world, you don't have anything! But if you have Jesus in your heart, there is no man on the face of the earth who is richer than you are!—Randy Smith.

SUNDAY: NOVEMBER TWENTY-THIRD

MORNING SERVICE

Topic: Thanks Be to God
TEXT: 1 Cor. 15:57.

My text is a cry of victory—Christian victory. "Thanks be to God, which giveth us the victory through our Lord Jesus Christ."

I. To live in fear is to live in the shadow of death, for God is love and love is life. Our fears, too, are either grounded or not grounded. Such fear resulting from insecurity is conquered by God-security; perfect love casts out fear. In all days but particularly in ours there is, however, real reason for fear. We all know how precarious life is. We feel the threat both of personal calamity and of political or military catastrophe. Yet even here we can trust God. If God is for us, who can be against us?

II. "That the length of his love outlasts the stubbornness of our sin! All of us have sinned and come short of the glory of God. We are never fully awake to reality until we wake up to self and determine to fight it. The more we know both the reality of Christ and of ourselves, the more we are overwhelmed by the depth and stubbornness of sin. Then we long to be rid of our load, to be free from the burden of sin.

III. "That the strength of his purpose is more durable than the straying of our aimlessness!" I am astonished how little time

and energy, let alone wisdom, we give deliberately to pursue the path of God. Even our efforts to promote the common good are exceedingly scattered. How much time do we spend as communities to discover and do the will of God? The planner and executor of most of our lives and of history as a whole is not we, but God. His great plan holds our lives together and directs the nations more deeply than conscious intention.

IV. "That the rest in his peace is more real than the restlessness of our conflicts!" How many of us are weary of wearing tensions at work, among friends when we are supposed to have fun, perhaps even at home. Without conflict and tensions there can be no growth either in persons or in community. Christ does not deliver us from conflict but makes us victorious in conflict by giving us his own self. This is the Christian victory, even our faith.

V. "That the height of his hope erases the depths of our hopelessness!" We live in an age largely bereft of hope. Gone is the old optimism. Come is the new despair. Contrast such feelings with those of another dark age when our faith was young: always abounding hope; a sure hope; "the God of hope fill you with all peace and joy in believing, that ye may abound in hope, through the power of the Holy Ghost" (Rom. 15:13). Without hope in God we have a right to despair, but standing on the promises of God, even when our hearts are weighted down, we repeat to ourselves: "Hope thou in God for I shall praise him who is the health of my countenance and my God" (Ps. 42:11).

VI. "That the surety of his promises is safer than the struggle of our doubts!" Doubt is good when it serves growth; doubt is bad when it results from sin. Most of our doubt has been due to spiritual rather than to intellectual causes. Intellectual doubt we must honor. The doubt that is a smoke screen, to shut God out of our lives, we must destroy. Our age is at least beginning to doubt its own doubts. It sees its own false certainties for what they are. Our idols stand impotent.

VI. "That the freedom of his service is more liberating than the fancy of our willfulness!" Those who have found the Christian victory know that in acceptance of God's will is freedom. Passivity gives power. To be free is to effect God's purpose for us and to express our whole nature. Freedom comes with fulfillment of self and society within the will of God for all men. True liberty is the one with which Christ has set us free. Seeking freedom for self we become slaves; becoming slaves of Christ we find ourselves startlingly free, and freely we exult.

VIII. "That the certainty of his health is more healing than the coddling of our sorrow!" The coddling of our sorrows increases our illness; the immortal medicine of God's love heals them. Even when there is no help from illness, either from doctor or from believing prayer, there is available a new heart of faith to bear up under illness and to know the Healer beyond every harm. Victorious faith should again know the strain of victory.

IX. "That the Light of Life everlasting refutes the lie of our death"! We know that we all die. The Christian faith takes death, as an event, with complete seriousness. We are not by nature immortal. By nature we are all bound for death. Nevertheless, when we know the Christian God, we know that he calls us back to life again. We know that for those who believe in Jesus' Resurrection, there is also resurrection for all. Death is birth! The New Testament speaks of "the birth pangs of death," of "the firstborn from the dead." God lets us all be born to newness of life in order to face his inexorable judgment and his illimitable grace. In his hands we are safe, for there is no condemnation for those who are in Christ Jesus; nothing shall ever separate us from the love of God in Christ Jesus our Lord; God is not the God of the dead but of the living, for all live unto him. —Nels F. S. Ferré.

Illustrations

REAL JOY.   This side of the Day of Judgment our joy is either counterfeit—forget that death is coming, forget inconstancy and halfheartedness, live for today alone with the fun it may provide for a time—or it is only under way—already we can see the God who is removing tears and death and planning the existence from which all evil will be subtracted. That is why we celebrate festivals in a time of waiting—every Sunday, every Christmas and Easter, every Advent—for they are reminders that the everlasting God has been on the job for a long time, and he isn't about to falter now. —Richard R. Caemmerer.

THE GOODNESS OF GOD.   My saintly mother, when once I was privileged to visit her, came to meet me at the door and before I had put my bags down, she queried, "Nels, is God all good; can I say anything too good about him?" My reply was instant. "No mother, you can't; God is all for us and for us all always!" "Thank you, dear," she replied, "what more can I need?"—Nels F. S. Ferré.

Sermon Suggestions

THE TRUE CHRISTIAN CHARACTER.   Text: Col. 2:7. (1) Rooted and building up in Christ. (2) Confirmed and steadied by faith. (3) Thankful in spirit.—Edwin C. Dargan.

A DIFFERENT KIND OF MESSIAH.   Gospel Text: Luke 23:35–43. (1) He did not have to save himself in order to do God's will. (2) He did not have to save only the good in order to do God's will.

Worship Aids

CALL TO WORSHIP.   "Thanks be to God, who gives us the victory through our Lord Jesus Christ" (1 Cor. 15:57, RSV).

INVOCATION.   O God, let this service be a service of true thanksgiving, an expression of gratitude and praise for what matters most in this our earthly pilgrimage. Open our eyes to blessings received in days past, blessings promised for the days to come, and blessings known and unrecognized in the here and now.

OFFERTORY SENTENCE.   "Freely ye have received, freely give" (Matt. 10:8).

OFFERTORY PRAYER.   This, now, is one way of thanking you, Lord, for all that you have so lavishly bestowed upon us—sins forgiven, hope established, love released, joy bestowed, and unnumbered blessings along life's way. You have already blessed us as we have received; now bless us and our offerings as we give.

PRAYER.   Almighty and everlasting God, Father of mercies and God of all comfort, we raise to thee our grateful praise. For the life we have from thee; for the good earth yielding grain and fruits for our sustenance; for the cattle upon a thousand hills; and for the manifold gifts of the sea, we humbly thank thee. For thy mercies bestowed through the nation to which we belong and especially for the freedoms won of old by our fathers and cherished and preserved even until now, we humbly thank thee. For thy prophets and saints whose vision of the Eternal has lighted our path and strengthened our hearts; for valiant souls who, keeping faith and hope in the midst of adversity, shame our doubt and our discouragement; for those near to us and dear who share our joys and our sorrows, and whose love to us never fails; and for all those our brethren whose daily task on land or sea ministers to our good, we praise and bless thy glorious name. Above all, we thank thee for thyself, O Lord, whose faithfulness is unto all generations. Give us grace, we beseech thee, to show forth thy praise not only in our words but in our lives, by committing ourselves wholly to thy service.—Ernest Fremont Tittle.

EVENING SERVICE

Topic: The Thanks-Full Life

TEXT: 1 Thess. 5:18.

I. What is your life full of anyway? I have been asking myself this question during the past few days and suggest that you do the same.

(a) As we look around us, we see some people who live lives that are full of fears: fear of risks, of new ventures, of illness; fear of exposing themselves to others; fear of what the future may bring to them and to the world in which we live.

(b) There are others whose lives are full of doubt and cynicism. They are suspicious and critical, trusting no one—and certainly no program or institution. To them anyone who appears to be decent or generous is suspect.

(c) Many people's lives seem to be full of runaway emotions today. They never take anything that happens calmly or serenely. One day they are on top of the world, the next down in the dumps. They hate and they love both life and people passionately and violently.

(d) Then there are, of course, many others whose lives are full of faith and trust and love and hopefulness. They never seem to be unwilling to reach out and to accept people of all kinds. They are always ready to give of themselves. They are willing to trust the promises and to seek the presence of God. These are the people who live in expectation—in expectation of new and better things, no matter what the situation may be now.

(e) It is well to remember, also, that when all is said and done, each one of us here in church today is actually all these people successively and interchangeably. Now we are one, now we are the other most of the time.

II. When we turn to the Bible we find the constant injunction to fill our lives with another quality—the quality of thankfulness. I believe that this is one of the most important injunctions of all.

(a) Thankfulness, you see, is an attitude and emotion that needs to be and should be claimed by everyone. "It is a good thing to give thanks unto the Lord," writes the psalmist. "From the rising of the sun to the going down of the same, the Lord's name is to be praised . . . At midnight I will rise to give thanks unto the Lord." Similarly, Saint Paul writes to the Ephesians as follows: "Be filled with the Spirit . . . always and for everything giving thanks in the name of our Lord Jesus Christ to God," and to the Thessalonians, "Give thanks in all circumstances, for this is the will of God in Christ Jesus for you."

(b) Let me submit that there is nothing more important to anyone than the achievement of a thanks-filled life. This is the first and most basic step along the pathway to a life that is filled with faith and trust and hopefulness. To give thanks "always and for everything" is to transform our daily experiences and to change and lift our lives.

III. The Christian life is a thanks-filled life. But how does the Christian keep his life filled with thanks in the world in which we must continue to live?

(a) I expect that the Christian keeps his life full of thanks in somewhat the same way the automobile driver successfully negotiates an automobile trip. I discover, at least, that I am most in danger whenever I take my eyes off the road, even if only for a moment. As soon as I begin to focus my attention on a person (do I know him or her, or not?), a billboard, or even a scenic wonder, I am in danger of running off the road or getting into the wrong lane of traffic.

(b) Just as the safe and successful driver keeps his eyes on the road, the Christian who would be thankful in all circumstances keeps his eyes on God. He lives "as seeing him who is invisible," as it was said of Moses. "The Lord is my strength and my shepherd," he says. "He is with me in adversity. He supplies my needs in such a way that I shall not lack. He restores my soul. Therefore, whatever may happen to me, even in the valley of the shadow of death, I can continue to live in the spirit of thankfulness.

(c) You see the thanks-full life thus becomes the joy-full life, which is a life that still lies open to all who are willing to enter it today. "Give thanks, then, in all circumstances; for this is the will of God in Christ Jesus for you" (1 Thess. 5:18). —Edward C. Dahl.

SUNDAY: NOVEMBER THIRTIETH

MORNING SERVICE

Topic: The Splendor of the Simple
Text: Matt. 25:1–13.
Jesus told a parable of the wise and foolish maidens who took their lamps and went to meet the bridegroom. Five foolish girls had not made proper preparation for the arrival of the bridegroom and we note the joy of those who were prepared and entered into the wedding celebration with joy and fullness. The theme of this most familiar and interesting parable is the often repeated theme of the necessity for preparation for the important events of life. The weeks before Christmas are such opportunities for preparation. The weeks that lie before us that we traditionally know as the season of Advent are the opportunities that we have to prepare ourselves for the holy event of Christmas once again.

I. What is there in the news of Advent to be heard today?

(a) A birth at midnight! Why did God not choose dawn with its bursting forth of variegated colors of the sun, or twilight when the hand of day reaches silently to pull down the purple curtain of night? Perhaps in the simplicity of Christmas, God wishes to remind us that there is no moment apart from him, no moment unknown to him, and no moment when he may not be known in our lives. The wonder and mystery of God's coming lies in the simplicity of it. The blessed Christmas story centers about the simple—not the prominent, nor the powerful, nor the supercolossal. In this holy event God was saying that life is a simple thing. The

Christmas story is really a very simple story. It is made up of the kind of universal experiences that everyone of us can recognize; an anxious father, a young mother who had experienced childbirth for the first time, a newborn baby.

(b) The Scriptures tell us that "the shepherds returned to their fields, glorifying and praising God for all they had heard and seen." I believe the shepherds were praising God because their happiness had been focused in something very simple and human. Once man had supposed God to be very distant, to reveal himself in terror and awe, to move among the clouds of Sinai, and to dwell in silence behind the curtain in the Holy of Holies. But in their worship the shepherds learned a more wonderful truth: God had entered the human situation through birth of a baby. Consequently, God is to be found in the experiences that are most common—friendship, affection, patience, love. Why do we look for God in the big events of life when we might better see him in the affairs of every day?

II. Lest we become too involved in the activities of the season, we must remember that in the holy event God was saying that love must be the most significant part of our living. The birth of the Child of Bethlehem introduced a new element into the human situation. It put love at the heart of the universe. When God's love was revealed in Jesus Christ, two conclusions were forced upon a reluctant world. First, since the act of the Creator in sending his Son was an act of divine love, it must be assumed that love is the way by which our life is to be lived. The other is closely related. Since God's method of revelation was a child become man, it can be concluded that human relationships are sacred.

(a) What is it, this love of which we speak? It is much deeper than we commonly and popularly make it. Love as it comes to us in Jesus Christ is like this. It is saying to another person I want, I will, and I work that you may come to life at its best. It is saying that the meaning of my whole life is the fulfillment of your life. This is love! To be sure, it can be most readily found in a loving family circle, but

it isn't there alone! It is that special quality of life that some of my teachers gave to me over the years. It is that quality of life that some of my physicians expressed to me in the course of this past summer. It is that quality of life that my friends and colleagues on the ministerial staff and members of this congregation express day by day. It is the love expressed by a woman who recently gave me a beautiful painting she had made of a peaceful, inviting meadow. It is our mutual ministry of concern for each other.

(b) The Word made flesh becomes a reality again and again as we, individual Christians, spearhead the gospel of love to the whole of another's existence. Love is the great power at work whenever we are lifting up a life that has fallen. It is that power that reaches out whenever we are sustaining life that is weakening, and awakening life that is asleep!

III. Lest we become too involved in the activities of the season, we must remember that in the holy event God was saying there is power in the gospel in response to our quest for the meaning of life.

(a) What are the thoughts that enter your mind and spirit as you turn your eyes into the heavens at night? Without the stars the night seems so dark and the dawn so far away. Men's hearts are warmed by the stars for they are a sign of God. Under the canopy of the sparkling heavens while camping, I hear God speaking to my inner self in strange and wonderfully deep ways.

(b) Clouds sometimes move in to block the view of the star-studded sky, and yet we know they are still high in the heavens. The movement of the clouds blocking out the stars is symbolic of the conflict between the idealism and realism of life. So much of life's experiences are filled with the thunder and lightning of each day's human relationships that we sometimes cannot see the stars of our beautiful ideals. Every day of our life the clouds appear along the horizon and angry voices thunder without reason, and threats like lightning break and crash over our heads. It is the realism of life that there are frequent conflicts between beautiful ideals and the brutal realities of living. Yet the message of Advent, like the North Star that holds the true direction under all circumstances, enables us to hope.

(c) It is small wonder that you and I are not of casual interest to God but of prime importance and concern. The gospel of Advent symbolizes, if it symbolizes anything, God's love for each one of us. The reason we celebrate Advent and Christmas is because God has invested the life of his eternal Son. God in the person of Jesus Christ came into human experience to touch and transform all of life. John's Gospel declares this truth in that "the Word became flesh and dwelt among us, full of grace and truth" (John 1:11). God reveals himself, not only in the world of space and nature, or in great cathedrals, or in the pageant of Bethlehem's manger, but in human life with its sin and struggle, its pain and sorrow, its guilt and shame, its birth and death.

(d) Like the foolish maidens in Jesus' parable, we may stand unprepared to hear and experience the good news of the Christmas gospel. Again, what is the news to be heard? One of the clearest words about Christmas is its simplicity. We must remember that God is saying that love is the most significant part of our living. We may hear in the Christmas gospel God saying to us, "I believe in you!" Spectacular? Yes, indeed, but very simple!—Donald L. Germain.

Illustrations

GOD FOR US.   We may count on the love of God—God's being for us—and should count on it. The Lord Jesus won this for us by taking upon himself suffering and the cross. Therefore, to him be praise and thanksgiving for this his inconceivable love! Therefore, we are determined to live anew in this love of his and even try to practice it in our own life, by putting up with our fellowmen, even if they get on our nerves, even if they are inclined to be unpleasant or hostile. That is the practical meaning of the story of Jesus' sufferings. But its truest meaning is this: God loves us in spite of ourselves.—Emil Brunner.

TO BE GOD'S CHILDREN.   If God does not go with us into our office, into the nursery and bedroom, into the vacation and the hospital, and finally to the deathbed and the cemetery, it really makes little difference whether we declare, "there is no God" or declare "of course, there is a God." This is what Paul means when he says to us, "For in Christ Jesus you are all sons of God through faith." He has this special relationship in mind. To be children of God is to be in a faith relationship to God through Christ. It means something real. It comes alive when our life seems empty, bleak, and useless, and when happiness and love of life are almost gone. As children of God we live our life with him step by step. In times of crisis, he stands inquiringly before us with his commands, and in times of trouble, he holds us close to himself.—Eduard Schweizer.

Sermon Suggestions

THREE CHARACTERISTICS OF PRAYER. Text: Col. 4:2. (1) Continuance. (2) Watchfulness. (3) Thankfulness.—Edwin C. Dargan.

HOW TO BE PREPARED FOR THE PAROUSIA. Gospel Text: Matt. 24:36–44. (1) Do not presume to know God's timetable. (2) Live from day to day in the freedom of faith. (3) Be at all times under the discipline of readiness.

Worship Aids

CALL TO WORSHIP.   "Lift up your heads; for your redemption draweth nigh" (Luke 21:28).

INVOCATION.   Gracious God, our Father, rich in your mercy and lavish in your care for us, we would praise your name this day. We thank you for blessings all around us: the clasp of a child's hand; the smile on a friend's face; the radiance of good health; the beauty of a crisp autumn day. In the quietness of this hour, O God, we would ask for a greater knowledge of who you are and of what you are about. We have come to worship today to learn of the One who knew what life was all about . . . Teach us. We have come to find a purpose for our existence and a motivation for our love . . . Inspire us. We have come to acknowledge the sins and failures of the week . . . Forgive us. We have come to be made new by the Christ who lived and died for us . . . Recreate us, and show us, we pray, the relevance of the gospel for our lives and for the world in which we live.—Reba Sloan Cobb.

OFFERTORY SENTENCE.   "Blessed be the Lord, who daily loadeth us with benefits, even the God of our salvation" (Ps. 68:19).

OFFERTORY PRAYER.   Our Father, we do not know how wonderfully we have been blessed: So many of thy blessings are beyond our knowledge or ability to appreciate. Open the eyes of our understanding and help us to recognize the marvelous gifts of thy grace and to walk in the assurance of the presence with us of thy unseen angels.

PRAYER.   Father, we find a bright spot in your presence. Enlighten our lives with your truth; brighten our relationships with your love. We thank you for one another, for your call that brings us together, for this place that your generous people have made possible, for your love in Jesus Christ—so overwhelming, so awesome, so compelling. We remember those in our larger family, Father, who need to be reminded of your love . . . and of ours, who are grieving, and who need your comforting and healing presence, and many others who are anxious and troubled and insecure and threatened. We pray, aaking your strong assurance. Now grant us the satisfaction of our own needs and the purification of our own desires.—J. Estill Jones.

EVENING SERVICE

Topic: Noah: The Promise of Mercy
TEXT: Gen. 9:8–17; Rom. 8:22–24.
Once again we have reached that most exciting time in the church year, the season of Advent. Advent is the time when we seek diligently to prepare our hearts for the coming of the Christ child once again. That is admittedly a very difficult thing for many of us to do. We tend to get so rushed

with shopping and parties and meetings that Christmas Day is here before we know it and only then do we realize that we have scarcely given a thought to how we should have prepared ourselves spiritually for this happy event.

I. Today we begin with one of the oldest covenants or promises of God in all of Scripture, the promise of mercy as it was given to all mankind through Noah.

(a) It is hard to believe that when the Lord looked down on all those peoole who lived before the flood, what he saw was any worse than what he would see if he looked down on us today. I doubt that they had any sins that haven't been reinvented since then and we probably have a few they didn't even think of. So if you take into account the remedy he used for getting the earth cleaned up in their day, it's enough to keep you awake at night. Just put yourself in Noah's place.

(b) Noah would be a long time forgetting all he had just been through. First, having to endure the ridicule of all his neighbors and friends, building a boat in the middle of the desert. It was small comfort later to know that he was right. He still had to watch as those he knew so well clung desperately to their rooftops, had to hear their cries as they banged on the sides of the ark.

(c) The voyage itself was no picnic either. The close quarters, the constant pitch and roll of the boat, the smells, the bad food, at times they were enough to make him wish that he had been left behind with the others. And then there was the sheer unendingness of it all. We always remember the 40 days of rain, but you have to remember that they were inside for 7 days before the rains began and it took 150 days for the waters to subside. When the bird came back to the boat, weak and exhausted because he could not find any place to land, Noah must have thought that living in that boat with all those animals was the way he was going to spend the rest of his days.

(d) Finally, of course, the waters did subside. The old man and his family and all the animals were able to walk out on dry ground. But even as Noah and his sons built the altar and prepared a sacrificial offering, a thought must have kept tugging at the back of his mind: If the Lord could do it once, what was to stop him from doing it again? And if Noah, a man who the Bible says found grace in the eyes of the Lord, asked a question like that, then there are probably a lot of people today asking the same question: If the peoole before the flood were destroyed for their evil, then why shouldn't the Lord wipe me off the face of the earth as well?

II. So if the Lord could do it once, what's to stop him from doing it again? Maybe he wouldn't wipe out everything and start over, but you have made such a mess of your life that he would be perfectly justified in finding some way to destroy you. So we kneel in the dirt with Noah, making our sacrifices, hoping that we can somehow stave off the inevitable, trying to avoid what we know we deserve. But sometime when we are doing all those things we try to do to appease an angry god, the real God speaks, and when he does he says the same thing to us that he said to Noah.

(a) "I'm going to make you a promise. This idea that I'm going to wipe every-thing out is getting us nowhere. Never again until the end of time am I going to destroy all the living creatures on the face of the earth. I am going to display a quality that evidently a lot of you forgot I had— mercy. And in case you think there might be a chance that one day I'll forget my promise, I will give you a sign. Every time you see the rainbow it will be as if I have tied a string around my finger to remind me of the covenant between us."

(b) Evidently even the Lord can learn something every once in a while and this is what he learned from the flood: It does precious little good to wipe out one set of human beings and start over with another set of human beings. Mankind is going to have the same kind of problem, no matter what. There is just no getting around it.

(c) If there was not some basic good at the core of man, then surely the Lord would have found an excuse and a way to get rid of us by now. And instead he keeps extending to us his mercy. But isn't the story of Advent that mercy is more than a promise, it's a reality? And isn't that what we need to know right now more than any-thing else?—James M. King.

SUNDAY: DECEMBER SEVENTH

MORNING SERVICE

Topic: Strange Delight

TEXT: Psalm 1.

We are so familiar with the first Psalm that it is difficult to appreciate the full force of its abrupt challenge. Yet, if we will study it for a moment, then study ourselves in the light of it, we shall see the sharp line it draws across our life as it lifts the ancient challenge: Choose ye this day! The psalmist holds that the blessed man will have a quite different attitude toward the law of God: He will make it the object of joyous contemplation at all times; he will delight in it. This, to our generation, must seem a strange delight. For law, to us, is not so much a delight as a sorrow.

I. This law of the Lord in which he de-lighted was no simple, single event; it was a broad all-inclusive thing, meaning, in fact, three different though closely related events or experiences.

(a) First, then, the law of God indicates the order of creation, the orderliness of the universe. This universe is no chance affair; it was created by God for his pur-pose and through his will and power. For the psalmist, man is no outsider in God's world; he belongs to the order of creation.

(b) The second broad fact that enters into the meaning of the law of the Lord in which the psalmist delights is the reality of Providence in human life and history. Like all Hebrews, he regards history as the me-dium through which God deals directly with men. He believes that the punish-ment of the ungodly man and the reward of the godly man are to be found to some extent in history.

(c) The third fact that composed the Law of the Lord to which the psalmist calls attention is the actual expression of his will in the Law book, the Torah and the Pentateuch—the first five books of our Bible. While they might differ on how literally to take its teachings, they agreed that it was God's covenant with them. One of the truly distinctive things about the life and culture of Israel is this conviction that they are a holy people and have been given a holy land in which, and a holy law by which, to live.

II. Though the psalmist set down this expression of faith two thousand years ago, his delight in the law of the Lord has not been disowned by subsequent generations.

(a) Generation after generation of skeptical, cynical, and proud peoples have turned away from it with a sneer, thinking to ignore it forever, only to grope their way back to it, blinded by the tragedy that eternally and irrevocably attends human folly. Many of the most powerful thinkers of our own time, whose interests lie quite outside the professions of the ministry or the church, are inclined to agree with the psalmist's faith in the law of God. The scientist, better than anyone else, knows that we live in a cosmos not a chaos, knows that we live in an essentially orderly universe.

(b) History is the medium through which God deals with us—deals, not as a billiard player cues the balls on a cosmic table, but as a father deals with his children. I myself am sure the psalmist had a good point when he delighted in the spiritual and moral heritage of his own faith and people. How can we avoid paying tribute to the indestructible power of that kind of heritage?

III. But there are those among us who object to the idea of external law, whether human or divine. They think it an invasion of their freedom. Before we mount that toboggan slide to sheer tragedy, we ought to reflect on the fact that law is positive as well as negative. The positive implications of the law of the Lord that we are studying can be summed up in two brief commandments.

(a) The first one can be phrased quite simply: Thou shalt think God's thoughts after him. This commandment is hard for some of us to take. It demands that we get

out of the limbo of ideas without action, of words without deeds. Still others among us reject the notion that there is anything ultimate or absolute about these great values; we want to feel that they are relative, through and through. Thou shalt think God's thoughts before him: believe this, and at a stroke, you become a committed person—committed to the conviction that you must seek truth, beauty, goodness, and love wherever they may be found because they are of God, because they are God's hand on man's shoulder leading him toward the abundant life.

(b) Believe in the reality of the law of the Lord, and you will be led to a second commandment: Thou shalt love God and man utterly. Easy to say but hard to do, isn't it? Most of us feel that a good many things have to be cleared up about both God and man before we can actually love them. The law of which we speak and in which we believe is not mechanical but moral; it is not a matter of routine, but of divine love. What God did and does by and through law was and is done with purpose and love and is fashioned from a sincere desire that men would know and understand the will of God. Man is no automaton, but a child —a child of God—a free moral agent to whom God must make a personal approach and a moral appeal. But, in the end, God must be God even as a father must be a father.

(c) This much seems to be clear about the law of God. We cannot break it, but we can break ourselves upon it. We can disobey it, but we cannot escape it. It is the literal Hound of Heaven to one who seeks to escape it. But to one who accepts and obeys it with joy in his soul, it is indeed a strange delight. It means strength, peace, joy.—Harold A. Bosley.

Illustrations

PROBLEMS WITH GOD. There are times when we may even feel as Clarence Day said his father seemed to feel in his praying: "He didn't actually accuse God of gross inefficiency but when he prayed, his tone was loud and angry, like that of a dissatisfied guest in a carelessly managed hotel."—Harold A. Bosley.

THE POWER OF HABIT. As we become permanent drunkards by so many separate drinks, so we become saints in the moral, and authorities and experts in the practical and scientific spheres, by so many separate acts and hours of work. Let no youth have any anxiety about the upshot of his education, whatever the line of it may be. If he keeps faithfully busy each hour of the working day, he may safely leave the final result to itself. He can with perfect certainty count on waking up some fine morning to find himself one of the competent ones of his generation, in whatever pursuit he may have singled out.—William James.

Sermon Suggestions

THE MINISTER AND HIS MINISTRY. Text: Col. 4:17. (1) The personal element—"say to Archippus." (2) The care needed—"take heed." (3) Sacredness of the trust—"in the Lord." (4) Magnitude of the work —"that thou fulfill it."—Edwin C. Dargan.

A PROPHETIC PARADOX. Gospel Text: Matt. 3:1–12. (1) Back to the basics (vv. 1–10). (2) Forward to the new age (vv. 11–12).

Worship Aids

CALL TO WORSHIP. "Blessed are they that hear the word of God, and keep it" (Luke 11:28).

INVOCATION. Father, through the ages your word has been a lamp unto the feet of your people and a light unto their path. The times are dark, and we need a sure word from you to push back the darkness and guide our way. So speak to us, we pray. Comfort us, challenge us, and show us the right road to follow.

OFFERTORY SENTENCE. "Be ye doers of the word, and not hearers only" (James 1:22).

OFFERTORY PRAYER. O God, in this moment we pray for the success of the gospel and at the same time we give our offerings to help bring that prayer to fulfillment.

Strengthen thy cause in the world beginning with us.

PRAYER. O God, help us find thee. Help us find thee through the wonders of the world—through the skies that color, heavens that tremble, hills that rise, mountains that soar, canyons that descend, mesas that spread, plains that extend, machines that produce, structures that tower, engines that fly. Help us find thee through nature—through a drop of water, the seven seas, massive mountains, high hills, pointed peaks, a blade of grass, the flight of birds, the harmony of flowers, the rhythm of life, the pulse beat of growth. Help us find thee through the arts —through the conflict of a drama, the grandeur of a cantata, the cheer of a carol, the joy of a hymn, the colors of a painting, the rhythm of the dance, the flow of words, the lines of a temple. Help us find thee through the lives of people—through the laugh of a child, the winsomeness of a lad, the glow of youth, the vigor of manhood, the understanding of womanhood, the wisdom of age. Help us find thee through Scripture—through the vision of Abraham, the wrestling of Jacob, the purity of Joseph, the strength of Deborah, the conscience of Amos, the faith of a centurion, the vigor of Peter, the humility of Mary, the forgiveness of Stephen, the love of Paul. But help us, O God, to find thee most through the life of the Man of Galilee, who walked the highways of the Holy Land, leaving behind pictures of thee, our Father.—Fred E. Luchs.

EVENING SERVICE

Topic: The Troublesome Bible
TEXT: Heb. 11:8–9, 39–40.
I have trouble when the Bible conflicts with my ideas, when it doesn't say what I think, when it counters my beliefs. It disturbs me and it irritates me and frustrates me. It can even make me angry. Let me tell you more specifically what I mean.
I. For one thing, I like to plan ahead.
(a) I do not like vague schedules or incomplete itineraries. I want my life organized, scheduled, and planned. I want to know when I will leave, when I am to ar-

rive, and when I will return. Give me a specific, detailed plan. That's what I like. But what do I get from the Bible? I get Abraham who, according to Hebrews 11, "bet his life on unseen realities."

(b) Unseen realities?! I want to see! I want a ticket that says I am confirmed to leave Ur of the Chaldees at 2:45 P.M. and will arrive in the Promised Land at 3:50 P.M. I search in vain for any such clairvoyant certainties in Abraham's story. And I am disturbed deeply by this. Is Abraham to be my guide and model for life? Abraham, who "set out without knowing where he was headed." It troubles me to consider that God may want me to believe like Abraham and live like him for I want exact details and not "unseen realities."

II. There is a second way in which the Bible confounds me. I like to be as certain as I can be about my doctrinal beliefs, about what the Bible teaches.

(a) But what do I get from the Bible? I get Paul, who "sees in a mirror dim shadows . . . [who] knows in part." I want no shadows in a mirror, but God in his pure essence. I want no partial knowledge, but pristine pure doctrine. What kind of God is this who gives me Paul? Why does the Divine seemingly beat around the bush of truth in parable, allegory, and inexhaustible metaphor? Doesn't God know that I must know in full? Why does he torture me?

(b) Shadows in a mirror? I want to know! I want a detailed vision of the truth and the future. I search in vain for such a map in the witness of Paul. And I am deeply disturbed by this. Is Paul to be my guide? Paul, who saw dim shadows of truth, who bounced around Europe and barely escaped with his life during his treacherous journeys, who lived by faith and not sight. It troubles me that God may want me to follow him in trust without knowing the future ahead of time, without understanding all there is to know of the Divine Mystery.

III. There is a third way in which the Bible perplexes me. I do not want to have any doubts about God's reality.

(a) Thus, I look for and want desperately a sign from the Lord that will guarantee my faith, that will make it unassailable.

I want a message in the sky, a supernatural miracle, or an appearance of an angel.

(b) But what do I get from the Bible? When I look to the Old Testament, I get Elijah. He looked toward the clouds; he listened to the thunder; he observed the fire. But, alas, there was no sign, no miracle, no angel. There was, however, something. Elijah heard the whisper of a voice like a distant memory speaking in an empty room. Is Elijah to be my guide? Elijah, who heard the still, small voice. It troubles me to consider that God would speak to me only in whispers.

(c) When I look to the New Testament for guarantees for my faith, I get the litany of heroes and heroines of Hebrews. I read of that great cloud of witnesses who lived by the assurance of things hoped for, by the conviction of things not seen, and who were not yet in possession of the things promised by God. Are these persons to provide patterns for my faith? It troubles me very much that they were so open and trusting with so few facts and proof.

IV. Here, then, are three ways in which the Bible troubles me. What do you do with a Bible like this?

(a) Many people dismiss its claims, find it out of touch with their needs and irrelevant to their lives. Others, and I would count myself among them, take another path. They struggle and wrestle with its audacious and surprising message. They try to hear it, understand it, and try it on as a way of seeing and living. Instead of looking for answers to their questions, they allow it to question and probe them.

(b) You listen as it says to you, "Let your mind be transformed." You ponder its imperative, "Live by faith and not by sight." You consider that "my ways are not your ways, nor are my thoughts your thoughts." You may discover, as I have, that authentic faith is more cloudy, opaque, and unfinished than you surmised. You may discover mystery instead of certain, dogmatic knowledge. You may find truth in living experience and not alone in wooden words, in the insight of the parable rather than in a hard-clad creed. The more you listen, the more you learn, but the deeper the mystery.—Donald W. Musser.

SUNDAY: DECEMBER FOURTEENTH

MORNING SERVICE

Topic: A Basis for Our Hope
TEXT: Rom. 15:4–13.

My purpose this morning is to show you that hope is one of the greatest activities you can engage in.

I. Basically, the Christian hope, based on Scripture, is that God is in control of the world. Of course, to you that is a debatable point, but the affirmation runs all through Scripture.

(a) We believe that life has meaning, that there is something in human nature that is beyond just eating and drinking and producing the next generation. We believe that God has an objective that we do not fully understand.

(b) Why do we believe all this? We believe it mostly because it is in the Holy Scripture. It is in the Scriptures because it is the actual history of human beings, largely in that tribe of Israel, who were chosen out of two hundred years of slavery to be God's special people. Somehow these tough people and their ideals have permeated life even among non-Judaic-Christian cultures. They are still the moral imperatives of our hearts' desires.

(c) The content of hope, then, is namely a philosophy of history that we hold. It is important to picture Jesus in that stream of history because in that perspective he gives to you a philosophy of history that God, the creator, is still at work. The God who saved Israel is at work. The God of Jesus Christ is at work. The God who made the Church, which has been buffeted around, at times by its own human faults, has still persevered. Finally, we have this hope: the hope that someday the kingdoms of this world shall be united under God, one God over all his people who made them and who will redeem them.

II. We live in hope! Some people just try to cope and balance missiles. They balance missile for missile to their own destruction, while others just throw up their hands and mope. We hope! We believe that love is greater than nuclear power.

(a) Look at the history of the world, and you can see how it changes. There is a greater world ahead of us, men and women. You say it is an illusion. The New World was an illusion once! By hope you involve yourself in the process and make it come to pass. You sweep away the cobwebs of illusion and discover deeper reality by living in hope.

(b) Do you see what I am saying? The Bible is the first basis of hope. The Bible is a spiritual recording of what actually happened in history. We are part of a history that is validated. You have the actual history of Jesus Christ, his manger birth, his crucifixion, his resurrection. You have a historical person who mastered Rome and all the powers that they said would smash him. He is the dominant figure of what it means to be a human being and to live a meaningful life.

III. Modern American people who expect peace, unity, righteousness, and integrity as a greater goal than self-destruction will actually help achieve it. We believe that you practice hope by action. How? By benevolence, by friendliness, by working, by praying. The Bible says of faith, hope, and love that the greatest is love. The three are really coefficients. Faith, hope, and love have this in common. They only exist when you throw yourself actively into them. Faith, hope, and love—all are throwing yourself into the process. That is what Jesus, the hope of the world, said. If anyone wants to be number one, let him be the servant of all and give himself in hope, in faith, in love. Men and women, the Christian Advent is a doctrine of hope for the whole world!
—Bryant M. Kirkland.

Illustrations

SHARING GOD'S VICTORY. The struggle with evil goes on "until Christ has put death under his feet." So far as we know, human history will always be the scene of contending powers. But the conception of the reign of Christ contains a hope that looks beyond all the particular victories that God continues to win. Our hope is that the good that comes to be is not lost but participates in the continuing life of God and thus shares in his ultimate victory. We believe that not only our present victories but even our failures can be transmuted into good. We believe that good is everlasting in God.—Daniel Day Williams.

THE LEAP OF FAITH.   Paul Tournier in his book *A Place for You* has most recently depicted the leap of faith by saying that we live in a rhythm of life between quitting one place in life and seeking another. He uses the analogy of a trapeze artist swinging on one bar to the utmost distance that it will take him and then turning loose and reaching hopefully and courageously for another bar. The breathless suspense in the "midair placelessness" is the anxiety of faith. One's breath and that of all who observe is held until the transition has been safely made, a transition that could never have been made if the person had not the courage to take "the leap."— Wayne E. Oates.

Sermon Suggestions

THE FOUNDATIONS OF FELLOWSHIP. Text: 1 Cor. 1:1–9. (1) The calling of God (vv. 1–3). (2) The grace of God (v. 4). (3) The enrichment of Jesus Christ (vv. 5–6). (4) The spiritual gifts (v. 7). (5) The sustaining power of Christ (v. 8). (6) The faithfulness of God (v. 9).—C. David Matthews.

OF GREATNESS AND THE KINGDOM.   Gospel Text: Matt. 11:2–11. (1) The mighty works of Jesus (vv. 2–6). (2) The significant role of John (vv. 7–11a). (3) The superior position of "the least" (vv. 11b).

Worship Aids

CALL TO WORSHIP.   "Hope we have as an anchor of the soul, both sure and steadfast" (Heb. 6:19).

INVOCATION.   O God, you bless us with a gift of new Light. Open our minds that we may respond to your word and share with others the full measure of your truth given to us in our Savior, Jesus Christ.— Harold A. Brack.

OFFERTORY SENTENCE.   "Every man shall give as he is able, according to the blessing of the Lord thy God which he hath given thee" (Deut. 16:17).

OFFERTORY PRAYER.   God, we don't like being used, or abused. We don't like being included only when there's no one else to include. We don't like being only a stepping-stone for someone to get somewhere else. We don't like being blamed by someone for his mistakes. Could it be, Lord, that you don't like these same things? Could it be that we ever treat you in a way we know we don't want to be treated? Could it be that we decide you will endure treatment that we will not tolerate for ourselves? Why do we pray when that's all we can do? Why don't we pray when we can do a lot of other things, none of them as good or important or helpful as praying? Why do we pray when everything has been taken away from us? Why don't we pray when we have so much, in abundance? Why do we pray when our world has caved in? Why don't we pray when we're on top of that world? Why do we pray when there's no justice, when everything's wrong and unfair? Why don't we pray when there is justice, when we are treated graciously, when we are shown kindness, when blessings without number flood our lives? Is an act of God a tornado, but not a talent; an earthquake, but not a baby; a dread disease, but not healing and health; a rampaging storm, but not calm and order; a natural disaster, but not the tiniest miracle? When God acts, do we see life, or death?—Gordon H. Reif.

PRAYER.   O God, we pray to thee for those who come after us, for our children, and the children of our friends, and for all the young lives that are marching up from the gates of birth, pure and eager, with the morning sunshine on their faces. We remember with a pang that these will live in the world we are making for them. We are wasting the resources of the earth in our headlong greed, and they will suffer want. We are poisoning the air of our land by our lies and our uncleanliness, and they will breathe it. O God, thou knowest how we have cried out in agony when the sins of our fathers have been visited upon us, and how we have struggled vainly against the inexorable fate that coursed in our blood or bound us in a prison house of life. Save us from maiming the innocent ones who come after us by the added cruelty of our sins. Help us to break the ancient force of evil by a holy and steadfast will and to endow our children with purer blood and nobler thoughts. Grant us grace to leave the earth fairer than we found it; to build upon it cities of God in which the cry of needless pain shall cease; and to put the yoke of Christ upon our business life that it may serve and not destroy. Lift the veil of the future and show us the generation to come as it will be if blighted by our guilt, that our lust may be cooled and we may walk in the fear of the Eternal. Grant us a vision of the far-off years as they may be if redeemed by the sons of God, that we may take heart and do battle for thy children and ours.—Walter Rauschenbusch.

EVENING SERVICE

Topic: God's Righteousness Among the Nations

TEXT: Isa. 42:1–4.

The coming of Christ has vast social and political consequences. The world into which Christ comes must become a different world because he enters into its life. Nothing shall be left the way it is. Everything shall be transformed by the power of this person's truth and grace.

I. Why is it that this innocent baby, lying in a stable's manger, is regarded as subversive, seditious, and revolutionary to the powers that be in the world?

(a) To Jesus, as to the Old Testament prophets, righteousness and justice had to do with championing the cause of the downtrodden and the powerless. God's justice is a social justice that has special concern for the widows and orphans who cannot get a fair day in court, for the poor and needy who are exploited by scheming moneylenders, for the aliens who are seen only as a cheap source of labor. God, far from being impartial in the affairs of the world, throws his weight against the privileged who have much and presses the cause of those victims of society who have little. There is a partiality in the heart of God toward those in need. This is not a sentimental kind of charitable warm feeling toward these persons, but a hard-as-nails insistence that they be treated as they should.

(b) Let us never forget that when Jesus pictured the Last Judgment he said that "when the Son of man comes in his glory . . . before him will be gathered all the *nations*, and he will separate them one from another as a shepherd separates the sheep from the goats." The one who comes into the world at Christmas is the Divine One who tests the righteousness of nations and judges them accordingly. He is the one who even now is at work to establish his kind of righteousness in the earth.

(c) No wonder the Herods of every age are disturbed by the pervasive working of God in Christ to support the victims of the status quo. The one who comes will not leave things as they are but is always rocking the boat of human affairs. He is seeking a new social order in which the victimized are liberated and made whole. Here is "the world's danger," for no one is safe till God's righteousness prevails among the nations.

II. We, of course, cannot be positive that the righteousness proclaimed shall, indeed, prevail in the liberation of all the earth. Ours is more of a hope to be expressed than a logic to be demonstrated. But it is not a hope that whistles in the dark for fear we may be wrong. It is a hope based in what we have already seen happening through the power of Christ's coming into the world.

(a) In the figure of this one who embodies love and righteousness we glimpse the reality of existence itself. Here in this one is what God himself intends for the world, and he shall have his way. We do not know how God shall effect his rule over all nations, for our thoughts are not his thoughts nor our ways his ways.

(b) He is the God of an open future who acts among us in surprising ways. The greatest surprise of all was his entrusting that future to an obscure couple named Joseph and Mary in the form of a tiny baby born in a stable. Out of that nonevent has come the one who grew up to overturn not petty Herods who sought to kill him, but mighty Caesars.

(c) Ours is a God of surprises that works out his righteousness in the most unex-pected ways. We know something about those surprises of God in our own day and time.

III. But we do not sit on our hands to await God's surprising future. In Christ's coming we glimpse where that future is headed and live into it with all the power God gives us. Confident of that future, glimpsed in Christ, we dare muster courage to do now what we can to aid the downtrodden in their liberation, offering it to God for his disposal.—Colbert S. Cartwright.

SUNDAY: DECEMBER TWENTY-FIRST

MORNING SERVICE

Topic: Meditations of a Foster Father
TEXT: Luke 2.

Who'd ever think that Joseph, the no-body carpenter from Nazareth, would be-come foster father to the Son of God? And a long six days' journey away from home? In a stable! And you, of all people, having an animal's feed box for a bassinet! When that prophet said, "God works in mysteri-ous ways his wonders to perform," that was the understatement of the ages!

I. Mary and Joseph childhood friends.

(a) Your mother and I have known each other since we were four. Everything had always fitted into the normal growing-up pattern for both of us.

(b) About the same time I started my own carpenter's shop, I began to see Mary as never before. Gradually, two thoughts dominated my mind. I sure loved that girl and wanted her to be my wife and, se-condly, "I'd better marry her before someone else does." My parents talked with hers and, after they had conferred with Mary, the arrangements were made for us to announce our engagement.

II. Mary visits Elizabeth.

(a) One day Mary seemed different. She greeted me with a puzzled expression and seemed surprised that I didn't know why she was puzzled, as though whatever thoughts she had I should have been hav-ing too. I didn't know about the angel's visit with her until later.

(b) When she announced she was going away for a visit, I was hurt. Mary had talked much of Elizabeth, an elderly cousin, mar-ried to a temple priest, and how Elizabeth prayed constantly for a child. I didn't un-derstand why Mary had to visit her now, when we were so busy and when I wanted to see her so much each day.

(c) Mary was gone three months. It seemed like three years. When she came back, her eyes were flashing. Her smile was radiant. The character and purity that had drawn me to her were more evident than ever before. She wore her goodness gracefully like a striking garment.

III. Mary conceives by the Holy Spirit.

(a) From these pure lips that I had never heard speak an evil or hurting thing there came words I could not believe. This cleanest of all the women of Nazareth and, I was sure, of all the girls in the world, told me she was going to have a baby.

(b) What now? What would I do? Our laws state that engagement is as binding as marriage and could only be dissolved by divorce. If I asked for a divorce, I would have to tell the elders the reason. They would ask Mary if she was with child. Then I would have to swear the child was not mine and the priests would judge her to be an adulteress. There is only one penalty for this crime. I could picture her being led to a high cliff and ordered to jump. If she refused, she would be pushed. I could see my Mary falling to the stony base of the cliff. The men, armed with stones, watch. If she moves, they throw the stones. If not, they go home and the body is left for the beasts and the birds. "No, no, I can't let that happen," my delirious heart shouted, "I love her."

IV. Joseph makes decision.

(a) Two other possibilities existed. For a great sum of money, to this poor carpenter, I could have sent her to some remote place, there to have the baby, and there to remain. Or I could swallow my pride, marry her, and hope there would not be too much comment about a six-month baby.

(b) The difficult decision was at last made. I would put her away. Even though I thought she had betrayed me, I could not let her die. Because I thought she had betrayed me, I could not be her husband.

(c) After making the decision—I don't remember going to sleep—I saw an angel standing by my bed.

V. After angel's visit Joseph understands.

(a) Suddenly I wasn't sleepy anymore. Not often do angels converse with carpenters! Did I dream that because I wanted to, I wondered? No, it was too real and, if made up, it would have been blasphemous, and I would not have dreamed a dream like that.

(b) I tell you, child, in that one angelic visit my crumbled world was rebuilt. As quickly as possible I went to Mary: "Now I know; now I understand," I said. She came to my home and became my wife.

VI. Joseph ponders problems.

(a) Suddenly the word came. Caesar Augustus had decided he was being cheated out of taxes because of our inadequate census. The public order stated that every mother's son alive would take his family and return to his ancestral city to register for taxing. How's that for a reason to take a trip? It said "family." "Would I have to take Mary?" I wondered. "The baby is almost here; she can't make a trip like that," I pleaded with the local official. He abruptly informed me that a watchdog for Rome in Nazareth could not make exceptions to an order of Caesar Augustus. Mary had to go to Bethlehem with me.

(b) After five days of hard travel we saw Jerusalem. It was a thrill to see the temple. I pondered the fact that it had been rebuilt by Herod. Strange that a man like that

would do a good thing. He claims to be a Jew, makes daily sacrifices, but he's not even a good hypocrite.

(c) It was when we saw Bethlehem that I finally remembered. That's why Mary had been so willing to take this journey; she had remembered. That little snatch of prophecy from Micah 5:2: "But thou, Bethlehem Ephratah, though thou be little among the thousands of Judah, yet out of thee shall he come . . . "

VII. Bethlehem already crowded.

(a) When I told the manager of the inn of our predicament, he was kind, in an easy sort of way, and I could tell in a minute he wasn't really listening. "There is no room," he said. "We have tents pitched in the alley and even cots on the roof." But his wife had been listening and she told us of the cave out back where the animals were kept. "I really wish we could do better," she said, "but that's all there is."

(b) While others were helping Mary, I waited, racing back and forth, wondering why things had not worked out better for your arrival. "Why a stable and a feed trough?" Isn't God a proud father? Why, I would have announced your arrival with giant letters across the sky on top of a rainbow. The orchestra of heaven would play a fanfare and Caesar's palace would be the only place.

VIII. Jesus Christ is born.

(a) Then I heard it. I heard silence. There was not so much as the bark of a dog. How can I say it? It was quiet, and yet there was music. It was the music of life that you almost hear in your good hours, but bless you, it was being played from every cloud bank last night. And the light —I felt that had I stood in the distance I would have seen that over Bethlehem some tremendous signal fire of glory had been set in the heavens.

(b) Now I could see it. Maybe you came into this life under these hard circumstances because God didn't intend his Son to be coddled or served, but for another reason altogether. Maybe you've come to show us that God is willing to get into this fouled-up life, not just with his breath but with himself, to face all our hardships and fears and temptations and maybe even death. Then we'd know that he knows what it's like here and what it will take to salvage us. And we'll know what he's like there and what we can expect from him.

(c) Now I understand why you chose to arrive incognito, just like the rest of us. Not in Caesar's palace, not in Herod's halls, but quietly, in a cowshed with a lowly carpenter for a foster father.—Frank Pollard.

Illustrations

THINKING HUMAN.   Henry Sloane Coffin once referred to a book written many years ago, entitled *Thinking Black*. The book was written by a man who had spent many years in central Africa. Said Coffin, "He had lived in the dark continent and shared the life of its people until he had acquired the native point of view, their ways of reasoning, their mental habit— "thinking black." May we not say that he who has impressed subsequent generations as belonging to another sphere—a visitor from heaven in our dark earth—so entered into the heart and mind of our race that his parables may be entitled "Thinking Human"? How feelingly he interprets the wistful father and the heartsick prodigal and the complacent and indignant elder brother! How movingly he voices the despair of the unemployed who have stood all day idle because no man hired them! How unerringly he sketches character after character in a few telling strokes—usually in a dozen words at the most—so that they live forever in the thoughts of men.

HOW GOD SPEAKS.   The authority of everything that Jesus said depends upon the eternity of his existence with God. He could never be the universal Savior of the whole race unless he was the eternal Son of God. So today when I look into a manger and find in the mystery of the love of God that God has become a baby, I look beyond it and behind it for centuries, before the foundation of the world, and I know that this is God speaking to my heart, and that this is not merely a man, but a God-man, who came out from the glory and humbled himself and took upon himself the form of sinful man. It is God speaking. The One who came in order that my religion might not be formality or legality, but might be life, liberty, victory, and joy in God—who became a baby!—Alan Redpath.

Sermon Suggestions

WHAT WE HAVE RECEIVED AND MUST RECEIVE.   Text: John 1:15–18. (1) Truth: beyond human powers and faculties; revealed in Jesus Christ, the Only Begotten Son; full of eternal light and life for us. (2) Grace: foreshadowed by the law; revealed in Jesus Christ, the Only Begotten Son; full of pardon and peace for us.—R. C. H. Lenski.

THE BIRTH OF JESUS.   Gospel Text: Matt. 1:18–25. (1) A human problem (vv. 18–19). (2) An angelic presence (vv. 20–21). (3) A divine prophecy (vv. 22–23). (4) An obedient protector (vv. 24–25).

Worship Aids

CALL TO WORSHIP.   "Let us now go even unto Bethlehem, and see this thing which is come to pass, which the Lord hath made known unto us" (Luke 2:15).

INVOCATION.   Lord, guide our thoughts and our hearts today as we return to our sacred shrines of faith and renew our worship and our commitment to your will.

OFFERTORY SENTENCE.   "And when they were come into the house, they saw the young child with Mary his mother, and fell down, and worshiped him: and when they had opened their treasures, they presented unto him gifts; gold, frankincense, and myrrh" (Matt. 2:11).

OFFERTORY PRAYER.   Lord Jesus Christ, shepherds and wise men of old came to worship you, and brought offerings of adoration and of gold, frankincense, and myrrh. Your coming has filled our hearts with joy and our lives with meaning, and we now bring to you our several gifts. Touch them with the wonder of your blessing, that they may honor you wherever your gospel is proclaimed.

PRAYER.   God and Father of our Lord Jesus Christ, God of grace and of glory, Lord of majesty and of mercy . . . we praise you for your goodness, for your gentleness, for your love. We thank you for this gathering produced by your gracious gift of the Christ Child, by his manly ministry to the children of men, by his strong sacrifice for man's sins, and by your raising him from the dead. We ask your continuing presence in this fellowship—mercifully forgiving our sins that we now confess to you, generously satisfying our needs that you know better than we, powerfully strengthening our wills, incisively sharpening our minds. Grant your healing to our sick, your comfort to our sorrowing, your presence to our lonely, your peace to our anxious. And, gravely we ask, Father, grant peace to your world. You loved it so much; we know that you love it yet.—J. Estill Jones.

EVENING SERVICE

Topic: A New Asceticism
    TEXT: Matt. 11:17.
    John was the true ascetic, the kind of ascetic that is healthy. His renunciation of the world had a legitimate purpose and it was not to save his own soul. In a culture gone soft and comfortable, what does this strange figure say? Well, Jesus talked about his friend John and he told a little parable. He said the people of his generation were like children playing on the green. Somebody played joyous music, and the children sat down and said we don't want to dance. And somebody played funeral music, and they said we don't want to weep. He is saying the people aren't listening; they aren't tuned in. They say we don't want to play seriously with life.

    I. Jesus is saying faith requires passionate response.

    (a) The dominant note of the New Testament is *rejoice*. Our faith requires the deepest passion, or I should say, it enables and empowers the deepest passion. Real faith does make us weep and lament over cruelty and life's injustice. At the same time we have a deep and abiding joy, for we know this is God's world and nothing can separate us from the love of Christ. But the many in the marketplace are like children who refuse to grow up, for growing up hurts; it brings both laughter and tears. But each of us says: I will not have it so. I will nurse my own ego. I will build up my defense against the world and its demands for my responsibility. I'll have it my way. I'll build up my security. I'll protect and caress it and keep it for myself.

    (b) We've forgotten the relationship that positive sacrifice has to life's real fulfillment. Have we become a self-indulgent, wasteful people? Affluence had tended to make us soft, and growing soft opens us to the furies. We need a new look at the austerity of John the Baptist. He represents what is positive in the ascetic aspects of our faith, something of the courage and toughness needed to redeem a cruel world.

    II. I know that few of us are going out in the world and become ascetics. People tend to take their affluence and a luxurious life as their right. But we may be in for a shock. We need a new form of asceticism to turn the tide of decadence.

    (a) We need a new kind of asceticism that is in this world for the sake of the world—one that recognizes a claim upon us not to turn away from the world but toward it, as Christ loved the world and gave himself for it. Nobody can do this without spiritual disciplines.

    (b) For today's world we need a new austerity and a new frugality that make the best use of everything. Christian discipleship requires a gentleness toward others and a severity toward oneself, for the Christian knows that it takes discipline to develop self-control, not to be controlled by our drives and emotions.

    (c) Our dominant secular philosophy is contradictory to this. The secular philosophies of self-realization tend to lead to self-indulgence. The human tendency is to have interest in what is easy and immediately gratifying. Some of the most essential learning comes out of conflict and struggle.

    (d) A certain amount of asceticism is required for doing anything great. Any great art requires pruning and cutting away excess. Anything done truly well requires giving up other things, a certain sacrifice. Except decadence, nothing ever comes of self-indulgence and a philosophy of immediate gratification. This applies to education as well as sex.

III. We need a new kind of asceticism, not to save our souls for heaven but to save this world for man—a new asceticism that conserves and trims, that practices austerity, not for austerity's sake but to develop endurance and fortitude. But we don't need to begin our austerity with the poor.

(a) We can all learn restraint and set a new tone, a new pace. Some people are beginning to practice fasting, and they are not as naive as some people mockingly say. At least it is a symbolic gesture and a symbolic gesture can fire the imagination.

(b) We need symbols of sacrifices and self-denial in a world where our dominant symbols comes from stimulating and conspicuous consumption. Prayer and fasting —are they nothing but gestures? Both John the Baptist and Jesus thought differently. In fact, it was after prayer and fasting that most of the prophets received their deepest insights. It seemed to clarify their vision and God knows that's what we need. We need to learn to be stern with ourselves, for we have become a wasteful and self-indulgent people. When we are challenged, we can respond and we usually do. We feel ever so much better when we demand more from ourselves. That's why John the Baptist is so fascinating. We admire him and are frightened by him, for we want a purity we don't have. We do want to love this world for God's sake. We are sick of decadence and crime. We come truly alive where the best is called forth from us. True faith requires a passionate response. It requires everything we have and are and more; and God our Father empowers the more.—Robert W. Greene.

SUNDAY: DECEMBER TWENTY-EIGHTH

MORNING SERVICE

Topic: You Are a Minister

TEXT: Luke 22:25–26.

If you are a Christian, you are a minister. This proposition is absolutely basic to any contemporary understanding of the Christian movement. A nonministering Christian is a contradiction in terms. The Christian faith is not made up of spectators listening to professionals and it is not for individuals who are seeking, primarily, to save their own souls. It is necessarily made up of persons who are called to serve as representatives of Christ in the world, and to serve means to minister. The ministry is intrinsic to the Christian life. The ministry is not something added or a means to an end; it is central and ineradicable.

I. The notion that a Christian must minister arose, in the beginning, from the example of Christ himself. Early Christians realized that they were called to minister because Christ ministered and they were called to follow him. "For I have given you an example," he said, "that you also should do as I have done to you" (John 13:15). Though this conception of what a Christian is was well understood in the beginning, it was lost, or at least neglected, for many years, and is now being rediscovered in a powerful way. The degree to which the idea of the universal ministry is being rediscovered in our generation is the most hopeful single factor in contemporary Christianity. If really understood and practiced, it would produce a new Reformation.

(a) One of the clear consequences of the proposition that if you are a Christian, you are a minister is the recognition that our ordinary distinction between ministers and lay Christians is wholly false and misleading. It may have significance for some religions, but it has no relevance to the Christian faith. If we take seriously the idea that all are called to be ministers, the old conception of a layman is as dated and quaint as is the surrey with the fringe on top. If we wish our Christianity to be contemporary, we should cease to talk about laymen at all.

(b) Once it was widely supposed that the

pastor of a church has a program to put into effect and that the ordinary members of the congregation perform their function by helping with this program. Thus the pastor might desire to promote an every-member canvass and the members would rally to provide the manpower for the canvass. Or the clergyman might desire to have a choir, and the members with musical talents were supposed to help make the choir a success. Though there are still situations in the church in which patterns of this kind are appropriate, the characteristic pattern needed in our time is utterly different. The new and revolutionary idea is that the ordinary member, because he is a servant of his fellowmen, begins to have a program in the world and the pastor becomes *his* helper in order to increase the value and probable success of the program. No matter how dedicated the ordinary Christian may be, he needs all the help that he can get, if he is to avoid pitfalls and be really effective. Who should be more helpful than his pastor? After all, this is where a pastor's major training should be applicable.

(c) Illustrations of such personal ministries are numerous and easy to find. Perhaps the Christian is a high school teacher and a loyal member of the church. He realizes that the school is his natural area of ministry. Here is a mission field if ever one existed. He would like to bring as much as possible of the spirit of Christ to bear on his teaching, on his personal relations among students and teachers, and in the general life in the school. How can he do this? Perhaps he needs the advice of a wise pastor in order to learn how far he can go and not trespass constitutional limits. Should he invite students to his house to form small groups devoted to study, witness, and sharing of personal problems? Should he lend books that have reached him, and thus stir up ideas? If so, which books are best as starters?

(d) It is obvious that all of the above questions that would face a high school teacher devoted to the ministry of his daily life are both relevant and hard to answer. It is precisely because there are no easy answers in the back of any manual of the ministry that the dedicated member needs

wise instructions. He should be able to get some of this from his pastor and some from his fellow members who have tried to follow the same road of humble service. This is why some of the most effective groupings of Christians in contemporary life are now based on occupations rather than upon geography. A modern church will necessarily be organized along the occupational lines if it means to take the universal ministry seriously.

II. We understand better the right relation between the ministering *member* and the ministering *pastor* if we think of the military equivalent. There is a strong reason for turning in this direction, as the military metaphors of the New Testament so eloquently indicate. The ordinary Christian soldier, that is, church member, is the one who fights on the front lines. The front lines of the Christian cause today are in factories, schools, legislatures, and homes. It is in these that the struggle is most fierce, because it is in these that the real opposition to the basic Christian witness is encountered. Those who are committed Christians are certainly a minority in any factory or office of any size. The person who undertakes to make a witness needs courage, for he will certainly meet ridicule, and he also needs wisdom, for foolish witnessing is energy that is wasted or is ultimately self-defeating.

(a) Since the ordinary Christian soldier is on the front line, he needs times of renewal in order to be ready for his task. His greatest support, intellectually and morally, must come from those operating chiefly in rear areas, who exist in order to strengthen the ones on the front lines. These supporters are the men who, in the New Testament, are called pastors and teachers. They exist for the wholly noble purpose of assisting those in whatever particular ministry these others may be called to perform, either individually or in groups. The good pastor, then, is really an "assistant in the ministry." That this is the meaning of the classic passage on the subject (Eph. 4:12) is shown with great clarity in this contemporary translation of the passage: "And these were his gifts . . . to equip God's people for work in his service, to the building up of the body of Christ" (NEB). No Christian who wishes to understand the ministry dares to omit a deep study of this passage.

(b) There is a temptation to suppose that there is conflict between the idea of a trained pastorate, on the one hand, and the idea of the ministry of every member, on the other. Some members tend to be anticlerical, feeling that they are forced to be second-class Christians, while some clergymen resent the general ministry, supposing that their own status is thereby threatened. This potential conflict is not at all necessary, providing we have a deeper understanding of what the Christian movement is. If we have a sacerdotal religion in which some can go into the holy of holies while others cannot, there is inevitable tension, but if the pastor is one of many ministers, with special gifts and consequent responsibilities, the reason for tension is entirely removed. Pastor and member both belong to the total ministry of Christ and do not threaten each other at all. The great ideal of the ministry of every Christian is one that cannot be put into actual effect unless there are skillful equippers who guide, inspire, and teach. What we have called the lay ministry needs the professional or separated ministry to bring it to fulfillment. Pastors become truly successful, not by attracting great audiences or by managing large budgets (though these are not to be despised) but only when the members whom they are guiding and teaching become effective witnesses in their daily lives in the world. The best pastors are those whose students in the ministry, the rank and file of the local church, have the courage and wisdom to be representatives of Christ in common life.

III. If we take this philosophy of the ministry seriously, it is obvious that the task of adult education is a tremendous one. If the plumbers and schoolteachers and salesmen are to discover and practice their ministry seven days a week, they need a vast amount of instruction and sound advice. They must know how to answer the honest inquiry of the man whose mother is dying of cancer, and they must be able to instruct the fellow worker who

would like to pray but does not know how to begin. They must be so familiar with the Bible that they can give guidance, on the spot, to the man who is baffled by Genesis. They must be clear enough in their own faith that they can both appreciate the problem of the person who doubts the miracles of the New Testament and provide answers in the light of reasonable conviction.

(a) The disgrace now is that the hungry sheep look up and are not fed. They will never get fed until the rank and file of Christians are themselves more thoroughly instructed. The needed instruction will never occur if all that we have is Sunday morning religion. In short, if we take the ministry seriously, we must expand our vision.

(b) It is important for Christians to realize how revolutionary the idea of the ministry is. Christ really turned existing ethical values upside down when he put on the garb of a servant and washed the feet of his followers. He knew that words were not really effective and that, consequently, he needed to engage in an acted parable. He had told his followers, earlier, that the struggle for prestige and personal eminence was wholly alien to his movement, but apparently they did not understand. It was after much powerful teaching that "an argument arose among them as to which of them was the greater" (Luke 9:46). His rebuke to them for even raising the question was the blunt statement that "he who is least among you all is the one who is great" (Luke 9:48). Later, when the same discussion arose, Christ was even more explicit, showing the contrast between Christian values and the values accepted by the world: "The kings of the Gentiles exercise lordship over them; and those in authority over them are called benefactors. But not so with you; rather let the greatest among you become as the youngest, and the leader as one who serves" (Luke 22:25, 26).

(c) It is doubtful if contemporary Christians have given these passages the attention they deserve. Because we tend to forget that minister means servant, there is always a temptation to reintroduce into the Christian society the very standards that Christ explicitly rejected. It is almost unbelievably fortunate that we have kept, through nearly two thousand years, the word *ministry*. It is so easy for a religion to become wholly dissociated from its roots and deny what it earlier affirmed. Part of our good fortune is found in the wonderful boon of the continung existence of the gospels. We may depart from them, but, because they are available, we are always in a position to return to our beginnings and to find a challenge to our waywardness.

(d) As long as we have the ideal of the ministry, there is real hope for the Christian movement. Whenever we return to this ideal, we have a potent challenge to our practices of selfishness and personal ease or comfort. As long as we know that we are called to be servants, we can realize that our religion is meant to be a stimulus to service rather than a means of self-gratification.

If you know truly that you are a minister, you will still have problems and the tasks are barely begun, but you are at least embarked on the most fruitful road that man knows. You will not be at your destination, but you will be on the way. It is Christ's way!—D. Elton Trueblood.

Illustrations

THE WAY WE WITNESS. There is a sense in which we witness by the way we do our job. A poor employee and a good witness never go together. We witness by the way we treat peoole. A person cannot live his Sundays listening to sermons on love and live his weekdays operating by the law of the jungle and be a witness. A person can be a witness by his interest in the persons with whom he works. We miss a lot if we only see the surface of those who spend most of their lives around us. They have families, fears, ambitions, frustrations, and a desire for meaning in their lives. Sometimes they wonder if anyone cares who they are or what they are or even *that* they are. A person can witness by how he relates to typical at-work discussions. The world of work is a world in which sex, government, football, kids, taxes, and almost everything else gets discussed. A

Christian who identifies with people cannot stand nervously by waiting for a lull in the conversation when he can give a commercial for the church.—Kenneth Chafin.

A MINISTERING PRESENCE. In a large public housing project live many members of a nearby congregation. How tragic if the congregation must organize a program of visitation evangelism in order to call on the people in that project. God has put members of that congregation into the various buildings precisely in order that they might be witnesses to Christ. They are the ones who live there naturally and whose daily lives either gossip the gospel or deny Christ. It is a sign of weakness if some special crusade must be organized in order that the church might begin to do what its members by rights should be doing by their presence there in the midst of the community already. A special calling program by the congregation as such may at times be in order and helpful, but basically the task of witness will be dependent on the work of those who live there. —George W. Webber.

Sermon Suggestions

THIS THING CALLED HAPPINESS. Happiness derives from: (1) Something to hope for. (2) Something to do. (3) Someone to love.—Edward Paul Cohn.

SAFE IN GOD'S CARE. Gospel Text: Matt. 2:13–15, 19–23. (1) A secret plan (vv. 13–15). (2) A brooding providence (vv. 19–22). (3) A special place (v. 23).

Worship Aids

CALL TO WORSHIP. "Come as living stones, and let yourselves be used in building the spiritual temple, where you will serve as holy priests to offer spiritual and acceptable sacrifices to God through Jesus Christ" (1 Pet. 2:5, TEV).

INVOCATION. Almighty God, who hast poured upon us the new light of thine incarnate Word: Grant that the same light, enkindled in our hearts, may shine forth in our lives; through the same Jesus Christ our Lord, who liveth and reigneth with thee, in the unity of the Holy Spirit, one God, now and forever.—*Book of Common Prayer*.

OFFERTORY SENTENCE. "He appointed some to be apostles, others to be prophets, others to be evangelists, others to be pastors and teachers. He did this to prepare all God's people for the work of Christian service, in order to build up the body of Christ" (Eph. 4:11–12, TEV).

OFFERTORY PRAYER. Father, we are all of us in ministry together if we belong to you. Help us to do all that we can, where we are, and wherever your Spirit leads us. Grant that we may not excuse ourselves from what we ought to be doing by merely helping to pay someone else to do our Christian service. Above all, may we give ourselves to you.

PRAYER. Thank you, Lord, for being alive in our lives enough so that when we do wrong, we don't feel right; when we sin against you and break your commandments, there is no happiness within us, no joyous celebration; when we do less than our best, as you make the best possible, we are discontented and miserable; when we pursue the easy—not the faithful—way, our conscience makes life very difficult for us. We want to worship you in such a life-changing way that we will know what is good in your sight, and do it; we will know what is evil in your sight, and refuse to have anything to do with it, no matter how attractive and enticing it may seem; we will feel deep within the satisfaction that comes from obeying you, the worthwhileness that comes from walking in your way, the strength that comes from letting your Spirit guide and direct us. We do not want just to hate what is evil: We want to love what is good. We do not want to know only what we are against: We want to know what we, as Christians, are for. We do not want simply to take up space and exist: We want to live with the purpose of eternity dwelling in our hearts, giving meaning to our days. We do not want to know only the things we will die for: We want to know, just as well, the things we will live for,

stand up and be counted for, strive for, struggle for, sacrifice for—pick up a cross for. And that is why we worship you now: so that we, as individuals, and as a church, want with all our being what you know we need.—Gordon H. Reif.

EVENING SERVICE

Topic: With Quiet Eyes
TEXT: Luke 2:22–25.

Who is he, this man who waits and looks out upon the temple with quiet eyes? Is this Simeon, the disinherited of the world, groaning under the weight of accumulated pains and longing, straining ears and eyes for sounds of hope and shafts of light? Is he a two-faced Janus figure, looking back through all the promise and anguish of his nation, and at once forward beyond the baby—that "still unspeaking and unspoken Word"—to the time when the thoughts of many are stripped clean and his people's pain is nailed tightly to a tree? Or is he everyman, chanting a Christmas litany of Godspell: "When will you save the people, O God of mercy, *when?*"

I. Lord, lettest thou thy servant depart in peace.

(a) What joys of growing can we imagine, took in his youth? How has he earned his bread? What anxieties does he know, what fears survive the passing of his years? Where are his wife and children? Gone? Or were they ever? Does he know hunger and thirst, and laughter and tears, guilt and boredom? Is he poor, or a man of means? He is tired, with few tomorrows, but what of his pain—does he have arthritis or cancer, or has his body just recently grown frail? We cannot know, but we can imagine for he is one of us—he too wears our mysterious flesh.

(b) If we were to meet him there at the temple where he belongs, what might he say to us? Would he speak to us of hope? Not a simpleminded hope that ignores the bleak realities of his urban life, but a prophet's hope of revealed glory, when all flesh shall see together. No, when he speaks there is reality in his words—the reality of unlove pressing against Jerusalem—the reality of rejection—the reality of the rise and fall of many—the reality of the anger of those who would confine the child always to a crib.

(c) Would he speak of other realities quite beyond Herod's knowing? Would he ask us in our modernity to tell him in what we place our hope? And after his listening can we hear him say, "You and I can do so many wonderful things, but can we be each other's hope?"

II. According to my word.

(a) Would he then, speak to us of salvation? Perhaps in his years, he has known the confusion that this word evokes. Perhaps he too sought it in the science, education, or machines of his time. Has he always been so sure as he is today?

(b) He would, I think, understand our doubt, our yearning. Yet, he would continue to speak to us of the one he holds, flesh of our flesh, understanding how hard it is sometimes to reach back to hold him too. I can hear him say, "You and I can do wonderful things, but we cannot save ourselves."

III. For mine eyes have seen your salvation.

(a) And would he finally speak tenderly to us of love? Of love that comes into the chaff of all his days—the pardoning, penetrating love bringing to his nostrils the very scent of God. It is a surprising love, an unexpected love, overpowering in its intensity and extent. He has encountered the expected—hope, peace, and salvation—they are the fruit of the promise, but such luminosity radiates beyond Israel to all who will see it. He can feel the child kicking joy to the farthest corners of the world and as he speaks, might he not then share the child with many standing in their anxiety firing flares for help?

(b) Would this old man in the "dry" months of his years tell the rejected, the guilt-ridden, the unlovely about the baby's tears, some already now full-grown, dropping on his sleeve, marking it indelibly with sacrificial love.

(c) There are other words he might have said to lift the ceiling of our hopes. Other words to give us comfort for our years—words of an infant's birthing, and ours, and his. In return he asks us only to find, to console, to release, to rebuild, to hope against hope, "to make music in our hearts —to made a deed to God of all our days, and look out on life with quiet eyes."—James M. Dodson.

SECTION XII. Ideas and Suggestions for Pulpit and Parish

COMPILED BY RACHEL TEDARDS

WAYS TO INCREASE CHURCH ATTENDENCE. After having two pastorates with steadily maintained attendance but little growth, John P. Jewell, Jr., of Plymouth Congregational Church in Racine, Wisconsin, served two churches in which attendance doubled after two-and-a-half years. He suggests these seven steps to increase attendance: (1) Develop programs that encourage *regular* attendance, beginning on a small scale and moving up. (2) Help the congregation experience success, to improve its self-esteem. (3) Organize campaigns into limited, measurable tasks. (4) Plan special events designed to make it easy to ask people to come. (5) Plan a year's calendar with at least one special event each month (Christmas and Easter are built-in special events). (6) Begin today; pick a theme or event, pay attention to detail, recruit helpers for specific tasks. The result is a group of people who know it can be done. (7) Create a task force of deacons to supervise a continuing effort.—*The Clergy Journal*.

"MINISTRIES BUILDING." Colonial Heights Church in Columbia, South Carolina, is renovating a four-story building, formerly unused, to provide community ministries. Respite House, an adult day-care center located there, provides physical therapy and exercise for older adults, giving families a break from twenty-four-hour-a-day care. The building also houses a food pantry, equipment for loan to handicapped people, an office and waiting room for a Christian counselor, a recrea-tional and youth facility, and a weekend shelter for out-of-town families visiting inmates at a nearby prison.

CLINIC. Crea Clinic provides free medical care for people outside the community health-care system. Doctors, nurses, and other volunteers of South Main Baptist Church in Houston provide services at the twice-a-week clinic, including laboratory work and prenatal care. The church provides space and utilities for the clinic, which receives some donations of medicine and supplies. The clinic's name comes from the Spanish word "crea," which means "I believe."

SYSTEMS FOR ORGANIZING PAPERWORK. With twenty-six file folders, you can create a system to organize your paperwork for an entire year in one file drawer.

First, label one This Year and one Next Year; place them in the file drawer with This Year first. Then, label twelve folders by month and place them directly behind the This Year folder, with the current month first.

Then, label five folders: Week 1, Week 2, Week 3, Week 4, and Week 5. These are inserted behind the current month folder, in their appropriate order. Seven folders, one for each day of the week, are placed behind the current week folder.

Items for this file system should be restricted to items requiring action by you or your church, and not materials for reference. Typical items would include correspondence to be answered, orders/ instructions you need to check later, projects that are coming due, lesson plans or sermon ideas you are expected to write, invitations to speaking engagements, and so on.

Each day, pull the file for that particular day and it should contain every item requiring your attention. At the end of the day, put all unfinished items into the next day's folder (or whenever you plan to return to it), and put the empty "today" folder at the end of the week. At the end of a week, sort through the file for the next week and distribute items into the proper days; and at the end of the month distribute items in next month's folder into the weekly folders.

The system can be expanded with special subject folders, including correspondence, mail orders/inquiries, travel file, newsletter, church boards, liturgical seasons, and an idea file.—*The Clergy Journal*.

HOLY WEEK SERVICES.   Churches desiring opportunities for worship with congregations of other denominations may plan ecumenical Holy Week services, meeting Monday through Friday during the lunch hour. If one church building is near the business district, services can be held there and opened to people from offices. Plan a half-hour Bible study or service, and a half-hour snack-lunch for participants, and enlist ministers from different congregations.

SERMON STUDY.   Evaluating sermons preached over the past six to nine months can be a good tool for keeping balance and variety in sermons. Use a simple form showing date, title, text, central idea, purpose, and sermon type (doctrinal, evangelistic, ethical, pastoral, and so on). The key question is how well did these sermons touch the needs of the hearers?

Remember that "balance" in sermon themes may not be desirable in the aftermath of events that deeply affect the church and/or community.

TEACHER PHONE-A-THON.   Teacher recruitment at First Presbyterian Church of Champaign, Illinois, began one spring with a letter to former teachers, likely parents, and new members who had indicated past experience in teaching. The letter spelled out expectations of teachers, the kind of curriculum used, training opportunities, and the flexibility of team teaching. The recipients were advised to expect a follow-up phone call on a particular evening.

On that date, the Christian Education Committee met at a business office of a member where they could use multiple phone lines. A large chart, listing all grades and names of returning teachers, was posted. Each potential teacher's name and phone number had been typed on a separate index card. After brief instructions and prayer, the callers divided the cards and began calling. "Yes" answers were noted on the poster, and all answers were noted on the cards. The cards of those not reached that evening were separated for later follow-up. All the cards were kept for future use, and lists were made of substitutes, workers for the evening youth program, and respondents who said, "Call me next year."—Cinda Gorman, *Church Teachers Magazine*.

MAKING THE MOST OF VOLUNTEERS. Groups with several volunteer workers need to designate one person to coordinate their work and supervise their training and orientation, according to Susan McCarter, business manager of *Seeds* magazine. Group training is sometimes possible, but usually each volunteer needs individual attention for thorough training. Show the value of volunteers' time and work by having tasks ready to begin when they arrive and by notifying them in advance when there is no work to be done. Make sure that workers in emotionally draining situations receive nurture and support to prevent burnout.

Show special appreciation with "fun nights" or recognition dinners, keep volunteers informed about the whole work or ministry, and provide times for their suggestions and input on decisions. Stay informed of significant things in their lives, praise them for their work, and provide them with opportunities for growth and education when possible.

EMPHASIZING TEAM MINISTRY.   Having the entire staff join the pastor at the front of the church during the invitation emphasizes commitment to team ministry, as well as increasing visibility for staff members whose regular responsibilities do not often involve the whole congregation.

TAPE RECORDERS LET STUDENTS HAVE THEIR SAY.   Concerned that teachers were doing all the talking in Sunday School classes, Brethren House in St. Petersburg, Florida, began providing tape recorders for children to talk into during activity time. Among the benefits of the practice: teachers are given opportunity to hear the children's fresh expressions and insights; misunderstandings can be discovered and noted for later correction; teachers can get to know pupils better; and tapes can help teachers know where to begin in future lessons. The children are given regular practice in tape-recording so that they feel confident and are taught to note their names and places on the tape. They can come, one at a time, to give their versions of a story, describe a picture, or express concerns. Privacy must be assured so they won't feel intimidated or "on stage."— Jean Lersch, *Church Teachers Magazine.*

MINISTRY WHEN A BABY DIES.   The death of a newborn or delivery of a stillborn infant needs special attention in ministry. To prepare for the eventuality, consider what your own feelings and reactions might be and try to come to terms with them. Then consider practical questions: what does an infant's funeral cost; how are such deaths handled for welfare parents; where can babies be buried; are birth and death certificates issued automatically in your county? What is different from the situation of an adult's death?

When a baby dies, try to help the parents deal with their feelings. Let them grieve and express their grief in ways that are comfortable to them. Encourage them to make necessary decisions for themselves, so that they regain influence over their lives and future. Let the mother decide whether to remain on the postpartum floor with other new mothers or to move to another part of the hospital. An autopsy may reveal information the parents will need in planning future pregnancies. Ask the funeral director to come to the hospital so both parents can be involved in planning. Advance information about hospital policies and/or legal requirements is helpful. Protect the parents from other people's "shoulds" and "shouldn'ts."

Seeing and holding the baby, even if seriously malformed, may allay the parents' imagined dread and make the loss more identifiable. Naming the baby and using the name personalizes him or her; secure remembrances such as pictures, a lock of hair, a baby bracelet, foot-and handprints, and a birth certificate (or nonlegal certificate acknowledging the baby's birth). Sibling participation in the grieving and the funeral will help keep even young children from feeling excluded or perhaps guilty. Allow the family to complete its "grief work," which many people will begin to deny them sooner than they need. Mark anniversaries of the baby's birth and death as times for special sensitivity.

INCORPORATING NEW SUNDAY SCHOOL MEMBERS.   Because established classes often have difficulty accepting new members, enlist popular teachers to offer ten-week courses on special topics, perhaps twice a year. Recruit two or three volunteers from existing classes to keep class records, serve as greeters, and organize refreshments. Invite inactive members of Sunday School and others in the community; at the end of the class, absorb newcomers into regular classes.

CODE OF CONDUCT FOR BOARDS. Ground rules for conflict have been established by the board of Fillmore (California) Baptist Church. They are (1) The relative attention given to any issue is in direct proportion to its prominence in Scripture. (2) Church members are encouraged to spend an hour each month in prayer for the pastor and board members. (3) Having a say is more important than having your way. (4) Withhold financial support only when the Lord stops blessing. (5) Stay in the thick of church life while serving on leadership boards. (6) A majority vote is a strong indication of God's will for us at this time. (7) Never keep silent in a meeting on an issue that won't be kept silent at home. (8) Every dissenting vote symbolizes a possible word of caution from the Lord. (9) People can love/respect each other while rejecting individual ideas. (10) Spiritual authority or knowledge will not be used as a club to force passage of an issue or program.— *Leadership.*

ADOPT A MISSION.   Calvary Church in Bel Air, Maryland, "adopted" the Asian mission of a Washington, D.C., mission church, contributing warm clothing, toys, and food over a period of two years.

SPEND A DAY WITH A MINISTER.   Deacons and other laypeople can benefit from arranging to spend a day at work with a church staff member, seeing and assisting with what is involved in the daily routine of staff ministry. Ministers also benefit from improved communication and deeper understanding of their work and their calling.   *Good*

SCHEDULE FOR VISITATION.   A pastor and elder organized a schedule of visitation, in which the elder selects families within a given geographical area, sends them a letter explaining the purpose of the pastor's visit about two weeks in advance, and telephones to confirm an appointment time. One day each week in the pastor's schedule is set aside for visitation in the afternoon and evening; a day or two in advance, the elder provides the names and addresses to the pastor for preparation. Before each call, the pastor reviews membership records, noting how and when they joined the church, names of children (with a note to confirm current addresses of grown children living away from home), and information on any other household members. During the visit, the usual agenda is to ask how they became members of that church, what have been the happiest/most satisfying and unhappiest/most disappointing experiences of life in that church, and suggestions for changing and improving church life. The final subject is "What would you like to do or par-

ticipate in, if someone asked or invited you, in the life of our congregation?" Each call is allotted forty-five minutes and is usually closed with a reading from Scripture and a prayer. Then during travel to the next visit, records are made of pertinent comments and impressions for facilitating future ministry to the family.—Gary J. Looman in *Sharing the Practice.*

TOY-LENDING LIBRARY.   Public libraries occasionally offer toys to be checked out, an idea church libraries might like to adopt. The toys attract children to the library and make them feel comfortable, with the benefit of stimulating a love of reading and learning. The libraries are also a learning resource for parents and a place to meet and discuss common problems, as well as relief for overloaded budgets. Training and experience lets workers suggest guidelines for purchases, and toys for handicapped and learning-disabled children can be stocked.

To start a toy library, select toys that are sturdy, waterproof, colorful, and designed for use by more than one age level. Save part of the budget until you learn which toys are most popular and how many borrowers will come. Store toys in file cabinets, bags, boxes or bins, on shelves or pegboards, arranged by type, by developmental stage, or by the skills they teach. Designate areas in which children may play without strict noise limits.

HOPE SEMINARS.   "Beginning Again: A Hope Seminar for the Formerly Married" is held four times a year in several local churches, meeting four Wednesday nights for two hours. The pastor leads the first session; a lay counselor leads two meetings on the grief process; and a lay member of the church leads the final program on setting goals. Each evening includes a presentation, refreshments, and a question-and-answer time.

The seminars are open to anyone in the community, for a small fee. Attendance in each case has ranged from 85 to 150 in the years the program has been in existence.

SUNDAY MORNING PRODUCE EXCHANGE.
When the next growing season rolls

around, consider setting up a produce table for parishioners to bring surplus food and flowers from their gardens for other members. Provide a container for cash donations, and apply the money to hunger relief. Have bags available for those taking food home. The exchange tables are a help to apartment dwellers and others who don't have opportunity to garden, a good after-church fellowship event, and a means of raising funds for the poor. —*Leadership 100.*

ENCOURAGE STAFF MEMBERS' GROWTH. Church staffs may select books to read together, with one person assigned to report on the book, or selected chapters, in staff meetings. Reporting assignments should rotate as new books are chosen.

FAITH JOURNALS.   Beginning in early childhood, churches can provide journals for children to write in at significant times such as special group events. Keep the journals at the church, accessible to teachers so they can be added to at any time. Give journals to students when they graduate from college, or when they leave the church and its young adult programs.

PART-TIME CHOIR.   A once-a-month "Praise Choir" at First Evangelical Covenant Church in Rockford, Illinois, creates an opportunity for people who cannot attend every week to participate in choir on a regular basis. The only requirement is a one-hour rehearsal the Wednesday evening before the last Sunday of each month; no long-term commitment is necessary. The Praise Choir sings simple arrangements that can be prepared quickly. Workers who have other commitments on Wednesday nights are excused to rehearse with the Praise Choir once a month. The experience has led some participants to join the regular choir, and new soloists and duet combinations have been discovered.—*Leadership 100.*

NEW PASTOR SURVEYS MEMBERS.   A pastor, when she begins a pastorate, hands out three-by-five cards at a Wednesday night service and asks those attending to tell her "What I would do first if I were

called to be the pastor." The survey not only adds to the pastor's knowledge of the church but also creates a context in which the pastor introduces herself and identifies her philosophy of ministry.

COMPUTER NETWORKS.   Growing use of computers in church administration has generated several nonprofit groups that help churches and ministers share effective ways to use computers. Among these groups are GRAPE (Gospel Resources and Program Exchange, P.O. Box 576, Keystone, WA 98345); Christian Computer Users' Association (1145 Alexander Street SE, Grand Rapids, MI 49507); and Church Computer Users Network (P.O. Box 1392, Dallas, TX 75221).

MAKING VISITORS FEEL AT HOME.   As a clergyperson with opportunity to visit congregations, Thomas W. Goodhue offers suggestions for making visitors feel welcome. First, remember that it takes courage to attend an unfamiliar congregation, especially for those who are in a strange city or who visit alone. Among the needs of visitors: clear signs giving directions; open access for handicapped persons; warm but not overwhelming greetings; singable opening hymns; some form of contact during the following week; good acoustics—ushers should direct visitors to seats where they can hear well; and sharing by laypeople during the service.

"CELEBRATION OF UNITY."   A communion service, consisting of readings from Old and New Testaments without interpretation, drew approximately eighty pastors to a North Carolina ministers conference where regular attendance had fallen to about twelve. Planners used the Imprimatur Revised Standard Version so Roman Catholics could take part, and the service drew Methodist, Lutheran, Baptist, Episcopal, Nazarene, and Quaker ministers and leaders.

SUPPER CLUB FOR YOUNG MARRIEDS. One local church reports that three dinners each fall and three each spring provide a dress-up event for young married couples. Programs relate to marriage enrichment, dealing with topics such as communication, finances, in-laws, parenting, and problem solving. Small group discussion during dessert helps create a community that helps young couples in adjusting to marriage.

Short-term Sunday School classes for couples in their first year of marriage can address similar issues and reinforce the supper club learnings and community building. Classes should be limited to twelve to fifteen couples and last for about six months; members can then be incorporated (back) into regular classes.

CHURCH ENERGY CONSERVATION.   Trinity Lutheran Church in Madison, Wisconsin, embarked in 1977 on a three-stage energy conservation program, spurred by the realization that their utility bills could total one million dollars over the next twenty-two years. Phase One focused on insulating and reroofing the sanctuary and educational buildings; other steps included installation of storm windows, a new boiler pump, and timers on thermostats. Phase Two primarily dealt with aesthetic improvements in the sanctuary but also replaced 260 light bulbs (75 watt) with four-foot, dimmable fluorescent lights that provide twice the light but cut operating costs by three-fourths. Phase Three included roofing a courtyard formed by the sanctuary and educational building, including vents to release hot air in the summer and skylights to trap solar heat in the winter. Volunteers managed the entire energy program and provided some of the less technical labor. Assistance from the American Lutheran Church included the creation of two books, *The Energy Efficient Church and Total Energy Management.—Leadership.*

VISITS TO HOSPITAL PATIENTS.   Friends In-Deed, a lay ministry program of an inner-city Houston church, organizes volunteers to visit cancer patients from other cities being treated at M. D. Anderson Medical Center. Volunteers are trained by the hospital chaplain as certified visitors.

An outgrowth of this ministry has been Sojourn House, which provides inexpensive housing to out-of-town families visiting hospital patients. The church currently leases eleven apartments, and members provide furnishings and supplies.

SECTION XIII. *A Little Treasury of Illustrations*

PILGRIMS AND STRANGERS. People who pass Lord Rothschild's mansion in Piccadilly are surprised to notice that the end of one of the cornices of his beautiful home is unfinished. Many think it strange that a rich man such as he could not afford to put the final touches on this otherwise superb residence. The explanation, however, is very simple. Lord Rothschild was an orthodox Jew; and every pious Jew's house, tradition says, must have some part unfinished to bear testimony to the fact that its occupants, like Abraham, are but pilgrims and strangers on earth. The incomplete cornice on the mansion says to all who understand its meaning: "This is not Lord Rothschild's final home; he is traveling to eternity."—M. R. DeHaan/H. G. Bosch.

TACTFULLY BOLD. John Woolman was an amazing eighteenth-century Quaker. He had a rare blend of personality traits—great zeal coupled with human compassion, a tremendous passion for righteousness teamed with an awareness of human frailty. Woolman became concerned in the 1700s that many Quakers were slaveholders. As a young man he determined to rid the Society of Friends of this ugly blight. His strategy was simple.

He did not picket.

He did not hold mass rallies.

He did not preach harsh sermons against slavery and slaveholders.

He did not gather names on petitions.

He did not go on a hunger strike.

He did not chastise or threaten.

He did not organize committees.

Rather, for thirty years he traveled up and down the country visiting with slaveholders. He would go into their homes, accept their gracious hospitality, and gain their respect. Then he would ask quite simply, "How does it feel to be a child of God and own slaves?" There was no condemnation in his approach because he believed the slaveholders were people of conscience who could be helped to make the right decision.—Mary Frances Bailey.

KNOWING GOD. My admired professor of theology, Daniel Evans, once preached a sermon on God. After the sermon a shoe manufacturer whom Dr. Evans knew well came up to him and objected, "I don't know any God. I don't know what you are talking about. Why don't you talk common sense?"

"Bill," responded Professor Evans, "what do you think about the first thing in the morning: shoes?"

"Well, that's my business, and of course I get ready for the day."

Continued Dr. Evans, "Then during the day you keep on with your business? You think all day of shoes?"

"I suppose so."

"Then at night," Dr. Evans persevered, "you often, no doubt, go out with business associates and your conversations stray off on shoes?"

"We shouldn't, but I guess we do talk shop all too often."

"Bill," said Dr. Evans, "the trouble with you is that your mind has turned into a last. You cannot know God by a last!"
—Nels F. S. Ferré.

RATIONING OUT GOD. Charles Swindoll, in his book *Improving Your Serve*, quotes the words of Wilbur Rees: "I would like to buy $3 worth of God, please, not enough to explode my soul or disturb my sleep, but just enough to equal a cup of warm milk or a snooze in the sunshine. I don't want enough of him to make me love a black man or pick beets with a migrant. I want ecstasy, not transformation; I want the warmth of the womb, not a new birth. I want a pound of the Eternal in a paper sack. I would like to buy $3 worth of God, please."—C. Neil Strait.

DANGEROUS FREEDOM. One of the largest and most successful manhunts in American history culminated in March 1984, with the roundup of 2,116 fugitives. U.S. marshals combined forces with California law enforcement agencies to create FIST (Fugitive Investigative Strike Team), which used such scams as a fake parcel delivery service to lure hunted criminals out of hiding. Most were being sought for violent crimes, each one apprehended having an average of five felony counts on his record.

Within weeks of their arrest, however, almost half of those rounded up were back on the street, either released on bail, placed on probation, or freed on their own recognizance. Ironically, many of them were fugitives precisely because they had previously jumped bond, violated parole, or failed to appear in court to face charges. For example, one twenty-five-year-old man from Oakland, California, who was set free had already accumulated twenty-six earlier arrests for grand theft and selling narcotics (*Time*, April 9, 1984, p. 29)!

It is always frustrating to discover how easily habitual criminals can secure their freedom, due in part to crowded prison conditions. But before we come down too hard on the courts, think how frequently we set free those very sins that we resolved so firmly to keep behind bars. Some vow to handcuff itchy fingers of greed, only to let selfishness run rampant just as soon as an opportunity arises. Others determine to incarcerate an unbridled tongue, only to unlock a torrent of gossip as soon as there is a tale to be told. On New Year's Day we resolve to round up our sins and shove them into the slammer, but long before Easter most of them are back on the prowl again. If you are *really* concerned about criminals on the loose, then try locking up your law-breaking habits and throwing away the key.—William E. Hull.

COURTING RISK. Dr. T. Glynn Williams, associate director of the Maryland Psychiatric Research Center, told me recently that he doesn't believe man was created to be safe and if there is no risk and danger in his life, he will create it. He sees this as a constructive urge rather than a destructive one. The need for danger and risk is universal to all of mankind—African bushmen, Australian aborigines, or urban dwellers in Brooklyn. Deprived of danger, man has a deep inner need to create some, or, like Homer Dodge, to put himself where "interesting things" can happen.—Bruce Larson.

CHRISTIAN WITNESS. On a trip to Dallas, I stopped at a restaurant in Missouri. A conversation opened with the waitress; she openly shared her guilt and domestic problems. Twenty-five minutes later, she prayed to receive Christ as her Savior. During the discussion, she said to me, "I used to attend a church, but they didn't care about us: We were not part of the group. And we couldn't afford the clothes they had, so we were not accepted. Why does a church exist if it doesn't love people?" An excellent question. Why does it?

The opportunity that the innkeeper in Bethlehem had is ours today. Christ can be invited to our home and enjoy his favorite meal. He can receive our hospitality, and we can quench his thirst. "Truly I say to you, to the extent that you did it to one of these brothers of mine, even the least of them, you did it to me" (Matt. 25:40).—Edwin W. Lutzer.

THE EVERLASTING WORD. One of the vivid memories of my youth is that of the period at the age of eight, when in the normal course of events in childhood, I became an atheist. Along with other philosophers of about the same age, I longed to make one grand gesture of heroic impiety, to do the wickedest thing we could think of. We decided that that would be to burn a Bible. So I got from the table in my father's study a large book bound in leather and a public burning of the Book was celebrated in the backyard. It was interrupted by the arrival of my father, who was a preacher. He did the meanest thing that could possibly be done to spoil the party. He gently pointed out that what we had on the fire, and that, like the burning bush, refused to be consumed, was not the Bible but the dictionary! And all the thrill was gone, when we discovered that it was not God we were defying but merely Noah Webster.—Halford E. Luccock.

PRACTICING THE GOSPEL.   The true pilgrim on the Christian way is still a shining wonder, because he follows a path that is absurdly out of step with those who follow their own paths. The lifestyle of a Tom Dooley or a Mother Theresa of Calcutta cuts entirely across the make-it-and-flaunt-it secular syndrome. Still, we are somehow inexorably drawn by the sheer, beautiful daring of their "absurdity." When we see the word of the gospel radically and literally practiced, we do instinctively recognize the "truth standing on its head."—Paul Liston.

MAKING DECISIONS.   The big clock in the courthouse tower struck twelve as the foreman of the jury said, "Well, let's take another vote." The results were unchanged from the previous vote: ten, guilty; one, not guilty; and one, undecided. It was the person who could not decide that arrested my attention. She was experiencing a great deal of discomfort by being in a situation where she had to decide. Her indecision was not without consequences, however, because the jury finally had to report that they were "hung" on the case. Everyone went home disappointed—the judge, the attorney, and the defendant, because the only decision we were able to make was the decision not to decide. "Not to decide is to decide," wrote Harvey Cox. It is impossible to escape decision making. We always decide, because even in our lack of responsi-ble decision making we decide to be irresponsible.—John Ishee.

CONTRADICTIONS IN CHARACTER.   One of my friends who has lived many years said to me, "The thing that amazes me about human beings is the goodness of some pretty bad people I have known, and on the other hand the surprising badness of some otherwise good people; if they would be one way or the other, I could find some way to work with them. But the minute I decide a guy is all bad, he does some noble deeds that seem all out of character. Or the very person I come to see as solid and trustworthy suddenly sells out his own mother or lets his children down."—R. Lofton Hudson.

AVAILABLE POWER.   I am told that when the great Hellgate bridge was being built over the East River in New York, the engineers came upon an old derelict ship, lying embedded in the river mud, just where one of the central piers of the bridge was to go down through to its bedrock foundation. No tugboat could be found that was able to start the derelict from its ancient bed in the ooze. It would not move, no matter what force was applied. Finally, one of the workers hit upon this scheme. He took a large flatboat, which had been used to bring stone down the river, and he chained it to the old sunken ship when the tide was low. Then he waited for the great tidal energies to do their work. Slowly the rising tide, with all the forces of the ocean behind it and the moon above it, came up under the flatboat, raising it inch by inch. And as it came up, lifted by irresistible power, the derelict came up with it, until it was entirely out of the mud that had held it. Then the boat, with its subterranean load, was towed out to sea where the old, waterlogged ship was unchained and allowed to drop forever out of sight and reach. There are *greater forces than those tidal energies waiting for us to use for our tasks*.—Rufus M. Jones.

CONVERSATIONAL PRAYER.   Rosalind Rinker was a missionary in China. She was trying to pray, yet the prayer meetings she went to "didn't mean anything" to her.

She found them boring because there were always the same "experts" praying those long, stilted prayers. She also felt threatened because she wanted to pray but feared she would make a fool of herself. She didn't know how to pray those beautiful stylized prayers. Out of all this "lack of meaning" she realized the need for a simple conversational prayer form in which everyone participated. After years of experimenting with this small group prayer, she found that structuring it into four steps helped people to be more comfortable praying. Those steps are (1) imagining Jesus present, (2) thanking Jesus, (3) asking Jesus for help and forgiveness, and (4) asking Jesus to help my brother.—Joseph Lange/Anthony J. Cushing.

THE GRACE OF FORGETTING.   Once a boy stood on a bridge watching the water currents go flowing by. Occasionally a piece of wood or debris would flow under the bridge and disappear from view. No matter what appeared on the surface of the water, the water slipped by as it had been doing for as long as anyone knew. As the boy contemplated the scene, a thought came into his mind. One day everything in life would pass under the bridge. The experience of that day was never forgotten. As the boy became a man, he learned to treat his mistakes and failures as "water under the bridge."—Larry Kennedy.

AFFIRMATION.   I have a quotation by Victor Hugo on the wall of my office that says, "Man lives by affirmation even more than by bread." Jesus is God's great affirmation of man. He loves us in our sins; he wants to change us, but he is totally on our side while we are yet sinners; and he calls us to enter into his great love and acceptance. When we have done this, then we go out and become this affirmation for others.—Bruce Larson.

TESTIMONY OF THE HOME.   For over a year, I served as the chaplain of a residential school for girls in Minnesota. I interviewed and counseled hundreds of girls. It gave me insight into the nature of delinquency. I discovered that in over 95 percent of the cases, the delinquency of young people could be attributed to delinquent homes and parents. It is the home that is all-important. Missionaries tell us that when they enter a new community in which the gospel of Christ has never been heard, the natives are most impressed at first not by the stories of Jesus or God but by the love and devotion they see in evidence in the homes of the missionaries.—Donald Norman Lindgren.

KINDNESS AND LOVE.   A story is told of a child who found a turtle and started to examine it, but the turtle closed his shell like a vise. The little boy then tried to pry open the turtle with a stick. His uncle nearby said, "No, no, that's not the way."

He took the creature inside and set him on the hearth. In a few minutes he began to get warm, stick out his head and feet, and calmly crawled toward the boy.

"People are sort of like turtles," his uncle said. "Never try to force a fella into anything. Just warm him with human kindness, and more than likely he'll come your way."—Cited by Ed Jansson.

THANKS "IN SPITE OF."   If our Pilgrim fathers had calculated their gratitude on the basis of a profit and loss statement, there never would have been instituted a Thanksgiving Day. By all the tokens that so many of us use to figure our cause for thanksgiving, the Pilgrims were quite pitifully in the red. They were poor, had not even had a good harvest. They were not in good health—half of them had died during the preceding winter and their one hope was that they might survive the next. They had no security of the kind that so many modern Americans would seemingly sell their souls and heritage to have given to them by law. They were not safe from their enemies—even the cemetery was disguised lest it betray their weakness. Yet they were the very ones who founded Thanksgiving Day. It was not done, however by a balance sheet list of advantages.—Hughes Wagner.

WHAT IS A CHRISTIAN.   Webster's unabridged dictionary lists four main definitions of the word *Christian*. (1) a person who professes belief in Jesus as the Christ

—or in the religion based on the teachings of Jesus; (2) the chief character in *Pilgrim's Progress*; (3) a decent, respectable person; (4) in a general sense, anyone born of Christian parents. How easily we drop from number one to number four. And what a price we pay for doing so!—Ernest T. Campbell.

CHRIST.   Wilbur Smith has written: "The latest edition of the Encyclopedia Britannica gives 20,000 words to this person, Jesus, and does not even hint that he did not exist—more words, by the way, than are given to Aristotle, Alexander, Cicero, Julius Caesar, or Napoleon Bonaparte."—Charles R. Swindoll.

LIFE'S PURPOSE.   Rabindranath Tagore, India's poet, said: "I have spent my life stringing and unstringing my instrument, and the song I came to sing remains unsung."—C. Neil Strait.

GIVING.   —When Mother Theresa visited Washington, D.C., she did not go to the centers of power and prestige. Instead, she went to the dark sides of poverty. Newsmen followed her and asked, "What do you hope to accomplish here?" She replied, "The joy of loving and being loved."

"That takes a lot of money, doesn't it?" a reporter asked.

Mother Theresa shook her head and said, "No, it takes a lot of sacrifice."—Charles Colson.

WORDS OF POWER.   A few years ago I met with military personnel in Berchtesgaden, West Germany. We were gathered there from all over Western Europe, and even as far away as Turkey—officers and enlisted men from all the services and some British soldiers as well. On the last night of our retreat, we gathered to celebrate the Lord's Supper. We met in the hotel where Joseph Goebbels and Hermann Goering used to stay when Adolf Hitler brought his high command together to plan various offenses. Outside the window, the Alps stood, reaching up into the twilight. It was an electric moment. Two words—"*Heil* Hitler!"—once

echoed through those halls, two words that once bloodied the face of Europe. But they could be heard no longer. They had been replaced by other words that night—older words, words with even more power: "This do in remembrance of me."—William J. Carl, III.

BIBLE PROMISES.   G. Ray Jordan tells of an old saint whose Bible was filled with notes written in the margin. Beside some of the verses the man had put the letters *T.P.* One day someone asked the old man what the letters meant. He responded, "Tried and Proved."—Ernest A. Fitzgerald.

CONVICTION.   After a businessman in the Pacific Northwest purchased a motel/restaurant, the first thing he did was to order the bar removed. He was told by those who thought they knew the business pattern and climate that he could not survive without the sale of liquor. But he did!

When he was questioned later about his courageous act, he said "Beliefs aren't worth much if a fella's not ready to live by them."—Charles Colson.

THE RANGE OF CHRISTIAN EXPERIENCE. Soon after he became a Christian, Jeb Magruder was sharing with Louie Evans some of the feelings and frustrations of his new walk with God. Evans told him: "But it isn't all joyful, Jeb. You'll become more sensitive to pain, and injustice, and frustration. That's Christ in us, too—opening us up to all the human vibrations."—Jeb Stuart Magruder.

GOD'S WITNESSES.   Mother Theresa, in speaking to her "sisters," said, "Make it a special point to become God's sign in your community."—Mother Theresa.

DUTY.   In 1805 the British navy was sent to battle the combined forces of Napoleon. The commander of the British fleet was Lord Nelson. Nelson chased the French fleet all the way from the West Indies to the coast of Spain. On the morning of October 21, Nelson finally managed to engage in battle. He sent a message to his forces that probably earned him that monument that stands in London's Trafalgar Square: "England expects every man to do his duty!" Few warriors have fought with greater bravery.—Ernest A. Fitzgerald.

SPIRITUAL LIGHT. When I was in high school, my biology class performed an experiment with bean sprouts. The class was divided into groups and each group grew several pots of beans, but each pot was treated differently. We wrapped a different color of cellophane paper around each pot. To our amazement, some of the beans grew thick and bushy, some were long and skinny, some turned pale and limp. We learned that the color of the paper filtered out that color of the spectrum. Plants need all eight colors of the spectrum to be healthy.

Every ray of light, no matter where it is in the world, has the same eight colors of the spectrum that blend together and appear white. Just as plants need all of light, people need all the components of spiritual light to be spiritually healthy. We cannot afford to filter out the spiritual truth that we may find uncomfortable shining on us. By filtering out the truth of God, we will become misshapen like the little bean sprouts.—Hal Poe.

STRUGGLE. At Chamonix in southeastern France at the foot of Mount Blanc, there is a stone that marks the grave of a guide who perished while climbing the Alps. On it are written these words: "He died climbing." To be victorious over the world does not mean that we will never stumble or fall. It means that after every fall we shall rise again—undaunted, undefeated, undismayed—and, still trusting God, shall climb and keep on climbing and *die climbing*.—Beau Colle.

COMMITMENT. An elderly gentleman who was nearly blind and deaf nevertheless found his way along the street with his cane regularly on Sundays to the church service. When asked why he continued attending when he could hear almost nothing spoken or sung, he replied, "I just want people to know which side I'm on."—Jim Martin.

THREE KINDS OF CHRISTIANS. While preaching on the power of the Holy Spirit, an elderly minister said there are three kinds of Christians. First, there is the *rowboat* Christian. He is pulling with all of his strength at his oars as he tries to row up the stream. He makes some progress. It is difficult going against the current. In his effort to row upstream, he gets all worn out. The old minister said, "There are a lot of Christians like that. They struggle and struggle in the energies of the flesh to get the job done for God."

Second, there are the *sailboat* Christians. When the winds of revival come, they really live as their sails are put up. The boat makes good progress as it sails along. For a time everything is wonderful. But when the wind stops blowing, the boat stops sailing and begins drifting. These people often get depressed and don't amount to much for the Lord until the wind of revival starts blowing again.

The old preacher went on to describe the third kind of Christian. He said that these are the *steamboat* Christians. The steamboat does not care about the current. It does not care about the wind. It is powered by fire and water that turns the great propellers and moves it to its destination, regardless of wind or weather. The old preacher stressed the fact that the power of the Holy Spirit makes the Christian a steamboat Christian.—Robert H. Wilson.

SPIRITUAL SURVIVAL. We had quite a little storm in our neighborhood. The winds gusted to gale velocity, the rains beat down in torrents, and even some hail pelted everything in its pathway. Result? A yard littered with enough broken limbs to fill two garbage cans with the debris.

As I stooped to pick up each of those fallen branches, I began to notice that most of them were barren of any foliage. Upon closer inspection I saw that, underneath the outer bark, many were dry and even rotten. Nature had, as it were, involuntarily "pruned" all of my trees, blowing the worthless limbs to the ground, leaving the healthy limbs to nourish their green leaves.

As I gazed into those garbage cans full

of dead sticks, I remembered John 15:2, "Every branch that bears no fruit, he takes away, and every branch that does bear fruit he prunes, that it may bear more fruit." The storm had lashed every limb with equal force, but only those without life were threatened by its fury. Just so, all of us are buffeted by storms of circumstance, but those who are spiritually alive deep within survive while those who are dead and brittle are destroyed.—William E. Hull.

THE PROMISED LAND OF THE CROSS. All three of Jesus' answers to the Tempter (Luke 4:1–13) are taken from Deuteronomy; all three recapture cohesively Israel's wanderings in the wilderness; and all three lead to the promised land where indeed Jesus shall reign, and from where he shall conquer the human heart in his good time —that is, all three lead to the promised land of the cross. Otherwise all three state emphatically, "No promises." That the gospel shall profit you anything on earth except, like the two thieves, places beside him, "ringside seats" or, like Peter, a topsy-turvy, upside-down crucifixion where indeed everything shall rightly go to your head and where you shall reign with him—your defeat your glory.—Peter Fribley.

LOVING ONESELF. One of my counselees told of going to her clergyman for counseling. After she told her story, he said, "The best I can hear you, you hate yourself. Why? Do you know that God loves and likes you? If you hate yourself, you are against God, on the opposite side of the fence."—R. Lofton Hudson.

RESPONSIBILITY. Pythagoras was once asked contemptuously by a Greek tyrant who he was and what was his particular business in the world. The philosopher replied that at the Olympic games some people came to try for the prizes, some to dispose of their merchandise, some to enjoy themselves and meet their friends, and some to look on. "I," said Pythagoras, "am one of those who come to look on at life." Bacon, in telling the story, adds: "But men must know that in this theater of

man's life it is reserved only for God and angels to be lookers-on."—James Moffatt.

CHRIST-LIKENESS. John Selwyn, once missionary bishop in Melanesia, on one occasion found it necessary to rebuke a native candidate for baptism. The man, only so recently a cannibal, enraged by the rebuke, struck the bishop a violent blow in the face. Selwyn, who had been a famous amateur boxer in his day, let the blow fall and quietly folded his arms. This so staggered the native that, turning away from the calm face that looked into his wild one, he ran headlong from the scene. Years later, long after Selwyn had returned to England, this same native came to another missionary and asked to be prepared for baptism. When asked what name he would like to take he replied: "Call me John Selwyn—for it was he who first taught me what Christ is like."—Joost de Blank.

INFLUENCE OF CHRIST. As Charles Dickens has shown in his immortal *Christmas Carol*, there is a light and warmth in the Christmas story that can melt the heart even of a Scrooge. Out of that story have grown little by little, but steadily on the whole, a new care for the child, a reverence for woman, a maintenance of the home, a service of the less fortunate the wide world over, a sorrow over wrong, and a striving after right.—Walter Russell Bowie.

MOTIVATION. In Christ every man is a new creation. One of the signs of this wonderful novelty is that duty is transformed into delight. In Christ men begin to get a kick out of righteousness. Justice becomes a thrill and mercy becomes a pleasure; and walking with God an ecstasy. In the vocabulary of men remade in Christ, the word *ought* vanishes. Conscience becomes a friend, or lover even. You never hear people say: "I ought to go to the pictures." Does a young man in love ever say to himself: "I *ought* to meet my lovely Jane tonight"? Never on your life! He will only begin to talk like that after he's been married a few years. So long as the dear delusion of being in love lasts, he will never use the word *ought*. Nothing will prevent him meeting Jane at 7:30—wind, rain, hail, snow. Let the universe do its worst, he will keep his 7:30 tryst at 7:00. Why? Because that is what he longs for with his whole being—with his unconscious as well as his conscious heart and mind. "As the hart *panteth* after the water-brooks, so panteth the heart of the lover for his beloved."—David R. Davies.

INNER RENEWAL.   So far as a man enters into real communion with our Lord, he rises thereby into a spirit superior to the ills and troubles of life. The very agencies that destroy the well-being and life of the faithless become the actual means by which the faithful make their steady ascent to God. Their communion with God endows them with enthusiasm, or at all events with trustfulness and calm, in circumstances where the faithless are overwhelmed with helplessness and despair, and where the mere moralist can at best only bow the head and submit. And just in proportion as he loses hold on the outer physical world, he is introduced into a new world of energy and joy. As the physical powers fail and the purely mental faculties lose the keenness of their edge, the spiritual life matures within him, his patience and tenderness grow deeper, his faith fuller, while his hopes reach out to the consummation of that blessedness of which he has already had a foretaste. Thus, while the outward man is daily perishing, the inner man is renewed in greater fullness day by day. Each stage in the process of physical decay marks another stage in spiritual growth, till at last the spirit annuls annihilation and under Christ's guidance enters into that good land that he had seen from afar—even into the gates of the city that hath foundations, the ever-blessed city of God.—R. H. Charles.

ASKING FOR HELP.   The story is told of a textile factory in which was found this sign on the wall over each machine: "If your threads get tangled, send for the foreman." A new employee went to work, and soon the threads became badly tangled. The more she attempted to untangle them, the more helpless she became. By

and by, in desperation, after wasting a lot of time, she did call for help. When the foreman came, he asked her why she had not sent for him earlier. She replied in self-defense, "I did my best." He answered with a smile, "Remember, doing your best is sending for me."—R. Lofton Hudson.

FRIENDSHIP EVANGELISM.   A Muslim student in a Christian school in Nigeria became a Christian. As a seminary student in the United States, he explained what led to his conversion. One of his professors had been instrumental in his decision: "He built a bridge of friendship to me, and Jesus walked across it."—Richard Cunningham.

SOLIDARITY OF CHRISTIANS AND JEWS. When Israel is led to the slaughter, the church goes with her—if things are as they should be.—Jürgen Moltmann.

PARENTING.   A superintendent of a large public school district made a profound statement: "Don, the problem so often is that parents are more concerned with passing on the product of their work than the formula for achieving the product."—Donald Gerig.

ROYAL COMPANY.   It is the clear testimony of the early church that a cross with Jesus is better than a crown without him. Peter was crucified upside down and would have sworn it was the world that was upside down, not he. At the marriage of the Prince of Wales and Lady Spencer in St. Paul's Cathedral, Archbishop Ramsey said, "Every couple is on its wedding day a royal couple." And it is the testimony of all the saints through all the ages that every company of souls that does not part company with Christ and Christ's people and Christ's causes is, in whatever circumstances, royal company.—Peter Fribley.

INTERPRETERS NEEDED.   Ten years ago I spent Easter in Vienna. What a magnificent city! It still reflects the splendor of the old Hapsburg empire. The Holy Roman emperors ruled an empire that stretched from Greece to Holland and included at one time Spain and all her New World possessions. As the center of such an empire, Vienna prospered and grew into one of the most magnificent cities on earth.

On Easter morning we decided to set out on foot for the oldest section of the city where the medieval churches and palaces still stand side by side. The first church we came to had the high gothic arches and stained glass windows of the late Middle Ages. Inside, a full orchestra played. When the service was over, we went on to another church built in the late seventeenth-century of polished marble with highly stylized frescoes on the ceiling. There we heard a huge choir present an oratorio. Throughout the day we went from church to church, heard magnificent music, and beheld the most beautiful of buildings. At the end of the day, however, I realized that I had understood none of what had happened.

People do not have to speak another language to miss the message of Easter. For many people Easter means new clothes, a week's vacation, eggs and candy, a family reunion—all of which are beautiful—but none of which have anything to do with Easter. Be an interpreter. Tell someone what it all means.—Hal Poe.

GOD'S CARE.   Corrie ten Boom tells of a time when her burdens weighed heavy on her and she discussed her concern with the Lord. "He showed me an empty suitcase, and said, 'You possess nothing, you have surrendered all, so you have no responsibilities at all. I carry all responsibilities, you are only my steward.'"—Corrie ten Boom.

CONSECRATION.   Someone asked Henry Drummond, "What does it cost to be a Christian?"

His reply: "The entrance fee is nothing, but the annual subscription is everything."—quoted by Corrie ten Boom.

CREATIVE   FRIENDSHIP.   Recently I talked to Dr. Paul Tournier, one of the best-known counselors and therapists of our time. When I asked him how he counsels people, he said, "I am very embar-rassed by all these people who come to see me. I don't know how to help people. I don't do anything at all. What is important is that people try to find their way and that I try to understand and support them, to welcome them. What is important is that people find me a true friend, someone to whom they confide everything. What a privilege to find someone to whom you can confide without fear of being judged." —Bruce Larson.

OUR IDENTITY.   During the Middle Ages, the countries of Europe developed the system of knighthood known as chivalry. The knights had personal symbols called coats of arms to identify themselves, which they often placed on their shield or armor. Those who knew these coats of arms could tell at a glance who someone was, even though his head was covered by a helmet, by the symbol he bore.

In Scotland, each clan or family also had a crest, or badge. One Sunday morning last year I stopped for a doughnut on my way to church, and in the shop I saw someone who had a tie with my family's crest on it. That morning I was wearing an identical tie. We immediately knew that we were members of the same clan. We spoke and talked about our family.

Jesus said that we could tell his disciples by the fruit of their lives. A good tree bears good fruit. The symbol of a Christian is not a charm we might wear around our neck. Instead, it is the very life we live.— Hal Poe.

WORLDLY WISDOM.   Very little else on earth can compare with the great American spectacle known as the presidential campaign. We drag our campaigns out for over a year between announcement of candidates and final election vote. Most nations devote a few weeks or months to the process at most. Each election the process lasts a little longer. The phenomenon has even created a new profession: the full-time campaign manager.

We have always had campaign managers, but they used to work just a few months before the election. As often as not it was something a person did as a sideline. With the urgency and intensity of politics today, however, campaign consultants work year round as though the election were only a day away.

Jesus advised his disciples to take a lesson from the children of the world. Do we have the same sense of urgency over our King's affairs as the modern politicoes do? —Hal Poe.

UNCONQUERED LIGHT.   In 1979, near Winnipeg, Canada, with a crew of physicists and astronomers from Minnesota, amid a large array of scientific equipment, long telescopes with tracking motors and short-wave communications equipment, I witnessed a complete solar eclipse. It was a cold, clear prairie winter day, and conditions were ideal.

It was the most eerie sight I have ever seen or likely ever will: fifteen degrees' drop in temperature in minutes, sudden high winds, the long skip of night communications coming up midday, birds nesting as if it were night, and most awesome of all, a 360-degree sunset. And then darkness.

And yet, all the while, light, the ring of refracted light from behind the blotting moon. Thus even during the time of so-called total eclipse, "the light shone in the darkness, and the darkness did not overcome it."—Peter Fribley.

A COMMAND TO REMEMBER.   We can only find our hope again if we resolve never to forget. It is only then that there is a future for us after Auschwitz. Anyone who suppresses this past, or who fails to stand up to the burden of our past, gives Hitler a posthumous victory.—Jürgen Moltmann.

TRUE ECONOMY.   His fellow students discovered in John Frederic Oberlin frugality and economy that they mistook for penuriousness, at the temporary cost of his personal popularity. One of them, while passing with him over a bridge in the city, determined to give his classmate a lesson, corrective of his supposed parsimony. Taking a coin from his pocket, he hurled it into the water, saying, "See that, Fritz?" There was no reply to this foolish performance, but later on, meeting a blind man, Oberlin gave him a coin such as the student had thrown away, simply saying to his companion, "See?" So early had he learned the lesson of regard for those who suffered in the hardships of life.—Augustus Field Beard (adapted).

GUIDANCE.   During World War II the Air Corps learned many things about flying and about the men who fly. They discovered one strange phenomenon when men were flying in total darkness, or in heavy fog, or clouds. As the flyers lost sight of any landmark or reference point, they became disoriented and unable to tell what direction they were going. In the void they could not feel the effects of gravity and would often emerge from the fog bank flying upside down or sideways. In the most extreme cases, pilots crashed into the ground, thinking they were flying straight. Now planes have sophisticated instruments that tell pilots their position so that they need not rely on their sensations.

People often find themselves in a spiritual void when life becomes confused and distorted. We lose sight of our direction and of landmarks that were once important in our life. Too often, we try to live by our feelings and find ourselves upside down. When our feelings only add to our confusion, we need to return to an objective guide and landmark. We need reliable instruments and we find this reliability in Scripture.—Hal Poe.

INDEX OF CONTRIBUTORS

SERMON TITLE INDEX

(Children's stories and sermons are identified cs; sermon suggestions ss)

SCRIPTURAL INDEX

INDEX OF PRAYERS

INDEX OF MATERIALS USEFUL AS CHILDREN'S STORIES AND SERMONS NOT INCLUDED IN SECTION X

INDEX OF MATERIALS USEFUL FOR SMALL GROUPS

INDEX OF SPECIAL DAYS AND SEASONS

TOPICAL INDEX

ACKNOWLEDGMENTS

Acknowledgment and gratitude are hereby expressed to the following for kind permission to reprint material from the books and periodicals listed below:

ABINGDON PRESS: Sermon excerpted from *He Died as He Lived*, by James T. Cleland, copyright © 1966 by Abingdon Press.

AFRICAN ENTERPRISE: Article, "Christ the Renewer," by Festo Kivengere, in *Outlook*, November 1984.

BAPTIST PROGRAM and author Mary Frances Bailey: Excerpt from article, "Tactfully Bold," in June–July, 1984, p. 7.

THE CHRISTIAN CENTURY FOUNDATION: Digest of sermon, "Our Homes and God," by George A. Buttrick, copyright © 1950 by Christian Century Foundation. Reprinted by permission from the October 1950 issue of (The Christian Ministry) *The Pulpit.*

CHURCH OF SCOTLAND: Material from *Thine Is the Kingdom*, by James S. Stewart; *Out of Nazareth*, by D. M. Bailie; and *To Whom Shall We Go?*, by D. M. Baillie.

CHURCH TEACHERS MAGAZINE: "Tape Recorders Let Students Have Their Say," by Jean Lersch, *Church Teachers Magazine*, June/July/August 1983, pp. 7–8. Used with permission. Published by National Teacher Education Program, 7214 E. Granada Road, Scottsdale, AZ 85257.

THE CLERGY JOURNAL: "Ways to Increase Church Attendance." Copyright © by Church Management, Inc., P.O. Box 1625, Austin, TX 78767. Used with permission. *The Clergy Journal*, LIX:9, from article by John P. Jewell. "Systems for Organizing Paperwork." Copyright © by Church Management, Inc., P.O. Box 1625, Austin, TX 78767. Used with permission. *The Clergy Journal* (November/December 1982 and March 1983), from columns by Steven R. Fleming.

CONSULTATION ON COMMON TEXTS: Bible references from the *Common Lectionary: The Lectionary Proposed by the Consultation on Common Texts*, copyright © 1983, James M. Schellman. Used with permission.

C.S.S. PUBLISHING COMPANY: Children's object lessons, "Faith Needs Work," by Wesley T. Runk, *Children's Sermon Service*, 30 September 1979; "No Good Until We Use It," by Wesley T. Runk, *Children's Sermon Service*, 6 May 1984; "I Know Who That Is!" by Wesley T. Runk, *Children's Sermon Service*, 13 May 1984; "You Can Trust Me," by Michael L. Sherer, *Children's Sermon Service Plus*, 2 September 1984; "Only God Is Good Enough," by Michael L. Sherer, *Children's Sermon Service Plus*, 28 October 1984. Used with permission from Children's Sermon Service, copyright © C.S.S. Publishing Company, Lima, OH 45804.

D. ELTON TRUEBLOOD: Address in a pamphlet, "You Are a Minister."

EXPOSITORY TIMES: A sermon, "The New Covenant," by James Stewart, from *Expository Times*, T. & T. Clark Limited, Publishers.

THE FAMILY CIRCLE, INC.: Extract from article, "Woman's World," by Gerri Hirshey. Reprinted from the Aug. 10, 1982, issue of *Family Circle Magazine*. copyright © 1982 *The Family Circle, Inc.* Appearing on page 303 of this volume, titled "Troy-Lending Library."

GUIDEPOSTS: Excerpt from "Words to Grow On," by Norman Vincent Peale, December 1984. Reprinted with permission from *Guideposts Magazine*. Copyright © 1984 by Guideposts Associates, Inc., Carmel, NY 10512.

HARPER & ROW, PUBLISHERS, INC.: Sermon by D. W. Cleverley Ford, from *An Expository Preacher's Notebook*, "When the King Refused," pp. 62–66 (1960). Sermon outline, John A. Broadus, "The Pleasures of Piety," in *The Favorite Sermons* of John A. Broadus, ed. by V. L. Stanfield (1959), pp. 130–32. Digest of sermon, "Relying on Our Spiritual Resources," Arnold H. Lowe, When God Moves In (1952), pp. 17–23. Digest of sermon by W. A. Cameron, "Saints in Strange Places," The Gift of God (Doran, 1925), pp. 153–65. Prayer by Paul Scherer, When God Hides, 1934, pp. 28. Digest of sermon by Arnold H. Lowe, Power for Life's Living, 1948, pp. 146–52. Digest of sermon by Halford E. Luccock, Marching off the Map, 1952, pp. 11–16. Digest of sermon by Walter Russell Bowie, Great Men of the Bible, 1937, pp. 100–14. Digest of sermon by Clovis G. Chappell, Sermons on Old & NT Characters, 1925, pp. 19–31. Prayer, Samuel Miller, Prayers for Daily Use, (1957), p. 49. Digest of "But if We suffer with God," a sermon by Robt. E. Luccock, in If God Be for Us, 1954, pp. 91–101. Digest of "Where Christianity Begins," a sermon by Harold A. Bosley, He Spoke to Them in Parables, 1963, pp. 115–23. Digest of a sermon, "Overcome Evil," Chas. R. Brown, Being Made Over, 1939, pp. 71–80. Prayer by Samuel H. Miller, Prayers for Daily Use, 1957, pp. 116f. Portion of prayer by Harry Emerson Fosdick in his Book of Public Prayers, 1959, pp. 154–55. Digest of sermon in W. A. Cameron, The Gift of God, 1925 (Doran), pp. 166–77. Digest of sermons, "Six Ways to Tell Right from Wrong," Harry Emerson Fosdick, The Hope of the World, 1933, pp. 126–135, and "Finding God in Unlikely Places," Harry Emerson Fosdick, What Is Vital in Religion, 1955, pp. 1–11. Sermon outline by John A. Broadus, Favorite Sermons of John A. Broadus, ed. by V. L. Stanfield, pp. 133–34. Digest of sermon, "Victory Over Death," Frederick W. Robertson, Robertson's Sermons, n.d., pp. 576–87. Portion of prayer, H. E. Fosdick, A Book of Public Prayers (1959), p. 134. Digest of sermon, Paul Scherer, The Word God Sent, 1965, pp. 169–77. An essay of about 1200 words, by Halford Luccock, Unfinished Business, 1956, pp. 26–27. A portion of a prayer, Harry Emerson Fosdick, in A Book of Public Prayers, 1959, pp. 88–89. Prayers by Samuel Miller, Prayers for Daily Use, 1957, p. 13, 15. Excerpts of lecture by Henry Drummond, "The Perfected Life," Henry Drummond: An Anthol-ogy, ed. by Kennedy, 1953, pp. 110–18. Prayer in Karl Barth, Deliverance to the Captives, 1961, pp. 124–25. Digest of sermon by Arnold Lowe, "We Must Confront Evil," The Importance of Being Ourselves, 1948, pp. 9–16. Excerpts from sermons by John A. Broadus in V. L. Stanfield, ed., Favorite Sermons of John A. Broadus (1959), pp. 111–13, 118–20, 115–17. Digest of sermon, "Teach Us to Number Our Days," by Karl Barth, Deliverance to the Captives, Harper: 1961, pp. 118–24. Digest of sermon, "When God Hides," by Paul Scherer, When God Hides, pp. 1–9, Harper: 1934.

HODDER & STOUGHTON LIMITED: Excerpt from sermon by D. W. Cleverley Ford, "When the King Refuses," from An Expository Preacher's Notebook, 1960. Reprinted with permission of Hodder and Stoughton Limited.

LAURENCE POLLINGER LIMITED: Four prayers by Samuel Miller from Prayers for Daily Use.

LEADERSHIP: Excerpts from article "Church Energy Conservation," copyright, © Leadership, 1982. Used with permission. Excerpt from article "Code of Conduct for Boards," Copyright © Leadership, 1983. Used with permission.

LEADERSHIP 100: Excerpt from article "Part-Time Choir," copyright © Leadership 100, 1983. Used with permission. Excerpt from article "Sunday Morning Produce Exchange," copyright © Leadership 100, 1983. Used with permission.

RANDOM HOUSE, INC.: Excerpt from "Saul" in The Poems and Plays of Robert Browning, by Random House, Inc.

REPORT FROM THE CAPITAL: Digest of sermon appearing in Report, Feb. 1984, p. 10, by Gerhard Claas. Used with permission of Report from the Capital.

REVIEW AND EXPOSITOR: Excerpts from article by Fred Craddock, Summer 1983, pp. 222–25, and digest of sermon by Nolan P. Howington, "The Liberating Christ," April 1958, pp. 196–202.

SCM PRESS LTS: Digest of sermon in The Hope of the World, by Harry Emerson Fosdick, pp. 126–35. SCM Press 1933.

SEEDS MAGAZINE: Excerpt from article, "Volunteers," by Susan McCarter, October 1984. Reprinted with permission from *SEEDS Magazine*. Copyright © 1984.

SHARING THE PRACTICE: Excerpt from article "Schedule for Visitation." Used with permission. Garry J. Looman, *Sharing the Practice*, copyright © 1983 by the Academy of Parish Clergy, Inc., Volume VI, no. 1, January/February 1983.

SUNDAY PUBLICATIONS, INC.: Sermon by James W. Cox, "Light for a New Life," *Word & Witness*, Mar. 5, 1978, Vol. 2, No. 4, p. 4, and an unnamed sermon by James W. Cox, *Word & Witness*, June 28, 1981, Vol. 5, No. 6, p. 4. *Word & Witness: Sunday Publications*, Lake Worth, FL 33461.

SUNDAY SCHOOL BOARD OF THE SOUTHERN BAPTIST CONVENTION: Devotional for Oct. 19 in *Open Windows*, Oct., Nov., Dec. 1984. Story, "A Bible for Biscuits," in Exploring I, from *Primary Leader*, April, May, June 1968, pp. 14–15. Devotional for March 7, *Open Windows*, Jan., Feb., Mar. 1985. Brief excerpt from "The Holy Spirit Works in People," *Exploring 2*, Oct., Nov., Dec. 1984, pp. 17–18. Devotional for Jan. 29, *Open Windows*, Jan., Feb., Mar. 1985. Devotional for Oct. 16, 1984, Open Windows, Oct., Nov., Dec. 1984, by Colleen Ralston. Excerpt from *Exploring 2*, "From a Devil to a Saint," Jan., Feb., Mar. 1985, pp. 42–43. Communion meditation, "The Lord's Presence—in Our Remembrance," *Proclaim*, July 1984, p. 14, by Alton McEachern. An essay by Arthur H. Criscoe, "The Ministry of the Spirit to the Believer," in *Facts & Trends*, Feb. 1984, pp. 7, 15. Sermon outline, "The Will to Witness," by Drew J. Grunnels, Jr., in *Proclaim*, Jan. 1985, p. 38. Excerpts from "How Does God Fight for Us?" by Jim England, *Ibid.*, pp. 22–23. Excerpts from articles by James W. Cox, "The Task of the Church," *Baptist Young People*, First Quarter, 1966, pp. 69–70. *Ibid.*, pp. 68–69, "The Signifi-cance of Worship." *Ibid.*, "The Way of Private Devotions," pp. 64–66. *Ibid.*, "How to Use the Bible," pp. 66–67. Outline of sermon, "Paradise Lost and Restored," by J. Dixon Free, *Proclaim*, July 1983, p. 20. Illustration by Gordon Clinard in *Proclaim*, Jan. 1982, p. 27. Illustrations in *Adult Life and Work Lesson Annual*, 1982–83, by Beau Colle, p. 164, by Jim Martin, p. 195, and by Robt. H. Wilson, p. 375. Sermon outline by James E. Carter, "What Death Does," *Proclaim*, July 1974, p. 13. Used with permission of The Sunday School Board of the Southern Baptist Convention.

THEOLOGY TODAY: Digest of sermon by George A. Buttrick, "Our Unshaken World and the Unshaken Kingdom," VII (Oct. 1950), pp. 301–07.

THE UPPER ROOM: Material from *Pockets*, "Pocketsful of Prayer," July 1984, p. 6., "Lent, etc." March 1984, pp. 6–7, "Pocketsful of Prayer," June 1984, p. 24, "Pocketsful of Prayer," September 1984, p. 24. From *Pockets*. Copyright © 1984 by The Upper Room, 1908 Grand Ave., P.O. Box 189, Nashville, TN 37202. Used with permission. Excerpts from *When Sorrow Comes*, by E. Stanley Jones. Copyright © 1944 by The Upper Room, 1908 Grand Ave., P.O. Box 189, Nashville, TN 37202. Used with permission. "God Is With Us," *The Upper Room*, March-April 1984. Copyright © 1984 by The Upper Room, 1908 Grand Avenue, P.O. Box 189, Nashville, TN 37202. Used with permission.

THE VESTRY-TRINITY CHURCH: Digest of "The Story of Two Giants," a sermon by Theodore Parker Ferris in *The New Life*, published by Seabury Press, 1961.

WAR CRY: Excerpt from article by Bramwell Trip, ". . . God With Us . . .", p. 23, 1984 Christmas *War Cry*, published by The Salvation Army.